# Heresy and the Formation of Medieval Islamic Orthodoxy

Between the eighth and eleventh centuries, many defining features of classical Sunni Islam began to take shape. Among these was the formation of medieval Sunnism around the belief in the unimpeachable orthodoxy of four eponymous founders and their schools of law. In this original study, Ahmad Khan explores the history and cultural memory of one of these eponymous founders, Abū Ḥanīfa. Showing how Abū Ḥanīfa evolved from being the object of intense religious exclusion to a pillar of Sunni orthodoxy, Khan examines the concepts of orthodoxy and heresy, and outlines their changing meanings over the course of four centuries. He demonstrates that orthodoxy and heresy were neither fixed theological categories nor pious fictions, but instead were impacted by everything from law and politics to society and culture. This book illuminates the significant yet often neglected transformations in Islamic social, political, and religious thought during this vibrant period.

Ahmad Khan is Assistant Professor of Islamic Studies at the American University in Cairo. He previously held positions at Oxford and Hamburg Universities and was the Arcapita Visiting Professor at Columbia University in New York. His publications include *Reclaiming Islamic Tradition: Modern Interpretations of the Classical Heritage* (2016). His research focuses on Islamic thought and history in the pre-modern and modern periods.

# Heresy and the Formation of Medieval Islamic Orthodoxy

## *The Making of Sunnism, from the Eighth to the Eleventh Centuries*

---

Ahmad Khan
*American University in Cairo*

CAMBRIDGE
UNIVERSITY PRESS

CAMBRIDGE
UNIVERSITY PRESS

Shaftesbury Road, Cambridge CB2 8EA, United Kingdom

One Liberty Plaza, 20th Floor, New York, NY 10006, USA

477 Williamstown Road, Port Melbourne, VIC 3207, Australia

314–321, 3rd Floor, Plot 3, Splendor Forum, Jasola District Centre, New Delhi – 110025, India

103 Penang Road, #05–06/07, Visioncrest Commercial, Singapore 238467

Cambridge University Press is part of Cambridge University Press & Assessment, a department of the University of Cambridge.

We share the University's mission to contribute to society through the pursuit of education, learning and research at the highest international levels of excellence.

www.cambridge.org
Information on this title: www.cambridge.org/9781009098373

DOI: 10.1017/9781009093033



First published 2023

*A catalogue record for this publication is available from the British Library.*

*Library of Congress Cataloging-in-Publication Data*
Names: Khan, Ahmad (Lecturer in Islamic studies), author.
Title: Heresy and the formation of medieval Islamic orthodoxy : the making of Sunnism, from the Eighth to the Eleventh Century / Ahmad Khan.
Description: 1. | New York : Cambridge University Press, 2022. | Includes bibliographical references and index.
Identifiers: LCCN 2022026169 | ISBN 9781009098373 (hardback) | ISBN 9781009096249 (paperback) | ISBN 9781009093033 (ebook)
Subjects: LCSH: Hanafites – History. | Sunna – History – To 1500. | Islamic heresies – History – To 1500. | Islam – History – To 1500.
Classification: LCC BP166.14.H2 K435 2022 | DDC 297.09/02–dc23/eng/20220622
LC record available at https://lccn.loc.gov/2022026169

ISBN 978-1-009-09837-3 Hardback

*Fā'idat al-tārīkh . . . fa minhā anna al-ʿāqil al-labīb idhā tafakkara fīhā wa ra'ā taqallub al-dunyā bi ahālīhā wa tatābaʿ nakabātihā ilā aʿyān qāṭinīhā wa annahā salabat nufūsahum wa dhakhā'irahum wa aʿdamat aṣāghirahum wa akābirahum fa lam tubqi ʿalā jalīl wa lā al-ḥaqīr wa lam yaslam min nakdihā ghanī wa lā faqīr zahida fīhā wa aʿraḍa ʿanhā wa aqbala ʿalā al-tazawwud li al-ākhira minhā wa raghiba fī dār tanazzahat ʿan hādhihi al-khaṣā'iṣ wa salima ahluhā min hādhihi al-naqā'iṣ wa laʿalla qā'il yaqūl mā narā nāẓir fīhā zahida fī al-dunyā wa aqbala ʿalā al-ākhira wa raghiba fī darajātihā al-ʿulyā al-fākhira fa yā layta shaʿrī kam ra'ā hādhā al-qā'il qāri' al-Qur'ān al-ʿAzīz alladhī huwa sayyid al-mawāʿiẓ wa afṣaḥ al-kalām yaṭlub bihi al-yasīr min hādhā al-ḥuṭām fa inna al-qulūb mūlaʿ bi ḥubb al-ʿājil.*

al-Sakhāwī, *al-Iʿlān bi al-tawbīkh li-man dhamma ahl al-tārīkh.*

L'histoire est anecdotique.

Paul Veyne, *Comment écrit l'histoire.*

*Lā siyyamā madhhab al-Imām al-Aʿẓam Abī Ḥanīfa . . . wujūh istinbāṭihi min al-Kitāb wa al-sunna tadiqqu ʿan ghālib al-ʿuqūl fa lā yakādu yaṭṭaliʿu ʿalayhā illā aṣḥāb al-kashf.*

al-Shaʿrānī, *Muqaddima fī dhamm al-ra'y wa bayān tabarrī al-a'imma al-mujtahidīn minhu.*

# Contents


*List of Figures and Tables* — *page* viii
*Preface* — ix
*Acknowledgements* — xii
*Notes on the Text* — xv

**Part I History of Orthodoxy** — 1
1 Introduction — 3
2 Discourses of Heresy I (800–850) — 20
3 Discourses of Heresy II (850–950) — 38

**Part II Heresy and Society** — 113
4 Regionalism and Topographies of Heresy — 117
5 Ethnogenesis and Heresy — 153
6 Politics: Rebellion and Heresy — 184
7 Religion and Society — 206

**Part III Unmaking Heresy: Orthodoxy as History Writing** — 261
8 *Manāqib*: Narratives of Orthodoxy I — 263
9 *Masānīd*: Narratives of Orthodoxy II — 313

**Part IV The Formation of Classical Sunnism** — 327
10 Consensus and Heresy — 329
11 Conclusion — 349

*Bibliography* — 365
*Index* — 413

# Figures and Tables

## Figures

3.1 Discourses of heresy in *Kitāb al-Sunna* *page* 97

## Tables

1.1 Evolving terminology of Sunnism 16
8.1 Overview of *ṭabaqāt* section within Ibn Abī al-ʿAwwām al-Saʿdī's *Faḍāʾil Abī Ḥanīfa* 281
8.2 The occurrence of *ṭabaqāt* sections within Ibn Abī al-ʿAwwām al-Saʿdī's *Faḍāʾil Abī Ḥanīfa* 282

# Preface

This monograph tells the story of how orthodoxy and heresy evolved alongside one another in a rich medieval religious tradition. It explores how discourses of heresy shaped in fundamental ways the development of orthodoxy in medieval Islamicate societies. In the following pages I examine this religious tradition during what may be considered its most diverse and unpredictable age, the eighth–eleventh centuries. It was during these exciting centuries that many defining features of classical Sunni Islam began to take shape. Among these, the formation of medieval Sunnism around a conviction concerning the unimpeachable orthodoxy of four eponymous founders and their subsequent schools of law must be regarded as one of the lasting achievements and legacies of Sunnism.

By the eleventh century, Abū Ḥanīfa, Mālik b. Anas, al-Shāfiʿī, and Aḥmad b. Ḥanbal were regarded as representatives par excellence of medieval Sunni orthodoxy. The legal schools that coalesced around them became markers of medieval Sunni orthodoxy, and they spawned a religious tradition that is paralleled in its relevance and longevity throughout Islamic history perhaps only by Sufism. The consensus that classical Sunni Islam was synonymous with the orthodox character of these four eponyms and schools of law was the cornerstone of medieval Sunnism's homeostatic structure that came to define and regulate interactions between diverse groups and movements in the post-formative period of Islamic history. This catholic character of medieval Sunnism was remarkable for its ability to have endured earlier periods of schism, factionalism, anathematisation, and deep communal fissures. We will see that orthodoxy and heresy in the eighth–eleventh centuries are best understood as processes; that is, shifting strategies of denunciation and approval which can elucidate how centuries of conflict and hostility evolved into a stable regime of consensus and negotiation.

Precisely how medieval Sunnism reached this accommodation is no simple story. Its very success demands that as historians we not only acknowledge its formation but seek to explain it and study its aetiology, without resorting to whiggish tendencies that lead us to describe such consequential developments in the history of medieval Sunni orthodoxy and heresy as inevitable. This book examines the evolution of discourses of heresy and orthodoxy between the late eighth and eleventh centuries to explain how, when, and why classical Sunnism formed around this diverse conception of orthodoxy. It contends that the evolution of heresy and orthodoxy in medieval Islamic history is a complex phenomenon, but that its epochal stages can be made intelligible through a combination of new methodological approaches and by working with a diverse range of primary sources.

This study argues that discourses of orthodoxy and heresy surrounding Abū Ḥanīfa (d. 150/767) provide us with original and important insights into the fluid formation of medieval Sunnism between the eighth and eleventh centuries, thereby furnishing considerable documentation for the complex evolution of orthodoxy and heresy in medieval Islam. Contestations over the orthodoxy of Abū Ḥanīfa provide the basis for a new account of medieval Sunnism's formation. The primary objective of this work is to document these two processes – the construction of discourses of heresy against Abū Ḥanīfa and his rehabilitation and subsequent apotheosis as an unrivalled representative of medieval Sunni orthodoxy – during the late eighth and eleventh centuries. This investigation of discourses of orthodoxy and heresy, I argue, provides a new window onto the fluid formation of proto-Sunni orthodoxy. We learn how medieval scholars and textual communities were engaged in constant and rapid efforts to develop an indigenous apparatus through which consensuses could be reached about orthodoxy and heresy; how orthodoxy was not a later 'communal fiction' but entailed stages and processes that can be identified and were identified by medieval Muslims. Above all, we gain an insight into how a formidable medieval society and religion negotiated conflict and disagreement without giving birth to a widespread culture of imperial councils, inquisitors, and persecutions.

This book is divided into four parts. Part I provides an introduction to the categories of orthodoxy and heresy in medieval Islam. Here, I outline a new approach in the field of Islamic studies and history towards understanding the role of discourses of heresy in the formation of medieval Sunnism. In the same section I write the mnemohistory of discourses of heresy around Abū Ḥanīfa, which aims to identify the central agents of proto-Sunni traditionalist orthodoxy. Part II contains a detailed analysis of how the discourse of heresy against Abū Ḥanīfa was framed in the context of religion, society, and politics in the late eighth and ninth centuries. Part III explains the processes through which Abū Ḥanīfa was defended against various charges of heresy, focusing on the functions of historical writing and memory towards rehabilitating him. Here,

I contend that the late ninth–tenth centuries marked a turning point in the history of Sunnism with the rise of new forms of writing dedicated to establishing Sunni orthodoxy. Part IV explains how the rehabilitation of Abū Ḥanīfa was a crucial factor in the great convergence in the eleventh century that, despite dissenting views, consolidated medieval Sunnism's ecumenical character. The final chapter summarises the main conclusions of this study and places them in the context of broader discussions about heresy and orthodoxy in the Islamic world and beyond.

# Acknowledgements

I should like to record my academic debt to Christopher Melchert. His supervision, unwavering support, and guidance have been instrumental to my training and career as an academic. Nicolai Sinai and Rob Gleave deserve special mention, too, for reading and commenting on an earlier draft of the entire manuscript. Their suggestions and criticisms were invaluable. The following friends and colleagues read or discussed various parts of this work with me, and I thank them all for their time and support: Talal Al-Azem, Jack Brown, Peter Brown, Michael Cook, Patricia Crone, Maribel Fierro, Andreas Görke, Wael Hallaq, Stefan Heidemann, Robert Hoyland, Christian Lange, Wilferd Madelung, Andrew Marsham, Hossein Modarresi, Harry Munt, Andrew Newman, Jürgen Paul, Judith Pfeiffer, Wadad Al-Qadi, Chase Robinson, Ahmed El Shamsy, Mathieu Tillier, Luke Treadwell, and Walter Young. Two anonymous reviewers provided exacting and detailed comments on an earlier version of this monograph, and I thank them for their gracious time and expertise. *Wa mā kāna min khaṭa' wa taḥrīf fa huwa minnī.*

I revisited some of the primary source material upon which this book is based during a graduate seminar on heresy and orthodoxy at the American University in Cairo. I should like to thank my exceptional graduate students at AUC for their contributions during these insightful seminars: Luke Barber, Mariam Ghorab, Yussif Khalifa, Menna Rashad, and Yasmin al-Wardany.

My own teacher, Christopher Melchert, has always impressed upon me the awareness that as scholars we are steeped in a long scholarly tradition, and that very often we owe more to our predecessors and contemporary peers than we sometimes care to admit. I should like to emphasise my debt and gratitude to scholars, past and present, whose writings I engage with throughout this monograph. Finally, I should like to record my debt to scholars and philologists who have been engaged in the thankless task of discovering, collecting, and editing manuscripts. From nineteenth- and twentieth-century Orientalists in Europe and America to editors in the Middle East, Iran, and the Indian subcontinent, our craft would be much impoverished were it not for their painstaking editorial efforts. I need not say anything further about them here since some time ago I decided that the best way to show my gratitude to them was to devote a scholarly study to their craft. Work on this has already begun, and I hope to return to it in the future.

My graduate study was made possible through the financial support of a number of institutions. First and foremost, I must thank the University of Oxford, Faculty of Oriental Studies for awarding me the three-year Sheikh Zayed graduate scholarship. Without this I might not have returned to an academic career. The British Institute of Persian Studies (BIPS) and the British Institute in Amman (BIA) provided additional funding for research abroad. Pembroke College supported me with a number of scholarships and prizes over the five years I was a member there. I am grateful to them for their constant support during my studies at Oxford, particularly to Josie Cobb and Alison Franklin. I should also like to thank the staff of the Oriental Institute, particularly Gemma Forster and Priscilla Lange, for being so very understanding and helpful. The librarians of the Oriental Institute (Oxford), Pembroke College (Oxford), Bodleian (Oxford), Firestone Library (Princeton), British Library (London), Chester Beatty (Dublin, Dr Frances Narkiewicz), Staatsbibliothek (Berlin), Dār al-Kutub (Cairo), National Library (Tehran), Dā'irat al-Maʿārif-i Buzurg-i Islāmī (Tehran), and the Staatsbibliothek and Asien Afrika Institut libraries (Hamburg) were all exemplary in their professionalism and kindness. This book would have looked very bare were it not for the generosity and knowledge of these librarians. I am particularly grateful to James Weinberger who guided my research at the Firestone Library in Princeton. Time and time again, I found everything I needed (and much more) at the Firestone Library. Additionally, I am indebted to those editors of pre-modern texts who ensured that their indices were comprehensive and reliable.

I should like to single out the invaluable technical assistance I received from my friend Kevin. Just as I was ready to submit my manuscript, my computer and the software I used to write this study failed me. I lost a substantial amount of my data and was unable to access the program with which I wrote this book. Kevin, a man with the patience of Job, intervened and spent hours upon hours trying to rectify the situation. I do not know what I would have done without his generous help and expertise.

I thank the Gang for having taken me under their gracious (and boisterous) wings: *yā lahu min ka'sin wa yā lahā min khamratin*.

I will never be able to record on paper my gratitude to my parents. They have done everything and more for my siblings and me. Both my mother and father have influenced me in ways I cannot possibly describe, but I am forever grateful to them for encouraging me to study history and not law, though I now recognise I am doing both. I would like to thank my paternal grandparents, for both of whom Islamic history was a very dear subject. I regard them as my first teachers. I should like to thank the Orchards, my maternal grandmother, and my three siblings and their families, especially Adam, for their cheerful company. I owe my elder brother an important debt, both metaphorically and literally. Somehow, I got him to agree to bring me back multi-volume editions of medieval texts from his work trips to Cairo and Amman, and all the whilst he refused to let me reimburse him. Finally, I cannot begin to express my gratitude to my wife and children. I shall be thanking them for the rest of my life.

# Notes on the Text

This monograph adopts the Library of Congress's transliteration system for Arabic and Persian, though specialists should note that there are occasional deviations. For example, I do not distinguish between the *alif* and *alif maqṣūra*. The *tā' al-marbūṭa* is not indicated except in *iḍāfa* constructions, where it is indicated with a *t*. The affixed masculine pronoun, which is lengthened in pronunciation if it follows a short vowel, shortened if it follows a long vowel, and marked in modern prints of the Quran by a small *wāw*, is not transliterated: so, *rasūluhu* and not *rasūluhū*; *fīhi* and not *fīhī*. The *hamzat al-waṣl* is not distinguished by an apostrophe. Arabic, Persian, and Urdu are transliterated according to similar rules, save that *wāw* is represented by *w* in Arabic and *v* in Persian (and Urdu). In transliterating Arabic, I use hyphens only for the definite article (*al-*) and not for conjunctions or prepositions (*wa*, *li*, *bi*). Were I now to rewrite this entire study, my transliteration style would show greater respect to Classical Arabic pronunciation: in particular, *ah* and not *a* for *tā' al-marbūṭa*; and distinguishing assimilated sun letters.

Major place names are not transliterated and are given in their Anglicised forms (e.g., Medina for Madina). They are transliterated when they appear in Arabic or Persian passages. Lesser-known towns and places are transliterated. All dynastic names are transliterated too. Transliterated words are italicised, except for proper nouns and words that appear in good English dictionaries (e.g., ḥadīth not *ḥadīth*; qadi not *qāḍī*, except when it appears with a name or in a primary source; Sunni and not Sunnī, etc.). For pointing names, I have usually relied on the expertise of Ibn Ḥajar and Ibn Mākūlā and, failing them, Fuat Sezgin. Where there are serious disputes I have tried to indicate them in the footnotes.

In passages that I have translated from Arabic and Persian, I have endeavoured to provide (as and when I have deemed it necessary and feasible) the corresponding original passages in the main text or in the footnotes. I consider this important because it allows the reader to understand and determine for him/herself the nature of my reasoning and interpretation. It also preserves, in my view, the integrity of the original text. Readers can see what the author of these passages was attempting to convey as well as my claims to understand their words. It is also on account of the text's integrity that I have translated all aspects of the passages I quote. Any and all invocations, salutations, honorific phrases, or curses have been rendered into English, as and when they occur in a given passage. I must confess my dissatisfaction with my translations of invocations and salutations, which are challenging to convey in English.

This monograph is the product of research and writing conducted in Princeton, Germany, Oxford, the British Library, Tehran, and Cairo. At different institutions I had access to particular editions of medieval texts. I have endeavoured to use scholarly editions of primary sources, but I have also checked these against other editions. This may strike some readers as pedantic. However, different editions of one text often rely on different manuscripts. Checking editions against one another goes a very small way towards dealing with the fluidity that marked the pre-modern manuscript tradition. Furthermore, I have checked editions against the original manuscripts where I have had access to them. I have provided corresponding references in alternative editions of the same work to which I had access for the facility of readers. Not all scholars have access to the kinds of resources provided by the Firestone Library, the Bodleian, and the British Library. I hope this convention will make it easier for scholars to study my references for themselves.

In writing this book, I have observed the stylistic conventions set out in *The Chicago Manual of Style* (16th edn.). All dates are given first according to the Hijri calendar, then according to the Gregorian; however, centuries are given only in the Common Era (e.g., the ninth century). Quranic citations are to the 1924 Egyptian edition based on the recension of Ḥafṣ from ʿĀṣim.

In citing works in the footnotes, certain journal titles and reference works have been abbreviated. These are as follows:

| | |
|---|---|
| *BSOAS* | *Bulletin of the School of Oriental and African Studies* = |
| $EI^2$ and $EI^3$ | *Encyclopaedia of Islam*, 2nd and 3rd editions |
| *GAL* | Brockelmann, *Geschichte der Arabischen Litteratur* |
| *GAS* | Sezgin, *Geschichte des Arabischen Schrifttums* |
| *IJMES* | *International Journal of Middle East Studies* |
| *ILS* | *Islamic Law and Society* |
| *JAOS* | *Journal of the American Oriental Society* |
| *JESHO* | *Journal of the Economic and Social History of the Orient* |
| *JNES* | *Journal of Near Eastern Studies* |
| *JRAS* | *Journal of the Royal Asiatic Society* |
| *JSAI* | *Jerusalem Studies in Arabic and Islam* |
| *ZDMG* | *Zeitschriften der Deutschen Morgenländischen Gesellschaft* |

*Part I*

# History of Orthodoxy

# 1 Introduction

This monograph tells the story of how orthodoxy and heresy evolved alongside one another in a rich medieval religious tradition. It explores how discourses of heresy shaped in fundamental ways the development of orthodoxy in medieval Islamicate societies. In the following pages I examine this religious tradition during what to this historian must be considered its most diverse and unpredictable age, the eighth–eleventh centuries. It was during these exciting centuries that many defining features of classical Sunni Islam began to take shape. Among these, the formation of medieval Sunnism around a conviction concerning the unimpeachable orthodoxy of four eponymous founders and their subsequent schools of law must be regarded as one of the lasting achievements and legacies of Sunnism. By the eleventh century, Abū Ḥanīfa, Mālik b. Anas, al-Shāfiʿī, and Aḥmad b. Ḥanbal were regarded as representatives par excellence of medieval Sunni orthodoxy. The legal schools that coalesced around them became markers of medieval Sunni orthodoxy, and they spawned a religious tradition that is paralleled in its relevance and longevity throughout Islamic history perhaps only by Sufism, Islam's mystical tradition. The consensus that classical Sunni Islam was synonymous with the orthodox character of these four eponyms and schools of law was the cornerstone of medieval Sunnism's homeostatic structure that came to define and regulate interactions between diverse groups and movements in the post-formative period of Islamic history. This catholic character of medieval Sunnism was remarkable for its ability to have endured earlier periods of schism, factionalism, anathematisation, and deep communal fissures. We will see that orthodoxy and heresy in the eighth–eleventh centuries are best understood as processes, which can elucidate how centuries of conflict and hostility evolved into a stable regime of consensus and negotiation.

Some scholars of Islam have tended to take for granted the extent of medieval Sunnism's accomplishment in regulating orthodoxy and heresy. As detailed portraits of the social, religious, and political milieu of the regions of the medieval Islamic world begin to emerge, Islamicists are becoming more aware of the cacophonous nature of competing religious movements and trends prior to the eleventh century. The religious, legal, political, theological, and cultural traditions of the Nile–Oxus region were marked by a sharp heterogeneity, and each province harboured its unique medley of religious ideas and practices.[1] By the beginning of the eleventh century the twenty-fifth ʿAbbāsid caliph, al-Qādir (r. 381–422/991–1031), had come to recognise that medieval Sunnism had arrived at some degree of consensus as to what constituted Sunni orthodoxy: the recognition of four schools of legal orthodoxy, represented by four eponyms of impeccable Sunni pedigree, was a defining feature of the religious policies of al-Qādir's reign.[2] The imperial recognition that religious orthodoxy was to be anchored in four schools of law marked not the inception of a new chapter in the formation of medieval Sunnism but rather an acknowledgement of the success of those religious communities and scholars who had made critical contributions towards the completion of this chapter. The state was in the business of following religious trends, not inaugurating them.[3]

[1] Some sense of the diverse ideas and practices against which medieval Sunnism developed can be gleaned from the following works: Sadighi, *Les mouvements religieux iraniens* = Sadighi, *Junbishhā-yi dīnī-yi īrānī*; Rekaya, 'Le Khurram-dīn et les mouvements khurramites sous les ʿAbbāsides'; Tucker, *Mahdis and Millenarians*; Haider, *The Origins of the Shīʿa*, esp. 189–284; Macuch, 'Die sasanidische Stiftung "für die Seele": Vorbild für den islamischen waqf?'; Macuch, 'Die sasanidische fromme Stiftung und der islamische waqf: Eine Gegenuberstellung'; János, 'The Four Sources of Law in Zoroastrian and Islamic Jurisprudence'; Jokisch, *Islamic Imperial Law*; Crone, *Roman, Provincial and Islamic Law*; Crone, *The Nativist Prophets*, 191–371; Cook, 'Early Muslim Dietary Law'.

[2] See Makdisi, *Ibn ʿAqīl: Religion and Culture in Classical Islam*, 299 ff.; Makdisi, *Ibn ʿAqīl et la résurgence*; Makdisi, 'The Significance of the Sunni Schools of Law'. On the emerging Sunnism under al-Qādir see also Glassen, *Der mittlere Weg*; Makdisi, 'The Sunni Revival'; Hanne, *Putting the Caliph in his Place*, 71–2. It was during the reign of al-Qādir that scholars explicitly identified the consolidation of Sunnism with the establishment of four legal schools of orthodoxy: Yāqūt al-Ḥamawī, *Muʿjam al-udabāʾ: Irshād al-arīb ilā maʿrifat al-adīb*, ed. Iḥsān ʿAbbās (Beirut: Dār al-Gharb al-Islāmī, 1993), 5: 1955; see both al-Māwardī, *al-Aḥkām al-sulṭāniyya wa al-wilāyāt al-dīniyya*, ed. Aḥmad Mubārak al-Baghdādī (Kuwait: Maktaba Dār Ibn Qutayba, 1989), 132; and al-Māwardī, *Adab al-qāḍī*, ed. Muḥyī Hilāl al-Sarḥān (Baghdad: Maṭbaʿat al-Irshād, 1971), 1: 184–88, where Ḥanafism is normalised and interchangeable with Shāfiʿism. For later declarations of Sunni orthodoxy corresponding to the four schools of law and their eponymous founders see Ibn Hubayra, *Ikhtilāf al-aʾimma wa al-umam*, ed. al-Sayyid Yūsuf Aḥmad (Beirut: Dār al-Kutub al-ʿIlmiyya, 2002), 2: 395; Ibn Rajab al-Ḥanbalī, 'al-Radd ʿalā man ittabaʿa ghayr al-madhāhib al-arbaʿa', in Ṭalʿat Fuʾād al-Ḥulwānī (ed.), *Majmūʿ rasāʾil al-ḥāfiẓ Ibn Rajab al-Ḥanbalī* (Cairo: al-Fārūq al-Ḥadītha, 2002), 2: 626; Ibn al-Jawzī, *al-Muntaẓam fī tārīkh al-mulūk wa al-umam*, ed. Muḥammad ʿAbd al-Qādir ʿAṭāʾ and Muṣṭafā ʿAbd al-Qādir ʿAṭā ʾ (Beirut: Dār al-Kutub al-ʿIlmiyya, 1992), 18: 31–2.

[3] This is not to undermine the impact that imperial measures such as al-Qādir's support for traditionalism and his specific measures for promoting four schools of law would have had on the social, religious, and political landscape of late ʿAbbāsid society. On caliphs supporting prevailing religious trends see Melchert, 'Religious Policies of the Caliphs', 342.

Precisely how medieval Sunnism reached this accommodation is no simple story. Its very success demands that as historians we not only acknowledge its formation but that we seek to explain it and study its aetiology, without resorting to Whiggish tendencies that lead us to describe such consequential developments in the history of medieval Sunni orthodoxy and heresy as inevitable.[4] It is against such essentialising tendencies that this book proposes to write a history of orthodoxy and heresy in medieval Islam.

This book examines the evolution of discourses of heresy and orthodoxy between the late eighth and eleventh centuries to explain how, when, and why classical Sunnism formed around this diverse conception of orthodoxy. It contends that the construction and evolution of heresy and orthodoxy in medieval Islamic history is a complex phenomenon, but that its epochal stages can be made intelligible through a combination of new methodological approaches and by working with a diverse range of primary sources. This study argues that discourses of heresy surrounding Abū Ḥanīfa (d. 150/767) provide us with original and important insights into the fluid formation of medieval Sunnism between the eighth and tenth centuries, thereby furnishing considerable documentation for the complex evolution of orthodoxy and heresy in medieval Islam. Contestations over the orthodoxy of Abū Ḥanīfa provide the basis for a new account of medieval Sunnism's formation.

I draw on the approach of mnemohistory (*Gedächtnisgeschichte*), a key historiographical technique developed by Jan Assmann, which reveals the processes of *making* Abū Ḥanīfa as a heretic among proto-Sunni traditionalists in the eighth and ninth centuries and *unmaking* Abū Ḥanīfa as a heretic among a more diverse coalition of proto-Sunnis from the tenth century onwards. Mnemohistory's central preoccupation is not with reconstructing the facts, beliefs, and details of historical persons. Instead, it investigates how the past is remembered.[5] In this sense, this study is not concerned with what Abū Ḥanīfa and his contemporaries in the eighth century did or did not believe. It explores the mnemohistory of Abū Ḥanīfa to yield valuable insights into the

[4] Examples of studies that gloss over these developments are Watt, *The Formative Period of Islamic Thought*, 142–3; Waines, *An Introduction to Islam*, 66; Brown, *A New Introduction to Islam*, 136–7; Weiss, *The Spirit of Islamic Law*, 9; Schacht, *An Introduction to Islamic Law*, 3; Rippin, *Muslims: Their Religious Beliefs and Practices*, 91; Bulliet, *The Patricians of Nishapur*, 35–8. This is in no way to suggest that these studies are incompetent. Scholarship is constantly evolving, and it is in this spirit that I draw attention to the need for more comprehensive research on medieval Sunni orthodoxy and heresy.

[5] Assmann, *Moses the Egyptian*, 8–17. For more perspectives on mnemohistory see Tamm (ed.), *Afterlife of Events*, 1–23, 115–33.

mechanisms by which the formation of Sunnism was contested and, gradually, consolidated.

The primary objective of this work is to document these two processes – the construction of discourses of heresy against Abū Ḥanīfa and his rehabilitation and subsequent apotheosis as an unrivalled representative of medieval Sunni orthodoxy – during the late eighth and eleventh centuries. This investigation of discourses of heresy, I argue, provides a new window onto the fluid formation of proto-Sunni orthodoxy. We learn how medieval scholars and textual communities were engaged in constant and rapid efforts to develop an indigenous apparatus through which consensuses could be reached about orthodoxy and heresy; how old orthodoxies were transformed into new heresies and vice versa. Above all, we gain an insight into how a formidable medieval society and religion negotiated conflict and disagreement without giving birth to a widespread culture of imperial councils, inquisitors, and persecutions.

There is no escaping the fact that this book is preoccupied with some central concepts in the study of medieval societies and religious history. It is tempting to set forth a theoretical framework that guides the precise empirical routes navigated throughout this work, but doing so risks reducing the study of complicated and unpredictable historical trajectories to the dogmas of medieval religious history and studies. This point is worth underscoring because one of the central conclusions of this book is that, in very significant ways, the development of orthodoxy and heresy in medieval Islamic history does not conform to the existing paradigms for understanding the formation of orthodoxy and heresy in medieval religious societies.

This is no excuse to set aside the labour involved in undertaking comparative and interdisciplinary research. In the appropriate places, this study explicitly reads the history of orthodoxy and heresy in medieval Islamic societies against and alongside scholarship in the fields of late antiquity, religious studies, institutional history, medieval history, and post-colonial theories of identity and difference. However, interdisciplinary work is valuable only after the philological, historical, and social and cultural peculiarities of one's specialist discipline have been documented. In the words of the greatest (fictional) researcher of our times, 'It is a capital mistake to theorise before one has data. Insensibly one begins to twist facts to suit theories, instead of theories to suit facts.'[6] In this way, theory and interdisciplinary methods can inform, rather than be superimposed onto, the study of medieval Islamic history and societies. This part of the Introduction is limited, therefore, to explaining how the book

[6] Doyle, *Sherlock Holmes*, 12.

defines terms such as orthodoxy and heresy, whilst later sections of the book, in particular Chapters 1 and 2, extend these definitions through a close reading of the primary sources.

The study of orthodoxy and heresy in medieval Islam has yet to develop into a systematic field of historical inquiry – so much so, in fact, that many treatments of these subjects in Islam show little engagement with the primary literature.[7] There are four noteworthy approaches in previous scholarship to deal with these problematic categories for the study of Islamic history. The first adopts a static, institutional interpretation of orthodoxy and heresy whose starting point is the obvious observation that Islam has neither church, councils, nor clergy. According to this view, the absence of such visible institutional structures vitiates the very value of such inquiries.[8] There is no doubt that the observation is an accurate one. But the lack of obvious parallel structures should not force us to abandon the search for similar mechanisms and agents by which orthodoxy and heresy were negotiated. This monograph argues that such an axiomatic assertion concerning the institutional apparatus of medieval Christendom and its absence in the medieval Islamic world cannot be used to dismiss the study of orthodoxy and heresy in medieval Islam. Such approaches no longer reflect the level of detail and sophistication now visible in scholarly treatments of orthodoxy and heresy in pre-modern European societies, and they also fall short in examining how non-European medieval societies developed indigenous attitudes and apparatuses for regulating their societies.[9]

Other approaches vacillate between broad conceptual essays on the subject of categories and detailed studies based on a restricted body of primary sources. A second approach, for example, proposes erudite but general assessments of the problems thrown up by the categories of orthodoxy and heresy. Alexander Knysh proposes sensible caveats to discussions of orthodoxy and heresy in Islamic history, noting that such terms should not be used indiscriminately.[10] Norman Calder presents another intelligent essay on the character of orthodoxy in Sunni Islam. Calder is not concerned with describing how orthodoxy and heresy were negotiated in the formative period of Islamic history, though he is keen to underline the importance of intellectual traditions over orthopraxy as defining the character of Sunni orthodoxy. Calder's essay presents an argument for how scholars today should conceive of orthodoxy, and his proposal is that the literary tradition of Islam, squeezed between the

[7] Henderson, *The Construction of Orthodoxy and Heresy*; Ames, *Medieval Heresies*.
[8] Wilson, 'The Failure of Nomenclature'.
[9] Goldziher, *Vorlesungen uber den Islam*, 183–4 = *Introduction to Islamic Theology and Law*, 162–3.
[10] Knysh, 'Orthodoxy and Heresy in Medieval Islam'.

bookcases of any traditional library, presents a snapshot of the vast parameters of orthodoxy in Islam.[11] In 1953 Bernard Lewis offered a valuable overview of the semantic field of heresy in Islamic history but, framing them as no more than observations, Lewis advanced too many generalisations.[12]

The third approach places far too much emphasis on (and trust in) the heresiographical sources to reconstruct how medieval Muslims defined orthodoxy and heresy. This tendency is apparent in Knysh's attempt to locate the sites of orthodoxy. Despite his careful and sophisticated reading of medieval heresiographers such as al-Shahrastānī (d. 548/1153) and al-Ashʿarī (d. 324/935–6), Knysh's article prioritises the heresiographical (*firaq*) genre to adumbrate the development of orthodoxy and heresy.[13] The focus on heresiography to write the history of orthodoxy and heresy in medieval Islam is reflected in a number of important studies.[14] A fourth approach views heresy through the lens of political history. In such studies, heresy and orthodoxy are viewed as mechanisms by which the state and the caliph regulated the social and religious order of medieval societies.[15] Historians who adopt this view succumb to the seductive historiographical framework that Peter Brown, in a not too dissimilar context, has criticised as reflecting an 'institutionalised egotism' – the conviction that real power resided in the emperor and the imperial apparatus.[16] My own study builds on the work of scholars such as George Makdisi, Christopher Melchert, Maribel Fierro, Muhammad Qasim Zaman, Eerik Dickinson, Josef van Ess, Wilferd Madelung, Jonathan Brown, Scott Lucas, Wael Hallaq, and Devin Stewart, all of whom have advanced the study of medieval Sunnism in significant ways by detailing its contested history.[17]

[11] Calder, 'The Limits of Islamic Orthodoxy'.

[12] Lewis, 'Some Observations on the Significance of Heresy'.

[13] Knysh, 'Orthodoxy and Heresy in Medieval Islam', 50–6.

[14] Watt, *The Formative Period of Islamic Thought*; van Ess, *Der Eine und das Andere*; Lewinstein, 'The Azāriqa in Islamic Heresiography'; Lewinstein, 'Making and Unmaking a Sect'; Judd, 'The Third Fitna'; Laoust, *Les schismes dans l'Islam*.

[15] Judd, 'The Third Fitna'; Turner, *Inquisition in Early Islam*; Hawting, 'The Case of Jaʿd b. Dirham'; Marsham, 'Public Execution in the Umayyad Period'.

[16] Brown, *Power and Persuasion in Late Antiquity*, 9.

[17] For their path-breaking work in the study of orthodoxy and the formation of medieval Sunnism and Shiʿism see Makdisi, 'Ṭabaqāt-Biography'; Melchert, *The Formation of the Sunni Schools of Law*; Melchert, 'Traditionist-Jurisprudents'; Stewart, *Islamic Legal Orthodoxy*; Madelung, *Religious Trends in Early Islamic Iran*; Madelung, 'The Early Murji'a'. On proto-Sunnism and the ḥadīth literature see Zaman, *Religion and Politics under the Early ʿAbbāsids*; Dickinson, *The Development of Early Sunnite Ḥadīth Criticism*; Hallaq, *Origins and Evolution*; Lucas, *Constructive Critics*; Brown, *The Canonization*; van Ess, *Theologie und Gesellschaft*. Maribel Fierro has pioneered the study of heresy and

The chief objective of this study is to identify the evolution of a discourse of heresy concerning Abū Ḥanīfa to demonstrate the epochal stages and shifts in the formation of Sunni orthodoxy. In contrast with some of the aforementioned approaches, this study proposes a new framework for the investigation of orthodoxy and heresy in medieval Islamic societies. There is a long tradition of describing what orthodoxy is in medieval Islam through theoretical essays and abstractions.[18] These certainly have their place; but it has been my preference to establish what orthodoxy and heresy meant in medieval Islam by documenting the very process of orthodoxy and heresy on the basis of medieval voices. Nevertheless, our work as historians must be intelligible to colleagues and readers unfamiliar with the particular details of medieval Islamicate society. For this reason, it is necessary that I explain how the framework of orthodoxy and heresy I propose relates to wider scholarship in the disciplines of medieval history and religious studies.

We should start with Walter Bauer's radical revisionist thesis published in 1943, which challenged the conventional ecclesiastical understanding of early Christian orthodoxy and heresy. In his *Rechtgläubigkeit und Ketzerei im ältesten Christentum* Bauer departed from the scholarly consensus that viewed heresies as genuine and concrete social movements which developed as deviations of earlier orthodox communities. He shifted the scholarly understanding of heresies away from one that saw in orthodox representations of heretics and heresies an accurate depiction of deviant

orthodoxy in medieval Andalus: Fierro, *La heterodoxia en al-Andalus*; Fierro, 'Heresy in al-Andalus'; Fierro, 'Accusations of zandaqa in al-Andalus'; Fierro, 'Religious Dissension in al-Andalus'.

18 Asad, *The Idea of an Anthropology of Islam*; and, more recently, Ahmed, *What Is Islam?* 270–97; Ahmed, *Before Orthodoxy*, 3–5. Ahmed has valuable insights about how modern scholarship accounts for Muslim orthodoxy, and his own interventions are very useful. However, it is one thing to posit something about medieval orthodoxy or argue about modern definitions of orthodoxy. It is another thing altogether to document the dynamics of orthodoxy based on the medieval sources themselves, which is what my study attempts. On a related note, readers of Ahmed's *What Is Islam?*, 113–52, might argue that my study reinforces a flawed paradigm that sees Islamic law as denoting orthodoxy. To be clear, my study contends that the schools of law represented one important dimension of medieval orthodoxy, but by no means the only one. I might have more sympathy for Ahmed's argument that *madhhab-i ʿishq* has been marginal to modern scholarly conceptions of what was 'meaningfully Islamic' to pre-modern Muslims were it not that his documentation for *madhhab-i ʿishq* and criticism of 'legal-supremacist' Islam rests on an old canard that sees Law as denoting orthodox Islam and Sufism as a manifestation of heterodox Islam. It amazes me that a scholar of Ahmed's analytical depth and acuteness for Orientalist readings of Islam in many respects attempted to rehabilitate such a patently flawed hypothesis. What is more, Ahmed marshals figures such as Saʿdī to buttress this hypothesis, who himself on at least one occasion was reluctant to distinguish between the two (*bar kafī jām-i sharīʿat bar kafī sindān-i ʿishq, har hawas-nākī nadānad jām va sindān bākhtan*). See Saʿdī, *Ghazalīyāt-i Saʿdī*, ed. Kāẓim Bargnaysī (Tehran: Fikr-i Ruz, 2002), 728 (ghazal no. 521).

movements to one that emphasised the processes by which orthodox communities projected heresies and heretics. In Bauer's retelling of early Christian history, major Christian communities in the Roman provinces practised 'heretical' forms of Christianity, whilst orthodoxy represented a limited and less widespread belief system adopted only by a particular form of the Church of Rome. That is to say, for Bauer, the ecclesiastical understanding of heresy as a secondary, deviant and fringe development was untenable. The historical evidence suggested that ecclesiastical conceptions of what constituted heresies represented the original and more diffuse understanding of early Christian belief.[19]

Bauer's re-imagining of the landscape of early Christian religious communities brought into sharp relief the problems posed by categories such as orthodoxy and heresy. There is no doubt that his work infused fresh doubts into medieval portrayals of heresies and heretics and made the precarious character of heresy the cornerstone of modern approaches to orthodoxy and heresy in early and medieval Christianity. Bauer's impact on the study of orthodoxy and heresy in late antique and medieval history has been immense. Yet his forceful dislodging of the Eusebian account of the origins of orthodoxy and heresy was still burdened by a reification of these categories nowhere more evident than in his essentialising of heresy and orthodoxy.

It is here that I adopt a different approach from Bauer's to the study of orthodoxy and heresy in medieval Islam. The spectacular work of Alain Le Boulluec is hard to imagine without Bauer's initial foray into the subject. For our book, the implications of Le Boulluec's work are far more promising. Le Boulluec's two-volume study, *La notion d'hérésie dans la littérature grecque IIe–IIIe siècles*, places 'représentations hérésiologiques' at the forefront of the study of orthodoxy and heresy in second- and third-century Greek patristic thought. Le Boulluec's work inaugurates a shift away from the value-laden character of much research into heresy and orthodoxy by revealing the discursive strategies involved in the construction of heresy by an array of gifted Christian heresiologists. For Le Boulluec, the writings of early Christian heresiologists such as Justin, Hegesippus, and Irenaeus reveal the precise strategies and mechanisms by which a discourse of heresy is constructed, articulated, and targeted at opponents.[20]

This last insight is crucial to the argument of this book, though in two contrasting ways: this monograph posits that heresy in the formative

[19] Bauer, *Rechtgläubigkeit und Ketzerei im ältesten Christentum* = trans. *Orthodoxy and Heresy in Earliest Christianity*.

[20] Le Boulluec, *La notion d'hérésie*.

centuries of Islam rested on the construction of discourses of heresy. The closer we examine such discourses, the more they reveal about the evolving nature of proto-Sunni orthodoxy, the influence of its promulgators, and the shifting fortunes of these discourses. On the other hand, Le Boulluec makes explicit claims to working within a Foucauldian framework in which notions of discourse acquire centre stage. But, for Foucault, one of the elementary requirements of identifying discourses was to read everything.[21] Had he any idea of the quantity of primary sources in Arabic and Persian, to say nothing of other Islamicate languages such as Ottoman Turkish, I am certain he would have exercised some flexibility in his formulation.[22] To be very clear, I lay no claim to having read everything. Nevertheless, I agree with the main thrust of Foucault's argument, which I interpret to be his concern that scholars would claim to locate discourses that in actual fact were visible in one genre only.[23] By placing discourses and not institutions at the centre of the study of orthodoxy and heresy in medieval Islam, I am arguing that the power to assert and establish narratives of orthodoxy or heresy depended on the construction of texts and textual communities. Books do not exist by their own powers. They represent existing and well-established networks and systems of references.[24] They are part of a discursive field, and deploying this Foucauldian analysis provides new insights into the actual work (and agents) of orthodoxy. We should remind ourselves, if only because the term 'discourse' has often been stripped of its original Foucauldian meaning, that Foucault defined discourse in the following way: 'Whenever one can describe, between a number of statements, concepts and thematic choices, one can define a regularity, we will say, for the sake of convenience, that we are dealing with a discursive formulation.'[25]

Discourses of heresy surrounding Abū Ḥanīfa in a wide range of texts and through mechanisms, strategies, and thematic choices that reoccur frequently signal a discursive formation that defined proto-Sunni traditionalist conceptions of orthodoxy. Studying the emergence of these discourses furnishes key insights into the formation of proto-Sunni traditionalist orthodoxy and its evolving hegemonic constellations. Perhaps more significantly, the failure to sustain discourses of heresy concerning

[21] Foucault, *Aesthetics*, 262–3, 303; Foucault, *Ethics*, 486.

[22] Foucault, *The Archaeology of Knowledge*, 146, where Foucault expresses the difficulty in describing all of a society's archive.

[23] Foucault, *Aesthetics*, 303.

[24] Foucault, *Aesthetics*, 304; Foucault, *The Archaeology of Knowledge*, 26.

[25] Foucault, *The Archaeology of Knowledge*, 41.

Abū Ḥanīfa as part of proto-Sunni traditionalism's vision of orthodoxy allows us to pursue the fascinating story of the failures and successes that shaped the evolution of proto-Sunnism. Finally, a primary advantage is gained by studying discourses of heresy and orthodoxy for its ability to orient scholars towards how and to what end such discursive positions are distributed. In this formulation, heresy and orthodoxy in the formative period of Islamic history are studied as shifting strategies of denunciation and approval. They are not seen as insuperable, hierarchical impositions on matters of doctrine and ritual. They do not function only in historical contexts that presume an ecclesiastical culture of councils, creeds, and inquisitions. Rather, discourses of heresy and orthodoxy appear to depend heavily on a combination of political life, social imaginaries (*mentalités*), ethno-racial identities, and religious ideas. In this study, therefore, I posit heresy not as a legal or theological category but as a process.

Based on a wider set of sources, one of the main contentions of this monograph is that discourses of heresy and orthodoxy should not be viewed through the prism of doxa and praxis alone. Discourses of heresy went far beyond this. They operated in the three quintessential spheres of medieval Islamic societies: religion, politics, and society. Also central to my argument about how discourses of orthodoxy and heresy functioned in medieval Islam is to posit orthodoxy at the end rather than the beginning of the process of community identity and formation. This allows us to identify local and temporal variations across the late eighth and eleventh centuries. Orthodoxy thus defines a temporary preponderance of significant and persistent views claiming to be representative. This power of consensus enables groups and movements to articulate and disseminate discourses of heresy. In turn, this gives birth to a discursive formation of terms, semantic fields, concepts, and attitudes that seek to identify and isolate heretics. Daniel Boyarin saw in discourses of orthodoxy and heresy in the second and third centuries a crucial site for excavating a genealogy of Judaism and Christianity in late antiquity. Boyarin, like Le Boulluec and other Islamicists, ascribes exceptional agency to heresiologists of the second century. The idea of orthodoxy, Boyarin argues, owes its origins to a group of Christian writers who compose heresiologies, which inscribe border lines, regulate, police, inspect, and enforce them. The consolidation of this discourse on boundaries, once adopted by any two groups, resulted in the establishment of palpable confessional identities and boundaries, the crossing of which signalled a move from one group to another. As anathematisers of heretics and heresies grew, those who were inside and those who were outside became clearly identified. For Boyarin, the very function of heresiology, therefore, was

Christian identity.[26] My own formulation is not nearly as dramatic as Boyarin's. However, the regularity of discourses of heresy against Abū Ḥanīfa, their system of dispersion, their common themes and statements denote the discursive formation of heresy. Above all, they help historians to catalogue the history of community formation and communal identity.

This is one of the chief points of departure between Le Boulluec's work and mine. Where heresiological texts form the basis of Le Boulluec's analysis of how orthodoxy and heresy are constructed, this study is more circumspect about the value of heresiographical sources for shedding light on when, how, and why orthodoxy and heresy evolved in the formation of medieval Sunnism. This, in fact, represents what I consider to be a weakness not just in Le Boulluec's approach but in the work of exceptional Islamicists who depend so heavily on the heresiographical genre in pursuit of studying orthodoxy and heresy in medieval Islam.

If our aim as historians is to reformulate conventional medieval accounts of documented heresies and orthodoxies, the heresiographical literature is likely to serve as our best guide. This is not my objective. The confessional demands of the genre are so explicit as to render them almost futile, except in a few specific cases, for historians seeking to locate subtle shifts and evolutions across the late eighth to eleventh centuries. They are valuable for their insights into how Sunni orthodoxy projected itself and reimagined its past from the tenth century onwards: in these works we are provided with a highly schematised narrative designed to adumbrate and organise a very complex history of social and religious movements into distinct typologies and tidy historical origins. This form of confessional narrative has been described by John Wansbrough as a procedure that historicised dogma:[27]

> Fundamental to the documentation of confessional identity was selection of appropriate insignia from the monotheist compendium of symbols, topoi, and theologoumena. What could be called the 'sectarian syndrome' exhibits a lingua franca composed of such elements, whose sole condition of employment is adaptability. These may be adduced as nomenclature (tags, eponyms, toponyms), as emblems (initiation rites, ritual acts), as creeds (membership rules), as catechisms (dogmatic formulae) and correspond functionally to the several stages of confessional elaboration.

Wansbrough's analysis reminds us of the pitfalls historians face if they limit themselves to, or depend too heavily upon, the heresiographical

[26] Boyarin, *Border Lines*.

[27] Wansbrough, *The Sectarian Milieu*, 99–100. In fact, ch. 3 of *The Sectarian Milieu* is inspired by Bauer's work on heresy and orthodoxy in early Christianity. The fate of Wansbrough's book is that it is a study often cited but seldom engaged with.

genre for the work of historical reconstruction, for the latter is concerned with delineating change over time. This study does not jettison the genre altogether, but nor does it assign the genre a central place in the reservoir of primary sources I draw upon. In this sense, I do not adopt the approach taken by A. H. M. Jones, who notoriously dismissed ecclesiastical or theological sources as 'chaff'.[28] I use heresiographical works as controls, indicating in the footnotes curious and relevant sections where these works shed light on arguments whose substance is found in non-heresiographical sources.

A study of discourses of heresy surrounding Abū Ḥanīfa has particular merit because it demonstrates the specific ways in which proto-Sunni orthodoxy evolved. It is vital, therefore, to clarify and define the terms I use to describe religious movements between the late eighth and eleventh centuries. By the beginning of the eleventh century medieval Sunnism had acquired a fairly stable identity that centred around schools of law, ideas about theology, mysticism, caliphs, dogmas about the past, and against other religious groups in Islam (Twelver Shiʿism, Zaydism, etc.). That we can speak of a stable medieval Sunni orthodoxy is underscored by the emerging doctrine that representatives of these schools and groups might have disagreed with each other but, nevertheless, viewed such disagreements as legitimate. Following modern scholars, I use the term proto-Sunni to refer to religious movements prior to medieval Sunnism, that is to say, between the eighth and tenth centuries. Proto-Sunni is a large and all-embracing term, however. It can refer to so large a constitution of Muslims, ideas, and groups that it can become futile in its heuristic employment.[29] For this reason, and to accentuate the existence of greater variety in the eighth–tenth centuries, I draw attention in this study to a literate and influential religious elite I term proto-Sunni traditionalists. There is no pure equivalent designation in the primary sources for this group, and here I submit my own dissatisfaction with such an incomplete resolution. The nearest equivalent would be the *aṣḥāb al-ḥadīth*, who are frequently referred to in the secondary literature as traditionalists.[30] My primary discomfort with using the term traditionalist

[28] Jones, *The Later Roman Empire, 284–602*, vi–vii.

[29] This is one common criticism of an otherwise impressive account of eighth–ninth-century religious movements: Zaman, *Religion and Politics under the Early ʿAbbāsids*.

[30] Hodgson, *The Venture of Islam*, 1: 386–92 and a discussion of Hodgson's 'ḥadīth folk' in Melchert, 'The Piety of the Hadith Folk', 425–7; Fück, 'Die Rolle des Traditionalismus im Islam'; Makdisi, 'Remarks on Traditionalism in Islamic Religious History'; Makdisi, 'Ashʿarī and the Ashʿarites in Islamic Religious History I', 49–50 (where we find a detailed definition of traditionalism, which I adhere to closely; though, the traditionalist–rationalist tension is central to Makdisi's article and subsequent research); Goldziher, *Die Ẓāhiriten*, 3–19 = *The Ẓāhirīs*, 3–19 (Goldziher's observation is astute, especially

is that it relies heavily on, or at least inadvertently invokes, a paradigmatic division in the primary sources of the ninth century onwards: *aṣḥāb al-ḥadīth* (traditionalists) and *aṣḥāb al-ra'y* (rationalists). It is an indisputable fact that our primary sources speak of serious divisions between these two groups. At the same time, however, this simple division became a mechanism for glossing over a broader set of divisions between these groups that did not pertain immediately to ḥadīth or jurisprudence. These readings viewed the formation of medieval Sunnism as a compromise between traditionalists and rationalists. A compromise was certainly reached, but not by traditionalists and rationalists of the ninth century, and not all traditionalists were open to rapprochement. One of the key tenets of proto-Sunni traditionalism was the exclusion of Abū Ḥanīfa as a heretic and deviant figure, and many proto-Sunni traditionalists made no concessions with respect to this doctrine. In short, proto-Sunnism is too broad a designation, and traditionalism/rationalism runs the risk of denoting a specific genealogy of medieval Sunnism that minimises earlier conflict and neglects what was really at stake (see Table 1.1).[31]

because he was writing at the end of the nineteenth century; nevertheless, it misses some very important elements in the broader conflict between traditionalism and rationalism, in part because of the dearth of published material to which Goldziher had access); Schacht, *The Origins of Muhammadan Jurisprudence*, esp. ch. 6; Graham, 'Traditionalism in Islam' (a broad interpretive essay on variations of traditionalism in Islamic history, which inadvertently highlights the problem that newcomers to the field, or outsiders, will confront when trying to determine what traditionalism is supposed to designate); Melchert, *The Formation of the Sunni Schools of Law*, 1–22 (which examines the conflict between traditionalism and rationalism in greater detail than previous scholarship and shows its manifestation beyond mere jurisprudential disagreement); Melchert, 'Traditionist-Jurisprudents' (which delineates more specific trends and groups on the traditionalist–rationalist spectrum); Hallaq, *Origins and Evolution*, 122–8 (which argues for a ninth-century synthesis or compromise among traditionalists and rationalists); El Shamsy, *The Canonization of Islamic Law*, 195–201 (which focuses on the compromise of traditionalists but without reference to the significant corpus of refutations against al-Shāfiʿī).

31 Recent attempts to use the appellation *ahl al-sunna* or *ṣāḥib al-sunna* to document the emergence of Sunnism leave me unconvinced. Gautier Juynboll first proposed this very method to understand the rise of Sunnism, and John Nawas has recently undertaken it (Juynboll, 'Some New ideas on the Development of *Sunna*'; Juynboll, 'An Excursus on the Ahl as-Sunna'; Nawas, 'The Appellation *Ṣāḥib Sunna* in Classical Islam'). Nawas's analysis leaves me entirely dissatisfied. It shows no sensitivity to the acute problem of using later sources to reconstruct eighth–ninth-century developments ('In principle all published classical Arabic biographical dictionaries, ranging from Ibn Saʿd (d. 230/845) to Ibn al-ʿImād (d. 1089/1679) were used for data collection': p. 4, n. 9). The method fails to consider the fact that our ninth–eleventh-century sources exhibit a good deal of geographical diversity. Readers of texts produced in Iraq and Khurāsān/Transoxiana from this period cannot fail to notice the lack of consistent terminology for groups and ideas in these regions. Nevertheless, Nawas is content with making grand claims upon the basis of this questionable method ('This feature of randomness . . . ensures that the results of our sample are generalisable. That is to say, the conclusions from this random sample very probably hold for the entire population under study, in the present case, all ulama of

Table 1.1 *Evolving terminology of Sunnism*

| Term | Period | Description |
|---|---|---|
| Proto-Sunnism | 8th–9th centuries | Comprising movements subsumed into classical Sunnism |
| Proto-Sunni traditionalism (*ahl al-ḥadīth, ahl al-sunna*) | 8th–9th centuries | One movement among proto-Sunnism |
| Proto-Ḥanafism (*ahl al-ra'y, aṣḥāb Abī Ḥanīfa, ahl al-Kūfa*) | 8th–9th centuries | Students affiliated with Abū Ḥanīfa and his circle |
| Ḥanafism | 10th century | Classical school of law |
| Classical Sunnism | 10th century | Based around the schools of law, accommodating opposing positions, and incorporating all of the above |

As I acknowledge, proto-Sunni traditionalism is not a satisfactory resolution, and it is for this reason that I have undertaken the effort of documenting proto-Sunni traditionalists (their writings, ideas, and networks), so that when I refer to proto-Sunni traditionalism readers can identify its adherents. Now, by the eleventh century, things had changed radically. Medieval Sunnism was now defined by its fidelity to four eponyms: Abū Ḥanīfa, Mālik b. Anas, al-Shāfiʿī, and Aḥmad b. Ḥanbal. Their legacies spawned, arguably, the defining religious institutions of the medieval Islamic world, the schools of law (*madhāhib*). Today, Thomas Carlyle's theory of history being commensurate with great heroes is out of vogue, but it is worth recalling that for medieval Muslims history was intimately tied to collective memories about a few great men.

Parts of this book may be misread as an attempt to deconstruct this historiographical edifice. It should be stated at the outset that this is not my objective. This study presents a historical explanation for the social, political, cultural, and religious forces that contributed to this impressive and long-standing feature of Islamic orthodoxy. As such, and contrary to trends in the field of religious studies, I contend that orthodoxy was not a later 'communal fiction' of medieval Muslims who suppressed earlier narratives of tension and conflict. Rather, they were transparent about orthodoxy being a contested process.

the first four centuries of Islam': p. 5). Nawas does not show his readers his sources, so there is little else I can say beyond this comment.

Though this book presents the first comprehensive treatment of discourses of heresy with respect to Abū Ḥanīfa, it is not the first to identify hostility towards Abū Ḥanīfa in the primary sources. Goldziher was the first scholar to draw attention to Abū Ḥanīfa's 'very poor reception from his conservative contemporaries'.[32] On the basis of the heresiographical literature, both Madelung and van Ess have attempted to reconstruct some of Abū Ḥanīfa's theological views.[33] The most significant references to anti-Ḥanafī material can be found in two publications of Christopher Melchert, and I see the present book as building upon his work on the history of medieval Sunnism.[34] The 'problem of Abū Ḥanīfa' is noted also by scholars such as Eerik Dickinson and Scott Lucas.[35] And, more recently, Jonathan Brown has emphasised the importance of studying how scholars such as al-Bukhārī and Abū Ḥanīfa achieved 'Sunni status'.[36]

Unlike some previous scholarship, this study is not concerned with reconstructing the life and thoughts of Abū Ḥanīfa. This decision is partly motivated by the problems presented by ninth-century sources in describing the outlook of an eighth-century scholar. As I have stated, this book argues that contestations surrounding Abū Ḥanīfa's shifting reputation as a heretic and then later as a pillar of Sunni orthodoxy bring into sharp relief the diverse forces and figures that defined the struggle over orthodoxy and heresy in Sunnism. It does not pretend to provide all the answers to the formation of medieval Sunni orthodoxy, but it seeks to contribute to issues that are found wanting in current scholarship. This monograph will, I hope, encourage new investigations into the contested history of orthodoxy and heresy in medieval Islam, paying particular attention to the cumulative role played by social, religious, political, and cultural factors in its formation. To this end, this study is divided into four parts. Part I writes the mnemohistory of discourses of heresy concerning Abū Ḥanīfa based on sources composed between the ninth and eleventh centuries. This section provides a comprehensive historical examination of how hostility towards Abū Ḥanīfa evolved in the space of three centuries. A central objective of this chapter is to explain the formation of proto-Sunni traditionalist networks connected through shared conceptions of orthodoxy and heresy. Discourses of heresy around Abū Ḥanīfa were

32 Goldziher, *Die Ẓāhiriten*, 13–16 = *The Ẓāhirīs*, 13–16.
33 Madelung, 'The Origins of the Controversy', 508–11; van Ess, *Theologie und Gesellschaft*, 1: 183–212.
34 Melchert, *The Formation of the Sunni Schools of Law*, 1–12, 48–60; Melchert, 'How Ḥanafism Came to Originate in Kufa', 332–3.
35 Dickinson, 'Aḥmad b. al-Ṣalt'; Lucas, *Constructive Critics*, 350–1.
36 Brown, *The Canonization*, 363.

central to the emerging corporate identity of proto-Sunni traditionalist scholars and textual communities, and by studying them in detail a clearer picture of the key agents of proto-Sunni traditionalist orthodoxy begins to emerge.

Part II proposes a typology of discourses of heresy. This section explores the themes and topoi within the vast range of primary sources studied in Part I to demonstrate that discourses of heresy went far beyond matters of doctrine and ritual. I contend that discourses of heresy concerning Abū Ḥanīfa show that conceptions of orthodoxy and heresy were woven into the very fabric of society and social imaginaries, religion, and politics. This section details precisely how heresy was framed in the context of broad developments in medieval Islamic societies during the late eighth–eleventh centuries.

One of the central aims of this book is to explain the changing nature of proto-Sunni traditionalist orthodoxy. How was it that a sustained and pervasive discourse of heresy against Abū Ḥanīfa failed to establish itself as part of medieval Sunnism's broad conception of orthodoxy by the beginning of the eleventh century? Parts III and IV are devoted to explaining these momentous changes in medieval Sunni orthodoxy. Part III explains the processes by which Abū Ḥanīfa was unmade as a heretic, focusing on the functions of historical writing and historical memory towards rehabilitating Abū Ḥanīfa. In this respect, I assign an important role to two genres of historical writing (*manāqib* and *masānīd* works), hitherto severely neglected in the study of medieval Islamic religious history, towards the successful integration of Abū Ḥanīfa among the select constellation of paragons of medieval Sunni orthodoxy. Part IV explains how the rehabilitation of Abū Ḥanīfa was a crucial factor in the great convergence in the eleventh century that, despite dissenting views, consolidated medieval Sunnism's ecumenical character.[37] The final chapter summarises the results of this monograph and places them in the context of broader discussions about heresy and orthodoxy in medieval societies and religions.

In general, this study will sketch the development of discourses of heresy and how they figured in the development of proto-Sunni traditionalist orthodoxy. I hope to show that dispensing with the concept of

[37] The modern process of editing of ninth–eleventh century texts, as part of nineteenth- and twenty-first-century efforts to identify, edit, and publish these sources, provoked new and old contestations regarding the legacy of discourses of heresy surrounding Abū Ḥanīfa and Ḥanafism. The modern reception and interpretation of medieval debates concerning Abū Ḥanīfa's rehabilitation signals just how impermeable the eleventh-century consensus of medieval Sunni orthodoxy was, for which see Khan, 'Islamic Tradition in an Age of Print'.

orthodoxy altogether, as Wilson suggests, before any substantial work has been done on the subject, is both rash and brazen. Similarly, declaring that there is no orthodoxy in Islam, as van Ess does, principally because medieval Islam lacked a church or centralising authority, ignores how different religious communities and groups cultivate and build social consensus and regulate activities and practices.

# 2 Discourses of Heresy I (800–850)

This chapter argues that the construction of heresy and orthodoxy in medieval Islamic history depended on the circulation of discourses of heresy among textual communities. In emphasising the agency of scholars, texts, and the informal communities that emerged around them, I am proposing that heresy and orthodoxy emerged organically and outside strict institutions and their mechanisms of regulation. This more informal regulation of heresy and orthodoxy through discourses shaped the development of medieval Sunni orthodoxy, but its informal dimension did not reduce its force or potency. As Foucault reminds us, 'Whenever one can describe, between a number of statements, concepts, and thematic choices, one can define a regularity, we will say, for the sake of convenience, that we are dealing with a discursive formulation.'[1] This chapter documents the regularity, wide dissemination, and systematic nature of discourses of heresy against Abū Ḥanīfa between the late eighth and eleventh centuries, and relies exclusively on sources composed during this period to write its history.

This brings us to the question of the sources, which has become the *leitmotif* of the academic study of medieval Islam. The pedigree of scholarship on the formative period of Islamic history often rests on the ability of the historian in successfully removing the cloud of suspicion that hangs over any research topic indebted to historical materials written centuries after the periods under study. The problems concerning even the most elementary sources for the study of early Islamic history extend far beyond the issue of how late texts were composed in relation to the events they purport to describe. If indeed empirical fundamentalism still guides positivist readings of contemporary sources narrating contemporary events, it is enough to unsettle such convictions by being reminded that the perfect historical document does not exist and no historical document can presume a state of innocence. These are literary problems that beset even scholars of documentary sources and state administration, where the

[1] Foucault, *The Archaeology of Knowledge*, 41.

potential power of imperial projection also forces us to resist any level of historical *naïveté*.[2] These historiographical problems are woven into the very fabric of the historian's craft, and in different places in this work I will be forced to respond to these challenges. In what follows, however, many of these destabilising and debilitating methodological issues have been neutralised because I use ninth-century texts to examine developments in the ninth century, and I do the same for the tenth and eleventh centuries. I do not attempt to write the history of the early eighth century, and I do not rely on later sources to document the history of the ninth–eleventh centuries. I should say something, too, about another distinct approach adopted in this study.[3]

I have characterised my approach to discourses of heresy around Abū Ḥanīfa as that of mnemohistory. Mnemohistory is a new approach to history that seeks to marry reception history with memory studies. It is best understood not as a separate discipline to history, but as one of its sub-disciplines. It is a historiographical technique employed not to understand the truth of traditions but to reveal how these discourses represent the phenomenon of collective memory. Mnemohistory's central preoccupation is not with reconstructing the facts, beliefs, and details of historical persons or events. Instead, mnemohistory investigates how the past is remembered. In this sense, this study is not concerned with what Abū Ḥanīfa and his contemporaries in the eighth century did or did not believe; rather, it explores the mnemohistory of Abū Ḥanīfa to yield valuable insights into the mechanisms by which the formation of Sunnism was contested in the ninth and tenth centuries, which is coterminous with the period in which our sources burst onto the scene. Despite my engagement with mnemohistory, I distance my work slightly from that of one of its foundational progenitors, Jan Assmann.[4] Collective memory

[2] A neat summary and critique of this body of scholarship, which, in my view, is an advance in our understanding of medieval Arabic sources, can be found in Al-Azmeh, *The Arabs and Islam in Late Antiquity*, 1–38.

[3] Nora, 'Comment écrire l'histoire de France?', 24: 'The road is open for a totally different history: instead of determinants, their effects; instead of actions remembered or commemorated, the marks they have left and the games of commemoration; not events for their own sake, but their construction in time, the gradual disappearance and reappearance of their significances; instead of the past as it was, its constant re-exploitation, utilisation and manipulation; not the tradition itself, but the way it was constituted and transmitted.' Cited in Tamm (ed.), *Afterlife of Events*, 7.

[4] Assmann, *Religion and Cultural Memory*; Assmann, *Moses the Egyptian*, 8–17. Assmann's exposition of mnemohistory can be narrow and restrictive. Its central concern is with the temporal orientation of mnemohistory from present to past: how memories of the past are remembered at any subsequent given moment. The literature on collective memory preceding and beyond Assmann is extremely insightful, too: Halbwachs, *On Collective Memory*; Halbwachs, *La topographie légendaire*. See also Marc Bloch's book review of Halbwachs's work in Bloch, 'Collective Memory'; for the social memory approach applied

forms an important component of this book, too, but I am equally committed to historiographical techniques that can complement mnemohistory and reassert the credibility of writing the history of developments in the ninth century. The mnemohistory of Abū Ḥanīfa goes beyond reconstructing the reception history of Abū Ḥanīfa in the eighth–eleventh centuries. Microhistorians of the past decade have showed us the merits of intensive study of particular places, events, and persons.[5] In this study I contend that mnemohistory can be more illuminating when it is combined with the historical ambition of microhistorians. Microhistory rests upon the potential that one singular episode or person's life has for revealing its exemplariness; that is to say, how an individual's life or, as in this case, contestations over their memory points to broader issues affecting whole cultures, societies, and religions. This chapter offers a detailed mnemohistory of Abū Ḥanīfa, which reveals the different stages in the process of making him a heretic among proto-Sunni traditionalists in the late eighth and ninth centuries, but this mnemohistory serves as a microhistory for appreciating the contested formation of medieval Sunnism. Taken together, these two approaches bring to light historical traces of the failures and successes of proto-Sunnism; they reveal acute antagonisms and their subsequent resolutions; they highlight competing orthodoxies, their progenitors, agents, and interlocutors; they shed light on social and mental structures (*mentalités*) of societies that otherwise seem negligible; and they bring into sharp relief significant social forces across the ninth and tenth centuries. Together, mnemohistory and microhistory move us away from the subject (Abū Ḥanīfa) and towards discourses of heresy, the construction of orthodoxy, and the formation of medieval Sunnism. In the words of microhistory's *éminence grise*, 'a close-up look permits us to grasp what eludes a comprehensive viewing, and vice versa'.[6]

This chapter places under the microscope an extensive range of primary sources composed between the ninth and tenth centuries. Using sources written during these centuries to describe the evolution

to the study of medieval history see Fentress and Wickham, *Social Memory*, 144–72; and Ricoeur, *Memory, History, Forgetting*, 204–33, 401–11. In general, Ricoeur's engagement with Halbwachs, de Certeau, Nora, Ginzburg, and Koselleck has been extremely helpful in developing my own ideas about the kinds of history that can be read and produced on the basis of medieval texts.

[5] Lepore, 'Historians Who Love Too Much', exposes some of the tensions that confront microhistorians and biographers. I do not always agree with her conclusions. Her forthright and sometimes curt dismissals of the differences between biography and microhistory rest upon very simple, selective presentations of important works in the field of microhistory.

[6] Ginzburg, 'Microhistory', 26.

of discourses of heresy within the same time frame permits us to engage creatively with a plenitude of contemporary primary sources without being forced to interrogate the sources for backward projection. In this way we are able to track the evolution of discourses of heresy. We can identify the growth, continuity, and shifts in contemporary formulations of orthodoxy and heresy. The explosion of literary activity in the ninth and tenth centuries presents a great advantage for this study's aim to write the history of orthodoxy and heresy in the ninth and tenth centuries. What is traditionally viewed to be an Achilles heel of modern history writing on the formative period of Islamic history becomes this book's escape from the historiographical conundrums of early Islamic history. This impressive period of literary production permits us to document the discourses of heresy surrounding Abū Ḥanīfa in sources as diverse as universal histories, local and regional histories, prosopographical sources (*ṭabaqāt*), works of transmitter criticism (*rijāl*), legal texts, ḥadīth compilations, *muṣannafs*, geographical sources, belles-lettres (*adab*), martyrologies (*maqātil* and *miḥan*), and 'hagiographical' sources. The substantive nature of the discourses studied in these sources are dialogic. They seek to speak about the other, and in this way they make their social identity explicit through differentiation.[7] The dialogic structure of our sources, whether explicit through actual dialogues or implicit through discourses of heresy being fundamentally a discourse of differentiation in face of the proximate other, can reveal insights that other sources might not. As Ginzburg states, 'in some exceptional cases we have a real dialogue: we can hear distant voices, we can detect a clash between different, even conflicting voices'. Along these lines, our monograph adopts the programmatic statement issued by Ginzburg: 'In order to decipher them, we must learn to catch, behind the smooth surface of the text, a subtle interplay of threats and fears, of attacks and withdrawals. We must learn to disentangle the different threads which form the textual fabric of these dialogues.'[8]

The methodological approach of this study to the sources and its precise application of the notion of discourses of heresy should now be clear: I do not use late sources (post-eleventh-century texts) to write the history of discourses of heresy and orthodoxy during the ninth–eleventh centuries;[9] ninth–eleventh-century sources shall be analysed to write the history of these centuries; contradictory reports, conflicting materials, and biased narratives are read not to be reconciled to uncover what really

[7] De Certeau, *The Writing of History*, 45.
[8] Ginzburg, 'The Inquisitor as Anthropologist', 160–1.
[9] Where I cite such primary sources I do so to relate information incidental or supplementary to our understanding of these periods.

happened in the eighth century but to analyse what did occur during the ninth–eleventh centuries. This chapter will provide a detailed historical account of how discourses of heresy concerning Abū Ḥanīfa evolved across the eighth and tenth centuries. I will draw attention to the mobility of such discourses to suggest that hostility towards Abū Ḥanīfa became integral to social, intellectual, anecdotal, and textual interactions between proto-Sunni traditionalists. This chapter will establish not only the centrality of discourses of heresy concerning Abū Ḥanīfa among proto-Sunni traditionalists, but it will also bring into sharp focus key agents of proto-Sunni traditionalist orthodoxy: the scholars and figures who articulated and promulgated discourses of heresy.

## 2.1 Agents of Orthodoxy

In 1070 al-Khaṭīb al-Baghdādī was putting the final touches to his monumental biographical dictionary of over 7,831 scholars who had some connection to the sprawling metropolis of Baghdad. Written in the eleventh century, al-Khaṭīb al-Baghdādī's *magnum opus* represented the culmination and vast accumulation of historical information concerning the social and religious history of the eighth–eleventh centuries. Much can and needs to be said about the motives and methods driving al-Khaṭīb al-Baghdādī's *History*, but what cannot be doubted is that he sought exhaustive comprehensiveness over piecemeal historical reconstruction.[10] Al-Khaṭīb al-Baghdādī's *Tārīkh Baghdād* offers the reader a panoptic view of the formative period of Islamic history, and for this reason alone his work is indispensable to historians of medieval Islam. This very strength of the work, however, poses a risk to the modern historian who seeks a detailed account of gradual, or abrupt, historical changes and developments over centuries. The case of the single most extensive biographical entry contained within the seventeen volumes of the published critical edition illustrates at once the strengths and risks I have in mind. Al-Khaṭīb al-Baghdādī's vast collection of hostile reports concerning Abū Ḥanīfa provides an immediate sense of just how widespread discourses of heresy against Abū Ḥanīfa had been before the eleventh century. What it does not allow for, however, is a more precise knowledge of how attitudes to Abū Ḥanīfa changed over the course of the eighth–eleventh centuries; nor does it allow us to reconstruct the proto-Sunni traditionalist textualist community that promulgated discourses of heresy against Abū Ḥanīfa. In

[10] A detailed study of al-Khaṭīb al-Baghdādī and his extensive oeuvre is now well overdue. Al-ʿUmarī, *Mawārid al-Khaṭīb al-Baghdādī* remains the most significant study of *Tārīkh Baghdād* in modern scholarship and, as the title indicates, is dedicated to studying how this comprehensiveness was achieved.

short, al-Khaṭīb al-Baghdādī's entry on Abū Ḥanīfa is no substitute for a more careful examination, century by century, text by text, and author by author, of the evolution of discourses of heresy. In fact, relying exclusively, or even primarily, on the *Tārīkh Baghdād* risks distorting the history of discourses of heresy and orthodoxy within proto-Sunnism.

This chapter reveals the results of a thorough investigation into a large and diverse corpus of texts composed between the ninth and eleventh centuries of discourses of heresy concerning Abū Ḥanīfa. I have identified three distinct stages in the development of hostility towards Abū Ḥanīfa during these centuries. During the first stage (800–850) discourses of heresy towards Abū Ḥanīfa were sharp, but they were limited to specific criticisms. These criticisms tended to be confined to Abū Ḥanīfa's legal views and his approach to ḥadīth. A more sustained and extensive discourse of heresy emerged only during the second stage (850–950). This period witnessed the emergence of a discourse of heresy designed to establish Abū Ḥanīfa as a heretic and deviant. It was, in my view, the very intensity of this discourse of heresy that occasioned a third shift (900–1000) in discourses of heresy against Abū Ḥanīfa. Proto-Sunni traditionalists now began to engender a more accommodating attitude towards Abū Ḥanīfa. This formed the groundwork for the wide embrace of Abū Ḥanīfa among the proto-Sunni community, culminating in his consecration as a saint-scholar and one of the four representatives of Sunni orthodoxy in medieval Islam.

Though I have been able to distinguish three important moments in the history of discourses of heresy against Abū Ḥanīfa, my periodisation is not without problems. There is significant overlap between stages two and three. Acute deprecations of Abū Ḥanīfa, which are a hallmark of stage two, survived into the tenth century (stage three). This should not necessarily diminish the validity of my periodisation. Ideas evolved from region to region and author to author. They were not sealed hermetically within strict chronological enclosures. The transmission of ideas was porous and contested, and my periodisation allows for changes in the tenor of discourses of heresy against Abū Ḥanīfa. I want to be even clearer about the evidence for these three stages and patterns in the development of discourses of heresy. The primary sources on which these results are based represent a substantial proportion of surviving texts from the ninth–eleventh centuries. The discourses of heresy are contained within some of the most prominent sources in the history of medieval Sunnism. The authors of these works, too, must be considered as some of the most influential figures in the development of medieval Sunnism. However, this evidence needs to be placed in its proper context. We must beware of assuming the exemplariness of the primary sources to which scholars have access today. There is a problem in asserting that these surviving sources are representative of the ideas and beliefs of the ninth–eleventh centuries. We must contend with the probability that most of what was written in this period has neither been published nor survived in manuscript form. Furthermore, the significance of these authors and their works does not mean that the views and ideas they expressed can be considered to represent the opinions of the majority of society. In fact, I argue that discourses of heresy against Abū Ḥanīfa were promulgated by an influential, enterprising, and outspoken but nevertheless discrete textual community of scholars. This was not an age or society that manufactured consent, and this fact alone has a bearing on what can be said specifically about the range and extent of discourses of heresy. My resolution, not wholly satisfactory, to this has been to identify both discourses of heresy against Abū Ḥanīfa and efforts to rehabilitate him as a figure of orthodoxy to assess what this material tells us about orthodoxy and heresy in medieval Islam. I have tried to immerse myself in the past by reading the sources closely; to go on reading until I can hear the people talking.[11] I am aware, nevertheless, that not everyone wanted to be heard, and that some did not care to lend their ears. This is simply one among many shortcomings that serve as a handicap to the historian's craft. The least we can do is to be explicitly conscious of it. More fundamentally, I propose to read these sources on the basis that I take their lack of neutrality extremely seriously. That is to say, the material I study consists of written sources and written records of oral speech, real and fictive. The hostility or warmth that they express, their tendency to clash or their inclination towards resolving differences – these reveal the formation of ideas and movements over time.[12]

Our earliest layer of Islamic historiography provides us with no material on discourses of heresy. The first phase of historical writing (610–730) reflects the demands of a fledgling state and a burgeoning religion. The Prophet Muḥammad's career is the central concern of the *sīra/maghāzī* literature.[13] It is reasonable to assume that these details, along with their kerygmatic component as *Heilgeschichte*, were coterminous with the requirements of organising a state and articulating the foundational moments and themes of a religion.[14]

[11] Young, *Last Essays*, 9.

[12] I take my cue from Carlo Ginzburg's remarkable exposition, which was penned as a response to Hayden White's ideas about the historian's craft. See Ginzburg, 'The Inquisitor as Anthropologist'.

[13] See Görke and Schoeler, 'Reconstructing the Earliest *sīra* Texts'; Wansbrough, *The Sectarian Milieu*, 1–49.

[14] For an overview of historical writing during this period see Robinson, *Islamic Historiography*, 20–4; Clanchy, *From Memory to Written Record*, 23–81 reaches similar conclusions about the growth of writing and state administration.

## 2.2 Stage One (800–850)

It is with Chase Robinson's second phase of historical writing that we see our first texts exhibiting hostility towards Abū Ḥanīfa. The proliferation of the written word during this period was combined with new developments in the social organisation of communities. This merger produced what Brian Stock termed 'textual communities'.[15] Social norms, practices, skills, expertise, and relations began to form around the written word and the community of authors that produced them. These texts gave rise to distinct relations and bonds, which, with the rise of increased specialisation, facilitated the formation of religious and social groups and loyalties.

### *Al-Shāfiʿī*

The first phase of discourses of heresy against Abū Ḥanīfa that can be identified with a good degree of confidence coincides with the formation of textual communities and the crystallisation of specialised disciplines. El Shamsy has described the canonisation of Islamic law as being among the foremost of these developments, spearheaded by the writings of Muḥammad b. Idrīs al-Shāfiʿī (d. 240/820). A systematic examination of al-Shāfiʿī's *magnum opus* remains a gap in the study of early Islamic law. El Shamsy's important contribution has laid the groundwork for a historian capable of obsessing over legal minutiae and explaining their implications for communities of jurists in the ninth century to tackle the *Kitāb al-Umm*.[16] As a mixed repository of religious trends and attitudes from the late eighth to mid-ninth centuries, the *Kitāb al-Umm* presents an early, but unique, insight into how proto-Sunni traditionalist communities understood the memory of Abū Ḥanīfa.[17] The mnemohistory of Abū Ḥanīfa reconstructed in this chapter draws on local histories, biographical

[15] Stock, *The Implications of Literacy*, 89–90.

[16] El Shamsy, *The Canonization of Islamic Law*, ch. 6, esp. with his work on al-Shāfiʿī's authorship, has laid the groundwork for such a study. There is an infrequent tendency to read the sources charitably when discussing al-Shāfiʿī's contribution. Adducing al-Karābisī's (d. 248/862) statement, 'We did not know what the Quran and Sunna were until we heard al-Shāfiʿī', for example, for verification of al-Shāfiʿī's paradigm shift in legal thinking is a step too far. Al-Karābisī, as El Shamsy himself states, was al-Shāfiʿī's student, and this form of praise is so paradigmatic as to be irrelevant as an independent witness to al-Shāfiʿī's contribution to Islamic legal theory: El Shamsy, *The Canonization of Islamic Law*, 70.

[17] For the dating and manuscript evidence of al-Shāfiʿī's corpus see Sezgin, *GAS*, 1: 486–90. Doubts have persisted concerning al-Shāfiʿī's authorship of the texts attributed to him. See Mubārak, *Iṣlāḥ ashnaʿ khaṭaʾ fī tārīkh al-tashrīʿ al-islāmī*; Calder, *Studies in Early Muslim Jurisprudence*, 67–85. For significant revisions to Mubārak and Calder see Lowry, 'The Legal Hermeneutics of al-Shāfiʿī and Ibn Qutayba'; Melchert, 'The Meaning of

dictionaries, *rijāl* works, ḥadīth collections, and many other sources. The *Kitāb al-Umm* differs from many of these works in ways important enough to exhibit a peculiar form and degree of hostility to Abū Ḥanīfa.

The individual treatises that make up some portion of the *Kitāb al-Umm* belong to a tradition of jurisprudential dialectic. Al-Shāfiʿī's aim in these treatises and in other legal works is fairly consistent. For al-Shāfiʿī, jurisprudential reasoning is a process that must be anchored in revelatory sources.[18] The communitarianism of forms of legal reasoning during his time greatly troubled al-Shāfiʿī. His legal works are concerned with defining a canon of legal sources, elementary linguistic proficiencies, and methods of legal reasoning that are, on the one hand, coherent and, on the other, derived from sacred sources.[19] In outlining his theory and method of jurisprudence, al-Shāfiʿī is responding to a number of alternative forms of legal reasoning to which he is deeply hostile.

*Kitāb Ibṭāl al-istiḥsān* is al-Shāfiʿī's refutation of one such form of legal reasoning.[20] *Istiḥsān* was a juristic technique associated with Abū Ḥanīfa and his associates in the late eighth century.[21] Definitions of *istiḥsān* are

"Qāla al-Shāfiʿī" in Ninth Century Sources'. Separately, both Mohyddin Yahia and El Shamsy have argued for the textual integrity and authenticity of al-Shāfiʿī's written corpus. See Yahia, *Šāfiʿī et les deux sources de la loi islamique*, ch. 3; El Shamsy, 'al-Shāfiʿī's Written Corpus'; El Shamsy, *The Canonization of Islamic Law*, ch. 6; and further details in El Shamsy, 'From Tradition to Law', ch. 6, esp. 265–77.

18 Al-Shāfiʿī, *Kitāb al-Umm*, ed. Rifʿat Fawzī ʿAbd al-Muṭṭalib (Mansoura: Dār al-Wafā', 2001), 1: 43. On al-Shāfiʿī's contribution to Islamic legal theory see Schacht, *The Origins of Muhammadan Jurisprudence*, 315–28; Goldziher, *The Ẓāhirīs*, 20–6; Yahia, *Šāfiʿī et les deux sources de la loi islamique*; El Shamsy, *The Canonization of Islamic Law*, esp. 69–87; Melchert, *The Formation of the Sunni Schools of Law*, 68–71; Lowry, *Early Islamic Legal Theory*; Lowry, 'Does Shāfiʿī Have a Theory of "Four Sources" of Law?'; Hallaq, 'Was al-Shāfiʿī the Master Architect of Islamic Jurisprudence?'; on the opposite side of the spectrum see Zayd, *al-Imām al-Shāfiʿī wa ta'sīs al-īdiyūlūgiyya al-wasaṭiyya*; Ali, *Imam Shafiʿi*, 47–78; Vishanoff, *The Formation of Islamic Hermeneutics*, ch. 2.

19 This is my reading of his work, but readers should consult El Shamsy, *The Canonization of Islamic Law*, esp. 84–7.

20 It is reported that al-Ṭabarī wrote a work with a similar title: Yāqūt al-Ḥamawī, *Muʿjam al-udabā'* (Beirut: Dār Iḥyā' al-Turāth al-ʿArabī, 1988), 18: 74. For Muḥammad b. Dāwūd al-Ẓāhirī's (d. 297/909) rejection of *istiḥsān* see al-Qāḍī al-Nuʿmān, *Ikhtilāf uṣūl al-madhāhib*, ed. S. T. Lockandwalla (Simla: Indian Institute for Advanced Study, 1972), 183–6, which reads as very similar to al-Shāfiʿī's criticisms.

21 There is more uncertainty surrounding the nascent circle of Abū Ḥanīfa than modern scholars of Islamic law care to admit. Staying with *Kitāb al-Umm*, consider for instance that al-Shāfiʿī speaks of Kufa as being a region divided between the legal doctrine (*qawl*) of Ibn Abī Laylā and the school (*madhhab*) and legal doctrine (*qawl*) of Abū Yūsuf: al-Shāfiʿī, *Kitāb al-Umm*, 9: 27. On the legal doctrine of *istiḥsān* see Zysow, *The Economy of Certainty*, 240–2, 399–402, but Zysow's lucid discussion is focused squarely on post-formative conceptions of *istiḥsān*; Makdisi, 'Ibn Taimīya's Autograph Manuscript on Istiḥsān'; Makdisi, 'Legal Logic and Equity in Islamic Law'; Makdisi, 'A Reality Check on Istihsan as a Method of Islamic Legal Reasoning', which examines case law applications of *istiḥsān* in al-Kāsānī's (d. 587/1191) *Badā'iʿ al-ṣanā'iʿ fī tartīb al-sharāʾiʿ*.

scarce in early Ḥanafī texts, and relying on opponents of *istiḥsān* for its definition is undesirable.[22] If we survey discussions of *istiḥsān* in the ninth century, it becomes clear that *istiḥsān* was a form of legal reasoning to arrive at legal rules. It was considered a departure from analogy (*qiyās*) and, as such, the deployment of either *qiyās* or *istiḥsān* resulted in different legal rulings.

There is evidence to suggest that the concept pre-dates Abū Ḥanīfa. One prominent exponent of *istiḥsān* seems to have been the Basran jurist Iyās b. Muʿāwiya (d. 122/740).[23] He is described as having urged the application of *istiḥsān* among qadis and at the level of provincial government.[24] Owing to the success and spread of proto-Ḥanafism, critics of *istiḥsān* regularly associated the method with Abū Ḥanīfa and his followers rather than with earlier jurists such as Iyās b. Muʿāwiya. In addition to this, scholars close to the circle of Abū Ḥanīfa were reputed to have authored works on the subject of *istiḥsān*.[25] Other proto-Ḥanafīs explicitly endorsed it. The *Kitāb al-Kharāj* attributed to Abū Yūsuf recommends *istiḥsān*: 'If the caliph or his governor (*al-imām aw ḥākimuhu*) sees a man commit theft, drink wine, or have sexual intercourse outside of marriage, the caliph should not stipulate a criminal

[22] Al-Shāfiʿī's curt definition of *istiḥsān* – he who adopts *istiḥsān* has legislated (*man istaḥsana fa qad sharraʿa*) – acquired iconic status in post-eleventh-century legal works: see al-Ghazālī, *al-Mankhūl min taʿlīqāt al-uṣūl*, ed. Muḥammad Ḥasan Ḥītū (Damascus: n.p., 1970), 374, who begins his chapter on *istiḥsān* with this alleged statement of al-Shāfiʿī's. Other scholars, Ḥanafīs and non-Ḥanafīs, sought to clarify that al-Shāfiʿī's followers had interpreted as a rebuke what was originally meant as a compliment of the highest nature (*inna maqṣūd al-Shāfiʿī min qawlihi hādhā madḥ al-mustaḥsin wa arāda anna man istaḥsana fa qad ṣāra bi manzilat nabī dhī sharīʿa wa atbāʿ al-Shāfiʿī lam yafhamū kalāmahu ʿalā wajhihi hādhā*). See ʿAbd al-ʿAlī al-Laknawī, *Fawātiḥ al-raḥamūt sharḥ musallam al-thubūt fī uṣūl al-fiqh*, ed. ʿAbd Allāh Maḥmūd Muḥammad ʿUmar (Beirut: Dār al-Kutub al-ʿIlmiyya, 2002), 2: 374; Ibn Rushd, *Bidāyat al-mujtahid wa nihāyat al-muqtaṣid*, ed. ʿAlī Muḥammad Muʿawwaḍ and ʿĀdil Aḥmad ʿAbd al-Mawjūd (Beirut: Dār al-Kutub al-ʿIlmiyya, 1996), 5: 251 = Ibn Rushd, *Bidāyat al-mujtahid wa nihāyat al-muqtaṣid*, ed. Muḥammad Ṣubḥī Ḥasan Ḥallāq (Cairo: Maktabat Ibn Taymiyya, 1994) 4: 61, where Ibn Rushd presents Mālik b. Anas's definition of *istiḥsān* as 'harmonising contradictory legal proofs' (*jamʿ bayna al-adilla al-mutaʿāriḍa*). To be clear, this is Ibn Rushd's interpretation of Mālik b. Anas's view of *istiḥsān*, which he presents after noting divergences on Mālik b. Anas's application of it.

[23] Iyās b. Muʿāwiya deserves a separate study, the starting point of which must be Wakīʿ, *Akhbār al-quḍāt*, ed. ʿAbd al-ʿAzīz Muṣṭafā al-Marāghī (Cairo: Maṭbaʿat al-Saʿāda, 1947–50; repr. Beirut: ʿĀlam al-Kutub, n.d.), 1: 361–88. For now, see Tillier, *L'invention du cadi*, 360–6.

[24] Wakīʿ, *Akhbār al-quḍāt*, 1: 214.

[25] Ibn al-Nadīm, *al-Fihrist*, ed. Riḍā Tajaddud (Tehran: Maṭbaʿāt Dānishgāh, 1971), 257 = *Kitāb al-Fihrist*, ed. Gustav Flügel (Leipzig: F. C. W. Vogel, 1872), 203–4 = *Kitāb al-Fihrist*, ed. Ayman Fu'ād al-Sayyid (London: Mu'assasat al-Furqān li al-Turāth al-Islāmī, 2009; 2nd edn. 2014), 2: 23. The latter is the superior edition. Devin Stewart is in the process of producing a new critical edition and translation (personal communication).

punishment (*ḥadd*) only if he has witnessed this and has no recourse to additional legal testimony. For the caliph or governor to act in this way is for him to exhibit *istiḥsān*.' The text goes on to distinguish carefully between *qiyās* and *istiḥsān*, which suggests not only that such clarification was important but also that proto-Ḥanafīs saw a clear distinction between the two forms of legal reasoning and their legal implications.[26]

The introductory passages of al-Shāfiʿī's legal treatise *Ibṭāl al-istiḥsān* present a clear dichotomy between sacred and false knowledge. In the first few lines of the work al-Shāfiʿī deftly sets out his stall: 'God sent Muḥammad with a mighty book, and no falsehood can creep into it (*baʿathahu bi kitāb ʿazīz lā ya'tīhi al-bāṭil min bayna yadayhi wa lā min khalfihi*).'[27] This choice selection of a Quranic verse employing a cognate of the root word *b-ṭ-l* provides an unambiguous early insight into al-Shāfiʿī's position on *istiḥsān*. He does not overdo the argument by quoting other passages in the Quran featuring the root *b-ṭ-l*. The rest of the introduction adduces Quranic verses in the hope of clarifying the nature and authority of revelatory sources.[28] In this sense, *Ibṭāl al-istiḥsān* openly adopts the broader ideological thrust of al-Shāfiʿī's oeuvre.[29]

Al-Shāfiʿī's critique of *istiḥsān* is severe. Individual jurists known to advocate the use of *istiḥsān* are not named, however. Abū Ḥanīfa, Abū Yūsuf, Iyās b. Muʿāwiya, and others are not directly attacked. This is not because they were not the main targets of al-Shāfiʿī's treatise. Such omissions are better understood in the light of the conventions of jurisprudential dialectic in the *Kitāb al-Umm*. As legal works, al-Shāfiʿī's treatises treat a number of jurisprudential controversies, but both the style and substance of these works is dialectical. Al-Shāfiʿī is seeking to draw distinctions between his own understanding of the law and those of his interlocutors. It is clear that he sees his interlocutors not as mere individuals and independent jurists, but that his writings are targeted towards legal communities located in the different provinces of the early Islamic empire. Al-Shāfiʿī's rhetoric is evidence of the level of social and religious organisation that jurists, scholars, and writers were cognisant of when they put ink to paper. Al-Shāfiʿī's criticisms of Abū Ḥanīfa are confined to a number of serious disputes concerning Abū Ḥanīfa's

[26] Abū Yūsuf (attr.), *Kitāb al-Kharāj* (Beirut: Dār al-Maʿrifa, 1979), 178. On dating the *Kitāb al-Kharāj* see Calder, *Studies in Early Muslim Jurisprudence*, 105–60, where the work is described, in my view unconvincingly, as being the product of a single redactional effort in the middle of the ninth century; Zaman, *Religion and Politics*, 91–4, provides a brief rebuttal of Calder's re-dating.

[27] Al-Shāfiʿī, *Kitāb Ibṭāl al-istiḥsān*, in *Kitāb al-Umm*, 9: 57–84.

[28] Al-Shāfiʿī, *Kitāb Ibṭāl al-istiḥsān*, in *Kitāb al-Umm*, 9: 57–8.

[29] At least on the subject of *istiḥsān*, much of the material found in the chapter on *istiḥsān* in *al-Risāla* is identical to *Ibṭāl al-istiḥsān*.

understanding of Islamic law, his methodology, and the sources upon which his legal understanding was based.[30] Jurisprudential treatises in al-Shāfiʿī's legal corpus are concerned with matters of method and hermeneutic. Another reason for this may be what El Shamsy calls the nature of al-Shāfiʿī's written work, which he describes as commentary notes and epistolary writing.[31]

This dimension to al-Shāfiʿī's work results in a different tradition of anti-Abū Ḥanīfa sentiment. Abū Ḥanīfa as an individual is not the subject of al-Shāfiʿī's scorn, but the methods and legal reasoning associated with Abū Ḥanīfa and his fellow jurists are attacked with great rigour and energy. Al-Shāfiʿī, for example, is explicit that *istiḥsān* is a heretical method of legal reasoning and rule determination. According to him, it undermines God's authority and that of the Prophet. It is distinctly outside the canon of sources one can draw upon legitimately to derive legal rules.[32] It is an arbitrary process of rule determination, and its universal acceptance would risk creating a chaotic and contradictory legal system.[33] Using al-Shāfiʿī's corpus as a benchmark for attitudes towards Abū Ḥanīfa in the late eighth and early ninth centuries, we cannot identify a discourse of heresy concerning Abū Ḥanīfa. Methods, legal devices, and legal opinions associated with Abū Ḥanīfa and proto-Ḥanafīs were attacked. But this was done at the level of jurisprudential dialectic, without broaching discourses of orthodoxy and heresy with

[30] Johansen, 'Casuistry: Between Legal Concept and Social Praxis'.

[31] El Shamsy, *The Canonization of Islamic Law*, 151.

[32] After listing the sources for rule determination, al-Shāfiʿī contrasts these with illegitimate methods for deducing rulings. See al-Shāfiʿī, *Kitāb Jimāʿ al-ʿilm*, in *Kitāb al-Umm*, 9: 14: 'It would not be permissible for us to state the permissibility of something on the basis of juristic preference, nor by any other arbitrary or subjective method (*fa lā yajūz lanā an naqūlahu bi mā istaḥsanā wa lā bi mā khaṭara ʿalā qulūbinā*)'; al-Shāfiʿī, *Kitāb Ibṭāl al-istiḥsān*, in *Kitāb al-Umm*, 9: 71 (*bi mā sanaḥa fī qulūbihim wa lā khaṭara ʿalā awhāmihim*). For al-Shāfiʿī, *ijtihād* and *qiyās*, sometimes conflated with *tashbīh*, are regarded as legitimate methods of rule determination because they rest upon legal evidences; *istiḥsān* is the very opposite, and because of this it is illegitimate (*wa kāna ʿalayhim an yajtahidū kamā amkanahum al-ijtihād. Wa kull amr Allāh jalla dhikruhu wa ashbāhu li hādhā tadullu ʿalā ibāḥat al-qiyās wa ḥaẓara an yaʿmala bi khilāfihi min al-istiḥsān, li anna man ṭalaba amr Allāh bi al-dalāla ʿalayhi fa innamā ṭalabahu bi al-sabīl allatī fuḍat ʿalayhi wa man qāla: astaḥsinu lā ʿan amr Allāh wa lā ʿan amr rasūlihi, fa lam yaqbal ʿan Allāh wa lā ʿan rasūlihi mā qāla*): see al-Shāfiʿī, *Kitāb Ibṭāl al-istiḥsān*, in *Kitāb al-Umm*, 9: 72–75. For *istiḥsān* as *taladhdhudh* see al-Shāfiʿī, *al-Risāla*, in *Kitāb al-Umm*, 1: 236.

[33] Al-Shāfiʿī, *Kitāb Ibṭāl al-istiḥsān*, in *Kitāb al-Umm*, 9: 75–6. It is possible that al-Shāfiʿī's attack on *istiḥsān* is motivated by his intuition that *istiḥsān* had the potential to wrest rule determination away from private jurisprudents to the state, caliph, and governors. For one, this is how Abū Yūsuf recommends *istiḥsān*; second, and of course because of this, al-Shāfiʿī discusses *istiḥsān* and criticises it using examples of where rulers are able to implement Islamic law and legal rulings as they see fit in their jurisdictions. See al-Shāfiʿī, *Kitāb Ibṭāl al-istiḥsān*, in *Kitāb al-Umm*, 9: 76. These passages are his most impassioned against *istiḥsān*.

respect to significant individuals. By the middle of the ninth century these two aspects began to merge, and it was this development that saw the rapid rise of discourses of heresy against Abū Ḥanīfa.

### *Ibn Saʿd*

Born in Basra around 168/784, Ibn Saʿd embarked on a journey familiar to many young and ambitious scholars of his day. He travelled to Baghdad. There, he quickly secured employment as a scribe with the historian and judge Muḥammad b. ʿUmar al-Wāqidī (d. 207/823). The earliest biographical sources present a sketchy history of Ibn Saʿd's career. He was known to have been a *muḥaddith* (ḥadīth transmitter) of good repute, employed in the service of more famous scholars, and adopted into the ʿAbbāsid family (*banū hāshim*) as a *mawlā* (client).[34] For some time in the late ninth and tenth centuries his name and reputation became embroiled in the events of the Miḥna, the inquisition introduced by the ʿAbbāsid caliph al-Ma'mūn (r. 198/813–218/833). The surviving part of Ibn Abī Ṭāhir Ṭayfūr's (d. 280/893) local history of Baghdad records that Ibn Saʿd was one of seven prominent scholars selected by al-Ma'mūn and his advisers to be tested about their belief in the created nature of the Quran.[35] His selection alongside prominent proto-Sunni traditionalists such as Yaḥyā b. Maʿīn[36] (d. 233/847), Abū Khaythama[37] (d. 234/848), and Aḥmad b. Dawraqī[38] (d. 246/860), as part of the first batch of scholars to be interrogated under the Miḥna, certainly points to his status among peers and the imperial administration.[39] Perhaps because of this Ibn Abī Ḥātim was keen to mention his father's testimony of Ibn Saʿd's scholarly integrity. 'He was truthful (*yaṣduq*),' Abū Ḥātim al-Rāzī (d. 277/890) was reported to have said.[40]

[34] For secondary sources see Sezgin, *GAS*, 1: 300–301; Fück, s.v. 'Ibn Saʿd', *EI*[3]; Loth, *Das Classebuch des Ibn Saʿd*; Cooperson, 'Ibn Saʿd'; Melchert, 'How Ḥanafism Came to Originate in Kufa', 324–31.

[35] Ibn Abī Ṭāhir Ṭayfūr, *Kitāb Baghdād*, ed. Muḥammad Zāhid al-Kawtharī (Cairo: ʿIzzat al-ʿAṭṭār al-Ḥusaynī, 1949), 183.

[36] Al-Bukhārī, *al-Tārīkh al-kabīr*, ed. Hāshim al-Nadwī et al. (Hyderabad: Maṭbaʿat Jamʿiyyat Dā'irat al-Maʿārif al-ʿUthmāniyya, 1941–63), 4.2: 307; Ibn Abī Ḥātim al-Rāzī, *al-Taqdima fī maʿrifa li al-kitāb al-jarḥ wa al-taʿdīl*, ed. ʿAbd al-Raḥmān b. Yaḥyā al-Yamānī (Hyderabad: Maṭbaʿat Jamʿiyyat Dā'irat al-Maʿārif al-ʿUthmāniyya, 1952–3), 314–19 ( Ibn Abī Ḥāṭim al-Rāzī, *al-Jarḥ wa al-taʿdīl*, ed. ʿAbd al-Rāḥmān b. Yaḥyā al-Muʿallimī (Hyderabad: Maṭbaʿat Dā'irat al-Maʿārif al-ʿUthmāniyya, 1953), 1.

[37] Al-Bukhārī, *al-Tārīkh al-kabīr*, 2.1: 429; Ibn Abī Ḥāṭim al-Rāzī, *al-Jarḥ*, 1.2: 591.

[38] Ibn Abī Ḥātim, *al-Jarḥ*, 1.1: 39.

[39] Al-Ṭabarī. *Tārīkh al-rusul wa al-mulūk*, ed. M. J. de Goeje et al. (Leiden: Brill, 1879–1901), 3: 1116 = 32: 204.

[40] Ibn Abī Ḥātim, *al-Jarḥ*, 3.2: 262.

Ibn Saʿd's literary fame is confined to his *al-Ṭabaqāt al-kubrā*, which is a well-ordered biographical dictionary composed between 820 and 845.[41] Any insights into discourses of heresy in the *ṭabaqāt* are constrained by the conventions and inner structure of prosopographical writing in early Islamic history.[42] Ibn Saʿd's *Ṭabaqāt* is typical of Wadad al-Qadi's description of biographical dictionaries of a general, not restricted, kind: 'a prose work whose primary structure is that of a series of biographies'.[43] Its system of arrangement is based predominantly on regions and generations, which helps to explain why Ibn Saʿd provides two separate notices for Abū Ḥanīfa: one in the section on jurisprudents and traditionists from Kufa and a second discussing those from Baghdad.[44]

The entries provide us with the standard biographical details one might expect in such works, but Ibn Saʿd also provides two qualitative statements that indicate proto-Sunni traditionalist attitudes towards Abū Ḥanīfa. We are informed that Abū Ḥanīfa was weak in ḥadīth (*ḍaʿīf al-ḥadīth*) and that he adhered to speculative jurisprudence (*ṣāḥib al-ra'y*). These specific criticisms of Abū Ḥanīfa are expanded in biographical notices for Abū Ḥanīfa's senior associates and students:[45]

> Abū Yūsuf al-Qāḍī: He has many ḥadīth on the authority of Abū Khuṣayf, Mughīra, Ḥuṣayn, Muṭarrif, Hishām b. ʿUrwa, al-Aʿmash, and others amongst the Kufans. He was known for his memorisation of ḥadīth ... then he adhered closely (*lazima*) to Abū Ḥanīfa, learnt jurisprudence (*tafaqqaha*) from him, and speculative jurisprudence (*ra'y*) overcame him (*ghalaba*). Consequently, he turned away (*jafā*) from ḥadīth.

Ibn Saʿd's capsule biography is otherwise rich in its rhetorical effect. Particular verbs denoting ideological developments are arranged according to a historical sequence of events. Abū Yūsuf's biography undergoes a temporalisation which begins with orthodoxy in the form of studying ḥadīth with proto-Sunni traditionalists and ends in deviancy under the domineering influence of Abū Ḥanīfa in the form of speculative legal

[41] For the editorial history of the text see Fück, s.v. 'Ibn Saʿd', *EI*[3]; Melchert, 'How Ḥanafism Came to Originate in Kufa', 325–6; Lucas, *Constructive Critics*, 206–7.

[42] Makdisi, 'Ṭabaqāt-Biography'; Gibb, 'Islamic Biographical Literature'; Hafsi, 'Recherhes sur le genre Tabaqat'; al-Qadi, 'Biographical Dictionaries'.

[43] Al-Qadi, 'Biographical Dictionaries', 94–5.

[44] Ibn Saʿd, *Ṭabaqāt al-kubrā* (Beirut: Dār al-Ṣādir, 1957–68), 6: 368 and 7: 322.

[45] Ibn Saʿd, *Ṭabaqāt al-kubrā*, 7: 330; see Melchert, 'How Ḥanafism Came to Originate in Kufa', 327 for other proto-Ḥanafīs in Ibn Saʿd's *Ṭabaqāt*. Ibn Saʿd's *al-Ṭabaqāt al-ṣaghīr* contains notices on both Abū Ḥanīfa and Abū Yūsuf under a section on scholars who moved to Baghdad after it was built and ended up dying there, but Ibn Saʿd provides no more than their names and years of death: see Ibn Saʿd, *al-Ṭabaqāt al-ṣaghīr*, ed. Bashshār ʿAwwād Maʿrūf and Muḥammad Zāhid Jawl (Beirut: Dār al-Gharb al-Islāmī, 2009), 2: 128 (Abū Ḥanīfa) and 2: 129 (Abū Yūsuf).

reasoning. This process of gradual decline ends in a fall encapsulated by Ibn Saʿd's concluding judgement that Abū Yūsuf turned away from the words of the Prophet.

### *Ibn Abī Shayba*

If al-Shāfiʿī's writings exhibit the incipient stages of discourses of heresy against Abū Ḥanīfa in the specialised genre of juristic writing, our next example reflects an intensification of criticisms against Abū Ḥanīfa that we found in Ibn Saʿd's biographical dictionary. Abū Bakr b. Abī Shayba (d. 235/849) belonged to a remarkable family of traditionalist scholars.[46] The family's talents were noticed by the highest authority of the day: in 234/848–9 the caliph al-Mutawakkil (r. 232/847–247/861) chose a select group of jurists and ḥadīth scholars to communicate the programme of proto-Sunni traditionalism widely in the regions of the Islamic empire. Taking care of their financial needs, expenses, and salaries, al-Mutawakkil dispatched ʿUthmān b. Muḥammad b. Abī Shayba to Baghdad. Here, ʿUthmān b. Abī Shayba (d. 239/853) was ordered to establish religious gatherings where ḥadīths refuting the Muʿtazila and the Jahmiyya would be read out. ʿUthmān was given a pulpit, where close to thirty thousand people gathered to listen to and write down ḥadīths narrated by him. His brother, Abū Bakr b. Abī Shayba, was sent to al-Ruṣāfa. We are told he was able to draw in crowds of the same magnitude in al-Ruṣāfa as ʿUthmān in Baghdad.[47] A third brother, Qāsim, fared less well and was one of the few members of the Shayba family not to have been considered an expert in ḥadīth.[48] Ibn Abī Shayba had a son, Ibrāhīm b. Abī Bakr, and a nephew, Abū Jaʿfar Muḥammad b. ʿUthmān b. Abī Shayba, both of whom lived up to the reputations of their fathers.[49] Ibn Abī Shayba is said to have transmitted pro-ʿAbbāsid ḥadīth.[50] During his first lecture in the mosque of al-Ruṣāfa, he related that 'the Messenger of God, may God pray over him and grant him peace, said: Remember me in al-ʿAbbās, for he is the last of my fathers. After all, the uncle of a man is like his father.'[51]

[46] Al-Khaṭīb al-Baghdādī. *Tārīkh Baghdād*, ed. Bashshār ʿAwwād Maʿrūf (Beirut: Dār al-Gharb al-Islāmī, 2001), 11: 259–67. For his and his brother's father see al-Khaṭīb al-Baghdādī, *Tārīkh Baghdād*, 2: 265–6.

[47] Al-Khaṭīb al-Baghdādī, *Tārīkh Baghdād*, 11: 261.

[48] Al-Khaṭīb al-Baghdādī, *Tārīkh Baghdād*, 11: 266, where Yaḥyā b. Maʿīn's dismissal of al-Qāsim's expertise is blunt: when asked about writing down traditions from Ibn Abī Shayba and ʿUthmān against those of al-Qāsim, Yaḥyā b. Maʿīn responded, 'write on the authority of those two'.

[49] Al-Khaṭīb al-Baghdādī, *Tārīkh Baghdād*, 11: 263.

[50] Al-Khaṭīb al-Baghdādī, *Tārīkh Baghdād*, 11: 262.

[51] Al-Khaṭīb al-Baghdādī, *Tārīkh Baghdād*, 11: 262 (*iḥfaẓūnī fī al-ʿAbbās fa innahu baqiyyatu ābāʾī, wa inna ʿamm al-rajul ṣinw abīhi*).

His scholarly reputation, however, stands largely on his fourteen-volume *Muṣannaf*, which is a compilation of Companion and Successor reports and, to a lesser degree, Prophetic reports arranged under legal headings. We observed in the case of al-Shāfiʿī that the nature of his criticisms of Abū Ḥanīfa were shaped by the demands of the genre in which he was writing. Juristic writing provided the necessary space to highlight Abū Ḥanīfa's juristic deficiencies. The *Muṣannaf*, too, belongs to a distinct genre, and thereby produces a specific range of criticisms against Abū Ḥanīfa. It consists of forty-one books. There are the usual range of legal subjects such as ritual purity (*al-ṭahāra*), marriage (*al-nikāḥ*), and sales (*al-buyūʿ*). In addition to these, the *Muṣannaf* contains books on doctrine (*al-īmān wa al-ru'yā*), history (*al-tārīkh*), eschatology (*ṣifat al-janna wa al-nār*), asceticism (*al-zuhd*), and the firsts (*al-awāʾil*). There is, also, the curious inclusion of one of the longest books, 'The Refutation of Abū Ḥanīfa'. The book does not deviate substantially from the style and format of the *Muṣannaf*'s other chapters. It is introduced with a sentence explaining that 'it describes all the instances in which Abū Ḥanīfa opposed reports (*al-athar*) that were transmitted from the Messenger of God'. Ibn Abī Shayba presents a total of 485 reports which he believes Abū Ḥanīfa contravened. The first report concerns the stoning to death of Jewish men and women and takes the following format:[52]

1. Sharīk b. ʿAbd Allāh < Samāk < Jābir b. Samura: the Prophet, God pray over him and grant him peace, stoned a Jewish man and a Jewish woman.
2. Abū Muʿāwiya and Wakīʿ < al-Aʿmash < ʿAbd Allāh b. Murra < al-Barā' b. ʿĀzib: the Messenger of God, God pray over him and grant him peace, stoned a Jewish man.
3. Ibn Numayr < ʿUbayd Allāh < Nāfiʿ < Ibn ʿUmar: the Prophet, God pray over him and grant him peace, stoned two Jews, and I was among the people who stoned them both.
4. Jarīr < Mughīra < al-Shaʿbī: the Prophet, God pray over him and grant him peace, stoned a Jewish man and a Jewish woman.
5. It is reported that Abū Ḥanīfa said: 'They are not to be stoned.'

The remaining 484 reports assume this very style of argumentation. The final report in Ibn Abī Shayba's refutation of Abū Ḥanīfa reads:[53]

[52] Ibn Abī Shayba, *al-Muṣannaf*, ed. Muḥammad ʿAwwāma (Jeddah: Dār al-Qibla li al-Thaqāfa al-Islāmiyya, 2006), 20: 53–4 = (Hyderabad: al-Maṭbaʿa al-ʿAzīziyya, 1966), 14: 148–9.

[53] Ibn Abī Shayba, *al-Muṣannaf*, 20: 216–17 = 14: 281–2.

1. Abū Khālid al-Aḥmar < Yaḥyā b. Sa'īd < 'Amr b. Yaḥyā b. 'Umāra < his father < Abī Sa'īd said: the Messenger of God, God pray over him and grant him peace, said: 'No charity (*ṣadaqa*) is due on anything less than five *aswāq*.'
2. Abū Usāma < Walīd b. Kathīr < Muḥammad b. 'Abd al-Raḥmān b. Abī Ṣa'ṣa'a < Yaḥyā b. 'Umāra and 'Ibād b. Tamīm < Abī Sa'īd al-Khudrī: he heard the Messenger of God, God pray over him and grant him peace, say: 'There is no charity due on anything less than five *aswāq* of dates.'
3. 'Alī b. Isḥāq < Ibn Mubārak < Ma'mar < Suhayl < his father < Abū Hurayra: The Prophet of God, God pray over him and give him peace, said: 'There is no charity due on anything less than five *aswāq*.'
4. It is reported that Abū Ḥanīfa said: 'Charity is due on anything that exceeds or is less than this.'

Despite the steady pattern of this kind of criticism against Abū Ḥanīfa, there are some alterations in the specific wording Ibn Abī Shayba chooses to describe Abū Ḥanīfa's contravention of Prophetic reports. We saw in the first report, for example, that Ibn Abī Shayba described Abū Ḥanīfa's legal views as being in direct contradiction to the Prophet's: where the Prophet stoned a Jewish man and woman, Abū Ḥanīfa ruled that they should not be stoned (*laysa 'alayhimā rajm*). This seems to represent the most frequent technique for describing Abū Ḥanīfa's opposition to Prophetic ḥadīth. Ibn Abī Shayba has Abū Ḥanīfa provide a legal opinion that is contrary to the one adumbrated by his selection of Prophetic reports. But there are other stock phrases Ibn Abī Shayba employs. When the Prophet forbade prayer in the resting places of camels, Abū Ḥanīfa declared that doing otherwise was not a problem (*lā ba's bi dhālika*). This specific phrase – *lā ba's bi dhālika* – appears in reports concerning the permissibility of travelling with the Quranic *muṣḥaf* to enemy lands (*al-safar bi al-muṣḥaf ilā arḍ al-'adūw*);[54] giving equally among one's offspring (*al-taswiya bayna al-awlād fī al-'aṭīya*);[55] on the prohibition of inheriting wine even if one intends to turn it into vinegar;[56] and many others. In other reports Abū Ḥanīfa is described as having opined against the verdict of a Prophetic ḥadīth (*qāla bi khilāfihi*).[57] Criticisms of Abū Ḥanīfa in Ibn Abī Shaybā's *Muṣannaf* assume a pattern consistent with the theme and central preoccupation of the work. Ḥadīth reports are the subject matter of the *Muṣannaf*, although as Christopher Melchert and Scott Lucas have pointed out, Companion

[54] Ibn Abī Shayba, *al-Muṣannaf*, 20: 58–9 = 14: 151–2.
[55] Ibn Abī Shayba, *al-Muṣannaf*, 20: 59–60 = 14: 152–3.
[56] Ibn Abī Shayba, *al-Muṣannaf*, 20: 90 = 14: 178.
[57] Ibn Abī Shayba, *al-Muṣannaf*, 20: 104 = 14: 188–9.

and Successor reports and not Prophetic ḥadīth constitute the mainstay of Ibn Abī Shayba's compilation.[58] In the light of the format and focus of the *Muṣannaf*, the way in which Ibn Abī Shayba articulates his opposition to Abū Ḥanīfa should not surprise us. Al-Shāfiʿī's hostility towards Abū Ḥanīfa was on account of the latter's legal method and juristic reasoning, and al-Shāfiʿī expressed them in works dedicated to juridical disputation. Ibn Saʿd was forced to use biography as a vehicle for conveying Abū Ḥanīfa and his students' deviation from ḥadīth to speculative jurisprudence. The biographical dictionary imposed this kind of constraint on the articulation of his ideas. Reports (*āthār*) are the focal point of Ibn Abī Shayba's work, and he found a way to use such reports to articulate what he deemed to be Abū Ḥanīfa's deviation from the words and deeds of the Prophet Muḥammad and his Companions.

[58] Melchert, 'Traditionist-Jurisprudents', 401–2; Lucas, 'Where are the Legal Ḥadīth?'.

# 3 Discourses of Heresy II (850–950)

## 3.1 Stage Two (850–950)

The second stage in discourses of heresy against Abū Ḥanīfa provides irrefutable evidence for this study's argument that a proto-Sunni traditionalist network of scholars and associates attempted to frame Abū Ḥanīfa as a heretic. It is in these shifting strategies of denunciation exhibited during this second phase that we learn precisely how orthodoxy worked in the ninth–tenth centuries. We begin to understand how such discourses of orthodoxy and heresy could become hegemonic. And, by focusing on the construction of heresiological discourses, we can develop a more accurate profile of the agents of orthodoxy.

Two of the most important voices among the proto-Sunni traditionalist community condemning Abū Ḥanīfa as a heretic and deviant were Abū Bakr al-Ḥumaydī and Isḥāq b. Rāhawayh. Their presence in discourses of heresy against Abū Ḥanīfa is ubiquitous; they are prominent as their promulgators, narrators, and progenitors. Their connections to subsequent proto-Sunni traditionalists, whose writings contain severe condemnations of Abū Ḥanīfa as a heretic and deviant scholar, warrant a closer examination of these two figures. The surviving works of al-Ḥumaydī and Isḥāq b. Rāhawayh are meagre and do not indicate any obvious or explicit attempts to cast Abū Ḥanīfa as a heretic. But this absence proves well the point that relying only on the surviving literary corpus does not permit one to capture the full extent of ninth–tenth-century religious developments.

### *Al-Ḥumaydī (d. 219/834)*

Al-Ḥumaydī was born into a Meccan family of some renown. His grandfather, al-Zubayr b. ʿUbayd Allāh b. Ḥumayd, belonged to the generation of the Successors.[1] Al-Ḥumaydī's father, al-Zubayr b. ʿĪsā, was a transmitter

[1] Al-Zubayr b. Bakkār, *Jamharat nasab quraysh wa akhbārihā*, ed. Maḥmūd Muḥammad Shākir (Cairo: Maktabat Dār al-ʿUrūba, 1962), 444–5; Ibn Ḥazm, *Jamharat ansāb al-ʿarab*, ed. ʿAbd al-Salām Hārūn (Cairo: Dār al-Maʿārif, 1962), 117 = *Jamharat ansāb al-*

of ḥadīth who had narrated traditions from Hishām b. ʿUrwa.[2] We must assume that his father's learning had a formative effect on al-Ḥumaydī's religious orientation. Residing in Mecca certainly reduced the usual demand on young students of ḥadīth to travel far and wide in search of ḥadīth masters. Though al-Ḥumaydī travelled to Egypt and Iraq, his residence in Mecca enabled him to benefit from the endless flow of scholarly traffic prompted by pilgrims flocking to the Ḥijāz. Post-classical sources have plenty to say about al-Ḥumaydī's proto-Sunni traditionalist credentials, but it seems wiser to limit ourselves first to his reception in ninth-century sources and among proto-Sunni traditionalists of that century.

Al-Ḥumaydī makes his first appearance in the literary record in the section on Meccan scholars in Ibn Saʿd's *al-Ṭabaqāt al-kubrā*. Ibn Saʿd's entries tend to give very little away, so we must assume that he deemed essential the following facts about al-Ḥumaydī's life: he was Sufyān b. ʿUyayna's disciple (*ṣāḥib*); he was a reliable (*thiqa*) ḥadīth scholar; and he had memorised a great many ḥadīth.[3] Ibn Qutayba also knew al-Ḥumaydī to be a member of the *aṣḥāb al-ḥadīth* and *ṣāḥib Ibn ʿUyayna*.[4] A more detailed picture of al-Ḥumaydī's importance begins to emerge in the work of one of his students. Al-Fasawī's *Kitāb al-Maʿrifa wa al-tārīkh* contains over 297 references to al-Ḥumaydī, 66 of which are reports al-Fasawī heard directly from al-Ḥumaydī.[5] Al-Fasawī's *History* is replete

*ʿarab*, ed. Évariste Lévi-Provençal (Cairo: Dār al-Maʿārif, 1948), 108; al-Samʿānī, *al-Ansāb*, ed. ʿAbd Allāh ʿUmar al-Bārūdī (Beirut: Dār al-Jinān, 1988), 4: 47–8.

2 Ibn Ḥibbān, *Kitāb al-Thiqāt* (Hyderabad: Dā'irat al-Maʿārif al-ʿUthmāniyya, 1973), 6: 331.

3 Ibn Saʿd, *Kitāb al-Ṭabaqāt al-kabīr [Biographien]*, ed. E. Sachau et al. (Leiden: Brill, 1904–40), 2: 368.

4 Ibn Qutayba, *Kitāb al-Maʿārif*, ed. Tharwat ʿUkāsha (Cairo: Dār al-Maʿārif, 1969), 526.

5 Al-Fasawī, *Kitāb al-Maʿrifa wa al-tārīkh*, 3rd ed., ed. Akram Ḍiyā' al-ʿUmarī (Medina: Maktabat al-Dār, 1989), 1: 185–6, 200, 203 (al-Fasawī enters a record of al-Ḥumaydī's passing in the year 219/834), 215, 216, 221, 223, 227, 229, 231, 234, 243 (al-Ḥumaydī's noble lineage), 280, 317, 346, 347, 348, 356, 361, 388, 396, 409, 415, 428 (al-Fasawī presents al-Ḥumaydī's autobiographical account of his studies in Medina), 431, 433, 438, 440, 445, 449, 456, 457, 458, 459, 489, 494, 496, 502, 513–14, 516, 517–18, 521, 540, 541, 543, 544, 549, 552, 555, 559, 560, 561, 565, 566, 572, 634–5, 647, 659, 661, 680, 681, 698, 702, 703, 706, 712, 725; 2: 5–6, 9, 10, 12–13, 15, 18–22, 24, 32, 45, 93, 94, 113 (report on al-Ḥumaydī's authority concerning Sufyān b. ʿUyayna's criticism of a ḥadīth transmitter, Ashʿath b. Siwār (according to Ibn Ḥajar al-ʿAsqalānī, *Tabṣīr al-muntabih bi taḥrīr al-Mushtabih*, ed. ʿAlī Muḥammad al-Bajāwī and Muḥammad ʿAlī al-Najjār (Beirut: al-Maktaba al-ʿIlmiyya, n.d.), 2: 699–700 other possibilities include Sawwār and Suwwār)), 177 (where we learn that al-Ḥumaydī lived in close proximity to Muṭarrif b. ʿAbd Allāh al-Yasārī, a student of and nephew of Mālik b. Anas, and an account of al-Ḥumaydī's counsel to al-Fasawī concerning the recensions of the *Muwaṭṭa'*), 178–9, 183 (al-Ḥumaydī tests two ḥadīth scholars claiming to have memorised ḥadīth from Sufyān b. ʿUyayna, and under al-Ḥumaydī's interrogation they both fail miserably), 187, 189, 190, 206, 207, 208, 209, 210, 211, 212, 214, 220, 226, 227, 229, 231, 236, 255, 256, 259, 279–80, 281, 294, 319, 320, 407, 421–2, 549, 550, 552, 556–7, 560, 561, 572, 574, 575,

with accounts of his encounters with al-Ḥumaydī. Al-Fasawī informs us that he arrived in Mecca at the beginning of Ramaḍān in 210/826. Once the month of fasting had finished, al-Ḥumaydī began teaching his *Musnad*. Al-Fasawī attended these lessons and heard the entire *Musnad*.[6] It is clear from the *Kitāb al-Maʿrifa wa al-tārīkh* that al-Fasawī and al-Ḥumaydī were intimate friends. In one account al-Fasawī tells us that he was in Mecca making his way towards the house of Muṭarrif b. ʿAbd Allāh (d. 210/825–6). On his way to meet Muṭarrif, al-Fasawī chanced upon al-Ḥumaydī, and the following conversation ensued:[7]

AL-ḤUMAYDĪ: Where are you going?
AL-FASAWĪ: I am going to see Muṭarrif to read the *Muwaṭṭaʾ* with him.
AL-ḤUMAYDĪ: Did you not hear the *Muwaṭṭaʾ* from ʿAbd Allāh b. Maslama b. Qaʿnab?
AL-FASAWĪ: Yes, I had heard it from him.
AL-ḤUMAYDĪ: In that case, go and perform the circumambulation (*al-ṭawāf*) and do not busy yourself with Muṭarrif.
AL-FASAWĪ: So, I walked with al-Ḥumaydī towards the Kaʿba, and he told me [about his reservations concerning Muṭarrif].[8]

577, 578, 579, 580, 581, 582, 583, 584–5, 587, 589, 590–1, 593, 595, 602, 606, 608, 611, 612, 613, 619, 620, 630, 635, 636, 637–8, 643, 652, 665, 667, 668, 669, 670–1, 671–2, 672, 673, 674, 675–6, 677, 678, 679, 680–1, 682, 683, 684, 685, 687, 688, 689–90, 690–1, 692 (al-Ḥumaydī distinguishing between Sufyān b. ʿUyayna's older (mistaken) and later narrations), 696, 697–708, 710, 711–25, 727–32, 734–45, 753, 755, 756, 757, 758, 778, 779 (anti-Abū Ḥanīfa report on al-Ḥumaydī's authority), 787 (anti-Abū Ḥanīfa report on al-Ḥumaydī's authority, containing al-Ḥumaydī's comment that anyone who holds the opinion attributed to Abū Ḥanīfa has committed heresy or unbelief (*fa qad kafara*)), 788 (anti-Abū Ḥanīfa report on al-Ḥumaydī's authority), 800–801, 800–817; 3: 5, 42, 48–9, 81, 85, 91, 102, 114, 115, 118, 119, 121, 122–3, 129, 130, 158, 160, 161, 166, 184 (report on al-Ḥumaydī's authority and al-Fasawī's remark about al-Ḥumaydī's unparalleled faithfulness to Islam and the people of Islam), 203, 217, 218, 220, 237, 263, 288, 333, 341, 343–4, 389, 391, 406, 408–9, 411, 421, 422, 473, 475, 490 (report on al-Ḥumaydī's authority from al-Fasawī's *Kitāb al-Sunna*), 495 (report on al-Ḥumaydī's authority from al-Fasawī's *Kitāb al-Sunna*), 498 (report on al-Ḥumaydī's authority from al-Fasawī's *Kitāb al-Sunna*), 501 (report on al-Ḥumaydī's authority from al-Fasawī's *Kitāb al-Sunna*), 511 (report on al-Ḥumaydī's authority from al-Fasawī's other works), 517 (report on al-Ḥumaydī's authority from al-Fasawī's other works), 527 (report on al-Ḥumaydī's authority from Ibn Abī ʿĀṣim's *Kitāb al-Sunna*), 531 (report on al-Ḥumaydī's authority from al-Ḥākim's *al-Mustadrak*), 537 (report on al-Ḥumaydī's authority from al-Bayhaqī's *al-Sunan al-kubrā*), 541 (report on al-Ḥumaydī's authority from al-Bayhaqī's *al-Sunan al-kubrā*), 542–3 (report on al-Ḥumaydī's authority from al-Bayhaqī's *al-Sunan al-kubrā*), 545 (report on al-Ḥumaydī's authority from al-Bayhaqī's *al-Sunan al-kubrā*), 547 (report on al-Ḥumaydī's authority from al-Bayhaqī's *al-Sunan al-kubrā*), 549 (report on al-Ḥumaydī's authority from al-Bayhaqī's *al-Sunan al-kubrā*), 560 (report on al-Ḥumaydī's authority from al-Bayhaqī's *Dalāʾil al-nubūwa*).

[6] Al-Fasawī, *Kitāb al-Maʿrifa wa al-tārīkh*, 1: 200.

[7] Al-Fasawī, *Kitāb al-Maʿrifa wa al-tārīkh*, 2: 177.

[8] Al-Ḥumaydī deemed ʿAbd Allāh b. Qaʿnab's (d. 221/836) recension of the *Muwaṭṭaʾ* to be more reliable than Muṭarrif's. Muṭarrif b. ʿAbd Allāh al-Yasārī (d. 220/835) was Mālik b. Anas's nephew.

Anecdotes such as these preserve the kinds of deep loyalties and friendships that existed among proto-Sunni traditionalists. Learning and knowledge was a friendship's greatest currency. When a fellow proto-Sunni traditionalist gave his word, it was as good as gold. There was no reason to question it. Al-Fasawī was ready to attend Muṭarrif's house for a lesson, but his reliable and trustworthy compatriot, al-Ḥumaydī, knew better. When he told al-Fasawī to change his plans abruptly, al-Fasawī made no further inquiries. He knew that al-Ḥumaydī and Muṭarrif were practically neighbours.[9] Eventually, al-Ḥumaydī gave his reasons. But not for a moment did al-Fasawī doubt his teacher's judgement. Traces of their friendship are scattered across al-Fasawī's ouevre. Al-Ḥumaydī figures in al-Fasawī's now lost *Kitāb al-Sunna*,[10] and the very first ḥadīth related by al-Fasawī in his *Mashyakha* is from al-Ḥumaydī, where al-Fasawī includes al-Ḥumaydī's running commentary on the ḥadīth in question.[11] Al-Ḥumaydī's role in the transmission and promulgation of discourses of heresy against Abū Ḥanīfa cannot be underestimated, and beyond this his contribution to the development of proto-Sunnism has yet to be acknowledged by modern scholars. This is understandable in the light of the tendency in modern scholarship to identify key changes and events in the religious and social history of medieval Islam with scholars whose written works have survived. It seems reasonable to assume that the survival of only two modest works by al-Ḥumaydī, neither of which has been examined in western scholarship, has something to do with the insufficient attention paid to him.[12]

Al-Ḥumaydī was a prolific author.[13] He composed a book on Quranic exegesis.[14] He wrote a work on the proofs of Muḥammad's prophethood.[15] A local history of Mecca is attributed to him.[16] Another literary

[9] Al-Fasawī, *Kitāb al-Maʿrifa wa al-tārīkh*, 2: 177.

[10] Al-Fasawī, *Kitāb al-Maʿrifa wa al-tārīkh*, 3: 490, 495, 498, 501.

[11] Al-Fasawī, *Mashyakhat Yaʿqūb b. Sufyān al-Fasawī*, ed. Muḥammad b. ʿAbd Allāh al-Sarrīʿ (Riyadh: Dār al-ʿĀṣima, 2010), 35–6.

[12] The only study I know of is the brief overview by al-Ṣuwayyān: Aḥmad b. ʿAbd al-Raḥmān al-Ṣuwayyān, *al-Imām ʿAbd Allāh b. al-Zubayr al-Ḥumaydī wa kitābuhu al-musnad* (Riyadh: Dār al-Miʿrāj al-Dawlīya li al-Nashr, 1996). Brief references to the *Musnad* appear in Juynboll, *Muslim Tradition*, 25, 27, 28, 112–13. Al-Ḥumaydī's potential leadership of the Shāfiʿī school upon al-Shāfiʿī's death is discussed by El Shamsy, *The Canonization of Islamic Law*, 119–20.

[13] Sezgin, *GAS*, 1: 101–2. [14] For his *al-Tafsīr* see Ibn Abī Ḥātim, *al-Jarḥ*, 4.1: 40.

[15] For *al-Dalāʾil* see Kātib Çelebi, *Kashf al-ẓunūn* (Beirut: Dār Iḥyāʾ al-Turāth al-ʿArabī, n. d.), 2: 1418; Ismāʿīl Pāshā, *Hadiyyat al-ʿārifin* (Beirut: Dār Iḥyāʾ al-Turāth al-ʿArabī, n. d.), 1: 439; ʿUmar Riḍā Kaḥḥāla, *Muʿjam al-muʾallifīn* (Beirut: Dār Iḥyāʾ al-Turāth al-ʿArabī, n.d.), 6: 54.

[16] For *Faḍāʾil Makka* see Ibn Ḥajar al-ʿAsqalānī, *Fatḥ al-bārī*, ed. ʿAbd al-ʿAzīz b. Bāz (Beirut: Dār al-Maʿrifa, 1970; repr. Beirut: Dār al-Kutub al-Salafiyya, n.d.), 3: 463.

contribution was a book, I assume, on rare ḥadīth reports.[17] His most important work is the *Musnad*. It is arranged, as was common for *masānīd* works of this period, according to the narrations of (182 male and female) Companions. This is not the place to examine what the *Musnad* and al-Ḥumaydī's career can tell us about the history of proto-Sunnism in the ninth century, but the *Musnad* is pertinent to the growth of discourses of heresy against Abū Ḥanīfa.

For one, the *Musnad* reveals al-Ḥumaydī's deep and personal relationship with Sufyān b. ʿUyayna (d. 198/814). Sufyān b. ʿUyayna was originally from Kufa, but he spent more than a decade in Mecca, and it was here that the two men struck up a productive and long-lasting friendship.[18] Al-Ḥumaydī alleged that he had spent close to twenty years in the learned company of Sufyān b. ʿUyayna.[19] Proto-Sunni traditionalists of the ninth century were aware of the proximity between the two scholars, and a number of them recognised al-Ḥumaydī's status as Sufyān b. ʿUyayna's most faithful and discerning student.[20] The connection between these two men is particularly important because both Sufyān b. ʿUyayna and al-Ḥumaydī appear in the sources as two of Abū Ḥanīfa's most severe detractors.

Moreover, a deeper appreciation of the *Musnad* gives us a more accurate understanding of the prominent influence al-Ḥumaydī had on leading members of the proto-Sunni traditionalist community and on the broader

[17] On *al-Nawādir* see Sezgin, *GAS*, 1: 101–2; Ibn Ḥajar al-ʿAsqalānī, *Fatḥ al-bārī*, 1: 180, 6: 248 (Ibn Bāz edn.). *Al-Nawādir* could denote a book on juridical opinions concerning rare issues (as in the case of Muʿallā b. Manṣūr's *al-Nawādir*) or, alternatively, a book on rare ḥadīth reports (as in the case of al-Ḥakīm al-Tirmidhī's *Nawādir al-uṣūl fī maʿrifat al-aḥādīth al-rasūl*, ed. Ismāʿīl Ibrāhīm ʿAwaḍ (Cairo: Maktabat al-Imām al-Bukhārī, 2008)).

[18] Ibn Ḥajar al-ʿAsqalānī, *Tahdhīb al-tahdhīb* (Hyderabad: Dā'irat al-Maʿārif al-Niẓāmiyya, 1907 and 1909), 4: 122 tells us that Sufyān moved from Kufa to Mecca in 163/779–80. I thank Christopher Melchert for this reference.

[19] Al-Bukhārī, *al-Tārīkh al-kabīr*, 3.1: 97 Ibn Abī Ḥātim, *al-Jarḥ*, 2.2: 57; Ibn Ḥibbān, *al-Thiqāt*, 8: 341. Later sources recount this: Ibn al-Qaysarānī, *al-Jamʿ bayna kitābay Abī Naṣr al-Kalābādhī wa Abī Bakr al-Iṣfahānī fī rijāl al-Bukhārī wa Muslim* (Hyderabad: Maṭbaʿat Majlis Dā'irat al-Maʿārif al-Niẓāmiyya, 1905; repr. Beirut: Dār al-Kutub al-ʿIlmiyya, 1984), 1: 265; al-Mizzī, *Tahdhīb al-kamāl fī asmā' al-rijāl*, ed. Bashshār ʿAwwād Maʿrūf (Beirut: Mu'assasat al-Risāla, 1983), 14: 514; al-Dhahabī, *Siyar aʿlām al-nubalā'*, ed. Shuʿayb al-Arnā'ūṭ et al. (Beirut: Mu'assasat al-Risāla, 1996), 10: 617; Tāj al-Dīn al-Subkī, *Ṭabaqāt al-Shāfiʿiyya al-kubrā*, ed. Maḥmūd Muḥammad al-Ṭanāḥī and ʿAbd al-Fattāḥ Muḥammad al-Ḥulw (Cairo: ʿĪsā al-Bābī al-Ḥalabī, 1964–76; repr. Cairo: Dār Iḥyā' al-Kutub al-ʿArabiyya, 1992), 2: 140; al-Samʿānī, *al-Ansāb*, ed. ʿAbd al-Raḥmān al-Muʿallimī al-Yamānī (Hyderabad: Dā'irat al-Maʿārif al-ʿUthmāniyya, 1979; repr. Cairo: Maktabat Ibn Taymiyya, 1981–4), 4: 233.

[20] Ibn Ḥajar al-ʿAsqalānī, *Tahdhīb al-tahdhīb* (Hyderabadedn.), 4: 118–19, 5: 215–16, 9: 25, 29; Ibn Abī Ḥātim, *al-Jarḥ*, 2.2: 57; Ibn ʿAbd al-Barr, *al-Intiqā' fī faḍā'il al-a'imma al-fuqahā'*, ed. ʿAbd al-Fattāḥ Abū Ghudda (Beirut: Dār al-Bashā'ir al-Islāmiyya, 1997), 104.

direction of proto-Sunni traditionalism in the middle of the ninth century. The relationship between al-Ḥumaydī and al-Bukhārī, which remains a blind spot in modern scholarship, illustrates why al-Ḥumaydī's contribution to the development of proto-Sunni traditionalism and its discourses of heresy against Abū Ḥanīfa must be accounted for. Al-Ḥumaydī was one of al-Bukhārī's greatest teachers. The friendship between teacher and student probably dates back to al-Bukhārī's visits to the Ḥijāz.[21] We learn from a fairly late source that al-Bukhārī, who apparently was eighteen years old at the time, came to see al-Ḥumaydī. Al-Ḥumaydī was in the middle of a discussion with another scholar concerning a particular ḥadīth. When al-Ḥumaydī saw al-Bukhārī, he declared al-Bukhārī fit and capable of arbitrating the scholarly disagreement. Al-Ḥumaydī and his interlocutor both presented their arguments to al-Bukhārī, and the latter ruled in favour of al-Ḥumaydī because his was the correct position.[22] There are also significant indications of al-Ḥumaydī's impact on al-Bukhārī's scholarship in the latter's *Ṣaḥīḥ*. At least seventy-five ḥadīths in the *Ṣaḥīḥ* are narrated on al-Ḥumaydī's authority.[23] Some of the greatest medieval readers of al-Bukhārī's *Ṣaḥīḥ* were of the view that his selection of the opening ḥadīth of the *Ṣaḥīḥ* was intended, among other things, to serve as a compliment to al-Ḥumaydī:[24]

> ʿAbd Allāh b. al-Zubayr al-Ḥumaydī > Sufyān > Yaḥyā b. Saʿīd al-Anṣārī > Muḥammad b. Ibrāhīm al-Taymī > ʿAlqama b. Waqqāṣ al-Laythī: I heard ʿUmar b. al-Khaṭṭāb on the minbar say: I heard the messenger of God, may God pray over him and grant him peace, say: All actions are in accordance only with their intentions. Thus, every person shall have only that which they intended. So, whomever's migration was for the sake of gaining some material benefit in this world, or for the sake of marrying a spouse, then their migration is for that which they intended.

Students of al-Bukhārī's *Ṣaḥīḥ*, such as Ibn ʿAdī (d. 365/976), Abū Naṣr Aḥmad al-Kalābādhī (d. 398/1008), and Ibn al-Qaysarānī (d. 507/1113), recognised the book's debt to al-Ḥumaydī, and they pointed to the first

[21] On al-Bukhārī's travels and his time in the Ḥijāz see Melchert, 'Bukhārī and his Ṣaḥīḥ', 427–8.

[22] Ibn Ḥajar al-ʿAsqalānī, *Taghlīq al-taʿlīq ʿalā Ṣaḥīḥ al-Bukhārī*, ed. Saʿīd ʿAbd al-Raḥmān Mūsā al-Qazafī (Beirut: al-Maktab al-Islāmī, 1985), 5: 404; Ibn Ḥajar al-ʿAsqalānī, *Hady [sic] al-sārī: muqaddimat Fatḥ al-Bārī*, ed. Muḥammad Fu'ād ʿAbd al-Bāqī and Muḥibb al-Dīn al-Khaṭīb (Beirut: Dār al-Maʿrifa, 1959), 1: 483.

[23] This was Ibn Ḥajar al-ʿAsqalānī's calculation in *Tahdhīb al-tahdhīb* (Hyderabad edn.), 5: 216. The modern authority on al-Ḥumaydī's *Musnad*, al-Ṣuwayyān, corroborates this number against Sezgin's figure of only thirty-three ḥadīths. See al-Ṣuwayyān, *al-Imām ʿAbd Allāh b. al-Zubayr al-Ḥumaydī*, 46 n. 3; Sezgin, *Buhârî'nin Kaynakları*, 213, no. 19. Scott C. Lucas seems aware of Sezgin's figure only: see Lucas, *Constructive Critics*, 363 n. 163.

[24] Al-Bukhārī, *Ṣaḥīḥ*, *kitāb bad' al-waḥy*, *bāb kayfa kāna bad' al-waḥy* 1.

ḥadīth of the *Ṣaḥīḥ* as evidence for this.[25] In al-Dhahabī's view, the first ḥadīth of al-Bukhārī's *Ṣaḥīḥ* was meant to deliver a statement about the book's integrity, and the esteem and pre-eminence of al-Ḥumaydī's transmission achieved precisely this.[26] Ibn Ḥajar al-ʿAsqalānī explained that al-Ḥumaydī was one of al-Bukhārī's greatest teachers. He tells us that al-Bukhārī began the *Ṣaḥīḥ* with al-Ḥumaydī's transmission because the latter was a Meccan, a Qurashī (and the Prophet had commanded that precedence be given to the people of Quraysh), and one of the greatest teachers from whom al-Bukhārī had learnt jurisprudence.[27]

Notwithstanding the prestige of beginning the *Ṣaḥīḥ* with al-Ḥumaydī's transmission, there may have been other reasons guiding al-Bukhārī's decision to open his *Ṣaḥīḥ* with this particular ḥadīth, transmitted by al-Ḥumaydī. It is possible that al-Bukhārī intended to announce at the very outset of his book his opposition to Abū Ḥanīfa and his followers. This very ḥadīth reappears in a number of places in the *Ṣaḥīḥ*, and it is cited by al-Bukhārī in his condemnation of *ḥiyal* (legal tricks), which further suggests that followers of Abū Ḥanīfa were the intended targets of al-Bukhārī's deployment of this tradition.[28] Al-Bukhārī's hostility to Abū Ḥanīfa will be discussed later in this chapter, but it is important to note that al-Ḥumaydī's *Musnad*, which must have been composed before al-Bukhārī's *Ṣaḥīḥ*, begins with the ḥadīth of

[25] Al-Kalābādhī, *Rijāl Ṣaḥīḥ al-Bukhārī*, ed. ʿAbd Allāh al-Laythī (Beirut: Dār al-Maʿrifa, 1987), 1: 406–7; Ibn al-Qaysarānī, *al-Jamʿ bayna kitābay*, 1: 265. Al-Ḥumaydī is mentioned in Ibn Manda, 'Tasmiyat al-mashāyikh alladhīna yarwī ʿanhum al-Imām Abū ʿAbd Allāh Muḥammad b. Ismāʿīl al-Bukhārī fī kitābihi al-jāmiʿ al-ṣaḥīḥ alladhī ṣannafahu', MS 1530, Idārat al-Makhṭūṭāt wa al-Maktabāt al-Islāmiyya bi Wizārat al-Awqāf al-Kuwaytiyya, fols. 1–23, at 14. The manuscript I had access to is a copy of the original Chester Beatty MS 5165, which was edited by Arberry: see 'Tasmiyat al-mashāyikh alladhīna yarwī ʿanhum al-Imām Abū ʿAbd Allāh Muḥammad b. Ismāʿīl al-Bukhārī', ed. Arberry in 'The Teachers of al-Bukhārī', 34–49; I did not have access to this article. This Ibn Manda may be identical to Abū Bakr al-Iṣfahānī, whose work Ibn al-Qaysarānī was collating in the source cited above. See Ibn ʿAdī, *Asāmī man rawā ʿanhum Muḥammad b. Ismāʿīl al-Bukhārī min mashāyikhihi alladhīna dhakarahum fī jāmiʿihi al-ṣaḥīḥ*, ed. ʿĀmir Ḥasan Ṣabrī (Beirut: Dār al-Bashā'ir al-Islāmiyya, 1994), 141, where he acknowledges al-Ḥumaydī's role as someone al-Bukhārī narrated ḥadīth reports from but is quick to note al-Ḥumaydī's close association with al-Shāfiʿī. Not all students of the *Ṣaḥīḥ* referred to the relationship between al-Bukhārī and al-Ḥumaydī. See, e.g., Abū Aḥmad al-Ḥākim (d. 378/988–9), *Kitāb al-Asāmī wa al-kunā*, ed. Yūsuf b. Muḥammad al-Dakhīl (Medina: Maktabat al-Ghurabā' al-Athariyya, 1994), 2: 176. On Abū Aḥmad al-Ḥākim see Khan, 'Before Shurūḥ'.

[26] Al-Dhahabī, *Siyar*, 10: 621.

[27] Ibn Ḥajar al-ʿAsqalānī, *Fatḥ al-bārī*, 1: 10 (Ibn Bāz edn.); Ibn Ḥajar al-ʿAsqalānī, *Tawālī al-ta'sīs li maʿālī Muḥammad b. Idrīs*, ed. Abū al-Fidā' ʿAbd Allāh al-Qāḍī (Beirut: Dār al-Kutub al-ʿIlmiyya, 1986), 244–5.

[28] Al-Bukhārī, *Ṣaḥīḥ*, *kitāb al-ḥiyal*, *bāb* 1. See Chapter 7 below for a discussion of *ḥiyal*.

intention.[29] It seems plausible that al-Bukhārī was framing his *Ṣaḥīḥ* against proto-Ḥanafīs and, in doing so, he was explicitly imitating the method and practice of his teacher, al-Ḥumaydī.

Al-Ḥumaydī's influence over al-Bukhārī's hostility towards Abū Ḥanīfa can be discerned elsewhere. In medieval and modern Arabophone scholarship, much has been made of al-Bukhārī's twenty-five references to 'some people' (*ba'ḍ al-nās*) in the *Ṣaḥīḥ*.[30] It has been pointed out that al-Bukhārī's use of the moniker *ba'ḍ al-nās* did not always imply Abū Ḥanīfa and was intended to denote rationalists and semi-rationalists such as 'Īsā b. Abān, al-Shāfi'ī, and al-Shaybānī.[31] Sunni traditionalists of the tenth century believed that the practice of employing oblique references to Abū Ḥanīfa as a veiled barb preceded al-Bukhārī. Ibn Ḥibbān (d. 354/965) writes:[32]

> I heard al-Ḥasan b. 'Uthmān b. Ziyād < Muḥammad b. Manṣūr al-Jawwār say: I saw al-Ḥumaydī reading the *Book of Refutation against Abū Ḥanīfa* in the sacred mosque, and I noticed that he would say: 'Some people say such and such.' I asked him, 'Why do you not mention them by name?' He replied, 'I dislike mentioning them by name in the sacred mosque.'

The historiographical obsession with al-Bukhārī and the canonisation of his *Ṣaḥīḥ* has contributed to the overshadowing of his teachers and influences. In this and other respects, al-Bukhārī's condemnation of Abū Ḥanīfa as a heretic and deviant owed much to al-Ḥumaydī's leadership. The salient point is not whether al-Ḥumaydī or al-Bukhārī was the first to

[29] Al-Ḥumaydī, *Musnad*, ed. Ḥabīb al-Raḥmān al-A'ẓamī (Karachi: al-Majlis al-'Ilmī, 1963; repr. Beirut: 'Ālam al-Kutub, 1988), 1: 16–17 = ed. Ḥusayn Salīm Asad (Damascus: Dār al-Saqqā, 1996), 1: 163. The line of transmission for the ḥadīth (*isnād*) in al-Ḥumaydī's *Musnad* is identical to the one provided by al-Bukhārī. There is a slight discrepancy in the content (*matn*). Present in al-Ḥumaydī's *Musnad* but absent in al-Bukhārī's *Ṣaḥīḥ* is the following phrase: *fa man kānat hijratuhu ilā Allāh wa rasūlihi, fa hijratuhu ilā Allāh wa rasūlihi.*

[30] For a nineteenth-century treatment of this topic see the treatise of al-Ghunaymī, *Kashf al-iltibās 'ammā awradahu al-imām al-Bukhārī 'alā ba'ḍ al-nās.*

[31] Melchert defines semi-rationalists as a middle party between rationalists and traditionalists of the ninth century: 'Its jurisprudence was formally based on textual sources but with heavier reliance on reason to combine texts than extreme traditionalists allowed; in theology, it upheld the essential traditionalist tenets but elaborated rationalist apologies for them and made concessions that appalled the extreme traditionalists': Melchert, *The Formation of the Sunni Schools of Law*, 70; Melchert, 'The Adversaries of Aḥmad Ibn Ḥanbal', 245–52. Brown has argued, *pace* Melchert, that al-Bukhārī was a traditionalist and not a semi-rationalist (Brown, *The Canonization*, 78–81), and the evidence presented here supports Brown's reading.

[32] Ibn Ḥibbān, *Kitāb al-Majrūḥīn min al-muḥaddithīn wa al-ḍu'afā' wa al-matrūkīn*, ed. Maḥmūd Ibrāhīm Zāyid (Beirut: Dār al-Ma'rifa, 1992), 3: 70 = *Kitāb al-Majrūḥīn min al-muḥaddithīn*, ed. Ḥamdī 'Abd al-Majīd al-Salafī (Riyadh: Dār al-Ṣumay'ī, 2009), 2: 411. On the discrepancies between the manuscripts and modern editions see Chapter 10 below.

use a certain phrase. Karl Mannheim has explained the problems with analyses of this kind and pointed towards the real significance of such phenomena:[33]

Just as it would be incorrect to attempt to derive a language merely from observing a single individual, who speaks not a language of his own but rather that of his contemporaries and predecessors who have prepared a path for him, so it is incorrect to explain the totality of an outlook with reference to its genesis in the mind of an individual. Only in quite a limited sense does the single individual create out of himself the mode of speech and thought we attribute to him. He speaks the language of his group.

Proto-Sunni traditionalists were creating a mode of speech and discourse against Abū Ḥanīfa unique to their network. In using *baʿḍ al-nās* in this particular fashion, al-Bukhārī and al-Ḥumaydī were speaking the language of their group. The decision to employ a generic term and not Abū Ḥanīfa's name was a conscious one and, as al-Ḥumaydī's earlier remark shows, this was probably not an indication of reverence.

The evidence in Ibn Ḥibbān's work also underscores the fact that al-Ḥumaydī may well be considered a pioneer in the promotion of discourses of heresy against Abū Ḥanīfa. There is reasonable evidence that he was one of the first proto-Sunni traditionalists to pen a refutation of Abū Ḥanīfa. Ibn Ḥibbān was not the only scholar aware of a book al-Ḥumaydī had penned attacking Abū Ḥanīfa. Ibn Abī Ḥātim, who had heard traditions from Abū Bakr al-Ṭabarī, stated that al-Ṭabarī transmitted al-Ḥumaydī's *The Refutation against al-Nuʿmān and the Book of Quranic Exegesis*.[34] Abū Bakr al-Ṭabarī, we are told, was a senior companion of Abū Zurʿa al-Rāzī (d. 264/878).[35] He was a truthful (*ṣadūq*) ḥadīth scholar, who adhered to the legal views of Abū Thawr. Abū Zurʿa al-Rāzī remembered al-Ḥumaydī's lessons wherein he read from *The Refutation against al-Nuʿmān*:[36]

The people of Rayy had become corrupted by Abū Ḥanīfa. We were young men, and we fell into this along with the rest of the people of Rayy. It got to a point where I asked Abū Nuʿaym about this, and it led me to realise that I had to do something. Al-Ḥumaydī used to read [to us] *The Refutation* and refer to Abū Ḥanīfa, and I also began to attack him; until, finally, God granted us favour, and we came to realise the deviation of the people.

[33] Mannheim, *Ideology and Utopia*, 2. [34] Ibn Abī Ḥātim, *al-Jarḥ*, 4.1: 40.
[35] On Abū Zurʿa al-Rāzī see Dickinson, *The Development of Early Sunnite Ḥadīth Criticism*, 18.
[36] Ibn Abī Ḥātim, *al-Jarḥ*, 4.1: 40 (*kāna ahl al-rayy qad uftutina bi Abī Ḥanīfa, wa kunnā aḥdāthan najrī maʿahum, wa la qad sa'altu Abā Nuʿaym ʿan hādhā, wa anā arā annī fī ʿamal. Wa la qad kāna al-Ḥumaydī yaqra'u Kitāb al-Radd wa yadhkuru Abā Ḥanīfa, wa anā ahummu bi al-wuthūb ʿalayhi ḥattā manna Allāh ʿalaynā wa ʿarafnā ḍalāta al-qawm*).

One can only speculate about the contents of al-Ḥumaydī's book condemning Abū Ḥanīfa. Might it have looked similar to Ibn Abī Shayba's *Radd ʿalā Abī Ḥanīfa*? One might suppose that al-Ḥumaydī was inspired by his teacher, al-Shāfiʿī, to compose *The Refutation against al-Nuʿmān*. Ibn Abī Ḥātim is again the source for a report that has al-Ḥumaydī express his gratitude for al-Shāfiʿī's intervention against the *aṣḥāb al-ra'y*: 'We desired to refute the *aṣḥāb al-ra'y* but we did not know how best to refute them until al-Shāfiʿī came to us and showed us the way.'[37] However, ascribing this motive to al-Ḥumaydī's authorship of a book condemning Abū Ḥanīfa may be too kind to pro-Shāfiʿī sources.[38]

Though we remain in the dark concerning the exact contents of al-Ḥumaydī's *Kitāb al-Radd ʿalā al-Nuʿmān*, there are traces in other texts of al-Ḥumaydī's contribution to discourses of heresy against Abū Ḥanīfa. The first indication comes from the work of al-Ḥumaydī's faithful student, al-Fasawī. The scene of the report is al-Ḥumaydī's home town, Mecca. We learn that Abū Ḥanīfa was in the Sacred Mosque when somebody asked him about a man who says: 'I testify that the Kaʿba is true, but I do not know whether it is this Kaʿba or not (*ashhadu anna al-kaʿba ḥaqq wa lā adrī hiya hādhihi am lā*).' To this hypothetical question, Abū Ḥanīfa responded: 'Such a person is a true believer (*mu'min ḥaqq*).' Then Abū Ḥanīfa was asked about a man who says: 'I testify that Muḥammad b. ʿAbd Allāh is a prophet, but I do not know whether he is the person whose body rests in Medina or not (*ashhadu anna Muḥammad b. ʿAbd Allāh nabī wa lākin lā adrī huwa alladhī qabruhu bi al-Madīna am lā*).' Abū Ḥanīfa gave the same answer: 'The person who says this is a true believer.' It seems that news of this travelled fast among the residents of the Ḥijāz. When al-Ḥumaydī came to learn of this he declared: 'Whoever holds such a doctrine has committed unbelief (*wa man qāla hādhā fa qad kafara*).'[39] This report belongs to a specific cluster of reports in which Abū Ḥanīfa is hereticised for making what his opponents deemed to be absurd and deviant declarations. It is difficult to identify a point of origin

[37] Ibn Abī Ḥātim, *Ādāb al-Shāfiʿī wa manāqibuhu*, ed. ʿAbd al-Ghanī ʿAbd al-Khāliq (Cairo: Maktabat al-Khānjī, 1993), 41–42 (*kunnā nurīd an narudda ʿalā aṣḥāb al-ra'y fa lam nuḥsin kayfa naruddu ʿalayhim ḥattā jā'anā al-Shāfiʿī fa fataḥa lanā*); al-Bayhaqī, *Manāqib al-Shāfiʿī*, ed. Aḥmad Ṣaqr (Cairo: Dār al-Turāth, 1970), 2: 154.

[38] On al-Ḥumaydī's relationship with al-Shāfiʿī see Ibn Abī Ḥātim, *Ādāb al-Shāfiʿī wa manāqibuhu*, 43–44 (al-Ḥumaydī with Aḥmad b. Ḥanbal and Sufyān b. ʿUyayna talking about al-Shāfiʿī), 97 (al-Shāfiʿī would sometimes pose questions to his son and to al-Ḥumaydī and offer a dinar to whomever gave the correct answer); Ibn Abī Ḥātim, *al-Jarḥ*, 3.2: 202–3; al-Bayhaqī, *Manāqib al-Shāfiʿī*, 2: 326; al-Subkī, *Ṭabaqāt al-shāfiʿiyya al-kubrā*, 2: 140; al-Nawawī, *Kitāb tahdhīb al-asmā'*, ed. F. Wustenfeld (Göttingen: London Society for the Publication of Oriental Texts, 1842–7), 1: 79.

[39] Al-Fasawī, *Kitāb al-Maʿrifa wa al-tārīkh*, 2: 287; al-Lālakā'ī, *Sharḥ uṣūl iʿtiqād ahl al-sunna*, ed. Aḥmad b. Masʿūd b. Ḥamdān (Riyadh: Dār al-Ṭayba, 2003), 5: 997–8.

for questions of this sort. We know that Abū Ḥanīfa and his students proposed accommodating solutions to new Muslims in the eastern provinces of the early Islamic empire, and these very overtures drew the ire of proto-Sunni traditionalists. One can imagine, then, that new Muslims in far-flung regions of the empire with no previous experience or understanding of Islam's Ḥijāzī origins or deep awareness of its founding Prophet's biography might have confessed their ignorance surrounding elementary facts of the religion. Still, Abū Ḥanīfa and his followers were unwilling to place such individuals outside the boundaries of belief. Proto-Sunni traditionalists such as al-Ḥumaydī, however, displayed no sympathy for confessions of ignorance and did not hesitate to assign the label of unbelief to anybody willing to entertain statements of this kind. Moreover, if we maintain our position that ninth-century reports illuminate ninth- and not mid-eighth-century developments, it seems likely that the original context of such questions and their eastern provenance were forgotten by ninth-century proto-Sunni traditionalists.

The study of discourses of heresy against Abū Ḥanīfa during its second iteration has revealed the prominence of a man who has barely featured even on the margins of modern histories of ninth-century proto-Sunnism. This reinforces the view that discourses of heresy concerning Abū Ḥanīfa can unveil key insights concerning the historical development of proto-Sunni traditionalist orthodoxy. The study of one is integral to the study of the other. Abū Bakr al-Ḥumaydī occupied a critical role in the development of proto-Sunni traditionalism. We have surveyed his ideas and activities against Abū Ḥanīfa and his followers. Of no less consequence, however, was al-Ḥumaydī's transmission of these ideas among members of the proto-Sunni traditionalist community. When al-Ḥumaydī declared defiantly that 'as long as I am in the Ḥijāz, Aḥmad [b. Ḥanbal] in Iraq, and Isḥāq [b. Rāhawayh] in Khurāsān, we will never be defeated', it was not intended as a mere rhetorical flourish.[40] Proto-Sunni traditionalists saw themselves as vanguards of orthodoxy, a transregional community engaged in a struggle against heresy.

### *Isḥāq b. Rāhawayh (d. 238/853)*

The transregional and empire-wide phenomenon of proto-Sunnism is neatly captured in the transition from al-Ḥumaydī in the Ḥijāz to Isḥāq b. Rāhawayh in Khurāsān. Isḥāq b. Rāhawayh was born in 161/777–8 in

[40] Al-Dhahabī, *Siyar*, 10: 619.

Marw.[41] He had lived in Khurāsān but he travelled widely, residing both in the Ḥijāz and in Iraq. One report states that he left for Iraq in 184/800 at the age of twenty-three. It was during his residence in Iraq that Isḥāq b. Rāhawayh become one of Aḥmad b. Ḥanbal's closest companions. Isḥāq b. Rāhawayh had studied with a number of prominent proto-Sunni traditionalists. He heard traditions from the likes of Sufyān b. ʿUyayna, Wakīʿ b. Jarrāḥ, and ʿAbd Allāh b. al-Mubārak. He returned to Nīshāpūr and lived out the rest of his life there.[42] He commanded immense respect among his proto-Sunni traditionalist peers. He was one of al-Bukhārī's teachers and is said to have been instrumental in al-Bukhārī's decision to compose his *Ṣaḥīḥ*.[43] Indeed, al-Bukhārī records his details in the *Tārīkh*

[41] There has long been confusion surrounding his name. The usual authorities for pointing ambiguous names, Ibn Ḥajar and Ibn Mākūlā, have nothing to say about this name. Al-Samʿānī, who was extremely well informed about names and places in Khurāsān and Transoxiana, states that his name should read 'Rāhuwayh' but that he was called 'Rāhawayh', seemingly owing to the difficulty of the *ḍamma* on the *hā'*: see al-Samʿānī, *al-Ansāb*, 3: 33–5 (Dār al-Jinān edn.). Ibn Khallikān, on the other hand, proposes 'Rāhwayh' and 'Rahūya'. Various stories surround the origins of his name. A report from his son, Abū al-Ḥasan ʿAlī, states that his father was born with holes in both of his ears. Isḥāq b. Rāhawayh's father was alarmed by this and made inquiries of al-Faḍl b. Mūsā al-Sīnānī, who replied that this was a harbinger of his being a leader of either good or sheer evil. On Isḥāq b. Rāhawayh's son Abū al-Ḥasan ʿAlī (d. 289/901–2), who served as the qadi of Marw and later Nīshāpūr, see al-Samʿānī, *al-Ansāb*, 3: 34 (Dār al-Jinān edn.). On Faḍl b. Mūsā al-Sīnānī (d. 192/808) see Ibn Saʿd, *Ṭabaqāt al-kabīr*, 7: 2, 104 (Leiden edn.); al-Bukhārī, *al-Tārīkh al-kabīr*, 4.1: 117; Ibn Abī Ḥātim, *al-Jarḥ*, 3.2: 28–9; Ibn ʿAdī, *al-Kāmil fī ḍuʿafāʾ al-rijāl*, ed. ʿĀdil Aḥmad ʿAbd al-Mawjūd and ʿAlī Muḥammad Muʿawwiḍ (Beirut: Dār al-Kutub al-ʿIlmiyya, 1997), 1: 195. See also Ibn ʿAbd al-Barr, *al-Intiqāʾ*, 113, where Isḥāq b. Rāhawayh speaks of Faḍl b. Mūsā al-Sinānī as being one of the most reliable scholars from whom he wrote down (or recorded) knowledge. The Ṭāhirid governor ʿAbd Allāh b. Ṭāhir was also said to have demanded an explanation from Isḥāq b. Rāhawayh about the genesis of his name. 'What is the meaning of this?', he asked. 'Do you dislike being addressed with this name?' Isḥāq b. Rāhawayh went on to explain that his father was born whilst travelling (presumably on a palfrey) and this is how he came to acquire the epithet 'Rāhuwī': see al-Khaṭīb al-Baghdādī, *Tārīkh Baghdād*, 7: 365–6. Ibn Khallikān gives a different version of a similar story: Isḥāq b. Rāhawayh's father was born on the road to Mecca. In Persian, 'road' is *rāh* and *wayh* means to find: the one found on the road. See Ibn Khallikān, *Wafāyāt al-aʿyān wa anbāʾ abnāʾ al-zamān*, ed. Iḥsān ʿAbbās (Beirut: Dār al-Ṣādir, 1978), 1: 199–201.

[42] The most comprehensive, though not the earliest, profile of Isḥāq b. Rāhawayh is provided by al-Khaṭīb al-Baghdādī, *Tārīkh Baghdād*, 7: 362–75. See also Ibn Qutayba, *Kitāb al-Maʿārif*, 287; al-Ṣafadī, *al-Wāfī bi al-wafayāt*, ed. Aḥmad al-Arnāʾūṭ and Turkī Muṣṭafā (Beirut: Dār Iḥyāʾ al-Turāth al-ʿArabī, 2000), 8: 251–2; al-Subkī, *Ṭabaqāt al-shāfiʿiyya al-kubrā*, 2: 83–93; Ibn ʿImād, *Shadharāt al-dhahab fī akhbār man dhahab*, ed. ʿAbd al-Qādir al-Arnāʾūṭ and Maḥmūd al-Arnāʾūṭ (Beirut: Dār Ibn Kathīr, 1986–9), 3: 172–3; al-Dhahabī, *Siyar*, 11: 379.

[43] Al-Khaṭīb al-Baghdādī, *Tārīkh Baghdād*, 2: 8; al-Dhahabī, *Tārīkh al-Islām wa wafayāt al-mashāhīr wa al-aʿlām*, ed. ʿUmar ʿAbd al-Salām Tadmurī (Beirut: Dār al-Kitāb al-ʿArabī, 1987–2000), 19: 248; al-Dhahabī, *Juzʾ fīhi tarjamat al-Bukhārī*, ed. Ibrāhīm b. Manṣūr al-Hāshimī (Beirut: Muʾassasat al-Rayyān, 2002), 39. For reports that Isḥāq b. Rāhawayh introduced al-Bukhārī to ʿAbd Allāh b. Ṭāhir, the governor of Khurāsān, see al-Khaṭīb al-Baghdādī, *Tārīkh Baghdād*, 2: 7, 9; al-Dhahabī, *Tārīkh al-Islām*, 19: 249.

*al-kabīr*.[44] Ibn Abī Ḥātim is more generous in telling us what contemporaries thought of Isḥāq b. Rāhawayh's learning. We are told that his father held Isḥāq b. Rāhawayh in great esteem.[45] We also learn in his biographical dictionary of ḥadīth transmitters that Ṣāliḥ b. Aḥmad b. Ḥanbal related that his father, Aḥmad b. Ḥanbal, declared Isḥāq b. Rāhawayh to be one of the leaders of the Muslims.[46] Ibn al-Nadīm described him as the author of three books: *Kitāb al-Sunan fī al-fiqh*, *al-Musnad*, and *Kitāb al-Tafsīr*.[47] In Khurāsān he was referred to as the king of kings (*shāhanshāh*) among the *ʿulamāʾ*.[48]

Like al-Ḥumaydī, Isḥāq b. Rāhawayh was central to the dissemination of discourses of heresy on account of his towering influence among proto-Sunni traditionalists and his active role in transmitting reports hostile to Abū Ḥanīfa. Early on in his career he was sympathetic to Abū Ḥanīfa and his followers. Abū Bakr al-Marrūdhī (d. 275/888) – another crucial contributor to discourses of heresy against Abū Ḥanīfa whose views we shall survey in this chapter – in his *Kitāb al-Waraʿ* presents the following account of Isḥāq b. Rāhawayh's dramatic volte-face:[49]

> I used to be an adherent of speculative jurisprudence (*ṣāḥib raʾy*). When I decided to embark on the greater pilgrimage (*al-ḥajj*), I studied deeply the books of ʿAbd Allāh b. Mubārak. I found therein close to three hundred ḥadīth which agreed with the jurisprudence of Abū Ḥanīfa (*mā yuwāfiq raʾy Abī Ḥanīfa*). I asked ʿAbd Allāh b. Mubārak's teachers in the Ḥijāz and in Iraq about them, and not for a moment did I think that any person would dare oppose Abū Ḥanīfa. When I arrived in Basra, I went to study with (*jalastu ilā*) ʿAbd al-Raḥmān b. Mahdī.

During their first meeting, the following conversation ensued between teacher and student:

ʿABD AL-RAḤMĀN B. MAHDĪ: Where are you from?
ISḤĀQ B. RĀHAWAYH: I am from Marw.
ISḤĀQ B. RĀHAWAYH: Upon hearing of this [that Isḥāq hailed from the same region as Ibn al-Mubārak], ʿAbd al-Raḥmān b. Mahdī prayed for God's mercy to descend upon (*fa taraḥḥama ʿalā*) Ibn al-Mubārak. He loved him a great deal (*wa kāna shadīd al-ḥubb lahu*). He then asked me whether I could recite an elegy (*marthiya*) to celebrate him. 'Yes,' I replied, and I recited the

[44] Al-Bukhārī, *al-Tārīkh al-kabīr*, 1.1: 379–80. [45] Ibn Abī Ḥātim, *al-Jarḥ*, 1.1: 209–10.
[46] Ibn Abī Ḥātim, *al-Jarḥ*, 1.1: 209–10.
[47] Ibn al-Nadīm, *Kitāb al-Fihrist*, 1: 230 (Flugel edn.) = *Kitāb al-Fihrist*, 1: 102 (A. F. al-Sayyid edn.).
[48] Al-Khalīlī, *al-Irshād fī maʿrifat ʿulamāʾ al-ḥadīth*, ed. Muḥammad Saʿid b. ʿUmar Idrīs (Riyadh: Maktabat al-Rushd, 1989), 909–11 (for him and his son).
[49] Abū Bakr al-Marrūdhī, *al-Waraʿ*, ed. Samīr al-Amīn al-Zuhayrī (Riyadh: Dār al-Ṣumayʿī, 1997), 131–5= (I did not have access to the following editions) ed. Muḥammad al-Saʿīd Basyūnī Zaghlūl (Beirut: Dār al-Kitāb al-ʿArabī, 1988) = ed. Zaynab Ibrāhīm al-Qārūṭ (Beirut: Dār al-Kutub al-ʿIlmiyya, 1983).

elegy of Abū Tamīla Yaḥyā b. Wāḍiḥ al-Anṣārī. Ibn al-Mahdī could not stop weeping as I was reciting the elegy, but he stopped abruptly when I recited: ' . . . and with the jurisprudence of al-Nuʿmān you [i.e. Ibn al-Mubārak] acquired knowledge and insight . . . '

ʿABD AL-RAḤMĀN B. MAHDĪ: Enough! You have sullied the elegy (*uskut! qad afsadta al-qaṣīda*).

ISḤĀQ B. RĀHAWAYH: But there are some wonderful verses that follow this.

ʿABD AL-RAḤMĀN B. MAHDĪ: Forget them. How dare you mention ʿAbd Allāh's transmission from Abū Ḥanīfa in the course of an elegy! Do you not know that for ʿAbd Allāh there is nothing more debased than the dirt of Iraq than his transmitting from Abū Ḥanīfa? How I wish he had not transmitted from him (*law wadadtu annahu lam yarwi ʿanhu*)! How I would have ransomed a great portion of my wealth to have ensured that (*wa innī kuntu aftadī dhālika bi ʿaẓm mālī*)!

ISḤĀQ B. RĀHAWAYH: O Abū Saʿīd, why are you so critical of Abū Ḥanīfa (*lima taḥmil ʿalā Abī Ḥanīfa kull hādhā*)? Is it because he would employ forms of speculative jurisprudence (*yatakallamu bi al-ra'y*)? Well, Mālik b. Anas, al-Awzāʿī, and Sufyān all employed forms of speculative jurisprudence.

ʿABD AL-RAḤMĀN B. MAHDĪ: I see, so you consider Abū Ḥanīfa to be in the same league as these people (*taqrunu Abā Ḥanīfa ilā hā'ulā'*)? Abū Ḥanīfa did not resemble these people in learning except in that he was a lone, deviant she-camel grazing in a fertile valley whilst all the other camels were grazing in a different valley altogether (*mā ashbaha Abā Ḥanīfa fī al-ʿilm illā bi nāqa shārida fārida turʿā fī wādī khaṣb wa al-ibl kulluhā fī wādī ākhar*).

ISḤĀQ B. RĀHAWAYH: After this, I started to reflect more deeply and discovered that the people's view of Abū Ḥanīfa's [orthodox] standing was completely at odds with what we in Khurāsān believed about him (*fa idhā al-nās fī amr Abī Ḥanīfa ʿalā khilāf mā kunnā ʿalayhi bi Khurāsān*).

Conversion narratives can be precarious sources of evidence. This particular account appears in a section of al-Marrūdhī's *Kitāb al-Waraʿ* highlighting scholars renowned for their scrupulous piety. The first two reports extol Ibn al-Mubārak and other reports in this section return to his piety and lofty standing. It seems that al-Marrūdhī's central motivation in relating this conversion narrative was to remind readers of Ibn al-Mubārak's regret over having transmitted reports on the authority of Abū Ḥanīfa. In my view, this affords the report greater credibility when considering what it informs us about Isḥāq b. Rāhawayh and discourses of heresy against Abū Ḥanīfa. This narrative account contains precious information about the formation of Isḥāq b. Rāhawayh's religious orientation. It comes from an author who would have been sympathetic to Isḥāq b. Rāhawayh, was intimately aware of his life and career, and was writing within a few decades of his death; yet this does not prevent the author from including material that exhibits Isḥāq b. Rāhawayh's religious *naïveté*.

Beyond the persons involved, we should also consider how important narratives such as these are for any social or religious history of the formation of medieval Sunni orthodoxy. The report shows, for example, that proto-Sunni traditionalists such as Isḥāq b. Rāhawayh recognised the fallacy of local or regional orthodoxies. Increasingly, they appealed to consensus formation with respect to orthodoxy above and beyond regional provincialism. Isḥāq b. Rāhawayh was disabused of the idea that Khurāsān represented the norms of proto-Sunni orthodoxy. A strikingly similar parallel can be observed in Abū Zurʿa al-Rāzī's account of the religious history of Rayy, which we shall encounter later in this study. Communities on the margins of the early Islamic empire were especially susceptible to being overrun by heretical and deviant ideas. Rayy, like Khurāsān, is described as being at odds with the norms of proto-Sunni orthodoxy in the centres of religious learning in early Islamic society. One cannot fail to notice, too, how the story of proto-Sunni orthodoxy in these narratives is the story of discourses of heresy against Abū Ḥanīfa. The agents of proto-Sunni orthodoxy – Abū Bakr al-Ḥumaydī and ʿAbd al-Raḥmān b. Mahdī – are none other than the severest critics of Abū Ḥanīfa. The mnemohistory of Abū Ḥanīfa (discourses of heresy), that is, represented the perfect foil for proto-Sunni traditionalists to define orthodoxy against heresy. Orthodoxy also has in these narratives a crucial disciplinary dimension. It was a process of disciplinary regulation: proto-Sunni traditionalists were successful in disabusing students and scholars of their commitment to deviant and heretical beliefs and practices. The disciplinary interventions of al-Ḥumaydī and ʿAbd al-Raḥmān b. Mahdī were integral to the dominance that orthodoxy established in the provinces of the medieval Islamic world.

This encounter with ʿAbd al-Raḥmān b. Mahdī must be considered to be the turning point of Isḥāq b. Rāhawayh's career. It might even be strengthened by the information we have that Isḥāq b. Rāhawayh's father was extremely close to the qadi of Marw, Faḍl b. Mūsā al-Sīnānī (d. 192/808), who seems to have been a proto-Ḥanafī.[50] We should be aware, nevertheless, that other sources maintain that it was al-Shāfiʿī who had a major impact on Isḥāq b. Rāhawayh's religious formation. Apparently, it was Isḥāq b. Rāhawayh's encounter with al-Shāfiʿī that led the former to abandon his heresy, and a number of scholars from Iraq were said to have made the same transition from heresy to orthodoxy on account of

[50] He appears in Ibn Abī al-ʿAwwām al-Saʿdī, *Faḍāʾil Abī Ḥanīfa wa akhbārihi wa manāqibihi*, ed. Laṭīf al-Raḥmān al-Bahrāʾijī al-Qāsimī (Mecca: al-Maktaba al-Imdādiyya, 2010), 213, 218; and he appears in a *manāqib* report for Abū Ḥanīfa in al-Muwaffaq al-Makkī, *Manāqib Abī Ḥanīfa* [printed with al-Kardarī, *Manāqib Abī Ḥanīfa*] (Hyderabad: Maṭbaʿat Dāʾirat al-Maʿārif al-ʿUthmāniyya, 1894), 1: 123–4.

al-Shāfiʿī's intervention.[51] Isḥāq b. Rāhawayh supposedly declared al-Shāfiʿī the leader of the scholars, adding that of the scholars who employed speculative jurisprudence none was less prone to getting it wrong than al-Shāfiʿī.[52] Another report alleges that Isḥāq b. Rāhawayh was so eager to get his hands on al-Shāfiʿī's books that he married a woman from Marw because he knew she possessed copies of al-Shāfiʿī's writings (by way of her deceased husband).[53] Ibn Abī Ḥātim speaks of Aḥmad b. Ḥanbal sending Isḥāq b. Rāhawayh the *Risāla* of al-Shāfiʿī.[54] There is even an allegation that Isḥāq b. Rāhawayh plagiarised parts of the book.[55] Some reports suggest that Isḥāq b. Rāhawayh had a more lukewarm attitude to al-Shāfiʿī and his ideas. It seems that it took some convincing by Aḥmad b. Ḥanbal to get Isḥāq b. Rāhawayh to give al-Shāfiʿī the time of day.[56] We learn that, after some reluctance, Isḥāq b. Rāhawayh finally agreed to a debate with al-Shāfiʿī concerning the permissibility of selling or renting houses in Mecca, a debate in which Isḥāq b. Rāhawayh outperformed al-Shāfiʿī.[57] These and other reports – that Isḥāq b. Rāhawayh asked a scholar he knew who had al-Shāfiʿī's corpus of writings from al-Buwayṭī to refrain from transmitting and

[51] Ibn Abī Ḥātim, *Ādāb al-Shāfiʿī wa manāqibuhu*, 65; al-Nawawī, *Kitāb Tahdhīb al-asmāʾ*, 78 (*qāla Abū Thawr: kuntu anā wa Isḥāq b. Rāhawayh wa Ḥusayn al-Karābīsī wa jamāʿa min al-ʿirāqiyyīn mā taraknā bidʿatanā ḥattā raʾaynā al-Shāfiʿī*).

[52] Ibn Abī Ḥātim, *Ādāb al-Shāfiʿī wa manāqibuhu*, 90; Fakhr al-Dīn al-Rāzī, *Manāqib al-Imām al-Shāfiʿī*, ed. Aḥmad Saqqā (Cairo: Maktabat al-Kulliyyāt al-Azhariyya, 1986), 64–5; Ibn ʿAbd al-Barr, *al-Intiqāʾ*, 130; al-Nawawī, *Kitāb Tahdhīb al-asmāʾ*, 78 (*al-Shāfiʿī imām al-ʿulamāʾ wa mā yatakallamu aḥad bi al-raʾy illā wa al-Shāfiʿī aqall khaṭaʾ minhu*) in the chapter *faṣl fī shahādat aʾimmat al-islām al-mutaqaddimīn fa man baʿdahum li al-Shāfiʿī bi al-taqaddum fī al-ʿilm wa iʿtirāfihim lahu bihi wa ḥusn thanāʾihim ʿalayhi wa jamīl duʿāʾihim lahu wa waṣfihim lahu bi al-ṣifāt al-jamīla wa al-khilāl al-ḥamīda.*

[53] Ibn Abī Ḥātim, *Ādāb al-Shāfiʿī wa manāqibuhu*, 64; al-Dhahabī, *Tārīkh al-Islām*, 14: 336 finds this to be far-fetched.

[54] Ibn Abī Ḥātim, *Ādāb al-Shāfiʿī wa manāqibuhu*, 62–3 (where Isḥāq b. Rāhawayh is said to have requested the book from Aḥmad b. Ḥanbal); Ibn Abī Ḥātim, *al-Jarḥ*, 3.2: 204.

[55] Ibn Abī Ḥātim, *Ādāb al-Shāfiʿī wa manāqibuhu*, 63; al-Dhahabī, *Tārīkh al-Islām*, 14: 336 doubts this, too.

[56] Ibn ʿAbd al-Barr, *al-Intiqāʾ*, 125; al-Rāzī, *Manāqib al-Imām al-Shāfiʿī*, 223.

[57] Ibn Abī Ḥātim, *Ādāb al-Shāfiʿī wa manāqibuhu*, 42–3, 82, 177–81; al-Bayhaqī, *Manāqib al-Shāfiʿī*, 1: 215; al-Rāzī, *Manāqib al-Imām al-Shāfiʿī*, 272–3; al-Subkī, *Ṭabaqāt al-shāfiʿiyya al-kubrā*, 2: 89–90; al-ʿAlmawī, *al-Muʿīd fī adab al-mufīd wa al-mustafīd*, ed. Aḥmad ʿUbayd (Damascus: al-Maktaba al-ʿArabiyya, 1930), 123–4, 125(for a transcript of a second disputation between Isḥāq b. Rāhawayh and al-Shāfiʿī); Ibn ʿAbd al-Barr, *al-Intiqāʾ*, 74; Ibn Jamāʿa, *Tadkhirat al-sāmiʿ wa al-mutakallim fī adab al-ʿālim wa al-mutaʿallim*, ed. Muḥammad b. Mahdī al-ʿAjmī, 4th edn. (Beirut: Dār al-Bashāʾir al-Islāmiyya, 2012), 102; Abū Shāma al-Maqdisī, *Mukhtaṣar al-muʾammal fī al-radd ilā al-amr al-awwal*, ed. Ṣalāḥ al-Dīn Maqbūl Aḥmad (Kuwait: Maktaba al-Ṣaḥwa al-Islāmiyya, n.d.), 30; al-Nawawī, *Kitāb Tahdhīb al-asmāʾ*, 1: 61; al-Dhahabī, *Tārīkh al-Islām*, 32; Yāqūt al-Ḥamawī, *Muʿjam al-udabāʾ*, 6: 2399–2402 (Dār al-Gharb al-Islāmī edn.). Yāqūt is quoting the debate from two earlier sources: al-Ḥākim's lost *Tārīkh Nīshāpūr* and al-Ābirī's *Kitāb Manāqib al-Shāfiʿī*.

teaching al-Shāfiʿī's books during the scholar's stay in Nīshāpūr, presumably because it might reveal Isḥāq b. Rāhawayh's debt to al-Shāfiʿī – seem designed to extol al-Shāfiʿī at the expense of one of the leading proto-Sunni traditionalists of the ninth century. One explanation for the ambivalence in the primary sources surrounding Isḥāq b. Rāhawayh's relationship to al-Shāfiʿī is implicit in the work of the eleventh-century historian of the *madhhab*s Ibn ʿAbd al-Barr (d. 463/1071), who seems to insinuate that Isḥāq b. Rāhawayh had a healthy scepticism towards al-Shāfiʿī during their time together in Mecca, but that later in Baghdad he studied under him.[58] Shāfiʿī authors of Shāfiʿī biographical dictionaries had other pressures and reasons for claiming Isḥāq b. Rāhawayh as one of their own. Highlighting the influence that al-Shāfiʿī might have had over someone as prominent and esteemed as Isḥāq b. Rāhawayh was certainly in the interests of al-Shāfiʿī's followers, many of whom were still struggling to fend off criticisms from proto-Sunni traditionalists.[59] So, on the one hand, the provenance of much of this material is explicitly favourable to al-Shāfiʿī. On the other hand, there is no reason why both ʿAbd al-Raḥmān b. Mahdī and al-Shāfiʿī could not have figured as important influences upon Isḥāq b. Rāhawayh.

His evolution from someone who respected and acknowledged Abū Ḥanīfa's learning to someone committed to anathematising him and his followers was a defining feature of his religious orientation. Proto-Sunni traditionalists who knew him well remarked on his visceral attacks on Abū Ḥanīfa and his followers. Ibn Qutayba was on close terms with Isḥāq b. Rāhawayh. He transmits material from Isḥāq b. Rāhawayh in a number of his works.[60] More to the point, Ibn

[58] Ibn ʿAbd al-Barr, *al-Intiqāʾ*, 167–8 (*wa mimman akhadha ʿan al-Shāfiʿī ayḍan bi Baghdād baʿd an raʾāhu wa jālasahu bi Makka Abū Yaʿqūb Isḥāq b. Ibrāhīm b. Makhlad, yuʿraf bi Ibn Rāhawayh*). The wording is vague, but my sense is that Ibn ʿAbd al-Barr was fully aware of what sources prior to him had stated about Isḥāq b. Rāhawayh's changing views towards al-Shāfiʿī. As a historian of the *madhhab*s committed to reconciling (though not whitewashing) eighth- and ninth-century conflicts, Ibn ʿAbd al-Barr suggests in a subtle manner that Isḥāq b. Rāhawayh's attitude to al-Shāfiʿī had evolved from when the two first met and debated in Mecca to their rapprochement in Baghdad; though I suspect that Ibn ʿAbd al-Barr was under pressure to relegate Isḥāq b. Rāhawayh to the status of al-Shāfiʿī's student and follower in the light of his writing after the establishment of the medieval Sunni consensus as to the orthodoxy of four Sunni schools and their eponymous founders, which might have the effect of exaggerating the influence of founders and minimising the independence of other jurists and scholars.

[59] On these criticisms see Melchert, 'The Adversaries of Aḥmad Ibn Ḥanbal', 248–9. I do not want to paint too simplistic a picture of pro-Shāfiʿī sources. Many of these works acknowledge, for example, that Isḥāq b. Rāhawayh outperformed al-Shāfiʿī twice in legal disputations. See Ibn Abī Ḥātim, *Ādāb al-Shāfiʿī wa manāqibuhu*, 178, 179; al-Bayhaqī, *Manāqib al-Shāfiʿī*, 1: 215; and Melchert, *The Formation of the Sunni Schools of Law*, 182.

[60] Ibn Qutayba, *Kitāb al-Maʿārif*, 287.

Qutayba knew Isḥāq b. Rāhawayh as a belligerent opponent of Abū Ḥanīfa and his followers:[61]

I have never seen anyone who, when the *aṣḥāb al-ra'y* were mentioned, would speak more reproachfully against them, fault them, instigate against their shameful teachings, and caution against them than Isḥāq b. Ibrāhīm al-Ḥanẓalī, known as Ibn Rāhawayh.

Ibn Qutayba's *Ta'wīl mukhtalif al-ḥadīth* claims to preserve some of Isḥāq b. Rāhawayh's attacks on the *aṣḥāb al-ra'y*. He writes that Isḥāq b. Rāhawayh used to say: 'They abandon (*nabadhū*) the Book of God the almighty and the practices (*sunan*) of His messenger, God pray over him and grant him peace, and instead they adhere to analogical reasoning (*qiyās*).' Ibn Qutayba reassures his readers concerning the sheer quantity of Isḥāq b. Rāhawayh's hostile material.[62] We learn, for example, that Isḥāq b. Rāhawayh attacked Abū Ḥanīfa and his followers for ruling that ritual cleansing (*wuḍū'*) is not required if a man falls into a heavy slumber whilst being seated. He was outraged, then, that the *aṣḥāb al-ra'y* also agreed that a loss of consciousness necessitated the performance of ritual cleansing. Isḥāq b. Rāhawayh failed to see the difference between these two situations.[63] He was equally perturbed by their neglect of Prophetic traditions obligating believers to perform the ritual cleansing upon falling into a state of slumber.[64] He, like many proto-Sunni traditionalists, was incensed by the contradictions that speculative jurisprudence was prone to producing, as well as its failure to acknowledge the authority of Prophetic reports. Ibn Qutayba does not reproduce all of Isḥāq b. Rāhawayh's criticisms, but he does relate Isḥāq b. Rāhawayh's dismay at the legal doctrines of the *aṣḥāb al-ra'y*: their legal views concerning the consequences of laughter during the prayer; the inheritance of grandchildren from their grandfather if their fathers death precedes that of their grandfather; Abū Ḥanīfa's position on raising the hands during the

[61] Ibn Qutayba, *Kitāb Ta'wīl mukhtalif al-ḥadīth*, ed. F. Zakī al-Kurdī (Cairo: Maṭba'at Kurdistān al-'Ilmiyya, 1908), 65 (*wa lam ara aḥadan alhaj bi dhikr aṣḥāb al-ra'y wa tanaqquṣihim wa al-ba'th 'alā qabīḥ aqāwīlihim wa al-tanbīh 'alayhā min* . . .) = ed. Muḥammad Zuhrī Najjār (Cairo: Maktabat al-Kulliyyāt al-Azhariyya, 1973); there seems to be no additional editorial work in this edition, and it seems to me no more than a reprint of the 1908 Cairene edition), 53 = ed. Abū al-Muẓaffar Sa'īd b. Muḥammad al-Sinnārī (Cairo: Dār al-Ḥadīth, 2006), 104 = trans. G. Lecomte as *Le traité des divergences du ḥadīṯ d'Ibn Qutayba (mort en 276/889)* (Damascus: Presses de l'ifpo, 1962), 59 (63), 60–1 (67), 119 (144), 192–3 (198), 317–18 (302), 335 (310).

[62] Ibn Qutayba, *Ta'wīl mukhtalif al-ḥadīth*, 65 (Zakī al-Kurdī edn.).

[63] This particular passage has been translated and analysed by Calder, *Studies in Early Muslim Jurisprudence*, 227–8. This comes in the context of Calder's useful account of legal hermeneutics.

[64] Ibn Qutayba, *Ta'wīl mukhtalif al-ḥadīth*, 65–6 (Zakī al-Kurdī edn.).

prayer; Abū Ḥanīfa's ruling that it is permissible to drink from silver vessels; and many other legal doctrines associated with Abū Ḥanīfa.[65] Isḥāq b. Rāhawayh was outspoken against Abū Ḥanīfa and his followers, and Ibn Qutayba states explicitly that were it not for the fact that the book would become too long he would have documented them all.[66] Among all the details of Isḥāq b. Rāhawayh's hostility towards Abū Ḥanīfa and his followers, it was their 'opposing the Book of God, as if they had never read it' that he found most abhorrent.[67]

Isḥāq b. Rāhawayh's anti-Ḥanafism was one of that lasting legacies that he bequeathed to many of his students and intimate colleagues. Abū al-ʿAbbās al-Sarrāj (d. 313/925) was one of Isḥāq b. Rāhawayh's most impressive students.[68] A towering figure in ḥadīth learning and a native of Khurāsān, al-Sarrāj must be considered one of the leading ḥadīth scholars of the ninth and tenth centuries. Although he was younger than al-Bukhārī and studied under him, there are indications that al-Bukhārī considered him to be a peer.[69] Al-Sarrāj was known to all the familiar historians of ḥadīth learning.[70] Unsurprisingly, no one was more thorough than al-Dhahabī in recording the details of al-Sarrāj's life.[71] There are hints of al-Sarrāj's hostility towards Abū Ḥanīfa and his followers in works prior to al-Dhahabī. However, it is from al-Dhahabī that we receive a precise account of his attitude towards Abū Ḥanīfa and his followers. There is every indication that al-Dhahabī's account was derived from al-Ḥākim's lost history of Nīshāpūr:[72]

[65] Ibn Qutayba, *Ta'wīl mukhtalif al-ḥadīth*, 66–9 (Zakī al-Kurdī edn.).

[66] Ibn Qutayba, *Ta'wīl mukhtalif al-ḥadīth*, 67 (Zakī al-Kurdī edn.).

[67] Ibn Qutayba, *Ta'wīl mukhtalif al-ḥadīth*, 67 (Zakī al-Kurdī edn.).

[68] His full name was Abū al-ʿAbbās Muḥammad b. Isḥāq b. Ibrāhīm al-Thaqafī al-Sarrāj.

[69] See Khalīlī, *al-Irshād*, 959 (Riyadh edn.) (al-Sarrāj transmitted ḥadīth from al-Bukhārī). Al-Sarrāj apparently wrote a *Kitāb al-Tārīkh*: al-Bukhārī studied this book, copied large quantities of the book with his own hand, and al-Sarrāj read the book to him. For this report see al-Khaṭīb al-Baghdādī, *Tārīkh Baghdād*, 2: 56–62, 59.

[70] See al-Khalīlī, *al-Irshād*, 828–30, 910 (Riyadh edn.); al-Khaṭīb al-Baghdādī, *Tārīkh Baghdād*, 2: 56–62; Ibn Abī Ḥātim, *al-Jarḥ*, 3.2: 196; Ibn Nuqṭa, *al-Taqyīd li maʿrifat al-ruwāt wa al-sunan wa al-masānīd* (Hyderabad: Dā'irat al-Maʿārif al-ʿUthmāniyya, 1983), 18–19. For his students in Jurjān see Ḥamza b. Yūsuf al-Sahmī, *Tārīkh Jurjān aw kitāb maʿrifat ʿulamā' ahl Jurjān*, ed. ʿAbd al-Raḥmān al-Muʿallimī (Hyderabad: Dā'irat al-Maʿārif al-ʿUthmāniyya, n.d.; repr. Beirut: ʿĀlam al-Kutub, 1987), 95, 172, 187, 260, 414, 513, 540, 546. For some of his writings see Ibn al-Nadīm, *Kitāb al-Fihrist*, 1: 477–8 (A. F. al-Sayyid edn.) (*Kitāb al-Akhbār*, which contains information on ḥadīth scholars (*al-muḥaddithīn*), viziers (*al-wuzarā'*), and governors (*al-wulāt*); *Rasā'il*; and *al-Ashʿār al-mukhtāra wa al-ṣaḥīḥa minhā wa al-muʿāra*).

[71] Al-Dhahabī, *Kitāb Tadhkirat al-ḥuffāẓ*, ed. ʿAbd al-Raḥmān b. Yaḥyā al-Muʿallimī (Hyderabad: Dā'irat al-Maʿārif al-ʿUthmāniyya, 1954), 2: 731–5; al-Dhahabī, *Tārīkh al-Islām*, 23: 462–4.

[72] Al-Dhahabī, *Tārīkh al-Islām*, 23: 463.

Al-Ḥākim said: Abū Aḥmad b. Abī al-Ḥasan said: 'Ibn Khuzayma sent me to Abū al-ʿAbbās al-Sarrāj, and he told me to pass on the following message to him: "Stop mentioning Abū Ḥanīfa and his followers [in a negative light] because the people of our region are becoming confused." I delivered this message to him [al-Sarrāj] and he scolded me (*amsik ʿan dhikr Abī Ḥanīfa wa aṣḥābihi fa inna ahl al-balad qad shawwashū fa addaytu al-risāla fa zabaranī*).'

Al-Sarrāj made further protests concerning the influence of the teachings of Abū Ḥanīfa in Nīshāpūr. He was disturbed by the widespread acceptance of Ḥanafī rituals and practices in his native province and sought to bring to an end the practice of pronouncing the *iqāma* (the final call to prayer) according to the Ḥanafī position. He decided to launch a complaint with the city's governor:

O governor, the *iqāma* has always been pronounced singly (*furādā*) [in contrast to the doubling in the *adhān*], and this is how it is in the Two Holy Sanctuaries [Mecca and Medina]. However, in our city's mosque it is pronounced in pairs (*mathnā mathnā*) [just as it is done in the *adhān*]. Now, our faith emerged from the Two Holy Sanctuaries, so I implore you to instruct that it be recited singly (*bi al-afrād*).

Al-Sarrāj's forthright protest astonished the governor and everyone else who was present. Al-Sarrāj had been brought into the governor's presence to provide some counsel concerning the (worldly) affairs of the city (*amr al-balad*), and here he was lecturing the governor about the history of the religion and its correct practices. As al-Sarrāj exited the governor's presence, the entire gathering condemned him. Al-Sarrāj himself felt no remorse, except that he was ashamed before God were he to speak to worldly matters (*amr al-dunyā*) and neglect matters of the religion (*amr al-dīn*).[73]

Later in our section treating discourses of heresy in Ibn Qutayba's *ouevre* we shall see the degree to which Isḥāq b. Rāhawayh's antipathy towards Abū Ḥanīfa is reflected in the religious thought of Ibn Qutayba. We must turn now to another one of Isḥāq b. Rāhawayh and al-Ḥumaydī's disciples, who occupied an important status as one of the agents of proto-Sunni traditionalist orthodoxy.

### *Al-Bukhārī (d. 256/870)*

Al-Bukhārī's condemnation of Abū Ḥanīfa is discussed in more than one place in this study. Chapter 5 contains an extensive treatment of al-Bukhārī's discourse of heresy against Abū Ḥanīfa and its relationship to ethnogenesis in early Islamicate societies. That section examines

[73] Al-Dhahabī, *Tārīkh al-Islām*, 23: 463–4.

al-Bukhārī's deprecation of Abū Ḥanīfa in his *Kitāb Raf' al-yadayn fī al-ṣalāt*. Since Chapter 3 is concerned with examining the role that ethnogenesis had in discourses of heresy against Abū Ḥanīfa, al-Bukhārī's biography and his upbringing are described in detail there. This section studies discourses of heresy against Abū Ḥanīfa and his followers in al-Bukhārī's *al-Tārīkh al-kabīr*, *al-Tārīkh al-awsaṭ*,[74] *al-Jāmi' al-Ṣaḥīḥ*, and *Kitāb Khalq af'āl al-'ibād*.

We learned in the section on al-Ḥumaydī that his influence on al-Bukhārī's religious formation and, in particular, the *Ṣaḥīḥ* was considerable. The very decision to begin the *Ṣaḥīḥ* with al-Ḥumaydī – an antagonist of Abū Ḥanīfa – and with the ḥadīth concerning the primacy of intentions in the performance of acts and rites raises the possibility that Abū Ḥanīfa and proto-Ḥanafīs were prime targets of al-Bukhārī's *al-Jāmi' al-Ṣaḥīḥ*. The ḥadīth of intention is cited by al-Bukhārī strategically in a number of places, and he seemed to have believed that it was a proof text against proto-Ḥanafī uses of *ḥiyal*.[75] The *Ṣaḥīḥ* was a landmark and controversial composition.[76] It made claims not just about the primacy of rigorously authenticated Prophetic reports. It entailed a statement about the sources of Islamic law, too. The comprehensive range of the *Ṣaḥīḥ* and its ordering around legal chapters provided al-Bukhārī with multiple opportunities to undermine the religious credibility of proto-Ḥanafīs. Let us consider, for example, al-Bukhārī's deployment of the moniker *ba'ḍ al-nās* for Abū Ḥanīfa and his disciples. We learned earlier that this label was shot through with subversive undertones and that it originated with al-Bukhārī's teacher, al-Ḥumaydī. Al-Bukhārī's *Ṣaḥīḥ* contains references to Mālik b. Anas, al-Shāfi'ī, and Aḥmad b. Ḥanbal.[77] Abū Ḥanīfa is not mentioned by name throughout the *Ṣaḥīḥ*. Mālik b. Anas, al-Shāfi'ī, and Aḥmad b. Ḥanbal are all referred to by al-Bukhārī on account either of their legal opinions or their transmissions of ḥadīth. Al-Bukhārī's

[74] This work has been published in different editions, though the preferred one is al-Bukhārī, *al-Tārīkh al-awsaṭ [Kitāb al-Mukhtaṣar]*, ed. Taysīr b. Sa'd Abū Ḥaymad (Riyadh: Dār al-Rushd, 2005).

[75] Al-Bukhārī, *al-Jāmi' al-Ṣaḥīḥ*, *kitāb al-ḥiyal; kitāb al-īmān, bāb mā jā'a anna al-a'māl bi al-niyyāt; kitāb al-'itq, bāb al-khaṭa' wa al-nisyān; kitāb al-manāqib al-anṣār, bāb hijrat al-nabī ilā al-madīna; kitāb al-nikāḥ, bāb man hājara aw 'amila khayran li yatazawwija imra'a; kitāb al-īmān wa al-nudhur, bāb al-niyya wa al-īmān; kitāb al-ḥiyal fī tark al-ḥiyal wa anna li kull imra'a mā nawā*.

[76] Brown, *The Canonization*, 93–6.

[77] Al-Bukhārī, *al-Jāmi' al-Ṣaḥīḥ*, *kitāb al-zakāt, bāb fī al-rikāz al-khums* (Mālik b. Anas and al-Shāfi'ī); *kitāb al-buyū', bāb tafsīr al-'arāyā* (Mālik b. Anas and al-Shāfi'ī); *kitāb al-maghāzī, bāb kam ghazā al-nabī ṣallā Allāhu 'alayhi wa sallama and kitāb al-nikāḥ, bāb mā yaḥillu min al-nisā' wa mā yaḥrumu* (Aḥmad b. Ḥanbal). As far as I have been able to ascertain, al-Bukhārī transmits no ḥadīth through al-Shāfi'ī, though he does transmit numerous ḥadīth reports through Mālik b. Anas and Aḥmad b. Ḥanbal.

*baʿḍ al-nās* moniker for Abū Ḥanīfa is reserved exclusively for cases where al-Bukhārī describes an opposing position. He cites *baʿḍ al-nās* on twenty-seven occasions. Abū Ḥanīfa and his followers were natural targets for al-Bukhārī's section on legal tricks (*kitāb al-ḥiyal*).[78] This book alone contains fourteen references to *baʿḍ al-nās*.[79] It opens with the same theme and ḥadīth report (with slight variations) with which al-Bukhārī opens his *Ṣaḥīḥ*:

> The chapter on abandoning legal tricks and that for every person is that which he intends with respect to oaths and other things. Abū al-Nuʿmān < Ḥammād b. Zayd < Yaḥyā b. Saʿīd < Muḥammad b. Ibrāhīm < ʿAlqama b. Waqqāṣ said: 'I heard ʿUmar b. al-Khaṭṭāb as he was giving a sermon say: "I heard the Prophet, God pray over him and grant him peace, say: 'O people. Actions are by intentions only. A man only obtains that which he intends. Whosoever's migration was to (and for) God and His Messenger, then his migration was to God and His Messenger. Whosever migrated for this world seeking to obtain something of it, or for the sake of marrying a woman, then his migration was for the sake of that which he migrated.'"'

At one point in the book on legal tricks al-Bukhārī drops this equivocating manner of criticising Abū Ḥanīfa and his followers:[80]

> The chapter on gifts and pre-emption. Certain persons have said: if someone gifts a gift of one hundred dirhams or more, and this gift has remained with the person for many years and the giver seeks a legal trick and then the gift-giver seeks to retrieve the gift, then there is no *zakāt* due on either of the two. He/they has opposed the messenger, God pray over him and grant him peace, in the matter of gifts; and he has eliminated [the obligation of] *zakāt* (*fa khālafa al-rasūl ṣallā Allāhu ʿalayhi wa sallama fī al-hiba wa asqaṭa al-zakāt*).

We see here a rapid transition of tone and style in the *Ṣaḥīḥ*. Al-Bukhārī accuses his interlocutor of opposing the Messenger in relation to the issue of gifts and he insists that his opponent's doctrine amounts to nothing less than vitiating altogether the obligation of *zakāt*. It is the shift in al-Bukhārī's mode of argumentation that adds weight to the view that *baʿḍ al-nās* was a reference to Abū Ḥanīfa and his followers, and that it was one that al-Bukhārī invoked whenever he sought to discredit proto-Ḥanafīs and their eponymous founder.

The earliest commentators on al-Bukhārī's *Ṣaḥīḥ* were not consistent in taking up the theme of the *Ṣaḥīḥ*'s opposition to proto-Ḥanafīs and Abū Ḥanīfa. The earliest extant commentary is al-Khaṭṭābī's

[78] On discourses of heresy against Abū Ḥanīfa on account of his alleged use of *ḥiyal* see Chapter 7 below.

[79] Sixteen references if one includes two references to *qāla baʿḍuhum*.

[80] Al-Bukhārī, *al-Jāmiʿ al-Ṣaḥīḥ*, *kitāb al-ḥiyal*, *bāb fī al-hiba wa al-shufʿa*.

(d. 388/998) *Aʿlām al-ḥadīth*.[81] There is good evidence to suggest that al-Khaṭṭābī was a Shāfiʿī in jurisprudence. He is described as a Shāfiʿī in almost all the main biographical dictionaries of the Shāfiʿī school.[82] He wrote a commentary on al-Muzanī's *Mukhtaṣar*. This work has not survived, but al-Subkī had access to it and al-Nawawī depended on it as one of his sources for his *Tahdhīb al-asmāʾ wa al-lughāt*.[83] Additionally, al-Khaṭṭābī wrote a biographical account of al-Shāfiʿī.[84] Despite these indications of al-Khaṭṭābī's loyalty to the Shāfiʿī school, Abū Ḥanīfa and his followers are not assailed in al-Khaṭṭābī's commentary. Abū Ḥanīfa appears only once by name in the work.[85] Al-Khaṭṭābī does, however,

[81] See Aḥmad ʿAbd Allāh al-Bātilī, *al-Imām al-Khaṭṭābī: al-muḥaddith al-faqīh wa al-adīb al-shāʿir* (Damascus: Dār al-Qalam, 1996). Both Brown (*The Canonization*, 134) and Tokatly ('The Aʿlām al-ḥadīth of al-Khaṭṭābī', 54) tell us that al-Khaṭṭābī was the first commentator on al-Bukhārī's *Ṣaḥīḥ*. In truth, al-Khaṭṭābī's is only the earliest surviving commentary. The earliest recorded commentaries are :1. Abū ʿAlī al-Ḥasan b. Muḥammad b. Ḥusayn b. al-Ḥasan b. Jaʿfar al-Ḥusaynī al-ʿAlawī al-Baghdādī (d. 358/969), *al-Kawkab al-nahārī fī sharḥ Ṣaḥīḥ al-Bukhārī*; 2. Abū Aḥmad Muḥammad b. Aḥmad b. al-Ḥusayn b. al-Qāsim b. al-Ghiṭrīf b. al-Jahm al-Ghiṭrīfī al-ʿAbdī al-Jurjānī al-Ribāṭī (d. 377/987–8), *al-Musnad al-ṣaḥīḥ ʿalā Ṣaḥīḥ al-Bukhārī* (see Muḥammad b. Jaʿfar al-Kattānī, *al-Risāla al-mustaṭrafa li bayān mashhūr kutub al-sunna al-masharrafa* (Beirut: Dār al-Bashāʾir al-Islāmiyya, 1993), 88; and al-Dhahabī, *Kitāb Tadhkirat al-ḥuffāẓ*, 3: 971–3); 3. Muḥammad b. Muḥammad b. Aḥmad b. Isḥāq al-Nīshāpūrī al-Ḥākim (d. 378/988), *Muṣannaf ʿalā al-Jāmiʿ al-Ṣaḥīḥ*; and 4. Abū ʿAbd Allāh Muḥammad b. al-ʿAbbās b. Aḥmad b. Muḥammad b. Abī Dhuhl al-Harawī (d. 378/988), *al-Muṣannaf al-ṣaḥīḥ ʿalā Ṣaḥīḥ al-Bukhārī*. For these and the most comprehensive account of commentaries on al-Bukhārī's *Ṣaḥīḥ* see ʿAbd Allāh Muḥammad al-Ḥibshī, *Jāmiʿ al-shurūḥ wa al-ḥawāshī: muʿjam shāmil li al-asmāʾ al-kutub al-mashrūḥa fī al-turāth al-Islāmī wa bayān shurūḥihā* (Abu Dhabi: al-Majmaʿ al-Thaqāfī, 2004), 1: 396–438. These are explicitly commentaries, but literary responses and interactions with al-Bukhārī's *Ṣaḥīḥ* go back to Ibn Abī Ḥātim who wrote a critical commentary, for which see al-Sakhāwī, *al-Iʿlān bi al-tawbīkh li man dhamma ahl al-tārīkh*, ed. Franz Rosenthal (Beirut: Mu'assasat al-Risāla, 1986), 207; Sezgin, *GAS*, 1: 179; and Dickinson, *The Development of Early Sunnite Ḥadīth Criticism*, 29–30. Al-Māsarjasī (d. 365/975–6) and Abū Aḥmad al-Ḥākim (d. 378/988) both authored *Mustakhraj*s. Al-Ḥākim's lost history is the first to mention their *Mustakhraj*s on al-Bukhārī and Muslim's *Ṣaḥīḥ*s, and we know this via the usual channel for such recondite matters in the history of ḥadīth, al-Dhahabī, *Siyar*, 16: 287–9; al-Dhahabī, *Tarājim al-aʾimma al-kibār aṣḥāb al-sunan wa al-āthār*, ed. Fahmī Saʿd (Beirut: ʿĀlam al-Kutub, 1993), 146; al-Ḥākim al-Nīshāpūrī, *Tārīkh Nīshāpūr*, ed. Muḥammad Riḍā Shafīʿī Kadkanī (Tehran: Āgāh, 1996), 187; al-Dhahabī, *Kitāb Tadhkirat al-ḥuffāẓ*, 3: 976–9. See Khan, 'Before Shurūḥ'.

[82] Al-Subkī, *Ṭabaqāt al-shāfiʿiyya al-kubrā*, 3: 282–90; al-Asnawī, *Ṭabaqāt al-shāfiʿiyya*, ed. ʿAbd Allāh al-Jubūrī (Riyadh: Dār al-ʿUlūm, 1981), 1: 467–8; Qāḍī Ibn Shuhba, *Ṭabaqāt al-shāfiʿiyya* (Hyderabad: Dāʾirat al-Maʿārif al-ʿUthmāniyya, 1978), 1: 140–1; al-ʿAbbādī, *Kitāb Ṭabaqāt al-fuqahāʾ al-shāfiʿiyya*, ed. Gösta Vitestam (Leiden: Brill, 1964), 94–6.

[83] Al-Subkī, *Ṭabaqāt al-shāfiʿiyya al-kubrā*, 3: 290; al-Nawawī, *Kitāb Tahdhīb al-asmāʾ*, 1: 8–9; al-Bātilī, *al-Imām al-Khaṭṭābī*, 1: 207–8.

[84] Al-Rāzī, *Manāqib al-Imām al-Shāfiʿī*, 225. And, as Christopher Melchert has reminded me (personal communication), al-Khaṭṭābī's commentaries regularly endorse al-Shāfiʿī's juridical views.

[85] Al-Khaṭṭābī, *Aʿlām al-ḥadīth fī sharḥ Ṣaḥīḥ al-Bukhārī*, ed. Muḥammad b. Saʿd b. ʿAbd al-Raḥmān al-Saʿūd (Mecca: al-Jāmiʿat Umm al-Qurā, 1988), 1415–19 (during a discussion on the obligation to obey rulers).

refer to the legal views of the *aṣḥāb al-ra'y* a number of times alongside other jurists, but not to criticise them.[86]

The same cannot be said of the second major commentator on al-Bukhārī's *Ṣaḥīḥ*. Al-Bukhārī's points of conflict with Abū Ḥanīfa and the Ḥanafīs acquire a prominent place in Ibn Baṭṭāl's (d. 449/1057) commentary. Ibn Baṭṭāl describes and refutes Abū Ḥanīfa's legal views on countless occasions.[87] Hostility towards Abū Ḥanīfa and his followers in al-Bukhārī's *Ṣaḥīḥ* would continue to occupy commentators from the High Middle Periods.[88] This discussion culminated in an intense debate between, arguably, the two greatest authorities on al-Bukhārī's *Ṣaḥīḥ* in the Mamlūk period.[89]

[86] Al-Khaṭṭābī, *A'lām al-ḥadīth*, 304 (alongside other jurists such as Mālik b. Anas, Aḥmad b. Ḥanbal, and Sufyān al-Thawrī), 512–13 (*bāb idhā raka'a dūna al-ṣaff*, alongside Mālik b. Anas and al-Shāfi'ī), 625 (*kitāb tafsīr al-ṣalāt, bāb mā jā'a fī al-taqṣīr wa kam yuqīm ḥattā yaqṣura*), 628 (*bāb fī kam yaqṣur al-ṣalāt*), 970 (*bāb man māta wa 'alayhi al-ṣawm*, mentioned alongside al-Shāfi'ī), 1246 (*bāb qismat al-ghanam*, mentioned in juxtaposition to the majority of scholars (*akthar al-'ulamā'*)); for mentions of the *fuqahā' al-'Irāq*: 114 (in juxtaposition to the Shāfi'īs), 216 (in juxtaposition to the *ahl al-Ḥijāz*), 282, 1031 (mentioned in the context of the *ahl al-'Irāq* opposing the outward meaning of the ḥadīth), 1110, 1197, 1855; for *ahl al-Kūfa*: 235 (*bāb isbāgh al-wuḍū'*, mentioned alongside Aḥmad b. Ḥanbal), 653 (*bāb idhā ṣallā khamsan*), 1416, 2086 (*bāb al-khamr min al-'inab wa ghayrihi*). I should add that I have major misgivings about Tokatly's understanding of al-Khaṭṭābī's commentary, and I have detailed these in my forthcoming re-examination of *A'lām al-ḥadīth*: see Khan, 'Ḥadīth Commentary and Philology in the Tenth-Century'.

[87] Ibn Baṭṭāl, *Sharḥ Ṣaḥīḥ al-Bukhārī*, ed. Abū Tamīm Yāsir b. Ibrāhīm (Riyadh: Maktabat al-Rushd, 2000), 1: 122, 227, 275, 408–10, 425–6; 2: 117–18, 163–4, 165, 267; 3: 5, 189, 453, 466–8, 484, 498, 530–1, 525, 568; 4: 21, 67, 101, 225, 255, 257, 314, 320, 340–1, 382, 402, 448, 492, 528–9; 5: 67, 157, 376; 6: 143, 167, 185–6, 233, 309, 314–15, 327, 380, 383, 419, 422, 426, 439, 446, 465, 474, 524–5; 7: 11, 120, 144, 256, 421, 456, 548; 8: 19–20, 25, 61, 148, 157–8, 192–4, 311–12, 321–3, 367–8, 451, 467, 469, 550, 623.

[88] This study is not concerned with post-classical debates about the perceived hostility between al-Bukhārī and Abū Ḥanīfa. So my references here (and for al-'Aynī and Ibn Ḥajar) are exemplary and not comprehensive. See Ibn al-Mulaqqin, *al-Tawḍīḥ li sharḥ al-Jāmi' al-Ṣaḥīḥ*, ed. Khālid al-Ribāṭ (Qatar: Wizārat al-Awqāf wa al-Shu'ūn al-Islāmiyya, 2008), 16: 456–7, 510; 17: 209; 25: 329; 30: 351; 32: 37, 63.

[89] See al-'Aynī, *'Umdat al-qārī fī sharḥ Ṣaḥīḥ al-Bukhārī* (Beirut: Idārat al-Ṭibā'a al-Munīriyya and Beirut: Dār al-Kutub al-'Ilmiyya, 2001), 24: 112; Ibn Ḥajar al-'Asqalānī, *Fatḥ al-bārī*, 3: 364 (Ibn Bāz edn.) (I have used three editions of this work at different institutions, among which the Būlāq edition is the preferred edition: ed. Naẓar al-Faryābī (Riyadh: Dār al-Ṭayba, 2005). Blecher, 'Revision in the Manuscript Age', 41, n. 14 is unaware of al-Faryābī's edition). On the rivalry see Ibn Ḥajar al-'Asqalānī, *Intiqāḍ al-i'tirāḍ fī al-radd 'alā al-'Aynī fī sharḥ al-Bukhārī*, ed. Ḥamdī b. 'Abd al-Majīd al-Salafī and Ṣubḥī b. Jāsim al-Sāmarrā'ī (Riyadh: Maktabat al-Rushd, n.d.). Joel Blecher's thesis does not treat commentarial debates surrounding al-Bukhārī's use of *ba'ḍ al-nās*. However, he has a brief discussion of Ḥanafī and Shāfi'ī rivalry as reflected in the commentaries of Ibn Ḥajar and al-'Aynī with respect to one particular ḥadīth. See Blecher, 'In the Shade of the Ṣaḥīḥ', 90–1.

Let us now turn to other venues where we can observe al-Bukhārī's denunciation of Abū Ḥanīfa. One major contention of this book is that discourses of heresy were weaponised in the process of constructing orthodoxy against the proximate other. The proximate other, as Jonathan Z. Smith has explained, posed an immense threat to pre-modern religious communities: 'The radically "other" is merely "other"; the proximate "other" is problematic, and hence, of supreme interest.'[90] Abū Ḥanīfa and his followers should be understood as the proximate other, and it is in this light that the discourse of heresy against Abū Ḥanīfa can be understood. In many ways Abū Ḥanīfa was a proto-Sunnī. But he and his followers differed in some important respects on questions of law, theology, and politics. As a proximate movement to proto-Sunnī traditionalism, these distinctions became inflated, and proto-Ḥanafism emerged as a problematic proximate other. More than one of the proto-Sunni traditionalists we have studied were at one time trained as proto-Ḥanafīs and thought highly of Abū Ḥanīfa. We do not know whether al-Bukhārī studied under proto-Ḥanafīs, but there can be little doubt that al-Bukhārī encountered proto-Ḥanafīs in Khurāsān, Transoxiana, and Baghdad.[91] There are other indications that al-Bukhārī had even memorised the books of proto- or semi-Ḥanafīs. Consider, for example, the narration of al-Firabrī on the authority of al-Bukhārī's copyist, Muḥammad b. Abī Ḥātim, that at the age of thirteen al-Bukhārī had memorised the books of Ibn al-Mubārak and Wakīʿ b. al-Jarrāh and that his familiarity with these works had endowed him with an intimate awareness of the ideas and writings of such people (*wa ʿaraftu kalām hāʾulāʾ*).[92] Later authors such as Ibn Ḥajar explained that *kalām hāʾulāʾ* was an oblique reference to proto- or semi-Ḥanafīs (*aṣḥāb al-raʾy*).[93] It seems, therefore, that, like the proto-Sunni traditionalists he studied with, al-Bukhārī's hostility towards Abū Ḥanīfa was informed by his interactions with proto-Ḥanafīs and their writings.[94] Agents of proto-Sunnī traditionalist orthodoxy, such as al-Bukhārī, were particularly sensitive to the differences they perceived to exist among the proximate other. These small differences were magnified by agents of orthodoxy and became of supreme interest to them, which is why the proximate other

[90] See Smith, 'What a Difference a Difference Makes'.

[91] Later historians report that al-Bukhārī met Muʿallā b. Manṣūr in 210/825–6 (see Ibn Ḥajar al-ʿAsqalānī, *Taghlīq al-taʿlīq*, 5: 389; al-Dhahabī, *Tārīkh al-Islām*, 19: 240).

[92] Al-Khaṭīb al-Baghdādī, *Tārīkh Baghdād*, 2: 325.

[93] Ibn Ḥajar al-ʿAsqalānī, *Hady* [*sic*] *al-sārī* (Bulaq edn.), 479. It seems the manuscript evidence establishes that Ibn Ḥajar entitled his work *Hudā al-sārī*.

[94] For the story that the Ḥanafī scholar Abū Ḥafṣ al-Bukhārī had al-Bukhārī expelled from Bukhārā, see al-Sarakhsī, *Kitāb al-Mabsūṭ* (Beirut: Dār al-Maʿrifa, 1989; repr. Cairo: Dār al-Saʿāda, 1906–1913), 30: 297.

(Abū Ḥanīfa and his followers) featured so heavily in discourses of heresy and orthodoxy.

In the light of the scarce background information on al-Bukhārī's interactions with proto-Ḥanafīs, we can turn directly to al-Bukhārī's *Histories* to examine his contribution to discourses of heresy against Abū Ḥanīfa. Al-Bukhārī composed three *Histories*: *al-Tārīkh al-kabīr*, *al-Tārīkh al-awsaṭ* (*Kitāb al-Mukhtaṣar*), and *al-Tārīkh al-ṣaghīr*. The first two have survived, but the third is no longer extant.[95] Al-Bukhārī also dedicated two works to the history of weak ḥadīth scholars: *Kitāb al-Ḍuʿafāʾ al-kabīr* and *Kitāb al-Ḍuʿafāʾ al-ṣaghīr*. The former is lost, whilst the latter has been published.[96] There are attacks on Abū Ḥanīfa and his students across all of these published works. Al-Bukhārī's *al-Tārīkh al-kabīr* devotes an entry to Abū Ḥanīfa. He dismisses Abū Ḥanīfa as belonging to a movement which proto-Sunni traditionalists deemed to be heretical, the Murjiʾa. He further explains that the scholarly community renounced (*sakatū ʿanhu*) Abū Ḥanīfa, his speculative jurisprudence, and his ḥadīth.[97] In the parlance of ḥadīth specialists, *sakatū ʿan* did not denote the silence of scholars. This particular phrase was a severe indictment of a scholar, and ḥadīth scholars understood al-Bukhārī's use of the term as his particular way of denouncing a scholar.[98] The religious deviancy of Abū Ḥanīfa is a theme to which al-

95 *Al-Tārīkh al-awsaṭ* (*Kitāb al-Mukhtaṣar*) has been published twice under the mistaken title of *al-Tārīkh al-ṣaghīr*: (Hyderabad: Maṭbaʿat Dāʾirat al-Maʿārif al-ʿUthmāniyya, n. d.) = ed. Maḥmūd Ibrāhīm Zāyid (Beirut: Dār al-Maʿrifa, 1986). *Al-Tārīkh al-awsaṭ* has been published properly as *al-Tārīkh al-awsaṭ*, ed. Muḥammad Ibrāhīm al-Luḥaydān (Riyadh: Dār al-Ṣumayʿī, 1998) and *al-Tārīkh al-awsaṭ [Kitāb al-Mukhtaṣar]*, ed. Saʿd Abū Ḥaymad (Riyadh: Maktabat al-Rushd, 2005), the latter being the superior edition and the one I try to cite. *Al-Tārīkh al-awsaṭ* was known to medieval authors as *Kitāb al-Mukhtaṣar*. This is how al-Bukhārī himself refers to it in *al-Tārīkh al-kabīr*, 4.1: 87. *Al-Tārīkh al-awsaṭ* has two recensions. Four manuscripts for the recension of Zanjawayh (d. 318/930) and one for al-Khaffāf (d. 294/906–7?). For more on the problems with previous editions of *al-Tārīkh al-awsaṭ* see al-Bukhārī, *al-Tārīkh al-awsaṭ [Kitāb al-Mukhtaṣar]*, 1: 114 ff. (Abū Ḥaymad edn.) (editor's introduction). Al-Kalābādhī, *Rijāl Ṣaḥīḥ Bukhārī*, 1: 253 (entry for Rafīʿ b. Mihrān) cites *al-Tārīkh al-kabīr* and *al-Tārīkh al-ṣaghīr*. Mughalṭāy b. Qalīj had access to all three histories: Mughalṭāy b. Qalīj, *Sharḥ Sunan Ibn Māja*, ed. Kāmil ʿUwayḍa (Mecca: Nizār Muṣṭafā al-Bāz, 1999), 1: 223; Mughalṭāy b. Qalīj, *Ikmāl Tahdhīb al-kamāl fī asmāʾ al-rijāl*, ed. ʿĀdil b. Muḥammad and Usāma b. Ibrāhīm (Cairo: al-Fārūq al-Ḥadītha li al-Ṭibāʿa wa al-Nashr, 2001), 1: 167 (entry on Abān b. Abī ʿAyyāsh). See also ʿAbd Allāh bt. Maḥrūs al-ʿAsālī, *Fihris Muṣannafāt al-imām ... al-Bukhārī ... al-mashhūra fīmā ʿadā ʻal-Ṣaḥīḥʼ*, arr. Muḥammad b. Ḥamza b. Saʿd (Riyadh: Dār al-ʿĀṣima, 1988), 28f.; ʿĀdil b. ʿAbd al-Shukr al-Zuraqī, *Tārīkh al-Bukhārī* (Riyadh: Dār al-Ṭuwayq, 2002), 8–29. He concludes that there were three histories and a fourth work, *Kitāb al-Ḍuʿafāʾ al-ṣaghīr*.

96 Al-Bukhārī, *Kitāb al-Ḍuʿafāʾ al-ṣaghīr*, ed. Maḥmūd Ibrāhīm Zāyid (Aleppo: Dār al-Waʿy, 1976) = *Majmūʿ fī al-ḍuʿafāʾ wa al-matrūkīn*, ed. ʿAbd al-ʿAzīz ʿIzz al-Dīn Sayrawān (Beirut: Dār al-Qalam, 1985), 405–503.

97 Al-Bukhārī, *al-Tārīkh al-kabīr*, 4.2: 81.

98 For the special meaning designated by *sakatū ʿanhu* in al-Bukhārī's writings and in *al-jarḥ wa al-taʿdīl* more widely see al-Dhahabī, *al-Mūqiẓa fī ʿilm muṣṭalaḥ al-ḥadīth*, ed. ʿAbd al-

Bukhārī returns in a number of related and unrelated entries. It is no surprise, for example, that al-Bukhārī's notice for Abū Yūsuf refers to Abū Ḥanīfa. Al-Bukhārī states there that Abū Yūsuf had studied with both al-Shaybānī and Abū Ḥanīfa. However, according to al-Bukhārī, Abū Ḥanīfa's most prominent disciples, al-Shaybānī and Abū Yūsuf, renounced Abū Ḥanīfa (*tarakūhu*).[99] Perhaps more surprising is Abū Ḥanīfa's appearance in the entry on the Medinese scholar Muḥammad b. Maslama Abū Hishām al-Makhzūmī. Al-Bukhārī states that Muḥammad b. Maslama once related that someone remarked to him, 'What is the business with Abū Ḥanīfa's speculative jurisprudence? It entered every single town save Medina.' To this, Muḥammad b. Maslama replied: 'He [Abū Ḥanīfa] was one of the anti-Christs, and the Prophet, God pray over him and grant him peace, said that neither the plague nor the anti-Christ shall enter Medina.'[100]

Al-Bukhārī's religious outlook in *al-Tārīkh al-kabīr* is constituted through a prosopographical lens. His judgements on thousands of individuals seek to produce a register of identifiable men in *isnād*s. This was not the primary venue for determining who was reliable and who was not, who was orthodox and who had deviant leanings.[101] In the light of this, it is all the more surprising that al-Bukhārī uses notices in *al-Tārīkh al-kabīr* on Abū Ḥanīfa and his students to convey to his readers that Abū Ḥanīfa stands outside the orthodox community.

When he is not constrained by the prosopographical vision, al-Bukhārī's discourse of heresy against Abū Ḥanīfa moves in different directions. Unlike *al-Tārīkh al-kabīr*, al-Bukhārī's *al-Tārīkh al-awsaṭ* is arranged chronologically. This seems to permit him a greater degree of flexibility with respect to expressing his animosity towards Abū Ḥanīfa and explaining the charges of heresy and deviance that proto-Sunni traditionalists levelled at Abū Ḥanīfa. In the entry for 150/767 al-Bukhārī records the death of Abū Ḥanīfa and notes that he was seventy years old when died.[102] This much is conventional in al-Bukhārī's

Fattāḥ Abū Ghudda (Aleppo: Maktab al-Maṭbūʿāt al-Islāmiyya, 1984–5), 83; al-Sharīf Ḥātim al-ʿAwnī, *Sharḥ Mūqiẓa li al-Dhahabī* (Dammām: Dār Ibn al-Jawzī, 2006), 238–9; al-Dhahabī, *Siyar*, 12: 439–41 (within al-Dhahabī's lengthy notice for al-Bukhārī); Ibn Kathīr, *al-Bāʿith al-ḥathīth: Sharḥ ikhtiṣār ʿulūm al-ḥadīth li al-Ḥāfiẓ Ibn Kathīr*, ed. and commentary Aḥmad Muḥammad Shākir (Beirut: Dār al-Kutub al-ʿIlmiyya, n.d.), 101; al-ʿIrāqī, *Sharḥ al-tabṣira wa al-tadhkira*, ed. ʿAbd al-Laṭīf al-Ḥāmīm and Māhir Yāsīn al-Faḥl (Beirut: Dār al-Kutub al-ʿIlmiyya, 2002), 1: 377 = *Sharḥ alfiyat al-ʿIrāqī*, ed. Muḥammad b. al-Ḥusayn al-ʿIrāqī al-Ḥusaynī (Beirut: Dār al-Kutub al-ʿIlmiyya, n.d.), 2: 11; Ibn Ḥajar al-ʿAsqalānī, *Hady al-sārī*, 1: 480.

99 Al-Bukhārī, *al-Tārīkh al-kabīr*, 4.2: 397.

100 Al-Bukhārī, *al-Tārīkh al-kabīr*, 1.1: 240.

101 Melchert, 'Bukhārī and Early Hadith Criticism', esp. 16–17.

102 Al-Bukhārī, *al-Tārīkh al-awsaṭ*, 4: 502 (Abū Ḥaymad edn.).

*al-Tārīkh al-awsaṭ*. What follows this, though, is a scathing description of the legacy that Abū Ḥanīfa represented in the eyes of proto-Sunni traditionalists:[103]

Nuʿaym b. Ḥammād < al-Fazārī said: 'I was with Sufyān when news of al-Nuʿmān's death arrived. He said: "Praise be to God. He was destroying Islam systematically. No one has been born in Islam more harmful than he [was]."'

The celebration of Abū Ḥanīfa's passing is ubiquitous in the literature produced by proto-Sunni traditionalists in the ninth and tenth centuries. Al-Bukhārī's decision to supplement the record of Abū Ḥanīfa's death date with a damning statement on the latter's legacy was designed to produce a categorical denunciation of Abū Ḥanīfa as a heretic. The semantic field of heresy may not be present in this statement, but the implications are clear enough. Abū Ḥanīfa was not merely an individual who dissented and deviated from proto-Sunni orthodoxy; in fact, his was an active heresy that threatened the very foundations of the religion. As such, proto-Sunni traditionalists believed that Abū Ḥanīfa's heresy represented an unprecedented danger to the Muslim community. Though this threat was perceived to manifest itself differently and widely, proto-Sunni traditionalists argued that there was an immediate sense in which Abū Ḥanīfa's heresies posed a grave threat to the Muslim polity. Al-Bukhārī's entry for the year 150 and for Abū Ḥanīfa's death continues with yet another narration from Ibrāhīm b. Muḥammad al-Fazārī. Al-Bukhārī narrates that al-Fazārī went to visit the caliph Hārūn al-Rashīd. Al-Fazārī entered the caliph's presence and noticed that Abū Yūsuf was also there. The caliph addressed al-Fazārī and asked, 'Are you one of those who wishes to see the sword raised against us?' The caliph's curt remark obviously annoyed al-Fazārī, and the attendance of Abū Yūsuf compounded al-Fazārī's sense of dismay. He suspected that Abū Yūsuf had had a hand in bringing al-Fazārī's name into disrepute with the caliph, and so rather than answering the caliph's question al-Fazārī insisted on revealing the views of Abū Yūsuf and Abū Ḥanīfa on the very issue of rebellion that the caliph had raised with him. Al-Fazārī told the caliph, 'I went on a raid in Ṭarsūs. When I returned, Abū Ḥanīfa said to me: "Where were you?" I replied, "I was raiding in Ṭarsūs." Then he said to me: "The rebellion of your brother with Ibrāhīm is more preferable to me than your raiding in Ṭarsūs."'[104]

Al-Bukhārī's insertion of this report corresponds neatly to his previous assertion that Abū Ḥanīfa was a pernicious force against Islam. In the

[103] Al-Bukhārī, *al-Tārīkh al-awsaṭ*, 4: 503 (Abū Ḥaymad edn.) = 2: 77 (al-Luḥaydān edn.).
[104] Al-Bukhārī, *al-Tārīkh al-awsaṭ*, 2: 100 (al-Luḥaydān edn.).

narrative told by al-Fazārī, Abū Ḥanīfa belittles al-Fazārī's frontier raiding against non-Muslims and encourages him to pursue the path taken by his brother in joining the rebellion of Ibrāhīm b. ʿAbd Allāh. For proto-Sunni traditionalists who believed that the kind of harm Abū Ḥanīfa posed to Islam was not merely intellectual, the implication of al-Fazārī's narration was that Abū Ḥanīfa was more supportive of Muslims raising the sword against other Muslims than their frontier campaigns against non-Muslims. Abū Ḥanīfa's ideas were an incitement to civil conflict among members of the Islamic polity, and proto-Sunni traditionalists such as al-Bukhārī sought to impress upon readers that this was a defining aspect of Abū Ḥanīfa's legacy to ninth-century Muslims.

There were other aspects of Abū Ḥanīfa's mnemohistory that al-Bukhārī seeks to highlight in *al-Tārīkh al-awsaṭ*. Al-Bukhārī was perturbed, for example, by the absence of certain pietistic norms and conventions in the religious teaching sessions of Abū Ḥanīfa. He recalls a comparison that Ibn al-Mubārak was said to have drawn between the study-circles of Sufyān (al-Thawrī) and those of an unnamed individual (*majlis ākhar*).[105]

> Whenever I wanted to see Sufyān, I saw him praying [upon the Prophet] or narrating ḥadīth, or engaged in abstruse matters of law (*fī ghāmiḍ al-fiqh*). As for the other gathering that I witnessed, no one prayed upon the Prophet in it.

The narrator, Ibn al-Mubārak, fails to mention the name of the scholar who convened the study-circle. However, al-Bukhārī claimed to know exactly to whom Ibn al-Mubārak was referring. He adds at the end of this report, 'he means [the gathering of] al-Nuʿmān'.[106] Al-Bukhārī is concerned with portraying the lack of basic religious piety in the study-circles of Abū Ḥanīfa. The report he cites is at pains to demonstrate that proto-Sunni traditionalists did not simply attack Abū Ḥanīfa for his speculative and casuistic jurisprudence. Abū Ḥanīfa was not the only scholar committed to tackling obscure legal conundrums. This was the inveterate practice of Sufyān al-Thawrī, too. However, Sufyān al-Thawrī's religious teaching sessions were characterised by the elementary norms of Muslim piety: he was either invoking blessings and prayers upon the Prophet or transmitting his words and deeds. According to his critics, these pietistic conventions were conspicuous by their absence in Abū Ḥanīfa's study sessions.

The final example of al-Bukhārī's condemnation of Abū Ḥanīfa underscores, once again, our view that discourses of heresy against Abū Ḥanīfa

[105] Al-Bukhārī, *al-Tārīkh al-awsaṭ*, 2: 113–14 (al-Luḥaydān edn.).
[106] Al-Bukhārī, *al-Tārīkh al-awsaṭ*, 2: 114 (al-Luḥaydān edn.).

represented a group phenomenon: that it was the constant chatter and communication between proto-Sunni traditionalists that gave birth to a discourse of heresy designed to exclude Abū Ḥanīfa from any emerging conception of proto-Sunni orthodoxy. Al-Bukhārī transmits the following story in his *al-Tārīkh al-awsaṭ*:[107]

> I heard al-Ḥumaydī say: Abū Ḥanīfa said: 'I came to Mecca and took from the cupper (*al-ḥajjām*) three *sunan*. When I sat in front of him, he said to me: "Face the Kaʿba." Then he began to shave the right side of my head and reached the two bones.'
>
> Al-Ḥumaydī said: 'How is it that a man who does not possess [knowledge of the] practices (*sunan*) of the Messenger of God, nor of the Companions, with regard to the rituals of pilgrimage (*al-manāsik*) and other things, can be followed in the commandments (*aḥkām*) of God concerning inheritance and other obligatory elements, [such as] prayer, alms-giving, and the rules of Islam?'

The source of al-Bukhārī and al-Ḥumaydī's outrage seems to be that Abū Ḥanīfa had to receive instructions from a cupper as to some of the basic rituals pertaining to the pilgrimage. Al-Ḥumaydī could not fathom why someone who was unfamiliar with the rituals of pilgrimage could be considered an authority and worthy of imitation with respect to any sphere of religious obligation. There is no attempt by proto-Sunni traditionalists to provide a wider background and context to the alleged anecdote about Abū Ḥanīfa. This certainly reads as a disjointed report, one dislodged from a broader narrative. Proto-Sunni traditionalists displayed no interest, for example, in entertaining the possibility that the anecdote referred to a pilgrimage Abū Ḥanīfa had undertaken as a young man.[108] This narration alone, regardless of its wider context, constituted further evidence for the proto-Sunni traditionalist belief that Abū Ḥanīfa could not be regarded as an exemplary figure of proto-Sunni orthodoxy.

Our final example of al-Bukhārī's discourse of heresy against Abū Ḥanīfa in this section comes from his *Kitāb al-Ḍuʿafāʾ al-ṣaghīr*. Al-Bukhārī's brief history of unreliable scholars is concerned with documenting the unreliability of scholars involved in the transmission or learning of ḥadīth.[109] Scholars are dismissed for various reasons. Al-Bukhārī brands certain

[107] Al-Bukhārī, *al-Tārīkh al-awsaṭ*, 3: 382 (Abū Ḥaymad edn.) = 2: 37–38 (al-Luḥaydān edn.). See also Yaḥyā b. Maʿīn, *al-Tārīkh* (al-Dūrī's recension), ed. Aḥmad Muḥammad Nūr Sayf (Mecca: Markaz al-Baḥth al-ʿIlmī wa Iḥyāʾ al-Turāth al-Islāmī, 1979), 2: 607.

[108] For this particular explanation see Ẓafar Aḥmad al-ʿUthmānī al-Tahānawī, *Muqaddimat iʿlāʾ al-sunan: Abū Ḥanīfa wa aṣḥābuhu al-muḥaddithūn* (Karachi: Idārat al-Qurʾān wa al-ʿUlūm al-Islāmiyya, 1984), 35.

[109] This work of al-Bukhārī's exhibits the influence of al-Ḥumaydī, too. See al-Bukhārī, *Kitāb al-Ḍuʿafāʾ al-ṣaghīr [wa yalīhi Kitāb al-Ḍuʿafāʾ wa al-matrūkīn li al-Nasāʾī]*, ed. Maḥmūd Ibrāhīm Zāyid (Beirut: Dār al-Maʿrifa, 1986), 69, 78, 81, 105, 107.

scholars as inveterate liars.[110] Others are discredited because of their association with heresies.[111] However, al-Bukhārī appears to give Abū Ḥanīfa special treatment. His entry on Abū Ḥanīfa relates three damning reports attacking Abū Ḥanīfa's religious credibility. The first report maintains that Abū Ḥanīfa repented from heresy twice. The second report states that when Sufyān al-Thawrī heard that Abū Ḥanīfa had passed away, he praised God, performed a prostration (of gratitude), and declared that Abū Ḥanīfa was committed to destroying Islam systematically and that nobody in Islam had been born more harmful than he. The third and final report, which al-Bukhārī also includes in his *al-Tārīkh al-kabīr*, describes Abū Ḥanīfa as one of the anti-Christs.[112]

We have seen that al-Bukhārī's denunciation of Abū Ḥanīfa as a heretic and deviant scholar emerged from different contexts and for various reasons. In Khurāsān and the Ḥijāz al-Bukhārī nurtured close and formative relationships with Abū Ḥanīfa's sternest critics. In Khurāsān he developed a life-long and definitive friendship with Isḥāq b. Rāhawayh. In Rayy he would have been exposed to staunch detractors of Abū Ḥanīfa. In Baghdad al-Bukhārī studied with Aḥmad b. Ḥanbal and Yaḥyā b. Maʿīn. In the Ḥijāz he studied with al-Ḥumaydī. Some historians with very good access to eastern sources believed that al-Bukhārī's expulsion from Bukhārā had been engineered by prominent Ḥanafīs in the region.[113] Al-Bukhārī's oeuvre exhibits a discourse of heresy against Abū Ḥanīfa that manifested itself in the spheres of law, rebellion, ḥadīth, piety, religious deviance, unbelief, heresy, ritual practice, and legal reasoning. There are many important dimensions of this discourse that have not been mentioned here, for they are treated at length in Chapter 3.

110 Al-Bukhārī, *Kitāb al-Ḍuʿafāʾ al-ṣaghīr*, 74, 120, 122 (Dār al-Maʿrifa edn.).

111 Al-Bukhārī, *Kitāb al-Ḍuʿafāʾ al-ṣaghīr* (Dār al-Maʿrifa edn.), for association with the Qadariyya see 17 (*kāna yarā al-qadar*), 43 (*fa afsadūhu bi al-qadar*), 98 (*kāna yarā al-qadar*), 101 (*kāna yuqāl fīhi al-qadar*), 111 (*kāna yarā al-qadar*), 124 (*yudhkar bi al-qadar*); for association with the Murjiʾa see 22 and 65 (*kāna yarā al-irjāʾ wa huwa ṣadūq*), where according to al-Bukhārī one could be a Murjiʾī and still be a moderately reliable transmitter of ḥadīth, 52 (*kāna yarā al-irjāʾ*), 78 (*kāna yarā al-irjāʾ*), 82 (*kāna yarā al-irjāʾ*); for association with the *aṣḥāb al-raʾy* see 24 (*ṣāḥib al-raʾy*); for association with the Muʿtazila see 39 (*kāna muʿtaziliyyan*); for association with the Ibāḍiyya see 40 (*kāna yarā raʾy al-ibāḍiyya*); for association with the Khārijīs see 85 (*kāna khārijiyyan*). On the question of ḥadīth scholars and sectaries see Melchert, 'Sectaries in the Six Books'.

112 Al-Bukhārī, *al-Ḍuʿafāʾ al-ṣaghīr*, ed. Abū ʿAbd Allāh Aḥmad b. Ibrāhīm b. Abī al-ʿAynayn (n.p.: Maktabat Ibn ʿAbbās, 2005), 132.

113 Ibn Abī al-Wafāʾ, *al-Jawāhir al-muḍiyya fī ṭabaqāt al-Ḥanafiyya*, ed. ʿAbd al-Fattāḥ Muḥammad Ḥulw (Cairo: Hajr li al-Ṭibāʿa wa al-Nashr, 1993), 1: 166; ʿAbd al-Qādir al-Tamīmī, *al-Ṭabaqāt al-saniyya fī tarājim al-Ḥanafiyya*, ed. ʿAbd al-Fattāḥ Muḥammad Ḥulw (Riyadh: Dār al-Rifāʿī, 1983), 1: 395.

### *Ibn Qutayba (d. 276/889)*

Ibn Qutayba's role in the development of proto-Sunni traditionalism is less secure than that of his contemporary al-Bukhārī. He has been described in modern scholarship as a follower of Aḥmad b. Ḥanbal, a member of Isḥāq b. Rāhawayh's 'school', and as a semi-rationalist.[114] There is no doubt that his career was more dexterous than those of other proto-Sunni traditionalists. To begin with, he moved in aristocratic and courtly circles. Ibn Qutayba found himself under the patronage of ʿUbayd Allāh b. Yaḥyā b. Khāqān (d. 247/861), the vizier of the caliph al-Mutawakkil.[115] At least one of his works is dedicated to him.[116] Proximity to political elites in the empire was not unknown among proto-Sunni traditionalists, and this connection to the empire's aristocrats need not undermine his proto-Sunni traditionalist credentials. For example, we find in the ninth-century biography of Aḥmad b. Ḥanbal written by his cousin Ḥanbal b. Isḥāq (d. 273/886), as well as in the earliest extant biographical dictionary of Ḥanbalīs, the claim that Yaḥyā b. Khāqān used to visit Aḥmad b. Ḥanbal very frequently, and that these visits were on the orders of al-Mutawakkil.[117] Furthermore, Aḥmad b.

[114] For Ibn Qutayba's contributions to proto-Sunni traditionalism see Melchert, 'Traditionist-Jurisprudents', 403–5; Lecomte, *Ibn Qutayba*, 215–74; Husaini, *Life and Works*, who considers Ibn Qutayba as adhering to Isḥāq b. Rāhawayh's school, which is a mistake in my view. At least one prominent medieval historian of ḥadīth scholars made room for Ibn Qutayba in his history of ḥadīth learning: al-Khalīlī, *al-Irshād fī maʿrifat ʿulamāʾ al-ḥadīth*, ed. Walīd Mutawallī Muḥammad (Cairo: al-Fārūq al-Ḥadītha li al-Ṭibāʿa wa al-Nashr, 2010), 250–1 = 626–7 (Riyadh edn.). According to my records, this citation has been overlooked by modern scholars (the *Irshād* had not been published when Lecomte published his book on Ibn Qutayba). When I first noticed Ibn Qutayba's entry in the *Irshād*, I interpreted this initially as further evidence of Ibn Qutayba's being ensconced in the annals of proto-Sunni traditionalism. However, after I made my way through the entire *Irshād*, I realised that al-Khalīlī's history of ḥadīth scholars has a weak spot for mavericks. Among the anomalies I found in the *Irshād* was the historian Abū Ḥanīfa al-Dīnawarī. In the light of this, scholars who view Ibn Qutayba as being on the fringes of proto-Sunni traditionalism would be well within their rights, therefore, to see his appearance in the *Irshād* as strengthening their position and not as evidence for his secure reputation as a proto-Sunni traditionalist.

[115] Sourdel, *Le vizirat ʿabbāside*, 2: 274–86, 305–9; Lecomte, *Ibn Qutayba*, 33.

[116] Ibn Qutayba, *Kitāb Adab al-kātib [Ibn Kutaiba's Adab al-kātib]*, ed. Max Grünert (Leiden: Brill, 1900), 6; Ibn Khallikān, *Wafayāt al-aʿyān*, 3: 43. The 'al-wazīr Abū al-Ḥasan' mentioned by Ibn Qutayba is ʿUbayd Allāh b. Yaḥyā b. Khāqān; not, as Sarah Savant claims, Fatḥ b. Khāqān. See Savant, *The New Muslims of Post-Conquest Iran*, 98. On this family see Gordon, 'The Khāqānid Families of the Early ʿAbbāsid Period'.

[117] Ibn Abī Yaʿlā, *Ṭabaqāt al-Ḥanābila*, ed. Muḥammad Ḥāmid al-Fiqī (Cairo: Maṭbaʿat al-Sunna al-Muḥammadiyya, 1952), 1: 401 = ed. ʿAbd al-Raḥmān b. Sulaymān al-ʿUthaymīn (Riyadh: al-Mamlaka al-ʿArabiyya al-Saʿūdiyya, al-Amāna al-ʿĀmma li al-Iḥtifāl bi Murūr Miʾat ʿĀm ʿalā Taʾsīs al-Mamlaka, 1999), 2: 524 (where Yaḥyā b. Khāqān has his own entry). Other officials such as ʿUbayd Allāh b. Yaḥyā b. Khāqān and ʿAlī b. Jahm would frequent Aḥmad b. Ḥanbal. See Ḥanbal b. Isḥāq, *Dhikr miḥnat al-imām Aḥmad b. Ḥanbal*, ed. Muḥammad Naghsh (Cairo: Dār al-Nashr al-Thaqāfa,

Ḥanbal's sons maintained affable relations with al-Mutawakkil and continued to accept gifts and stipends from the imperial purse despite their father's protests.[118]

It was probably the combination of Ibn Qutayba's competent religious and judicial learning in addition to his access to important officials in the imperial entourage of the caliph that saw him occupy the judgeship of the city of Dīnawār. This, too, was not breaking with proto-Sunni traditionalist conventions and norms. Some proto-Sunni traditionalists felt that being in the employ of the state as a judge could compromise their moral integrity. It seems that Aḥmad b. Ḥanbal considered even being employed by the state as illegitimate.[119] He dismissed outright any discussion of being appointed to a judgeship in Yemen[120] and would not accept a delegation of state judges who presumably came to pay their respects in the final hours of his life (*wa jā'a qawm min al-quḍāt wa ghayrihim, fa lam yu'dhan lahum*).[121] Others clearly believed it was possible to overcome any such moral conundrums, or they simply conceded that they could not sustain such scrupulousness in the face of the harsh social and economic realities of everyday life. Three of Aḥmad b. Ḥanbal's sons – ʿAbd Allāh, Ṣāliḥ, and Saʿīd – accepted judgeships. Their decision to work as judges for the state prompted Aḥmad b. Ḥanbal's refusal to pray behind his sons.[122] Aḥmad b. Ḥanbal represented one end of the spectrum among proto-Sunni traditionalists, and his sons and men like Ibn Qutayba the other.

If there is something to distinguish Ibn Qutayba from the proto-Sunni traditionalist community it may well be that his published works exhibit a literary adroitness not altogether common among proto-Sunni traditionalists. Books such as *Kitāb al-Maʿārif*, *Adab al-kātib*, and *ʿUyūn al-akhbār* speak to the intellectual and moral edification of a burgeoning secretarial and literary class; and Ibn Qutayba is sometimes explicit that it is this particular audience he is addressing. When he wrote the *Kitāb al-Maʿārif*, he explained: 'I have compiled in this book the things that should be known to those who have been blessed with positions of social prestige, who have

1983), 87. See also Melchert, *Aḥmad ibn Hanbal*, 14–16; Cook, *Commanding Right and Forbidding Wrong*, 101–5.

118 Ḥanbal b. Isḥāq, *Dhikr miḥnat al-imām Aḥmad b. Ḥanbal*, 87–9.

119 Al-Khallāl, *Kitāb al-Siyar*, *apud* Ibn Abī Yaʿlā, *Ṭabaqāt al-Ḥanābila*, 1: 223 (al-Fiqī edn.) = ed. ʿAbd al-Raḥmān b. Sulaymān al-ʿUthaymīn, 2: 123–4.

120 Ibn al-Jawzī, *Manāqib al-Imām Aḥmad b. Ḥanbal*, ed. Muḥammad Amīn Khānjī (Cairo: Maktabat al-Khānjī, 1931), 270.

121 Al-Dhahabī, *Tarjamat al-imām Aḥmad min Tārīkh al-Islām li al-Ḥāfiẓ al-Dhahabī* (Aleppo: Dār al-Waʿy, n.d.), 73; al-Dhahabī, *Tārīkh al-Islām*, 18: 139.

122 Ṣāliḥ b. Aḥmad, *Sīrat al-imām Aḥmad b. Ḥanbal*, ed. Fu'ād ʿAbd al-Munʿim Aḥmad (Riyadh: Dār al-Salaf, 1995), 108–9; Abū Nuʿaym al-Iṣfahānī, *Ḥilyat al-awliyā' wa ṭabaqāt al-aṣfiyā'* (Cairo: Maktabat al-Khānjī and Maṭbaʿat al-Saʿāda, 1932–8), 9: 176.

been lifted out from the ranks of *hoi polloi* on account of their literary and social education and risen through learning and eloquence above the general populace.'[123] His *'Uyūn al-akhbār* appears to speak to a broader coalition of educated readers. 'I have composed this book, *'Uyūn al-akhbār*', Ibn Qutayba writes, 'as an illumination for the person ignorant of a proper literary education, as a reminder to religious scholars, to refine the education of rulers and ruled, and for the pleasure of kings.'[124] Still, even in these books Ibn Qutayba can be seen to be advocating proto-Sunni traditionalist ideas. These ideas are often the mainstay of his other books, such as *Ta'wīl mukhtalif al-ḥadīth*, *Gharīb al-ḥadīth*, and *Kitāb al-Ashriba*.

We have already seen that a closer look at his writings points us towards one of his pivotal proto-Sunni traditionalist mentors and teachers, Isḥāq b. Rāhawayh. Our discussion of Isḥāq b. Rāhawayh's discourse of heresy against Abū Ḥanīfa examined some of the passages in Ibn Qutayba's work where the latter transmits Isḥāq b. Rāhawayh's attacks on Abū Ḥanīfa. Ibn Qutayba made a conscious effort to include Isḥāq b. Rāhawayh's severe criticism of Abū Ḥanīfa, though he explained that he had omitted much of this material in order to keep the length of *Ta'wīl mukhtalif al-ḥadīth* reasonable. Ibn Qutayba's relationship with Isḥāq b. Rāhawayh does raise questions about the extent of the former's connections to the proto-Sunni traditionalist community.[125] One modern historian, Michael Cook, has stated, for example, that Ibn Qutayba had probably not even heard of al-Bukhārī.[126] Cook believed that there was 'no compelling reason' to suggest that Ibn Qutayba knew al-Bukhārī. Ibn Qutayba does not cite al-Bukhārī, and nor should we expect him to. However, Cook might have been unaware of Isḥāq b. Rāhawayh's proximity to Ibn Qutayba and al-Bukhārī, who were both his students, and it seems likely that Ibn Qutayba would have heard about al-Bukhārī. Ibn Qutayba was not a ḥadīth critic, but he was aware of their methods and relied upon

[123] See, for example, Ibn Qutayba, *Kitāb al-Ma'ārif*, 1 (*hādhā kitāb jama'tu fīhi min al-ma'ārif mā yaḥiqqu 'alā man an'ama 'alayhi bi sharaf al-manzila wa ukhrija bi al-ta'addub 'an ṭabaqat al-ḥushwa wa fuḍḍila bi al-'ilm wa al-bayān 'alā al-'āmma*).

[124] Ibn Qutayba, *'Uyūn al-akhbār*, 1: yā (numbering by letters: this corresponds to p. 2) (*wa hādhihi 'uyūn al-akhbār naẓẓamtuhā li mughfil al-ta'addub tabṣiratan wa li ahl al-'ilm tadhkiratan wa li sā'is al-nās wa masūsihim mu'addiban wa li al-mulūk mustarāḥan*). See also the remarks about *adab* and history writing in Khalidi, *Arabic Historical Thought in the Classical Period*, 108–11, though one might wish to ignore Khalidi's highly subjective judgements about Ibn Qutayba's literary originality and flair.

[125] Lecomte, *Ibn Qutayba*, 45–83 recognises Isḥāq b. Rāhawayh as one of Ibn Qutayba's 'maîtres'. Lecomte's profile of Isḥāq b. Rāhawayh hardly goes far enough and does not appreciate fully his role in the development of proto-Sunni traditionalism and how this might have impacted Ibn Qutayba. Still, Lecomte must be credited with having done the most thorough work to date on Ibn Qutayba's teachers.

[126] Cook, 'Ibn Qutayba and the Monkeys', 61.

them in his works. Both Ibn Qutayba and al-Bukhārī penned treatises on the controversy surrounding *lafẓ al-Qur'ān*, though there is no evidence that either was aware of the other's work on this subject. There are other significant similarities and overlapping themes, and whilst they might not provide categorical proof that Ibn Qutayba knew al-Bukhārī, it seems to me that Isḥāq b. Rāhawayh constitutes a compelling intermediary through whom Ibn Qutayba would have come to hear of al-Bukhārī.

The precise nature of Ibn Qutayba's proto-Sunni connections notwithstanding, his decision to incorporate Isḥāq b. Rāhawayh's indictments of Abū Ḥanīfa speaks to his commitment to the proto-Sunni traditionalist endeavour to promulgate discourses of heresy against Abū Ḥanīfa, which aimed at excluding him and his followers from any emerging orthodoxy. That is to say, Ibn Qutayba signed up to a central tenet of proto-Sunni traditionalism. One can see this operating in *Kitāb al-Maʿārif*, where classifications and lists become important vehicles for articulating proto-Sunni traditionalist orthodoxy. His chapter on the *aṣḥāb al-ra'y* contains nine entries, whilst the chapter on the *aṣḥāb al-ḥadīth* contains ninety-eight biographies. One can surmise that Ibn Qutayba is using quantity to make his argument: members of one group deserve more exposure and greater attention. Competing groups to which Ibn Qutayba is already hostile warrant curt dismissal. There is a danger that historians of Islamic legal history will read too much into the organisation of Ibn Qutayba's *Kitāb al-Maʿārif*. Norman Calder argued that the chapter on the *aṣḥāb al-ra'y* had been placed after the chapter on Successors and before the chapter on the *aṣḥāb al-ḥadīth* so 'as to mark the deviation of the jurists from the tradition'. Calder continues: 'Transmission was from the Successors to the Transmitters; the jurists, dominated by *ra'y*, failed to take up and pass on the cultural baton.'[127] This interpretation of Ibn Qutayba's *Kitāb al-Maʿārif* cannot be sustained upon closer scrutiny. Ibn Qutayba's chapter on Successors indeed lists speculative jurists such as Ibrāhīm al-Nakhaʿī (d. 96/714) and Rabīʿat al-Ra'y (d. 136/753).[128] Rabīʿat al-Ra'y also makes an appearance in the chapter on the *aṣḥāb al-ra'y*,[129] whilst Ibrāhīm al-Nakhaʿī is listed as a Shiʿi in the chapter on *asmā' al-ghāliya*.[130] Similarly, the chapter on Successors contains the biographies of sectaries such as Ghaylān al-Dimashqī, who is described

[127] Calder, *Studies in Early Muslim Jurisprudence*, 187. It is worth mentioning that Calder's weak argument concerning Ibn Qutayba's chapter arrangement in the *Kitāb al-Maʿārif* occurs in an otherwise illuminating account of the social and cultural contexts under which ninth-century literature developed (Calder, *Studies in Early Muslim Jurisprudence*, 161–97) – an account that has been neglected by modern historians writing about the legal writing, literature, and canonisation in the ninth century.

[128] Ibn Qutayba, *Kitāb al-Maʿārif*, 462. [129] Ibn Qutayba, *Kitāb al-Maʿārif*, 496.

[130] Ibn Qutayba, *Kitāb al-Maʿārif*, 624.

as a Qadarī,[131] ʿAmr b. ʿUbayd, who is described as a Muʿtazilī,[132] and Ḥammād b. Abī Sulaymān, who is listed as a Murjiʾī.[133] There are other, more accurate ways to demonstrate the *Kitāb al-Maʿārif*'s hostility towards Abū Ḥanīfa and his followers. First, we have the fact that the *Kitāb al-Maʿārif* places Abū Ḥanīfa, Abū Yūsuf, al-Shaybānī, and Misʿar b. Kidām as belonging to the Murji'a, one of four groups listed in the chapter on *asmāʾ al-ghāliya min al-rāfiḍa*.[134] Second, we can turn to the entries in the *Kitāb al-Maʿārif* for Abū Ḥanīfa and his two foremost students, Abū Yūsuf and al-Shaybānī. These entries we can deal with very quickly. Ibn Qutayba describes both of them as having been overcome by speculative jurisprudence (*ra'y*) on account of their association with Abū Ḥanīfa. When it comes to Abū Ḥanīfa himself, Ibn Qutayba is more forthcoming in expressing his opposition to proto-Ḥanafism and adopts a more mocking tone by choosing to cite a lyrical battle between a supporter and a detractor of Abū Ḥanīfa:[135]

> When the people test us by means of analogical reasoning
> presenting before us novel legal issues,
> We place before them a correct measurement
> inherited from the model of Abū Ḥanīfa,
> When the jurist hears it, he memorises it
> and has it inscribed on a sheet of paper

The response from Abū Ḥanīfa's detractor is then cited by Ibn Qutayba:

> When the people of speculative jurisprudence quarrel over analogical reasoning
> it produces heretical innovations, insignificant and absurd,
> We place before them the word of God on the matter
> along with noble reports which are superior [to *ra'y*],
> So how many a chaste virgin has been illegitimately breached
> the prohibited is made permissible only by Abū Ḥanīfa

The *Ta'wīl mukhtalif al-ḥadīth* adopts a more urgent and hostile approach to Abū Ḥanīfa. Unlike the *Kitāb al-Maʿārif*, the *Ta'wīl mukhtalif al-ḥadīth* was composed explicitly to defend proto-Sunni traditionalism against competing groups.[136] Among these, the *aṣḥāb al-kalām* are his main opponents. There are so many digressions in the book, however, that

[131] Ibn Qutayba, *Kitāb al-Maʿārif*, 494.
[132] Ibn Qutayba, *Kitāb al-Maʿārif*, 493.
[133] Ibn Qutayba, *Kitāb al-Maʿārif*, 474.
[134] Ibn Qutayba, *Kitāb al-Maʿārif*, 625.
[135] Ibn Qutayba, *Kitāb al-Maʿārif*, 495.
[136] Ibn Qutayba, *Ta'wīl mukhtalif al-ḥadīth*, 2, 14–15, 103–4 (Zakī al-Kurdī edn.). The editors of Ḍirār b. ʿAmr, *Kitāb al-Taḥrīsh*, ed. Hüseyin Hansu and Mehmet Kaskin (Istanbul: Shirkat Dār al-Irshād; Beirut: Dār Ibn Ḥazm, 2014), 18–22 have argued that Ibn Qutayba's *Ta'wīl mukhtalif al-ḥadīth* is a response to the *Kitāb al-Taḥrīsh*.

Abū Ḥanīfa, and the kind of jurisprudence associated with him, also becomes a target. Ibn Qutayba writes:[137]

We turn now to the *aṣḥāb al-ra'y*. We find them, too, disagreeing and relying upon analogical reasoning, invoking analogy and juristic preference. They arrive at a legal view and issue rulings on it, but then they retract from them.

Ibn Qutayba's supporting evidence for this rebuke against the *aṣḥāb al-ra'y* comes from Abū Ḥanīfa. He cites the case of a man from Khurāsān who had recorded in a notebook the legal opinions of Abū Ḥanīfa when the two men were in Mecca. After a year had passed, the man returned to Abū Ḥanīfa and recited his legal opinions back to him (*ʿaraḍa ʿalayhi*). Abū Ḥanīfa retracted every single ruling the book contained (*rajaʿa ʿan dhālika kullihi*). The man could not contain himself. Exasperated and astonished, he took a handful of dust, placed it over his head, and cried: 'O people, I came to this man a year ago, and he issued me all the legal rulings contained in this book. [I returned to Khurāsān, where] on the basis of his book, I permitted the shedding of blood and made licit sexual relations. Now a year later this man has changed his mind on these matters.' Ibn Qutayba tells us that onlookers were disturbed by the man's revelations and asked Abū Ḥanīfa about this. When he appeared nonplussed about changing his opinions, one observer invoked the curse of God against him.[138] The theme of Abū Ḥanīfa's jurisprudence dominates Ibn Qutayba's discourse of heresy, but he uses a statement attributed to the Syrian scholar al-Awzāʿī (d. 157/774) to explain the emergence of proto-Sunni traditionalist discourses of heresy against Abū Ḥanīfa:[139]

We do not loathe (*lā nanqimu*) Abū Ḥanīfa because he employs speculative jurisprudence, for all of us to do this (*kullunā yarā*). However, we loathe him because when a ḥadīth comes to him on the authority of the Prophet, God pray over him and grant him peace, he opposes it (*yukhālifuhu*) in preference for something else.

This explanation paves the way for a series of examples whereby Ibn Qutayba demonstrates what he perceives to be Abū Ḥanīfa's disregard for Prophetic ḥadīth.[140] Ibn Qutayba then gives ample space to Isḥāq b. Rāhawayh's censure of Abū Ḥanīfa, where he describes seven instances of Abū Ḥanīfa's 'unforgivable opposition to the Quran and unforgivable opposition to the Messenger of God, upon one's having been acquainted with his statement'.[141]

137 Ibn Qutayba, *Ta'wīl mukhtalif al-ḥadīth*, 62 (Zakī al-Kurdī edn.).
138 Ibn Qutayba, *Ta'wīl mukhtalif al-ḥadīth*, 62–3 (Zakī al-Kurdī edn.).
139 Ibn Qutayba, *Ta'wīl mukhtalif al-ḥadīth*, 63 (Zakī al-Kurdī edn.).
140 Ibn Qutayba, *Ta'wīl mukhtalif al-ḥadīth*, 63–5 (Zakī al-Kurdī edn.).
141 Ibn Qutayba, *Ta'wīl mukhtalif al-ḥadīth*, 65–8 (Zakī al-Kurdī edn.).

What has this review of discourses of heresy against Abū Ḥanīfa in the writings of Ibn Qutayba demonstrated? There should be no shame in admitting that texts cannot be bent to say what the historian expects them to say. Ibn Qutayba's hostility to Abū Ḥanīfa does not, in my view, correspond to the vitriolic discourse of heresy contained in the writings of scholars included in this second phase of proto-Sunni traditionalist orthodoxy. Ibn Qutayba certainly depicts Abū Ḥanīfa as being opposed to and outside his vision of proto-Sunni traditionalist orthodoxy. He does not, however, anathematise Abū Ḥanīfa. He does not employ the semantic field of heresy (*kufr*, *murūq*, *bidaʿ*, *ahwāʾ*) against him. Nor does he cultivate a wider discourse of heresy against Abū Ḥanīfa that goes beyond the spheres of jurisprudence and ḥadīth. In Ibn Qutayba we have a version of discourses of heresy against Abū Ḥanīfa that lies somewhere in between the first and second phases identified in this study. Historical research is judged, and rightly so, on the art of a forceful argument. But it must be equally concerned with coming to terms with the ambivalence of our medieval sources, and Ibn Qutayba's oeuvre forces us to do just that. He is not the only one, and perhaps now is the right occasion to review the case of one notable proto-Sunni traditionalist who seems to have dissented against proto-Sunni traditionalism's discourse of heresy against Abū Ḥanīfa.

The case of Yaḥyā b. Maʿīn as someone who repudiated discourses of heresy against Abū Ḥanīfa is all the more surprising given his outstanding credentials as a proto-Sunni traditionalist. He had an unimpeachable record as a scholar and was an intimate companion of Aḥmad b. Ḥanbal.[142] Yet the literary record from the ninth–tenth centuries suggests that Yaḥyā b. Maʿīn regretted the attacks his peers were making on Abū Ḥanīfa. The books that his students transmitted from him establish Yaḥyā b. Maʿīn's exceptional sympathy for Abū Ḥanīfa and proto-Ḥanafism. Al-Dūrī said that he heard Yaḥyā b. Maʿīn admit: 'We will not lie before God, sometimes we hear something from the *raʾy* of Abū Ḥanīfa and we find it to be to our liking, so we adopt it.'[143] The wording is somewhat reluctant, but Yaḥyā b. Maʿīn appears to want to put his view on the public record. Another student, Ibn al-Junayd, asked Yaḥyā b. Maʿīn what he thought of someone who relied on speculative jurisprudence. 'Whose *raʾy* do you have in mind?' Yaḥyā asked. 'That of al-Shāfiʿī and Abū Ḥanīfa,' replied Ibn al-Junayd. Yaḥyā b. Maʿīn told his student

[142] Al-Khaṭīb al-Baghdādī, *Tārīkh Baghdād*, 16: 263–76.

[143] Yaḥyā b. Maʿīn, *al-Tārīkh* (al-Dūrī's recension), 3: 517; Ibn al-Junayd, *Suʾālāt Ibn al-Junayd li Yaḥyā b. Maʿīn*, ed. Aḥmad Muḥammad Nūr Sayf (Medina: Maktabat al-Dār, 1988), 368; Yaḥyā b. Maʿīn, *Maʿrifat al-rijāl*, ed. Muḥammad Kāmil al-Qaṣṣār (Damascus: Majmaʿ al-Lugha al-ʿArabiyya, 1985), 2: 56.

that he should avoid al-Shāfiʿī's *ra'y* because he himself found Abū Ḥanīfa's *ra'y* preferable.[144] On yet another occasion he went even further: 'There is no problem with Abū Ḥanīfa, and he never lied. In our view, Abū Ḥanīfa was of the people of truth (*ahl al-ṣidq*) and the charge of lying cannot be ascribed to him. Ibn Hubayra beat him in order to get him to accept a judgeship, but still Abū Ḥanīfa refused.'[145] These views certainly put him at odds with his peers. It dismayed Yaḥyā b. Maʿīn, for example, when one scholar prayed against Abū Ḥanīfa.[146] What exceptions such as Yaḥyā b. Maʿīn indicate is that discourses of heresy against Abū Ḥanīfa were slow to develop and that resistance to them existed among some proto-Sunni traditionalists. Ibn Qutayba did not go as far as Yaḥyā b. Maʿīn. Whilst Ibn Qutayba's works lack a fully developed discourse of heresy against Abū Ḥanīfa, there is no doubt that Ibn Qutayba – a perceptive observer of the social dynamics of medieval Muslim societies – had a conception of orthodoxy. There is one passage, in particular, where his description of proto-Sunni traditionalism approximates an argument of orthodoxy, in so far as he speaks of orthodoxy as a majoritarian phenomenon with the capacity to yield wide and far-reaching social consensus. He explains that the consensuses reached by proto-Sunni traditionalists represent the doctrines and views of the general population in all the major provinces of the empire. He contends that 'if one were to proclaim the doctrines of the *aṣḥāb al-ḥadīth* – and we have already explained that there was an overwhelming consensus concerning these doctrines – in public gatherings and markets, one would be met with neither objection nor aversion'.[147] According to Ibn Qutayba, the orthodoxy of proto-Sunni traditionalists was the orthodoxy of medieval Islamic society at large.

### *Al-Fasawī (d. 277/890)*

Al-Fasawī devotes an entire chapter to discourses of heresy against Abū Ḥanīfa, and this is immediately after a chapter describing Iraq, Abū Ḥanīfa's region of birth, as an unholy region.[148] His chapter concerning the heresies and unholiness of Iraq closes with a pithy description of religious learning in Iraq. The Iraqis are described as being unparalleled in asking so many questions yet equally so in turning their backs upon hearing the answers. Another observer recounts his experience of the

[144] Ibn al-Junayd, *Su'ālāt Ibn al-Junayd*, 295.
[145] Yaḥyā b. Maʿīn, *Maʿrifat al-rijāl*, 1: 79.
[146] Ibn al-Junayd, *Su'ālāt Ibn al-Junayd*, 318.
[147] Ibn Qutayba, *Ta'wīl mukhtalif al-ḥadīth*, 20 (Zakī al-Kurdī edn.).
[148] This is the subject of Chapter 4 of this study.

people of Iraq: 'I have never seen a people ask so many questions concerning insignificant matters and yet more prone to committing grave sins.'[149]

His chapter on discourses of heresy against Abū Ḥanīfa gives us a very good idea of just how systematic proto-Sunni traditionalist hostility towards Abū Ḥanīfa had become by the middle of the ninth century. Scattered throughout al-Fasawī's *History* are anecdotes about Abū Ḥanīfa, most of which are sharply critical of him. There are two exceptions to this. There is one neutral report noting his death in the year 150/767.[150] The other anomaly is the only report in the *History* that presents Abū Ḥanīfa in a positive light. Al-Fasawī transmits a set of reports critical of the use of analogical reasoning (*qiyās*). One of these reports is attributed to Wakīʿ b. al-Jarrāḥ:[151] 'Abū Ḥanīfa said: Some uses of analogical reasoning are more vile than urinating in the mosque (*min al-qiyās qiyās aqbaḥu min al-bawl fī al-masjid*).' His contemporary and associate Abū Zurʿa al-Dimashqī remembered having heard Wakīʿ say something similar to Yaḥyā b. Ṣāliḥ al-Wuḥāẓī:[152] 'O Yaḥyā, beware of speculative jurisprudence (*ra'y*), for I have heard Abū Ḥanīfa say: "Urinating in the mosque is better than some of their analogical reasoning."'

Our proto-Sunni traditionalists were aware of reports that praised Abū Ḥanīfa, and they seemed to cite them only seldom. Still, its context here is unclear. Our agents of orthodoxy may be attacking analogical reasoning by suggesting that even someone so closely associated with it as Abū Ḥanīfa found abhorrent some instances of analogical reasoning. Wakīʿ b. al-Jarrāḥ exhibits all the signs of a proto-Sunni traditionalist. Ninth–tenth-century ḥadīth critics considered him a master of ḥadīth (*ḥāfiẓ*). Like proto-Sunni traditionalists, he considered Irjā' to be a heretical doctrine.[153] He played a prominent role in the transmission and circulation of discourses of heresy against Abū Ḥanīfa.[154] The list of books attributed to him

[149] Al-Fasawī, *Kitāb al-Maʿrifa wa al-tārīkh*, 2: 772.
[150] Al-Fasawī, *Kitāb al-Maʿrifa wa al-tārīkh*, 1: 135.
[151] Al-Fasawī, *Kitāb al-Maʿrifa wa al-tārīkh*, 1: 673; also cited in Ḥanafī sources such as Ibn Abī al-ʿAwwām al-Saʿdī, *Faḍā'il Abī Ḥanīfa*, 159.
[152] Abū Zurʿa al-Dimashqī, *Tārīkh*, ed. Shukr Allāh b. Niʿmat Allāh al-Qūjānī (Damascus: Majmaʿ al-Lugha al-ʿArabiyya, 1990), 2: 507.
[153] See al-Bukhārī, *Khalq afʿāl al-ʿibād wa radd ʿalā al-jahmiyya wa aṣḥāb al-taʿṭīl* (Beirut: Mu'assasat al-Risāla, 1990), 12 = ed. ʿAbd al-Raḥmān ʿAmīra (Riyadh: Dār ʿUkāẓ, n. d.), 34.
[154] Al-Khaṭīb al-Baghdādī, *Tārīkh Baghdād*, 13: 370 (where Wakīʿ expresses his dismay at Abū Ḥanīfa's view on how one ought to express verbally that one is a believer (*mu'min*).

resonates with what we know about patterns of proto-Sunni traditionalist authorship in the ninth century:

1. *Kitāb al-Zuhd.*[155]
2. *Kitāb al-Musnad.*[156]
3. *al-Muṣannaf.*[157]
4. *al-Sunan.*[158]
5. *Kitāb al-Maʿrifa wa al-tārīkh.*[159]
6. *Kitāb Faḍāʾil al-ṣaḥāba.*[160]

Moreover, proto-Sunni traditionalists certainly saw Wakīʿ b. al-Jarrāḥ as one of their own.[161] On the other hand, al-Fasawī's report has Wakīʿ placing Abū Ḥanīfa in a good light, and there are some indications of a connection to proto-Ḥanafism. First, both early and late Ḥanafī biographical dictionaries class him as a Ḥanafī.[162] One proto-Sunni traditionalist, who himself appears to have dissented from the view of his proto-Sunni traditionalist peers with respect to Abū Ḥanīfa, claimed that Wakīʿ issued legal rulings in line with the opinions of Abū Ḥanīfa.[163]

Returning to al-Fasawī's discourse of heresy against Abū Ḥanīfa, more material can be found outside the chapter targeting Abū Ḥanīfa. In the course of a discussion concerning what ought to be done in the case of a female apostate, al-Fasawī reports two opinions attributed to Abū Ḥanīfa.[164] Al-Fasawī transmits a number of sayings attributed to Ayyūb al-Sakhtiyānī (d. 131/748–9). Among these was that Ayyūb despised Abū Ḥanīfa, Rabīʿa, and al-Battī, presumably on account of their association with speculative jurisprudence. Another report on the following page makes this very clear, in which the downfall of the Jews is explained by the emergence among them of bastard foreigners who relied on speculative jurisprudence, and a parallel development is identified among the

[155] One of two works attributed to him which have been published: Wakīʿ b. al-Jarrāḥ, *Kitāb al-Zuhd*, ed. ʿAbd al-Raḥmān ʿAbd al-Jabbār al-Farīwāʾī (Riyadh: Dār al-Ṣumayʿī, 1994); the other is *Nuskhat Wakī b. al-Jarrāḥ*, ed. Fahd al-Ḥammūdī (Beirut: al-Shabaka al-ʿArabiyya, 2014).

[156] Al-Samʿānī, *al-Taḥbīr fī al-muʿjam al-kabīr*, ed. Munīra Nājī Sālim (Baghdad: al-Irshād Press, 1975), 2: 181(a very rich list of books al-Samʿānī was authorised to teach or transmit by his teacher Abū al-Faḍl al-Bukhārī).

[157] Ibn Khayr al-Ishbīlī, *Fihrist*, ed. Bashshār ʿAwwād Maʿrūf and Maḥmūd Bashshār ʿAwwād (Beirut: Dār al-Gharb al-Islāmī, 2009), 172.

[158] Ibn al-Nadīm, *al-Fihrist*, 2: 89–90 (A. F. al-Sayyid edn.); Sezgin, *GAS*, 1: 96–7.

[159] Discussed in Chapter 4 below.

[160] Al-Dhahabī, *Siyar*, 7: 43.

[161] Aḥmad b. Ḥanbal respected him greatly for many reasons, one of which was Wakīʿ's refusal to mix with rulers: Ibn Abī Ḥātim, *Taqdima*, 223; al-Khaṭīb al-Baghdādī, *Tārīkh Baghdād*, 13: 477.

[162] Ibn Abī al-ʿAwwām al-Saʿdī, *Faḍāʾil Abī Ḥanīfa*, 143, 159; Ibn Abī al-Wafāʾ, *al-Jawāhir al-muḍiyya*, 2: 208.

[163] Al-Khaṭīb al-Baghdādī, *Tārīkh Baghdād*, 13: 470–1 (citing Yaḥyā b. Maʿīn's view).

[164] Al-Fasawī, *Kitāb al-Maʿrifa wa al-tārīkh*, 3: 14.

nascent Muslim community, the instigators of which are these three jurists.[165] Let us now turn to al-Fasawī's chapter dedicated solely to discourses of heresy against Abū Ḥanīfa.

In this chapter we find forty-three reports severely critical of Abū Ḥanīfa. I shall present and discuss those reports that represent the most extreme tendencies within proto-Sunni traditionalist discourses of heresy against Abū Ḥanīfa, placing particular emphasis on reports that invoke the semantic field of heresiological discourses. One of the very first reports in this chapter establishes the general tone of al-Fasawī's conception of heresy and Abū Ḥanīfa's place within it. He reports from Aḥmad b. Khalīl, who had heard ʿAbda b. Sulaymān al-Marwazī say the following: 'I heard ʿAbd Allāh b. al-Mubārak mention Abū Ḥanīfa, when a person interjected and asked him: "Did Abū Ḥanīfa adhere to any form of heresy?" "Yes, the doctrine of Irjā'."'[166] Al-Fasawī wanted this allegation to stick, for he supplies further data to corroborate Abū Ḥanīfa's association with movements that proto-Sunni traditionalists considered anathema. In this case, it is Abū Ḥanīfa's disciple Abū Yūsuf to whom the questions are posed:[167]

QUESTIONER: Was Abū Ḥanīfa a murji'ī?
ABŪ YŪSUF: Yes, he was.
QUESTIONER: Was Abū Ḥanīfa a jahmī?
ABŪ YŪSUF: Yes, he was.
QUESTIONER: So where do you stand in relation to him (*fa ayna anta minhu*)?
ABŪ YŪSUF: Abū Ḥanīfa was nothing more than a teacher. As such, whatever we found from his teachings to be correct, we accepted; whatever we found to be repugnant, we left with him (*innamā kāna Abū Ḥanīfa mudarrisan fa mā kāna min qawlihi ḥasanan, qabilnāhu; wa mā kāna qabīḥan taraknāhu ʿalayhi*).

Al-Fasawī wanted his readers to believe that Abū Ḥanīfa was implicated in heresies not simply by his opponents but by his closest students and companions. The idea that Abū Yūsuf acknowledged Abū Ḥanīfa's adherence to heretical doctrines seems far-fetched. Abū Yūsuf's attempt to justify his association with Abū Ḥanīfa on the grounds of a sensible distinction between Abū Ḥanīfa's correct and deviant teachings sounds too neat. Muslim scholars of the late eighth and ninth centuries knew of the dangers of associating with scholars with supposed heretical leanings, and it seems unlikely that Abū Yūsuf would have relied on so neat a distinction to exculpate him from alleged charges of heresy. On the other hand, al-Fasawī's was not a voice in the wilderness. ʿAbd Allāh b. Aḥmad

165 Al-Fasawī, *Kitāb al-Maʿrifa wa al-tārīkh*, 3: 20–1.
166 Al-Fasawī, *Kitāb al-Maʿrifa wa al-tārīkh*, 2: 783 (*hal kāna fīhi min al-hawā shay'? Naʿam, al-irjā'*).
167 Al-Fasawī, *Kitāb al-Maʿrifa wa al-tārīkh*, 2: 783.

b. Ḥanbal was able to produce a similar report, as was a local historian of Jurjān.[168] I do not think we can deduce from this anything concrete concerning Abū Yūsuf's views about his teacher.[169] The controversy surrounding Abū Ḥanīfa's proto-Sunni status had now extended to the alleged views held by influential religious scholars. Proto-Sunni traditionalists were happy to present Abū Yūsuf in a credible and positive light in order to discredit Abū Ḥanīfa as a figure of orthodoxy, and this would force later Ḥanafīs to assert that Abū Yūsuf had acquitted Abū Ḥanīfa of having any association with such repugnant heresies. That these reports contradict each other provides us with good evidence that by the ninth century religious crevices were opening up among religious groups on the question of Abū Ḥanīfa's religious orthodoxy. Opposing parties were ascribing contradictory material to scholars of significant social standing.[170] We should not make the mistake of assuming that al-Fasawī was trying to improve the image of Abū Yūsuf. This report is concerned solely with disparaging Abū Ḥanīfa. Elsewhere in al-Fasawī's *History*, for example, we see that he turns on Abū Yūsuf. In the chapter against Abū Ḥanīfa, al-Fasawī refers to an incident in which a man asked ʿAbd Allāh b. al-Mubārak about a legal matter. After Ibn al-Mubārak had given his answer, the man replied that he had asked Abū Yūsuf the same question and his answer contradicted the one Ibn al-Mubārak had given. Ibn al-Mubārak's response was curt: 'If you have prayed any of the obligatory prayers behind Abū Yūsuf, secure them by repeating them.'[171] It is clear in this instance that al-Fasawī uses material against Abū Yūsuf in an attempt to discredit Abū Ḥanīfa, just as earlier he had employed material placing Abū Yūsuf in a positive light to discredit Abū Ḥanīfa. Proto-Sunni traditionalists simply wanted the charge of heresy against Abū Ḥanīfa to stick, and they would marshal whatever

[168] ʿAbd Allāh b. Aḥmad b. Ḥanbal, *Kitāb al-Sunna*, ed. Muḥammad Saʿīd b. Sālim al-Qaḥṭānī (Riyadh: Dār ʿĀlam al-Kutub, 1996), 181; al-Sahmī, *Tārīkh Jurjān*, 219.

[169] Zaman, *Religion and Politics*, 60, on the other hand, interprets material ascribed to Abū Yūsuf as evidence of his views.

[170] See Wakīʿ, *Akhbār al-quḍāt*, 3: 258 and al-Khaṭīb al-Baghdādī, *Tārīkh Baghdād*, 15: 530 (Saʿīd b. Sālim said to Abū Yūsuf: 'I have heard the people of Khurāsān say that Abū Ḥanīfa was a jahmī and murji'ī.' Abū Yūsuf replied: 'They speak the truth. He also believed in rebellion against rulers (*yarā al-sayf ayḍan*).' So I said to him: 'Where do you stand in relation to him?' He said: 'We only went to Abū Ḥanīfa to learn jurisprudence from him. We did not follow him in our religious outlook'). Elsewhere (al-Khaṭīb al-Baghdādī, *Tārīkh Baghdād*, 15: 514), Abū Yūsuf relates that Abū Ḥanīfa declared the Jahmiyya to be one of the most evil groups in Khurāsān. Furthermore, see al-Khaṭīb al-Baghdādī, *Tārīkh Baghdād*, 15: 518 (where Abū Yūsuf is alleged to have said that Abū Ḥanīfa was the first person to declare that the Quran was created; but this is contradicted at 15: 517).

[171] Al-Fasawī, *Kitāb al-Maʿrifa wa al-tārīkh*, 2: 789.

evidence they could find to build a case against Abū Ḥanīfa's orthodoxy.[172]

We must consider that proto-Sunni traditionalists such as al-Fasawī were motivated to compile chapters dedicated to discourses of heresy against Abū Ḥanīfa so that this evidence could be accessed easily. Al-Fasawī had amassed a large repository of reports concerning Abū Ḥanīfa and decided to locate them in a single place. However, proto-Sunni traditionalists would have wished to demonstrate that these discourses of heresy were not the product of a particular regional or ideological persuasion. Abū Ḥanīfa's heresy had to be portrayed as a phenomenon recognised by a wide array of scholars and evident to communities residing everywhere in early Islamic societies. This made the views of proto-Sunni traditionalists of excellent standing, such as Abū Bakr al-Ḥumaydī, integral to al-Fasawī's broadside against Abū Ḥanīfa. It is in this context that al-Fasawī cites al-Ḥumaydī to argue that Abū Ḥanīfa was a heretic. Al-Ḥumaydī reports that Abū Ḥanīfa was teaching at the Sacred Mosque (*al-masjid al-ḥarām*) in Mecca when a man posed him a hypothetical question. The questioner was interested in Abū Ḥanīfa's verdict concerning a man who testifies that the Kaʿba is true but does not know whether the Kaʿba being referred to is the one located in Mecca or not. Abū Ḥanīfa replied that he considered such a person a true believer (*mu'min ḥaqq*). The questioner followed this up with a similar scenario: what did Abū Ḥanīfa think about a man who testifies that Muḥammad b. ʿAbd Allāh is a prophet but does not know whether he is the one whose grave is located in Medina. Again, Abū Ḥanīfa returned the answer that a person who held this opinion must be considered a true believer. Al-Ḥumaydī, on the other hand, considered this to be clear heresy (*fa qad kafara*).[173] In the eyes of al-Fasawī, al-Ḥumaydī represented proto-Sunni traditionalist orthodoxy in Mecca, and his local perspective on orthodoxy and religious deviance in the context of Mecca could complement the emerging consensus of proto-Sunni traditionalism in the rest of the empire.

One theme that was of particular interest to al-Fasawī was the purported inquisition at which Abū Ḥanīfa was made to repent from heresy.[174] He cites two important Kufan scholars of the eighth century, Sufyān al-Thawrī and Sharīk b. ʿAbd Allāh, to the effect that Abū Ḥanīfa

[172] Ibn Ḥibbān, *Kitāb al-Majrūḥīn*, 3: 64–5 (Beirut edn.) = 2: 406 (Riyadh edn.).
[173] Al-Fasawī, *Kitāb al-Maʿrifa wa al-tārīkh*, 2: 786. Another contemporary of Abū Ḥanīfa reported that he heard him say that 'if a man worshipped this sandal and, by doing so, drew closer to God, then I do not see any problem with this (*law anna rajul ʿabada hādhihi al-naʿl yataqarrabu bihā ilā Allāh, lam ara bi dhālika ba's*)'. Saʿīd b. ʿAbd al-ʿAzīz al-Tanūkhī heard this and remarked that this was manifest heresy (*hādhā al-kufr ṣurāḥ*). See al-Fasawī, *Kitāb al-Maʿrifa wa al-tārīkh*, 2: 784.
[174] This inquisition is treated at length in Chapter 7.

was made to repent from heresy (*kufr* and *zandaqa*).[175] Moreover, he relates that it was the notorious governor of Iraq, Khālid al-Qasrī, who oversaw the proceedings of the inquisition and demanded Abū Ḥanīfa's repentance. This is not an insignificant detail. Al-Fasawī, it seems, wants to confer legitimacy upon this episode by arguing that it was carried out by responsible authorities and confirmed by men in good standing such as Kufa's qadi, Sharīk b. ʿAbd Allāh. The majority of reports surrounding Abū Ḥanīfa's inquisition explain that the inquisition was led by a group of Khārijīs in Kufa. That is to say, Abū Ḥanīfa was on the receiving end of a trial initiated by a deviant religious community. Al-Fasawī's reports convey a very different picture of the local circumstances surrounding the inquisition. The inquisition was not the result of a chaotic political situation that was exploited by a wing of Khārijīs. Rather, Kufa was in the able hands of Khālid al-Qasrī. He determined that an inquisition was necessary and that Abū Ḥanīfa must repent formally from heresy. Moreover, men of local prestige (qadis and scholars) could corroborate this.

Before al-Fasawī, proto-Sunni discourses of heresy against Abū Ḥanīfa were scattershot. In al-Fasawī's *History* we can observe the maturation of proto-Sunni traditionalist orthodoxy. Discourses of heresy against Abū Ḥanīfa were now being collected in one place. A composite case was being built against Abū Ḥanīfa in order to demonstrate to readers and listeners that Abū Ḥanīfa and his followers were corrupted by heresy. This conscious form of orthodoxy formation depended on the construction of discourses of heresy. And al-Fasawī, as an author of *The Sunna and Avoiding the People of Heresy*, was well placed to cultivate proto-Sunni traditionalist orthodoxy by pitting it against the purported heresies of Abū Ḥanīfa.[176]

### *Abū Zurʿa al-Dimashqī (d. 280/893)*

It can scarcely be doubted that al-Fasawī and Abū Zurʿa al-Dimashqī belonged to the same proto-Sunni traditionalist community. A fourteenth-century source, probably relying on an earlier source now lost to us, presents us with Abū Zurʿa al-Dimashqī's encounter with Yaʿqūb b. Sufyān al-Fasawī:[177]

175 Al-Fasawī, *Kitāb al-Maʿrifa wa al-tārīkh*, 2: 786.

176 Al-Samʿānī, *al-Taḥbīr fī al-muʿjam al-kabīr*, 2: 83 (who has the title as *al-Sunna wa majāniyat ahl al-bidaʿ*, but I read *mujānaba* for *majāniya*).

177 Ibn Ḥajar al-ʿAsqalānī, *Tahdhīb al-tahdhīb* (Hyderabad edn.), 387 (*qadima ʿalaynā rajulān min nubalāʾ al-nās: aḥaduhumā wa arḥaluhumā Yaʿqūb b. Sufyān, yuʿjazu ahl al-ʿIrāq an yaraw mithlahu rajulan wa kāna Yaḥyā fī al-Tārīkh yantakhibu minhu wa kāna*

Two men of the greatest moral character came to study with us. One of them, who also happened to have travelled more widely [in search of ḥadīth], was Yaʿqūb b. Sufyān. The people of Iraq shall never see a man like him. Yaḥyā [b. Maʿīn] would quote from him in his *History*. He was a man of great piety and mighty standing. Once, I was sitting in the mosque [of Damascus] when a man of the people of Khurāsān came to me and said: 'Are you Abū Zurʿa?' 'I am,' I replied. He then began to ask me about some very subtle and acute matters [of learning]. I asked the man, 'Where on earth did you gather this learning from?' 'We wrote it down from Yaʿqūb b. Sufyān, who transmitted it from you.'

Abū Zurʿa al-Dimashqī was one of al-Fasawī's teachers.[178] But the master displayed no inhibition in extolling his student's learning and moral character. In turn, al-Fasawī's debt to Abū Zurʿa al-Dimashqī is recorded in his *Kitāb al-Maʿrifa wa al-tārīkh*, where al-Fasawī transmits reports directly from him.[179] These two men had met, respected, and viewed each other as legitimate religious authorities. Many of the reports al-Fasawī cites on the authority of Abū Zurʿa al-Dimashqī appear in the latter's *Tārīkh*.[180] We have, therefore, both anecdotal and textual evidence for the exchange of religious information between them.

This connection is important in so far as we should not underestimate one of proto-Sunni traditionalism's greatest strengths – namely, the ability to generate a set of coherent values and ideas that linked communities that were otherwise separated from each other by large distances and terrains.[181]

*nabīlan jalīl al-qadr fa bayna anā qāʾid fī al-masjid idhā jāʾanī rajul min ahl Khurāsān fa qāla lī: anta Abū Zurʿa? Qultu: naʿam. Fa jaʿala yasʾalunī ʿan hādhihi al-daqāʾiq fa qultu lahu: min ayna jamaʿta hādhihi? Qāla: hādhihi katabnāhā ʿan Yaʿqūb b. Sufyān ʿanka).*

178 I have chosen to add 'al-Dimashqī' to his name consistently to differentiate him from Abū Zurʿa al-Rāzī, who is also mentioned in this study.

179 For some of these reports see al-Fasawī, *Kitāb al-Maʿrifa wa al-tārīkh*, 1: 117 (Asad b. Wadāʿa), 121 (ʿAmr b. Muhājir's death date), 129 (Asad b. Wadāʿa), 130 (ʿAmr b. Muhājir's death date taken up again), 132 (al-Zabīdī; ʿUthmān b. Abī al-ʿĀtika), 134 (al-Waḍīn b. ʿAṭāʾ), 137 (Ibn Isḥāq), 143–4 (the number of legal questions al-Awzāʿī answered), 148 (martyrdom of Ḥarmala b. ʿImrān b. Qurrān), 151 (death dates for four scholars), 153 (dates of birth and death for ʿAbd Allāh b. al-ʿAlāʾ and Ibn Thawbān), 155 and 157 (Saʿīd b. ʿAbd al-ʿAzīz al-Tanūkhī), 177 (death date of one Sulaymān), 180–1 (in the year 189 the alms-tax was collected and distributed properly), 200 (funeral prayer of Muḥammad b. al-Mubārak al-Ṣūrī), 208 (death date of Muḥammad b. Dāwūd b. ʿĪsā), 2: 336 (ʿUmar b. ʿAbd al-ʿAzīz), 374 (Makḥūl and Rabīʿa b. Yazīd), 398 (ʿUbayda b. Qays al-ʿUqaylī), 399–400 (Makḥūl), 403 (ʿAṭiyya b. Qays), 405 (wise sayings of Saʿīd b. ʿAbd al-Raḥmān b. Ibrāhīm), 408 (the number of legal questions al-Awzāʿī answered, again).

180 Abū Zurʿa al-Dimashqī, *Tārīkh*, 1: 255 (report no. 334), 256 (report no. 335), 259 (report no. 352), 260 (report no. 355), 261 (report no. 361), 262 (report no. 362), 273 (reports no. 393 and 394), 281 (report no. 436), 282 (report no. 441), 284 (report no. 452), 286 (report no. 466), 2: 721 (report no. 2303).

181 The point is made very well by Robinson, *Empire and Elites after the Muslim Conquest*, 166: 'but no less important in tying province to capital was a network of learning, which emerged during the second century as the study of ḥadīth began to crystallise'.

Al-Fasawī was in many ways a representative of proto-Sunni traditionalism in the eastern provinces of the empire, but he had travelled to Shām in order to establish affinities and loyalties with proto-Sunni traditionalists there. Abū Zurʿa al-Dimashqī's career was formed in this proto-Sunni traditionalist milieu.[182] Both his father and paternal uncle had studied with a number of Shām's leading traditionists such as al-Awzāʿī.[183] Abū Zurʿa seems to have spent a number of years under the tutelage of Abū Mushir al-Ghassānī (d. 218/833).[184] Al-Ghassāni was very highly regarded by ninth-century proto-Sunni traditionalists. Yaḥyā b. Maʿīn was remembered to have considered it utterly shameful to teach or narrate ḥadīth in a place where the likes of Abū Mushir resided, whilst Aḥmad b. Ḥanbal told Abū Zurʿa that Shām was home to three proto-Sunni traditionalists, one of whom was Abū Mushir.[185] Apart from Shām, Abū Zurʿa spent periods of study in Egypt and Iraq. In Iraq he studied with Yaḥyā b. Maʿīn and Aḥmad b. Ḥanbal, and even transmitted a *Masāʾil* collection from the latter;[186] additionally, Abū Zurʿa's *Tārīkh* preserves a number of discussions he had with these two leading proto-Sunni traditionalists.[187] The *Tārīkh* bears witness to Abū Zurʿa's relations and encounters with other members of the proto-Sunni traditionalist community, particularly those who played a prominent role in circulating discourses of heresy against Abū Ḥanīfa. Abū

[182] For an overview of his life and career see Abū Zurʿa al-Dimashqī, *Tārīkh*, 1: 10–94 (al-Qūjānī's introduction); and Rotter, 'Abū Zurʿa al-Dimashqī und das Problem'. Rotter's analysis of Abū Zurʿa al-Dimashqī's *Tārīkh* is based on its manuscript; there was no published edition when he was writing.

[183] Ibn ʿAsākir, *Tārīkh madīnat Dimashq*, ed. ʿUmar b. Gharāma al-ʿAmrawī (Beirut: Dār al-Fikr, 1996), 9: 182–3.

[184] On Abū Mushir al-Ghassānī see Ibn Abī Ḥātim, *Taqdima*, 286–92; al-Khaṭīb al-Baghdādī, *Tārīkh Baghdād*, 11: 72–5; Ibn ʿAsākir, *Tārīkh madīnat Dimashq*, 33: 421–44; Khalek, *Damascus after the Muslim Conquest*, 66–72; Cobb, *White Banners*, 53, 60, 62 (where a picture emerges of Abū Mushir as a local qadi and very much a member of the Damascene elite); Rotter, 'Abū Zurʿa al-Dimashqī und das Problem', 99–100, with special attention to Abū Mushir's works constituting sources for Abū Zurʿa's *Tārīkh*; Ibn al-Jawzī, *Manāqib al-Imām Aḥmad b. Ḥanbal*, ed. ʿAlī Muḥammad ʿUmar (Cairo: Maktabat al-Khānjī, 2009), 389 = ed. ʿAbd al-Muḥsin al-Turkī (Giza: Dār Hajr, 1988), 538–9, where Abū Mushir is summoned to al-Maʾmūn during the inquisition and initially refuses to submit to the caliph's doctrine until he is threatened with physical punishment. According to Ibn al-Jawzī, not even this was enough to spare him imprisonment, and he languished in jail until he died.

[185] Ibn ʿAdī, *al-Kāmil*, 1: 209 (*idhā ḥaddathtu fī balad fīhi mithl Abī Mushir fa yajibu li liḥyatī an tuḥlaqa*); Abū Zurʿa al-Dimashqī, *Tārīkh*, 1: 384 (*qāla Abū Zurʿa: qāla lī Aḥmad b. Ḥanbal: kāna ʿindakum thalāth aṣḥāb al-ḥadīth: Marwān, al-Walīd, wa Abū Mushir*).

[186] Al-Khallāl, *Ṭabaqāt*, *apud* Ibn Abī Yaʿlā, *Ṭabaqāt al-Ḥanābila*, 1: 205–6 (al-Fiqī edn.). Al-Qūjānī supposes that the *Masāʾil* work is, in fact, the *Fāwāʾid* (see Abū Zurʿa al-Dimashqī, *Tārīkh*, 1: 64). I do not believe this is correct based on my perusal of a manuscript of the *Fawāʾid*.

[187] Abū Zurʿa al-Dimashqī, *Tārīkh*, 1: 285 and 305 (where Abū Zurʿa records that they were together in 214/829–30?), 2: 460–4. This is also corroborated by Abū Zurʿa, 'al-Fawāʾid al-muʿallala', MS Feyzullah 2169, Millet Kütüphanesi, 48a.

Zurʿa describes his encounters with al-Ḥumaydī and Ibn Abī Shayba, for example.[188] Now that we have a better idea of Abū Zurʿa's proto-Sunni traditionalist education and connections, we can turn to the discourses of heresy against Abū Ḥanīfa found in his *Tārīkh.*[189]

In the light of what I have said about Abū Zurʿa's proto-Sunni traditionalism we should expect to find a general tenor of hostility towards perceived forms of heresies in his writings. The *Tārīkh* seems to be operating within a framework of proto-Sunni traditionalism that is committed to consciously shaping conceptions of orthodoxy and heresy. This is clear when, for example, Abū Zurʿa proposes distinctions between people of orthodoxy and heresy. In a section discussing the reputation of Ḥammād b. Abī Sulaymān (d. 120/738), Abū Zurʿa quotes someone as telling Ḥammād: 'You were once a leader of the Sunna [read: orthodoxy] and now you have become a sinner embroiled in heresy (*al-bidaʿ*).'[190] Abū Zurʿa is careful to clarify the nature of this perceived heresy. He writes, 'I heard Abū Nuʿaym say, "Ḥammād was a murji'ī."'[191] The scholar Abū Zurʿa discusses after Ḥammād is Dharr b. ʿAbd Allāh. He, too, is identified as a Murji'ī.[192] Any association with Irjā' is indeed a marker of heresy for Abū Zurʿa.

Abū Zurʿa's source for these two reports concerning orthodoxy and heresy is someone called Aḥmad b. Shabbuwayh (d. 229/843).[193] Perhaps the greatest pre-modern historian of Sunni traditionalism recognised Ibn Shabbuwayh as a proto-Sunni traditionalist. Al-Dhahabī adorns him with the esteemed epithet of Shaykh al-Islām.[194] What do we know of Ibn Shabbuwayh on the basis of sources composed in the ninth century, and to what extent was he an agent of proto-Sunni traditionalist orthodoxy? It seems that al-Bukhārī transmits ḥadīth from him in the *Ṣaḥīḥ*.[195] In his *Histories*, al-Bukhārī provides brief biographical

[188] Abū Zurʿa al-Dimashqī, *Tārīkh*, 2: 462, 466, 472 (Ibn Abī Shayba) and 1: 194, 2: 511, 557, 569, 583 (al-Ḥumaydī).

[189] Shukr Allāh b. Niʿmat Allāh al-Qūjānī, the editor of Abū Zurʿa's *Tārīkh*, has identified him as the author of twenty-five works (see Abū Zurʿa al-Dimashqī, *Tārīkh*, 1: 48–77). I am aware of two of these works having survived: the *Tārīkh* and the *Fawā'id*. The *Fawā'id* does not seem to contain any attacks on Abū Ḥanīfa.

[190] Abū Zurʿa al-Dimashqī, *Tārīkh*, 2: 675.

[191] Abū Zurʿa al-Dimashqī, *Tārīkh*, 2: 675.

[192] Abū Zurʿa al-Dimashqī, *Tārīkh*, 2: 675–6.

[193] I rely on al-Samʿānī's pointing for his name (Shabbuwayh as opposed to Shabbawayh): al-Samʿānī, *al-Ansāb*, 7: 284–5 (Maktabat Ibn Taymiyya edn.).

[194] Al-Dhahabī, *Siyar*, 11: 7–8; al-Dhahabī, *Kitāb Tadhkirat al-ḥuffāẓ*, 2: 464–5 (as *shaykh waqtihi*).

[195] For his appearance as 'Aḥmad b. Muḥammad' in the *Ṣaḥīḥ* see al-Bukhārī, *al-Jāmiʿ al-Ṣaḥīḥ*, *kitāb al-wuḍū', bāb mā yaqaʿu min al-najāsāt fī al-samn wa al-mā'* 72; *kitāb al-aḍāḥī, bāb idhā baʿatha bi hadyihi li yudhbaḥa lam yaḥrum ʿalayhi shay'* 15; *kitāb al-jihād, bāb al-rukūb ʿalā al-dābba al-ṣaʿba wa al-fuḥūla min al-khayl* 50. Later scholars who

notices for Ibn Shabbuwayh.[196] Ibn Abī Ḥātim relates the opinions of his father and uncle concerning Aḥmad b. Shabbuwayh. Both of them knew Ibn Shabbuwayh, and Abū Ḥātim confirms that he met and studied with him (*adraktuhu*). Neither of them, however, wrote traditions on his authority.[197] Al-Dāraquṭnī noted some of his teachers and students. Among the latter was Abū Dāwūd al-Sijistānī.[198] Ibn Shabbuwayh had studied with proto-Sunni traditionalists from his native Marw and Khurāsān.[199] He also travelled with his son to Baghdad.[200] It was in Baghdad that he studied with Aḥmad b. Ḥanbal.[201] In one account we learn that he came to Baghdad to see the caliph to reprimand him ('command good and forbid wrong'). Before doing so he decided to consult Aḥmad b. Ḥanbal. Ibn Ḥanbal gave Ibn Shabbuwayh a reality check and told him, 'I fear that you won't be up to the task.'[202]

specialised in identifying al-Bukhārī's informants and transmitters did express some uncertainty as to this transmitter's identity: see the discussions in Mughalṭāy b. Qalīj, *Ikmāl Tahdhīb al-kamāl fī asmā' al-rijāl*, 112–14; Ibn Mākūlā, *al-Ikmāl fī raf' al-irtiyāb 'an al-mu'talif wa al-mukhtalif fī al-asmā' wa al-kunā wa al-ansāb*, ed. 'Abd al-Raḥmān b. Yaḥyā al-Mu'allimī al-Yamānī (Hyderabad: Dā'irat al-Ma'ārif al-'Uthmāniyya, 1962–7), 5: 21–2; al-Mizzī, *Tahdhīb al-kamāl*, 1: 433–6; Ibn Khalfūn, *al-Mu'lim bi shuyūkh al-Bukhārī wa Muslim*, ed. Abū 'Abd al-Raḥmān 'Ādil b. Sa'd (Beirut: Dār al-Kutub al-'Ilmiyya, 2000), 43; al-Kalābādhī, *Rijāl Ṣaḥīḥ Bukhārī*, 42 (as Aḥmad b. Ma'mar b. Mūsā, Abū al-'Abbās, *yuqāl lahu* Mardawayh al-Simsār al-Marwazī); Ibn al-Qaysarānī, *al-Jam' bayna kitābay*, 11–12; Ibn 'Asākir, *Tārīkh madīnat Dimashq*, 71: 167–70; Ibn 'Asākir, *al-Mu'jam al-mushtamil 'alā dhikr asmā' al-shuyūkh al-a'imma al-nabal*, ed. Sukayna al-Shihābī (Damascus: Dār al-Fikr, 1981), 57 (Aḥmad b. Muḥammad b. Thābit b. 'Uthmān b. Mas'ūd b. Yazīd, Abū al-Ḥasan al-Khuzā'ī al-Marwazī al-Mākhuwānī, *al-ma'rūf bi* Ibn Shabbuwayh).

196 Al-Bukhārī, *al-Tārīkh al-kabīr*, 1.2: 5; al-Bukhārī, *al-Tārīkh al-awsaṭ*, 4: 1018 (Abū Ḥaymad edn.) = 2: 252 (al-Luḥaydān edn.).

197 Ibn Abī Ḥātim, *al-Jarḥ*, 1.1: 55.

198 Al-Dāraquṭnī, *al-Mu'talif wa al-mukhtalif*, ed. Muwaffaq b. 'Abd Allāh b. 'Abd al-Qādir (Beirut: Dār al-Gharb al-Islāmī, 1986), 3: 1417–18.

199 Al-Sam'ānī, *al-Ansāb*, 7: 285 (Maktabat Ibn Taymiyya edn.). Ibn Ḥibbān, *Kitāb al-Thiqāt*, 8: 13 (Hyderabad edn.) (Ibn Shabbuwayh studied under al-Faḍl b. Mūsā al-Sīnānī (the editor has his name as Shaybānī, an easy mistake to make)).

200 Al-Khaṭīb al-Baghdādī, *Tārīkh Baghdād*, 11: 6–8. Al-Sam'ānī, *al-Ansāb*, 7: 285 (Maktabat Ibn Taymiyya edn.) describes his son as one of the leading proto-Sunni traditionalists (*min a'immat ahl al-ḥadīth*), who had studied under the likes of Isḥāq b. Rāhawayh.

201 Ibn Abī Ya'lā, *Ṭabaqāt al-Ḥanābila*, 47–8 (al-Fiqī edn.) (*naqala 'an imāminā ashyā'*).

202 Ibn Abī Ya'lā, *Ṭabaqāt al-Ḥanābila*, 47–8 (al-Fiqī edn.). Both Cook (*Commanding Right and Forbidding Wrong*, 101 n. 152) and Laoust (*La profession de foi d'Ibn Baṭṭa*, 53) record this incident. Cook adds a reference to Ibn Mufliḥ's *al-Ādāb al-shar'iyya* (Cairo: n.p., 1348–9), 3: 492, which contains a more detailed account (I have not seen the edition Cook cites). It adds that Ibn Shabbuwayh told Aḥmad b. Ḥanbal that he was resigned to the likelihood of being beaten to death. Aḥmad b. Ḥanbal told him to go and seek Bishr al-Ḥāfī's counsel. Bishr al-Ḥāfī gave Ibn Shabbuwayh the same advice Aḥmad b. Ḥanbal had supplied. Ibn Shabbuwayh emphasised the fact that he had accepted the fate awaiting him. Finally, he changed his mind when Bishr al-Ḥāfī suggested that Ibn

In short, Ibn Shabbuwayh was both well connected to and well regarded by ninth- and tenth-century proto-Sunni traditionalists. Perhaps because of this it is no surprise to learn that he contributed to the growing hostility towards Abū Ḥanīfa and his followers. First of all, he appears in our sources as particularly fastidious with respect to circulating reports that sought to demarcate the boundaries of orthodoxy and heresy. He tells of one instance in which a teacher of his asked Ibn al-Mubārāk, 'Who is the majoritarian group [of orthodoxy]?'[203] Ibn al-Mubārak gave the name of three people who embodied proto-Sunni traditionalist orthodoxy. Aḥmad b. Shabbuwayh corroborates Ibn al-Mubārak's identification of these men as proto-Sunni traditionalists by remarking that 'none of these men was tainted by Irjā''.[204] He also emphasised the wide gulf between the kind of religious learning and piety serviced by ḥadīth, on the one hand, and speculative jurisprudence, on the other. In a tradition transmitted by his son, who had studied with Isḥāq b. Rāhawayh, Ibn Shabbuwayh declared that those interested in attaining salvation in the afterlife should study Prophetic traditions, whilst those interested in attaining knowledge of this world should concern themselves with *ra'y*.[205]

Furthermore, Aḥmad b. Shabbuwayh is a frequent source for invective against Abū Ḥanīfa in ninth- and tenth-century sources. In ʿAbd Allāh b. Aḥmad b. Ḥanbal's *Kitāb al-Sunna* Aḥmad b. Shabbuwayh narrates a

Shabbuwayh's actions would lead to his death and that this, in turn, would condemn the caliph to hellfire. Even Aḥmad b. Ḥanbal was amazed by Bishr al-Ḥāfī's reasoning. See Ibn Mufliḥ, *al-Ādāb al-sharʿiyya*, ed. Shuʿayb al-Arna'ūṭ and ʿUmar al-Qayyām (Beirut: Mu'assasat al-Risāla, 1999), 3: 463. Ibn al-Mufliḥ is quoting from al-Khallāl, so I am assuming that Ibn Abī Yaʿlā quoted a short excerpt from al-Khallāl's now lost work. A small portion of al-Khallāl's *Ṭabaqāt aṣḥab al-Imām Aḥmad b. Ḥanbal* (Riyadh: Markaz al-Malik Fayṣal li al-Buḥūth wa al-Dirāsāt al-Islāmiyya, 2019) has survived and been published (names beginning with *alif* to *khā'*), but it does not contain an entry on Aḥmad b. Shabbuwayh.

203 Ibn Ḥajar al-ʿAsqalānī, *Tahdhīb al-tahdhīb* (Beirut: Mu'assasat al-Risāla, 1995), 1: 438 (*man al-jamāʿa?*).

204 Ibn Ḥajar al-ʿAsqalānī, *Tahdhīb al-tahdhīb*, 1: 438 (Mu'assasat al-Risāla edn.) (*laysa fīhim shay' min al-irjā'*). Ibn Ḥajar's report is probably based on a slightly longer account contained in Abū Zurʿa al-Dimashqī's *Tārīkh*.

205 Al-Khaṭīb al-Baghdādī, *Kitāb Sharaf aṣḥāb al-ḥadīth*, ed. Muḥammad Saʿīd Khaṭīb Ughlī (Ankara: Jāmiʿat Anqara, 1969), 75; reproduced in al-Dhahabī, *Siyar*, 11: 7–8 (*man arāda ʿilm al-qabr fa ʿalayhi bi al-athar wa man arāda ʿilm al-khubz fa ʿalayhi bi al-ra'y*). I am interpreting *ʿilm al-khubz* to refer to worldly learning. A further insight into Ibn Shabbuwayh's commitment to proto-Sunni traditionalism might be gained from a report his son transmits that quotes a certain Yūnus b. Sulaymān al-Saqaṭī as having said: 'I found in the ḥadīth the mention of the Lord almighty and His lordship, mightiness, and exaltedness, mention of the throne and descriptions of Paradise and Hell, and mention of the prophets and messengers, the licit and illicit, and incitement towards good relations with one's relatives, and much else of good in the ḥadīth; and when I looked into *ra'y*, I found that it was concerned with deception and how to sever family relations (*al-makr wa al-ghadr*) and much else of evil in *ra'y*.'

story in which Ibn al-Mubārak describes his study with Abū Ḥanīfa as a source of affliction. He was asked, 'Did you relate knowledge from Abū Ḥanīfa?' He replied, 'Yes, and I was afflicted by it.'[206] Again, Ibn Shabbuwayh quotes Ibn al-Mubārak as having declared highway robbery to be better than some of Abū Ḥanīfa's doctrines.[207] Ibn Shabbuwayh's son transmitted reports of a more caustic nature through Isḥāq b. Rāhawayh. In an apparent reference to Abū Ḥanīfa, a Khurāsānī scholar is reported to have said that 'the issuing of religious opinions in Bukhārā of that so and so Jahmī is more harmful to the Muslims than the appearance of the Beast or the anti-Christ'.[208] Ibn Shabbuwayh (and his son) also circulated scornful reports about Abū Ḥanīfa's leading disciple, Abū Yūsuf, which criticised the latter for the ends to which he utilised his learning, and suggested that Mālik b. Anas refused to take questions from him because he regarded the chief judge as unorthodox.[209]

Specific attacks against Abū Ḥanīfa are grouped together in Abū Zurʿa's *Tārīkh*. One report appears to cast doubt on Abū Ḥanīfa's belonging to the generation of the Successors.[210] Once again, Aḥmad b. Shabbuwayh is his source for a report that almost certainly alludes to Abū Ḥanīfa, which warns against a man in Kufa who answers questions concerning the most enigmatic issues (*muʿḍilāt*).[211] Another report transmitted by Aḥmad b. Shabbuwayh has al-Awzāʿī reprimand Ibn al-Mubārak when the latter sought his counsel after he had praised Abū Ḥanīfa in passing: 'Yes, I was going to give you some advice regardless of your asking for it, for I heard you praise a man who permitted rebellion against the Muslims.'[212] Abū Zurʿa's *Tārīkh* seeks to amplify a wider initiative to isolate and exclude Abū Ḥanīfa from the proto-Sunni community. He reminds his readers that not only did proto-Sunni traditionalists admonish one another about praising Abū Ḥanīfa, but he cites occasions in which proto-Sunni traditionalists avoided speaking to or sitting with Abū Ḥanīfa. The *Tārīkh* claims that Sufyān (al-Thawrī?) refused to discuss matters with Abū Ḥanīfa, and that when a group of scholars in Mecca were interrupted by the arrival of Abū Ḥanīfa, they got

206 ʿAbd Allāh b. Aḥmad b. Ḥanbal, *Kitāb al-Sunna*, 215.

207 ʿAbd Allāh b. Aḥmad b. Ḥanbal, *Kitāb al-Sunna*, 214.

208 ʿAbd Allāh b. Aḥmad b. Ḥanbal, *Kitāb al-Sunna*, 214.

209 Al-ʿUqaylī, *Kitāb al-Ḍuʿafāʾ*, ed. Ismāʿīl al-Salafī (Riyadh: Dār al-Ṣumayʿī, 2000), 4: 1544–5 (entry on Abū Yūsuf).

210 Abū Zurʿa al-Dimashqī, *Tārīkh*, 2: 505 (*anā akbar man raʾa Abā Ḥanīfa*).

211 Abū Zurʿa al-Dimashqī, *Tārīkh*, 2: 505. For reasons why this report alludes to Abū Ḥanīfa, see Chapter 7 below.

212 Abū Zurʿa al-Dimashqī, *Tārīkh*, 2: 505 (*kuntu ʿinda al-Awzāʿī fa aṭraytu Abā Ḥanīfa, fa sakata ʿannī. Fa lammā kāna ʿinda al-wadāʿ qultu lahu: awṣinī. Qāla: Ammā innī aradtu dhāka wa law lam tasʾalnī samiʿtuka tuṭrī rajulan kāna yarā al-sayf fī al-umma*). See also al-Khaṭīb al-Baghdādī, *Tārīkh Baghdād*, 15: 528.

up and left, 'fearful of catching his disease'.[213] The *Tārīkh* hosts the usual criticisms of Abū Ḥanīfa and his speculative jurisprudence, but it also entertains more severe criticisms.[214] Abū Zur'a quotes Sufyān al-Thawrī as writing off Abū Ḥanīfa as untrustworthy and unreliable because he was made to repent from heresy twice.[215] In addition, a report that points to the wide dissemination of discourses against Abū Ḥanīfa states that a local qadi prayed during a sermon that God would show no mercy to Abū Ḥanīfa, for he was the first to claim that the Quran was created.[216] Resembling this spirit of broad condemnation is another report in the *Tārīkh* that no birth was more harmful to Islam than the birth of Abū Ḥanīfa.[217]

This digression from Abū Zur'a al-Dimashqī's discourses of heresy against Abū Ḥanīfa to the background of a source he cites frequently in his local history of Damascus exemplifies the subtle formation of a proto-Sunni traditionalist orthodoxy defined through a collective effort to construct heresiological discourses against Abū Ḥanīfa. A reference to Aḥmad b. Shabbuwayh is not an incidental fact in Abū Zur'a's text. He is a source of information in so far as the information he provides represents a broader religious outlook that Abū Zur'a and other proto-Sunni traditionalists share.[218] Even in the section on the judges of Marw, Aḥmad b. Shabbuwayh corroborates the orthodoxy of one particular judge by exonerating him from any association with either Irjā' or Abū Ḥanīfa's doctrines.[219] This might be lost on modern (and early modern) readers unfamiliar with Aḥmad b. Shabbuwayh's contribution to proto-Sunni traditionalist orthodoxy, especially in the form of discourses of heresy against Abū Ḥanīfa. Many of Abū Zur'a's contemporaries and readers, on the other hand, would have been familiar with what united men such as Abū Zur'a and Ibn Shabbuwayh.

### *'Abd Allāh b. Aḥmad b. Ḥanbal (d. 290/903)*

Aḥmad b. Ḥanbal's son 'Abd Allāh was a good example of the kind of ninth-century scholar who would have recognised Aḥmad b.

[213] Abū Zur'a al-Dimashqī, *Tārīkh*, 2: 505 (Sufyān and Abū Ḥanīfa), 507 (Abū Ḥanīfa's disease).
[214] Abū Zur'a al-Dimashqī, *Tārīkh*, 2: 507, 508 (x 3).
[215] Abū Zur'a al-Dimashqī, *Tārīkh*, 2: 505–6 (*ustutība Abū Ḥanīfa marratayn*), 507 (*Abū Ḥanīfa ghayr thiqa wa lā ma'mūn, ustutība marratayn*).
[216] Abū Zur'a al-Dimashqī, *Tārīkh*, 2: 506.
[217] Abū Zur'a al-Dimashqī, *Tārīkh*, 2: 507.
[218] The information on judges in Marw is provided by Ibn Shabbuwayh: see Abū Zur'a al-Dimashqī, *Tārīkh*, 1: 206–8.
[219] Abū Zur'a al-Dimashqī, *Tārīkh*, 1: 208.

Shabbuwayh as a fellow Sunni traditionalist. There are reasons internal to the texts ʿAbd Allāh b. Ḥanbal composed that indicate such an awareness, but let us first consider the contexts in which the two men might have known each other by way of ʿAbd Allāh's biography. ʿAbd Allāh b. Ḥanbal was one of seven children from three of Aḥmad b. Ḥanbal's marriages. The two best known sons were ʿAbd Allāh and Ṣāliḥ, a fact which must have something to do with their prominent role in transmitting their father's teachings and works. Of the two, Ṣāliḥ was the elder and issued from his father's marriage to ʿĀ'isha bt. al-Faḍl, whilst ʿAbd Allāh was born to Aḥmad b. Ḥanbal's second wife, Rayḥāna.[220]

Despite their father's hostility to state employment, almost all of Aḥmad b. Ḥanbal's sons worked as judges in the empire's provinces.[221] Ṣāliḥ served as a judge in Ṭarsūs and Iṣfahān and performed certain diplomatic duties on behalf of the caliph al-Muwaffaq.[222] Saʿīd served as a judge in Kufa.[223] Our central protagonist, ʿAbd Allāh, occupied the judgeship in Khurāsān and Ḥimṣ.[224] As a young man ʿAbd Allāh had studied with proto-Sunni traditionalists such as Yaḥyā b. Maʿīn and Ibn Abī Shayba. In the *Masā'il*, for instance, we find ʿAbd Allāh in the company

220 The third wife was called Ḥusn, and bore Aḥmad six children.

221 See Melchert, *The Formation of the Sunni Schools of Law*, 140; Melchert, *Aḥmad ibn Ḥanbal*, 15–16; and for changing Ḥanbalī attitudes towards state employment see the vast amount of data amassed by Cook, *Commanding Right and Forbidding Wrong*, 123–8.

222 For Ṣāliḥ's judgeships in Ṭarsūs and Iṣfahān, where he is reported as disgusted with himself and speaks of being compelled to accept the judgeship in order to settle his debts, see Ibn Abī Yaʿlā, *Ṭabaqāt al-Ḥanābila*, 1: 174–5 (al-Fiqī edn.) = 1: 463–6 (al-ʿUthaymīn edn.); al-Khallāl, *Adab al-qaḍā'*, *apud* al-Khaṭīb al-Baghdādī, *Tārīkh Baghdād*, 10: 433–5 (for Ṣāliḥ's anguished account of his inauguration as qadi of Iṣfahān); Ibn Ḥazm, *Jamharat*, 319 (ʿAbd al-Salām Hārūn edn.) (*qāḍī al-thaghr*); Ibn al-Jawzī, *Manāqib*, 302 (Maktabat al-Khānjī edn.). For Ṣāliḥ being dispatched by Muwaffaq to Aḥmad b. Ṭūlūn, perhaps as part of a delegation of proto-Sunni traditionalists (*aṣḥāb al-ḥadīth*), see the eyewitness account of Abū al-Ḥasan Muḥammad b. al-Fayḍ al-Ghassānī, *Akhbār wa ḥikāyāt*, ed. Ibrāhīm Ṣāliḥ (Damascus: Dār al-Bashā'ir, 1994), 41. The author of this overlooked work was a ninth–tenth-century proto-Sunni traditionalist from Damascus.

223 For Saʿīd's judgeship see Ibn Abī Yaʿlā, *Ṭabaqāt al-Ḥanābila*, 2: 49 (al-Fiqī edn.) = 3: 89–90 (al-ʿUthaymīn edn.) (the detail is tucked away in the entry on Aḥmad b. Ḥanbal's grandson Zuhayr b. Ṣāliḥ, and contains a highly informative family account of Aḥmad b. Ḥanbal's marriage and family history; the editor's conjectural objection to Saʿīd's ever having been a qadi because the historical sources are silent about this is baseless given the reference that follows). Saud al-Sarhan follows Ibn al-Jawzī (*Manāqib*, 304–5 (Maktabat al-Khānjī edn.)) in the view that Saʿīd did not work as a judge: see al-Sarhan, 'Early Muslim Traditionalism', 209 n. 44. However, the earliest reference to Saʿīd's judgeship is in a source overlooked by both al-Sarhan and Hurvitz (*The Formation of Hanbalism*, 35): Wakīʿ, *Akhbār al-quḍāt*, 3: 199. Al-Khaṭīb al-Baghdādī, *Tārīkh Baghdād*, 10: 137 has an entry on Saʿīd but does not mention his judgeship, although he mentions al-Qāḍī Abū ʿImrān Mūsā b. al-Qāsim b. al-Ashyab as his student (*rawā ʿanhu*).

224 For ʿAbd Allāh's judgeship in Khurāsān and Ḥimṣ see Ibn Abī Yaʿlā, *Ṭabaqāt al-Ḥanābila*, 1: 188 (al-Fiqī edn.) = 2: 20 (al-ʿUthaymīn edn.); Ibn Ḥazm, *Jamharat*, 319 (ʿAbd al-Salām Hārūn edn.).

of Ibn Abī Shayba's son, ʿAbd Allāh, in Kufa in 230/844–5.[225] Evidently he studied with his father, and later biographers emphasised Aḥmad b. Ḥanbal's high regard for the quality of ʿAbd Allāh's religious learning.[226] Even in the earliest sources ʿAbd Allāh comes across as a dedicated and keen student. The *Masāʾil* collection he compiled, for example, describes him making notations whilst journeying with his father to Mecca.[227] ʿAbd Allāh comes across as a precocious student whose juridical opinions are confirmed by his father.[228] The *Masāʾil* collection was one of many of his father's books that ʿAbd Allāh transmitted. It, too, exhibits the proto-Sunni traditionalist tendency of defining orthodoxy against heresy, particularly in the following exchange between ʿAbd Allāh and his father:[229]

ʿABD ALLĀH: I said to my father: 'What is your opinion concerning people belonging to the *aṣḥāb al-ḥadīth* who go to a shaykh who is either a Murjiʾī, a Shiʿi, or simply holds some doctrine that is opposed to the Sunna (*aw fīhi shayʾ min khilāf al-sunna*)? Should I remain quiet and not warn against him, or should I warn people about him?'

AḤMAD B. ḤANBAL: If he calls people to heresy (*bidaʿ*) and he is a leader among them and invites others to that heresy, then, yes: you must warn against him.

Proto-Sunni traditionalists were certainly conscious of a group identity, which formed in opposition to perceived heresies. It was not enough, however, to simply insist on the demarcations and boundaries between orthodoxy and heresy. It was equally the work of orthodoxy to oppose very publicly figures they saw as representatives of deviant movements. Proto-Sunni traditionalists were not simply venting against Abū Ḥanīfa. They knew that presenting Abū Ḥanīfa as a heretical and deviant scholar was integral to the formation of orthodoxy. This was an essential task of orthodoxy, and it is within this context that we must understand the profusion of discourses of heresy against Abū Ḥanīfa in the ninth century.

225 ʿAbd Allāh b. Aḥmad b. Ḥanbal, *Masāʾil al-Imām Aḥmad b. Ḥanbal riwāyat ibnihi ʿAbd Allāh b. Aḥmad*, ed. Zuhayr al-Shāwīsh (Damascus: al-Maktab al-Islāmī, 1981), 41. Although, on this occasion, ʿAbd Allāh relates his father ʿAbd Allāh b. Abī Shayba's view that saying *yahdīkum Allāh* in the series of responses after one sneezes was an innovation of the Khawārij. Aḥmad b. Ḥanbal finds this untenable. For ʿAbd Allāh's meetings with Ibn Abī Shayba, as recorded in the *Masāʾil*, see 93, 185, 344, 364.

226 Ibn Abī Yaʿlā, *Ṭabaqāt al-Ḥanābila*, 1: 180 (al-Fiqī edn.); al-Khaṭīb al-Baghdādī, *Tārīkh Baghdād*, 11: 13–14.

227 ʿAbd Allāh b. Aḥmad b. Ḥanbal, *Masāʾil*, 199.

228 ʿAbd Allāh b. Aḥmad b. Ḥanbal, *Masāʾil*, 55 (ʿAbd Allāh decided to hit his servant because he had missed a prayer intentionally. His father agreed that he should do so until the servant returned to praying).

229 ʿAbd Allāh b. Aḥmad b. Ḥanbal, *Masāʾil*, 439. A similar point regarding heretics who preach their heretical doctrines is made in al-Marrūdhī, *Kitāb al-ʿIlal wa maʿrifat al-rijāl li Aḥmad b. Muḥammad b. Ḥanbal: riwāyat al-Marrūdhī*, ed. Waṣī Allāh b. Muḥammad ʿAbbās (Bombay: al-Dār al-Salafiyya, 1988; repr. Cairo: Dār al-Imām Aḥmad, 2006), 126.

The book most relevant to our discussion of discourses of heresy against Abū Ḥanīfa is the *Kitāb al-Sunna*, though one other work attributed to ʿAbd Allāh b. Aḥmad b. Ḥanbal mentions thc followers of Abū Ḥanīfa as a source of misguidance for many people.[230] The *Kitāb al-Sunna* belongs to a genre of proto-Sunni traditionalist writing that was crucial to emergence of a public discourse designed to establish orthodoxy by explicating heresy.[231] His work was preceded by or was coterminous with a number of books authored by proto-Sunni traditionalists bearing similar titles. An early work, the *Kitāb al-Taḥrīsh*, speaks to the cacophonous nature of the Muslim community in the eighth to early ninth century, though this may have been our author's main intention. The *Kitāb al-Taḥrīsh* was authored from the opposing perspective of proto-Sunni traditionalism. Its author, Ḍirār b. ʿAmr, was associated with the early Muʿtazila. His genealogy of sect formation in early Islam is highly deterministic, which makes it difficult to use for historians, and is replete with idealised tropes.[232] Nevertheless, there is an awareness of the

[230] Aḥmad b. Ḥanbal (attrib.), *Kitāb al-Radd ʿalā al-jahmiyya wa al-zanādiqa*, ed. Daghīs b. Shubayb al-ʿAjmī (Kuwait: Gharās, 2005), 207. There is much uncertainty regarding the attribution of this text to both Aḥmad b. Ḥanbal and his son ʿAbd Allāh. The manuscripts do not resolve the issue: at least nine manuscripts of the work exist, but the earliest copy was made in 1418. I know of six editions of the text: ed. Daghīs b. Shubayb al-ʿAjmī (Kuwait: Gharās, 2005), based on MS Ẓāhiriyya, and eight other manuscripts = ed. Ṣabrī Salāma Shāhīn (Riyadh: Dār al-Thibāt li al-Nashr wa al-Tawzīʿ, 2002), the editor does not say which manuscripts serve the basis of the edition = ed. Muḥammad Ḥasan Rāshid (Cairo: al-Maṭbaʿa al-Salafiyya, 1973), based on MS. Ẓāhiriyya maj. 116 = ed. ʿAbd al-Raḥmān ʿUmayra (Riyadh: Dār al-Liwā', 1982) = ed. Muḥammad Fahr Shafqa (Ḥamā: Maktabat Ibn al-Haytham, 1967) = ed. Qiwām al-Dīn, 'Imam Ahmed'in bir eseri. İslâmın en kadim iki mezhebinin münakaşası', Darülfünun İlâhiyat Fâkültesi Mecmuası, 2: 5/6 (1927), 278–327, based on MS. Revan Köşki, Istanbul 510/4 (I owe my knowledge of this last work to Christopher Melchert). For a discussion of the work's authenticity with respect to its transmission history see al-Sarhan, 'Early Muslim Traditionalism', 48–54. Abū Ḥanīfa, Abū Yūsuf, and al-Shaybānī are also mentioned in the (blameworthy) context of composing books in ʿAbd Allāh b. Aḥmad b. Ḥanbal, *Masā'il*, 437.

[231] This edition is based on six manuscripts: The *aṣl* is al-Ẓāhiriyya, MS 1047, copied in 644/1246–7; Maktabat al-Shaykh ʿAbd Allāh b. Ḥasan Āl al-Shaykh, now in Jāmiʿat Umm al-Qurā, MS 1497, copied in 783/1381–2; al-Maktaba al-ʿĀmma, MS 288, copied in 1283/1866–7; Dār al-Kutub al-Miṣriyya, MS 1747; al-Maktaba al-Taymūriyya, MS 335, copied in 1329/1911, Khudā Bakhsh, MS 3700, copied in 1300/1882–3. Another edition of the work has been prepared by ʿĀdil Ḥamdān (n.p.: n.p., 2015). This edition also uses al-Ẓāhiriyya, MS 1047 as the *aṣl*. There are significant discrepancies between the manuscripts, none more pertinent than the complete absence of the chapter on Abū Ḥanīfa in Jāmiʿat Umm al-Qurā, MS 1497. See also ʿĀdil Ḥamdān's polemical critique of earlier editions of the *Kitāb al-Sunna*: ʿĀdil Ḥamdān, *Silsilat taʿlīqātī ʿalā taḥqīqāt kutub al-sunna: Kitāb al-Sunna* (n.p.: Dār al-Naṣīḥa, n.d.).

[232] Consider the following explanation: Ḍirār b. ʿAmr, *Kitāb al-Taḥrīsh*, 41 (*wa minhum man akfarahum jamīʿan wa minhum man tawallā baʿḍan wa minhum man tawallāhum jamīʿan wa minhum man waqafa fīhim wa minhum man jazama al-kalām fīhim. Fa hādhā awwal sabab mā ikhtalafa fīhi ahl al-ṣalāt wa minhu tashaʿʿabū*). Another early

concept of religious deviance (*ahl al-bidaʿ wa al-ḍalāl*). The problem is that our author seeks to argue that every single religious denomination classifies other groups as belonging to the *ahl al-bidaʿ wa al-ḍalāl.*[233] Our author is vaguely aware of a majoritarian orthodoxy: on one occasion he speaks of *ṣāḥib sunna wa al-jamāʿa*, and twice he refers to the *jamāʿa.*[234] *Kitāb al-Taḥrīsh* conveys the sheer diversity of the early Islamic community, with no single group dominating and shaping religious orthodoxy. When the author wants to speak of the generality of Muslims – there being no indisputable majoritarian group in his view – he speaks of those who pray towards the Kaʿba (*ahl al-qibla*).[235] In conclusion, what is patently absent in the eighth and early ninth centuries is a mature formulation of religious orthodoxy, particularly one that is defined against heresy.

It is in the *kutub al-sunna* of the mid- to late ninth century that we can observe a maturation of proto-Sunni traditionalist orthodoxy, whereby conceptions of orthodoxy are articulated in direct opposition to perceived heresies. It is through this mechanism, then, that fields of heresy are also demarcated. For example, the first chapter of Ibn Abī ʿĀṣim's (d. 287/900) *Kitāb al-Sunna* raises the spectre of heresy (*ahwāʾ*);[236] another chapter quotes a tradition encouraging believers to seek protection from heresy;[237] and the subsequent chapter speaks of the deviant nature of heresy.[238] Towards the end of the book Ibn Abī ʿĀṣim makes it clear that the phenomenon of proto-Sunni traditionalist orthodoxy was, by definition, majoritarian.[239] Quietism was also an integral component of proto-Sunni traditionalist conceptions of orthodoxy, but it made space for speaking truth to power.[240] Other *Kitāb al-Sunna* books exhibit similar

work is al-Kinānī's *Kitāb al-Ḥayda*, but its attribution is uncertain and it resembles a disputation treatise: ʿAbd al-ʿAzīz al-Kinānī, *Kitāb al-Ḥayda* (Giza: Maktabat al-Nawʿiyya al-Islāmiyya li al-Iḥyāʾ al-Turāth al-Islāmī, n.d.). I thank Ahmed El Shamsy for bringing this text to my attention. The authenticity of the text has been disputed by van Ess, *Theologie und Gesellschaft*, 3: 504–8 and El Omari, 'Kitāb al-Ḥayda'. Van Ess's most recent examination of *Kitāb al-Taḥrīsh*, this time based on the published edition, reiterates the uncertainty surrounding the text's integrity.

233 Ḍirār b. ʿAmr, *Kitāb al-Taḥrīsh*, 46, 51, 52, 56. 57, 58, 59, 61, 69, 72, 73, 74, 75, 76, 77, 79, 84, 90, 91, 92, 97, 101.

234 Ḍirār b. ʿAmr, *Kitāb al-Taḥrīsh*, 72, 75, 104. As van Ess has observed, the *aṣḥāb al-ḥadīth* are not mentioned once: van Ess, *Kleine Schriften*, 3: 2497–8 ('Das K. At-Taḥrīš des Ḍirār b. ʿAmr: Einige Bemerkungen zu Ort und Anlaβ seiner Abfassung').

235 Ḍirār b. ʿAmr, *Kitāb al-Taḥrīsh*, 99.

236 Ibn Abī ʿĀṣim, *Kitāb al-Sunna*, ed. Bāsim b. Fayṣal al-Jawābara (Riyadh: Dār al-Ṣumayʿī, 1998), 35–41.

237 Ibn Abī ʿĀṣim, *Kitāb al-Sunna*, 44 (citing Ibn Abī Shayba).

238 Ibn Abī ʿĀṣim, *Kitāb al-Sunna*, 44–5 (citing Ibn Abī Shayba).

239 Ibn Abī ʿĀṣim, *Kitāb al-Sunna*, 617–22.

240 Ibn Abī ʿĀṣim, *Kitāb al-Sunna*, 696 ff. (quietism), 731–9 (speaking truth to power).

developments.[241] Abū ʿUbayd al-Qāsim b. Sallām (d. 224/838–9) begins his treatise on faith (*īmān*) by articulating proto-Sunni traditionalist orthodoxy in contrast to those who deviate from it.[242] Muḥammad b. Naṣr al-Marwazī's (d. 294/906) *Kitāb al-Sunna* is an odd work and stands apart from the *kutub al-sunna*, though it is noteworthy that he authored a refutation against Abū Ḥanīfa.[243]

In terms of discourses of heresy against Abū Ḥanīfa, ʿAbd Allāh b. Aḥmad b. Ḥanbal's *Kitāb al-Sunna* was a watershed moment in the evolution of proto-Sunni traditionalist orthodoxy. It represents the kind of religious information that was being circulated among the proto-Sunni traditionalist community in different regions of the early Islamic world in the middle of the ninth century.[244] My cursory reading of the text suggests a *terminus post quem* of 231/845–6.[245] The majority of the reports originate with ʿAbd Allāh's main proto-Sunni traditionalist teachers.[246] Among these illustrious figures are Aḥmad b. Ḥanbal, Aḥmad b. Ibrāhīm al-Dawraqī, Ibn Abī Shayba, and Aḥmad b. Shabbuwayh.[247] Evidence

[241] Al-Ḥumaydī, *Uṣūl al-sunna*, ed. Mashʿal Muḥammad al-Ḥaddādī (Kuwait: Dār Ibn al-Athīr, 1997), 43 is no more than a few folios and displays on one occasion only an attempt to define orthodoxy against heresy (*wa an lā naqūl kamā qālat al-khawārij*).

[242] Abū ʿUbayd al-Qāsim b. Sallām, *Kitāb al-Īmān*, ed. Muḥammad Nāṣir al-Dīn al-Albānī (Riyadh: Maktabat al-Maʿārif, 2000), 9 (*wa tadhkur annaka aḥbabta maʿrifat mā ʿalayhi ahl al-sunna min dhālika wa mā al-ḥujja ʿalā man fāraqahum fīhi*), 53 (*wa zaʿama man khālafanā anna al-qawl dūna al-ʿamal, fa hādhā ʿindanā mutanāqiḍ*), 59 (*qad dhakarnā mā kāna min mufāraqat al-qawm iyyānā [fī anna] al-ʿamal min al-īmān, ʿalā annahum wa in kānū lanā mufāriqīn, fa innahum dhahabū ilā madhhab qad yaqaʿu al-ghalaṭ fī mithlihi*), 66–7 (*wa ʿalā mithl hādhā al-qawl kāna Sufyān wa al-Awzāʿī wa Mālik b. Anas wa man baʿduhum min arbāb al-ʿilm wa ahl al-sunna alladhīna kānū maṣābīḥ al-arḍ wa a'immat al-ʿilm fī dahrihim min ahl al-ʿIrāq wa al-Ḥijāz wa al-Shām wa ghayrihā zārīn ʿalā ahl al-bidaʿ kullihā wa yarawna al-īmān qawlan wa ʿamalan*). It is interesting to note that passages like these, which speak to the burgeoning confidence of a proto-Sunni traditionalist orthodoxy, are absent in the earlier work of Ibn Abī Shayba, *Kitāb al-Īmān*, ed. Muḥammad Nāṣir al-Dīn al-Albānī (Damascus: al-Maktab al-Islamī, 1983), 157–85. I have not undertaken a systematic comparison between this *Kitāb al-Īmān* and the Kitāb al-Īmān that appears in Ibn Abī Shayba, *al-Muṣannaf*, 6: 157–84. The ordering of traditions certainly differs in both texts.

[243] Al-Dhahabī, *Siyar*, 14: 38. Muḥammad b. Naṣr al-Marwazī, *al-Sunna*, ed. ʿAbd Allāh b. Muḥammad al-Buṣīrī (Riyadh: Dār al-ʿĀṣima, 2001). His *Ikhtilāf al-fuqahā'* makes no explicit reference to Abū Ḥanīfa by name, but he does refer frequently to the *aṣḥāb al-ra'y* and their leader (*shaykuhum*): see Muḥammad b. Naṣr al-Marwazī, *Ikhtilāf al-fuqahā'*, ed. Muḥammad Ṭāhir Ḥakīm (Riyadh: Maktaba Aḍwā' al-Salaf, 2000), 169.

[244] The *Kitāb al-Sunna* refers occasionally to the places where he received or heard reports: see ʿAbd Allāh b. Aḥmad b. Ḥanbal, *Kitāb al-Sunna*, 493 and 559 (Medina), 495–6 and 563 and 624 (Basra), and 627 (Kufa).

[245] I have noticed three occasions in the text where ʿAbd Allāh refers to the year in which he received a report: ʿAbd Allāh b. Aḥmad b. Ḥanbal, *Kitāb al-Sunna*, 161 (226/840–1), 479 and 495–6 (231/845–6), 550 (231/845–6).

[246] A complete list of teachers is given in ʿAbd Allāh b. Aḥmad b. Ḥanbal, *Kitāb al-Sunna*, 40–7 (editor's introduction).

[247] For a list of ʿAbd Allāh's informants, and the number of times they are cited, see ʿAbd Allāh b. Aḥmad b. Ḥanbal, *Kitāb al-Sunna*, 61–2 (editor's introduction).

internal to *Kitāb al-Sunna* suggests that most of the information was received by ʿAbd Allāh through oral transmission, but we do learn of instances where ʿAbd Allāḥ's information was extracted from written texts. In one passage, for example, we are told that ʿAbd Allāh reproduced material from his father's handwritten notes.[248] The *terminus post quem* helps to explain *Kitāb al-Sunna*'s principal target: those who believe in the createdness of the Quran, described by our author as the Jahmiyya. The year 231/845–6 witnessed Aḥmad b. Naṣr al-Khuzāʿī's execution by the caliph al-Wāthiq. Modern historians have interpreted this incident as a manifestation of al-Wāthiq's energetic commitment to the Miḥna, which al-Mutawakkil would bring to an end in 849 or 851–2, as well as evidence for the caliph's role as somebody who shaped and enforced religious orthodoxy.[249] Aḥmad b. Naṣr's refusal to assent to the caliphal doctrine of a created Quran did play a role in his trial and execution.[250] However, it would be a mistake to view this as the principal cause behind the caliph's pursuit of him. Aḥmad b. Naṣr may have been a proto-Sunni traditionalist, but he represented a distinct brand of proto-Sunni traditionalism. Unlike Aḥmad b. Ḥanbal, for example, Aḥmad b. Naṣr was in the process of raising a rebellion against the caliph.[251] As we shall see in our analysis of discourses of heresy against Abū Ḥanīfa in the *Kitāb al-Sunna*, Aḥmad b. Ḥanbal found the idea of rebelling against the state not only repugnant but a sign of heresy. In circumstances such as these, Ibn Ḥanbal believed that men could speak truth to power, but a more brazen challenge to the caliphal office was unconscionable. Within a year of Aḥmad b. Naṣr's execution, change was in the air. Al-Mutawakkil had ascended the throne. Caliphal interest in pursuing the Miḥna went from waning to a complete reversal. Aḥmad b. Ḥanbal was now receiving invitations to visit the caliph in Samarra.[252]

These dramatic events and turbulent changes must have been stirring in ʿAbd Allāh's mind when he began to compose the *Kitāb al-Sunna*. But proto-Sunni traditionalist conceptions of orthodoxy were not limited to debates concerning the createdness of the Quran. Other themes that appear prominently in the *Kitāb al-Sunna* are Irjā', the nature of faith (performance, action, or both), destinarianism, the probity of the first four caliphs, and attitudes to the state. But we can measure the

248 ʿAbd Allāh b. Aḥmad b. Ḥanbal, *Kitāb al-Sunna*, 512 (*wajadtu fī kitāb abī bi khaṭṭ yadihi mimmā yuḥtajju bihi ʿalā al-jahmiyya min al-Qur'ān al-Karīm*).

249 Turner, 'The Enigmatic Reign of al-Wāthiq'.

250 Al-Ṭabarī, *Tārīkh*, 3: 1412 = 9: 190–1. For other indicators of al-Wāthiq's Miḥna policy see Melchert, 'Religious Policies of the Caliphs', 320.

251 Al-Ṭabarī, *Tārīkh*, 3: 1412 = 9: 190–1. Though, for the record, Aḥmad b. Naṣr did object to the notion that he was planning to rebel.

252 Melchert, 'Religious Policies of the Caliphs', 326–7.

importance of discourses of heresy against Abū Ḥanīfa to proto-Sunni traditionalists by the fact that ʿAbd Allāh's *Kitāb al-Sunna* devotes almost fifty pages to portraying Abū Ḥanīfa as a heresiarch.[253] ʿAbd Allāh's method for depicting Abū Ḥanīfa as a heretic and deviant observes the norms of religious authority current among proto-Sunni traditionalists of the ninth century. Rather than communicating his own thoughts and ideas about Abū Ḥanīfa, ʿAbd Allāh proposes to relate information he heard from a select group of religious authorities. His first point of reference is, naturally enough, his father. At the very outset of the chapter ʿAbd Allāh relates that his father believed that hostility to Abū Ḥanīfa and his followers was a source of divine reward.[254] This sanguine interpretation of displays of enmity towards Abū Ḥanīfa helps to explain the virulent and profuse nature of discourses of heresy against Abū Ḥanīfa in the *Kitāb al-Sunna*. It provided the necessary pretext, if one was needed, for any emerging orthodoxy to rally against perceived heretics. He then refers to the authority of a constellation of proto-Sunni traditionalists, all of whom were integral to the transmission and circulation of discourses of heresy against Abū Ḥanīfa: Ḥammād b. Abī Sulaymān; al-Awzāʿī; Abū Ayyūb al-Sakhtiyānī; Ibn ʿAwn; al-Aʿmash; Mughīra al-Ḍabbī; Sufyān al-Thawrī; Mālik b. Anas; Ḥammād b. Zayd; ʿAbd Allāh b. al-Mubārak; Sufyān b. ʿUyayna; Abū Isḥāq al-Fazārī; and many others.

The *Kitāb al-Sunna* evidences a number of themes that form the basis of discourses of heresy against Abū Ḥanīfa (see Figure 3.1). I have counted a total number of 184 anti-Abū Ḥanīfa reports in this section of the *Kitāb al-Sunna*.

There are six overarching (and overlapping) themes in the material ʿAbd Allāh b. Aḥmad b. Ḥanbal collects against Abū Ḥanīfa. Most of the (forty-one) reports fall into the category of general curses against Abū Ḥanīfa. Within this category we have reports describing Abū Ḥanīfa as the greatest source of harm to Islam and Muslims; the most wretched person to be born in the religion of Islam; prayers and curses against Abū Ḥanīfa; and expressions of joy at the news of his death. The second prominent theme is the opposition between Abū Ḥanīfa's *ra'y* and Prophetic ḥadīth (thirty-two reports). This is followed closely by the theme of heresies (thirty-one reports). This category refers to reports wherein the semantic field of heresy (*kufr*, *kāfir*; *zandaqa*, *zindīq*; *murūq*, *māriq*, etc.) is employed against Abū Ḥanīfa. Examples of reports from this category include a report in which a proto-Sunni traditionalist encouraged his colleague to declare Abū Ḥanīfa an unbeliever (*kāfir*)

[253] ʿAbd Allāh b. Aḥmad b. Ḥanbal, *Kitāb al-Sunna*, 180–228.
[254] ʿAbd Allāh b. Aḥmad b. Ḥanbal, *Kitāb al-Sunna*, 180.

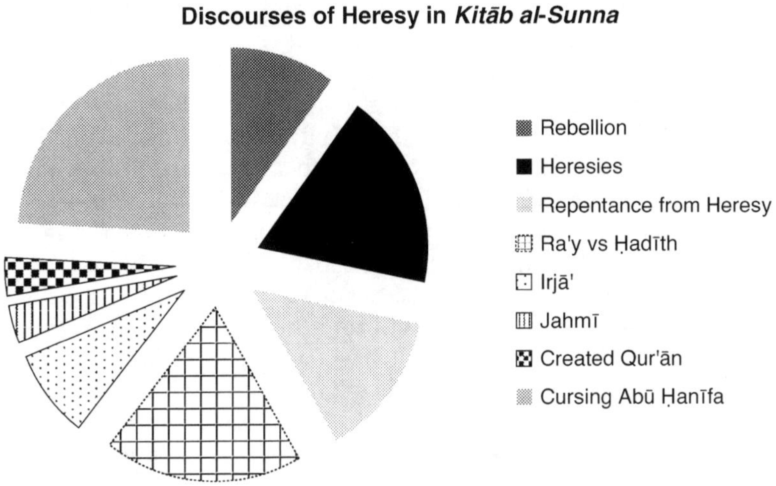


Figure 3.1 Discourses of heresy in *Kitāb al-Sunna.*

and heretic (*zindīq*) because he believed the Quran to be created;[255] students of Mālik b. Anas alleged that he declared Abū Ḥanīfa to be beyond the pale of the religion;[256] on a separate occasion, when someone proposed one of Abū Ḥanīfa's solutions to a legal question, it was dismissed curtly as the view of 'that apostate'.[257] The fourth theme refers to reports that describe Abū Ḥanīfa as having repented publicly from heresy (twenty-three reports). Another prominent theme is rebellion (seventeen reports). ʿAbd Allāh collects reports in which proto-Sunni traditionalists drew attention to the heretical nature of Abū Ḥanīfa's support for rebellion against Muslim rulers. A sixth theme is Abū Ḥanīfa's adherence to the heresy of Irjā' (fourteen reports). Little is made of Abū Ḥanīfa's views on the Quran (six reports) and his connection to the Jahmiyya (six reports), which is especially surprising given the historical background of the Miḥna and the involvement of the author's father, Aḥmad b. Ḥanbal, in that inquisition. There is no doubt that the *Kitāb al-Sunna* represented the culmination of proto-Sunni traditionalist attempts to place Abū Ḥanīfa outside the realm of orthodoxy and that the close

255 ʿAbd Allāh b. Aḥmad b. Ḥanbal, *Kitāb al-Sunna*, 184–5.

256 ʿAbd Allāh b. Aḥmad b. Ḥanbal, *Kitāb al-Sunna*, 199 (*samiʿtu Mālik yaqūl fī Abī Ḥanīfa qawlan yukhrijuhu min al-dīn*).

257 ʿAbd Allāh b. Aḥmad b. Ḥanbal, *Kitāb al-Sunna*, 211 (*samiʿtu Abī yaqūl: kunnā ʿinda Ḥammād b. Salama fa dhakarū mas'ala fa qīla: Abū Ḥanīfa yaqūl bihā. Fa qāla: hādhā wa Allāhi qawl dhāka al-māriq*).

students of Aḥmad b. Ḥanbal were at the forefront of disseminating discourses of heresy against Abū Ḥanīfa.

One such student was Abū Bakr al-Marrūdhī (d. 275/888). He originated from Marw-i rūdh, one of the five principal cities of Khurāsān, but it was in Baghdad that he established his reputation as one of Aḥmad b. Ḥanbal's foremost students. He was sufficiently close to Aḥmad b. Ḥanbal to have performed the ritual washing of his body before his burial.[258] Another measure of his proximity is his transmission of Aḥmad b. Ḥanbal's legal opinions, along with a book recording his master's assessments of ḥadīth critics.[259] Like ʿAbd Allāh b. Aḥmad b. Ḥanbal, al-Marrūdhī belonged to the circle of proto-Sunni traditionalists emerging from the circle of Aḥmad b. Ḥanbal who were particularly fervent in their opposition to Abū Ḥanīfa and his followers. Al-Marrūdhī's contribution to discourses of heresy against Abū Ḥanīfa appears in a somewhat unlikely source: *Akhbār al-shuyūkh wa akhlāquhum*, a book he wrote in order to urge religious scholars to keep their distance from rulers.[260]

It is unclear, therefore, why al-Marrūdhī includes three reports in the *Akhbār al-shuyūkh* severely critical of Abū Ḥanīfa. The first report is one we encountered earlier in this book. It has Isḥāq b. Rāhawayh explain the moment he came to the realisation that Abū Ḥanīfa stood outside the orthodoxy of proto-Sunni traditionalists.[261] A second report declares that no tribulation descended from the heavens to the earth more harmful

[258] Al-Khaṭīb al-Baghdādī, *Tārīkh Baghdād*, 6: 104–6, 104; Ibn Abī Yaʿlā, *Ṭabaqāt al-Ḥanābila*, 1: 56–63 (al-Fiqī edn.).

[259] Al-Khaṭīb al-Baghdādī, *Tārīkh Baghdād*, 6: 104. Some parts of the *Masāʾil* have been published in the form of doctoral dissertations submitted to Umm al-Qurā University, Mecca: al-Marrūdhī, *Masāʾil al-Imām Aḥmad al-fiqhiyya bi riwāyat al-Marrūdhī min al-nikāḥ ḥattā nihāyat al-qaḍāʾ wa al-shahādāt*, ed. ʿAbd al-Muḥsin b. Muḥammad al-Maʿyūf (Mecca: Jāmiʿat Umm al-Qurā, 2011) and *Masāʾil al-Imām Aḥmad fī al-ʿibādāt bi riwāyat Abī Bakr al-Marrūdhī*, ed. ʿAbd al-Raḥmān b. ʿAlī al-Ṭarīqī (Mecca: Jāmiʿ Umm al-Qurā, 2011). ʿAbd al-Raḥmān b. ʿAlī al-Ṭarīqī has also edited other chapters from Marrūdhī's *Masāʾil*: see *Majallat al-Jāmiʿa al-Islāmiyya bi al-Madīna al-Munawwara*, 1; *Majalla Jāmiʿat al-Malik Saʿūd li al-ʿUlūm al-Tarbawiya wa al-Dirāsāt al-Islāmiyya*, 2, 20 (2008); *Majallat Jāmiʿat Umm al-Qurā li ʿUlūm al-Sharīʿa wa al-Lugha wa Ādābihā*, 33 (2005). The book on ḥadīth criticism is al-Marrūdhī, *Kitāb al-ʿIlal*. The text was dictated by al-Marrūdhī when he was in Ṭarsūs and it was being read and transmitted in Isfarāʾīn (Nīshāpūr) by Abū ʿAwāna al-Isfarāʾīnī (d. 316/929) near the beginning of the tenth century. The work provides valuable insights into the proto-Sunni traditionalist network: 189, 193, 253, 255 (interactions with al-Fasawī), 175 (one anti-Abū Ḥanīfa report, a version of which occurs in ʿAbd Allāh b. Aḥmad b. Ḥanbal, *Kitāb al-Sunna*, 192).

[260] The manuscript consisted of three sections. The second section of the book (*al-juzʾ al-thānī*) has not survived, though the editor of the book has managed to locate some passages from the lost section in later works. The edition itself is based on a unicum manuscript: al-Marrūdhī, *Akhbār al-shuyūkh wa akhlāquhum*, ed. ʿĀmir Ḥasan Ṣabrī (Beirut: Dār al-Bashāʾir al-Islāmiyya, 2005), 27–9 (editor's introduction).

[261] Al-Marrūdhī, *Akhbār al-shuyūkh wa akhlāquhum*, 160–1.

than that of Abū Ḥanīfa.[262] The third and fourth reports echo a widely circulated attack on Abū Ḥanīfa, which locates the origins of the Muslim community's deviance in the influence of Abū Ḥanīfa, among others, and his ancestral and social origins. The fourth report seeks to further explain this deviance. A ninth-century proto-Sunni traditionalist observes that in his time people showed great keenness in performing good deeds, prayers, paying the charitable tax, and doing other virtuous actions such as commanding good. He is disturbed by a more recent trend that sees this religious devotion being replaced by an infatuation with speculative jurisprudence.[263] A fifth report does not mention Abū Ḥanīfa directly. It presents Ibn al-Mubārak's outrage over the contents of *Kitāb al-Ḥiyal*, leading him to declare its author an unbeliever (*kāfir*). *Kitāb al-Ḥiyal*, as I establish later in this study, was produced from within Abū Ḥanīfa's circle. Al-Marrūdhī (or Ibn al-Mubārak) does not give us the author's name, but his inclusion of the report certainly highlights his intransigent opposition to Abū Ḥanīfa and his followers.

ʿAbd Allāh b. Aḥmad b. Ḥanbal and al-Marrūdhī conclude stage two of proto-Sunni traditionalist discourses against Abū Ḥanīfa. In this and the previous chapter we have seen how stage two represented a turning point in the history of proto-Sunnism. Between roughly 850 and 900 there was a concerted attempt in the different provinces of the early Islamic empire to cast Abū Ḥanīfa as a heretic who stood outside proto-Sunni traditionalist conceptions of orthodoxy. By excluding Abū Ḥanīfa from the proto-Sunni traditionalist community, his opponents sought to undermine the religious orthodoxy and standing of his students and followers. The language and tone of this discourse of heresy is remarkable for the degree of hostility it exhibits towards a figure whose memory would spawn the most widespread legal school in Islamic history. Even though discourses of heresy certainly began to wane in the late ninth to eleventh centuries, for reasons I document in Part III of this study, one obvious consequence of this caustic discourse of heresy was that it continued to find some scattered supporters in the tenth and eleventh centuries. In fact, inhibitions towards proto-Sunni traditionalist discourses of heresy among its members can be observed in the work of Ibn Abī Ḥātim al-Rāzī. He is my

[262] Al-Marrūdhī, *Akhbār al-shuyūkh wa akhlāquhum*, 160–2 (*mā ḥabaṭat fitnatun min al-samāʾ ilā al-arḍ aḍarra min Abī Ḥanīfa*).

[263] Al-Marrūdhī, *Akhbār al-shuyūkh wa akhlāquhum*, 163 (*adraktu al-nās wa hum yataḥāththūn ʿalā al-aʿmāl: al-ṣalāt wa al-zakāt wa fiʿl al-khayr wa al-amr bi al-maʿrūf wa naḥwi hādhā, wa innahum al-yawm yataḥāththūn ʿalā al-raʾy*); Ibn Abī Ḥātim al-Rāzī, *Kitāb al-ʿIlal*, ed. Saʿīd b. ʿAbd Allāh al-Ḥumayd and Khālid b. ʿAbd al-Raḥmān al-Juraysī (Riyadh: Maktabat al-Malik Fahd al-Waṭaniyya, 2006), 359–60.

starting point for stage three of proto-Sunni discourses of heresy against Abū Ḥanīfa.

Quite unlike many proto-Sunni traditionalists studied in this chapter, Ibn Abī Ḥātim has been the subject of a monograph in modern western scholarship.[264] A detailed reconstruction of his life and career is provided by Eerik Dickinson, so I shall limit myself to some preliminary biographical remarks before directly addressing Ibn Abī Ḥātim's contribution to the mnemohistory of Abū Ḥanīfa. Despite the obvious merits of Dickinson's monograph, it must be admitted that there is so much material in his *Taqdima*, *Kitāb al-Jarḥ wa al-taʿdīl*, and other works that is relevant to the history of proto-Sunnism in general, yet remains to be excavated. Nowhere is this clearer than in the information these works yield for the history of proto-Sunni traditionalist orthodoxy and the consolidation of discourses of heresy against Abū Ḥanīfa. We can illustrate this by focusing on Ibn Abī Ḥātim's primary religious teachers, his father, Abū Ḥātim (d. 277/890), and Abū Zurʿa al-Rāzī, both of whom receive scant attention in Dickinson's otherwise rigorous guide to ḥadīth criticism.[265]

As we have learnt by now, some of Abū Ḥanīfa's sharpest critics were once adherents of the *ahl al-ra'y*. In this respect, Abū Zurʿa al-Rāzī was no different. As a young man in Rayy, Abū Zurʿa al-Rāzī went along with what he described as the orthodoxy of the masses, which was aligned with the ideas of Abū Ḥanīfa. Abū ʿUthmān al-Bardhaʿī (d. 292/905) was a student of Abū Zurʿa al-Rāzī. As we can see in the following accounts, his work provides important commentary on the religious milieu of Rayy in the mid- to late ninth century.[266] Abū Zurʿa remembered the

[264] Dickinson, *The Development of Early Sunnite Ḥadīth Criticism*.

[265] For a painstaking study of Abū Zurʿa al-Rāzī see Saʿdī al-Hāshimī, *Abū Zurʿa al-Rāzī wa juhūduhu fī al-sunna al-nabawiyya maʿa taḥqīq kitābihi al-Ḍuʿafāʾ wa ajwibatihi ʿalā as'ilat al-Bardhaʿī* (Medina: al-Maktaba al-ʿArabiyya al-Saʿūdiyya al-Jāmiʿa al-Islāmiyya, n. d.). Non-Arabic readers can consult the brief paragraph on his biography in Dickinson, *The Development of Early Sunnite Ḥadīth Criticism*, 18 and Sezgin, *GAS*, 1: 145. For Abū Zurʿa's works, Sezgin notes the existence only of a fragment of his *Kitāb al-Zuhd* cited by Ibn Ḥajar, *al-Iṣāba fī tamyīz al-ṣaḥāba*, ed. ʿAbd Allāh b. ʿAbd al-Muḥsin al-Turkī and ʿAbd al-Samad Ḥasan Yamāma (Cairo: Dār al-Ḥijr, 2008), 12: 288 in the entry for Abū Suʿād al-Ḥimṣī. For a more comprehensive account of his works see al-Hāshimī, *Abū Zurʿa al-Rāzī*, 1: 183–203.

[266] I should point out that al-Bardhaʿī studied with Abū Zurʿa al-Dimashqī, another proto-Sunni traditionalist whose contribution to heresiological discourses against Abū Ḥanīfa has been surveyed in this chapter. See al-Bardhaʿī, *Kitāb al-Ḍuʿafāʾ wa al-kadhdhābīn wa al-matrūkīn min aṣḥāb al-ḥadīth*, in *Abū Zurʿa al-Rāzī wa juhūduhu fī al-sunna al-nabawiyya maʿa taḥqīq kitābihi al-Ḍuʿafāʾ wa ajwibatihi ʿalā as'ilat al-Bardhaʿī*, ed. Saʿdī al-Hāshimī (Medina: n.p., 1989), 2: 725–6, particularly where he provides several reports told to him directly by Abū Zurʿa al-Dimashqī and where al-Bardhaʿī writes: 'Abū Zurʿa [al-Rāzī], Abū Ḥātim, and Abū Zurʿa al-Dimashqī said . . . '.

proto-Ḥanafī Muḥammad b. Muqātil saying upon his arrival in Rayy that it was the waning influence of Abū Ḥanīfa and his followers in Iraq that strengthened his resolve to gain the upper hand for proto-Ḥanafism in Rayy by any and all means necessary (*fa la anṣurannahu bi ghāyat al-naṣr*). Abū Zurʿa insisted: 'We succeeded in gaining the upper hand over Muqātil in Rayy.'[267] It was only later, after being exposed to proto-Sunni traditionalist critics of Abū Ḥanīfa such as Abū Nuʿaym and al-Ḥumaydī, that Abū Zurʿa recognised the misguided nature of his earlier ways.[268] There is a strong likelihood that Isḥāq b. Rāhawayh played the most pivotal role in Abū Zurʿa's shift away from Abū Ḥanīfa. Ibn Abī Ḥātim speaks on more than one occasion of written correspondence between the two men. Isḥāq b. Rāhawayh's letter, which was written in response to a letter he received from Abū Zurʿa, read as follows:[269]

My joy for you increases day by day. Praise be to God, for He has made you into one of those who master his Sunna, and there is nothing more urgent than this for the student of knowledge today. Aḥmad b. Ibrāhīm continues to speak very highly of you, so highly in fact that it borders on the excessive, even though, by the grace of God, there is no sign of excessiveness in you. He read to me your letter to him containing that which I counselled you with respect to manifesting the Sunna and abandoning hypocrisy. May God reward you with good. Engross yourself in what I have counselled you, and know that falsehood goes round and round and then it fades away. You are from among those whose piety and religion is beloved to one. I hear from our foremost brothers the [noble] path of learning and memorisation that you are upon, and I am indeed overjoyed by it.

We have seen in the cases of so many proto-Sunni traditionalists how instrumental Isḥāq b. Rāhawayh's influence was, especially with respect to discourses of heresy against Abū Ḥanīfa. Now it emerges that he also cast his shadow over the development of a figure who would become one of Rayy's indisputable leaders of proto-Sunni traditionalism. This letter,

267 Al-Bardhaʿī, *Kitāb al-Ḍuʿafāʾ*, 2: 755–6 (*fa sulliṭa alayhi minnā mā qad ʿalimta*).

268 Al-Bardhaʿī, *Kitāb al-Ḍuʿafāʾ*, 2: 754–6.

269 Ibn Abī Ḥātim, *Taqdima*, 329 (*innī azdādu bika kulla yawm surūran, fa al-ḥamd li Allāh alladhī jaʿalaka mimman yaḥfaẓu sunnatahu wa hādhā min aʿẓam mā yaḥtāju ilayhi al-yawm ṭālib al-ʿilm wa Aḥmad b. Ibrāhīm lā yazālu fī dhikrika al-jamīl ḥattā yakāda yufriṭu wa in lam yakun fīka bi ḥamd Allāh ifrāṭ wa aqraʾanī kitābaka ilayhi bi naḥw mā awṣaytuka min iẓhār al-sunna wa tark al-mudāhana fa jazāka Allāh khayran fa ḍumm ʿalā mā awṣaytuka fa inna li al-bāṭil jawlan thumma yaḍmaḥillu wa innaka mimman uḥabbu ṣalāḥuhu wa dīnuhu* [reading *dīnuhu* for *zīnuhu*] *wa innī asmaʿu min ikhwāninā al-qādimīn mā anta ʿalayhi min al-ʿilm wa al-ḥifẓ wa innī asurru bi dhālika*). The letter implies previous correspondence, and a fragment of this earlier correspondence may be found elsewhere in the *Taqdima*: see Ibn Abī Ḥātim, *Taqdima*, 342, where Abū Zurʿa states: 'Isḥāq b. Rāhawayh wrote to me saying, "Do not be terrified by falsehood, for falsehood goes round and round and then it disappears."' If we take seriously Isḥāq b. Rāhawayh's letter in which he speaks of his earlier correspondence and counsel, which I do, then this might be a fragment from an earlier letter.

which I regard as authentic, reinforces our hypothesis of a proto-Sunni traditionalist community operating and communicating with orally and via texts across the regions of the early Islamic empire. This is evident not only in the correspondence between Isḥāq b. Rāhawayh and Abū Zurʿa al-Rāzī, but also in the claim that other proto-Sunni traditionalists were corresponding with one another and keeping one another informed of the activities of their colleagues and peers. Furthermore, we might deduce with good reason that Isḥāq b. Rāhawayh's role in the development of Abū Zurʿa's proto-Sunni traditionalism would not have precluded a transference of the former's determined opposition to Abū Ḥanīfa to Abū Zurʿa.

Abū Zurʿa al-Rāzī's initial fondness for Abū Ḥanīfa and the *ahl al-ra'y* meant that he had an insider's knowledge of proto-Ḥanafism.[270] It was this early exposure, then, that provided him with the necessary material to attack Abū Ḥanīfa's religious credibility. Abū ʿUthmān al-Bardhaʿī (d. 292/905), who took care to record his conversations with both Abū Ḥātim and Abū Zurʿa, preserves some of this anti-Abū Ḥanīfa material.[271] Al-Bardhaʿī relates that he heard Abū Zurʿa declare Abū Ḥanīfa and his two premier disciples to be Jahmīs (a heretical label).[272] He tells another anecdote in which his teacher, Abū Zurʿa al-Rāzī, caught a glimpse of his book and saw that it contained a ḥadīth transmitted by Abū Ḥātim on the authority of Abū Ḥanīfa. This prompted a long dialogue between Abū Zurʿa and al-Bardhaʿī in the presence of Abū Ḥātim:[273]

ABŪ ZURʿA: Who should be blamed for [citing] this ḥadīth, you or Abū Ḥātim?[274]

AL-BARDHAʿĪ: I [am to blame].

ABŪ ZURʿA: How so?

AL-BARDHAʿĪ: I forced him [Abū Ḥātim] to relate the tradition, and there was a relevant chapter, so he read it to me with some reluctance. I do remember, however, that Abū Ḥātim followed this up with some very harsh words which I omitted from my book at that time (*li annī jabartuhu ʿalā qirā'atihi wa kāna bāban fa qara'ahu ʿalayya baʿd juhd fa qāla lī qawlan ghalīẓan ansītuhu fī kitābī dhālika al-waqt*).

270 Al-Bardhaʿī insinuates as much in *Kitāb al-Ḍuʿafā'*, 2: 723.

271 Al-Khalīlī, an important historian of ḥadīth learning in the eastern regions of the medieval Islamic world, considered al-Bardhaʿī a scholar of great standing and wide acclaim: see al-Khalīlī, *al-Irshād*, 2: 782 (Riyadh edn.).

272 Al-Bardhaʿī, *Kitāb al-Ḍuʿafā'*, 2: 570.

273 Al-Bardhaʿī, *Kitāb al-Ḍuʿafā'*, 2: 717–22 (*wa ra'ā Abū Zurʿa fī kitābī ḥadīthan ʿan Abī Ḥātim ʿan shaykh lahu ʿan Ayyūb b. Suwayd ʿan Abī Ḥanīfa ḥadīthan musnidan, wa Abū Ḥātim jālis ilā janbihi fa qāla lī*).

274 *Man yuʿātab ʿalā hādhā, anta aw Abū Ḥātim?*

At this point, al-Bardhaʿī made a half-hearted attempt to justify to Abū Zurʿa the inclusion of a ḥadīth on the authority of Abū Ḥanīfa. He said to his teacher:

AL-BARDHAʿĪ: Ibrāhīm b. Arūma used to regard Abū Ḥanīfa's *isnād*s to be reliable (*inna Ibrāhīm b. Arūma kāna yaʿnī bi isnād Abī Ḥanīfa*).

ABŪ ZURʿA: What a calamity! It was for this reason that our problem with Ibrāhīm became so grave. On what grounds did he [Ibrāhīm] consider him [Abū Ḥanīfa] to be reliable? Was it on account of his [Abū Ḥanīfa's] large following or because of his mastery (*innā li Allāh wa innā ilayhi rājiʿūn! ʿaẓumat muṣībatunā fī Ibrāhīm yaʿnī bihi. Li ayy maʿnā yuṣaddiquhu? Li atbāʿihi? Li itqānihi*)?

AL-BARDHAʿĪ: At this point, Abū Zurʿa made some extremely harsh comments about Ibrāhīm which I have omitted here. Then he said (*thumma dhakara kalāman ghalīẓan fī Ibrāhīm lam ukhrijhu hāhunā thumma qāla*).

ABŪ ZURʿA: May God have mercy upon Aḥmad b. Ḥanbal. I have heard that his heart was tormented by the ḥadīths he had from Muʿallā b. Manṣūr, which he was in desperate need of. After all, Muʿalla resembled the people of learning, for he was an ardent student of knowledge who travelled in search of ḥadīth, and he was well respected on account of this. Aḥmad showed the utmost forbearance with respect to these ḥadīths by not hearing a single letter of them, and this in spite of the fact that ʿAlī b. al-Madīnī, Abū Khaythama, and the rest of our companions heard ḥadīth from him. And in what respect does al-Muʿallā resemble Abū Ḥanīfa? Muʿallā was truthful (*ṣadūq*), whilst Abū Ḥanīfa would combine different ḥadīths (*raḥima Allāh Aḥmad b. Ḥanbal. Balaghanī annahu kāna fī qalbihi ghuṣaṣ min aḥādīth ẓaharat ʿan al-Muʿallā b. Manṣūr kāna yaḥtāju ilayhā wa kāna al-Muʿallā ashbaha al-qawm bi ahl al-ʿilm wa dhālika annahu kāna ṭallāban li al-ʿilm wa raḥila wa ʿuniya bihi fa ṣabura Aḥmad ʿan tilka al-aḥādīth wa lam yasmaʿ minhu ḥarfan wa ammā ʿAlī b. al-Madīnī wa Abū Khaythama wa ʿāmmat aṣḥābinā samiʿū minhu wa ayy shay' yashbihu al-Muʿallā min Abī Ḥanīfa: al-Muʿallā ṣadūq wa Abū Ḥanīfa yaṣilu al-aḥādīth*).

AL-BARDHAʿĪ: I think this is what Abū Zurʿa said or something to its effect (*aw kalima qālahā Abū Zurʿa hādhā maʿnāhā*).

ABŪ ZURʿA: Abū Ḥanīfa related from Mūsā b. Abī ʿĀ'isha from ʿAbd Allāh b. Shaddād from Jābir from the Prophet, May God pray over him and grant him peace. Then he added to the ḥadīth on Jābir's authority: 'The Quran is created.' He [Abū Ḥanīfa] opposed the Messenger of God, may God pray over him and grant him peace, he disparaged the traditions, and he called people to heresy and misguidance. So only an ignoramus would consider someone who does all this to have reliable ḥadīths (*ḥaddatha ʿan Mūsā b. Abī ʿĀ'isha ʿan ʿAbd Allāh b. Shaddād ʿan Jābir ʿan al-nabī ṣallā Allāh ʿalayhi wa sallama, fa zāda fī al-ḥadīth ʿan Jābir, yaʿnī ḥadīth al-qirā'a khalfa, wa yaqūl: 'al-Qur'ān makhlūq.' Wa yaruddu ʿalā rasūl Allāh ṣallā Allāh ʿalayhi wa sallama wa yastahzi'u bi al-āthār wa yadʿū ilā al-bidaʿ wa al-ḍalālāt. Thumma yaʿnī bi ḥadīthihi mā yafʿalu hādhā illā ghabī jāhil*).

AL-BARDHAʿĪ: He said something along these lines. Then he began to vent his fury against Ibrāhīm, he mentioned the ḥadīths related by Abū Ḥanīfa and showed that they had no basis. . . . Finally, he said to me:

ABŪ ZURʿA: Whoever says the Quran is created is an unbeliever, and only the unbelievers consider reliable that which the unbelievers have transmitted (*aw naḥwu mā qāla wa jaʿala yuharridu ʿalā Ibrāhīm wa yadhkuru aḥādīth min riwāyat Abī Ḥanīfa lā aṣl lahā . . . thumma qāla lī: man qāla al-Qurʾān makhlūq fa huwa kāfir, fa yaʿnī bimā asnada al-kuffār ayy qawm hāʾulāʾ*).

This long anecdote preserves one example of the countless interactions that proto-Sunni traditionalists must have had with each other, peer to peer and student to master. Ḥadīth scholars kept notebooks and jotted down whatever information they deemed relevant and from authorities that the ḥadīth community regarded as orthodox. Al-Bardhaʿī made the mistake of recording information transmitted by Abū Ḥanīfa. He himself did not consider this to be a gross oversight, though he was cognisant of proto-Sunni traditionalist unease with Abū Ḥanīfa's probity. He tells us how he compelled his teacher, Abū Ḥātim, to relate a tradition from Abū Ḥanīfa to him and speaks of Abū Ḥātim's qualms over doing so. More than this, he recalls how Abū Ḥātim narrated the tradition and then launched an attack on Abū Ḥanīfa. Abū Zurʿa's intervention provides an excellent illustration of the kind of self-regulation of orthodoxy that was common in early Islamic society. Abū Zurʿa begins with a direct and probing question, which signals his disapproval of what he finds in his student's notebook. Al-Bardhaʿī, though, is an intrepid student and proposes a justification for his inclusion of a ḥadīth from Abū Ḥanīfa on the basis of another proto-Sunni traditionalist's positive assessment of Abū Ḥanīfa's transmission of ḥadīths. This riposte from al-Bardhaʿī only makes matters worse, as Abū Zurʿa recites an invocation typically said upon hearing disastrous news, such as the death of a pious person. Here, Abū Zurʿa demonstrates his mastery as a proto-Sunni traditionalist. It was, he tells his jejune student, for this very reason that he and his colleagues took umbrage with Ibrāhīm b. Arūma. This kind of assessment was enough to impugn Ibrāhīm b. Arūma's credibility as a ḥadīth scholar.[275] Abū Zurʿa even seems to suggest that Ibrāhīm's judgement was motivated by public pressure: namely, Abū Ḥanīfa's large following. Curiously, al-Bardhaʿī chooses to omit a more serious diatribe that Abū Zurʿa launched against Abū Ḥanīfa. We might suppose that al-Bardhaʿī had slightly more sympathy than his peers for Abū Ḥanīfa and his followers, for this is the second admission from him that he chose

[275] He receives a positive entry in Abū Nuʿaym al-Iṣfahānī, *Dhikr akhbār Iṣfahān*, ed. S. Dedering (Leiden: Brill, 1931), 1: 184–5.

to omit vitriolic remarks made by his teachers against Abū Ḥanīfa. Nevertheless, Abū Zurʿa's masterful tutorial in proto-Sunni traditionalism continues. He cites the illustrious example of Aḥmad b. Ḥanbal. Even when other proto-Sunni traditionalists around him agreed to hear and transmit traditions from a prominent proto-Ḥanafī, al-Muʿallā b. Manṣūr (d. 211/826–7), who unlike many other proto-Ḥanafīs had an admirable grasp of ḥadīth, still Aḥmad b. Ḥanbal would hear not even a single tradition from him. As much as this pained Aḥmad b. Ḥanbal, he could not bring himself to transmit traditions from someone who happened to be truthful but was tainted by his association with Abū Ḥanīfa. It seems that Abū Zurʿa practised what he preached, for we learn that he rebuked a scholar for citing a ḥadīth from Abū Ḥanīfa and then got up and left.[276]

Al-Bardhaʿī's work reminds us, though, that Abū Zurʿa himself was a student before he became a master. He was once in al-Bardhaʿī's shoes, seeking the guidance of his teachers concerning the religious credibility of figures such as Abū Ḥanīfa. Al-Bardhaʿī recalls how he heard Abū Zurʿa say that he asked Abū Nuʿaym about some ḥadīths transmitted by Abū Ḥanīfa.[277] Likewise, al-Bardhaʿī had learnt from Abū Ḥātim that Abū Ḥanīfa was incompetent in the science of transmitting ḥadīth and regularly made mistakes in their *isnād*s, even in the few ḥadīths that Abū Ḥanīfa claimed to know.[278] In the end, Abū Zurʿa resorts to a simple and plain message: Abū Ḥanīfa was a misguided heretic, and only people belonging to this category will transmit his traditions or teachings. This conversation between Abū Zurʿa and al-Bardhaʿī gives some sense of how deep proto-Sunni traditionalist opposition to Abū Ḥanīfa went. It is a classic account of how orthodoxy regulated and disciplined religious ideas and of how, ultimately, orthodoxy worked.

## 3.2 Stage Three (900–1000)

### *Ibn Abī Ḥātim al-Rāzī (d. 327/938)*

A central argument in this study is that orthodoxy was never static. Something had changed between the time of Abū Ḥātim and Abū Zurʿa, on the one hand, and Ibn Abī Ḥātim, on the other. Ibn Abī Ḥātim's oeuvre does exhibit a discourse of heresy against Abū Ḥanīfa,

[276] Al-Bardhaʿī, *Kitāb al-Ḍuʿafāʾ*, 2: 716–17.
[277] Al-Bardhaʿī, *Kitāb al-Ḍuʿafāʾ*, 2: 753–4.
[278] Al-Bardhaʿī, *Kitāb al-Ḍuʿafāʾ*, 2: 756 (Abū Ḥātim relates an account he heard from Sufyān b. ʿUyayna, wherein Abū Ḥanīfa narrated these traditions incorrectly to Sufyān).

but it does not display the acerbic character visible in the views of his two teachers. He signals this at the outset of the *Taqdima* when he describes the conflict between proto-Sunni traditionalists and Ḥanafīs as 'disagreement with respect to method'.[279] Ibn Abī Ḥātim is advancing a new perspective on the mnemohistory of Abū Ḥanīfa. What was in the ninth century undoubtedly a discourse of heresy against Abū Ḥanīfa is being read by Ibn Abī Ḥātim in the tenth century as a methodological disagreement. The ninth-century sources this book has examined do not frame hostility towards Abū Ḥanīfa as a consequence of differing methods. Rather, they exhibit a unified chorus of discourses of heresy against Abū Ḥanīfa circulating among proto-Sunni traditionalists and ringing out from different corners of the early Islamic empire. The emerging conclusion in the ninth century was that Abū Ḥanīfa and his followers stood outside proto-Sunni traditionalist conceptions of orthodoxy. Ibn Abī Ḥātim's comparatively accommodating reading of discourses of heresy against Abū Ḥanīfa is largely absent from the writings of earlier proto-Sunni traditionalists.[280]

Ibn Abī Ḥātim presents Abū Ḥanīfa and his followers as subordinate members of the broad proto-Sunni orthodoxy of the early tenth century. This much is clear in his programmatic introduction to his massive biographical dictionary of ḥadīth transmitters. The *Taqdima* seeks to justify the discipline of ḥadīth criticism and to establish the religious superiority of ḥadīth critics. In order to do this, he argues that Abū Ḥanīfa and his followers acknowledged the religious superiority of the ḥadīth critics over themselves. Ibn Abī Ḥātim cites the example of Sufyān al-Thawrī, who was reported to have gone on record to say that he never once went to Abū Ḥanīfa with a question but that Abū Ḥanīfa would visit him and seek out his response to a range of religious questions. Ibn Abī Ḥātim draws the following conclusion from this report:[281]

> This proves clearly that Abū Ḥanīfa had this [esteemed] image (*ṣūra*) of Sufyān al-Thawrī, such that Abū Ḥanīfa would have recourse to al-Thawrī to ask him questions that otherwise puzzled him. Abū Ḥanīfa was pleased to regard al-Thawrī as a religious authority for himself and for others (*raḍiyahu imāman li nafsihi wa li ghayrihi*).

Ibn Abī Ḥātim is clearly reading an established discourse of heresy from which he carefully selects and omits information. Ibn Abī Ḥātim

[279] Ibn Abī Ḥātim, *Taqdima*, 3 (*al-ikhtilāf fī al-madhhab*). My reasons for interpreting the *ahl al-Ḥijāz* as proto-Sunni traditionalists and *ahl al-Kūfa* as Ḥanafīs are based on the subsequent sentences in the *Taqdima*.

[280] See my note on Yaḥyā b. Maʿīn on pp. 75-76 above.

[281] Ibn Abī Ḥātim, *Taqdima*, 3.

interprets this material in a manner that conforms to his broader thesis about where religious authority and orthodoxy is located. He does the same for another figure central to proto-Sunni traditionalism, Mālik b. Anas. First, he cites a report that presents Abū Ḥanīfa as eagerly jotting down material attributed to Mālik b. Anas and dictated to him by one of Mālik b. Anas's students, which he again interprets as evidence that Abū Ḥanīfa considered Mālik b. Anas as a superior religious authority (*raḍiyahu imāman li nafsihi wa li ghayrihi*).[282] Second, he furnishes reports in which al-Shaybānī admits that Mālik b. Anas was more knowledgable than Abū Ḥanīfa about the Quran, Prophetic Sunna, and the views of the Companions.[283] To make his point, he draws on a dialogue between al-Shāfiʿī and Abū Ḥanīfa's student al-Shaybānī:[284]

AL-SHAYBĀNĪ: Who was more knowledgeable, our master, meaning Abū Ḥanīfa, or your master, meaning Mālik b. Anas?
AL-SHĀFIʿĪ: Truthfully?
AL-SHAYBĀNĪ: Yes, truthfully.
AL-SHĀFIʿĪ: I implore you by God, tell me, who had more knowledge of the Quran, our master or your master?
AL-SHAYBĀNĪ: Your master, Mālik b. Anas.
AL-SHĀFIʿĪ: Who had more knowledge of the Sunna, our master or your master?
AL-SHAYBĀNĪ: By God, your master, Mālik b. Anas.
AL-SHĀFIʿĪ: I implore you by God, tell me, who had more knowledge of the sayings of the Companions of the messenger of God, God pray over him and grant him peace, and the sayings of the early scholars, our master or your master?
AL-SHAYBĀNĪ: Your master.
AL-SHĀFIʿĪ: There you have it. Nothing remains [for your master] except analogical reasoning. But, even there, analogical reasoning is non-existent unless it is based on these three sources. What is there for someone to employ analogical reasoning upon if he does not even know the foundations?

Ibn Abī Ḥātim claims that this conversation was witnessed by ʿAbd al-Raḥmān, who extrapolated from it that al-Shaybānī had recognised the superior religious learning of Mālik b. Anas over Abū Ḥanīfa.[285] Third, he contrasts the religious authority that Mālik b. Anas had acquired among communities in the ninth century with that of Abū Ḥanīfa. Again, Ibn Abī Ḥātim employs the voice of Abū Ḥanīfa's pre-eminent disciple, al-Shaybānī, to drive home his point. He tells us that Shaybānī would recall how whenever he would transmit ḥadīth from Mālik b. Anas,

[282] Ibn Abī Ḥātim, *Taqdima*, 3–4.
[283] Ibn Abī Ḥātim, *Taqdima*, 4, 12–13 and in Ibn Abī Ḥātim, *Ādāb al-Shāfiʿī wa manāqibuhu*, 159–60, 201.
[284] Ibn Abī Ḥātim, *Taqdima*, 4.
[285] Ibn Abī Ḥātim, *Taqdima*, 4, 11 (where a similar point is made).

people would flock to him in droves and the place would fill up. However, whenever he transmitted from other teachers only a small group would gather.[286]

I would argue that the shift we see with Ibn Abī Ḥātim's writings reflects a new development in the religious history of proto-Sunnism at the beginning of the tenth century. The issues so central to the heresy-making discourse of the ninth century are absent in Ibn Abī Ḥātim's writings.[287] We have no reports labelling Abū Ḥanīfa a heretic. There is no employment of the language of disease to allude to Abū Ḥanīfa's heresies. Reports concerning Abū Ḥanīfa's repentance from heresy and supposed inquisition are nowhere to be seen. The semantic field of heresy is not cited against Abū Ḥanīfa. References to Abū Ḥanīfa's views on rebellion, which proto-Sunni traditionalists roundly attacked, are omitted. Both the substance and style of Ibn Abī Ḥātim's attitudes to Abū Ḥanīfa point to a conciliatory approach towards late ninth- and early tenth-century Ḥanafīs. There seems to be an overt attempt by Ibn Abī Ḥātim to write with Abū Ḥanīfa's followers in mind. He seems to be trying to convince them not of Abū Ḥanīfa's status as a heretic or deviant scholar but rather as someone whose religious authority was subordinate to a constellation of exemplars of proto-Sunni orthodoxy; men such as Sufyān al-Thawrī, al-Shāfiʿī, and Mālik b. Anas. The aim of reaching out to contemporary Ḥanafīs, I would argue, motivated his adoption of softer themes within earlier discourses of heresy (juristic opinions and insufficient knowledge of ḥadīth). It was out of this same desire that Ibn Abī Ḥātim's works jettison so many aspects integral to ninth-century discourses of heresy against Abū Ḥanīfa. Ibn Abī Ḥātim thus represents a shift among some, though not all, proto-Sunni traditionalists in their criticism of Abū Ḥanīfa. This was a discourse that portrayed Abū Ḥanīfa as inferior to other proto-Sunnis but did not anathematise or exclude him from the emerging proto-Sunni orthodoxy. As such, it was a major development towards the gradual evolution in proto-Sunni views of Abū Ḥanīfa, which would culminate in the tenth century with the apotheosis of Abū Ḥanīfa as a representative of medieval Sunni orthodoxy.

However, the history of discourses of heresy against Abū Ḥanīfa did not disappear with Ibn Abī Ḥātim, and they certainly do not end in this monograph. Chapters 8 and 9 will explain some of the reasons for shifts in

[286] Ibn Abī Ḥātim, *Taqdima*, 4–5; Ibn Abī Ḥātim, *Ādāb al-Shāfiʿī wa manāqibuhu*, 173–4.

[287] That is to say, they are not found in all thirty-four anti-Ḥanafī reports in Ibn Abī Ḥātim, *Ādāb al-Shāfiʿī wa manāqibuhu*, 13–15, 36, 55, 73, 90, 102, 103, 105, 108, 110–12, 140, 153, 155, 164, 166, 170–4, 176, 201–3, 211, 212, 228, 239, 281, 282, 285, 286, 288, 290, 297–9, 301, 304, 306.

proto-Sunni attitudes towards Abū Ḥanīfa, in the way in which we have seen with Ibn Abī Ḥātim; whilst Chapter 10 will fill in the details concerning episodic attempts in the tenth–twelfth centuries to contest the new consensus that secured Abū Ḥanīfa's reputation as an orthodox Sunni among a wider coalition of proto-Sunnis. At this point, however, I should like to bring this long chapter to a close with some reflections on my argument that the emergence of textual communities of orthodoxy owed itself in large part to a conscious enterprise to articulate notions of orthodoxy and heresy.

This chapter has drawn attention to the formation of orthodoxy through the construction of discourses of heresy against Abū Ḥanīfa. In turn, this has shed new light on the emergence of a proto-Sunni traditionalist community as a network of shared interests distributed across the regions of the early Islamic empire. The importance of proto-Sunni traditionalism lay in the fact that it represented a textual community of orthodoxy, and to appreciate the implications of its textual dominance we must reflect on the fact that the rise of discourses of heresy against Abū Ḥanīfa dovetailed with a social and technological revolution in medieval Islamicate societies.[288] The introduction and spread of paper in the eighth and ninth centuries precipitated a massive growth in the writing of texts. Caliphs, wealthy patrons, bureaucrats, poets, theologians, jurists, subalterns, and landowners all contributed to this new cultural formation. They all participated in a discursive sphere whose currency was not so much the power of domination as the power of persuasion. Large-scale book production gave a definitive character to new crafts, professions, and markets. In fact, an entire economy emerged around this that necessitated paper mills, booksellers, libraries, and scribes. It is in this literary milieu that we can make better sense, too, of the range of diverse opinions concerning the social merits of writing and book production.[289] From clarion calls among traditionalists to destroy books to al-Jāḥiẓ's paean of books, the formation of textual communities fostered new intellectual exchanges.[290] This had

[288] For a preliminary overview see Pedersen, *The Arabic Book*. A more critical account of the introduction of paper into the medieval Islamic world can be found in Bloom, *Paper before Print*, 42–89. See also Beeston, 'Background Topics', 22–6, though, *pace* Beeston, note Bloom's important note of caution regarding historical explanations for the introduction of paper into the Islamic world.

[289] For the argument against writing, see Cook, 'The Opponents of the Writing of Tradition in Early Islam'; Schoeler, *The Oral and the Written in Early Islam*, 111–41; Kister, '. . . Lā taqra'ū l-qur'āna'. Concerning the destruction of books, see Melchert, 'The Destruction of Books by Traditionists'.

[290] Goody, *The Domestication of the Savage Mind*, 36–51. For more general remarks on this issue see Goody and Watt, 'The Consequences of Literacy', esp. 326 ff. A good deal of Goody's characterisations are overdrawn, and his suggestions for deep cognitive

profound effects on religious movements, community formation, and ideas about orthodoxy and heresy.

The production of written works generated new opportunities for articulating competing notions of religious orthodoxy. Discourses of heresy against Abū Ḥanīfa, for example, reflected two different modes for articulating notions of heresy and orthodoxy. One level of criticism occurred at the level of anecdotes and oral communication. As these anecdotes moved from memory to the written record, they added a new dimension to the way notions of orthodoxy and heresy could be articulated, scrutinised, and expanded among social and religious networks. Even after their movement from the oral to the written, anecdotes continued to circulate. However, the ability to record such material in written compositions opened up new potentialities. Fleeting anecdotes that in their oral mode assumed only a semi-permanent character were transformed as they moved into texts to form stable propositions.[291] The tyranny of conceptual dichotomies such as oral and written has entered into Islamic historiography, and this has unnecessarily reduced complex historical processes to simple dichotomies. The transition from oral to written was never complete, and al-Jāḥiẓ's attempt to convince his readers of the benefits of writing over audition does not do away with the latter altogether. His argument, to be clear, is that book reading should outweigh one's book hearing (*fa al-insān lā yaʿlamu ḥattā yakthura samāʿuhu wa lā budda min an takūna kutubuhu akthar min samāʿihi*).[292] This is one development that seems to elude al-Jāḥiẓ in his otherwise elegant paean of books. In *Kitāb al-Ḥayawān* al-Jāḥiẓ presents a manifesto for books and their role in the formation of cohesive societies and social practices. As

changes are radical. Similarly, Goody's polarisation between oral and written modes of communication is problematic (as is Schoeler's). This has substantial ramifications for the context that concerns us. Oral conventions were not swept aside during the peak of religious writing in the ninth century, for example. This complementarity between the oral and written is slightly closer to Clanchy and Stock's perspectives (Clanchy, *From Memory to Written Record*, 9; Stock, *The Implications of Literacy*, 13–18); but the theoretical or interdisciplinary nature of scholarship on literacy, unsurprisingly, fails to speak to the specific circumstances of early Islamic societies. Clanchy's interpretation of writing and its spread being linked to the ultimate trust and prestige accorded to it over oral communication is in open contradiction to scholarly and professional norms throughout the Islamic Middle Ages: see Clanchy, *From Memory to Written Record*, 294–327.

291 Schoeler's research has often been taken to be the final word on orality and literacy in early Islam, despite the fact that his findings tend to be under-theorised and move across the disciplines of medieval Islam too swiftly. This is not the occasion to enter into a fuller treatment, but my discussion here tries to fill in some of the gaps. Al-Azmeh, *The Arabs and Islam in Late Antiquity*, 87–100 presents a convincing re-evaluation of Schoeler's distinction between *hypomnēma* and *syngramma*.

292 Al-Jāḥiẓ, *Kitāb al-Ḥayawān*, ed. ʿAbd al-Salām Muḥammad Hārūn (Beirut: Dār al-Kitāb al-ʿArabī, 1966), 1: 50–102. See now the indispensable companion to al-Jāḥiẓ's oeuvre: Montgomery, *al-Jāḥiẓ*, 161–7.

attentive as he is to the social implications of writing, al-Jāḥiẓ says nothing about the relationship between writing and orthodoxy. I would suggest, though, that al-Jāḥiẓ was well aware of the consequences of writing for group formation and discourses of orthodoxy and heresy in the ninth century. Towards the end of *Kitāb al-Ḥayawān* he is forced to clarify that his book does not serve the purpose of articulating notions of orthodoxy and heresy, matters that otherwise overwhelmed the book market in a moment of intense factionalism in ʿAbbāsid society.[293] He fails to mention this in the first volume because it undermines his thesis that books and their composition provided an escape from intense factionalism and participation, and were the hallmark of cohesive societies.

The growth of writing encouraged a culture of examination that necessitated a consistent vocabulary that permeated the intellectual culture of religious communities as far as Khurāsān and North Africa. It demanded deliberate steps of logic, explanation, and critique. New rules for intellectual engagement were slowly being formed.[294] With written compositions, textual communities were developing techniques to argue and build consensus. Textual communities, as we have seen in the case of proto-Sunni traditionalists, were sharing, exchanging, disseminating, meeting, and copying from one another at a time when proto-Sunnism was less a bland consensus than a scene of ferocious contention and debate. That it to say, textual communities were caught up in the process of community and identity formation.[295] And whilst orthodoxy may not have necessitated written modes of communication, these nevertheless extended the orthodoxy of the statement to the orthodoxy of the book.[296]

In conclusion, the formation of textual communities is so important to the evolution of Sunnism in general, and to discourses of heresy specifically, because it ensured that memories and anecdotes were recorded in texts. One view is that these writings were written by religious elites and therefore

[293] Al-Jāḥiẓ, *Kitāb al-Ḥayawān*, 7: 7–8.

[294] This is evident in the granularity with which scholars addressed the rules of dialectics. See Karabela, 'The Development of Dialectic and Argumentation'; Young, *The Dialectical Forge*.

[295] The implications of writing and texts that I am emphasising here are not treated in the secondary literature I have consulted, though important discussions on tangential issues can be found in Calder, *Studies in Early Muslim Jurisprudence*, 161–97; Toorawa, *Ibn Abī Ṭāhir Ṭayfūr*, 11–34; Schoeler, *The Genesis of Literature in Islam*, 40–53; and Rosenthal, '"Of Making Many Books There is no End"'.

[296] I have benefited immensely from the magisterial work of Stock, *The Implications of Literacy*, 88–150 ('Literacy and early heresy'), esp. 98–101. Christopher Melchert's analysis of the role of texts and the teaching of doctrine approaches this phenomenon from a different angle: Melchert, *The Formation of the Sunni Schools of Law*, 60–8.

represent the views of a single layer of early Islamic society. On the other hand, Louis Gernet (and, more recently, Peter Brown) has reminded us in his study of piety in ancient Greece that religious elites and their writings function as exemplifications of the broader trends and ideas permeating a society. That is to say, religious elites do not invent as much as they render explicit what many others think.[297] We do not have to look further than the great social commentator of the tenth century al-Tanūkhī to understand the consequences of texts, as well as their relationship to the wider beliefs held by members of early Islamic societies. He writes in his *Nishwār al-muḥāḍara*: 'It is my purpose to collect in this work such stories as are current on men's lips and which have not yet been transferred from the custody of their memories to perpetuation in notebooks.'[298] Proto-Sunni traditionalists of the ninth century who were committed to articulating a conception of orthodoxy through focusing on discourses of heresy against Abū Ḥanīfa exhibited a self-awareness of the opportunities this opened up for proto-Sunni traditionalist orthodoxy. Al-Humāydī's defiant statement, 'as long as I am in the Ḥijāz, Aḥmad [b. Ḥanbal] is in Iraq, and Isḥāq [b. Rāhawayh] is in Khurāsān, we will never be defeated', is sufficient evidence of this.[299] It is no coincidence that these three men were all friends and on good terms with one another, wrote books, articulated a transregional vision of proto-Sunni orthodoxy, played a pivotal role in discourses of heresy against Abū Ḥanīfa, and believed that the fight for orthodoxy would be fought to the death.

[297] Gernet, *Le génie grec dans la religion*, 306; Brown, *Through the Eye of a Needle*, xxiii–xxiv. This understanding of religious elites and their relationship to society is relevant and particular to the study of texts produced by religious elites. Sociological theories of elites in the context of politics and government, however, operate on an entirely different understanding as to the role of governing and non-governing elites in the age of mass society. See Mosca, *The Ruling Class*; Pareto, *The Rise and Fall of Elites*.

[298] Al-Tanūkhī, *Nishwār al-muḥāḍara wa akhbār al-mudhākara*, ed. ʿAbbūd al-Shāljī (Beirut: Dār Ṣādir, 1995 [1973]), 7 = *The Table-Talk of a Mesopotamian Judge*, trans. D. S. Margoliouth (London: Royal Asiatic Society, 1922), 1. As readers of al-Tanūkhī's introduction will recognise, he frames his own work explicitly as an attempt to transfer the oral to the written. Readers should note that I have followed Margoliouth's translation: he added supplements in italics because of the fragmentary nature of the first page of the manuscript.

[299] Al-Dhahabī, *Siyar*, 10: 619.

*Part II*

# Heresy and Society

So far we have gained some understanding of the extent and range of discourses of heresy concerning Abū Ḥanīfa. We have sketched its historical evolution, its main progenitors, and the connections between them. The aim of subsequent chapters is to document the ways in which discourses of heresy and orthodoxy were embedded in wider social and historical phenomena. This is a departure from the manner in which the history of orthodoxy and heresy in Islam is typically written.

The traditional framework for studying orthodoxy and heresy in Islamic history remains beholden to the heresiographical sources, an approach exemplified by Josef van Ess's monumental survey of the genre.[1] Medieval heresiography, however, proposes neat historicisations of confessional dogmas, and nowhere is this clearer than in theological genealogies of heresies and heresiarchs that heresiographers sketch. Heresiographers and heresiographies are by no means uniform. Still, the majority of such texts adhere to certain forms and literary structures which do not lend themselves to an examination of the complex and wide-ranging evolution of discourses of heresy and orthodoxy in medieval Islamicate societies.[2] This has not prevented both Islamicists and non-Islamicists writing comparative histories of orthodoxy and heresy from using heresiography as their central guide to orthodoxy and heresy in Islam.[3]

[1] Van Ess, *Der Eine und das Andere*.

[2] Patricia Crone has written a fine study of religion and rebellion in medieval Iran (Crone, *The Nativist Prophets of Early Islamic Iran*), but I find it astonishing that a historian who has done so much to caution students and colleagues about the perils of early Islamic sources relies so heavily on medieval Muslim heresiography to write the history of nativist rebellions in medieval Iran. Crone would probably respond (as she did to me during our conversations in Princeton in 2012) that heresiographers were some of the only people interested in telling us about the beliefs of these otherwise enigmatic personalities and movements. Still, this approach has serious shortcomings. It is telling, for instance, that taxation and the economy are almost entirely absent in her history of revolts and social unrest in eighth–ninth century Iran. Find me a heresiographer interested in taxation.

[3] Henderson, *The Construction of Orthodoxy and Heresy*; Ames, *Medieval Heresies*.

I approach the history of orthodoxy from a study of discourses of heresy, and I do so from the vantage point of a historian. This part of the monograph is concerned with teasing out the connections between discourses of heresy and social developments and beliefs in medieval Islamicate societies. This may sound like a straightforward historical exercise but the fact is that, unlike colleagues in the field of late antique studies or medieval history, I do not have the benefit of a running start. Consider, for example, that even a classic as dated as Ernst Troeltsch's *Die Soziallehren der christlichen Kirchen und Gruppen* has no equivalent in the field of Islamic Studies and History.

It is important for historians of Islam to remind themselves that, though modern disciplinary boundaries between the religious, the social, and the political are necessary for the growth of knowledge and specialisation in the modern academy, imposing them onto medieval societies is a patent error.[4] It is an almost irresistible impulse for historians to impose the artificial boundaries that distinguish modern professional disciplines in the academy from each other onto the map of medieval Islamicate societies. This has the result of treating medieval poetry as a subject of literature, heresy and orthodoxy as subjects of theology and religious studies, rebellion as a matter of interest for the political historian, legal debates the purview of legal historians, and ethnicity and language as belonging to the realm of the social and cultural historian. This study, but in particular this part of it, insists on the artificiality of such boundaries in medieval Islamicate societies. Where I am forced to distinguish my discussion of discourses of heresy pertaining to jurisprudence, ḥadīth, theology, and piety it is purely for organisational purposes. Although it should be clear to readers of this section, it bears reminding that this study does not support artificial boundaries between social and religious spheres of life.[5]

In what follows, I document ways in which discourses of heresy and the formation of orthodoxy cannot be disentangled from medieval mentalités and regional historical developments (Chapter 4); from constructions of ethnicity, genealogy, and language, as well as developments in conversion to Islam and the effect this had on ritual prayer in the eastern provinces of the early Islamic empire (Chapter 5); from the history of the medieval state, rebellions, and the rise of provincial dynasties in eastern Iran

[4] Abbott, *Chaos of Disciplines*, 121–56.

[5] A similar approach can be seen in two classics of medieval European history: Troeltsch, *Gesammelte Schriften I*, 370 = *The Social Teachings of the Christian Churches*, 1: 336; Ladurie, *Montaillou*. For a succinct review of the historiographies of heresy in medieval European history see Stock, *The Implications of Literacy*, 92–101.

(Chapter 6); nor from developments in jurisprudence, ḥadīth, doctrine, and conceptions of piety (Chapter 7).

A detailed examination of discourses of heresy against Abū Ḥanīfa documents a total view of the history of orthodoxy and heresy in medieval Islamicate societies in which social, political, cultural, and religious themes do not exist independently of one another. The fact that these themes cohere in proto-Sunni traditionalist discourses of heresy is a strong indication of this total view of heresy and orthodoxy. It is the task of these subsequent chapters to document the wider relationship between discourses of heresy and society.

# 4 Regionalism and Topographies of Heresy

Our failure to explore the deeper mentalités that governed medieval Islamicate societies has limited our understanding of how the categories of orthodoxy and heresy were deployed in the eighth and ninth centuries. The rigid structures of the heresiographical genre, which have informed most contemporary scholarship on medieval heresy and orthodoxy, have much to say about the central roles of law and doctrine (orthodoxy), on the one hand, and ritual and practice (orthopraxy), on the other.[6] This is one reason why the debate about conceptions of orthodoxy and heresy in medieval Islam has centred around orthopraxy and orthodoxy and determining which of these two approaches best characterises medieval Islam. It is important to remember, though, that these practices and beliefs were embedded within an emerging cultural order that, in turn, rested upon a particular social construction of reality.[7] Law and ritual are more recognisable to historians today as boundary markers and fields of distinction because they still resonate strongly with modern conceptions of how societies and groups operate. The long labour of 'disenchantment', which for Max Weber was the fundamental chasm between pre-modernity and modernity, has made redundant many medieval structures of reality. The world that (most) medieval Muslims inhabited and imagined constitutes a foreign country for modern historians.[8] Our conception of the categories of orthodoxy and orthopraxy, narrowly defined as *doxa* and *praxis*, represents only one aspect of the framework of heresy that dominated medieval religions and societies.[9]

[6] See this study's Introduction. [7] Bourdieu, *Outline of a Theory of Practice*, 164.

[8] For medieval dissenting voices on medieval mentalités that were deemed to be 'irrational' and 'mythical', see, as an example, Abū al-Faḍl Bayhaqī, *Tārīkh-i Bayhaqī*, ed. ʿAlī Akbar Fayyāḍ (Mashhad: Mu'assasah-i Chāp va Intishārāt-i Dānishgāh-i Firdaws, 1963), 666–67.

[9] This attempt to capture aspects of the representation and social construction of reality, based on the writings of medieval Muslims, has been the common thread of a long tradition of sociological thought, where it has sometimes acquired both an analytical and a programmatic function. See Bourdieu, *Distinction*, 482–3; Berger and Luckmann, *The Social Construction of Reality*, 110–46, where the analysis establishes the propinquity

As historians of the medieval world, we risk misreading the societies and groups we study – the discourses of heresy that form the subject of this chapter – if we fail to examine what role wider aspects of medieval Muslim mentalités played in the construction of heresy and heresiological discourses. This chapter, therefore, examines the broader relationship between heresy and society. It explains how discourses of heresy concerning Abū Ḥanīfa were articulated around a wider set of themes and intertwined with a range of social motifs and discursive mentalités.[10] My investigation concentrates on the extent to which discourses of heresy were anchored in beliefs about the sacred and profane nature of places and regions, which in turn drew on medieval beliefs about holy and unholy regions, the divine curse, and the devil's role in society.

To illustrate the connection between regionalism and heresy, I analyse al-Fasawī's chapter on Kufa and Abū Ḥanīfa in his ninth-century history, *Kitāb al-Maʿrifa wa al-tārīkh*. Chapter 3 of this book included an examination of the discourse of heresy against Abū Ḥanīfa in al-Fasawī's history. As I mentioned there, al-Fasawī's discourse of heresy comprises forty-three hostile reports against Abū Ḥanīfa. Six of these explicitly accuse Abū Ḥanīfa of heresy (*kufr* and *zandaqa*). The reports on Abū Ḥanīfa belong to a chapter entitled 'What has been related about Kufa, Abū Ḥanīfa, al-Aʿmash, and others'. The attack on Abū Ḥanīfa is prefaced by a lengthy description of Kufa as an unholy region. The strategy of establishing a link between unholy regions and deviant scholars is nowhere clearer than in al-Fasawī's chapters on specific regions of the early Islamic empire.

In this chapter, I argue that al-Fasawī's description of Kufa as an unholy region is designed to provide a framework for his invective against Abū Ḥanīfa in the same chapter. In al-Fasawī's work we can discern a

between conceptual machineries of the symbolic universe and their social structures, but is too dogmatic in its emphasis on legitimisation in the social world, which serves to draw too sharp a distinction between mentalités and society. Such sharp distinctions do not represent how many medieval religious communities conceived of the organisation of the world: see the brief remarks of von Martin, *The Sociology of the Renaissance*, 19. The origins of this broader structure and its eventual collapse were sketched by Karl Jaspers. See Jaspers, *The Origin and Goal of History*, 4, 55 for its emergence, and 127 for a dramatic obituary: 'The essential fact is: There is no longer anything outside. The world is closed. The unity of the earth has arrived.' The study of such mentalités in the humanities and social sciences are the subject of three excellent chapters in Bellah and Joas (eds.), *The Axial Age*, 146–90, 277–93, and 430–66.

[10] My approach to medieval mentalités is informed by the following works: Hutton, 'The History of Mentalities'; Burke, 'Reflections on the Historical Revolution in France'; Hobsbawm, 'Comment'; Le Goff, 'Mentalities'. The relationship between cultural history and the history of mentalités is disputed. See Darnton's criticisms of French historiography in 'Intellectual and Cultural History'. Christian Lange has made an important contribution to the history of mentalités in the field of medieval Islamic history: Lange, *Justice, Punishment and the Medieval Muslim Imagination*, 15–18.

kind of historiography that specialists of local-history writing in the medieval Islamic world have neglected. Al-Fasawī's dismissal of Kufa as an unholy region articulates a number of key features of medieval Islamic mentalités, and my chapter explores how these social motifs and beliefs helped to determine conceptions of heresy in al-Fasawī's ninth-century history. I hope it will impress upon historians the necessity to formulate a broader conceptualisation of heresy: one that accounts for the porous boundaries between religion, society, and the imagination in medieval Islamic societies. Since this chapter aims to demonstrate how al-Fasawī depicts Kufa as an unholy region that cultivated heretical figures and ideas, we must begin by exploring how medieval Muslims conceived of the routes and realms of the medieval Islamicate world as sacred or profane.

There is a degree of homogeneity in the way in which medieval local historians and scholars wrote about cities and towns.[11] When local historians composed works about particular regions, they did so because they wanted to communicate the virtues and merits of their particular locales.[12] If it was not a selfless act of regional patriotism, provincial rulers were always ready to support and extend patronage to scholars writing about the lands that they governed.[13] In addition to rulers, we can reasonably assume that indigenous populations would have welcomed celebratory accounts of their towns' sacred and holy past, fine production of religious scholars and saints, and mesmerising accounts of their landscapes and landmarks.[14] Historians and geographers also were keen to add flavour and intrigue to their accounts of regions by highlighting peculiarities and fascinating details about particular places and their inhabitants.[15]

[11] The objectives of medieval administrative geographers differed from those of local historians, and even among the former group motives diverged. Al-Muqaddasī, for example, wanted to be remembered by posterity, and realised that aiming for the widest possible readership was the best way to go about achieving this, 'so that travellers, merchants, righteous and elect individuals, kings and élites, judges and jurists, laity and leaders would find the book to be indispensable (*wa ʿalimtu annahu bāb lā budda minhu li al-musāfirīn wa al-tujjār . . . al-ṣāliḥīn wa al-akhyār . . . al-mulūk wa al-kubarā' . . . al-quḍāt wa al-fuqahā' . . . al-ʿāmma wa al-ru'asā'*)': al-Muqaddasī, *Aḥsan al-taqāsīm fī maʿrifat al-aqālīm*, 2nd ed., ed. M. J. de Goeje (Leiden: Brill, 1906), 2.

[12] For a list of local histories see Ibn Funduq, *Tārīkh-i Bayhaq*, ed. Aḥmad Bahmanyār (Tehran: Kitābfurūshī Furūghī dar Chāpkhāneh-yi Islāmiyya, 1938), 20–1. On motives for composing such works see Shaykh al-Islām al-Wā'iẓ and ʿAbd Allāh b. Muḥammad b. al-Qāsim al-Ḥusaynī, *Faḍā'il-i Balkh*, ed. ʿAbd al-Ḥayy Ḥabībī (Tehran: Intishārāt-i Bunyād-i Farhang-i Irān, 1971), 9–10; al-Sahmī, *Tārīkh Jurjān*, 43–4; Anon., *Tārīkh-i Sīstān* (Tehran: Kitābkhāna-i Zawwār, n.d), 1–2.

[13] For al-Jaʿfar al-Narshakhī's (d. after 322/943) dedication to the Sāmānid ruler Nūḥ b. Naṣr (r. 331–43/942–54) see al-Narshakhī, *Tārīkh-i Bukhārā*, ed. Mudarris Riẓavī (Tehran: n.p, 1984), 1.

[14] Abū Nuʿaym al-Iṣfahānī, *Dhikr akhbār Iṣfahān*, 1.

[15] Zakariyyā' b. Muḥammad b. Maḥmūd al-Qazwīnī, *Āthār al-bilād wa akhbār al-ʿibād* (Beirut: Dār Ṣādir, n.d.).

Increasingly, between the ninth and eleventh centuries, this interest in producing local histories acquired a new sense of urgency as the notion of a strong, centralised state gave way to the fractious reality of the Islamic commonwealth.[16] Zayde Antrim has argued convincingly that this new political reality, the fragmentation of political power, had an important role to play in the genesis of a discourse of place, which gave Muslims a powerful language with which to assert connectivity and belonging.[17] Still, as important as such political upheavals might have been, it is worth recognising that we can assign to political fragmentation too important a role in the making and production of local history writing. Connectivity and belonging can be interpreted more broadly.

This would require positing a more complex relationship between political centres and regional provinces in such a way that historians avoid reducing articulations of regional pride to vibrant responses to the enervated presence of the imperial centre. We might have to assert for the imperial centre a more muted role when studying the construction of holy and unholy discourses about regions – without, however, relegating political developments to the margins. After all, this chapter, too, raises the relationship between political upheaval in Iraq and discourses of unholy regions and heretics in the ninth century. Nonetheless, we might wish to reassert the centrality of social ideas and beliefs about particular regions. In so doing, we will see that expressions of fealty to particular places and deep hostility to others owed as much to potent medieval beliefs and mentalités about physical locations, the inhabitants of specific towns, antediluvian histories, and medieval mentalités about the sacred and profane as they did to the disembodiment of the early Islamic empire and the emergence of a commonwealth of regionalisms in its place; and it is the importance of these elements in al-Fasawī's depiction of Kufa that I want to demonstrate in the rest of this chapter.

## 4.1 Holy and Unholy Regions in al-Fasawī's *History*

Yaʿqūb b. Sufyān al-Fasawī's (d. 277/890) *Kitāb al-Maʿrifa wa al-tārīkh* shows a lively interest in local towns and cities.[18] Both the organisation and content of the history demonstrate an acute concern with the peculiarities

[16] On this process see Kennedy, *The Prophet and the Age of the Caliphates*, 156–210; Hodgson, *The Venture of Islam*, 2: 12–62; Morgan, *Medieval Persia*, 19–24.

[17] Antrim, *Routes and Realms*, 144.

[18] Al-Fasawī's *Kitāb al-Maʿrifa wa al-tārīkh* certainly belongs to the genre of traditionalist history, but there remains a puzzle over the work's organisation and diverse content. Its title is an associated problem, but there is a possibility that works of this kind were common among proto-Sunni traditionalists. Some bibliographical sources attribute to Wakīʿ b. al-Jarrāḥ (d. 196–7/812–13) a work with the identical title: see Ziriklī, *al-Aʿlām: qāmūs tarājim li ashhar al-rijāl wa al-nisāʾ min al-ʿArab wa al-mustaʿribīn wa al-mustashriqīn* (Beirut: Dār al-ʿIlm

of towns, regional differences, holy and unholy places, and the role of the *ʿulamāʾ* in adding to (or detracting from) the prestige and sanctity of regions. Al-Fasawī's early life and career help to explain this alertness to the power and pedigree of particular regions. Abū Yūsuf Yaʿqūb b. Sufyān b. Juwwān al-Fasawī was born in the small town of Fasā in the last decade of the eighth century. Fasā was a small district in the province of Fārs, located to the south-west of Shīrāz and to the west of Dārābjird.[19] According to some historians, Fasā was home to only a few notable scholars, although it was considered to be a veritable domain of proto-Sunnism (*fa inna Shīrāz wa Iṣṭakhr wa Fasā al-ghālib ʿalayhim madhāhib ahl al-jamāʿa*).[20] For most historians and geographers of Fārs, al-Fasawī stood out as a man of vast learning and deep piety. But he would also gain a reputation for his wide travels as a young student and, later, as a learned scholar in the regions of the early Islamic empire.[21]

li al-Malāyīn, 1979), 8: 177–8; Ismāʿīl Pāshā al-Baghdādī, *Hadiyyat al-ʿārifīn: asmāʾ al-muʾallifīn wa al-muṣannifīn* (Beirut: Dār Iḥyāʾ al-Turāth al-ʿArabī, 1955), 2: 500.

19 Al-Muṭahhar b. Ṭāhir al-Maqdīsī, *Kitāb al-Badʾ wa al-tārīkh*, ed. M. C. Huart (Paris: Ernest Leroux, 1907), 4: 50–1; Ibn al-Athīr, *al-Kāmil fī al-tārīkh* (Beirut: Dār Ṣādir, 1966), 9: 650, where Ibn al-Athīr notes the original Persian pronunciation, Basā; Ibn Khurradādhbih, *Kitāb al-Masālik wa al-mamālik*, ed. M. J. De Goeje (Leiden: Brill, 1889), 45–6; Yāqūt al-Ḥamawī, *Jacut's Geographisches Wörterbuch: aus den Handschriften zu Berlin (Kitāb Muʿjam al-buldān)* (Leipzig: In Commission bei F. A. Brockhaus, 1886–73), 1: 608–9, 2: 560, 3: 891–2, where Yāqūt provides a fuller description of Fasā and singles out al-Fasawī by way of illustrating the town's production of scholars; Abū Isḥāq al-Fārisī al-Iṣṭakhrī, *Kitāb al-Masālik wa al-mamālik*, ed. M. J. De Goeje (Leiden: Brill, 1870), 108, 127–8, who adds that Fasā was the second largest province of Fārs after Shīrāz.

20 On Fasā's scholars see al-Samʿānī, *al-Ansāb*, 10: 222–5 (Hyderabad edn.) = 9: 305–8 (Maktabat Ibn Taymiyya edn.). On the region's hospitality to proto-Sunnism see al-Iṣṭakhrī, *Kitāb al-Masālik wa al-mamālik*, 139. Al-Muqaddasī shows some enthusiasm for Fasā in his *Aḥsan al-taqāsīm*, 420–1.

21 On al-Fasawī see Yāqūt al-Ḥamawī, *Kitāb Muʿjam al-buldān*, 3: 892; al-Rāmahurmuzī, *al-Muḥaddith al-fāṣil bayn al-rāwī wa al-wāʿī*, ed. Muḥammad ʿAjāj al-Khaṭīb (Beirut: Dār al-Fikr, 1971), 230 (*jamaʿa bayn al-ʿIrāq wa al-Jazīra wa Miṣr wa al-Shām*); Ibn Nuqṭa, *al-Taqyīd*, 2: 314–16 (*ṭāfa al-bilād*). Ibn Nuqṭa provides a detailed itinerary of al-Fasawī's studies and teachers. It is very likely that Ibn Nuqṭa was relying on al-Fasawī's *Mashyakha* for this information. Ibn Ḥajar al-ʿAsqalānī, *Tahdhīb al-tahdhīb*, 11: 386 (Hyderabad edn.); al-Mizzī, *Tahdhīb al-kamāl*, 32: 324–35; Ibn Yūnus al-Ṣadafī, *Tārīkh Ibn Yūnus al-Ṣadafī [Tārīkh al-Miṣriyyīn and Tārīkh al-Ghurabāʾ]*, ed. ʿAbd al-Fattāḥ Fatḥī ʿAbd al-Fattāḥ (Beirut: Dār al-Kutub al-ʿIlmiyya, 2000), 2: 258; Ibn Ḥibbān, *Kitāb al-Thiqāt*, 9: 287; al-Dhahabī, *Tadhkirat al-ḥuffāẓ*, 2: 582–3; al-Dhahabī, *Siyar*, 13: 180–4; Ibn Kathīr, *al-Bidāya wa al-nihāya* (Damascus: Dār Ibn Kathīr, 2010), 11:320–1; Ibn Abī Ḥātim, *al-Jarḥ*, 4.2: 208; al-Nābulusī, *Ikhtiṣār Ṭabaqāt al-Ḥanābila*, ed. Aḥmad ʿUbayd (Damascus: al-Maktaba al-ʿArabiyya, 1930), 2: 432; Ibn al-Athīr, *al-Lubāb fī tahdhīb al-ansāb* (Baghdad: Maktabat al-Muthannā, n.d.), 2: 432; Ibn al-Athīr, *al-Kāmil fī al-tārīkh*, ed. Abū al-Fidāʾ ʿAbd al-Qāḍī (Beirut: Dār al-Kutub al-ʿIlmiyya, 1987), 6: 360, where, in this edition, he is described as Yaʿqūb b. Sufyān b. Ḥawwān al-Sarī; Ibn al-Jazarī, *Ghāyat al-nihāya fī ṭabaqāt al-qurrāʾ*, ed. Gotthelf Bergsträßer (Cairo: Maktabat al-Khānjī, 1932–3; repr. Beirut: Dār al-Kutub al-ʿIlmiyya, 2006), 2: 339; Ibn Manẓūr, *Mukhtaṣar Tārīkh Dimashq li Ibn ʿAsākir*, ed. Sukayna al-Shihābī (Damascus: Dār al-Fikr, 1989), 28:

Al-Fasawī left Fasā and began his travels to collect ḥadīth in his late teens. According to ḥadīth manuals from the tenth and eleventh centuries, ḥadīth study in earnest would begin most commonly between the ages of fifteen and twenty, so al-Fasawī's career is nothing out of the ordinary.[22] Al-Fasawī tells us of his journey to Mecca in 216/831, where his scholarly sojourn extended to four months. After this, he departed for Egypt. He moved on to Damascus in 217/832, but he was back in Mecca for the greater pilgrimage in 218/833. He returned to Damascus and spent time in the region of Shām. For the next thirty years al-Fasawī would study and collect ḥadīth in Mecca, Egypt, Damascus, Ḥimṣ, Palestine, ʿAsqalān, Basra, Balkh, and Khurāsān. He seems to have remained aloof from political life, but he became embroiled, unwittingly, in some controversy during his stay in the province of Fārs during the reign of the Ṣaffārid ruler Yaʿqūb b. Layth (r. 265/879–287/900), where he was summoned to clarify his views regarding the third caliph, ʿUthmān b. ʿAffān. As it turned out, Yaʿqūb b. Layth's concern was misplaced. Our sources tell us that, upon realising that al-Fasawī had said something untoward about ʿUthmān b. ʿAffān, Yaʿqūb dismissed the matter, revealing that he was worried only because he thought al-Fasawī had disparaged Abū Muḥammad ʿUthmān b. ʿAffān al-Sijzī: 'What concern do I have for the companion of the Prophet?', said Yaʿqūb; 'I thought he [al-Fasawī] was speaking about ʿUthmān b. ʿAffān al-Sijzī.'[23] Al-Fasawī died in Basra in 277/890.[24]

44–6; Ibn ʿImād, *Shadharāt al-dhahab*, 3: 321–2; al-Samʿānī, *al-Ansāb*, 9: 305 (Cairo edn.) and 10: 222–5 (Hyderabad edn.). Christopher Melchert has published an important article in which he examines al-Fasawī's *Kitāb al-Maʿrifa wa al-tārīkh* to document the development of different regional trends in early Islamic law: see Melchert, 'How Ḥanafism Came to Originate in Kufa'. Tor, *Violent Order*, 145–6, mentions al-Fasawī in the context of an incident involving him and the Ṣaffārids.

[22] On the age of ḥadīth study see al-Rāmahurmuzī, *al-Muḥaddith al-fāṣil*, 185–200; al-Khaṭīb al-Baghdādī, *al-Kifāya fī ʿilm al-riwāya* (Hyderabad: Dāʾirat al-Maʿārif al-ʿUthmāniyya, 1938), 54–6, where both authors are keen to point out regional variations with respect to the age of ḥadīth study. See also Bulliet, 'The Age Structure of Medieval Islamic Education', esp. 108–9. It is worth noting that Bulliet's conclusions about the age of ḥadīth study, based on his statistical interpretation of a twelfth-century biographical dictionary of Nīshāpūr, are completely at odds with both al-Rāmahurmuzī and al-Khaṭīb's discussions. Additionally, Bulliet's failure to cite any primary sources throughout the article makes his conclusions difficult to accept.

[23] On al-Sijzī see al-Khaṭīb al-Baghdādī, *al-Muttafiq wa al-muftariq*, ed. Muḥammad Ṣādiq (Damascus: Dār al-Qādirī, 1997), 3: 1615–16; Ibn al-Jawzī, *Kitāb al-Ḍuʿafāʾ wa al-matrūkīn* (Beirut: Dār al-Kutub al-ʿIlmiyya, 1986), 2: 170–1; Ibn al-Jawzī, *Talqīḥ fuhūm ahl al-athar fī ʿuyūn al-tārīkh wa al-siyar* (Cairo: Maktabat al-Ādāb, 1975), 619. This anecdote reads like an anti-Ṣaffārid story stemming from Ṭāhirid–Ṣaffārid rivalry over claims to superior Sunnism in Khurāsān in the ninth century.

[24] There are conflicting opinions about both his death date and where he died. See Ibn Manẓūr, *Mukhtaṣar Tārīkh Dimashq*, 28: 46.

We know a good deal about his travels and studies because al-Fasawī was diligent enough to record this information in his *Kitāb al-Maʿrifa wa al-tārīkh*. There are two prominent regions missing from this otherwise impressive register of scholarly travels in the ninth century: al-Fasawī is silent on whether he visited Kufa and Baghdad.[25] The second major work of his that survives, the *Mashyakha*, does reveal some of his connections to scholarly networks in Kufa, Basra, and Baghdad.[26] The *Mashyakha* was a valuable source for later scholars and historians. Presumably, al-Fasawī's simple arrangement and classification of his ḥadīth teachers according to their towns and cities provided the basis for a useful snapshot of ḥadīth learning in the ninth century.[27] *Kitāb al-Maʿrifa wa al-tārīkh* has sections devoted to the history of many of these regions, and these sections represent the coming together of two major concerns in al-Fasawī's history, regionalism and prosopography.[28]

Al-Fasawī records details about scholars on the basis of their association with a particular region, which suggests that his central aim was to document the range and pedigrees of a region's scholars. One consequence of this approach to traditionalist history was that the prestige of any given region was tied to its success or failure in generating a healthy production line of scholars. The care taken by historians to detail the vitae of numerous scholars and to identify their contribution to scholarly learning and religious piety suggests that the region was to be the *Gestalt* of the holy and scholarly labours of its individuals and communities. In this way, historians of regions and their scholars contributed towards making places into sacred ideas. This process is familiar to historians of other parts of the medieval world. Under the Carolingians, for example, the history of Christianity was presented as a history of Rome for the very reason that Rome had become the resting place of martyrs, saints, and

[25] As we shall in this chapter, there are good reasons for this omission.

[26] For his Kufan teachers see al-Fasawī, *Mashyakhat*, 96–126, 154–6, 177–8, 145–54, 176–7 (Basran teachers), 157–8, 178–9 (Baghdadian teachers).

[27] See al-Sakhāwī, *al-Iʿlān*, 222–5, where, in his section on *Muʿjam*s and *Mashyakha*s, al-Sakhāwī refers to al-Fasawī as a pioneer in their composition and geographical arrangement: *wa min al-qudamāʾ fī dhālik Abū Yūsuf Yaʿqūb al-Fasawī, rattabahum ʿalā al-buldān allatī dakhalahā*. The edited text has been wrongly transcribed: *rattabahum* appears as *wa tabbahum*.

[28] Al-Fasawī's interest in regions extends to Miṣr. He has sections on the virtues of Miṣr and its scholars, which have now been placed side by side by Akram Ḍiyāʾ al-ʿUmarī in his edition of the work. See al-Fasawī, *Kitāb al-Maʿrifa wa al-tārīkh*, 2: 487, n. 2 (editor's note), 2: 483–7 (virtues), 2: 487–533 (scholars). See Robinson, *Islamic Historiography*, 66–74 (prosopography), 85–102 (historiography and traditionalism). On Sunnī historiography see now Andersson, *Early Sunnī Historiography*, esp. 90–104.

holy relics; it was the city of emperors; and it was home to a galaxy of bishops.[29] A similar process can be seen with respect to Jerusalem, too. Reacting against Mircea Eliade's understanding of the sacred place as the site of divine manifestation, scholars have highlighted the creative construction of Jerusalem as a holy land. Jonathan Z. Smith has drawn attention to the importance of ritual action in producing sacred and holy places.[30] Robert Wilken, in what is probably the most comprehensive history of the idea of Palestine as a holy place in late antiquity, has documented the central role of 'tactile piety' in establishing the holiness of Jerusalem.[31] Peter Walker has used the writings of Eusebius of Caesarea (d. 339) to examine shifts in the fourth century with respect to the notion of Jerusalem as a holy region. Walker's work has demonstrated that, for late antique scholars such as Eusebius, holy cities and places could lose their status as sacred sites and diminish in standing.[32]

The relationship, then, between regionalism and prosopography meant that discourses of heresy and orthodoxy, particularly when involving specific scholars, were dependent on a contentious process of consensus building about the reputation and status of specific regions. This is precisely what we see in al-Fasawī's account of Kufa and one of its most controversial scholars, Abū Ḥanīfa. First, al-Fasawī's history of Kufa reflects a vision of topography and regional history writing deeply connected to mentalités that hinge on social beliefs and motifs about the devil, divine curses, antediluvian histories, and social and political upheavals. Second, these interconnected themes about the moral malaise of Kufa are woven into a coherent narrative about Kufa's heretical and unholy past. Moreover, this narrative serves to consolidate the unholy connection between Kufa and Abū Ḥanīfa and makes explicit the common thread of religious deviancy between the two that al-Fasawī is so keen to emphasise. We are given an insight, therefore, into the relationship between discourses of heresy and society, between moral topographies and conceptions of orthodoxy and heresy.

[29] McKitterick, *Perceptions of the Past*; McKitterick, *Charlemagne*, 292–381. On this theme see Noble, 'Topography, Celebration, and Power'. For the wider recognition of episcopal power in particular cities see Moore, *A Sacred Kingdom*, 21–51. In the other direction see Maier, 'The Topography of Heresy', on the territoriality of dissenting communities in fourth-century Rome.

[30] Smith, *To Take Place*, 74–95; Eliade, *The Sacred and the Profane.*

[31] Wilken, *The Land Called Holy*, 115–16.

[32] Walker, *Holy City, Holy Places?* On sacred topography and the construction of Jerusalem as a holy region see also Halbwachs, *La topographie légendaire*; Markus, 'How on Earth Could Places Become Holy?'; MacCormack, 'Loca Sancta'.

## 4.2 Heresies and Heretics

The power of place in the medieval Islamic world, even in an age of transregional learning and regional displacement, was inseparable from the power of persons and communities. In *Kitāb al-Maʿrifa wa al-tārīkh*, al-Fasawī's section on each region is preceded by an account of the region's sacred and (un)holy character, drawing on Prophetic and Companion traditions, which establishes a framework within which to describe the communities and scholars that constituted the region's members. Al-Fasawī's history of Basra is dedicated to describing the reputations of more than fifty scholars from Basra and recording traditions associated with them.[33] He opens with a set of reports in which the virtues of Basra are contrasted with the vices of Kufa. The first report sets a scene all too familiar to historians who have worked on Kufan and Basran rivalry.[34]

A group of scholars are engaged in a light-hearted session of regional patriotism. Among them are al-Aḥnaf b. Qays (d. *c.*72/691) and al-Shaʿbī (d. between 103/721 and 109/727).[35] They begin to trade remarks and quips about the merits of Basra over Kufa and vice versa. Addressing the Kufans, al-Aḥnaf says: 'You are our servants, we rescued you from your slaves (*antum khawalunā, istanqadhnākum min ʿabīdikum*).'[36] Not to be

[33] Al-Fasawī, *Kitāb al-Maʿrifa wa al-tārīkh*, 1: 211. On Basra's intellectual and religious milieu see Pellat, *Le milieu basrien*. For the town's urban history see AlSayyad, *Cities and Caliphs*. This is a problematic work, but one can (cautiously) recommend his comments on the town's urban and architectural features. See Cobb, 'Review of Nezar AlSayyad'.

[34] On this kind of rivalry see van Gelder, 'Kufa vs. Basra'. On similar rivalries see Selove, 'Who Invented the Microcosm?' For an early account of the social and political climate of these two towns see Ibn al-Muqaffaʿ, *Āthār Ibn al-Muqaffaʿ*, ed. Muḥammad Kurd ʿAlī (Beirut: Dār al-Kutub al-ʿIlmiyya, 1989), 315–17; Ibn al-Muqaffaʿ, *Rasāʾil al-bulaghāʾ*, ed. Muḥammad Kurd ʿAlī (Cairo: Dār al-Kutub al-ʿArabiyya al-Kubrā, 1913), 125–7.

[35] On al-Aḥnaf b. Qays see Ibn Ḥajar al-ʿAsqalānī, *Taqrīb al-tahdhīb*, ed. ʿĀdil Murshid and Ibrāhīm al-Zaybaq (Beirut: Mu'assasat al-Risāla, 1995), 1: 121; Ibn Ḥajar al-ʿAsqalānī, *Tahdhīb al-tahdhīb*, ed. Ibrāhīm al-Zaybaq and ʿĀdil Murshid (Beirut: Mu'assasat al-Risāla, n.d.), 1: 99. All references to the *Tahdhīb* in this chapter are to this edition and not to the Hyderabad edition.

[36] See Abū al-Faraj al-Iṣfahānī, *Kitāb al-Aghānī* (Beirut: Dār al-Iḥyā' al-Turāth al-ʿArabī, 1994), 6: 313–14, 328–89. The text differs slightly in Iḥsān ʿAbbās's edition: Abū al-Faraj al-Iṣfahānī, *Kitāb al-Aghānī*, ed. Iḥsān ʿAbbās (Beirut: Dār Ṣādir, 2002), 6: 43 (*wa hal ahl al-Kūfa illā khawalunā? Istanqadhnāhum min ʿabīdihim*). As an interrogative phrase implying negation, the exception, *khawal*, may be put either in the accusative or permutative, although the latter is preferred. See Ibn al-Anbārī, *Kitāb al-Inṣāf fī masāʾil al-khilāf bayn al-naḥwiyyīn al-baṣriyyīn wa al-kūfiyyīn*, ed. Gotthold Weil (Leiden: Brill, 1913), 120. I interpret *ʿabīd* as a reference to al-Mukhtār's rebellion and the social background of his supporters. The two editions of al-Iṣfahānī's *Kitāb al-Aghānī* that I have consulted both take *ʿabīd* to be a reference to the Khawārij. Another possibility, suggested to me by Christian Julien Robin, is that the phrase *ʿabīdikum* might be a reference to the ʿIbād of al-Ḥīra, in which case the translation would read: 'You are our servants, we delivered you from the Christian ʿIbād of al-Ḥīra.' This is possible, since this reading would preserve the notion of a slight against the Kufans on account of their social status. There is a

outdone, al-Shaʿbī recites a stirring panegyric in praise of Kufa from the poetry of his brother-in-law al-Aʿshā Hamdān (d. *c.*83/702).[37]

Al-Aḥnaf's reaction to al-Aʿshā's panegyric in praise of Kufa over Basra is a turning point in the gathering, as the playful ambience of the scholars' gathering is injected with a more serious tone. Al-Aḥnaf curtly orders his slave-girl to fetch a notebook and insists that his Kufan guest, al-Shaʿbī, read out its contents. Al-Shaʿbī reads the letter.[38] It turns out to be from the Kufan rebel al-Mukhtār (d. 67/687) to al-Aḥnaf, in which al-Mukhtār claims to be a prophet.[39] Despite al-Shaʿbī's having read the letter, al-Aḥnaf is determined to drive the point home to the entire group.

AL-AḤNAF: Tell me, does this come from a Kufan or a Basran?

AL-SHAʿBĪ: God forgive you Abū Baḥr, we were speaking in jest and intended no offence.[40]

further complication, however, in so far as Ibn Manẓūr in his dictionary cautioned against scholars confusing the plurals *ʿabīd* ('slaves', pl. of *ʿabd*) and *ʿibād* ('devotees', pl. of *ʿabd*). Though the meaning of the singular can be ambiguous, Ibn Manẓūr insists that the plural form discriminates between the two possible meanings: Ibn Manẓūr, *Lisān al-ʿArab* (Beirut: Dār Ṣādir, n.d.), 2: 270. Now it is possible that someone in the eighth–ninth centuries made the very mistake that Ibn Manẓūr would later caution against. For more on the ethnic and confessional composition of al-Ḥīra, particularly with regard to the ʿIbād of al-Ḥīra and an explanation for the appellation *ʿibād* to the Christians of al-Ḥīra, see al-Yaʿqūbī, *Kitāb al-Buldān*, ed. M. J. De Goeje (Leiden: Brill, 1892), 371. This passage does not belong to this edition of Yaʿqūbī's *Kitāb al-Buldān*, but the editor, De Goeje, has included it as an appendix to the work, containing extracts from Yaʿqūbī's works not found in his writings but in later sources. The source is al-Bakrī, *Muʿjam mā istaʿjama min al-asmāʾ al-bilād wa al-mawāḍiʿ*, ed. Muṣṭafā al-Saqqā (Beirut: Dār al-Kutub al-ʿIlmiyya, n.d.), 24–5, where al-Bakrī lists a number of other etymological possibilities. In the secondary literature see Rothstein, *Dynastie der Laḥmiden in al-Ḥīra*, 18–20; and for a detailed portrait of the *ʿibād* of al-Ḥīra see Toral-Niehoff, *al-Ḥīra*, 88–105; Toral-Niehoff, 'The ʿIbād of al-Ḥīra'; Morony, *Iraq after the Muslim Conquest*, 221–2, 375–8; Donner, *The Early Islamic Conquests*, 233. See also Chapter 5 below.

[37] Al-Shaʿbī was married to al-Aʿshā's sister, and al-Aʿshā was married to al-Shaʿbī's sister. See al-Iṣfahānī, *Kitāb al-Aghānī*, 6: 313–14, 326–8; al-Dhahabī, *Tārīkh al-Islām*, 6: 41. On al-Shaʿbī see also Juynboll, *Encyclopedia of Canonical Ḥadīth*, 463–71; and Judd, *Religious Scholars and the Umayyads*, 41–51.

[38] Ibn al-Faqīh refers to the correspondence between al-Mukhtār and al-Aḥnaf: see Ibn al-Faqīh, *Kitāb al-Buldān*, ed. M. J. de Goeje (Leiden: Brill, 1885), 185.

[39] For further medieval documentation of al-Mukhtār's 'heretical' claims see al-Balādhurī, *Ansāb al-ashrāf*, ed. Maḥmūd al-Firdaws al-ʿAẓm (Damascus: Dār al-Yaqẓa al-ʿArabiyya, 1999), 6: 59–60; al-Ṭabarī, *Tārīkh*, 2: 520–37, 598–640; al-Bayhaqī, *Dalāʾil al-nubūwa wa maʿrifat aḥwāl ṣāḥib al-sharīʿa*, ed. ʿAbd al-Muʿṭī Qalʿajī (Beirut: Dār al-Kutub al-ʿIlmiyya, 1988), 6: 482–4. On al-Mukhtār see von Gelder, *Muhtar de valsche Profeet*; Crone, 'The Significance of Wooden Weapons'; Wellhausen, *Religio-Political Factions in Early Islam*, 121–59; Wellhausen, *Die religiös-politischen Oppositionsparteien im alten Islam*, 87–89; Rotter, *Die Umayyaden und der zweite Bürgerkrieg*, 93–106, 214–20; Sellheim, *Der zweite Bürgerkrieg im Islam*; Anthony, *The Caliph and the Heretic*, 256–90; al-Dīnawarī, *al-Akhbār al-ṭiwāl* (Leiden: Brill, 1888), 300–14.

[40] Al-Aḥnaf's full name was al-Aḥnaf b. Qays b. Muʿāwiya b. Ḥuṣayn al-Tamīmī al-Saʿdī Abū Baḥr al-Baṣrī. See Ibn Ḥajar al-ʿAsqalānī, *Taqrīb al-tahdhīb*, 1: 121; Ibn Ḥajar al-ʿAsqalānī, *Tahdhīb al-tahdhīb*, 1: 99 (Beirut edn.).

AL-AḤNAF: Tell me, who is it from?
AL-SHAʿBĪ: God forgive you.
AL-AḤNAF: Tell me.
AL-SHAʿBĪ: He is from Kufa.

The session is brought to an abrupt end, we are told, when al-Aḥnaf declares, 'We Basrans do not have anyone like that among us.'[41] This was not the only occasion where Aḥnaf, in particular, was involved in Kufan and Basran literary jostling.[42] Rivalry between Kufa and Basra was a common feature of regional attitudes among scholars, students, and inhabitants. In the social sphere of ninth-century learning and education, regional practices and trends mattered. The organisation of ninth-century prosopographical and historical works along regional lines exemplifies the tendency to conceptualise regions as repositories not just of ordinary inhabitants but of particular views and beliefs. This is observable in the work of medieval geographers, too, where authors such as al-Muqaddasī (d. 380/991) have as much to say about a region's inclination to orthodox or heretical movements as about its demography and economy.[43]

Al-Fasawī's description of this intimate and hostile exchange between Kufan and Basran scholars is designed to illustrate Kufa's unholiness as a region that produced heretics and was remembered for having done so. Normally we would not be in a position to determine whether al-Fasawī's deep-seated enmity towards Kufa resulted in a careful narrative readjustment of an encounter between al-Shaʿbī and al-Aḥnaf. In this particular case, however, we can compare al-Fasawī's narrative with that of Abū al-Faraj al-Iṣfahānī (d. 363/972) contained in the latter's tenth-century literary masterpiece, *Kitāb al-Aghānī.*

Al-Aʿshā is one of the literary personalities whom al-Iṣfahānī surveys in the *Book of Songs.*[44] Al-Iṣfahānī's account differs in very few places. We learn that the social gathering took place in a mosque during the time of

[41] Al-Fasawī, *Kitāb al-Maʿrifa wa al-tārīkh*, 2: 30–2. This report also appears in al-Bayhaqī, *Dalāʾil al-nubūwa*, 6: 483, where al-Bayhaqī simply ends with al-Aḥnaf declaring that no character similar to al-Mukhtār was to be found among the Basrans. This version is one of two different reports mentioned by al-Fasawī, and it is al-Fasawī's report that turns up in al-Bayhaqī's work. Ibn ʿAsākir narrates al-Fasawī's version alongside an alternative account in Ibn ʿAsākir, *Tārīkh Madīnat al-Dimashq*, ed. ʿAbd al-Bāqī b. Aḥmad and ʿAbd al-Raḥmān b. Qaḥṭān (Beirut: Dār al-Fikr, 1996), 34: 482–5. See also the version in al-Balādhurī, *Ansāb al-ashrāf*, 6: 74.

[42] Al-Masʿūdī, *Les prairies d'or. Texte et traduction par C. Barbier de Meynard et Pavet de Courteille [Murūj al-dhahab]* (Paris: Société Asiatique, 1861–77), 6: 275–6; al-Masʿūdī, *Murūj al-dhahab wa maʿādin al-jawhar*, ed. Kamāl Ḥasan Marʿī (Beirut: al-Maktaba al-ʿAṣriyya, 2005), 3: 274–5.

[43] Al-Muqaddasī, *Aḥsan al-taqāsīm*, 32–43.

[44] On al-Iṣfahānī's survey of al-Aʿshā's literary corpus see Kilpatrick, *Making the Great Book of Songs*, 190–2.

Ibn al-Zubayr's (d. 73/692) rebellion, which places the alleged encounter some time during the last two decades of the seventh century. For our purposes, the most significant discrepancy is al-Iṣfahānī's account of al-Aḥnaf's response to al-Shaʿbī's recitation of al-Aʿshā's poetry. Contrary to al-Fasawī's transmission, there is no indignant reaction. The gathering maintains its jaunty mood, as al-Aḥnaf recognises al-Shaʿbī's deft deployment of the great Kufan's poetry and proceeds to taunt his fellow Basrans for having been outwitted by al-Shaʿbī.[45] In al-Iṣfahānī's account we have a description of a merry social occasion in which Basrans and Kufans engage in polite exchanges about the virtues of their respective regions, and the Kufans are congratulated on their literary triumph over their hosts. Al-Fasawī's account is very different. What started as a playful and social gathering is transformed into a caustic deprecation of Kufa as a breeding ground for heretics and false prophets.

Kufa's reputation for breeding heretics and false prophets was known to other sources. Ibn al-Faqīh (d. *c.*289/902) provides further glimpses into the social and religious tensions between Kufa and Basra. He records a long debate between Abū Bakr al-Ḥudhalī (d. 159/775–6), a Basran, and Ibn ʿAyyāsh (d. 193/809), a Kufan, in the presence of the first ʿAbbāsid caliph, Abū al-ʿAbbās al-Saffāḥ (r. 132/750–136/754), during which Abū Bakr al-Ḥudhalī raises the matter of the number of false prophets in Kufa. He says to Ibn ʿAyyāsh mockingly: 'You have more prophets than we do. We have but one prophet: Muḥammad, may God bless him. All your prophets are weavers ... I have not seen prophets crucified except in the town of Kufa.' Ibn ʿAyyāsh even acknowledges the factual accuracy of Abū Bakr's rebuke, but he interprets it in a positive light: 'You deprecate the people of Kufa on account of three mad men of *hoi polloi* who, in their madness, claimed to be prophets, and so God let them be crucified in Kūfa.'[46]

The two remaining reports in al-Fasawī's discussion of Basra's merits pursue an identical strategy of praising Basra at the expense of Kufa. Once again, al-Fasawī describes an encounter. He recalls a scene in Mecca's mosque, where ʿAbd Rabbih b. Rāshid was passing as a lesson was being held. As he approached the circle of students, he found among them Ibn ʿUmar. Ibn ʿUmar bluntly asked ʿAbd Rabbih, 'Where do you come from?' 'From Basra,' he answered. Ibn ʿUmar ended the brief encounter by reassuring ʿAbd Rabbih: 'The people of Basra are more virtuous than the people of Kufa.'[47] A third unpropitious report about Kufa brings to a

[45] Al-Iṣfahānī, *Kitāb al-Aghānī*, 6: 328–9.
[46] Ibn al-Faqīh, *Kitāb al-Buldān*, 167–8, 185. See also van Gelder, 'Kufa vs. Basra', 350.
[47] Al-Fasawī, *Kitāb al-Maʿrifa wa al-tārīkh*, 2: 32.

close al-Fasawī's collection of reports in praise of Basra. Al-Fasawī produces a report in which Yūnus b. ʿUbayd (d. 140/757), a Basran scholar, counts not having been raised in Kufa as one of the great favours of God upon him.[48]

The history of Shām manifests a more familiar approach to documenting the sacred history of a holy region. Unlike Basra, the regions of Shām developed a strong tradition of local historiography.[49] Al-Fasawī's history of Shām has a wealth of material to draw upon to describe its sacred topography.[50] Readers of al-Fasawī's history of Shām are treated to a succession of no less than forty reports and traditions that describe the sanctity of Shām. Shām's holiness is established first through al-Fasawī's citation of a report in which the Prophet declares his favour for Shām as he responds to a request to choose a destination for migration. 'Choose Shām,' the Prophet responds without any hesitation.[51] In the same section, Shām is declared to be the best of God's lands;[52] it contains God's elect servants;[53] it is the fount of God's light;[54] God has guaranteed the safety of Shām and its inhabitants;[55] faith is to be found only in Shām during the time of civil strife (*fitna*);[56] Damascus is declared to be the fortress of the Muslims on the day of massacre (*yawm al-malḥama*);[57] 'If the people of Shām become corrupt, then there is no good to be found among any of you,' says another Prophetic report;[58] Shām, along with Mecca and Medina, is identified as one of the places where the Prophet is

48 Al-Fasawī, *Kitāb al-Maʿrifa wa al-tārīkh*, 2: 32. Anti-Kufa reports make a haphazard appearance, once again, in al-Fasawī's chapter on Basra, where a version of this report is recorded. See al-Fasawī, *Kitāb al-Maʿrifa wa al-tārīkh*, 2: 255–8. On Yūnus b. ʿUbayd see Ibn Ḥajar al-ʿAsqalānī, *Tahdhīb al-tahdhīb*, 11: 442–5 (Hyderabad edn.).

49 Dahhan, 'The Origins and Development of the Local Histories of Syria'; Borrut, *Entre mémoire et pouvoir*, 120–6; Khalek, *Damascus after the Muslim Conquest*, ch. 2; Elad, *Medieval Jerusalem*, 6–22, 147–58; Bianquis, *Damas et la Syrie sous la domination fatimide*, 1–34. On history-writing in Damascus see Conrad, 'Das Kitāb al-Ṭabaqāt des Abū Zurʿa al-Dimašqī'; Conrad, *Abū 'l-Ḥusain al-Rāzī*; Rotter, ' Abū Zurʿa al-Dimashqī und das Problem'.

50 On Shām's *faḍāʾil* traditions see Kister, 'A Comment on the Antiquity of Traditions Praising Jerusalem'; Cobb, *White Banners*, 52–5; Cobb, 'Virtual Sacrality'; Meri, *The Cult of Saints*, 14–16; Khalek, *Damascus after the Muslim Conquest*, 139–50; Madelung, 'Apocalyptic Prophecies'; Abū al-Ḥasan ʿAlī b. Muḥammad al-Rabaʿī, *Faḍāʾil al-Shām wa al-Dimashq*, ed. Salāḥ al-Dīn al-Munajjid (Damascus: al-Majmaʿ al-ʿIlmī al-ʿArabī, 1950).

51 Al-Fasawī, *Kitāb al-Maʿrifa wa al-tārīkh*, 2: 287–8.

52 Al-Fasawī, *Kitāb al-Maʿrifa wa al-tārīkh*, 2: 289–90.

53 Al-Fasawī, *Kitāb al-Maʿrifa wa al-tārīkh*, 2: 289.

54 Al-Fasawī, *Kitāb al-Maʿrifa wa al-tārīkh*, 2: 289.

55 Al-Fasawī, *Kitāb al-Maʿrifa wa al-tārīkh*, 2: 289.

56 Al-Fasawī, *Kitāb al-Maʿrifa wa al-tārīkh*, 2: 291.

57 Al-Fasawī, *Kitāb al-Maʿrifa wa al-tārīkh*, 2: 290.

58 Al-Fasawī, *Kitāb al-Maʿrifa wa al-tārīkh*, 2: 295–6.

said to have received prophecy;[59] Damascus is named as one of the five places of paradise on earth.[60]

For medieval scholars like al-Fasawī, the physical landscape of the world and the worldly fortunes of individual regions were embedded deeply within medieval mentalités that governed society's attitudes to the holy, unholy, moral, supernatural, and eschatological. Society was ordered around a wider set of medieval mentalités that were thought to interact with the social, political, and moral framework of medieval Islamic societies. The reports above are pregnant with social and political overtones. The attempt to establish Shām as a holy sanctuary in times of insecurity, civil strife, and corruption resonates most obviously with the anxieties of Umayyad Syria in the eighth century. The narratives about Shām's impervious sacrality were designed to provide reassurances during a crisis of control and confidence.[61] However, our sources also are keen to establish an *Entstehungsgeschichte* for beliefs about the holiness and unholiness of regions that emancipate such narratives from their sociopolitical historical contexts. We find in al-Fasawī's history the following report:[62]

> God apportioned good (*qassama Allāh al-khayr*) in the world into ten tenths. He placed nine-tenths of it in Shām, and the remaining portion was distributed among the other regions (*wa baqiyyatuhu fī sā'ir al-araḍīn*). Likewise, He apportioned evil (*al-sharr*) in the world into ten tenths, of which only a small portion was allotted to Shām; the overwhelming portion of evil was distributed among all the other regions.

This is an emphatic illustration of how recent or contemporary attitudes towards certain towns and regions were anchored in a distant and immutable past. It provides an important insight into how and why attitudes towards regions and places were cultivated in the medieval Islamic world. The narrative articulates a plan of history and the fundamental agency of divine providence in the division of holy and unholy regions, good and evil, order and chaos. This is a conception of history in which discourses of regions and discourses of heresy and orthodoxy were collapsed into what Erich Auerbach described as the 'figural interpretation of history':[63]

[59] Al-Fasawī, *Kitāb al-Maʿrifa wa al-tārīkh*, 2: 298.
[60] Al-Fasawī, *Kitāb al-Maʿrifa wa al-tārīkh*, 2: 305.
[61] For an overview of the political history and memory of Umayyad Syria see Cobb, *White Banners*, 1–9; and Borrut, *Entre mémoire et pouvoir*, 61–78.
[62] Al-Fasawī, *Kitāb al-Maʿrifa wa al-tārīkh*, 2: 295. This report is also mentioned in al-Ṭabarānī, *al-Muʿjam al-kabīr*, ed. Ḥamdī ʿAbd al-Majīd al-Silāfī (Cairo: Maktabat Ibn Taymiyya, 1983), 9: 198.
[63] Auerbach, *Mimesis*, 73–5. It is hardly incidental that Auerbach's piercing analysis is applied to the writings of the Latin Church Fathers, particularly those of Jerome and Augustine.

The horizontal, that is the temporal and causal, connection of occurrences is dissolved; the here and now is no longer a mere link in an earthly chain of events, it is simultaneously something which has always been, and which will be fulfilled in the future; and strictly, in the eyes of God, it is something eternal, something omni-temporal, something already consummated in the realm of fragmentary earthly event.

By incorporating this tradition into his section on Kufa, al-Fasawī is blurring the lines between doctrine and discourses of holy and unholy regions. The regional sanctity of Shām is anchored in a doctrinal certainty that belongs to the antediluvian period, the epoch before epochs; a pre-historical moment when God determined the nature of the world and the division of good and evil. Al-Fasawī is positing a pre-earthly distribution of the holy and unholy in the regions and realms of the world. Any predisposition that a region might have to the sacred is dependent on a supernatural scheme that allows for no renegotiation. In Auerbach's words, the 'connection of occurrences is dissolved'.

We learn more about this doctrine concerning the distribution of good and evil in the regions of the early Islamic empire. Towards the beginning of his account execrating Kufa, al-Fasawī relates a tradition that develops the idea of a preternatural distribution of evil and good. Kufa, it seems, is described to ʿAlī b. Abī Ṭālib as a region nine-tenths occupied by evil, devils, and rebellious demons (*tisʿat aʿshār al-sharr wa shayāṭīn al-ins wa maradat al-jinn*).[64] Al-Fasawī combines two ideas – the 'omni-temporal' doctrine of earthly events and the view that Kufa was a unique site of demonological activity – to dismiss Kufa as an unholy region. These themes continue to find currency throughout al-Fasawī's chapter on Kufa, where their relationship to the social conditions and historical circumstances of the eighth–ninth centuries becomes more apparent. Al-Fasawī adduces a report attributed to the Prophet's most prominent Companion in Kufa, ʿAbd Allāh b. Masʿūd (d. *c.*33/653):[65]

You are in the place where the tongues were confused [as a manifestation of God's displeasure] between Babel and Ḥīra (*tabalbalat al-alsun bayn Bābil wa al-Ḥīra*). Nine-tenths of good is to be found in Shām, whilst the remaining tenth portion is to be found in other places; and nine-tenths of evil is to be found in other places, with only the tenth portion of evil remaining in Shām.

Whilst his readers would have needed little help in deciphering the location of the place between Babel and Ḥīra, the placement of the report a

64 Al-Fasawī, *Kitāb al-Maʿrifa wa al-tārīkh*, 2: 750–1. The report does not mention Kufa explicitly, but its placement in the chapter on Kufa makes this a reasonable inference.

65 Al-Fasawī, *Kitāb al-Maʿrifa wa al-tārīkh*, 2: 750. For ʿAbd Allāh b. Masʿūd, see Ibn Ḥajar al-ʿAsqalānī, *Tahdhīb al-tahdhīb*, 2: 431–2 (Beirut edn.).

few folios into the section 'What has been related about Kufa' leaves little room for doubt as to the region in question. More importantly, the report invokes the primeval biblical pericope about the confusion of tongues at Babel, an event which in Islamic and pre-Islamic Near Eastern sources signified an instance of God's punishment upon the people of Babel. This was part of the cultural memory of Near Eastern communities in Mesopotamia and Iraq, and a ninth-century historian's record of it in his chapter on Kufa demonstrates that Muslim communities were acutely aware of the implications of their topography and conscious of its sacred or profane nature.[66] Moreover, the tradition cleverly reflects a degree of anxiety about the cultural, social, ethnic, and religious hybridity that would have characterised Kufa's demographic constitution in the eighth and ninth centuries.[67] The tradition seems to suggest a congruity between foreign ethnicities and non-Muslim confessional communities, on the one hand, and the high risk of exposure to evil, demons, doctrinal and ritual deviancy, and heresy, on the other. This relationship between

[66] Arno Borst's monumental six-volume history of western and eastern accounts of the Tower of Babel remains the authoritative work on the subject, though his discussion of Islamic materials is limited to works in translation. See Borst, *Der Turmbau von Babel*, 1: 325–54, esp. 331–50. See also Geiger, *Judaism and Islam*, 89–93. On the primeval history of the confusion of the tongues at Babel in the primary sources see al-Ṭabarī, *Tārīkh*, 1: 319–23; al-Bīrūnī, *al-Āthār al-bāqiya ʿan al-qurūn al-khāliya [Chronologie Orientalischer Völker]*, ed. Eduard Sachau (Leipzig: Otto Harrassowitz, 1923), 87; al-Bakrī, *Muʿjam mā istaʿjama min al-asmāʾ al-bilād wa al-mawāḍiʿ*, 218–19; Jalāl al-Dīn al-Suyūṭī, *al-Muzhir fī ʿulūm al-lugha wa anwāʿihā* (Cairo: Dār Iḥyāʾ al-Kutub al-ʿArabiyya, 1958), 1: 32; and for non-Islamic materials see Ginzberg, *Legends of the Jews*, 1: 16–64; Sherman, *Babel's Tower Translated*; Rubin, 'The Language of Creation or the Primordial Language'. On Babel and Ḥīra see Morony, *Iraq after the Muslim Conquest*, 143–55. The history of Ḥīra in the early Islamic period has yet to be written. The most thorough account of its history during late antiquity stops at the eve of Islam, although it reinforces the conventional scholarly assessment that Ḥīra anticipated the dynamism and cultural hybridity that defined Kufa, Basra, and Baghdad: see Toral-Niehoff, *al-Ḥīra*, 221. Bertold Spuler's classic account is more forthcoming on Ḥīra in the early Islamic period: Spuler, *Iran in früh-islamischer Zeit*, 7–9, 298 n. 2. Al-Ṣarrāf attempts to say more about Ḥīra in the first two centuries of Islam, but unfortunately her study lacks detail and often resorts to generalisations: al-Ṣarrāf, 'al-Ḥīra fī al-qarnayn al-awwal wa al-thānī al-hijrayn'.

[67] No local history of early Islamic Kufa has survived. The prosopographical sources do permit a one-sided reconstruction of Kufa's residents, for which see Khalīfa b. Khayyāṭ, *Kitāb al-Ṭabaqāt*, ed. Akram Ḍiyāʾ al-ʿUmarī (Baghdad: Baghdad University and Maṭbaʿat al-ʿĀnī, 1967), 126–73; Morony, 'Religious Communities in Late Sasanian and Early Muslim Iraq'; Morony, *Iraq after the Muslim Conquest*, chs. 3 and 4; Donner, *The Early Islamic Conquests*, 239–45. See Spuler, *Iran in früh-islamischer Zeit*, 297–8, for his use of economic data (*kharāj* and *jizya*) for the early Islamic provinces to infer ethnic and confessional composition. A good overview of confessional and ethnic hybridity in the early period is provided by Hoyland, *In God's Path*, 157–69. I know of no comprehensive treatment of ethnicity and ethnic composition in the regions of the early Islamic empire. Meanwhile, Peter Webb has offered a thought-provoking study of Arab ethnogenesis in the early Islamic period. His discussion of ethnicity in eighth–ninth-century Iraq is particularly relevant: Webb, *Imagining the Arabs*, ch. 5.

regions, their confessional and ethnic constitution, and their propensity for religious deviance and heresy is a recurring theme in the discourse of heresy surrounding both Abū Ḥanīfa and Kufa. As such, it will be treated in the next chapter, but already we can begin to see that al-Fasawī's histories of Basra and Shām are deeply embedded with anti-Kufan narratives.

This aspect of al-Fasawī's history stands out in some respects from medieval universal, regional, and local history writing.[68] A number of important publications have documented the rise of local historiography and its contribution to a discourse of sanctity around places and regions.[69] This body of scholarship has come to dominate our understanding of medieval perspectives on holy places.[70] The regions and realms of the medieval Islamic world were undoubtedly invested with notions of sanctity and sacrality, but there was also a darker side to the historical and cultural memory of towns and cities. The positive gloss on regions leaves unexamined the more unpalatable and, occasionally, graphic discourses about unholy places. This aspect of the memory of towns and places comes to the forefront in this chapter because it is understood to be an

[68] On universal histories see Springberg-Hinsen, *Die Zeit vor dem Islam in arabischen Universalgeschichten*; Radtke, 'Towards a Typology of Abbasid Universal Chronicles'; Radtke, *Weltgeschichte und Weltbeschreibung*; Robinson, *Islamic Historiography*, 134–8; Rosenthal, *A History of Muslim Historiography*, 114–30.

[69] Much of the scholarly interest in local and regional historiography can be traced to a historical curiosity for viewing Islam from the edge, an approach neatly captured by Richard Bulliet's work on medieval Iran. In a number of publications Bulliet led the call for a shift away from the centre. He urged Islamicists to resist the gravitational pull of the imperial cities of the caliphs on historians, which had had the effect of making historians over-reliant on medieval universal histories for sketching a portrait of medieval Islamdom. See Bulliet, *The Patricians of Nishapur*; Bulliet, *Islam: The View from the Edge*; Bulliet, 'City Histories in Medieval Iran'. See also Frye, 'City Chronicles of Central Asia and Khurasan', 405. Bulliet's work prompted a group of historians to turn their attention to charting the rise of local historiography in medieval Iran: Melville, 'Persian Local Histories'; Melville, 'The Caspian Provinces'; Bosworth, 'Sistan and Its Local Histories'; Pourshariati, 'Local Historiography in Early Medieval Iran'; Pourshariati, 'Local Histories of Khurasan'; Paul, 'The Histories of Isfahan'; Paul, 'The Histories of Herat'; Paul, 'The Histories of Samarqand'; Paul, *Herrscher, Gemeinwesen, Vermittler*, 21–3; Weinberger, 'The Authorship'; Miller, 'Local History in Ninth/Fifteenth Century Yazd'. See also Lambton, 'Persian Local Histories'; Lambton, 'An Account of the Tārīkhi Qumm'; Meisami, *Persian Historiography*, 79–108, 209–29; Drechsler, *Die Geschichte der Stadt Qom*; Shimamoto, 'Some Reflections on the Origin of Qom'. Some of these local histories are used to good effect in Savant, *The New Muslims of Post-Conquest Iran*, 90–129.

[70] Kister, 'Sanctity Joint and Divided'; Elad, *Medieval Jerusalem*; Livne-Kafri, 'The Early Shīʿa and Jerusalem'; Azad, *Sacred Landscape*; Munt, *The Holy City of Medina*; Toral-Niehoff, *al-Ḥīra*; Haider, *The Origins of the Shīʿa*; Friedman, '"Kufa Is Better"'. Neither Haider nor Friedman mention the presence of anti-Kufan material. An exception is Melchert, 'How Ḥanafism Came to Originate in Kufa', 336–7, where he discusses several anti-Iraqi reports in the context of ḥadīth learning in Iraq.

important element of ninth-century discourses of heresy. The relationship between making heretics and framing regions as unholy allows us to assess precisely how towns were desacralised and framed as breeding grounds for heretics and heresies. For example, what mechanisms were utilised for dismissing regions as unholy? What were the strategies of desanctification? Why were certain regions more vulnerable than others to such techniques? Above all, what were the inter-relationalities between the framing of heretics and the framing of regions?

Al-Fasawī's attempt to discredit Kufa as an unholy region is tied to his long diatribe against Abū Ḥanīfa contained in the same section on Kufa. His attack on Kufa involves a creative form of history writing that draws on a repertoire of medieval mentalités. Al-Fasawī draws on eschatology, ethnicity, politics, scripture, the devil, demons, ritual, and supernatural beliefs in order to characterise Kufa as an unholy and heretical region. The very first report in his chapter on Kufa aims to establish a Prophetic justification for the belief that it was a seat of heresy in the medieval Islamic world:[71]

> ʿAbd Allāh b. Maslama b. Qaʿnabī (d. 221/835, Basra)[72] < Mālik (d. 179/795, Medina)[73] < ʿAbd Allāh b. Dīnār (d. 127/744, Medina)[74] < ʿAbd Allāh b. ʿUmar (d. 73/692, Mecca)[75] said: I saw the Messenger of God point to the East and say: 'From there, indeed the tribulation shall come from there. Indeed, the tribulation shall come from there, from where the horn of the devil shall rise.'

This is followed by a second tradition in which the Prophet is reported as having said that 'the seat of heresy is in the East'.[76] For al-Fasawī there was no doubt that these ominous pronouncements about the East were directed towards Kufa.[77] In the same chapter al-Fasawī cites different versions of a similar report in which al-Mashriq is replaced with ʿIraq.[78] Al-Fasawī's motivations for using this tradition become a little clearer when we consider how versions of this report were handled by some of his contemporaries and predecessors. Muḥammad b. Ismāʿīl al-Bukhārī (d. 256/870) died a few decades before al-Fasawī. Al-Bukhārī's *al-Jāmiʿ al-ṣaḥīḥ* presents an alternative version of this report in his chapter on the

[71] Al-Fasawī, *Kitāb al-Maʿrifa wa al-tārīkh*, 2: 749.
[72] Ibn Ḥajar al-ʿAsqalānī, *Tahdhīb al-tahdhīb*, 2: 433–4 (Beirut edn.).
[73] Ibn Ḥajar al-ʿAsqalānī, *Tahdhīb al-tahdhīb*, 4: 6–8 (Beirut edn.).
[74] Ibn Ḥajar al-ʿAsqalānī, *Tahdhīb al-tahdhīb*, 2: 328 (Beirut edn.).
[75] Ibn Ḥajar al-ʿAsqalānī, *Tahdhīb al-tahdhīb*, 2: 389–90 (Beirut edn.).
[76] Al-Fasawī, *Kitāb al-Maʿrifa wa al-tārīkh*, 2: 749.
[77] In medieval geographies 'al-Mashriq' referred to the eastern lands of the ʿAbbāsid caliphate. See al-Muqaddasī, *Aḥsan al-taqāsīm*, 260.
[78] Al-Fasawī, *Kitāb al-Maʿrifa wa al-tārīkh*, 2: 747.

beginning of creation, under the sub-heading 'The best of a man's wealth is cattle which he takes to the peak of the mountain':[79]

The seat of unbelief is in the East; pride and haughtiness is among the people who have horses and camels; the loud-voiced people are the people of the tents; and tranquility is with the people who have cattle.

Al-Bukhārī's placement of this report in a chapter on wealth and property does indeed raise the question of how central the association of Kufa with unbelief was for al-Fasawī's contemporaries.[80] There is nothing in al-Bukhārī's presentation of this report that refutes al-Fasawī's insistence that Iraq was to be the breeding ground of heresy and unbelief. However, the different ways in which our two authors select, omit, and arrange information can tell us about the strategies that medieval writers adopted when articulating specific religious ideas. We find other versions of the 'unbelief in al-Mashriq' report towards the end of al-Bukhārī's *al-Jāmiʿ al-ṣaḥīḥ* in his chapter on trials and tribulations (*fitan*). Again, there is no suggestion that the region of Iraq is intended.[81] Al-Bukhārī's earliest commentator, al-Khaṭṭābī, was more confident about how to interpret the geographical

[79] Al-Bukhārī, *al-Jāmiʿ al-ṣaḥīḥ, kitāb bad' al-khalq* 59, *bāb khayr māl al-muslim ghanam yatbaʿu bihā shaghaf al-jibāl* 15, no. 3301 (numbering after ʿAbd al-Bāqī's edn.) (*ra's al-kufr naḥwa al-mashriq; wa al-fakhr wa al-khuyalā' fī ahl al-khayl; wa al-ibl wa al-faddādīn ahl al-wabar; wa al-sakīna fī ahl al-ghanam*).

[80] This version also appears in al-Bukhārī, *Kitāb al-Adab al-mufrad*, ed. Samīr b. Amīn al-Zuhayrī (Riyadh: Maktabat al-Maʿārif li al-Nashr wa al-Tawzīʿ, 1998), 296; Muslim, *al-Jāmiʿ al-ṣaḥīḥ, kitāb al-īmān* 1, *bāb tafāḍul ahl al-īmān fīhi wa rujḥān ahl al-Yaman fīhi* 21, no. 85, 86, 90 (numbering after ʿAbd al-Bāqī's edn.); Aḥmad b. Ḥanbal, *al-Musnad li Aḥmad b. Ḥanbal*, ed. Muḥammad Aḥmad Shākir (Cairo: Dār al-Ḥadīth, 1995), 9: 508–9, 623–4; Abū Yaʿlā al-Mawṣilī, *Musnad Abī Yaʿlā al-Mawṣilī*, ed. Ḥusayn Salīm Asad (Beirut: Dār al-Ma'mūn li al-Turāth, 1987), 11: 226–7; Abū ʿAwāna, *Musnad Abī ʿAwāna*, ed. Ayman b. ʿĀrif al-Dimashqī (Beirut: Dār al-Maʿārif, 1998), 1: 61–3, where at least ten versions of this report are collected in the chapter, *bayān al-akhlāq wa al-aʿmāl al-maḥmūda allatī jaʿalahā rasūl Allāh min al-īmān wa nasabahā ilā ahl al-Ḥijāz wa mā yalīhā, wa al-akhlāq wa al-aʿmāl al-madhmūma allatī nasabahā ilā al-kufr wa annahā qibal al-Mashriq*; Ibn Manda, *Kitāb al-Īmān*, ed. ʿAlī b. Muḥammad b. Nāṣir al-Faqīhī (Beirut: Mu'assasat al-Risāla, 1985), 2: 524–8; al-Ṭaḥāwī, *Sharḥ mushkil al-āthār*, ed. Shuʿayb al-Arna'ūṭ (Beirut: Mu'assasat al-Risāla, 1994), 2: 270. For attempts in the Higher Middle Ages to discern the exact location and meaning of this tradition see al-ʿAynī, *ʿUmdat al-qārī sharḥ Ṣaḥīḥ al-Bukhārī* (Beirut: Dār al-Fikr, n.d.), 15: 190–2; Ibn Ḥajar al-ʿAsqalānī, *Fatḥ al-bārī bi sharḥ ṣaḥīḥ al-Bukhārī*, ed. ʿAbd al-Qādir Shaybat al-Ḥamd (Riyadh: Maktabat al-Malik Fahd al-Waṭaniyya Athnā' al-Nashr, 2001), 6: 402–3; al-Nawawī, *Sharḥ al-Nawawī ʿalā Muslim* (Cairo: al-Maṭbaʿa al-Miṣriyya bi al-Azhar, 1929), 2: 29–35, where the tradition appears under the chapter on the superior faith of the people of Yemen.

[81] Al-Bukhārī, *al-Jāmiʿ al-ṣaḥīḥ, kitāb al-fitan* 92, *bāb qawl al-nabī al-fitna min qibal al-mashriq* 16.

location of al-Mashriq. His commentary focuses on the following tradition that appears in al-Bukhārī's *al-Jāmiʿ al-ṣaḥīḥ*:

ʿAlī b. ʿAbd Allāh (d. 234/849, Basra)[82] < Azhar b. Saʿd (d. *c.*203/818, Basra)[83] < Ibn ʿAwn (d. 150/767, Basra)[84] < Nāfiʿ (d. *c.*117/735, Medina)[85] < Ibn ʿUmar: The Prophet of God said: 'O my lord, bless for us our Shām, bless for us our Yemen.' Some people said: 'And in our Najd, O messenger of God.' I think on the third occasion, he [the Prophet] said: 'There you will find upheavals and tribulations and from there the horns of the devil shall appear.'

After citing this, al-Khaṭṭābī adds: 'Najd is a region in the east (*nāḥiyat al-mashriq*). Someone located in Medina will find that Najd for that individual is the desert region of Iraq (*bādiyat al-ʿIrāq*) and its surrounding regions, which is Mashriq to its people. The original meaning of the word Najd is elevated ground (*wa aṣl al-Najd mā irtafaʿa min al-arḍ*).'[86] Al-Khaṭṭābī mentions this tradition in 'The chapter regarding the saying of the Prophet: "The tribulation will appear from the direction of the East"'. In his commentary on al-Bukhārī's chapter 'The best of a man's wealth is cattle which he takes to the peak of the mountain' al-Khaṭṭābī does not cite the version of the tradition that states that 'the seat of unbelief is in the East'. The point is that al-Khaṭṭābī's commentary tells us that he interpreted references to al-Mashriq in al-Bukhārī's *al-Jāmiʿ al-ṣaḥīḥ* as denoting the region of Iraq. In this respect he shares al-Fasawī's convictions about the geographical location of al-Mashriq. But al-Fasawī goes further than even al-Khaṭṭābī by insisting on a direct connection between ḥadīth reports about heresy and unbelief in al-Mashriq and Kufa.

A century before al-Fasawī, Mālik b. Anas, like al-Bukhārī, incorporated the report into his chapter on cattle (*ghanam*).[87] The connection between al-Mashriq, Iraq, and heresy looms large in the *Muwaṭṭaʾ*. The

[82] Ibn Ḥajar al-ʿAsqalānī, *Tahdhīb al-tahdhīb*, 3: 176–80 (Mu'assasat al-Risāla edn.). Better known as ʿAlī b. al-Madīnī.

[83] Ibn Ḥajar al-ʿAsqalānī, *Tahdhīb al-tahdhīb*, 1: 104–6 (Mu'assasat al-Risāla edn.).

[84] Ibn Ḥajar al-ʿAsqalānī, *Tahdhīb al-tahdhīb*, 2: 398–9 (Mu'assasat al-Risāla edn.). I follow Ibn Ḥajar's preference for 150 as his year of death.

[85] Ibn Ḥajar al-ʿAsqalānī, *Tahdhīb al-tahdhīb*, 2: 210–12 (Mu'assasat al-Risāla edn.). On Nāfiʿ, his historicity, and his traditions from Ibn ʿUmar, see Juynboll, 'Nāfiʿ, the Mawlā of Ibn ʿUmar' and Motzki's response in Motzki, 'Quo vadis Ḥadīth-Forschung?'.

[86] Al-Khaṭṭābī, *Aʿlām al-ḥadīth*, 2329–30. Note the dominance of Basran traditionists in the *isnād*. It is significant to note that al-Khaṭṭābī's citations from al-Bukhārī are sometimes at odds with current editions of al-Bukhārī's *Ṣaḥīḥ*. For example, in al-Khaṭṭābī's *Aʿlām al-ḥadīth*, *qarn* in *wa bihā yaṭlaʿu qarn al-shayṭān* has been inserted in parenthesis by the editor. For more on al-Khaṭṭābī and his commentary see Tokatly, 'The Aʿlām al-ḥadīth of al-Khaṭṭābī'. Al-Khaṭṭābī receives a brief mention in Brown, *The Canonization*, 134.

[87] Mālik b. Anas, *al-Muwaṭṭaʾ bi riwāyat Yaḥyā b. Yaḥyā al-Laythī*, *kitāb al-istiʾdhān* 54, *bāb mā jāʾa fī amr al-ghanam* 6, no. 15 (numbering after ʿAbd al-Bāqī's edn.).

*Muwaṭṭa'* contains a specific chapter on reports about the Mashriq.[88] It contains two traditions: the first is identical both in its chain of transmission and its wording to the tradition included in al-Fasawī's history: 'I saw the messenger of God point to the East and say: "From there, indeed the tribulation shall come from there. Indeed, the tribulation shall come from there, from where the horn of the devil shall rise."'[89] The second report, of which a variation appears in al-Fasawī's history, describes an exchange between the second caliph ʿUmar and Kaʿb al-Aḥbār (d. *c.*35/656).[90] ʿUmar b. al-Khaṭṭāb was planning to go to Iraq (*arāda al-khurūj ilā al-ʿIrāq*). Kaʿb al-Aḥbār caught wind of this and warned ʿUmar: 'Do not set out for Iraq, O Commander of the Believers, for that land contains ninth-tenths of sorcery (*tisʿat aʿshār al-siḥr*), godless demons (*fasaqat al-jinn*), and the incurable disease (*al-dā' al-ʿuḍāl*).'[91] The explicit connection made between Iraq and al-Mashriq in these traditions in the *Muwaṭṭa'* reinforces the idea that in the ninth century Iraq was believed to have been uniquely receptive to heresy, demons, and religious deviation. That such reports about the Mashriq being a place of heresy, unbelief, tribulation and civil strife, the devil, and demons were collected and arranged into specific sections indicates the extent to which negative reports about Iraq had captured the imagination of ninth-century scholars and audiences.

The careful process of selection, variation, and textual fluidity shows how medieval historians and scholars exploited the geographical ambiguity of traditions referring to heresy, unbelief, and upheaval in the East. In this case, al-Fasawī uses the tradition's geographical malleability to interpret the report as a pointed rebuke against Kufa. This technique of interrupting and isolating fluid reports, which are then recycled for specific purposes, suggests that the discourse surrounding Kufa's unholiness was critical to al-Fasawī and his readership. Kufa's desanctification could rest on a reconstruction of material taken from a pool of reports which might have little direct correlation to the discourse of holy and unholy places. The process by which material was dislocated from its origins and

[88] Mālik b. Anas, *al-Muwaṭṭa'*, *kitāb al-isti'dhān* 54, *bāb mā jā'a fī al-mashriq* 11.

[89] Mālik b. Anas, *al-Muwaṭṭa'*, *kitāb al-isti'dhān* 54, *bāb mā jā'a fī al-mashriq* 11, no. 29.

[90] Kaʿb al-Aḥbār was reportedly a Yemeni Jewish convert to Islam. His name features in many early Islamic biblical narratives and apocalyptic traditions. There are a number of recent studies on Kaʿb al-Aḥbār, but I have consulted only Rubin, *Between Bible and Qur'an*, 13–23; Tottoli, *Biblical Prophets in the Qur'ān*, 89–91; Wolfensohn, *Kaʿb al-Aḥbār*; Ibn Ḥajar al-ʿAsqalānī reckoned him among the *muʿammarūn* (*wa qad zāda ʿalā al-mi'a*): see Ibn Ḥajar al-ʿAsqalānī, *Taqrīb al-tahdhīb*, 812 (under Kaʿb b. Mātiʿ). Remarkably, Fuat Sezgin attributes six works to his name: Sezgin, *GAS*, 1: 304–5.

[91] Mālik b. Anas, *al-Muwaṭṭa'*, *kitāb al-isti'dhān* 54, *bāb mā jā'a fī al-mashriq* 11, no. 30. It is conceivable that *tisʿat aʿshār al-siḥr* is an incorrect transcription of *tisʿat aʿshār al-sharr*, which appears in other reports. Other sources tell us that Mālik b. Anas described Abū Ḥanīfa as *al-dā' al-ʿuḍāl*. This issue is treated in Chapter 7 below.

reimagined in new and different contexts gives us a very precise insight into how, when, and where discourses around unholy places emerged. To this extent, we should be sensitive to the different histories told by conflicting forms of presentation and selection.

## 4.3 The Devil in Kufa

As we have seen, al-Fasawī is committed to establishing the presence of an incorrigible apparatus of heresy and deviance in Kufa. He does this not only in his chapter on Kufa, but also in his sections on Basra and Shām. He singles out Kufa for its production of heretics. He suggests that being raised anywhere other than in the region of Kufa ought to be considered a sign of God's immense grace and favour. Al-Fasawī attempts to seal his argument by presenting evidence to the effect that Kufa's status as an unholy region has its origins in an irrevocable, pre-earthly uneven distribution of good and evil. Al-Fasawī extends this web of unholiness around Kufa by advancing a special affinity between Kufa and the devil:[92]

> The devil descended to the East [Iraq], and there he defecated. Then he set out for the holy land of Shām, but he was prevented from entering it, so he went to Busāq and continued on until he reached the West, and there he established his presence and unfolded his machinations.

We can see just how dramatically the devil is woven into the very landscape and topography of the medieval Islamic world. Al-Fasawī's conception of the devil as a well-travelled social actor, whose actions have real implications for the social, religious, and political history of towns and cities, reflects a widespread medieval belief.[93] We find al-Fasawī mentioning it again in his *History*, this time referring explicitly to Iraq rather than the Mashriq:

Abū Ḥafṣ Ḥarmala b. ʿImrān (d. 243/858, Miṣr)[94] < Ibn Wahb (d. 197/812, Miṣr)[95] < Yaḥyā b. Ayyūb (d. 168/785, Miṣr)[96] and Ibn Lahīʿa (d. 174/790,

[92] Al-Fasawī, *Kitāb al-Maʿrifa wa al-tārīkh*, 2: 305–6 (*nazala al-shayṭān bi al-Mashriq fa qaḍā qaḍā'ahu thumma kharaja yurīd al-arḍ al-muqaddasa al-Shām fa muniʿa fa kharaja ʿalā Busāq ḥattā jā'a al-Maghrib fa bāḍa bayḍahu wa basaṭa bihā ʿaqbariyyahu*).

[93] For two provocative reflections on the decline of this 'belief see Douglas, *Mary Douglas: A Very Personal Method*, 95–9, esp. 95; and Lefebvre, *Introduction to Modernity*, 56–64.

[94] Ibn Ḥajar al-ʿAsqalānī, *Tahdhīb al-tahdhīb*, 1: 372–3 (Mu'assasat al-Risāla edn.). This is Ḥarmala b. Yaḥyā b. ʿAbd Allāh b. Ḥarmala b. ʿImrān al-Tujībī; not to be confused with his grandfather, Ḥarmala b. ʿImrān b. Qurād al-Tujībī. Both were known as Abū Ḥafṣ al-Miṣrī.

[95] Ibn Ḥajar al-ʿAsqalānī, *Tahdhīb al-tahdhīb*, 2: 453–5 (Mu'assasat al-Risāla edn.).

[96] Ibn Ḥajar al-ʿAsqalānī, *Tahdhīb al-tahdhīb*, 4: 342–3 (Mu'assasat al-Risāla edn.).

Miṣr)[97] < ʿAqīl [b. Khālid al-Aylī] (d. *c.*144/761, Miṣr)[98] < Ibn Shihāb (d. *c.*124/742, Medina)[99] < Yaʿqūb b. ʿAbd Allāh b. al-Mughīra b. al-Akhnas (d. 128/745, Medina)[100] < Ibn ʿUmar: the Prophet said: 'Iblīs entered Iraq, where he defecated; then he entered Shām, where he was driven out by its inhabitants to the borders of Busāq; finally, he entered Miṣr, and there he established himself and spread and unfolded his machinations (*dakhala iblīs al-ʿIrāq fa qaḍā ḥājatahu, thumma dakhala al-Shām fa ṭaradūhu ḥattā balagha Busāq thumma dakhala Miṣr fa bāḍa bihā wa farrakha wa basaṭa ʿaqbariyyahu*).'[101]

Mapping the devil, writing him into and out of the history and topography of specific regions, characterised an essential component of medieval mentalités. The devil was conceived of as a real actor with important agency in the regional dramas of the medieval Islamic world. The degree to which certain regions are hospitable to his presence serves as an indicator of the sacred nature of some regions and the unholy character of others. The dominance of narrators from Miṣr in the *isnād* of a tradition that implicates Miṣr, along with Iraq, is further evidence that such traditions were not only products of regional rivalry; these beliefs were strong enough to move narrators to transmit traditions against their native regions. It is clear, then, from this report that medieval Muslims invested both holiness and unholiness in specific regions. And this became especially significant as a way to frame the emergence of deviance and heresy in particular regions. To this extent, it is no surprise that the role of the devil appears prominently in discourses about regions and their heresy and orthodoxy. What is surprising is the reluctance of social historians to take stock of the salience of the devil in medieval Islamicate societies.

97 Ibn Ḥajar al-ʿAsqalānī, *Tahdhīb al-tahdhīb*, 2: 411–14 (Mu'assasat al-Risāla edn.).

98 According to Ibn Ḥajar, ʿUqayl b. Khālid b. ʿAqīl al-Aylī: Ibn Ḥajar al-ʿAsqalānī, *Tahdhīb al-tahdhīb*, 3: 130–1 (Mu'assasat al-Risāla edn.).

99 Ibn Ḥajar al-ʿAsqalānī, *Tahdhīb al-tahdhīb*, 3: 696–9 (Mu'assasat al-Risāla edn.).

100 Ibn Ḥajar al-ʿAsqalānī, *Tahdhīb al-tahdhīb*, 4: 444–5 (Mu'assasat al-Risāla edn.). This person might not be identical to the figure in the *isnād*. Ibn Ḥajar describes a Yaʿqūb b. ʿUtba b. al-Mughīra b. al-Akhnas.

101 Al-Fasawī, *Kitāb al-Maʿrifa wa al-tārīkh*, 2: 748–9. For the location of Busāq see Yāqūt al-Ḥamawī, *Jacut's Geographisches Wörterbuch (Kitāb Muʿjam al-buldān)*, 1: 609–10. Translated literally, the phrase *qaḍā ḥājatahu* would be rendered as 'Iblīs executed his responsibilities'. However, the phrase was commonly used in medieval Arabic to refer to defecation (*ghawaṭa*), excrement, and faeces. See Muḥammad b. Abī Bakr al-Rāzī, Mukhtār al-ṣiḥāḥ (Beirut: Maktabat Lubnān, 1986), 202 (under gh-w-ṭ: *wa kāna al-rajul minhum idhā arāda an yaqḍiya al-ḥāja atā al-ghā'iṭ wa qaḍā ḥājatahu*); al-Ṭabarī, *Tafsīr al-Ṭabarī: jāmiʿ al-bayān ʿan ta'wīl āy al-Qur'ān*, ed. Maḥmūd Muḥammad Shākir and Aḥmad Muḥammad Shākir (Cairo: Dār al-Maʿārif, 1954), 8: 388–5. Here, al-Ṭabarī explains the meaning of the expression *aw jā'a aḥadun minkum min al-ghā'iṭ* in Quran 5:43 to refer to defecation by way of the Arabic phrase *qaḍā ḥājatahu*: *yaqūl aw jā'a aḥadun minkum min al-ghā'iṭ, qad qaḍā ḥājatahu wa huwa musāfir ṣaḥīḥ … wa al-ghā'iṭ … wa jaʿala kināya ʿan qaḍā' ḥājat al-insān li anna al-ʿarab kānat takhtār qaḍā' ḥājatihā fī al-ghīṭān.*

Devils, demons, and spirits have been the subject of fascinating social histories in the fields of late antiquity, medieval studies, and early modern history.[102] Any reluctance to investigate the history of the devil in medieval Islamicate societies cannot justify itself by a dearth of primary source material.

The early centuries of Islamic history boast a considerable production of books that emphatically present the devil as a social and historical actor in the earthly dramas and episodes of everyday medieval life. In the ninth century, during al-Fasawī's time, the devil became a subject of intense inquiry. One scholar and author, in particular, was responsible for popularising such narratives and beliefs. Ibn Abī Dunyā's (d. 281/894) *Makā'id al-shayṭān* represents one of the most significant ninth-century monographs on the devil. In fact, Ibn Abī Dunyā's exceptionally large oeuvre shows a special interest in eschatology and macabre subjects. He is known to have authored books such as the book of graves (*kitāb al-qubūr*), remembrance of death (*dhikr al-mawt*), the book of grief (*kitāb al-aḥzān*), beings who live after death (*man ʿāsha baʿd al-mawt*), the book of fear (*kitāb al-wajal*), and a second book on the devil (*maṣā'id al-shayṭān*).[103]

The *Makā'id al-shayṭān* mirrors al-Fasawī's portrayal of the devil as a social and historical agent in community life. Ibn Abī Dunyā suggests that the physical movement of the devil is the direct cause of earthquakes. We are told that the devil cries when he fails in bringing about sedition. We also learn that the devil, Iblīs, is the father of five children, each of whom is assigned a specific task. Thibir is dedicated to causing destruction and tribulation, uncovering the breasts of women, jolting their living quarters, and inciting behaviour reminiscent of the age of ignorance. Al-Aʿwar, the second son, encourages people to fornicate. Masūṭ is responsible for spreading lies. Dāsim causes discord among families and communities. Zilnabūr ignites disputes in the market places.[104]

Ibn al-Mufliḥ (d. 763/1362), also inquisitive about the devil's social life, points out his more mundane activities: the types of foods he eats; where he urinates and excretes; and more details about the precise nature of his stool.[105] Indeed, the social and religious implications of

[102] Pagels, *The Origin of Satan*; Forsyth, *The Old Enemy*; Russell, *Satan*; and Thomas, *Religion and the Decline of Magic*.

[103] On Ibn Abī Dunyā see Brockelmann, *GAL*, 1: 160 and supp. 1: 247–8; Ismāʿīl Pāshā al-Baghdādī, *Hadiyyat al-ʿārifīn: asmā' al-mu'allifīn wa al-muṣannifīn* (Istanbul: n.p., 1955), 1: 442; and Kinberg, 'Interaction between This World and the Afterworld in Early Islamic Tradition'.

[104] Ibn Abī al-Dunyā, *Makā'id al-shayṭān* (Cairo: Maktabat al-Qur'ān, 1991), 54–5.

[105] Ibn Mufliḥ, *Maṣā'ib al-insān min makā'id al-shayṭān* (Cairo: Maktabat al-Khānjī, 1943), 59–62.

the latter are hinted at in al-Fasawī's reports about the devil defecating in Iraq.[106]

Finally, we should note that early beliefs and narratives about the devil in Kufa and Iraq may have had their origins in the historical memory of confessional communities in the Fertile Crescent stretching back to the religious and cultural life of late antiquity. It appears that there was a resolute tradition of antediluvian narratives in ancient Mesopotamia that focused on demonology and the devil;[107] and Quran 2:102 demonstrates that the early Muslim community was aware of this memory and indeed perpetuated it:

And they followed what the devils (*shayāṭīn*) had recited during the reign of Solomon. It was not Solomon who disbelieved, but the devils disbelieved, teaching people magic and that which was revealed to the two angels at Babylon (Bābil), Hārūt and Mārūt. But the two angels do not teach anyone unless they say, 'We are a trial, so do not disbelieve.' And they learn from them that by which they cause separation between a man and his wife. But they do not harm anyone through it except by permission of God. And the people learn what harms them and does not benefit them. But the Children of Israel certainly knew that whoever purchased the magic would not have in the Hereafter any share. And wretched is that for which they sold themselves, if they only knew.

[106] The social and religious consequences of the devil's defecation seem to find resonance in the reports we find in al-Fasawī's history. Two similar phrases appear in al-Fasawī's reports about the devil's activities in Iraq: *qaḍā ḥājatahu* and *qaḍā qadā'ahu*. These two phrases became the most common synonyms for the act of defecation (see above, note 95). There is a possibility that such phrases as they appear in al-Fasawī's reports about Kufa contain a veiled barb. By the ninth century, stools and urine had been incorporated into strict purity laws. They were both held to be ritually impure. But they were also embedded within certain social and moral conceptions of impurity, which was why scatology was closely linked to ideas about devils and demons. It is possible that al-Fasawī was presenting narratives that bring together scatology, demonology, and regionalism to cast an even darker shadow over the moral topography of Kufa. On defecation and its meanings see Morrison, *Excrement in the Late Middle Ages*; Bayless, *Sin and Filth in Medieval Culture*; Dominique Laporte has written creatively about secular and cultural conceptions of defecation, but a history of holy and unholy defecation has yet to be written. See Laporte, *History of Shit*. On ritual impurity see Reinhart, 'Impurity/No Danger'; Katz, 'The Study of Islamic Ritual and the Meaning of Wuḍū''; Maghen, 'First Blood'; Maghen, 'Close Encounters'; Reid, *Law and Piety in Medieval Islam*, 163–4.

[107] Here, I am relying on the following works: Kvanvig, *Primeval History*, esp. 504–8; Kvanvig, *Roots of Apocalyptic*; Haas, *Magie und Mythen in Babylonien*. The argument for a Mesopotamian origin for antediluvian narratives is also made in Bautsch, *A Study of the Geography of I Enoch*. There are channels of communication between late antique narratives and early Muslim accounts of antediluvian episodes, and Joseph Witztum has attempted to identify them. His intertextual analysis of Quranic retellings of Jewish–Christian narratives covers the Fall of Adam and Eve but stops just short of their and Satan's descent: Witztum, 'The Syriac Milieu of the Quran', 65–107.

Memories of Mesopotamia's antediluvian and demonological past were vibrant among its multi-confessional communities in the eighth century. Muḥammad al-Qazwīnī (d. 682/1283) relates the following story about Babel which he attributes to the Kufan al-Aʿmash. Al-Aʿmash relates that Mujāhid b. Jabr (d. 104/722) had a fascination for strange and fantastical stories, but he would refuse to listen to such stories and would prefer to travel to places to examine their veracity. So, when he arrived in Babel he met the governor, al-Ḥajjāj. Al-Ḥajjāj inquired about Mujāhid's motives for coming to Babel, to which Mujāhid responded that he had a matter to discuss with the exilarch (*ra's al-jālūt*). 'What is it exactly that you want?' al-Ḥajjāj asked. 'I want somebody to show me Hārūt and Mārūt.' Al-Ḥajjāj then ordered some of the Jews to take Mujāhid and show him the two fallen angels. Mujāhid went along with this Jewish guide and they continued on until they reached a certain place. The man lifted a boulder, which revealed a tunnel of some sort (*sarab*). The Jewish man said to Mujāhid: 'Go down and look at the two fallen angels, but do not mention the name of God (*inzil wa unẓur ilayhimā wa lā tadhkur Allāh*).' Mujāhid made his way down, and the Jewish man continued to walk with him until he saw the two fallen angels, and he found them to look like two great mountains, hanging upside down, their heads barely above the ground, and chained from their ankles to their knees in iron shackles (*fa ra'āhumā mithl al-jabalayn al-ʿaẓīmayn mankūsayn ʿalā ra'sayhimā wa ʿalayhimā al-ḥadīd min aʿqābihimā ilā rukabihimā muṣaffadayn*). When Mujāhid saw them he could not control himself, and he uttered the name of God, whereupon the two fallen angels shook so violently that they almost broke loose from their shackles. Both Mujāhid and the Jewish man passed out at the sight of the two fallen angels. When they both came round, the Jewish man raised his head and said to Mujāhid: 'I had said to you not to mention God's name. We almost lost our lives.' Mujāhid held on tightly to the Jewish man, and he would not let go of him as they climbed up together until they exited the lair.[108]

[108] Al-Qazwīnī, *Āthār al-bilād*, 304–6. Mujāhid b. Jabr (attr.), *Tafsīr Mujāhid*, ed. Muḥammad ʿAbd al-Islām Abū al-Nayl (Cairo: Dār al-Fikr al-Islāmī al-Ḥadītha, 1989), 209–10 comments on some features of Quran 2:102, but says nothing about Hārūt and Mārūt. See also Littmann, 'Hārut and Mārut'. Littmann gathers and translates accounts of the Hārūt and Mārūt story mainly from al-Ṭabarī's *Tafsīr*. After comparing the accounts in al-Ṭabarī's Quranic exegesis with some other sources, Littmann concludes that the story has its origins in Persia and, on the way to Arabia, came into contact with Jewish communities in Babel ('Somit werden auch die persischen Elemente der alten Sage, ehe sie nach Arabien kam, in Babylonien mit den judischen eine Einheit eingegangen sein'). Littmann then attempts to extract the Bablyonian elements of the story. Al-Ṭabarī includes a report in which Mujāhid explains the story of Hārūt and Mārūt, but there is no reference to the episode described above. See al-Ṭabarī, *Tafsīr al-Ṭabarī*, 2: 434–5. The Persian version of al-Ṭabarī's *Tafsīr* does refer to

The survival of a number of reports about the devil in Iraq in contexts different than the one provided by al-Fasawī provides further documentation for a unique propinquity between the devil and Iraq in medieval mentalités. Al-Fasawī's chapter on Kufa contains more than a dozen traditions that speak very graphically about the devil's physical presence in Kufa. It would be a mistake to think that these narratives depended only on events contemporary with al-Fasawī. Rather, these narratives belong to a cluster of memories about the antediluvian past that would have been familiar to religious communities in the Fertile Crescent, particularly because they narrate what for these communities would have been the origins of human history: the moment when Adam, Eve, and the devil were believed to have been cast down to earth.

There is some evidence that some of al-Fasawī's predecessors and contemporaries believed that the devil was exiled to Iraq in the aftermath of the cosmic confrontation between God and the devil. ʿAbd al-Razzāq al-Ṣanʿānī (d. 211/827) has a chapter entitled *bāb al-ʿIrāq* in his *Muṣannaf* in which he relates that Basra was the place where Iblīs first set foot and that he later settled in Miṣr.[109] Some sources state that the devil was banished to the region of Baysān. Another source tells us that it was the region of Ubulla.[110] Reports in al-Fasawī's history and in a large number

a small passageway under the earth (*dar zīr-i zamīn*) in Babel, Mount Damāvand, and mentions an account of a certain individual who visited the two fallen angels at this location. See *Tarjama-i tafsīr-i Ṭabarī*, ed. Ḥabīb Yaghmā'ī (Tehran: Dānishgāh-i Ṭihrān, 1960), 95–8, executed by a cohort of scholars under the orders of the Sāmānid ruler Manṣūr b. Nūḥ (r. 350/961–365/976). See also the long and unstructured discussion in al-Jaṣṣāṣ, *Aḥkām al-Qur'ān*, ed. Muḥammad al-Ṣādiq al-Qamḥāwī (Beirut: Dār Iḥyā' al-Turāth al-ʿArabī, 1996), 1: 64–9. See also Jung, *Fallen Angels*, 126–38; de Menasce, 'Une légende indo-iranienne'. For some brief but illuminating comments on the Mesopotamian origins of fallen angels narratives in general, and Hārūt and Mārūt narratives in particular, see Crone, 'The Book of Watchers', esp. 27–31, 47.

109 ʿAbd al-Razzāq al-Ṣanʿānī, *al-Muṣannaf*, ed. Ḥabīb al-Raḥmān al-Aʿẓamī (n.p. [South Africa]: al-Majlis al-ʿIlmī, 1970), 11: 251 (*mawḍiʿ qadima Iblīs bi al-Baṣra wa farrakha bi Miṣr*), 11: 334 (also on Iraq and Miṣr).

110 Muqātil's *Tafsīr* is forthcoming about the details of the exile. He too identifies Ubulla in Basra as the devil's place of exile. See (pseudo?-) Muqātil b. Sulaymān al-Balkhī, *Tafsīr Muqātil b. Sulaymān*, ed. ʿAbd Allāh Maḥmūd Shiḥāta (Beirut: Mu'assasat al-Tārīkh al-ʿArabī, 2002), 1: 99–100. On Muqātil and his *tafsīr* see Gilliot, 'Muqātil, grand exégète'; van Ess, *Theologie und Gesellschaft*, 2: 516–32; Versteegh, 'Grammar and Exegesis'; al-Rāzī surveys all the possibilities, in the course of which he refers to the devil's descent to Basra: Fakhr al-Dīn al-Rāzī, *al-Tafsīr al-kabīr* (Beirut: Dār al-Fikr, 1981), 3: 27–8; Abū Ḥayyān al-Andalūsī, *Tafsīr baḥr al-muḥīṭ* (Beirut: Dār al-Kutub al-ʿIlmiyya, 1993), 1: 315. On Ubulla see Yāqūt al-Ḥamawī, *Kitāb Muʿjam al-buldān*, 1: 96–8, 2: 560, 3: 891–2. There are sources, too, that place the devil in Kufa in an encounter with Noah: see Ismāʿīl Ḥaqqī al-Būrsawī, *Rūḥ al-bayān fī tafsīr al-Qur'ān* (Istanbul: al-Maṭbaʿa al-ʿUthmāniyya, n.d.), 4: 21–2, 127. On the devil's descent and the meaning of *ihbiṭū* (Q 2:36), see Ibn Qayyim al-Jawziyya, *Ḥādī al-arwāḥ ilā bilād al-afrāḥ*, ed. Zā'id b. Aḥmad al-Nushayrī (Beirut: Dār ʿĀlam al-Fawā'id, 2007), 57–65. On the descent see also Gimaret, *Une lecture muʿtazilite du Coran*, 85; Ibn ʿAṭiyya, *al-Muḥarrar al-wajīz fī tafsīr*

of early sources about the horns of the devil rising in the East should be seen as yet another feature of the devil's emplotment into the history of Kufa and Iraq in the eighth and ninth centuries.[111] What they all share is a representation of Iraq that depends on doctrines about the devil as an agent of disorder in the chaotic political history and social memory of Iraq.

Like their Near Eastern late antique neighbours, early Muslims had a rich pool of resources for putting together narratives about the antediluvian past. This connection that medieval Muslims drew between antediluvian events in the 'otherworld' and their continuation in the earthly life was a cornerstone of late antique ideas about the porous boundaries between prehistory and human history, this world and the otherworld, the natural and the supernatural.[112] It is understandable, therefore, that these

*al-kitāb al-ʿazīz*, ed. ʿAbd al-Salām ʿAbd al-Shāfī Muḥammad (Beirut: Dār al-Kutub al-ʿIlmiyya, 2001), 1: 131; Beck, 'Iblis und Mensch'. Beck's article fails to consider the view, put forward by exegetes, that the command *ihbiṭū* extends to the devil: Ginzberg, *Legends of the Jews*, 1: 62–4. On the devil more generally see Goldziher, *Abhandlungen zur arabischen Philologie*, 1: 106–7, 107–17, 205–12; Goldziher, 'Die Ginnen der Dichter'; Eichler, *Die Dschinn, Teufel und Engel im Koran*.

111 For similar reports and variants see al-Ṭaḥāwī, *Aḥkām al-Qur'ān al-karīm* ed. Saʿd al-Dīn Awnāl (Istanbul: Markaz al-Buḥūth al-Islāmiyya, 1998), 1: 174; al-Ṭaḥāwī, *Sharḥ mushkil al-āthār*, 2: 270; al-Dawlābī, *al-Kunā wa al-asmā'* (Beirut: Dār al-Kutub al-ʿIlmiyya, 1999), 1: 368; Abū al-Shaykh, *Ṭabaqāt al-muḥaddithīn bi Iṣfahān wa al-wāridīn ʿalayhā*, ed. ʿAbd al-Ghafūr ʿAbd al-Ḥaqq Ḥusayn al-Balūshī (Beirut: Mu'assasat al-Risāla, 1996), 4: 106–7; al-Fākihī, *Akhbār Makka fī qadīm al-dahr wa ḥadīthihi*, ed. ʿAbd al-Malik ʿAbd Allāh b. Duhaysh (Beirut: Dār Khiḍr, 1994), 2: 85 (mentioned in his description of the springs of Zamzam); al-Khaṭīb al-Baghdādī's decision to place this tradition in his section on ambiguous and clear traditions (*al-mujmal wa al-mubayyan*) is an indication of the geographical ambiguity entailed in this tradition: al-Khaṭīb al-Baghdādī, *Kitāb al-Faqīh wa al-mutafaqqih*, ed. Abū ʿAbd al-Raḥmān and ʿĀdil b. Yūsuf al-ʿAzzāzī (Riyadh: Dār Ibn al-Jawzī, 1996), 1: 325–6.

112 The proximity between paradise and earth and the precise topographic relationship between them is the subject of an entire volume, but it is worth pointing out two chapters that are particularly relevant: Reed, 'Heavenly Ascent, Angelic Descent, and the Transmission of Knowledge'; and Schäfer, 'In Heaven as It Is in Hell'. Narratives about the antediluvian past were invoked frequently in order to establish connections between antediluvian rebellion and evil and late antique and medieval heresy, deviance, and social and political crises. See Reed, 'The Trickery of the Fallen Angels'; Orlov, *Divine Scapegoats*. More widely, demons and devils were woven into the fabric of everyday social, political, and religious life in the medieval Islamic world. There is, quite possibly, another dimension that has negatively impacted scholarship on the centrality of the devils, demons, and the supernatural in medieval Islamicate societies. An excessive focus on the 'rationality' of the Islamic tradition seems to have dissuaded scholars from studying devils and demons: von Grunebaum, *Medieval Islam*, 23–4; Dols's fascinating study is an exception to this trend, though it, too, emphasises the popularity of demons and devils among laymen, which recalls a distinction that has to be demonstrated with respect to 'laymen' and 'elites' as opposed simply to being invoked: Dols, *Majnūn*, 213–15. An important investigation into the possible sources of early Islamic narratives about the antediluvian past is Crone, 'The Book of Watchers'. Less helpful is McCants, *Founding Gods, Inventing Nations*, 53–5.

narratives formed part of the multi-faceted process of history writing in the ninth century. The history of regions and places was inseparable from the ideas and beliefs that were shared by society. The devil as the sower of discord and heresy occupies a central role in the great Near Eastern trope of rebellion and evil. The way in which al-Fasawī frames Kufa as an accursed, heretical, and unholy region that had endeared itself to the devil is an indication that memories of the antediluvian past were vibrant in early Islamic societies and that they persisted long afterwards.

## 4.4 Kufa's Curse

Al-Fasawī's ability to draw on the rich semiotic koine of late antique religions, mentalités, and beliefs in order represent Kufa as an unholy region is greatly dependent upon the way in which the holy and the supernatural were seen to manifest themselves in the events of the eighth and ninth centuries. One of the most powerful mechanisms for desacralising Kufa was the device of the curse. The power of the curse in late antiquity has been examined by Peter Brown. Brown's analysis is concerned with who wields the power to pronounce divine imprecations. For him, the curse is yet another marker of the social and communal demand for holy men who, through the device of the curse, would resolve the social tensions of their communities.[113] Brown is right to focus our attention on the authorities who acquired the social power and prestige to pronounce the curse. On the other hand, we must also consider the implications of such curses being directed at discrete audiences and recipients. Agents of curses should be no more important than their recipients. In what follows, I shall briefly discuss the use of the curse in al-Fasawī's history as a device to frame Kufa as an unholy region.

It is of no small significance that al-Fasawī commences his chapter on Kufa with three slightly different versions of a Prophetic curse against Iraq:[114]

Muḥammad b. ʿAbd al-ʿAzīz al-Ramlī (d. 232/847, Wāsiṭ)[115] < Ḍamra b. Rabīʿa (d. 202/818, Damascus)[116] < Ibn Shawdhab (d. 144/761, Khurāsān)[117] < Tawbat al-ʿAnbārī (d. *c.*131/749, Basra)[118] < Sālim (d. 106/725, Medina)[119] <

[113] Brown, *Society and the Holy in Late Antiquity*, 302–22.

[114] Al-Fasawī, *Kitāb al-Maʿrifa wa al-tārīkh*, 2: 746–7.

[115] Ibn Ḥajar al-ʿAsqalānī, *Tahdhīb al-tahdhīb*, 3: 633 (Mu'assasat al-Risāla edn.). See also al-Samʿānī, *al-Ansāb*, 6: 164 (Cairo edn.).

[116] Ibn Ḥajar al-ʿAsqalānī, *Tahdhīb al-tahdhīb*, 2: 229–30 (Mu'assasat al-Risāla edn.).

[117] Ibn Ḥajar al-ʿAsqalānī, *Tahdhīb al-tahdhīb*, 2: 354 (Mu'assasat al-Risāla edn.). Ibn Shawdhab settled in Basra and Damascus.

[118] Ibn Ḥajar al-ʿAsqalānī, *Tahdhīb al-tahdhīb*, 1: 261 (Mu'assasat al-Risāla edn.).

[119] Ibn Ḥajar al-ʿAsqalānī, *Tahdhīb al-tahdhīb*, 1: 676–7 (Mu'assasat al-Risāla edn.).

Ibn ʿUmar said: The messenger of God, God pray over him and grant him peace, said: 'O my Lord, grant sanctity to us in our Medina, and in every measure (*Ṣāʿinā wa Muddinā*), and in our Yemen, and in our Shām.' Then a man said: 'O messenger of God, what about our Iraq?' The messenger of God responded: 'There you will find earthquakes and tribulations and from there shall rise the horns of the devil.'

Saʿīd b. Asad (d. ?/?)[120] < Ḍamra < Ibn Shawdhab < Tawbat al-ʿAnbārī < Sālim < Sālim's father said: The messenger of God, God pray over him and grant him peace, said: 'O my Lord, grant sanctity to us in our Medina, and in every measure, and in our Yemen, and in our Shām.' Then a man said: 'O messenger of God, what about our Iraq?' The prophet of God, God pray over him and grant him peace, said again: 'O my Lord, grant sanctity to us in our Medina, and in every measure (*Ṣāʿinā wa Muddinā*), and in our Yemen, and in our Shām.' Once more, the man asked: 'O messenger of God, and our Iraq?' The prophet, upon him be peace, said: 'O my Lord, grant sanctity to us in our Medina, and in every measure (*Ṣāʿinā wa Muddinā*), and in our Yemen, and in our Shām.' The third time, the man asked, 'and our Iraq?' The prophet, God pray over him and grant him peace, said: 'From there will appear earthquakes and tribulations and from there shall rise the horns of the devil.' Ibn Shawdhab said: 'You see that Mecca in this ḥadīth is referred to as Yamāniyya.'

ʿĪsā b. Muḥammad (d. 256/869, Ramla)[121] < al-Walīd b. Mazīd (d. 207/822, Beirut)[122] < ʿAbd Allāh b. Shawdhab < ʿAbd Allāḥ b. al-Qāsim (d. ?/?)[123] < Maṭar (d. 125/743, Khurāsān)[124] < Kathīr (d. ?/?, Basra)[125] < Abū Sahl (d. ?/?)[126] < Tawbat al-ʿAnbārī < Sālim b. ʿAbd Allāh < Sālim's father said: The prophet of God, God pray over him and grant him peace, recited a prayer in which he said: 'O my Lord, sanctify for us our Mecca; sanctify for us our Medina; sanctify for us our Shām; and sanctify for us our Yemen. O my Lord, sanctify for us in every measure.' Then a man said: 'And in our Iraq?' The prophet turned away from him. The prophet responded in this way three times: Whenever the man would say 'and in our Iraq', the prophet would turn away from him. Finally, he [the

[120] I have been unable to find an entry for him in the biographical sources. I take him to be the great-great-grandson of the Umayyad caliph al-Walīd. For al-Walīd's grandson, Asad b. Mūsā b. Ibrāhīm b. al-Walīd b. ʿAbd al-Malik b. Marwān (d. 212/827, Miṣr), see Ibn Ḥajar al-ʿAsqalānī, *Tahdhīb al-tahdhīb*, 1: 133 (Mu'assasat al-Risāla edn.). Ibn Ḥajar transmits a report stating that Asad's son, Saʿīd b. Asad, authored a two-volume work, *Faḍā'il al-tābiʿīn*. Al-Sakhāwī mentions his full name, Saʿīd b. Asad b. Mūsā, and his authorship of a work on the Successors. See al-Sakhāwī, *Fatḥ al-mughīth bi sharḥ alfiyat al-ḥadīth* (Riyadh: Maktabat Dār al-Minhāj, 2005), 4: 104.

[121] Ibn Ḥajar al-ʿAsqalānī, *Tahdhīb al-tahdhīb*, 3: 366–7 (Mu'assasat al-Risāla edn.).

[122] Ibn Ḥajar al-ʿAsqalānī, *Tahdhīb al-tahdhīb*, 4: 324 (Mu'assasat al-Risāla edn.).

[123] Ibn Ḥajar al-ʿAsqalānī, *Tahdhīb al-tahdhīb*, 2: 404 (Mu'assasat al-Risāla edn.).

[124] Ibn Ḥajar al-ʿAsqalānī, *Tahdhīb al-tahdhīb*, 4: 87–8 (Mu'assasat al-Risāla edn.) (under Maṭar b. Ṭahmān al-Warrāq). He settled in Basra. There is a possibility that Maṭar might be Maṭar b. ʿAbd al-Raḥmān al-ʿAnbarī al-Aʿtaq (see Ibn Ḥajar al-ʿAsqalānī, *Tahdhīb al-tahdhīb*, 4: 88 (Mu'assasat al-Risāla edn.)).

[125] Ibn Ḥajar al-ʿAsqalānī, *Tahdhīb al-tahdhīb*, 3: 458 (Mu'assasat al-Risāla edn.). He settled in Balkh.

[126] Ibn Ḥajar al-ʿAsqalānī, *Tahdhīb al-tahdhīb*, 3: 458 (Mu'assasat al-Risāla edn.). He settled in Balkh.

Prophet] said: 'From there will appear earthquakes and tribulations and from there shall rise the horns of the devil.'

In these opening reports in al-Fasawī's chapter on Kufa, holy and unholy regions are demarcated through the device of prayer and curse. The Prophet makes a heartfelt prayer for the sanctification of a number of key regions of the early Islamic world. Not only is Iraq excluded from this prayer, but the Prophet refuses to submit to the petition of a certain individual to include Iraq. Three times the Prophet ignores the man's petition and turns away from him. On the third and final occasion the Prophet invokes the power of the curse by withholding the prestige of divine favour and sanctification for Iraq and declares that Iraq will be the site of grave upheavals and of the devil's appearance.

Kufa is written out of God's divine favour in the physical landscape of the medieval Islamic world. Elsewhere in al-Fasawī's history it is the recipient of any number of divine curses. Al-Fasawī mentions five variations of two specific incidents in which ʿAlī b. Abī Ṭālib and ʿUmar b. al-Khaṭṭāb imprecate Kufa and its inhabitants. ʿAlī, we are told, has this to say about the Kufans:

ʿAbd al-ʿAzīz b. ʿAbd Allāh al-Uwaysī (d. 236/850, Medina)[127] < Ibrāhīm b. Saʿd (d. *c.*182/798, Baghdad)[128] < Shuʿba (d. 160/776–7, Basra)[129] < Abī ʿAwn Muḥammad b. ʿUbayd Allāh al-Thaqafī (d. 116/734, Kufa)[130] < Abī Ṣāliḥ al-Ḥanafī (d. ?/?, Kufa)[131]: I saw ʿAlī b. Abī Ṭālib take the *muṣḥaf* and place it upon his head, whereupon I saw its pages moving. He said: 'O my lord, they have prevented me from establishing among the community that which should be there, so grant me the reward of that which should be there.' Then he said: 'O my lord, I have become impatient with them and they with me, and I loathe them and they loathe me; they have imposed upon me things which are contrary to my disposition, character, and ethics, such that were unknown to me. Send me in their place a people better than them, and send to them in my place one more evil than me. O my lord, make their hearts perish just as salt perishes in water.'

127 Ibn Ḥajar al-ʿAsqalānī, *Tahdhīb al-tahdhīb*, 2: 588–9 (Mu'assasat al-Risāla edn.).
128 Ibn Ḥajar al-ʿAsqalānī, *Tahdhīb al-tahdhīb*, 1: 66–7 (Mu'assasat al-Risāla edn.).
129 Ibn Ḥajar al-ʿAsqalānī, *Tahdhīb al-tahdhīb*, 2: 166–70 (Mu'assasat al-Risāla edn.).
130 Ibn Ḥajar al-ʿAsqalānī, *Tahdhīb al-tahdhīb*, 3: 637 (Mu'assasat al-Risāla edn.) (under Muḥammad b. ʿUbayd Allāh b. Saʿīd), 4: 567 (under Abū ʿAwn al-Thaqafī).
131 Ibn Ḥajar al-ʿAsqalānī, *Tahdhīb al-tahdhīb*, 2: 546 (Mu'assasat al-Risāla edn.) (under ʿAbd al-Raḥmān b. Qays Abū Ṣāliḥ al-Ḥanafī), 4: 539 (under Abū Ṣāliḥ al-Ḥanafī). I found no death date recorded for him in the biographical or historical sources; simply references to him as a Successor (*tābiʿī*). For his traditions from ʿAlī b. Abī Ṭālib see Ibn Kathīr, *Jāmiʿ al-masānīd wa al-sunan al-hādī li aqwam sunan*, ed. ʿAbd al-Muʿtī Amīn Qalʿajī (Beirut: Dār al-Fikr, 1994), 20: 293–5 (vol. 20 consists of the *Musnad* of ʿAlī b. Abī Ṭālib).

The report ends with confirmation from Ibrāhīm b. Saʿd that this curse was intended for the people of Kufa.[132] Al-Fasawī's section on Kufa features a second report that has ʿAlī invite God's curse against the Kufans: 'Abase their homes and fill their hearts with terror.'[133]

A careful examination of these works shows just how intensely (and graphically) the devil was seen to operate in the social, religious, and political history of the early Muslim community. Al-Fasawī's history assigns to the devil a good number of functions and roles. In so doing, there is little to distinguish his treatment of the devil from those that appear in similar sources. It is, however, al-Fasawī's specific emplotment of the devil into the landscape and politics of Kufa that emerges as an important strategy in his efforts to dismiss Kufa as an unholy region.[134]

> Abū ʿUdhba reported that a man came to ʿUmar b. al-Khaṭṭāb and informed him that the people of Iraq had attacked their governor with pebbles. ʿUmar was furious and came out to lead the congregation in prayer. During the prayer, ʿUmar made a mistake, which prompted members of the congregation to offer the corrective remark, *subḥāna Allāh.* Upon performing the final salutation, ʿUmar turned to the congregation and said: 'Who among you is from the people of Shām?' One man stood up, then another, then I (Abū ʿUdhbah) stood up as the third and then a fourth. ʿUmar said: 'O people of Shām, prepare yourself against the people of Iraq, for the devil established himself among them and from there spread out. O my lord, they have certainly deceived me, so seize them, and quickly unleash upon them al-Ghulām al-Thaqafī, who will rule over them with the reign of ignorance. He will accept neither from the best of them nor will he let the worst of them go unpunished.'[135]

The events of the great civil war (35–41/656–61) that resulted in the murder of the third caliph, ʿUthmān, were still etched in the memory of eighth- and ninth-century Muslims. As Tayeb El-Hibri has shown, Kufa

[132] Al-Fasawī, *Kitāb al-Maʿrifa wa al-tārīkh*, 2: 751; Ibn Kathīr, *al-Bidāya wa al-nihāya*, 8: 12; al-Masʿūdī, *Les prairies d'or [Murūj al-dhahab]*, 5: 327–8.

[133] Al-Fasawī, *Kitāb al-Maʿrifa wa al-tārīkh*, 2: 752.

[134] The devil appears in the foundation narratives of other towns and cities. See, e.g., Ḥasan b. Muḥammad Qummī, *Tārīkh-i Qum*, ed. Muḥammad Riḍā Anṣārī Qummī (Qum: Kitābkhāneh-yi Buzurg-i Hazrat-i Āyat Allāh al-ʿUẓmā Marʿashī Najafī, 2006), 51.

[135] Al-Fasawī, *Kitāb al-Maʿrifa wa al-tārīkh*, 2: 754–5. A number of al-Fasawī's contemporaries cite a version of this tradition: Ibn Qutayba, *Kitāb al-Maʿārif*, 397, where it appears in Ibn Qutayba's profile of al-Ḥajjāj b. Yūsuf; al-Bukhārī, *Kitāb al-Kunā juz' min al-Tārīkh al-kabīr* (Hyderabad: Dā'irat al-Maʿārif al-ʿUthmāniyya, 1978), 62. For later versions see al-Lālakā'ī, *Sharḥ uṣūl iʿtiqād ahl al-sunna wa al-jamāʿa*, ed. Aḥmad b. Masʿūd b. Ḥamdān (Riyadh: Dār al-Ṭayba, 2003), 125; Ibn Kathīr, *al-Bidāya wa al-nihāya*, 9: 152; Ibn Mākūla, *Ikmāl*, 6: 165–6; al-Suyūṭī, *Khaṣā'is al-kubrā aw kifāyat al-ṭālib al-labīb fī khaṣā'iṣ al-ḥabīb*, ed. Muḥammad Khalīl Hirās (ʿAbdūn: Dār al-Kutub al-Ḥadītha, 1967), 2: 472–3; al-Dhahabī, *Mīzān al-iʿtidāl fī naqd al-rijāl*, ed. ʿAlī Muḥammad al-Bijāwī (Beirut: Dār al-Maʿrifa, 1963), 4: 551; Ibn Ḥajar, *Lisān al-mīzān*, ed. ʿAbd al-Fattāḥ Abū Ghudda (Beirut: Maktabat al-Maṭbūʿāt al-Islāmī, 2002), 9: 121.

took centre stage in the story of the first civil war.[136] The ensuing conflict between the powerful governor of Shām, Muʿāwiya, and the fourth caliph, ʿAlī, in Iraq resulted in an intensification of hostilities between the two regions. A century later Kufa again became the launching site for Hāshimī revolutionary activity that would culminate in the ʿAbbāsid overthrow of the Umayyads. These two formative and violent events contributed to Kufa's constituting a *lieu de mémoire* for sedition and rebellion, a reputation recorded in al-Ḥajjāj's eloquent and scathing address to the people of Iraq, whom he was sent to suppress.[137] If Kufa was the stage for this earthly drama of violence, al-Fasawī's history suggests that the devil's pervasive presence in Kufa had an important part to play.

In such narratives, Kufa's unholiness is juxtaposed with ʿUmar's concern for the people of Shām. This direct comparison between Kufa and Shām reflects the deep regional commitments of members of the early Islamic polity. Religious and political affiliations were entrenched in particular regions. Most importantly, as this report claims, the devil's physical residence in Kufa and his activities therein were seen to be critical to Kufa's fate. The belief that the devil took up residence in Kufa is, as we have seen, a recurring theme in al-Fasawī's history. But it reflects wider religious beliefs and social attitudes about the function of the devil in medieval Islamic societies. After all, this narrative about the devil's activities in Iraq is not peculiar to mechanisms for dismissing regions as unholy places. If we expand our discussion beyond al-Fasawī's history to conceptions of the devil's role in medieval Islamic society, we see that this kind of documentation of the devil's mundane activities in medieval regions is part of a wider understanding of his deep and graphic role as a social actor. The political overtones of these instances of divine curse against Kufa and its inhabitants take us into the heart of the political instability and insurrection in Kufa under ʿUthmān. Sedition and treachery were to become important socio-cultural themes in Kufa's history, as it became the fomenting ground for a succession of failed insurrections and ʿAlid rebellions against the Umayyads and ʿAbbāsids.[138]

We must recall that this moral topography of Kufa as a town of heretics, the devil, the curse, evil, and demons was articulated against the background of a succession of political and social crises in Kufa. Founded in 17/638 during ʿUmar's rule by Saʿd b. Abī Waqqāṣ, Kufa became the

[136] El-Hibri, *Parable and Politics*, 128–33, 154–7.
[137] Nora, 'Between Memory and History'. For al-Ḥajjāj's speech see al-Balādhurī, *Anonyme arabische Chronik [Ansāb al-ashrāf]*, ed. W. Ahlwardt (Greifswald: Selbstverlag, 1883), 11: 267–70.
[138] El-Hibri, *Parable and Politics*, 128–33.

caliphal capital under ʿAlī. Towards the end of the seventh century it was the scene of al-Mukhtār's rebellion. In 82/701 Ibn Ashʿath's rebellion struck the town during the reign of ʿAbd al-Malik b. Marwān (r. 72–86/691–705) and the latter's governor, Ḥajjāj b. Yūsuf al-Thaqafī, was sent to suppress the uprising. In 122/740 Zayd b. ʿAlī rebelled, and within a decade the town witnessed the Khārijite uprising of al-Ḍaḥḥāk b. Qays and the rebellion of ʿAbd Allāh b. Muʿāwiya. Under al-Saffāḥ, Kufa became the ʿAbbāsid capital until 145/762, but during al-Manṣūr's reign (r. 136–8/754–6) Muḥammad al-Nafs al-Zakiyya and his brother Ibrāhīm b. ʿAbd Allāh rebelled in 145/763.[139]

Despite these tumultuous political events, we must be wary of taking too simplistic a view of anti-Kufan narratives or describing them as representing dynastic rivalries in which invective against Kufa is seen to reflect pro-Umayyad sentiments. As we have seen, anti-Kufan reports are mentioned across a variety of ninth-century sources, and their *isnād*s tend to defy the Shām versus Iraq framework. Perhaps more pertinent than the events of the eighth and ninth centuries was the political and social background against which al-Fasawī was writing. In 250/864 Kufa was the scene of Yaḥyā b. ʿUmar's Zaydī revolt and the uprising of al-Ḥusayn b. Muḥammad. In 255/868–9 two Ḥasanids rebelled in Kufa.[140] The ʿAbbāsids faced the revolt of the Zanj in 255/869.[141] Perhaps most dramatically, Yaʿqūb b. Layth marched on Iraq in 262/875 against the caliph al-Muʿtamid (r. 256–79/870–92).[142]

We cannot ignore the political upheaval that Kufa and Iraq experienced during al-Fasawī's lifetime and the memory of Kufa's political and social turbulence during the seventh–ninth centuries. Nor can we underestimate the salience and spread of mentalités and beliefs about Kufa. Our understanding of discourses of heresy around Kufa and Iraq has to incorporate ninth-century mentalités and beliefs about the devil, discourses about holy and unholy regions, and the region's social and political history. It is important to recall, for example, that the political circumstances surrounding Kufa's political alignments are articulated through the device of the curse. The divine curse is afforded a powerful degree of agency to set the course of Kufa's subsequent history during the

[139] For the political history of Kufa between the seventh and eighth centuries see Hinds, 'Kufan Political Alignments'; Djaït, *al-Kūfa*; and Kennedy, *The Prophet and the Age of the Caliphates*, 94–103.

[140] Newman, *The Formative Period of Twelver Shīʿism*, 9.

[141] Popovic, *The Revolt of African Slaves*. For a sense of how contemporaries responded to the devastation in Iraq see Ibn al-Rūmī's elegy in Ibn al-Rūmī, *Dīwān Ibn al-Rūmī*, ed. Ḥuṣayn Naṣṣār (Cairo: Dār al-Kutub al-Wathā'iq al-Qawmiyya, 2003), 3: 2377–82.

[142] Abū Saʿīd Gardīzī, *Zayn al-akhbār*, ed. ʿAbd al-Ḥayy Ḥabībī (Tehran: Dunyā-yi Kitāb, 1944), 310–11; Anon., *Tārīkh-i Sīstān*, 231–2.

ninth and tenth centuries. We are presented here with an *aspect théâtral*, whose protagonists, plots, heroes, and villains were many. Kufa simply serves as a synecdoche for the unholy and heretical. The supernatural power of prophecy and curse, its ability to orchestrate events in Iraq, represents the very blurring of the borderline between society and the supernatural.[143] This, arguably, is the hallmark of medieval Islamic society. And it is a recurring theme of al-Fasawī's history of Kufa which is presented in its most dramatic form by al-Fasawī in the central role that he assigns the devil in the history of Kufa. In a region that al-Fasawī has depicted, quite literally, as godforsaken, the devil naturally comes to occupy a crucial role in the town's history. Invective belonged to the discourse not just of heresy, but to historians and scholars with a penchant for local and regional history.

## 4.5 Conclusion

In the work of historians such as al-Fasawī we are able to see how medieval scholars in their depiction of reality weaved a contiguous and intricate tapestry of social and religious life. Its threads do not simply connect historical periods, they contract historical time. Human history is telescoped as memories of prehistory, the Fall, and antediluvian periods are brought into sharp relief in al-Fasawī's ninth-century reconstruction of Kufa's history. Kufa's history is dependent upon a structure of reality that owes as much to seventh- and eighth-century developments (Kufa's curse) as it does to memories of an ancient past in which the devil was cast down to earth, good and evil were unevenly distributed among the realms of the Islamic world, and in which the Prophet was reported to have warned about Kufa's dark and unholy prospects.

My aim in this chapter has been to show that discourses of heresy around particular regions – in this case Kufa – depended upon a range of socio-religious motifs and mentalités. The power of such discourses and ideas about unholy regions facilitated the reception of heresiological discourses about Abū Ḥanīfa. Establishing the religious deviance of certain scholars became all the more simple through the process of narrating the unholiness of their home town. Unholy regions were likely to produce

[143] The supernatural was essential to the societies that historians of medieval Islam study. In the light of its importance, it is remarkable that more work has not been done on this subject. Contrast this with scholarship on the late antique world, executed with exemplary clarity by Brown, *Society and the Holy in Late Antiquity*, 302–32, and I am indebted to his discussion in that book. See also Brown's comments on St. Augustine's *de civitate Dei* and the sack of Rome in Brown, *Augustine of Hippo*, 311–12. For curses see Kirschner, 'The Vocation of Holiness in Late Antiquity', 116–17; Langer, *Cursing the Christians?* for a fascinating history of liturgical curse texts.

deviant ideas and scholars. For al-Fasawī the logic was clear enough, for his diatribe against Kufa ends where his attack on Abū Ḥanīfa begins.

The objective of historians was not limited to the detailing of fact. Facts were incorporated into historical narratives, and in doing so historians aimed to insert moral, religious, and supernatural phenomena into the basic facts and matters of medieval life. The moral imagination was the social imagination. Medieval historians such as al-Fasawī did not depict our historical reality, but they described their world. Al-Fasawī had a total view of society. Heresy was not simply the product of human error or ritual deviancy. When framing heresies and heretics, historians such as al-Fasawī collapsed distinctions and boundaries between society and the supernatural, physical regions and holy and unholy devices. Against this social and moral topography of Kufa, al-Fasawī's discourse of heresy against Abū Ḥanīfa was a logical extension of his bleak vision of Kufa's past and present. As we shall see in the next chapter on ethnogenesis and discourses of heresy, holy and unholy regions constituted just one social dimension of heresiological discourses against Abū Ḥanīfa. Like regionalism, ethnicity became a source of deep social and religious anxiety in the eighth and ninth centuries, and this was reflected in the way in which discourses of heresy against Abū Ḥanīfa incorporated slights against Abū Ḥanīfa's ethnic and ancestral origins. Consequently, both regionalism and ethnicity evolved into strategies of distinction between heresy and orthodoxy.[144]

[144] Pohl, 'Introduction: Strategies of Distinction'.

# 5 Ethnogenesis and Heresy

Ethnogenesis, regionalism, and heresy are all tools of otherness and, as such, they belong to what Jonathan Z. Smith has termed the 'discourse of difference'.[1] The relationships between regionalism and heresy (the subject of the previous chapter) and between ethnogenesis and heresy (the focus of this chapter) differ in some important respects. Where regionalism and heresy operate on an understanding of topography and territoriality, ethnogenesis and heresy construct imagined and perceived boundaries of difference.[2] This creative aspect of constructing ethnicity, language, and foreignness in the service of discourses of heresy serves a fundamental role in the consolidation of group identities, and the formation of proto-Sunnism was no exception to such social dynamics. In the eighth–ninth centuries ethnicity (and ethno-racial reasoning) was a banal feature of social, political, economic, and religious life in early Islamicate societies. It should not surprise us, therefore, that ethno-racial reasoning became an important mechanism in discourses of orthodoxy and heresy in medieval Islam.

This chapter argues that ethnogenesis had a considerable impact on religious developments in the late eighth–tenth centuries.[3] Processes of ethnogenesis in the diverse and multi-ethnic milieu of the early Islamic empire dovetailed with emerging discourses of heresy and orthodoxy.

[1] Smith, 'What a Difference a Difference Makes'; Burke, *History and Social Theory*, 57–60. Hartog, *The Mirror of Herodotus*, 212–59 has called this the 'rhetoric of otherness'.

[2] On the construction of ethnic identities see the important contributions of Amory, *People and Identity in Ostrogothic Italy*, esp. 314: 'Ethnographic discourse did not merely describe society: it attempted to order and reorder it'; Gillet, 'Ethnogenesis'; Pohl, 'Conceptions of Ethnicity'. For a wide range of contributions on the subject of ethnic communities in medieval societies, see Pohl and Reimitz (eds.), *Strategies of Distinction*.

[3] In reading ethnogenesis alongside religious developments I am following a well-trodden path in the field of religious history: Hodge, *If Sons, Then Heirs* has shown how crucial kinship and ethnicity were to Paul's attempt to forge religious identities; Johnson, *Ethnicity and Argument* analyses Eusebius' use of 'ethnic argumentation' to explore how Christian otherness rested on representations of ethnic identities; and Lieu, *Christian Identity*, 239–68, esp. 259–67, 272–4, 309–10 identifies a central role for ethnicity in the articulation of Christian identities.

This fusion of two concomitant historical developments helps to explain why proto-Sunni traditionalists deployed forms of ethno-racial reasoning, often in a seamless manner, to cast Abū Ḥanīfa as a heretic. This chapter draws attention to a set of specific, but interconnected, strategies of distinction.

I analyse five social and cultural themes that characterise the ethno-racial dimensions of discourses of heresy against Abū Ḥanīfa: the first theme concerns the confessional ambiguity of Abū Ḥanīfa's ancestors; the second relates to conflicting accounts of his (ethnic) genealogy; the third theme displays attempts to establish his servile social status by linking his ancestors to the institution of slavery and captivity; the fourth theme surveys the semantic field of foreignness utilised by proto-Sunni traditionalists to label Abū Ḥanīfa; and the fifth theme is an extension of ethno-racial labelling, and is anchored in claims both that Abū Ḥanīfa's knowledge of the Arabic language was deficient and that he considered Persian to be a sacred language suitable for ritual performance and scriptural recital. A closer examination of such strategies of distinction establishes a clearer history of how identity was constructed among religious movements and why the formation of religious orthodoxy cannot be divorced from the social and cultural history of the eighth–tenth centuries. It is to this history that we now turn.

## 5.1 Ethnogenesis in Early Islamicate Societies

It is important to recall the myriad ways in which ethnicity was implicated in the everyday social life of medieval Islamicate societies. Islam's foundational scripture is explicit about having been revealed in the language of the Arabs. The Quran emphasises the primacy of the Arabic language as a unique receptacle of God's word on more than one occasion.[4,5] The Quran also mentions the Arabian Peninsula and its longer role in the history of monotheism. Peter Webb has argued that these discrete and specific features of the Quran have been misread frequently as evidence for the convergence of religion (Islam) and *ethnos* (Arabness).[6] On the other hand, the *éminence grise* of ethnicity studies, Anthony D. Smith, identified ethnicity as a constant in Arab conceptions of the religion of Islam. For Smith, myths of divine election were so obviously anchored in Arabness as to require little in the way of demonstration. Christianity, on

4 Quran 12.2, 13.37, 16.103, 20.113, 26.195, 39.28, 41.3, 41.44, 42.7, 43.3, 46.12.

5 Consider passages relating to Abraham (Quran 2.127) and the people of ʿĀd and Thamūd, for which see Hoyland, *Arabia and the Arabs*, 68–9, 223–4; Retsö, *The Arabs in Antiquity*, 34–40.

6 Webb, *Imagining the Arabs*, 115–26.

the other hand, neutralised the potential for ethnicity to become a strategy of distinction, difference, or contention. Despite the prominence and influence of Smith's work, there can be little doubt that his understanding of the relationship between religion and ethnicity for the history of both early Islam and early Christianity is untenable.[7] Whilst historians of early Christianity have discredited Smith's ahistorical and broad thesis of the role that ethnicity played in the construction of Christian identities, scholarly works on ethnicity and medieval Islam continue to appeal to Smith's authority.

Sarah Bowen Savant's recent monograph exploring the formation of 'Persian ethnic identity' after the Muslim conquests is one such example. In an otherwise valuable study, Savant places Smith's influential thesis that the myth of ethnic election is absolutely integral to ethnic survival at the heart of her investigation into how Persian ethnic identity was constructed and remembered in medieval Islam. She argues, for example, that the incorporation of Persians into sacred Arab genealogies is a manifestation of Smith's theory of divine ethnic election.[8] For Smith, such myths of election were obvious in the case of the Arabs and Islam.[9] Smith has no primary sources to support his claim.[10] Still, Savant transforms Smith's undocumented and general assertion into a hypothesis about ethnogenesis in medieval Islam:[11]

> From an early date, the Arabs often espoused a missionary sense of chosenness when they sought new converts, first among other Arabs and then among their neighbours. Arabic literature is filled with claims representing them as a people of religion, set apart from others. A common identity, documented through tribal genealogies, was nurtured, and it was also their election that made Arabs out of former non-Arabs. An ideology of election was supported by the Prophet as well

[7] See Buell, *Why This New Race*, 1, where Smith is cited as one of a number of scholars who considers ethnicity to be nugatory to the history of early Christianity. As Buell shows, it is not just anthropologists who dismiss ethnicity. Buell is critical of historians of early Christianity, such as Guy Stroumsa, for asserting that 'ethnic terms were deeply irrelevant for the Christians'. See Stroumsa, *Barbarian Philosophy*, 156. Stroumsa's more recent work suggests a significant departure from this earlier position. See, e.g., Stroumsa, 'Barbarians or Heretics?'.

[8] Smith's theory of divine election is articulated in Smith, 'Chosen Peoples', 441 ('the creation and dissemination by specialists of the belief that "we are a 'chosen people'"').

[9] Smith, 'Chosen Peoples', 444: 'We need not dwell at length on the powerful myths of election that have surfaced periodically among the Arabs and their kingdoms, notably during the Islamic conquests and in the period of the Crusades.'

[10] Smith cites Armstrong, *Nations before Nationalism*, ch. 3 for 'medieval Islamic identities'. Armstrong says almost nothing regarding the importance of Arab ethnicity. In fact, he argues that Arab predominance was undermined in the early Islamic period. Smith also provides two references for the 'Arab dimensions of Islam', but provides no pagination: see Smith, 'Chosen Peoples', 452.

[11] Savant, *The New Muslims of Post-Conquest Iran*, 50–1.

as by the supreme importance of the Arabic language in Muslim religion and ritual.

Like Smith, Savant's bold hypothesis about the 'missionary sense of chosenness', a requirement of Smith's theory of ethnicity, lacks any supporting evidence. There are no footnotes pointing to this missionary form of divine election. Despite the claim that Arabic literature is filled with such claims, nothing other than a passage from al-Jāḥiẓ describing the Arabs is cited to refer to 'a mature sense of Arabness'.[12]

In fact, ethnogenesis was a complicated and tense process in early Islamicate societies, and it is difficult to discern in our texts any one single conception of ethnic chosenness. Arabs and Persians were not static ethnic categories. In the eighth and ninth centuries they underwent many transformations and came to denote very different identities depending on where one was in the early Islamic empire. This is to be expected in a society marked by a high degree of religious, ethnic, cultural, and linguistic diversity. Simplistic notions of ethnic survival and stratification produced in an age of nationalism are ill suited to medieval societies as diverse as the medieval Near East. Historians are on safer grounds studying specific examples of ethno-racial forms of reasoning.

The everyday significance of ethnogenesis in the social life of medieval Islamicate societies meant that conceptions of ethnicity and religious orthodoxy and heresy were destined to come into conversation with one another. Discourses of heresy and orthodoxy were anchored in specific social and cultural processes. Like regionalism, ethnogenesis in the diverse, multi-confessional, and multi-ethnic provinces of the early Islamic empire had the potential to induce crevasses among religious movements. Ethno-racial reasoning played an important analytical role in how society understood, interpreted, and articulated the political mobilisation of groups and communities. Military life, on so many levels, was stratified along ethnic and racial lines. The recruitment of military personnel was configured according to perceived characteristics of ethnicity. Salaries were subject to fluctuations depending on the social and ethnic nature of soldiers and units.[13] Populations were settled, resettled, and surveyed, and this process rested on conceptions of ethnicity, race, and tribe.[14]

Ethnicity, therefore, operated at every level of social interaction in medieval Islamicate societies. These are the circumstances against which discourses of heresy evolved in the eighth–tenth centuries. As we

[12] Savant, *The New Muslims of Post-Conquest Iran*, 50–1.
[13] Kennedy, *The Armies of the Caliphs*, 62 ff.; Kennedy, 'Military Pay'.
[14] Al-Qadi, 'Population Census and Land Surveys'.

shall now see, conceptions of ethnicity became part of the religious rhetoric of orthodoxy and heresy, uprightness and deviance.

## 5.2 Genealogy

The construction of genealogy is more than just a social fact of kinship. It has a legitimising role in societies in which traditional structures of kinship, tribalism, and religion dominate.[15] Bringing a scholar's genealogy into disrepute was a powerful means of discrediting them and reducing their standing among Muslim communities.[16] Biographical dictionaries were the perfect venue for this. Ibn Ḥibbān's biographical dictionary of unreliable and weak ḥadīth transmitters commences his entry on Abū Ḥanīfa in conventional fashion. He describes him as an upholder of speculative jurisprudence; mentions the names of two transmitters from whom he narrated traditions; and gives his date and place of birth. Ibn Ḥibbān then turns to the issue of Abū Ḥanīfa's ancestry and genealogy:[17]

> Abū Ḥanīfa's father was a slave captive (*mamlūk*) to a man from the tribe of Banū Rabīʿa Taym Allāh Najd.[18] They were known as the tribe of Banū Qafal. His father was freed (*uʿtiqa*) and became a bread-maker (*khabbāz*) for ʿAbd Allāh b. Qafal.[19]

It is worth remembering that the entry on Abū Ḥanīfa is the lengthiest and most captious biography in Ibn Ḥibbān's multi-volume work. His decision to anchor his long diatribe in the context of Abū Ḥanīfa's servile social and ancestral origins exemplifies the connections that proto-Sunni traditionalists sought to establish between ethno-social statuses and heretical ideas.

This strategy seems to have had wider appeal among proto-Sunni traditionalists. Al-Khaṭīb al-Baghdādī's *Tārīkh Baghdād* is the largest

[15] The point is obvious enough, but it is discussed in detail by Szombathy, 'Genealogy in Medieval Muslim Societies'. A broader perspective on the role of genealogies throughout Islamic history is provided in Savant and de Felipe, *Genealogy and Knowledge in Muslim Societies*.

[16] There is a brief paragraph on Abū Ḥanīfa's ethnicity in van Ess, *Theologie und Gesellschaft*, 1: 186–7, though van Ess acknowledges that his account derives mainly from U. F. ʿAbd-Allāh, s.v. 'Abū Ḥanīfa', *Encyclopaedia Iranica*, 1: 295–301.

[17] Ibn Ḥibbān, *Kitāb al-Majrūḥīn*, 3: 61–3 (Beirut edn.) = 3: 405–6 (Riyadh edn.).

[18] On this tribe see Ibn al-Kalbī, *Jamharat al-nasab*, ed. Nājī Ḥasan (Beirut: ʿĀlam al-Kutub, 1986), 3: 517–21 = *Ǧamharat an-nasab: Das genealogische Werk des Hišām ibn Muḥammad al-Kalbī*, ed. Werner Caskel (Leiden: Brill, 1966), 150.

[19] On ʿAbd Allāh b. Qafal see Ibn al-Kalbī, *Jamharat al-nasab*, 3: 518; Yāqūt al-Ḥamawī, *Kitāb al-Muqtaḍab min kitāb Jamharat al-nasab*, ed. Nājī Ḥasan (Beirut: al-Dār al-ʿArabiyya li al-Mawsūʿāt, 1987), 190, where at least one of the manuscripts mentions that Abū Ḥanīfa was the *mawlā* of Banū Qafal.

repository of discourses of heresy against Abū Ḥanīfa in medieval Islamic sources, which is why near-contemporaries of his who happened to be Ḥanafīs produced a string of refutations.[20] It is the lengthiest entry from a total of 7,831 in the *Tārīkh Baghdād*, running into 142 pages in the most recent critical edition. Ethno-racial reasoning plays a crucial role in al-Khaṭīb al-Baghdādī's wide-ranging survey of discourses of heresy against Abū Ḥanīfa. At the outset, al-Khaṭīb al-Baghdādī presents eleven reports concerning Abū Ḥanīfa's genealogy and ancestry. The first report provides a neutral statement on Abū Ḥanīfa's genealogy.[21]

Ḥamza b. Muḥammad b. Ṭāhir < al-Walīd b. Bakr < ʿAlī b. Aḥmad b. Zakariyyā' al-Hāshimī < Abū Muslim Ṣāliḥ b. Aḥmad b. ʿAbd Allāh b. Ṣāliḥ al-ʿIjlī < al-ʿIjlī's father said: Abū Ḥanīfa al-Nuʿmān b. Thābit was a Kūfan from the Taym tribe of Rahṭ Ḥamza al-Zayyāt. He was a silk merchant.

Next, al-Khaṭīb al-Baghdādī presents a report stating that when Abū Ḥanīfa was born his father was still a Christian (*wulida Abū Ḥanīfa wa abūhu naṣrānī*).[22] This created yet another context of deviance. Abū Ḥanīfa's opponents were able to use elements from his fluid and uncertain genealogical history to insist on the confessional impurity of Abū Ḥanīfa and his immediate family.

The careful manner in which al-Khaṭīb al-Baghdādī arranges his information seems designed to discredit and unravel Abū Ḥanīfa's dubious social and ethnic origins. The next report adduced by al-Khaṭīb al-Baghdādī sketches a slightly different family trajectory:[23]

Al-Ḥasan b. Muḥammad b. al-Khallāl < ʿAlī b. ʿAmr al-Ḥarīrī < al-Qāsim ʿAlī b. Muḥammad b. Kās al-Nakhaʿī < Muḥammad b. ʿAlī b. ʿAffān < Muḥammad b. Isḥāq al-Bakkā'ī < ʿUmar b. Ḥammād b. Abī Ḥanīfa said: Abū Ḥanīfa al-Nuʿmān b. Thābit b. Zūṭā. As for Zūṭā, he was from the people of Kābul. Thābit was born a Muslim. Zūṭā used to be a slave captive for the tribe of Banī Taym Allāh b. Thaʿlaba. He was freed and made a client of the tribe of Banī Taym Allāh b. Thaʿlaba and then after of the tribe of Banī Qafal.

According to this report, Abū Hanīfa's grandfather was a slave captive from Kābul in Khurāsān. He served as a slave in a family from the tribe of Banū Taym Allāh b. Thaʿlaba. He was freed, presumably on account of converting to Islam. As a new convert to the religion of Islam, he was integrated as a client (*mawlā*) of the same tribal family and then underwent the same process with a family from the tribe of Banū Qafal. Zuṭā's

[20] A refutation was penned by an Ayyūbid prince: see al-Malik al-Muʿaẓẓam Abū Muẓaffar ʿĪsā b. Abī Bakr, *al-Sahm al-muṣīb fī kabid al-Khaṭīb* (Cairo: Maṭbaʿat al-Saʿāda, 1932).

[21] Al-Khaṭīb al-Baghdādī, *Tārīkh Baghdād*, 15: 446.

[22] Al-Khaṭīb al-Baghdādī, *Tārīkh Baghdād*, 15: 446.

[23] Al-Khaṭīb al-Baghdādī, *Tārīkh Baghdād*, 15: 446.

son, Thābit, was born a Muslim. Converts were vehicles for the mobility of ideas from foreign regions and cultures, as well as from old and competing religions. The process of conversion served as a catalyst for new tensions over ethnicity and community formation. The institution of *walā'* is a transparent case in which the process of ethnogenesis in the nascent empire gave rise to new pressures on religious and political elites to regulate the status of recent converts and freedmen.[24] The business of incorporating new converts and freedmen into social ties with an Arab Muslim patron was one solution to the vexing problem that faced an imperial Arab elite seeking to maintain its privileged status amidst an influx of new converts seeking membership within a religious community that displayed no obvious scriptural basis for the domination or supremacy of any one particular ethnic group.

The diverse ethnic composition of the *amṣār*, too, complicated an already volatile social situation. These *amṣār* were the birthplace of some critical discussions concerning legal, political, and economic regulation. Religious ideas evolved, therefore, alongside new institutions. Furthermore, the nature and success of the conquests also meant that the Arab ruling elite had to draw on the industry of competent native administrators, bureaucrats, and elites. The demand created new opportunities, and many converts readily took advantage of these openings. The absorption of non-Arab elites into favourable social structures was a selective process. By the Marwānid period there was enough of a correlation between ethnic, social, and political tensions for historians to describe al-Mukhtār's rebellion as a revolt against the degradation of the *mawālī*.[25] The *mawālī* came to symbolise political and social strife. Soon, their opponents would begin to cast them as religious deviants, too. Nowhere is this clearer than in the following reaction to al-Mukhtār's revolt:[26]

[24] On *walā'* and *mawālī* see Urban, 'The Early Islamic Mawālī', 86–112, now published as *Conquered Populations in Early Islam*; Enderwitz, *Gesselschaftlicher Rang und ethnische Legitimation*; Cooperson, '"Arabs" and "Iranian"'; Elad, 'Ethnic Composition'; Elad, 'Mawālī in the Composition of al-Ma'mūn's Army'. Our understanding of the importance of the *mawālī* has been enhanced by Crone's fascination with the subject throughout her career, though Urban's thesis provides an important corrective to some of Crone's work. See Crone, *Slaves on Horses*, ch. 8; Crone, 'The Significance of Wooden Weapons'; Crone, 'Mawālī and the Prophet's Family'; Crone, *The Nativist Prophets*; Nawas, 'The Birth of an Elite'; Nawas, 'The Contribution of the Mawālī'; Nawas, 'A Profile of the Mawālī Ulama'; Retsö, *The Arabs in Antiquity*, 66–9.

[25] Al-Ṭabarī, *Tārīkh*, 2: 649, 719.

[26] Al-Ṭabarī, *Tārīkh*, 2: 750; al-Balādhurī, *Ansāb al-ashrāf*, 6: 135 (al-ʿAẓm edn.). On al-Mukhtār and the *mawālī* see Dixon, *The Umayyad Caliphate*, 5; Fishbein, 'The Life of al-Mukhtār b. Abī ʿUbayd', 3–4, 36; Crone, 'The Significance of Wooden Weapons', 178.

When the news of the killing of al-Mukhtār's supporters reached Kufa, ʿUbayd Allāh b. al-Ḥurr [a Kufan *sharīf*] said: 'As for me, I think that the amīr [Muṣʿab b. Zubayr] should return every tribal group (*qawm*) who was with that liar to their people, for we have use for them on our frontiers; and that he should return our slaves to us, for they are for our widowers and our weak ones; and that the mawālī should have their heads struck off for their unbelief and the magnitude of their arrogance, and the paucity of their thankfulness has become apparent. I do not trust them with religion.'

Similarly, the *mawālī* appear as an acrimonious constituency in the rebellion of Ibn Ashʿath; and the *ʿajam* serve the same role in historical accounts of al-Ḥārith b. Surayj's revolt.[27]

Proto-Sunni traditionalists were aware of this context when they portrayed heresies and heretics as outsiders threatening to undermine the religion of Islam from within. Proto-Sunni traditionalists raised the issue of Abū Ḥanīfa's servile status to add another layer of foreignness to his questionable genealogy, even if, as one report tells us, Abū Ḥanīfa reassured his patron that he should deem himself privileged to have Abū Ḥanīfa as his client.[28] Not only did this root Abū Ḥanīfa and his family in a debased social status, but it connected him to an important social group that was maligned frequently in the eighth and ninth centuries: the *mawālī*.

A third report confirms that Abū Ḥanīfa's grandfather hailed from Kābul.[29] In the next report al-Khaṭīb al-Baghdādī suggests a more sinister explanation for much of the confusion surrounding Abū Ḥanīfa's ancestral origins, namely, that Abū Ḥanīfa falsified his genealogy. His real name, we are told, was ʿAtīk b. Zūṭara, but he invented a false genealogy, and he adopted a false name for himself (al-Nuʿmān) and for his father (Thābit).[30]

[27] Ibn al-Aʿtham al-Kūfī, *Kitāb al-Futūḥ*, ed. Muḥammad ʿAbd al-Muʿīd Khān *et al.* (Hyderabad: Dā'irat al-Maʿārif al-ʿUthmāniyya, 1968–75), 7: 146–7 (for Ibn Ashʿath) and 8: 164 (for al-Ḥārith b. Surayj). On this source see Conrad, 'Ibn Aʿtham and his History'; and Lindstedt, 'al-Madā'inī's *Kitāb al-Dawla*'; Lindstedt, 'Sources for the Biography of the Historian Ibn Aʿtham al-Kūfī'.

[28] The Arabic is concise, curt, and conforms entirely with Abū Ḥanīfa's reputation for devastating wit: *samiʿtu rajulan min Banī Qafal min khiyār Banī Taym Allāh yaqūl li Abī Ḥanīfa: anta mawlayya. Qāla: anā wa Allāhi ashrafu laka minka lī.* See Ibn ʿAbd al-Barr, *al-Intiqā'*, 191.

[29] Muḥammad b. ʿAlī b. ʿAffān: al-Faḍl b. Dukayn said: *Abū Ḥanīfa al-Nuʿmān b. Thābit b. Zūṭā aṣluhu min Kābul* (al-Khaṭīb al-Baghdādī, *Tārīkh Baghdād*, 15: 446).

[30] This report appears in Abū Nuʿaym al-Iṣfahānī, *Musnad al-Imām Abī Ḥanīfa*, ed. Naẓar Muḥammad al-Fāryābī (Riyadh: Maktabat al-Kawthar, 1994), 19. Its *isnād* is: Abū Nuʿaym al-Ḥāfiẓ < Abū Muḥammad al-Ghiṭrīfī < al-Sājī < Muḥammad b. Muʿāwiya al-Ziyādī < Abū Jaʿfar said: *kāna Abū Ḥanīfa ismuhu ʿAtīk b. Zūṭara, fa sammā nafsahu al-Nuʿmān wa abāhu Thābit.*

A further four reports present yet more contradictory accounts. One connects his ancestry to the people of Bābil in Iraq.[31] A second states that Abū Ḥanīfa's father was from Nasā.[32] A third purports that Abū Ḥanīfa's ancestors were from Tirmidh.[33] The fourth report points to Anbār as the home of Thābit, Abū Ḥanīfa's father.[34]

Abū Ḥanīfa's ancestry and genealogy, as constructed by proto-Sunni traditionalists, is characterised by deep contradictions. This in itself upset a pietistic and scholarly convention in medieval Islam. Genealogies were a matter of great religious and social significance. They had to be transparent. Abū Ḥanīfa's genealogical ancestry is presented by proto-Sunni traditionalists as obscure and spurious. The exact geographical origins of his family are unknown. The confessional status of his father and grandfather is brought into disrepute. Allegations are made that Abū Ḥanīfa conjured up a false name and invented a false genealogy. The story of the social and ethnic status of Abū Ḥanīfa and his ancestors is one that vacillates between extremes. According to his detractors, he descends from slave captives. Defenders of Abū Ḥanīfa, notably his grandson Ismāʿīl b. Ḥammād b. Abī Ḥanīfa, repudiated the allegation that his grandfather was a slave. 'We are sons of free Persians.'[35] In addition to this, Ismāʿīl presented an entirely different narrative regarding his grandfather's social and religious status. He maintained that his grandfather went to ʿAlī b. Abī Ṭālib and sought his blessings on him and his descendants. Abū Ḥanīfa's family was clearly perturbed by the ethno-racial smears against their ancestors. ʿUmar b. Ḥammād relates that his brother, Ismāʿīl b. Ḥammād, made the following declaration: 'I am Ismāʿīl b. Hammād b. Abī Ḥanīfa al-Nuʿmān b. Thābit b. al-Marzubān, among the sons of the kings of Persians. By God, slavery befell us never.' According to family accounts, the ancestral connections that proto-Sunni traditionalists made concerning the servile status of Abū Ḥanīfa's family, first as slaves, then as clients, then as freedmen, were completely at odds with their genealogical history. They descended from Persian kings, not

[31] Al-Khaṭīb al-Baghdādī, *Tārīkh Baghdād*, 15: 447. Its *isnād* is: Aḥmad b. ʿUmar b. Rawḥ al-Nahrawānī < al-Muʿāfā b. Zakariyyā' < Aḥmad b. Naḍr b. Ṭālib < Ismāʿīl b. ʿAbd Allāh b. Maymūn < Abū ʿAbd al-Raḥmān al-Muqrī'.

[32] Al-Khaṭīb al-Baghdādī, *Tārīkh Baghdād*, 15: 447. Its *isnād* is: al-Khallāl < ʿAlī b. ʿAmr al-Ḥarīrī < ʿAlī b. Muḥammad b. Kās al-Nakhaʿī < Abū Bakr al-Marrūdhī < al-Naḍr b. Muḥammad < Yaḥyā b. al-Naḍr al-Qurashī.

[33] Al-Khaṭīb al-Baghdādī, *Tārīkh Baghdād*, 15: 447. Its *isnād* is: al-Nakhaʿī < Sulaymān b. Rabīʿ < al-Ḥārith b. Idrīs.

[34] Al-Khaṭīb al-Baghdādī, *Tārīkh Baghdād*, 15: 447. Its *isnād* is: al-Nakhaʿī < Abū Jaʿfar Aḥmad b. Isḥāq b. Buhlūl al-Qāḍī < father < grandfather.

[35] Al-ʿIjlī, *Tārīkh al-thiqāt*, ed. ʿAbd al-Muʿṭī al-Qalʿajī (Beirut: Dār al-Kutub al-ʿIlmiyya, 1984), 1: 450.

as slave captives and bread-makers for Arab tribesmen.[36] The only comfort provided to historians by accounts as contradictory as these is that they demonstrate how much was at stake in constructing genealogies of men of orthodoxy or heresy.

## 5.3 The Heresy of Foreigners

The use of ethno-racial forms of reasoning in discourses of heresy against Abū Ḥanīfa provides further support for this study's thesis that orthodoxy and heresy transcended the sphere of belief and practice.[37] Ninth-century texts exemplify a fascination with ethnography, and this has to be seen in the context of multifarious communities undergoing processes of ethnogenesis in a multi-ethnic empire underpinned by a confession with no definitive overtures to one ethnic community.[38] This complex situation solicited a number of reactions, but above all it created a semantic field which provided the basis for ethno-racial forms of reasoning. It was with such words that proto-Sunni traditionalist movements articulated conceptions of orthodoxy and heresy in the semantic field of foreignness, and this shows how discourses of heresy were entangled in the formation of ethnic and social identities.

### *Nabaṭī*

*Nabaṭī* was a term with ethno-racial connotations, and was used to disparage Abū Ḥanīfa. The term was a pejorative one usually used as an ethnic designation for Iraqi Aramaeans. Ibn al-Manẓūr's definition of the term describes it as referring to a generation that settled in Iraq (*jīl yanzilūn al-sawād*), and he cites yet another authority to add that they settled in valleys between the two Iraqs (*yanzilūn bi al-baṭā'iḥ bayn al-ʿIrāqayn*).[39]

This seems to be the context in which it was used in discourses of heresy against Abū Ḥanīfa. Proto-Sunni traditionalists were engaged in

[36] Al-Khaṭīb al-Baghdādī, *Tārīkh Baghdād*, 15: 447–8. His source is a report in al-Ṣaymarī, *Akhbār Abī Ḥanīfa wa aṣḥābihi*, ed. Abū al-Wafā' al-Afghānī (Beirut: ʿAlam al-Kutub, 1985), 16.

[37] 'Ethnic reasoning' is the term used by Buell, *Why This New Race*.

[38] For examples of medieval ethnography see al-Jāḥiẓ, *Thalāth rasā'il [Tria Opuscula Auctore]*, ed. G. van Vloten (Leiden: Brill, 1903), 1–56 (*Risāla ilā al-Fatḥ b. Khāqān fī manāqib al-turk wa ʿāmmat jund al-khilāfa*), 57–85 (*Kitāb fakhr al-sūdān ʿalā al-bīḍān*); Ibn Qutayba, *Faḍl al-ʿarab wa al-tanbīh ʿalā ʿulūmihā*, ed. Walīd Maḥmūd Khāliṣ (Abū Dhabi: al-Majmaʿ al-Thaqafī, 1998); al-Qazwīnī, *Āthār al-bilād*, 6, where he announces his ethnographic intentions; al-Masʿūdī, *Kitāb al-Tanbīh wa al-ishrāf*, ed. M. J. de Goeje (Leiden: Brill, 1894). See also Silverstein, 'The Medieval Islamic Worldview'.

[39] Ibn al-Manẓūr, *Lisān al-ʿArab* (Cairo: Dār al-Maʿārif, n.d.), 4326 cites other authorities regarding their residence in Iraq (*sukkān al-ʿIrāq*).

deliberate attempts to interpret Abū Ḥanīfa's religious deviance in this ethno-racial framework.[40] Ethno-racial words and discourses of heresy were channelled to discredit scholars, and, in a multi-ethno-racial empire in which words had legal consequences, forms of ethno-racial labelling were libellous. The *Kitāb al-Umm*'s chapter on slander (*bāb al-firya*) opens with a legal discussion concerning the consequences of unkind ethnic or tribal labelling and produces the views of Abū Ḥanīfa and al-Shāfiʿī on inaccurate uses of the label *nabaṭī*.[41]

The legal implications of inaccurate and underhand ethno-racial classification did not necessarily dissuade proto-Sunni traditionalists from making use of them in religious polemics against Abū Ḥanīfa. ʿAbd Allāh b. Ḥanbal, for example, includes in his capacious assortment of discourses of heresy concerning Abū Ḥanīfa this perspective on the relationship between Abū Ḥanīfa's deviance and his ethnic background: 'Sufyān b. Wakīʿ < I heard my father say: whenever Abū Ḥanīfa was mentioned in a gathering, Sufyān would say: "We seek refuge in God from the evil of the *nabaṭī* when he becomes an Arab."'[42] In the same section ʿAbd Allāh b. Ḥanbal produces a charientism, cleverly manipulating the double entendre possible with the root n-b-ṭ: 'Abū Ḥanīfa was a *nabaṭī* who interpreted (*istanbaṭa*) religious matters on the basis of his own speculative opinion.'[43] Then there is the story in Ibn Waḍḍāḥ's work:[44]

Muḥammad b. Waḍḍāḥ < Muḥammad b. ʿAbd Allāh al-Sahmī < al-Malaṭī < Ibn Jurayj < ʿAṭā' b. Abī Rabāḥ said: a man who seemed peculiar passed by ʿAlī b. Abī Ṭālib, and ʿAlī asked him: 'Are you of the people of Khurāsān?'

MAN: No.
ʿALĪ: Are you from the people of Fārs?
MAN: No.
ʿALĪ: So where do you come from?
MAN: I am from the people of the earth (*ahl al-arḍ*).
ʿALĪ: Indeed, I heard the messenger of God say: 'The religion will continue to remain upright and virtuous as long as the *nabaṭ* of Iraq do not become Muslims. When the *nabaṭ* of Iraq become Muslims, however, they will corrupt the religion and they will speak about the religion without any knowledge, and when this happens Islam will be defiled and destroyed.'

40 Al-Khaṭīb al-Baghdādī, *Tārīkh Baghdād*, 15: 447.
41 Abū Yūsuf (attrib.), *Ikhtilāf Abī Ḥanīfa wa Ibn Abī Laylā*, ed. Abū al-Wafā' al-Afghānī (Hyderabad: Dā'irat al-Maʿārif al-ʿUthmāniyya, 1938–9), 163; al-Shāfiʿī, *Kitāb al-Umm* (Bulaq: al-Maṭbaʿa al-Kubrā al-Amīriyya, 1907), 7: 141.
42 ʿAbd Allāh b. Aḥmad b. Ḥanbal, *Kitāb al-Sunna*, 198.
43 ʿAbd Allāh b. Aḥmad b. Ḥanbal, *Kitāb al-Sunna*, 197.
44 Ibn Waḍḍāḥ, *Kitāb al-Bidaʿ [Tratado contra las innovaciones]*, ed. M. Isabel Fierro (Madrid: Consejo Superior de Investigaciones Cientificas, 1988), 213.

The material in Ibn Waḍḍāḥ's work provides us with an insight into the broader connotations involved in the act of labelling scholars as *nabaṭī*s. To use this term among proto-Sunnī traditionalists was to invoke the religious deviance of a particular individual. It was to argue that they were culpable of corrupting the religion. It is unclear whether this meaning was understood to later authors who cited reports that labelled Abū Ḥanīfa as a *nabaṭī*,[45] but there can be little doubt that proto-Sunnī traditionalists of the ninth century were cognisant of its implication.

### *Muwallad*

Another term of reference for foreigners in early Islamicate societies was *muwallad*. The *muwalladūn* were a class of acculturated Arabs whose parents and ancestors had been non-Arabs. In the words of Ibn Manẓūr, these were Arabs not of pure breed (*wa rajul muwallad idhā kāna ʿarabiyyan ghayr maḥḍ*). Ibn Manẓūr lists other definitions, all of which reinforce this sense of ethnic and cultural diffusion: a *muwallad* refers to someone born in a place to which either one of their parents belongs (*wulidat bi arḍ wa laysa bihā illā abūhā aw ummuhā*); a person born among the Arabs, raised with the children of Arabs, and acculturated according to ways of the Arabs (*wulidat bayn al-ʿarab wa nasha'at maʿa awlādihim wa ta'addabat bi ādābihim*).[46] When applied to scholars like Abū Ḥanīfa, the term signalled more than simply an ethnic category. The *muwalladūn* denoted an ethnic category of scholars of dubious confessional and social status (*abnā' sabāyā al-umam*).[47] These were scholars who, in the view of proto-Sunni traditionalists, had been advocates of deviant and heretical views. In support of these views they would sometimes adduce reports to the effect that the Arabs would perish on encountering the sons of Persian women.[48]

ʿAbd Allāh b. Ḥanbal's corpus, as we observed in Chapter 3, is replete with excoriating discourses of heresy against Abū Ḥanīfa. Among other things, his *Kitāb al-ʿIlal wa maʿrifat al-rijāl* purports to reproduce many assessments of individuals that ʿAbd Allāh heard from his father, Aḥmad b. Ḥanbal, and Yaḥyā b. Maʿīn. In one report he recalls that his father said that Ibn ʿUyayna once remarked: 'There are

[45] Al-Ṣaymarī, *Akhbār Abī Ḥanīfa*, 75–6.
[46] Ibn Manẓūr, *Lisān al-ʿArab*, 3: 469–70 (Dār Ṣādir edn.). On the *muwalladūn* see also Fierro, *ʿAbd al-Rahman III*, 30–1; Guzman, 'Ethnic Groups and Social Classes'.
[47] De Wet, *Preaching Bondage* would describe this as doulogy: *doulos* (slave) and *logos* (discourse), a discourse of slavery.
[48] See Ibn Abī Shayba, *al-Muṣannaf*, 21: 264.

three individuals whose speculative jurisprudence is shocking: In Basra, ʿUthmān al-Battī; in Medina, Rabīʿat al-Raʾy; and in Kufa, Abū Ḥanīfa.' After hearing this from his father, ʿAbd Allāh relates that he thought his father added the following interpretation: 'The point Ibn ʿUyayna was making was that these three individuals were sons of foreign captive slave women.'[49] The idea that heresy and religious deviance were related to the penetration of *muwalladūn* actually precedes ʿAbd Allāh b. Ḥanbal. One of the earliest extant literary texts in early Islamic history exhibits an awareness of this concept. Ḍirār b. ʿAmr's *Kitāb al-Taḥrīsh* opens with an attempt to explain the origins of disagreement and sectarianism in early Islamic history. In one passage he remarks that the religious community of Muslims will not perish until the sons of foreigners and the *muwalladūn* become a significant demographic, and they shall be a source of their misguidance.[50]

Al-Khaṭīb al-Baghdādī, who took it upon himself to gather as many vilifications of Abū Ḥanīfa as he could find in ninth–tenth century sources, begins his section on the condemnation by scholars of Abū Ḥanīfa with three reports. Each report combines ethno-racial reasoning and discourses of heresy to explain Abū Ḥanīfa's religious deviancy, and each report identifies him as a *muwallad*:

> Abū Nuʿaym al-Ḥāfiẓ < Muḥammad b. al-Ḥasan al-Ṣawwāf < Bishr b. Mūsā < al-Ḥumaydī < Sufyān < Hishām b. ʿUrwa < my father said: the religion of the Children of Israel remained upright until there appeared among them the *muwalladūn*, the sons of captive slave women from foreign peoples. They spread the practice of speculative opinion among the Children of Israel, which led them to go astray and caused others to deviate. Sufyān said: 'Likewise, the religion of the people remained upright until this was transformed by Abū Ḥanīfa in Kufa, al-Battī in Basra, and Rabīʿa in Medina. We did some digging around only to discover that these three individuals were descendants of captive slave women from foreign peoples.'[51]

[49] ʿAbd Allāh b. Aḥmad b. Ḥanbal, *Kitāb al-ʿIlal wa maʿrifat al-rijāl ʿan Yaḥyā b. Maʿīn*, ed. Waṣī Allāh b. Muḥammad ʿAbbās (Riyadh: Dār al-Khānī, 2001), 3: 156 (*wa rubbamā qāla Abī qāla: thalāthat awlād sabāyā al-umam. Hādhā maʿnāhu*). Also found in Abū Zurʿa al-Dimashqī, *Tārīkh*, 2: 508.

[50] Ḍirār b. ʿAmr, *Kitāb al-Taḥrīsh*, 39. In my opinion, the editors have misread the manuscript, or the manuscript contains a scribal error: the editors have *mā halakat umma ḥattā yakthura fīhā anbāʾ al-umam wa al-muwalladūn min ghayr rushdihim* where I would read *mā halakat umma ḥattā yakthura fīhā abnāʾ al-umam wa al-muwalladūn min ghayr rushdihim*. Likewise, their suggestion in the footnote for reading *anbāʾ al-umam for abnāʾ al-ithm* seems incorrect.

[51] Al-Khaṭīb al-Baghdādī, *Tārīkh Baghdād*, 15: 543. Note that this *isnād* places Aḥmad b. Ḥanbal's nephew and al-Ḥumaydī together.

Ibn Rizziq < ʿUthmān b. Aḥmad al-Daqqāq < Ḥanbal b. Isḥāq < al-Ḥumaydī said: I heard Sufyān say: 'Our religion remained on the right path until Abū Ḥanīfa emerged in Kufa, Rabīʿa in Medina, and al-Battī in Basra.' He said: Sufyān then turned to me and said: 'As for your province, it was based on the religious teachings of ʿAʾṭā.' Then Sufyān said: 'We thought about this issue for some time and we came to the conclusion that it was exactly as Hishām b. ʿUrwa had said on the authority of his father: the religion of the Children of Israel remained upright until there appeared among them the *muwalladūn*, the sons of captive slave women from foreign peoples. They spread the practice of speculative opinion among the Children of Israel, which led them to go astray and caused others to deviate.' Sufyān said: 'We investigated this and discovered that Rabīʿa was the son of a female slave captive, al-Battī was the son of a female slave captive, and Abū Ḥanīfa was the son of a female slave captive. We realised then that this was exactly how it happened with the Jews.'[52]

Al-Qāḍī Abū al-Ḥasan b. al-Ḥusayn b. Rāmīn al-Istirābādhī < Abū al-Ḥasan Aḥmad b. Jaʿfar b. Abī Tawba al-Ṣūfī in Shīrāz < ʿAlī b. al-Ḥusayn b. Maʿdān < Abū ʿAmmār al-Ḥusayn b. Ḥurayth < al-Ḥumaydī < Sufyān b. ʿUyayna: we thought among ourselves and came to the realisation that the first people who altered this [upright] state of affairs (*awwal man baddala hādhā al-sha'n*) were Abū Ḥanīfa in Kufa, al-Battī in Basra, and Rabīʿa in Medina. We investigated this and discovered that they were *muwallad*s of foreign female slave captives (*muwalladī sabāyā al-umam*). Al-Barqānī < Muḥammad b. ʿAbd Allāh b. Khamīrawayh al-Harawī < al-Ḥusayn b. Idrīs < Ibn ʿAmmār < Sufyān b. ʿUyayna said: we pondered over this phrase [*muwalladī sabāyā al-umam*] in that ḥadīth [concerning the Children of Israel and speculative jurisprudence], when it finally struck us who they were: Abū Ḥanīfa in Kufa, ʿUthmān al-Battī in Basra, and Rabīʿat al-Ra'y in Medina.[53]

What we have here is copious evidence for how a number of proto-Sunni traditionalists interpreted the birth of heresy and religious deviance in medieval Islam. Ethno-racial forms of reasoning were a critical prism through which conceptions of orthodoxy and discourses of heresy developed. The spread of heretical deviants and movements in the provinces of the early Islamic empire is explained in terms of the penetration of foreigners into the ranks of the Muslim community. These were not just any foreigners. They were, in the view of proto-Sunni traditionalists, products of servile social and religious circumstances, born in the midst of war, conquest, slavery, and concubinage. In disparaging Abū Ḥanīfa (and others), proto-Sunni traditionalists marshalled and circulated these ethno-racial accounts. Ethno-racial reasoning became an indispensable component of discourses of heresy against Abū Ḥanīfa.

[52] Al-Khaṭīb al-Baghdādī, *Tārīkh Baghdād*, 15: 543.
[53] Al-Khaṭīb al-Baghdādī, *Tārīkh Baghdād*, 15: 543.

## 5.4 Ethnogenesis, Orthodoxy, and Orthopraxy in Transoxiana

This section assesses the impact that regional circumstances, such as language and ethnicity, had on constructions of Abū Ḥanīfa's religious deviancy. It takes as its starting point a particular thread of proto-Sunni traditionalist attacks on Abū Ḥanīfa. Al-Bukhārī is the protagonist who best exemplifies this particular strain of proto-Sunni traditionalism. His life, career, and writings highlight why ethnogenesis, language, and the performance of the ritual prayer featured in proto-Sunni traditionalist constructions of orthodoxy and heresy with respect to Abū Ḥanīfa. In this section I argue that al-Bukhārī's criticisms of Abū Ḥanīfa cannot be divorced from certain anxieties arising out of wider social and religious developments in the eighth and ninth centuries, chief among them being: (i) conversion and the spread of Islam in Khurāsān and Transoxiana; (ii) the diffusion of proto-Ḥanafism in these same regions; (iii) the process of ethnogenesis; and (iv) debates concerning prayer and language.

The third ethno-racial label that appears in discourses of heresy against Abū Ḥanīfa is the term *ʿajam*. It was used in early Islamic literature to denote Persians and, when speaking of episodes in the first century, non-Muslim Persians.[54] We have already observed that opponents of Abū Ḥanīfa relied on the art of genealogy to discredit him as a foreigner from the land of Persia.[55] The case of al-Bukhārī establishes a wider spectrum of strategies for how and why ethnogenesis impacted the formation of orthodoxy and heresy in early Islam.

The first and most obvious context for al-Bukhārī's castigation of Abū Ḥanīfa's association with the *ʿajam* is the Shuʿūbiyya controversy. The phenomenon of Shuʿūbism refers to a concerted effort by some writers during the eighth–twelfth centuries to accentuate the prestige of Persians and minimise the distinction of Arabs. Beyond this basic feature of Shuʿūbism it is difficult to speak of a specific programme or movement, and we should probably regard the controversy as reflecting a range of sentiments emerging out the changing social, economic, professional, and religious circumstances of both Arab and non-Arab Persian Muslims in the eighth and ninth centuries. On the other hand, regarding Shuʿūbism as no more than a literary movement does not do justice to the

[54] On the *ʿajam* see E. C. Bosworth, s.v. '*ʿAjam*', *Encyclopaedia Iranica*, 1.7: 700–701; Goldziher, *Muslim Studies*, 1: 40–4, 137; Savant, *The New Muslims of Post-Conquest Iran*, 79–81.

[55] In Chapters 8 (*Manāqib*) and 9 (*Masānīd*) of this study we shall see how defenders of Abū Ḥanīfa used his Persian ethnicity and genealogy to establish his incontrovertible orthodoxy.

chronological consanguinity between history and literature.[56] The eighth and ninth centuries saw the *mawālī* rise to positions of high social standing and importance. The middle of the eighth century was the moment when Arabs were dropped from the registry of state pensions.[57] In the seventh and eighth centuries, non-Arabs were instrumental in the development of the nascent state's fledgling bureaucracy, especially in the light of the fact that the Arabicisation of the administration was not complete until the middle of the eighth century.[58] The Arabicisation of the language of administration occurred in provinces at different times in the mid- to late eighth century. It must have affected the short-term economic and social status of non-Arabs employed by the state. All this is to say that the literature that speaks of the merits of the Shuʿūbiyya was in some part a reflection of the perceived grievances of different ethnic communities.

In other areas of society, people of Persian stock were making substantial contributions to disciplines unhindered by the ebb and flow of state administration. Persian scholars were at the forefront of the disciplines of philology (al-Sibawayh (d. *c.* 177/793)), ḥadīth (Isḥāq b. Rāhawayh), belles-lettres (Ibn Qutayba and Abū al-Faraj al-Iṣfahānī), and history (al-Ṭabarī (d. 310/923) and al-Dīnawārī (d. *c.* 281/894)). Their regional and ethnic associations did not, however, determine where they situated themselves during the Shuʿūbiyya controversy. In fact, as Islamicists well know, one of the peculiar features of tracts responding to the Shuʿūbiyya is that their authors were scarcely Arabs themselves. These scholars had Persian genealogies, but they were not moved to marshal arguments for the cultural superiority of Persians over Arabs.[59] Their reluctance to do so is probably due to more than one factor. For one thing, many of these

[56] In an otherwise perceptive article, Mottahedeh pays little attention to historical developments and their surviving echo in literature. See Mottahedeh, 'The Shuʿūbiyyah Controversy'; Lecomte, *Ibn Qutayba*, xiii; Goldziher, *Muslim Studies*, 1: 98–198; Gibb, 'The Social Significance of the Shuubiya'.

[57] In some instances in Khurāsān, *mawālī* soldiers were being paid the same as Arab soldiers: see Ibn al-Aʿtham al-Kūfī, *Kitāb al-Futūḥ*, 6: 146. Arabs were also being dropped from the *dīwān al-ʿaṭāʾ*: see Abū ʿUmar Muḥammad b. Yūsuf al-Kindī, *Kitāb al-Wulāt wa kitāb al-quḍāt [The Governors and Judges of Egypt]*, ed. Rhuvon Guest (Leiden: Brill, 1912), 193–4; Sharon, *Black Banners*, 102 n. 14, 272–6.

[58] For these centuries 'non-Arab' could refer to the employment of non-Muslims. Both the ethnic and confessional hybridity of the early Islamic state is treated in Hoyland, *In God's Path*, esp. 209–18; Borrut and Donner (eds.), *Christians and Others in the Umayyad State*; Yarbrough, *Friends of the Emir*, though this work treats attitudes to and theories of Muslim employment as opposed to its practice under the Umayyads and ʿAbbāsids. For the Arabicisation of the state administration see al-Jahshiyārī, *Kitāb al-Wuzarāʾ wa al-kuttāb*, ed. Muṣṭafā Saqqā et al. (Cairo: Maktabat al-Bābī al-Ḥalabī, 1938), 38, 67. Abbott, *The Qurrah Papyri*, 11–12 has a useful discussion of this issue.

[59] Though Pourshariati, 'The Akhbār al-ṭiwāl', argues that al-Dīnawārī's history represents a layer of Shuʿūbī historical writing. See also Savant, *The New Muslims of Post-Conquest Iran*, 148–56 for Persian themes in al-Dīnawārī's history.

scholars were aware of the fact that a scholar's achievements could be recognised irrespective of his cultural ancestry. For many scholars this was proof of the insignificance of one's ethnic background. Alternatively, Mottahedeh has argued, Persian critics of the Shuʿūbiyya sought to reassert the prestige of noble genealogies, both Arab and non-Arab, whilst assimilating this view within a story of the success of Islam as a religion. This is why, for example, both al-Jāḥiẓ and Ibn Qutayba remained critical of appeals to pre-Islamic Persian nobilities when employed as reproaches against Islam.[60]

Al-Bukhārī's ancestral pedigree was, in many respects, representative of legal and ḥadīth scholars of his day. He was born in Bukhārā in 194/810 during a tumultuous period in the city's history. A few decades earlier Bukhārā had been among one of the many provincial cities of Khurāsān and Transoxiana swept away by a succession of nativist revolts.[61] Al-Bukhārī's grandfather had converted to Islam from Zoroastrianism. As a *mawlā*, he took the name of his Arab patron, Yamān al-Juʿfī, the governor of Bukhārā.[62] His father, Ismāʿīl b. Ibrāhīm b. Mughīra, turns up in some biographical dictionaries as a ḥadīth scholar.[63] The family of al-Bukhārī was wealthy. Modern scholars, basing themselves on information from later historians such as al-Dhahabī and Ibn Ḥajar al-ʿAsqalānī, describe al-Bukhārī's family as *dihqān*s, but the primary sources speak mainly of wealth derived from mercantile activities.[64] It was from his

[60] Mottahedeh, 'The Shuʿūbiyyah Controversy', 178–80.

[61] See Crone, *The Nativist Prophets*; Karev, *Samarqand et le Sughd* is the definitive account of Transoxiana's history from the beginning of the conquests to the tenth century.

[62] For modern biographies of al-Bukhārī see Brown, *The Canonization*, 65–9; Abdul-Jabbar, *Bukharī*, 9–23; Sezgin, *Buhârî'nin Kaynakları*, 210. However, the most careful and detailed reconstruction of al-Bukhārī's life and career has been provided by Melchert, 'Bukhārī and his *Ṣaḥīḥ*', 426–31. Melchert's article refers to the most relevant primary and modern sources (in Arabic and European languages). One important source for al-Bukhārī that Melchert does not mention is Ghunjār's *History*. For this reason, I discussed this work in some detail in Chapter 1. Another early and now partially lost source for al-Bukhārī's biography was Abū Aḥmad al-Ḥākim's *Kitāb al-Asāmī*. The work is incomplete and al-Bukhārī's biography seems to be missing from the four-volume work. It must have contained an entry on al-Bukhārī, not least because al-Dhahabī cites the work in his biography of al-Bukhārī in al-Dhahabī, *Tārīkh al-Islām*, 19: 258–9. For the earliest extant biographies see the following: Ibn Abī Ḥātim, *al-Jarḥ*, 4.1: 182–3; Ibn ʿAdī, *al-Kāmil*, 1: 226–7; Ibn ʿAdī, *Asāmī man rawā ʿanhum*, 47–63; al-Khaṭīb al-Baghdādī, *Tārīkh Baghdād*, 2: 322–59; al-Khalīlī, *al-Irshād*, 958–66 (Riyadh edn.); al-ʿAbbādī, *Kitāb Ṭabaqāt al-fuqahāʾ*, 53–4.

[63] Ibn Ḥibbān, *Kitāb al-Thiqāt*, 8: 98; al-Bukhārī, *al-Tārīkh al-kabīr*, 1.1: 342–3; Ibn Ḥajar al-ʿAsqalānī, *Tahdhīb al-tahdhīb*, 1: 140 (Mu'assasat al-Risāla edn.) = *Tahdhīb al-tahdhīb*, 1: 274–5 (Hyderabad edn.).

[64] Brown, *The Canonization*, 65–6 describes the Bukhārīs as '*dehqān*s', but his source (Ibn ʿAdī al-Jurjānī) mentions neither the term nor the ownership of estates and properties. Brown's source is Ibn ʿAdī, *Asāmī man rawā ʿanhum Muḥammad b. Ismāʿīl al-Bukhārī min mashāyikhihi alladhīna dhakarahum fī jāmiʿihi al-ṣaḥīḥ*, ed.

father's inheritance that al-Bukhārī is said to have come into significant wealth.[65] Much of the detailed biographical information we have for al-Bukhārī's personal life comes from Ghunjār's (d. 412/1021) lost history of Bukhārā. Excerpts of this work survive in a number of later Muslim sources. Taken together, these reports suggest that Ghunjār's history was a key source for al-Bukhārī's life and career.[66]

It is also Ghunjār's work that preserves a number of contemporary accounts about al-Bukhārī from the latter's companion and secretary, Muḥammad b. Abī Ḥātim al-Warrāq. These biographical accounts combine themes of economic prosperity, austerity, and piety in al-Bukhārī's

Badr b. Muḥammad al-ʿAmmāsh (Medina: Dār al-Bukhārī, 1994–5), 59= Beirut edn. 47–8. See al-Dhahabī, *Tārīkh al-Islām*, 19: 238–74 for the entry on al-Bukhārī, whilst 263–4 speaks of al-Bukhārī's owning an estate (*qiṭʿat al-arḍ*) that brought in a yearly income of 700 dirhams. On *dihqāns* as tax collectors and landowners see Morony, *Iraq after the Muslim Conquest*, 200–206; Paul, 'Where did the Dihqāns go?'; Zakeri, *Sāsānid Soldiers in Early Muslim Society*, 101–11, 203–64; Tafazzoli, *Sasanian Society*, 38–53.

65 Ibn Ḥajar al-ʿAsqalānī, *Taghlīq al-taʿlīq*, 5: 394–5.

66 Ibn Ḥajar al-ʿAsqalānī, *Taghlīq al-taʿlīq*, 5: 395. On Ghunjār's lost history see Sezgin, *GAS*, 1: 353; al-Sakhāwī, *al-Iʿlān*, 239–40, who possessed an abridgement by al-Silafī of Ghunjār's *Dhayl* = Rosenthal, *A History of Muslim Historiography*, 461; al-Khaṭīb al-Baghdādī, *Tārīkh Baghdād*, 11: 206; Ibn al-Ṣalāḥ al-Shahrazūrī, *ʿUlūm al-ḥadīth*, ed. Nūr al-Dīn ʿItr (Beirut: Dār al-Fikr, 1986), 340 (*wa Ghunjār muta'akhkhir wa huwa Abū ʿAbd Allāh Muḥammad b. Aḥmad al-Bukhārī al-Ḥāfiẓ ṣāḥib Tārīkh Bukhārā*); Kâtip Çelebi, *Lexicon bibliographicum et encyclopaedicum [Kashf al-ẓunūn ʿan asāmī al-kutub wa al-funūn]*, ed. and trans. Gustav Flügel (Leipzig: Oriental Translation Fund of Great Britain and Ireland, 1835–58), 2: 116–17; Ibn Bashkuwāl, *al-Ṣila fī tārīkh a'immat al-Andalus wa ʿulamā'ihim wa muḥaddithīhim wa fuqahā'ihim wa udabā'ihim*, ed. Bashshār ʿAwwād Maʿrūf (Beirut: Dār al-Gharb al-Islāmī, 2010), 1: 283 (s.v. 'Saʿīd b. Naṣr b. ʿUmar b. Khalfūn'); Ibn Ḥajar, *Lisān al-Mīzān*, 4: 258–9 (Hyderabad edn.) (s.v. 'ʿAlī b. Muḥammad Abū Aḥmad al-Ḥanīnī al-Marwadhī') = Ibn Ḥajar, *Lisān al-Mīzān*, 6: 22–3 (Abū Ghudda edn.) (s.v. 'ʿAlī b. Muḥammad Abū Aḥmad al-Ḥabībī al-Marwadhī'); Ibn Ḥajar, *Taghlīq al-taʿlīq*, 5: 388; al-Subkī, *Ṭabaqāt al-Shāfiʿiyya al-kubrā*, 2: 216; al-Sakhāwī, *al-Ḍaw' al-lāmiʿ li ahl al-qarn al-tāsiʿ* (Beirut: Dār al-Jīl, 1992), 9: 119; al-Samʿānī, *al-Ansāb*, 9: 177–8, 363 (Maktabat Ibn Taymiyya edn.) = al-Samʿānī, *al-Ansāb*, 1: 108, 217, 4: 311–12 (Dār al-Jinān edn.); Ibn ʿImād, *Shadharāt al-dhahab*, 5: 173 speaks of a continuation (*dhayl*) of al-Ghunjār's *Tārīkh Bukhāra* by Ibn Nāṣir al-Dīn Abū Ḥāmid Aḥmad b. Muḥammad b. Aḥīd b. ʿAbd Allāh b. Māmā al-Iṣfahānī (d. 436/1045); Ibn al-Athīr, *al-Lubāb*, 3: 156 for his *tarjama*, but without any mention of his *Dhayl*; al-Dhahabī, *Siyar*, 17: 580, though, unlike al-Samʿānī, al-Dhahabī had no direct access to the *Dhayl*; Ziriklī, *al-Aʿlām*, 1: 213; Ziriklī, *al-Aʿlām*, 15th edn. (Beirut: Dār al-ʿIlm li al-Malāyīn 2002) (s.v. 'Ibn Māmā'); Ismāʿīl Pāshā al-Baghdādī, *Hadiyyat al-ʿārifīn*, 1: 74 (s.v. 'Ibn Māmā'); al-Dhahabī, *Kitāb Tadhkirat al-ḥuffāẓ*, 3: 1117–18; al-Ṣafadī, *Kitāb al-Wāfī bi al-wafāyāt*, ed. H. Ritter et al. (Leipzig, Istanbul, and Beirut: German Oriental Institute, 1962–97), 7: 361 (s.v. 'al-Ḥāfiẓ al-Māmā'ī, Aḥmad b. Muḥammad b. Aḥīd') = al-Ṣafadī, *Kitāb al-Wāfī bi al-wafāyāt*, 7: 236 (Dār al-Iḥyā' al-Turāth al-ʿArabī edn.) (s.v. 'al-Ḥāfiẓ al-Māmā'ī, Aḥmad b. Muḥammad b. Aḥīd'); Yāqūt had access to Ibn Māmā's work, for which see Yāqūt b. ʿAbd Allāh al-Ḥamawī, *Muʿjam al-udabā'*, 5: 2349 (Dār al-Gharb al-Islāmī edn.) = *The irshād al-arīb ilā maʿrifat al-adīb: or Dictionary of Learned Men of Yāqūt*, ed. D. S. Margoliouth, 2nd edn. (London: Luzac, 1923–31), 6: 329.

life. One report from al-Warrāq narrates the following from al-Bukhārī: 'I departed to go and see Ādam b. Abī Iyās, my money having been delayed (*ta'akhkharat nafaqatī*), so I was reduced to eating weeds from the ground (*ḥashīsh al-arḍ*). On the third day, a man unknown to me came by and gifted me a purse with money inside it.' Another report tells us that al-Warrāq heard al-Bukhārī say: 'I would receive five hundred dirhams every month, which I would spend in the way of seeking knowledge, for what is with God is greater and more lasting.'[67]

Al-Bukhārī's relationship with Abū Ḥanīfa has been addressed in detail in Chapter 1. The central concern here is to highlight another aspect of al-Bukhārī's opposition to Abū Ḥanīfa and proto-Ḥanafism in the context of Khurāsān and Transoxiana's social history. Scholars such as al-Bukhārī lived in societies in which religious, ethnic, social, ancestral, and political loyalties were tugging at one another. These two provinces, perhaps more than any other region of the Islamicate world, became the central scenes for the playing out of these tensions. A concatenation of rebellions in Khurāsān in the late eighth–ninth centuries saw rebels mobilise ethnic (what Crone calls Iranian nativism), social, ancestral, and religious sentiments against the state's provincial authorities, in order to break away from the empire. This was a delicate moment in the religious and cultural history of the period.

This social, political, and religious discontent was matched by al-Bukhārī's grievances against certain religious trends in proto-Sunnism. Al-Bukhārī's vitriolic condemnation of Abū Ḥanīfa encapsulates these discontents by pointing to the conversion and spread of Islam, the spread of proto-Ḥanafism, the process of ethnogenesis, and disputes over core aspects of religious life (prayer and liturgical languages).

Our sources are not always so generous in revealing the anxieties that such historical events engendered, but al-Bukhārī's combining of religion, ritual, ethnicity, language, orthodoxy, and heresy in an otherwise quotidian treatise on Islamic ritual bring us closer to the climate of his society. These are the first lines of al-Bukhārī's book regarding the performance of the ritual prayer and the obligation, according to al-Bukhārī, that one raise one's hand during the *takbīrāt*:[68]

[67] Ibn Ḥajar, *Taghlīq al-ta'līq*, 5: 395; al-Dhahabī, *Tārīkh al-Islām*, 19: 236, with slightly different wording.

[68] Al-Bukhārī, *Kitāb Raf' al-yadayn fī al-ṣalāt*, ed. Badī' al-Dīn al-Rāshidī (Beirut: Dār Ibn Ḥazm, 1996), 17–20 (*al-radd 'alā man ankara raf' al-aydi fī al-ṣalāt 'inda al-rukū' wa idhā rafa'a ra'suhu min al-rukū', wa abhama 'alā al-'ajam fī dhālika takallufan limā lā ya'nīhi fīmā thabata 'an rasūl Allāh min fi'lihi wa qawlihi wa min fi'l aṣḥābihi wa riwāyatihi ka dhālika, thumma fi'l al-tābi'īn wa iqtidā' al-salaf bihim fī ṣiḥḥat al-akhbār ba'ḍ al-thiqa 'an al-thiqa min al-khalaf al-'udūl raḥimahum Allāh ta'ālā wa anjaza lahum mā wa'adahum 'alā ḍaghīnat ṣadrihi wa ḥajarat qalbihi nifāran 'an sunan rasūl Allāh mustaḥiqqan/mustakhiffan*

[This book is] A refutation of him who rejected raising the hands in the ritual prayer before bowing and upon raising his head after the cycle of prostration. He confused the non-Arabs on this issue out of his endeavour to disregard utterly that which was established from the Messenger of God of his actions and sayings; and he had the same disregard for that which was established from the actions of his Companions and their narrations; and then the generation of the Successors and the adherence of the pious ancestors to them with respect to narrations that had been authenticated, transmitted from one reliable authority to another from the upright generation that came after, may God be pleased with them all and may He grant them what He has promised them. [And this was all done] out of the spitefulness of his breast, the rancour of his heart, departing from the practices of the Messenger of God, showing contempt for what he transmitted out of his arrogance and enmity for its people [*ahl al-sunan*], because heresy had contaminated his flesh, bones, and mind and made him delight in the non-Arabs' misguided celebration of him.

Al-Bukhārī is not merely asserting his opposition to a contrary legal position. He frames his opposition in the context of one notable individual's enterprise to undermine the ḥadīth, the Sunna, the probity of the Companions, and the legal opinions of the Successors. In short, al-Bukhārī is articulating his conviction that Abū Ḥanīfa's jurisprudence represents the extreme opposite of the doctrines and methods that underpinned proto-Sunni traditionalism. For al-Bukhārī this represents nothing short of heretical innovation which he then proceeds to depict graphically as having permeated the very flesh and bones of Abū Ḥanīfa. But it is a heresy, he argues, that became widespread because of Abū Ḥanīfa's popularity among the *ʿajam*. Orthopraxy, orthodoxy, and ethnic forms of reasoning come together in this compact criticism of Abū Ḥanīfa.

In this report al-Bukhārī pays Abū Ḥanīfa the courtesy of not naming him directly. However, the references to Abū Ḥanīfa later in the same work indicate who the subject of al-Bukhārī's tirade is. Right before naming Abū Ḥanīfa, al-Bukhārī returns to the very contentious themes he raised at the outset of his book. He refers to Wakīʿ b. Jarrāḥ's definition of orthodoxy and heresy: 'Whoever studies ḥadīth as they have come down to us, he is a man of orthodoxy; but whoever studies ḥadīth in order to strengthen his whims, he is a man of heresy.'[69] Al-Bukhārī then adds his own explanation: 'He means by this that it is imperative that

*limā yaḥmiluhu istikbāran wa ʿadāwatan li ahlihā li shawb al-bidʿat laḥmihi wa ʿidhāmihi wa mukhkhihi wa anasathu bi iḥtifāl al-ʿajam ḥawlahu ightirāran*).

[69] Al-Bukhārī, *Kitāb Rafʿ al-yadayn*, 105 (*man ṭalaba al-ḥadīth kamā jā'a fa huwa ṣāḥib sunna, wa man ṭalaba al-ḥadīth li yuqawwiya hawāhu fa huwa ṣāḥib bidʿa*). Note that I translate *ṣāḥib sunna* as a man of orthodoxy because it contrasted to *ṣāḥib bidʿa* (a man of heresy).

a person adjust his opinion in accordance with the ḥadīth of the Prophet, and when the ḥadīth is confirmed he does not seek to weaken it with defects nor to authenticate it in order to strengthen his whims.' This, al-Bukhārī continues, is articulated in the ḥadīth of the Prophet: 'None of you believes until his views are in accordance with what I have come with.'[70] In order to illustrate the disparity between orthodoxy and heresy, al-Bukhārī cites an incident involving Abū Ḥanīfa which by the ninth century had become widespread:[71]

IBN AL-MUBĀRAK: I was praying next to al-Nuʿmān [b. Thābit] and I raised my hands.

ABŪ ḤANĪfa [after the prayer had finished, as another source tells us]: Did you not fear that you would fly?

IBN AL-MUBĀRAK: If I did not fly away the first time I raised my hands at the opening *takbīr* of prayer, why would I fly away the second time?

Al-Bukhārī expresses his delight at this quip of Ibn al-Mubārak's by adding Wakīʿ's acknowledgement of Ibn al-Mubārak's condign response: 'God bless Ibn al-Mubārak. He was someone of quick wit.'[72]

Al-Bukhārī's account invites us into competing visions of proto-Sunni orthodoxy. For learned agents of orthodoxy such as al-Bukhārī, certain practices, however insignificant and mundane they may appear to modern readers, betrayed one's commitment to particular visions of orthodoxy. Quick wit and humour could be deployed to underscore the triumph of one conception of orthodoxy over another. The next report has Ibn ʿUmar's description of the Prophet's performance of the ritual prayer: 'I saw that when the Messenger of God stood for the start of prayer he raised his two hands until they would be placed identically by his shoulders, and then he would pronounce the *takbīr*; and he would do this when he would raise his head after the cycle of prostration and also when he would say *samiʿa Allāh li man ḥamidahu*, but he would not raise [his hands] after raising his head from the prostration of the forehead [to the sitting position].'[73] This is what al-Bukhārī appears to have in mind when he refers at the start of his book in such belligerent a tone to Abū Ḥanīfa's alleged contempt for transmissions concerning the Prophet's

[70] Al-Bukhārī, *Kitāb Rafʿ al-yadayn*, 105–6 (*lā yu'min aḥadukum ḥattā yakūna hawāhu tabaʿan limā ji'tu bihi*).

[71] Al-Bukhārī, *Kitāb Rafʿ al-yadayn*, 107. See, e.g., Ibn Qutayba, *Ta'wīl mukhtalif al-ḥadīth* (Zakī al-Kurdī edn.), 66–7 = ed. Muḥammad ʿAbd al-Raḥīm (Beirut: Dār al-Fikr, 1995), 59 = al-Sinnārī edn., 106–7 = *Le traité*, 66; al-Khaṭīb al-Baghdādī, *Tārīkh Baghdād*, 15: 535. The *isnād* is Isḥāq b. Rāhawayh < Wakīʿ b. al-Jarrāḥ; ʿAbd Allāh b. Aḥmad b. Ḥanbal, *Kitāb al-Sunna*, 1: 276; Ibn Ḥibbān, *Kitāb al-Thiqāt*, 8: 45.

[72] Al-Bukhārī, *Kitāb Rafʿ al-yadayn*, 107 (*kāna ḥāḍir al-jawāb*).

[73] Al-Bukhārī, *Kitāb Rafʿ al-yadayn*, 108–9.

actions and sayings. The playful barb that Abū Ḥanīfa is reported to have delivered to Ibn al-Mubārak is, in al-Bukhārī's view, an attack on the Prophet's performance of the ritual prayer. This is a carefully crafted argument designed to discredit Abū Ḥanīfa's claim to orthodoxy.

The correct performance of the ritual prayer was a matter of utmost importance for early Muslims.[74] Early Islamic juridical and ḥadīth works are replete with discussions seeking to clarify different aspects of the ritual prayer. The ambiguity regarding the very first ritual act of the prayer was a disturbing fact for some religious scholars, and certainly for al-Bukhārī. Al-Bukhārī's treatise is an attempt to establish, beyond any doubt, the validity of the raising of the two hands at the point of bowing (*rukūʿ*) and upon raising one's head after the bowing (*idhā arāda an yarkaʿa wa idhā rafaʿa ra'sahu ʿmin al-rukūʿ*).[75] For this purpose, he gathers a copious amount of narrations. It is worth remembering that ninth-century society in Khurāsān and Transoxiana was still largely non-Muslim. Not only was proto-Sunni orthopraxy not uniform, but these Muslim communities were in the process of consolidating their religious identities, beliefs, and practices. The wave of ninth-century conversion, too, reinforced the urgency and relevance of treatises on elementary features of the ritual prayer. We must reckon with the very likely possibility that al-Bukhārī was writing for an eager and receptive audience. This also puts into perspective the acrimony that al-Bukhārī expresses for Abū Ḥanīfa and other scholars who believed that the raising of the two hands was not to be performed.

[74] On the fluidity of the ritual prayer see Goldziher, *Muslim Studies*, 2: ch. 2, esp. 39–40; a response to Goldziher's hypotheses about the ritual prayer in al-Azami, *On Schacht*, 12–15. For more on the fluidity of the ritual prayer see Sijpesteijn, 'A Ḥadīth Fragment on Papyrus'. El Shamsy, 'Debates on Prayer', has criticised Sijpesteijn's interpretation of the papyrus. There is one turn of phrase in Sijpesteijn's article that seems far-fetched based on the nature and content of the papyrus. She writes that ḥadīth fragments 'reflect an environment in which believers were unsure about how to execute the most basic religious obligations either because these were still being discussed, or because they were new to the religion. Either explanation fits of course the second-third/eighth-ninth-century environment of our papyrus very well.' El Shamsy's response focuses mainly on this sentence. I agree with El Shamsy that Sijpesteijn's speculation on the basis of this fragment is unwarranted, but one should note that Sijpesteijn's conclusion seems to favour a different reading, namely, that the papyrus 'is an informal recording of some ḥadīths for personal or educational use'. So, whilst El Shamsy's criticisms seem sound, it should not surprise us that in some provinces such as Khurāsān and Transoxiana aspects of the ritual prayer were being debated and indeed practised differently in the eighth century. Haider, *The Origins of the Shīʿa*, 57–94, 95–137, has argued that differences in the ritual prayer (the *basmala* and *qunūt* prayer) played a decisive role in the formation of sectarian identity in the eighth century. In the case of the Imāmīs, these differences point to an independent sectarian identity, but less so in the case of the Zaydīs.

[75] Al-Bukhārī, *Kitāb Rafʿ al-yadayn*, 22.

Al-Bukhārī's assessment of Abū Ḥanīfa must be placed alongside other circumstances specific to Khurāsān and Transoxiana's history. This anxiety over the influence of Abū Ḥanīfa in the eastern provinces of the early Islamic empire is borne out by what little early evidence we have for the spread of proto-Ḥanafism in the eighth and ninth centuries. This is already attested to in the earliest Ḥanafī biographical dictionary. Ibn Abī al-ʿAwwām al-Saʿdī's tenth-century work, *Faḍā'il Abī Ḥanīfa wa akhbāruhu wa manāqibuhu*, lists twenty-three Ḥanafīs in the eastern provinces: four from Rayy and nineteen from Khurāsān. This would have been a choice selection only of the most prominent Ḥanafīs.[76] Information from later sources also testifies to the earlier spread of Ḥanafism in the eastern provinces.[77] Both proto-Shāfiʿism and proto-Ḥanbalism appear to have gained some influence in Khurāsān only in the second half of the ninth century,[78] and in the first half of the ninth century various other strands of proto-Sunnism, such as the Karrāmiyya, existed in Khurāsān and Transoxiana.[79] Of these different trends, al-Bukhārī's remarks in *Rafʿ al-yadayn fī al-ṣalāt* are aimed most obviously at followers of Abū Ḥanīfa and possibly at the followers of Ibn Karrām.[80] Though we know very little of Karrāmī legal doctrines, it seems that their *fiqh* sought to accommodate the wave of conversion to Islam in the ninth century.[81] Ibn Ḥibbān describes Ma'mūn b. Aḥmad al-Sulamī as one of the many anti-Christs who seemed to adhere to the Karrāmī *madhhab*.

76 Ibn Abī al-ʿAwwām al-Saʿdī, *Faḍā'il Abī Ḥanīfa*, 212–22. See also Melchert, 'The Spread of Ḥanafism'.

77 Such as in al-Wāʿiẓ, *Faḍā'il-i Balkh*; Melchert, 'The Spread of Ḥanafism'; Madelung, 'The Early Murji'a', 32–9; Madelung, 'The Spread of Māturīdism'; Azad, *Sacred Landscape*, 132–8.

78 For proto-Shāfiʿism see Halm, *Die Ausbreitung*; for proto-Ḥanbalism see the patchy account in Hurvitz, *The Formation of Hanbalism*, 73–83; Madelung, *Religious Trends in Early Islamic Iran*, 22.

79 On the Karrāmiyya see Massignon, *Essai sur les origines*, 260–8; van Ess, *Ungenützte Texte zur Karrāmīya*; Bosworth, 'The Rise of the Karāmiyyah in Khurasan'; Bulliet, *The Patricians of Nishapur*, 62–4; Chabbi, 'Remarques sur le développement historique', 41–5; Melchert, 'Sufis and Competing Movements', 240–2; Madelung, *Religious Trends in Early Islamic Iran*, 39–45.

80 The author of *al-Nutaf* states that Muḥammad b. Karrām's (Abū ʿAbd Allāh in *al-Nutaf*) position was identical to Abū Ḥanīfa's. See al-Sughdī, *al-Nutaf fī al-fatāwā*, ed. Ṣalāḥ al-Dīn al-Nāhī (Baghdad: al-Maktaba al-Waṭaniyya, 1976), 1: 67. On the legal affiliation of the Karrāmiyya see Zysow, 'Two Unrecognised Karrāmī Texts'.

81 Al-Muqaddasī, *Aḥsan al-taqāsīm*, 365; ʿAbd al-Qāhir al-Baghdādī, *al-Farq bayn al-firaq*, ed. Muḥammad Muḥyī al-Dīn ʿAbd al-Ḥamīd (Beirut: al-Maktaba al-ʿAṣriyya, 1995), 223–4; Abū al-Muẓaffar al-Isfarā'īnī, *al-Tabṣīr fī al-dīn*, ed. Muḥammad Zāhid al-Kawtharī (Cairo: al-Maktaba al-Azhariyya li al-Turāth, 1940), 93–9 (most of which is concerned with theological matters), 97–9 (for their legal doctrines); Sayyid Murtaḍā Ibn Dāʿī, *Tabṣirat al-ʿawāmm fī maʿrifat maqālāt al-anām*, ed. ʿAbbās Iqbāl, 2nd edn. (Tehran: Maṭbaʿah-yi Majlis, 1964), 64–74, esp. 67, where he describes Ibn Karrām's legal (and theological) teachings based on purported access to his writings.

Ibn Ḥibbān lists a number of shocking doctrines he was reputed to have espoused and attributed to the Prophet Muḥammad, including that faith necessitated only an utterance; the prayer of anyone who raises their hands during the prayer is void; reciting the *fātiḥa* behind the imam is to fill one's tongue with fire. These are all doctrines that were associated with proto-Ḥanafīs, at least in the eastern provinces. Ibn Ḥibbān also identifies him with more outrageous 'forgeries': 'There will appear a man in my community who will be known as Muḥammad b. Idrīs, and he will cause more harm to my community than Satan. There will appear another man in my community known as Abū Ḥanīfa, and he is the shining light of my community.' For Ibn Ḥibbān, the consanguinity between the Karrāmīs and Ḥanafīs of Khurāsān was both disturbing and tragic.[82] The similarities did not end there. As we shall see, like Abū Ḥanīfa, Abū ʿAbd Allāh Muḥammad b. Karrām (d. 255/869) is reported to have opined in favour of Persian as a liturgical language in Islamic ritual.[83]

It was left to jurists and religious scholars to provide solutions to the changing environment that saw members of diffuse religious communities slowly commit to the new religion of Islam. Khurāsān was a province that saw Arabs acculturate themselves to the region's languages, cultures, and customs. But with the process of conversion gaining ground in the ninth century, the local population, in turn, was coming to terms with the norms and practices of the religion of Islam. This was no straightforward evolution of religious tradition. Conversion was seldom a neat transition from an old confession to a new one, and the wave of nativist revolts in the eighth and ninth centuries was an indication of how idiosyncratic the religious milieu of Khurāsān had become. A central challenge for scholars and jurists was to make the new religion commensurable with the life of the native population.

For this to happen, new converts were faced with the obstacles of liturgy and prayer. At the centre of this new religion was God's word, the Quran, revealed in clear, unadulterated Arabic. The religion's integral rituals were elaborated and performed in Arabic. Above all, the ritual prayer demanded basic literacy in Arabic. How might a Persian-speaking population converting to the religion of Islam deal with this demand for basic familiarity with Arabic?

[82] Ibn Ḥibbān, *Kitāb al-Majrūḥīn*, 3: 45–6 (Beirut edn.).

[83] See al-Sughdī, *al-Nutaf*, 1: 49–50. Abū Ḥafṣ al-Nīshāpūrī, 'Rawnaq al-majālis', MS Berlin 8855, gives no further information about Karrāmī views on this subject. For this work see Ahlwardt, *Die Handschriften-Verzeichnisse*, 7: 733–4; Brockelmann, *GAL*, supp. 2: 285; Hatoum, 'An Eleventh Century Karrāmī Text'; van Ess, *Ungenützte Texte zur Karrāmīya*, 35.

It is difficult to be precise about how much Arabic local Persian-speaking populations would have known. At a first glance, there is no reason to assume that non-Muslim Khurāsānians would have any knowledge of how to read or speak Arabic. Consider, for example, the well-documented tradition of Middle Persian inscriptions on Arab Sasanian coins in the last decade of the seventh century. Our earliest record for the testification of Islam (*shahāda*) is from a Zubayrid coin, where the *shahāda* appears in Pahlavi.[84] Administrative changes at the heart of the early Islamic empire in the eighth century did create new incentives for the proliferation of Arabic among the local population. Al-Jahshiyārī gives us some insight into one very significant administrative reform: the Arabicisation of the *dīwān* from Persian:[85]

> Most of the secretaries of Khurāsān at that time were Magians. The accounts were kept in Persian. So Yūsuf b. ʿUmar, who was then the governor of Iraq in the year 142/759 sent a letter to Naṣr b. Sayyār . . . ordering him not to resort to any of the polytheists in his government and for the purposes of correspondence. The first person to translate writing from Persian into Arabic was Isḥāq b. Ṭulayq, the scribe.

In a separate passage, al-Jahshiyārī gives a slightly different account of the same phenomenon but locates this during the governorship of al-Ḥajjāj. He informs us that the last person to keep accounts in Persian was the head of the *dīwān al-kharāj*, a certain Zādhān Farrūkh.[86] A settled and acculturated generation of Arab migrants, an increase in conversion to Islam, and the professional and economic incentives of Arab literacy all contributed to an increased level of familiarity with Arabic in the eighth and ninth centuries. Above all, the vast scale on which provincial authorities produced written documentation for the province's taxpayers reinforces the view that Arab literacy was expanding.[87]

Still, these facts do not translate into a wider dissemination of the Arabic language among Khurāsān's population. And the ensuing controversy surrounding Abū Ḥanīfa's views on the recitation of the Quran and

[84] Mochiri, 'A Pahlavi Forerunner'; Curiel and Gignoux, 'Un poids arabo-sasanide'; Shaked, 'Mihr the Judge'. The demand for an increasing religious, linguistic, and cultural fusion between the new religion of Islam and Persian-speaking provinces created a certain degree of commensurability. Consider the similarity between the Persian *basmala* and the beginning invocation of Zoroastrian texts, discussed by Gignoux, 'Pour une origine iranienne du bi'smillah'.

[85] Al-Jahshiyārī, *Kitāb al-Wuzarāʾ*, 67.

[86] Al-Jahshiyārī, *Kitāb al-Wuzarāʾ*, 38.

[87] Eighth-century documents from Khurāsān show that local officials communicated with local non-Arab landowning elites in Arabic. See Khan, *Arabic Documents from Early Islamic Khurasan*.

the performance of the ritual prayer in Persian highlights the social and religious gravity of these debates in the ninth century, especially.[88]

Though we shall focus on debates concerning the language of liturgy, it would be careless to ignore the fact that some proto-Sunni traditionalists believed the spread and frequent use of Persian (among Arabic speakers, I presume) to constitute a major social and religious defect. Ibn Abī Shayba's book on proper social and religious conduct, the *Kitāb al-Adab*, explains that speaking in Persian, presumably when one knew how to speak Arabic, was disliked, though he added that some scholars had allowed exceptions to this social and religious norm.[89] Abū Ḥanīfa's views on language, liturgy, and prayer appear on the record in the ninth century. This is not, in and of itself, a decisive fact since almost all of our earliest extant legal texts date from this period. The important point here is that the debate is as old as the extant sources. Abū Ḥanīfa's student al-Shaybānī informs us that Abū Ḥanīfa was of the opinion that 'opening the prayer in Persian and performing the rest of the ritual prayer in Persian, even if one knows Arabic, was permissible'.[90] Al-Shaybānī's redactor follows this up with quotations from both Abū Yūsuf and al-Shaybānī to the effect that they both disagreed with Abū Ḥanīfa. They contended that the liturgical use of Persian in the ritual prayer was only permissible if one had no knowledge of Arabic.[91] Al-Narshakhī describes this exact phenomenon in his local history of Bukhārā, new Muslims performing the ritual prayer and reciting the Quran in Persian because they were unable to understand Arabic.[92]

[88] Zadeh, *The Vernacular Qur'an*; Katz, *Prayer in Islamic Thought and Practice*, 27–9.

[89] Ibn Abī Shayba, *Kitāb al-Adab*, ed. Muḥammad Riḍā al-Qahwajī (Beirut: Dār al-Bashā'ir al-Islāmiyya, 1999), 153–6. There is a *Kitāb al-Adab* that contains these reports in Ibn Abī Shayba, *al-Muṣannaf*, 13: 402–4 (Jeddah edn.), but there are discrepancies between the two books.

[90] Al-Shaybānī, *al-Jāmiʿ al-ṣaghīr* [published with the commentary of al-Laknawī, *al-Nāfiʿ al-Kabīr*] (Karachi: Idārat al-Qur'ān wa al-ʿUlūm al-Islāmiyya, 1990), 94; al-Shaybānī, *al-Aṣl*, ed. Mehmet Boynukalin (Qatar: Wizārat al-Awqāf and Beirut: Dār Ibn Ḥazm, 2012) 1: 16 = al-Shaybānī, *Kitāb al-Aṣl*, ed. Abū al-Wafā' al-Afghānī (Hyderabad: Majlis Dā'irat al-Maʿārif al-ʿUthmāniyya, 1966; repr. Beirut: ʿĀlam al-Kutub, 1990), 1: 15.

[91] On the question of al-Shaybānī's authorship of texts see Sadeghi, 'The Authenticity of Two 2nd/8th-Century Legal Texts'; Sadeghi, *The Logic of Law Making in Islam*, 177–200 (Appendix: The Authenticity of Early Ḥanafī Texts: Two Books of al-Shaybānī). Sadeghi's discussions deal only with the *Kitāb al-Āthār* and the *Muwaṭṭa'*.

[92] Al-Narshakhī, *Tārīkh-i Bukhārā*, ed. Mudarris Riẓavī (Tehran: Intishārāt-i Tūs, 1967), 67 (*va mardumān-i Bukhāra bih avval-i Islām dar namāz Qur'ān bih pārsī khwāndandī va ʿarabī natuvānastandī āmūkhtan, va chūn vaqt-i rukūʿ shudī mardī būdī keh dar pas-i īshān bāng zad ībknytā nkyntā' va chūn sajdeh khwāstandī kardan bāng kardī nikūnyā nikūnī*). See the notes of Richard Frye (and W. B. Henning) on Sogdian phrases used to inform the congregation when to bow and when to prostrate in al-Narshakhī, *The History of Bukhara*, trans. Richard N. Frye (Cambridge, MA: Medieval Academy of America, 1954), 135–6.

Law and jurisprudence adapted to local customs and social pressures. Despite Abū Yūsuf and al-Shaybānī's protestations, the Ḥanafī scholars and communities of Khurāsān and Transoxiana advanced a number of different arguments in favour of Abū Ḥanīfa's position on Persian as a language of liturgy in prayer and Quranic recitation, and these can be tracked century by century in the writings of al-Māturīdī (d. 333/944), al-Zandawasītī (d. 382/992), al-Sughdī (d. 461/1068), and al-Sarakhsī. In his *Ta'wīlāt al-Qur'ān* al-Māturīdī establishes a Quranic basis for Abū Ḥanīfa's opinion concerning the permissibility of performing the prayer in Persian. His argument rests on an interpretation of the phrase *muṣaddiqan limā ma'akum* in Quran 4.44.

God's saying, *muṣaddiqan limā ma'akum*, means that which is in agreement with that which is with you. It [the Book] is agreement with that which is with you in respect of the pursuant meanings and the injunctions in it, not in respect of its style and language. Similarly, all of God almighty's revealed books (*kutub Allāh*) are in agreement with each other in their meanings and injunctions, even if they differ with respect to style and language. This proves that they were revealed by God almighty. Had it originated from anyone other than God, they would have been divergent. Consider His saying: 'Had it been from anyone besides God they certainly would have found in it much divergence.' And herein lies a proof for the opinion of Abū Ḥanīfa as to his permitting the performance of the ritual prayer in Persian, for the change of the style and the difference of the language does not occasion a change in the meanings and nor does it produce different injunctions (*ikhtilāf al-aḥkām*), since God, mighty and majestic, has declared that it [the Book] is in agreement with what is with you, yet in its language and style it is different, whereas the meanings are in agreement.[93]

According to al-Māturīdī, performing the ritual prayer in Persian or reciting verses from the Quran in Persian was compatible with the divine word. Language and style do not determine God's revelations, meanings and injunctions do. In this view, and in very specific circumstances, the language of liturgy was not confined to Arabic. Al-Māturīdī can be said to represent one strain in Transoxanian Ḥanafism. Al-Zandawasītī, a much-neglected figure in modern scholarship, provides us the view from tenth-century Bukhārā. In his unpublished *Rawḍāt al-'ulamā'* he reasserts Abū Ḥanīfa's verdict on performing the prayer in Persian: 'Abū Ḥanīfa permitted the reading of the Quran in Persian during the ritual prayer, but if a person knows how to recite in Arabic it is impermissible to recite in

[93] Abū al-Manṣūr al-Māturīdī, *Ta'wīlāt al-Qur'ān*, ed. Ahmed Vanlioğlu and Bekir Topaloğlu (Istanbul: Dār al-Mīzān, 2005), 3: 254–5 (*fa fīhi dalīl li qawl Abī Ḥanīfa raḍiya Allāh 'anhu ḥaythu ajāza al-ṣalāt bi al-qirā'a bi al-fārisiyya li anna taghyīr al-naẓm wa ikhtilāf al-lisān lam yūjab taghyīr al-ma'ānī wa ikhtilāf al-aḥkām ḥaythu akhbara 'azza wa jalla annahu muwāfiq limā ma'ahum wa huwa fī al-lisān wa al-naẓm mukhtalif wa al-ma'ānī muwāfiq*).

Persian. If he does not know Arabic, recital in Persian is permissible.'[94] Towards the end of the work, in the chapter on the ritual prayer, its merits, and its legal issues, al-Zandawasītī gives a fuller account of the legal debates in Khurāsān and Transoxiana. He cites Abū Ḥanīfa's opinion, as found in Abū Ḥafṣ al-Kabīr's *Masā'il*, in the case of someone who opens the prayer in Persian (*kabbara bi al-fārisiyya*) by saying *khudā buzurg ast* (God is great). By saying this, a person has entered the ritual prayer. Al-Zandawasītī adds that this opinion derives from an analogy with Abū Ḥanīfa's deeming it valid for the Quran to be recited in Persian during the ritual prayer.[95]

The eleventh-century Ḥanafī qadi al-Sughdī gives the same account of this legal doctrine, adding that Abū Ḥanīfa's legal doctrine on Persian as a liturgical language extended to the *takbīr*, the *adhān*, the *iqāma*, the *tashahhud*, the *dhibḥ*, the *khuṭba*, and the recital of the Quran in prayer. Al-Sughdī treats Quranic recital during the prayer separately. He begins by surveying the views of different jurists (al-Shāfiʿī and Ibn Karrām) before turning to the positions of Abū Ḥanīfa, Abū Yūsuf, and al-Shaybānī.[96]

The legacy of Abū Ḥanīfa's views concerning Persian as a liturgical language in the Persian-speaking provinces of the empire occupied the mind of a more prominent Ḥanafī jurist a century later. Al-Sarakhsī discusses the matter in two places. He explores this issue at greater length in his *al-Mabsūṭ*. He discusses the permissibility of Persian as the language of liturgy with reference to eight ritual acts: the opening of the prayer (*iftitāḥ*); reciting the invocations of the ritual prayer (*qara'a fī ṣalātihi bi al-fārisiyya*); testification whilst sitting in the prayer (*tashahhud bi al-fārisiyya*); delivering the Friday sermon (*khaṭaba al-imām yawm al-jumʿa bi al-fārisiyya*); testifying to one's belief (*wa law āmana bi al-fārisiyya kāna mu'minan*); reciting the liturgical invocation necessary for ritual sacrifice (*ʿinda al-dhibḥ*); performing the *talbiya* required during the Ḥajj ritual (*labba bi al-fārisiyya*); and performing the call to prayer (*adhdhana bi al-fārisiyya*). According to al-Sarakhsī, Abū Ḥanīfa permitted the use of Persian in all eight circumstances.[97]

94 Al-Zandawasītī, 'Rawḍat al-ʿulamā' wa bahjat al-fuḍalā'', MS Syria, Maktabat ʿUyūn al-Sūd, MS 707, fol. 1b = 'Rawḍat al-ʿulamā' wa nuzhat al-fuḍalā'', MS Dublin, Chester Beatty, MS 6820, fols. 1a–b, where this passage is missing. On the manuscripts see Brockelmann, *GAL*, supp. 1: 361; Sezgin, *GAS*, 1: 670. On the author see Ibn Abī al-Wafā', *al-Jawāhir al-muḍiyya*, 4: 222; Ibn Quṭlūbughā, *Tāj al-tarājim*, ed. Muḥammad Khayr Ramaḍān Yūsuf (Beirut: Dār al-Qalam, 1992), 164–5.

95 Al-Zandawasītī, 'Rawḍat al-ʿulamā'', MS 707, fols. 99b–100a = MS 6820, fol. 53b.

96 Al-Sughdī, *al-Nutaf*, 1: 49–51. Al-Sughdī refers to Abū Yūsuf's notes on Abū Ḥanīfa's lessons (*wa dhakara Abū Yūsuf fī al-Amālī ʿan Abī Ḥanīfa annahu qāla*).

97 Al-Sarakhsī, *Kitāb al-Mabsūṭ* (Beirut: Dār al-Maʿrifa, 1989; repr. Cairo: Dār al-Saʿāda, 1906–13), 1: 36–7.

Al-Sarakshī proceeds to provide explanations for Abū Ḥanīfa's juridical opinion. At one point he states that Abū Ḥanīfa's view was based on the early precedent of the companion Salmān al-Fārisī, who was asked by the people of Fārs to provide a Persian translation of the *fātiḥa*. Accordingly, they recited the *fātiḥa* in the ritual prayer in Persian until they became acquainted with Arabic.[98]

Al-Sarakhsī takes up the issues in a work written after *al-Mabsūṭ*. The *Uṣūl* appears to be responding to similar objections at the heart of al-Māturīdī's discussion. Al-Sarakhsī begins by presenting the view of 'many of our scholars' that the inimitability of the Quran lies both in its style (*naẓm*) and meanings (*al-maʿānī*). This was the view of Abū Yūsuf and al-Shaybānī, and for this reason they both deemed the recitation of the Quran in Persian to invalidate the prayer. The obligation to recite the Quran in the prayer is an obligation to recite the inimitable, and inimitability lies in the combination of the style and the meaning. According to al-Sarakhsī, the inimitable is the word of God, which is neither *muḥdath* nor *makhlūq*, whereas all languages, be they Arabic, Persian, or other languages, are *muḥdath*. According to this reasoning, Abū Ḥanīfa's permitting the recitation of the Quran in Persian during the prayer is sound and is no affront to the Quran's inimitability nor to the prayer's validity.[99]

We have examined proto-Sunni traditionalist hostility towards Abū Ḥanīfa on account of his proximity to non-Arabs, the diffusion of proto-Ḥanafism in Khurāsān and Transoxiana, Abū Ḥanīfa's ethnic origins, his family's confessional background and ancestral social status, and his legal

98 Al-Sarakhsī, *Kitāb al-Mabsūṭ*, 1: 37 (*wa Abū Ḥanīfa istadalla bi mā ruwiya anna al-furs katabū ilā Salmān an yaṭluba lahum al-fātiḥa bi al-fārisiyya fa kānū yaqra'ūn dhālika fī al-ṣalāt ḥattā lānat alsinatuhum li al-ʿarabiyya*). On Salmān al-Fārisī's translation, particularly its role in modern debates concerning the translation of Quran into different languages, see Zadeh, 'The Fātiḥa of Salmān al-Fārisī'; al-Laknawī, *Aḥkām al-nafā'is fī adā' al-adhkār bi lisān al-fāris*, in *Majmūʿat al-rasā'il al-Laknawī*, ed. Naʿīm Ashrāf Nūr Aḥmad (Karachi: Idārat al-Qur'ān wa al-ʿUlūm al-Islāmiyya, 1998–9), 4: 333–92.

99 Al-Sarakhsī, *Uṣūl al-Sarakhsī*, ed. Abū al-Wafā' al-Afghānī (Hyderabad: Lajnat Iḥyā' al-Maʿārif al-Nuʿmāniyya, 1953–4), 2: 281–2 (under *faṣl fī bayān al-kitāb wa kawnihi ḥujja*). There are four extant editions of this work: al-Sarakhsī, *Uṣūl al-Sarakhsī* (Hyderabad edn.) = *al-Muḥarrar fī uṣūl al-fiqh*, ed. Abū ʿAbd al-Raḥmān Ṣalāḥ b. Muḥammad b. ʿUwayḍa (Beirut: Dār al-Kutub al-ʿIlmiyya, 1996) = *Uṣūl al-Sarakhsī*, ed. Rafīq al-ʿAjam (Beirut: Dār al-Maʿrifa, 1997) = *Tamhīd al-fuṣūl fī al-uṣūl*, ed. ʿAbd Allāh b. Sulaymān b. ʿĀmir al-Sayyid (Mecca: Umm al-Qurā University, 2011), which is a comprehensive study, though an incomplete edition, of al-Sarakhsī and the *Uṣūl*. I rely on Abū al-Wafā' al-Afghānī's edition because of his scrupulous editorial practices, which the two other complete editions do not exhibit: Abū al-Wafā' al-Afghānī relies on four manuscripts; the other two editors either fail to mention the manuscripts they rely upon (as in ʿUwayḍa) or simply rely on the painstaking editorial efforts of Abū al-Wafā' al-Afghānī (as in Rafīq al-ʿAjam). For a critique of these editions, see al-Sayyid in *Tamhīd al-fuṣūl fī al-uṣūl*, 6–8 (editor's introduction).

views concerning the validity of Persian as a liturgical language. There was yet another tributary to this overflowing stream of proto-Sunni agitation. This 'discourse of difference' was reinforced by the notion that Abū Ḥanīfa's grasp of the Arabic language was insufficient. Mastery of the Arabic language was a fundamental prerequisite for any scholar. No one had a made a stronger case for this than al-Shāfiʿī in the eighth century.[100] The dissemination of reports that Abū Ḥanīfa's grammar was weak (*yalḥanu*),[101] that he did not know his broken plurals,[102] that his vocabulary was lacking,[103] and his knowledge of declensions was deficient provided further evidence for the view that Abū Ḥanīfa's religious deviance was not unconnected to the linguistic, cultural, and ethnic background that his opponents constructed.[104]

## 5.5 Conclusion

This chapter has argued that proto-Sunni traditionalist attacks on Abū Ḥanīfa were a product of the social and cultural environment of the eighth and ninth centuries. Whilst the discourse of heresy against Abū Ḥanīfa does not represent a body of social facts pointing to his heresy, social facts and ideas were used to discredit Abū Ḥanīfa and build up a discourse of heresy surrounding his memory. The social and cultural facts studied in this chapter all pertain to the ways in which Abū Ḥanīfa's relationship with the province of Khurāsān and Transoxiana was interpreted to represent forms of religious deviance. I have argued that ethnogenesis was central to the way in which proto-Sunni traditionalists interpreted the history of heresy. Discourses of heresy depended on ethnic reasoning and argumentation. Genealogy and geography were mechanisms by which trajectories of heresy and orthodoxy were understood. Religious demands upon Persian-speaking communities and societies produced new

[100] See Lowry, *Early Islamic Legal Theory*, 294–8; El Shamsy, *The Canonization of Islamic Law*, 71–4, 116 n. 98, 215–16.

[101] Al-Khaṭīb al-Baghdādī, *Kitāb al-Faqīh wa al-mutafaqqih*, 2: 55 (*innaka aḥwaju ilā iṣlāḥ lisānika min jamīʿ al-nās*); al-Khaṭīb al-Baghdādī, *al-Jāmiʿ li al-akhlāq al-rāwī wa ādāb al-sāmiʿ*, ed. Maḥmūd al-Ṭaḥḥān (Riyadh: Maktabat al-Maʿārif, 1983), 2: 26.

[102] In al-Khaṭīb al-Baghdādī, *Tārīkh Baghdād*, 15: 455–6 two reports are adduced to demonstrate Abū Ḥanīfa's weak grasp of Arabic grammar (*lam yakun lahu ʿilm bi al-naḥw*), in particular its broken plurals (*kulūb* instead of *kilāb*) and declensions (*law annahu ḥattā yarmīhi bi Abā Qubays* instead of *bi Abī Qubays*).

[103] Al-Zajjājī, *Majālis al-ʿulamāʾ*, ed. ʿAbd al-Salām Hārūn (Cairo: Maktabat al-Khānjī, 1999), 181. It should be borne in mind that al-Zajjājī's book is a witty, playful, erudite, and (some might say) pretentious display of grammatical virtuosity. Very often religious scholars are on the receiving end of his derision.

[104] Al-Khaṭīb al-Baghdādī, *Tārīkh Baghdād*, 15: 455–6.

religious controversies in which proto-Sunni communities sought to define the rules of liturgy, prayer, and Quranic recitation. The categories of heresy and orthodoxy were by no means oblivious to the ethnographic gaze, the process of ethnogenesis in early Islamicate world, and forms of ethnic argumentation.[105]

[105] Berzon, *Classifying Christians*.

# 6 Politics: Rebellion and Heresy

Readers have already been introduced to my argument that Abū Ḥanīfa's politics – that is, his support for rebellions in the late eighth century – represented what was most reprehensible to proto-Sunni traditionalists of the ninth–tenth centuries. This chapter will present evidence for the hypothesis that it was Abū Ḥanīfa's perceived violation of a tenet of proto-Sunni orthodoxy that served as a catalyst for the sheer volume of discourses of heresy against Abū Ḥanīfa, which emphasised his support for rebellion against a legitimate state. I shall begin by examining our earliest sources that refer to Abū Ḥanīfa's involvement in three rebellions. This is necessary not only because it enhances our understanding of the evolution of proto-Sunni traditionalist ideas about heresy and orthodoxy and how central politics was to them, but also because no systematic study of Abū Ḥanīfa's support for rebellions has been undertaken by modern scholars.[1] I shall then demonstrate how Abū Ḥanīfa's support for these movements flew in the face of a basic fact of proto-Sunni traditionalist orthodoxy in the late eighth and ninth centuries; namely, quietism and obedience to the state. This chapter will close with a discussion of how and why proto-Sunni traditionalists gave so much attention in discourses of heresy against Abū Ḥanīfa to what they saw as his heretical views on

[1] In a number of publications, Cook has used his footnotes to refer to Abū Ḥanīfa's sympathy with ʿAlid uprisings: *Early Muslim Dogma*, 172 n. 7 and *Commanding Right and Forbidding Wrong*, 9 n. 29, 51. Similar references are found in Crone, *Medieval Islamic Political Thought*, 137 ('most early Murji'ites, probably including Abū Ḥanīfa, were activists who "believed in the sword"'); Crone and Zimmermann, *The Epistle of Sālim Ibn Dhakwān*, 240–1 n. 91; Madelung, *Der Imam al-Qāsim ibn Ibrāhīm*, 74, 234 n. 38; Zaman, 'The Nature of Muḥammad al-Nafs al-Zakiyya's Mahdiship'; Zaman, *Religion and Politics*, 73 n. 13, 74 n. 14; Tsafrir, *The History of an Islamic School of Law*, 25 (where she mentions in passing Abū Ḥanīfa's 'public incautious remarks at the time of the appearance of the ʿAlid rebels al-Nafs al-Zakiyya and his brother Ibrāhīm'); Abou El Fadl, *Rebellion and Violence*, 72–3, 77–8 (where he relies on a very late source); van Ess, *Theologie und Gesellschaft*, 1: 187–8. Jokisch, *Islamic Imperial Law*, fails to mention the episode, and had he done so it would have caused insurmountable problems for his overarching thesis about Ḥanafism as imperial Islamic law. So many of these references cite van Arendonk's pathbreaking research on the ʿAlids: *De Opkomst*, 281, 288 = *Les débuts de l'imāmat Zaidite au Yemen*, 307, 315.

rebellion against legitimate rulers, in addition to highlighting the role that provincial political elites and representatives of the state might have had in fostering proto-Sunni traditionalism.

## 6.1 Abū Ḥanīfa and Rebellion

Zayd b. ʿAlī was the great-grandson of ʿAlī b. Abī Ṭālib and Fāṭima, and he was a younger brother to the fifth imam of the Twelver Shiʿa, Muḥammad al-Bāqir. As the head of the Ḥusaynid branch of the ʿAlids, Muḥammad al-Bāqir had entrusted Zayd b. ʿAlī with dealings over the litigation concerning the *ṣadaqāt* (land endowments) of ʿAlī between the families of al-Ḥasan and al-Ḥusayn. ʿAbd Allāh b. al-Ḥasan, the father of Muḥammad al-Nafs al-Zakiyya and Ibrāhīm b. ʿAbd Allāh, accused Zayd of harbouring ambitions for the caliphate. The Umayyads were happy to use these disputes between the Ḥasanids and Ḥusaynids to discredit the family of the Prophet in front of the Medinan populace. Sensing that things were not going his way, Zayd broke off from negotiations. Matters became worse for Zayd as he was accused of being in possession of Khālid al-Qasrī's deposits. These accusations swirling around the person of Zayd b. ʿAlī and his disputes with competing ʿAlids resulted in the caliph Hishām ordering the governor of Iraq to dispatch Zayd b. ʿAlī to the Ḥijāz. Hishām feared that the current atmosphere coupled with Zayd's residence among the Kufans would prompt Zayd to rebellion. The caliph's fears were soon realised. After some deliberation, a promise of support from the Kufans convinced Zayd to stay in the town, and he began to make preparations for a rebellion. Supporters were found in the Sawād, al-Madā'in, Basra, Wāsiṭ, Mawṣil, Rayy, Jurjān, and Upper Mesopotamia. Support for Zayd b. ʿAlī was less forthcoming from other places. In particular, it was patchy among the religious scholars. Even more reluctant in their support were the different ʿAlid families. The later tradition identifies Zayd's refusal to condemn Abū Bakr and ʿUmar as a major reason for the lukewarm support from the ʿAlids. In 122/740 Zayd was forced to rebel. Yūsuf b. ʿUmar led the army against him. On the third day one of Yūsuf's men shot an arrow towards Zayd, killing him. Zayd's head was sent to Hishām in Damascus and paraded in Medina. His was body was crucified in Kufa.[2]

Abū Ḥanīfa's support for Zayd b. ʿAlī's rebellion is not explicitly referred to in proto-Sunni traditionalist discourses of heresy. In fact,

[2] There has been a tendency to portray Zayd b. ʿAlī's rebellion as a Shiʿite revolt: see Sharon, *Black Banners*, 145–7, 174–7; Blankinship, *The End of the Jihād State*, 102, 190. In my view a more accurate interpretation has been advanced by Haider, *The Origins of the Shīʿa*, 189–214.

only Abū Ḥanīfa's support for the rebellion of Ibrāhīm b. ʿAbd Allāh is cited. Otherwise, criticisms of Abū Ḥanīfa's views on rebellion are general. They refer broadly to his support for rebellion against the state and its legitimate rulers (*khurūj ʿalā al-a'imma or kāna yarā al-sayf fī al-a'imma*).[3] Our earliest reference to Abū Ḥanīfa's involvement with Zayd b. ʿAlī's revolt appears in al-Balādhurī's *Ansāb al-ashrāf*, a key source for the history of ʿAlid revolts, not least because of its incorporation of earlier *maqtal* sources now lost to us.[4] We are told there that Zayd b. ʿAlī had written to people in the provinces. In his letters he described the tyrannical rule of the Umayyads and incited the provinces to rise up against them. He had one of his deputies, ʿAṭā' b. Muslim, visit Abū Ḥanīfa. The news of Zayd's ambitions perturbed Abū Ḥanīfa (*fa kāda yughshā ʿalayhi faraqan*). His first response was to inquire about scholars (*fuqahā'*) who had pledged their support to Zayd. He was told that Salama b. Kuhayl, Yazīd b. Abī Ziyād, Hishām al-Burayd, Abū Hāshim al-Rummānī, and others had all thrown in their lot with Zayd. Abū Ḥanīfa was reticent, however. 'I am not able to rebel (*lastu aqwā ʿalā al-khurūj*),' he told ʿAṭā' b. Muslim. Instead, he sent him money with which Zayd could empower himself.[5] Al-Balādhurī's account is located in his section on Zayd b. ʿAlī, but it is introduced without an *isnād*. Zaydī historiography, on the other hand, provides further details concerning the nature of Abū Ḥanīfa's involvement in the rebellion. The *Maqātil al-ṭālibiyyīn* of Abū al-Faraj al-Iṣfahānī (d. 363/972) belongs to a genre of Arabic historical writing that, as Sebastian Günther and James Bellamy have shown, developed in the first half of the eighth century.[6] ʿAlid uprisings and the involvement of proto-Sunni scholars are key themes in the *Maqātil al-ṭālibiyyīn*, and so it is not altogether surprising that a version similar to al-Balādhurī's report can be found in the section treating Zayd b. ʿAlī's rebellion. The only difference is that Abū al-Faraj provides us with an *isnād*: ʿAlī b. al-Ḥusayn < al-Ḥusayn < ʿAlī b. Ibrāhīm < ʿAmr < Faḍl b. al-Zubayr:[7]

ABŪ ḤANĪFA: Who among the scholars of the people has come forward for Zayd in this matter?

[3] This has been misunderstood to mean 'he was a sword in the side of the umma'. See Judd, 'Competitive Hagiography', 26 n. 2.

[4] On ʿUmar b. Shabba see Shaltūt, 'Ta'rīkh al-Madīna'; for Abū Mikhnaf's *maqtal* reports see Sezgin, *Abū Mihnaf*, 59–62. See the lengthy entry on him in Bujnūrdī (ed.), *Dā'irat al-Maʿārif-i buzurg-i Islāmī*, 6: 213–20.

[5] Al-Balādhurī, *Ansāb al-ashrāf*, ed. W. Madelung (Berlin and Beirut: Klaus Schwarz, 2003), 2.28: 620–1.

[6] Günther, *Quellenuntersuchungen*, 110–230; Bellamy, 'Sources'.

[7] Abū al-Faraj al-Iṣfahānī, *Maqātil al-ṭālibiyyīn*, ed. al-Sayyid Aḥmad Ṣaqr (Qum: Intishārāt al-Sharīf al-Riḍā, 1996), 141.

FAḌL B. AL-ZUBAYR: Salama b. Kuhayl, Yazīd b. Abī Ziyād, Hishām b. al-Burayd, Abū Hāshim al-Rummānī, Ḥajjāj b. Dīnār, and others.

ABŪ ḤANĪfa: Tell Zayd that I can provide you with support and power for jihād against your enemies, so ensure that you and your companions benefit from it by acquiring horses and weapons (*ʿindī maʿūna wa quwwa ʿalā jihād ʿaduwwika, fa-'astaʿin bihā anta wa aṣḥābuka fī al-kurāʿ wa al-silāḥ*).

FAḌL B. AL-ZUBAYR: Then he sent that [money?] with me to Zayd, and Zayd took it.

What can we deduce from the report's *isnād*? First, we have ʿAlī b. al-Ḥusayn, who is the text's author, Abū al-Faraj al-Isfahānī. The second name in the *isnād*, al-Ḥusayn, is to be identified with al-Ḥusayn b. al-Qāsim al-Ibrāhīm (d. 246/860), the well-known Zaydī Muʿtazilī.[8] ʿAlī b. Ibrāhīm is unknown to me. The fourth individual is ʿAmr b. ʿAbd al-Ghaffār b. ʿUmar (d. 202/817–18). The ninth-century proto-Sunni ḥadīth scholar ʿAlī b. al-Madīnī knew ʿAmr b. ʿAbd al-Ghaffār as a traditionist but refused to transmit ḥadīths from him because he was inclined to Shiʿism (*rāfiḍī*).[9] Our main informant is Fuḍayl (not Faḍl) b. Zubayr al-Rassān (d. *c.* 140/759), a Jārūdī supporter of Zayd b. ʿAlī.[10] It seems we are dealing with a Zaydī *isnād*.

The story of Abū Ḥanīfa's support for Zayd b. ʿAlī found a regular place in subsequent Zaydī historiography. Abū Ṭālib Yaḥyā b. al-Ḥusayn al-Hārūnī (d. 424/1033) explained that Abū Ḥanīfa was among a number of prominent scholars (*fuqahā'*) who lent financial support to Zayd b. ʿAlī's rebellion (*wa aʿānahu bi māl kathīr*).[11] Finally, Abū al-Faraj al-Iṣfahānī gives us a sense of how an eclectic community of Zaydīs and proto-Sunni traditionalists of the eighth and ninth centuries remembered Abū Ḥanīfa's support for Zayd b. ʿAlī:[12]

[8] Van Arendonk, *De Opkomst*, 323. On him see Madelung, *Der Imam al-Qāsim ibn Ibrāhīm*.

[9] Al-Khaṭīb al-Baghdādī, *Tārīkh Baghdād*, 14: 107–9. See also Aḥmad b. ʿĪsā b. Zayd, Amālī *apud* ʿAlī b. Ismāʿīl al-Mu'ayyad al-Ṣanʿānī, *Kitāb Ra'b al-ṣadʿ* (Beirut: Dār al-Nafā'is, 1990), 1: 292.

[10] Al-Qummī, *Maqālāt wa al-firaq*, ed. Muḥammad Jawād Mashkūr (Tehran: Maṭbaʿat Ḥaydarī, 1923), 74; Ibn al-Nadīm, *Kitāb al-Fihrist*, 1: 640 (A. F. al-Sayyid edn.) (classed as a Zaydī rationalist theologian (*mutakallim*)) = 178 (Flügel edn.); al-Ṭūsī, *Rijāl al-Ṭūsī*, ed. Jawād al-Qayyūmī al-Iṣfahānī (Qum: Mu'assasat al-Nashr al-Islāmī, n.d.), 143 (as a follower of Muḥammad al-Bāqir), 269 (as a follower of Jaʿfar al-Ṣādiq); al-Ṭūsī, *Kitāb al-Amālī*, ed. Baharād Jaʿfarī and ʿAlī Akbar Ghaffārī (Tehran: Dār al-Kutub al-Islāmiyya, 1961), 682 and 729 (transmitting traditions); Ibn Qūlūwayh, *Kāmil al-ziyārāt* (Qum: Nashr al-Faqāha, 2009), 150–1 (transmitting a tradition); al-Tustarī, *Qāmūs al-rijāl* (Qum: Mu'assasat al-Nashr al-Islāmī, 2009), 8: 344–5; van Arendonk, *De Opkomst*, 281–2.

[11] Abū Ṭālib Yaḥyā b. al-Ḥusayn al-Hārūnī, *al-Ifāda fī tārīkh al-a'imma al-sāda*, ed. Muḥammad Kāẓim Raḥmatī (Tehran: Mīrāth-i Maktūb, 2008), 13–14.

[12] Abū al-Faraj al-Iṣfahānī, *Maqātil al-ṭālibiyyīn*, 140. I admit that the final sentence is somewhat laconic and may be read differently. For example, 'He did something to Ibn al-Mubārak over the latter's refusal to acknowledge their virtues and imprecated him.'

ʿAlī b. al-Ḥusayn < ʿAlī al-ʿAbbās < Aḥmad b. Yaḥyā < ʿAbd Allāh b. Marwān b. Muʿāwiya said: 'I heard Muḥammad b. Jaʿfar b. Muḥammad in the governor's palace say, "May God have mercy upon Abū Ḥanīfa. His love for us was evidenced by his support for Zayd b. ʿAlī (*la qad taḥaqqaqat mawaddatuhu lanā fī nuṣratihi Zayd b. ʿAlī*)." He even persuaded Ibn al-Mubārak in secret of our virtues and called him to it (*wa faʿala bi Ibn al-Mubārak fī kitmānihi faḍā'il anā wa daʿā ʿalayhi*).'

The *isnād* combines a number of individuals with mixed sectarian backgrounds. Our author's informant is Abū al-Ḥasan ʿAlī b. al-ʿAbbās b. al-Walīd al-Maqāniʿī (d. *c.*306/919), who was a Kufan scholar reckoned by medieval Sunni scholars as a trustworthy and truthful ḥadīth scholar but among medieval Imāmī Shiʿa as a Shiʿi transmitter.[13] Aḥmad b. Yaḥyā seems to be Zayd b. ʿAlī's grandson. ʿAbd Allāh b. Marwān b. Muʿāwiya al-Fazārī (d. 193/810) was another Kufan scholar and traditionist, who was considered to have been a teacher to proto-Sunni traditionalists such as al-Ḥumaydī, Yaḥyā b. Maʿīn, Isḥāq b. Rāhawayh, Ibn Abī Shayba, and Yaʿqūb al-Dawraqī.[14] Not everyone, however, was content with his reputation as a proto-Sunni ḥadīth scholar. Yaḥyā

[13] Interestingly, the Sunni literary tradition remains silent on al-Maqāniʿī's Zaydī and proto-Shiʿi inclinations: al-Ḥākim al-Nīshāpūrī, *Su'ālāt al-Ḥākim al-Nīshāpūrī li Dāraquṭnī fī al-jarḥ wa al-taʿdīl*, ed. Muwaffaq b. ʿAbd Allāh b. ʿAbd al-Qādir (Riyadh: Maktabat al-Maʿārif, 1984), 126; al-Sahmī, *Su'ālāt Ḥamza b. Yūsuf al-Sahmī li al-Dāraquṭnī wa ghayrihi min al-mashāyikh fī al-jarḥ wa al-taʿdīl*, ed. Muwaffaq b. ʿAbd Allāh b. ʿAbd al-Qādir (Riyadh: Maktabat al-Maʿārif, 1984), 227; Abū Bakr al-Ismāʿīlī, *Kitāb al-Muʿjam fī asāmī shuyūkh Abī Bakr al-Ismāʿīlī*, ed. Ziyād Muḥammad Manṣūr (Medina: Maktabat al-ʿUlūm wa al-Ḥikam, 1990), 740; Ibn al-Jazarī, *Ghāyat al-nihāya*, 1: 484; al-Samʿānī, *al-Ansāb*, 5: 361 (Dār al-Jinān edn.); Ibn al-Athīr, *al-Lubāb*, 3: 245; al-Dhahabī, *Siyar*, 14: 430–1; al-Dhahabī, *Tahdhīb siyar aʿlām al-nubalā'*, ed. Shuʿayb al-Arna'ūṭ (Beirut: Mu'assasat al-Risāla, 1991), 2: 41. For al-Maqāniʿī in Shiʿi sources see al-Ṭūsī, *Kitāb al-Amālī*, 213, 321, 349, 359, 379, 633, 1009; al-Ṭūsī, *al-Fihrist* (Qum: al-Sharīf al-Riḍā, n.d.), 98 (where a *Kitāb Faḍl al-Shīʿa* is attributed to him); al-Shaykh al-Mufīd, *al-Irshād fī maʿrifat ḥujaj Allāh ʿalā al-ʿibād* (Beirut: Mu'assasat Āl al-Bayt li Iḥyā' al-Turāth, 1995), 2: 193; Ibn Shahrāshūb, *Maʿālim al-ʿulamā'*, ed. al-Sayyid Muḥammad Ṣādiq Āl Baḥr al-ʿUlūm (Beirut: Dār al-Aḍwā', n.d.), 69.

[14] For early, and overwhelmingly proto-Sunni, sources see Ibn Saʿd, *al-Ṭabaqāt al-kabīr*, 7.2: 73 (Leiden edn.); ʿUthmān b. Saʿīd al-Dārimī, *Tārīkh [ʿan Yaḥyā b. Maʿīn]*, ed. Aḥmad Muḥammad Nūr Sayf (Damascus: Dār al-Ma'mūn li al-Turāth, 1980), 203 (where he is classed as trustworthy (*thiqa*)); al-Bukhārī, *al-Tārīkh al-kabīr*, 4.1: 372; Abū Zurʿa al-Dimashqī, *Tārīkh*, 2: 461–2 (where Yaḥyā b. Maʿīn rates Marwān b. Muʿāwiya below the latter's paternal uncle, Abū Isḥāq al-Fazārī). For later sources see al-Khaṭīb al-Baghdādī, *Tārīkh Baghdād*, 13: 149; Ibn Manda, *Fatḥ al-bāb fī al-kunā wa al-alqāb*, ed. Abū Qutayba Naẓar Muḥammad al-Fārayābī (Riyadh: Maktabat al-Kawthar, 1996), 1: 268 (s.v. 'Abū Ḥudhayfa'); al-ʿIjlī, *Tārīkh al-thiqāt*, 1: 424; Ibn Ḥibbān, *Kitāb al-Thiqāt*, 8: 350; Ibn Ḥajar al-ʿAsqalānī, *Taqrīb al-tahdhīb*, ed. Muṣṭafā ʿAbd al-Qādir ʿAṭā' (Beirut: Dār al-Kutub al-ʿIlmiyya, 1993), 2: 172; Ibn Ḥajar al-ʿAsqalānī, *Tahdhīb al-tahdhīb*, 10: 96–8 (Hyderabad edn.); al-Mizzī, *Tahdhīb al-kamāl*, 27: 403–10; al-Dhahabī, *Tārīkh al-Islām*, 16: 245; al-Dhahabī, *Siyar*, 9: 51.

b. Maʿīn, for one, got into an argument with Marwān b. Muʿāwiya about his reliance on *'rāfiḍī'* transmitters. He also criticised his tendency to describe proto-Sunni traditionalists as Shiʿis.[15] Finally, Muḥammad b. Jaʿfar b. Muḥammad b. ʿAlī, nicknamed Dībāja, appears to be the son of Jaʿfar al-Ṣādiq. Shiʿa scholars of the Middle Ages remembered Dībāja as a courageous and pious man, who adopted the doctrine of the Zaydīs concerning the permissibility of open rebellion.[16]An intriguing aspect of these *isnād*s is the assorted background of the transmitters. In the late eighth and ninth centuries, boundaries were porous enough for scholars to teach and study with proto-Sunni traditionalists whilst adhering to proto-Shiʿi or Zaydī beliefs; yet these movements were also distinct enough for proto-Sunni traditionalists to highlight what they believed to be these traditionists' unorthodox views.[17]

As I have stated, discourses of heresy against Abū Ḥanīfa are coy on the question of his involvement with Zayd b. ʿAlī's rebellion. On the one hand, proto-Sunni traditionalists were working round the clock to publicise Abū Ḥanīfa's support for rebellions because it was further evidence of his heresy. On the other hand, they were reluctant to highlight the evidence connecting him to Zayd b. ʿAlī's rebelllion. How might we explain this? Proto-Sunni traditionalists of the late eighth and ninth centuries had either encouraged, witnessed, or experienced the ʿAbbāsid revolution, and others were now prospering under their rule. A good number of them had cordial relations with ʿAbbāsid caliphs.[18] Zayd b. ʿAlī's rebellion against the Umayyads was viewed by the ʿAbbāsids as an important epoch in the tradition of legitimate and necessary revolt against their dynastic predecessors, and his execution as a rebel by the caliph Hishām became an iconic feature of ʿAbbāsid-era annals. It would hardly work against Abū Ḥanīfa for his opponents writing under the ʿAbbāsids to draw attention to his role in supporting Zayd b. ʿAlī in

[15] Yaḥyā b. Maʿīn, *Tārīkh*, ed. Aḥmad Muḥammad Nūr Sayf (Medina: Maktaba al-Mukarrama, 1979), 2: 556–7.

[16] Al-Shaykh al-Mufīd, *al-Irshād*, 2: 211; al-Najāshī, *Rijāl al-Najāshī*, ed. Mūsā al-Shabīrī al-Zanjānī (Qum: Mu'assasat al-Nashr al-Islāmī, 1998), 367; al-Ṭūsī, *Rijāl al-Ṭūsī*, 275; al-Ṣanʿānī, *Kitāb Ra'b al-ṣad'*, 3: 1698–9. It is not entirely unlikely that Muḥammad b. Jaʿfar Dībāja was able to make this remark at the governor's residence. When his rebellion in 199/815 failed, al-Ma'mūn was serving as governor of the province. Muḥammad b. Jaʿfar Dībāja was delivered to al-Ma'mūn, but the future caliph honoured him and incorporated him into his provincial court setup: see al-Shaykh al-Mufīd, *al-Irshād*, 2: 212–13, where a moving account of al-Ma'mūn's actions during Muḥammad b. Jaʿfar Dībāja's funeral is also given.

[17] A good example of this is the case of Jaʿfar al-Ṣādiq's brother, ʿAbd Allāh: 'He opposed his father's beliefs, mixed with the Ḥashawiyya, and inclined to the doctrines of the Murji'a; nevertheless, he claimed the *Imāma* after his father's death' (al-Shaykh al-Mufīd, *al-Irshād*, 2: 210–11).

[18] In general, see Zaman, *Religion and Politics*, 70–118.

the latter's struggle against the Umayyads. As we shall see shortly, proto-Sunni traditionalists adopted a completely different stance when it came to Abū Ḥanīfa's involvement with ʿAlid uprisings against the ʿAbbāsids.

Before we turn to the ʿAlid rebellion of Ibrāhīm b. ʿAbd Allāh, we should review a report implicating Abū Ḥanīfa in a revolt led by al-Ḥārith b. Surayj in Khurāsān. Though this incident finds no explicit mention in discourses of heresy against Abū Ḥanīfa, it does implicate him in yet another revolt against the Umayyads. In fact, only one source seems to record this episode.[19] Al-Ṭabarī's *Tārīkh* gives considerable attention, and rightly so, to a significant rebellion in Khurāsān in 116/734 led by al-Ḥārith b. Surayj. It represented a tumultuous movement in Khurāsān opposed to provincial policies and conduct during which al-Ḥārith b. Surayj managed to attract a wide coalition of Muslims, subalterns (*mawālī*), and non-Muslim Turgesh troops. Al-Ḥārith managed to capture Balkh from Naṣr b. Sayyār, but the important city of Marw proved elusive. He remained a thorn in the side of Khurāsān's governors for more than a decade, but he was finally defeated and killed in 128/746.

According to al-Ṭabarī, the initiative for offering safe conduct to al-Ḥārith b. Surayj came from the governor of Khurāsān, Naṣr b. Sayyār. Two men, Khālid b. Ziyād and Khālid b. ʿAmr, travelled to Kufa to petition the caliph Yazīd b. al-Walīd (r. 125–743/126–744) for a pardon. When they reached Kufa, they sought out Abū Ḥanīfa and asked him to write to one of Yazīd b. al-Walīd's associates. Abū Ḥanīfa wrote to a man called al-Ajlaḥ, who was a close companion of the caliph. Abū Ḥanīfa's intervention proved successful, and the two men were granted an audience with Yazīd b. al-Walīd. In 126/744 Yazīd b. al-Walīd resorted to a common strategy when faced with rebels who failed to acquiesce: he decided to grant al-Ḥārith b. Surayj a safe conduct, which served as an official amnesty from the Umayyad state.[20] I have not seen proto-Sunni traditionalist writings express an interest in Abū Ḥanīfa's relationship with al-Ḥārith b. Surayj's rebellion. I would not say that the episode would have been unknown to them, for there are some suggestions that the heresiarch Jahm b. Ṣafwān served as the intermediary between Abū Ḥanīfa and al-Ḥārith b. Surayj.[21]

Ibrāhīm b. ʿAbd Allāh was one of two ʿAlid revolutionaries who challenged the authority of the ʿAbbāsid caliph al-Manṣūr. Modern scholars

[19] Al-Ṭabarī, *Tārīkh*, 2: 1866–8 = 26: 234–6. Ibn ʿAsākir (*Tārīkh madīnat al-Dimashq*, 16: 31 (al-ʿAmrawī edn.)) repeats the story and cites al-Ṭabarī's account.

[20] Al-Ṭabarī, *Tārīkh*, 2: 1866–8 = 26: 234–6. See Madelung, 'The Early Murji'a', 34; Melchert, 'The Spread of Ḥanafism', 23–4. For the strength of both Ḥanafism and Murji'ism in Balkh see al-Wāʿiẓ, *Faḍā'il-i Balkh*, 28–9.

[21] See section 7.5 below.

know him primarily through his association with his brother, Muḥammad al-Nafs al-Zakiyya. Muḥammad al-Nafs al-Zakiyya's rebellion has always loomed large for both pre-modern and modern scholars, resulting in some serious neglect of Ibrāhīm b. ʿAbd Allāh's involvement.[22] The present study is not the place to settle this imbalance in the modern literature, but it is important to emphasise that Ibrāhīm b. ʿAbd Allāh's rebellion posed a more serious threat to the ʿAbbāsids than that of his brother, even if the two were coordinated to some degree.

The evidence connecting Abū Ḥanīfa to Ibrāhīm b. ʿAbd Allāh's rebellion is abundant by the ninth century. Major figures of proto-Sunni traditionalism refer to Abū Ḥanīfa's support for the ʿAlid rebellion in order to depict Abū Ḥanīfa as a heretic.[23] Abū Ḥanīfa's support for Ibrāhīm's rebellion was known to writers who had no interest in contributing to the discourse of heresy against him. Abū al-Faraj al-Iṣfahānī's *Maqātil al-ṭālibiyyīn* contains thirteen reports to this effect and helps us to sketch some of the details of Abū Ḥanīfa's involvement in the rebellion. Abū Ḥanīfa expressed his backing for Ibrāhīm's uprising publicly.[24] He ordered the people to rebel with him.[25] He and his compatriot, Misʿar b. Kidām, wrote to Ibrāhīm and invited him to come to Kufa, whence they could provide him with the requisite support and assistance. They guaranteed Ibrāhīm that the Kufans would rebel with him.[26] When this came to the attention of the Murji'a in Kufa, they were enraged. They castigated both Abū Ḥanīfa and Misʿar b. Kidām for supporting Ibrāhīm's rebellion and for encouraging him to rebel from Kufa.[27] We might infer from this that the Kufan Murji'a of the late eighth century were indeed politically quietist and were perturbed by what they

[22] Elad, *The Rebellion of Muhammad al-Nafs al-Zakiyya*, the most authoritative work on al-Nafs al-Zakiyya's rebellion, says little about Ibrāhīm, although Elad has stated that Ibrāhīm's rebellion deserves a separate study (private communication).

[23] Al-Khaṭīb al-Baghdādī, *Tārīkh Baghdād*, 15: 528–30 (a total of nine reports); al-Bukhārī, *al-Tārīkh al-awsaṭ*, 2: 100 (cited in the Luḥaydān edn.) = 3: 562 (cited in the footnote in the Abū Ḥaymad edn.); al-Fasawī, *Kitāb al-Maʿrifa wa al-tārīkh*, 2: 788 (*aḥalla lahum al-khurūj ʿalā al-a'imma*); ʿAbd Allāh b. Aḥmad b. Ḥanbal, *Kitāb al-Sunna*, 213, 218, 219 (a total of six reports); al-ʿUqaylī, *Kitāb al-Ḍuʿafā' al-kabīr*, ed. ʿAbd al-Muʿṭī Amīn Qalʿajī (Beirut: Dār al-Kutub al-ʿIlmiyya, 1984), 4: 282 = *Kitāb al-Ḍuʿafā'*, 4: 1409 (al-Salafī edn.) (support for Ibrāhīm's rebellion) = *Kitāb al-Ḍuʿafā'*, ed. Bashshār ʿAwwād Maʿrūf and Muḥammad Bashshār Maʿrūf (Tunis: Dār al-Gharb al-Islāmī, 2015), 4: 322–3.

[24] Abū al-Faraj al-Iṣfahānī, *Maqātil al-ṭālibiyyīn*, 310 (*kāna Abū Ḥanīfa yajharu fī amr Ibrāhīm jahran shadīdan*); al-Azdī, *Tārīkh Mawṣil*, ed. ʿAlī Ḥabība (Cairo: Lajnat Iḥyā' al-Turāth al-Islāmī, 1967), 188 (where he is also reported to have said, 'Were I able to see, I would certainly rebel with Ibrāhīm, but what prevents you all from rebelling?').

[25] Abū al-Faraj al-Iṣfahānī, *Maqātil al-ṭālibiyyīn*, 310 (*yuftī al-nās bi al-khurūj maʿahu*).

[26] Abū al-Faraj al-Iṣfahānī, *Maqātil al-ṭālibiyyīn*, 310 (reported by Abū Ḥanīfa's student Zufar b. Hudhayl), 314 (reported by ʿUmar b. Shabba).

[27] Abū al-Faraj al-Iṣfahānī, *Maqātil al-ṭālibiyyīn*, 310, 314. For classifications of both Misʿar b. Kidām and Abū Ḥanīfa as Murji'īs see Ibn Qutayba, *Kitāb al-Maʿārif*, 481.

perceived to be Misʿar b. Kidām and Abū Ḥanīfa's revival of an earlier strand of Murji'ī activism.[28] Both proto-Sunni traditionalists and later Ḥanafīs would describe Abū Ḥanīfa as one of the Murji'a who advocated for armed rebellion.[29]

Further details about Abū Hanīfa's backing for Ibrāhīm's revolt are given in Zaydī histories. We are informed that Abū Ḥanīfa tried to garner support for Ibrāhīm b. ʿAbd Allāh's rebellion, albeit clandestinely. Crucially, one source speaks of written correspondence that took place between Abū Ḥanīfa and Ibrāhīm b. ʿAbd Allāh, and even produces what purports to be a letter Abū Ḥanīfa sent to Ibrāhīm in which he told him:[30]

So when God grants you victory over ʿĪsā b. Mūsā and his army, do not deal with them in the manner in which your father dealt with the people of al-Jamal. For, indeed, he did not slay the defeated, he did not take the booty, he did not pursue from the rear, nor did he harry the wounded. For, in truth, it was not for the people that they take the booty. Instead, deal with them in a manner akin to his conduct on the day of Ṣiffīn, for there he harried the wounded and distributed the booty, as the people of Shām had a right to it.

According to *al-Ifāda*, the letter never reached Ibrāhīm. The caliph al-Manṣūr managed to obtain the letter, and on the basis of this he had Abū Ḥanīfa brought to Baghdad and poisoned to death.[31] It seems that the connection between Ibrāhīm b. ʿAbd Allāh's rebellion and Abū Ḥanīfa may have been so strong that the caliph intended to make a point when he

[28] This unsettles the view proposed at one point by Cook, *Early Muslim Dogma*, 26: 'All this begins by now to look straightforward. On the one hand we have a quietism well-attested in classical – or at least Ḥanafī – Murji'ism. On the other we have the evidence of a proto-Murji'ite hostility towards the rulers of the day. It is a simple and attractive hypothesis that the political stance of the Murji'a was initially hostile to the regime, and subsequently softened.' On the political views of the Murji'a see the comprehensive and, generally, balanced discussion in Crone and Zimmermann, *The Epistle of Sālim Ibn Dhakwān*, 236–43, though there too the authors assume the authenticity of texts attributed to Abū Ḥanīfa; and for a thorough review of Murji'ism in general and in Kufa in particular, see van Ess, *Theologie und Gesellschaft*, 1: 154–83, esp. 179–83 (where van Ess discusses the full range of Murji'ī quietist and activist views), 182–3 (on Misʿar b. Kidām), and 187–8 (remarks on Abū Ḥanīfa and ʿAlid rebellions). I am in favour of treating the history of Irjā' in Kufa separately from that of Irjā' in Khurāsān. For the latter see Madelung, 'The Early Murji'a'; and more recently, Melchert, 'The Spread of Ḥanafism', 23–4. For Irjā' and Ḥanafism see also Melchert, *The Formation of the Sunni Schools of Law*, 56–60.

[29] Al-ʿUqaylī, *Kitāb al-Ḍuʿafā' al-kabīr*, 4: 283 (two reports) (Qalʿajī edn.) = 1409, 1410 (al-Salafī edn.); Abū Zurʿa al-Dimashqī, *Tārīkh*, 2: 506 (with no mention of Irjā'); ʿAbd Allāh b. Aḥmad b. Ḥanbal, *Kitāb al-Sunna*, 213, 218, 219; al-Khaṭīb al-Baghdādī, *Tārīkh Baghdād*, 15: 529–30 (al-Khaṭīb cites three reports that connect Abū Ḥanīfa's Murji'ism to rebellion (*murji'ī yarā al-sayf*), one of which has al-Fazārī in the *isnād*); al-Jaṣṣāṣ, *Aḥkām al-Qur'ān*, 1: 86–7 (for a fascinating defence of Abū Ḥanīfa's views on rebellion).

[30] Abū Ṭālib al-Hārūnī, *al-Ifāda*, 22; Abū al-Faraj al-Iṣfahānī, *Maqātil al-ṭālibiyyīn*, 315.

[31] Abū Ṭālib al-Hārūnī, *al-Ifāda*, 22; Abū al-Faraj al-Iṣfahānī, *Maqātil al-ṭālibiyyīn*, 315 and 316 (where two similar reports are provided).

decided to deposit the decapitated heads of Ibrāhīm and his brother near the house of Abū Ḥanīfa. Even in death, so it seems, Ibrāhīm b. ʿAbd Allāh's legacy was inseparable from Abū Ḥanīfa.[32]

Indeed, Abū Ḥanīfa seems to have been very forthright to a number of people about the necessity of joining Ibrāhīm's rebellion. One man recalled seeing Abū Ḥanīfa standing on the steps of his house, when two men approached him and asked his opinion about rebelling (*al-khurūj*) with Ibrāhīm. 'Go and rebel (*ukhrujā*),' he told them.[33] Another man reported that he went to Abū Ḥanīfa during the rebellion of Ibrāhīm, because Abū Ḥanīfa was someone he held in great esteem. He asked Abū Ḥanīfa what action he deemed most preferable after one had completed the greater pilgrimage, and whether joining Ibrāhīm's rebellion was preferable to going on another pilgrimage. 'Holy war after one has performed the greater pilgrimage is equal to fifty pilgrimages,' Abū Ḥanīfa replied.[34] On yet another occasion a woman came up to Abū Ḥanīfa during the days of Ibrāhīm's rebellion and said to him, 'My son wishes to join this man [in his rebellion], but I forbid him to do so.' 'Let him join,' Abū Ḥanīfa told the woman.[35] Perhaps the most notorious incident, however, was one that proto-Sunni traditionalists highlighted in order to disparage Abū Ḥanīfa as a heretic; and it was one involving one of their own, Abū Isḥāq al-Fazārī (d. *c.*185/802).

## 6.2 Proto-Sunni Traditionalism and Quietism

Abū Ḥanīfa's vocal support for ʿAlid rebellions fell foul of proto-Sunni traditionalist orthodoxy, which maintained that revolt against the state was impermissible and tantamount to heresy. An authoritative and illuminating study of rebellion in Islamic law insists that quietism was not the dominant view among proto-Sunni jurists.[36] This position is in response to the work of a previous scholar who contended that proto-Sunni scholars adopted largely quietist positions vis-à-vis the legitimacy of the state.[37] In what follows, I argue that by the ninth century proto-Sunni

[32] Al-Balādhurī, *Ansāb al-ashrāf*, 2.28: 535–6 (Berlin edn.) (*wa ḥumila ra's Muḥammad wa ra's Ibrāhīm ilā Khurāsān thumma ruddā fa dafanahumā alladhī ḥamalahumā taḥta daraja fī manzilihi bi darb Abī Ḥanīfa fī madīnat Abī Jaʿfar bi Baghdād*).

[33] Abū al-Faraj al-Iṣfahānī, *Maqātil al-ṭālibiyyīn*, 313.

[34] Abū al-Faraj al-Iṣfahānī, *Maqātil al-ṭālibiyyīn*, 324 (*ghazwa baʿda ḥijjat al-Islām afḍal min khamsīn ḥijja*).

[35] Abū al-Faraj al-Iṣfahānī, *Maqātil al-ṭālibiyyīn*, 325.

[36] Abou El Fadl, *Rebellion and Violence*.

[37] Zaman, *Religion and Politics*. Abou El Fadl, *Rebellion and Violence* is a learned book, but the author's impressive intellectual history of pre-modern rebellion is also designed to explore its potentialities for the modern world. This causes him to make some puzzling claims, and he often does so on the basis of thin and late documentation: Abou El Fadl

traditionalists began to articulate explicitly a conception of orthodoxy that adopted a stern stance against rebellion. First, and as an extension to the discussion of Abū Ḥanīfa's part in Ibrāhīm b. ʿAbd Allāh's rebellion, we shall consider the example of a proto-Sunni traditionalist who became embroiled in controversy with Abū Ḥanīfa at the time of Ibrāhīm's uprising.

Al-Fasawī relates the following encounter between al-Fazārī and Abū Ḥanīfa:[38]

AL-FAZĀRĪ: My brother was slain with Ibrāhīm al-Fāṭimī in Basra. I travelled there in order to collect his belongings (inheritance). I met Abū Ḥanīfa. He said to me:

ABŪ ḤANĪfa: Where have you come from and where are you going?

AL-FAZĀRĪ: I told him that I had come from Maṣṣīṣa because my brother had been killed with Ibrāhīm. He said to me:

ABŪ ḤANĪfa: It would have been better for you had you been killed with your brother than the place from which you have just come.

AL-FAZĀRĪ: So I said to him:

AL-FAZĀRĪ: What prevented you from fighting in the rebellion?

ABŪ ḤANĪfa: I would not have hesitated had it not been for the fact that I was entrusted with people's property.

Abū Isḥāq al-Fazārī was a proto-Sunni traditionalist. Ibn Abī Ḥātim al-Rāzī's summary of his career is conclusive about this: 'If you see a Shāmī who loves al-Awzāʿī and Abū Isḥāq al-Fazārī, then know that he is a man of proto-Sunni traditionalist orthodoxy (*ṣāḥib sunna*).'[39] Al-Khalīlī also

disagrees with Zaman's thesis that proto-Sunnism adopted quietism after the mid-second century, but he fails to muster up the evidence against this hypothesis. He is correct in pointing out that juristic positions on rebellion are necessarily going to err on the side of conservative quietism and that, consequently, this material is not so promising when the scholarly debate rests on a simply dichotomy between quietism and activism. In my view, where Zaman's thesis runs into problems (and what Abou El Fadl fails to recognise) is his attempt to envision a broad proto-Sunni consensus. As I stated at the outset of this study, proto-Sunnism is too broad a category to be of any great utility, and in my discussion of rebellion and quietism I have limited my conclusions to the proto-Sunni traditionalist community. As for thin and late sources in Abou El Fadl's book, the discussion of Abū Ḥanīfa's history with ʿAlid uprisings is both incomplete and consistently relies on late sources (Abou El Fadl, *Rebellion and Violence*, 77 n. 72); the survey of al-Thawrī's views on rebellions rests on evidence from al-Dhahabī, al-Ṣafadī, and Ibn al-ʿImād (Abou El Fadl, *Rebellion and Violence*, 96–7).

38 Al-Fasawī, *Kitāb al-Maʿrifa wa al-tārīkh*, 2: 788.

39 Ibn Abī Ḥātim, *Taqdima*, 1: 284–6. The same view was held by Abū al-ʿArab al-Tamīmī, *Kitāb al-Miḥan*, ed. Yaḥyā al-Jabbūrī (Beirut: Dār al-Gharb al-Islāmī, 2006), 296. The fullest biography can be found in Ibn ʿAsākir, *Tārīkh madīnat Dimashq*, 7: 119–33 (al-ʿAmrawī edn.); but see also al-Dhahabī, *Siyar*, 8: 539–43; al-Dhahabī, *Tadhkirat al-ḥuffāẓ*, 1: 273–4. It should be obvious to readers that 'proto-Sunni traditionalist orthodoxy' is contextual and not a literal translation for *ṣāḥib sunna*.

saw him as a representative of orthodoxy.[40] His *al-Irshād fī maʿrifat ʿulamāʾ al-ḥadīth* includes a story where al-Ḥumaydī recalls Sufyān b. ʿUyayna's anger when a man came to him saying that he had heard al-Fazārī transmit traditions from Sufyān b. ʿUyayna. Now he wanted to hear them from the latter directly. 'Woe unto you,' he told the visitor. Sufyān b. ʿUyayna deemed it entirely superfluous given that the man had heard these traditions from a scholar of al-Fazārī's standing.[41] These proto-Sunni traditionalist credentials are borne out by al-Fazārī's personal history of militant piety, his relations with the rulers of his time, and his role in circulating discourses of heresy against Abū Ḥanīfa. We read in al-Bukhārī's *al-Tārīkh al-awsaṭ* that al-Fazārī said: 'I was with Sufyān when the news of al-Nuʿmān's [b. Thābit] death came. He said: "Praise be to God. He was destroying Islam systematically. No one was born in Islam more accursed than him."'[42] Putting aside whatever personal animosity al-Fazārī might have had towards Abū Ḥanīfa, it seems very likely that he objected to Abū Ḥanīfa's views concerning rebellion against legitimate rulers. Al-Fazārī, like many proto-Sunni traditionalists, had a long and prestigious record of fighting on the frontiers against the Byzantines.[43] Not only did he die on one of these frontiers (al-Maṣṣīṣa), but he even composed a book dedicated to the subject, *Kitāb al-Siyar*. Al-Ḥumaydī recalls hearing al-Shāfiʿī tell him that no one had produced a book on the subject of *siyar* quite like al-Fazārī's.[44]

Other sources add weight to the view that al-Fazārī considered Abū Ḥanīfa's position on Ibrāhīm's rebellion to be at odds with proto-Sunni traditionalist orthodoxy because the ʿAbbāsid caliph, al-Manṣūr, was a legitimate ruler; and rebelling against a legitimate ruler was tantamount to heresy.[45] According to one ninth-century source, al-Fazārī

[40] Al-Khalīlī, *al-Irshād*, 442–5 (Riyadh edn.).

[41] Al-Khalīlī, *al-Irshād*, 443 (Riyadh edn.).

[42] Al-Bukhārī, *al-Tārīkh al-awsaṭ [Kitāb al-Mukhtaṣar]*, 3: 503 (Abū Ḥaymad edn.).

[43] On proto-Sunni traditionalism and militant piety see Sizgorich, *Violence and Belief*, 180–95 (where the focus is on Ibn al-Mubārak); Bonner, *Aristocratic Violence*, esp. 157–84; Tor, *Violent Order*, though I think the latter goes too far in conflating the phenomenon of religious violence (and the *ʿayyārūn*, in particular) with Sunni traditionalism, where the evidence is thin, and, in turn, underestimates the importance of urban militias.

[44] Al-Khalīlī, *al-Irshād*, 443 (Riyadh edn.). On the *siyar* see Muranyi, 'Das Kitāb al-Siyar'; Bonner, *Aristocratic Violence*, 113–18.

[45] Naturally, this raises doubts about Bonner's (*Aristocratic Violence*, 110) or his source's characterisation of al-Fazārī as someone who 'banned from these sessions all those who had dealings with the government'. The source, I believe, is Ibn ʿAsākir, *Tārīkh madīnat Dimashq*, 7: 120–1 (al-ʿAmrawī edn.) (*man kāna man yaʾtī al-sulṭān fa lā yaḥḍur majlisanā*). On a related note, Bonner arrives at the conclusion that al-Fazārī marked a shift in notions of authority. For Fazārī, authority 'now inheres in the religious scholar, rather than in the imam/caliph and his delegated representatives' (Bonner, *Aristocratic Violence*, 119). What is Bonner's evidence for al-Fazārī's views on religious authority vis-à-vis scholars and rulers?

once had an altercation with a ruler that resulted in him receiving 200 lashes.[46] Otherwise, the sources pretty much agree that al-Fazārī was on good terms with political authorities. One source distinguishes him as belonging to a group of religious scholars who accepted gifts or stipends from rulers, if only to distribute the money among the local population.[47] Hārūn al-Rashīd cited al-Fazārī, along with Ibn al-Mubārak, as an exemplary religious authority when engaged in an argument with a heretic (*zindīq*).[48] There is reason to assume that al-Fazārī visited Hārūn al-Rashīd more than just once. When the caliph remarked that al-Fazārī had a considerable reputation among the Arabs, al-Fazārī was unmoved by the comment. 'This will not help me one bit in front of God on the Day of Reckoning,' he told the caliph.[49] Also during Hārūn al-Rashīd's reign al-Fazārī was one of several scholars counselling the governor about treaties with non-Muslims.[50] Then there is al-Aṣmaʿī's eyewitness account of al-Fazārī's meeting with Hārūn al-Rashīd and Abū Yūsuf:[51]

AL-AṢMAʿĪ: I was sitting in the company of Hārūn al-Rashīd reciting some poetry for him. The judge Abū Yūsuf was seated beside him. Shortly after, al-Faḍl b. al-Rabīʿ entered the room.

AL-FAḌL B. AL-RABĪʿ: Abū Isḥāq al-Fazārī is at the door.

HĀRŪN AL-RASHĪd: Let him in.

AL-AṢMAʿĪ: When he entered, he said [to the caliph].

AL-FAZĀRĪ: Peace be upon you along with God's mercy and grace, Commander of the Faithful.

It is one report (Bonner, *Aristocratic Violence*, 116–17), which, as far as I can see, represents no significant comment on the authority of scholars against that of rulers, even when interpreted against al-Awzāʿī's response to a similar issue. In my view, Bonner has read into this report the issue of caliphal authority versus scholarly authority, which seems entirely unwarranted. I discovered in the final stages of writing this monograph that Cook's summary of al-Fazārī's career (*Commanding Right and Forbidding Wrong*, 66) agrees with my own reading and serves to correct Bonner's account.

46 Abū al-ʿArab al-Tamīmī, *Kitāb al-Miḥan*, 296, 357; repeated in Yāqūt al-Ḥamawī, *Muʿjam al-udabāʾ*, 1: 95 (Dār al-Gharb al-Islāmī edn.).

47 Ibn ʿAsākir, *Tārīkh madīnat Dimashq*, 7: 129 (al-ʿAmrawī edn.); Yāqūt al-Ḥamawī, *Muʿjam al-udabāʾ*, 1: 93 f., esp. 95–6 (Dār al-Gharb al-Islāmī edn.).

48 Ibn ʿAsākir, *Tārīkh madīnat Dimashq*, 7:127 (al-ʿAmrawī edn.); Yāqūt al-Ḥamawī, *Muʿjam al-udabāʾ*, 1: 95 (Dār al-Gharb al-Islāmī edn.).

49 Abū Nuʿaym, *Ḥilyat al-awliyāʾ* (Cairo: Maktabat al-Khānjī, 1996; repr. Beirut: Dār al-Fikr, n.d.), 8: 253–65, esp. 253 (I owe my knowledge of this reference to the editor of Ibn ʿAsākir's *Tārīkh*): Ibn ʿAsākir, *Tārīkh madīnat Dimashq*, 7: 128–9 (al-ʿAmrawī edn.).

50 Abū ʿUbayd al-Qāsim b. Sallām, *Kitāb al-Amwāl*, ed. Muḥammad Ḥāmid al-Fiqī (Cairo: n.p., 1975), 171.

51 Ibn ʿAsākir, *Tārīkh madīnat Dimashq*, 7: 129–30 (al-ʿAmrawī edn.); Yāqūt al-Ḥamawī, *Muʿjam al-udabāʾ*, 1: 96 (Dār al-Gharb al-Islāmī edn.).

HĀRŪN AL-RASHĪd: May God grant you no peace, may He banish your house, and may He make desolate your resting place.[52]

AL-FAZĀRĪ: Why is that, Commander of the Faithful?

HĀRŪN AL-RASHĪd: Are you not the person who declared the [wearing of] black to be illicit (*anta alladhī tuḥarrimu al-sawād*)?

AL-FAZĀRĪ: Commander of the Faithful, who told you this? Perhaps it was that person – al-Fazārī pointed in the direction of Abū Yūsuf and made a remark. By God, Commander of the Faithful, when Ibrāhīm had rebelled against your grandfather al-Manṣūr, my brother rebelled with him. Meanwhile, I had made an intention to go [to the Byzantine frontier] to raid, so I went to Abū Ḥanīfa and I mentioned this [my brother's joining Ibrāhīm's rebellion and my plans to go raiding] to him. He told me: 'Your brother's rebelling is more beloved to me than your intention to go raiding.' By God, I never declared the [wearing of] black to be illicit (*yā amīr al-mu'minīn, man akhbaraka bi hādhā? La'alla hādhā akhbaraka – wa ashāra ilā Abī Yūsuf wa dhakara kalima – wa Allāhi yā amīr al-mu'minīn la qad kharaja Ibrāhīm 'alā jaddika al-Manṣūr fa kharaja akhī ma'ahu wa 'azamtu 'alā al-ghazw fa ataytu Abā Ḥanīfa fa dhakartu lahu dhālika fa qāla lī: 'makhraj akhīka aḥabbu ilayya mimmā 'azamta 'alayhi min al-ghazw.' Wa wa Allāhi mā ḥarramtu al-sawād*).

HĀRŪN AL-RASHĪd: In that case, may God grant you peace, may He bring peace to your abode, and may He breathe life into your resting place. Sit down, Abū Isḥāq, [be] happy.[53] Three thousand dinars are to be given to Abū Isḥāq.

AL-AṢMA'Ī: The money was brought and placed in al-Fazārī's hand. He left the room and then departed.

According to al-Aṣma'ī, Abū Isḥāq did not need the money. Both he and Ibn al-Mubārak distributed all of the money to charitable causes in al-Rāfiqa. This detail is of tertiary interest to us, however. More pertinent to this chapter are the following points. Al-Fazārī, a proto-Sunni traditionalist, is at the court of the caliph, seeking to maintain cordial relations with him, and accepting a stipend from him. He is outraged by the caliph's suggestion that he is disloyal to the 'Abbāsids. Suspecting that Abū Yūsuf is the source of the rumour that al-Fazārī has declared the donning of black – the colour of the 'Abbāsids – impermissible, he cannot help but use this occasion to articulate the irony of Abū Yūsuf comfortably ensconced in Hārūn al-Rashīd's court trying to drive a wedge in between al-Fazārī and the caliph. The implication is that al-Fazārī, if indeed he believes the donning of black to be impermissible, is undermining the legitimacy of the 'Abbāsids. This is not lost on al-Fazārī. He reminds the

[52] This is a particular expression in the literary sources but usually the prerogative of caliphs and governors alone. For instances where this phrase is employed either as a curse or to signal approval see al-Jāḥiẓ, *Kitāb al-Ḥayawān*, 4: 64; al-Balādhurī, *Ansāb al-ashrāf*, ed. Suhayl Zakkār (Beirut: Dār al-Fikr, 1996), 9: 67.

[53] *Yā Masrūr* may be a reference to one of the caliph's courtiers or eunuchs ordered by the caliph to fetch al-Fazārī his money.

caliph that it was Abū Yūsuf's teacher, Abū Ḥanīfa, who supported the rebellion against the caliph's grandfather, counselled his brother to do the same, and tried to convince him that participation in Ibrāhīm's rebellion was more meritorious than raiding against the Byzantines.

A similar story is told by al-Bukhārī in the ninth century, this time with al-Fazārī as the narrator. Al-Fazārī explains that he went to see Hārūn al-Rashīd and found Abū Yūsuf sitting there next to him. The caliph saw al-Fazārī and accused of him advocating rebellion against him (*anta alladhī tarā al-sayf ʿalaynā*)? Al-Fazārī suspected Abū Yūsuf of feeding this idea to Hārūn, and so he decided to tell the caliph about his run-in with Abū Ḥanīfa during the rebellion of Ibrāhīm.[54] Al-Fazārī's aim is to assure the caliph of his own loyalty whilst casting aspersions on the fidelity of Abū Ḥanīfa, Abū Yūsuf, and possibly other proto-Ḥanafīs. Al-Fazārī was probably aware that his family history revealed a certain sympathy for rebellions against the state: his nephew Marwān b. Muʿāwiya, whom we discussed above, may have been a Zaydī; his brother had espoused rebellion against the ʿAbbāsids and died fighting for Ibrāhīm against the caliph al-Manṣūr. The loyal proto-Sunni traditionalist that he was, al-Fazārī was keen to put to rest any doubts about his own views on the legitimacy of the ʿAbbāsids.

Proto-Sunni traditionalists rallied hard against those whom they believed advocated rebellion against rulers. This is evidenced by the reports we have cited that castigate Abū Ḥanīfa for the fact that he supported open rebellion against rulers (*kāna yarā al-sayf ʿalā al-aʾimma*). It can be seen also in the history of other individuals who were discredited for similar views. We have the example, for instance, of Muḥammad b. Rāshid al-Makḥūlī (d. *c.*160/776), a Damascene traditionist with a decent reputation for transmission who fled to Iraq and was known for his heretical views on doctrine and rebellion.[55] ʿImrān

[54] Al-Bukhārī, *al-Tārīkh al-awsaṭ*, 2: 100 (cited in the Luḥaydān edn.) = 3: 562 (cited in the footnote in the Abū Ḥaymad edn.). This report is present in ʿAbd Allāh b. Aḥmad b. ʿAbd al-Salām al-Khaffāf's (d. 294/907) recension only. It is missing in Abū Muḥammad Zanjawayh b. Muḥammad al-Nīshāpūrī's (d. 318/930) recension.

[55] Abū Zurʿa al-Dimashqī, *Tārīkh*, 1: 401 (reliable but someone who inclined towards heresy (*thiqa wa kāna yamīlu ilā hawā*) and when Abū Mus'hir was asked why it was that he did not write traditions from Muḥammad b. Rāshid, he replied: because he advocated rebellions against rulers (*kayfa lam taktub ʿan Muḥammad b. Rāshid? Qāla: kāna yarā al-khurūj ʿalā al-aʾimma*)); al-Fasawī, *Kitāb al-Maʿrifa wa al-tārīkh*, 2: 395–6; Yaḥyā b. Maʿīn, *al-Tārīkh*, 4: 446 (al-Dūrī's rescension); Ibn al-Junayd, *Suʾālāt Ibn al-Junayd*, 306, 337, 472; al-Nasāʾī, *Kitāb al-Ḍuʿafāʾ wa al-matrūkīn* [published with *Kitāb al-Ḍuʿafāʾ al-ṣaghīr*], ed. Maḥmūd Ibrāhīm Zāyid (Beirut: Dār al-Maʿrifa, 1986), 235 (weak (*laysa bi al-quwwa*)); Ibn ʿAdī, *al-Kāmil fī ḍuʿafāʾ al-rijāl*, ed. al-Ghazzāwī and Suhayl Zakkār (Beirut: Dār al-Fikr, 1988), 8: 201–2 esp. 201 (*kāna yarā al-khurūj ʿalā al-aʾimma*); al-Jūzajānī, *Aḥwāl al-rijāl*, ed. ʿAbd al-ʿAlīm ʿAbd al-ʿAẓīm al-Bastawī (n.p. [Pakistan]: Ḥadīth Academy, n.d.), 278; al-Khaṭīb al-Baghdādī, *Tārīkh Baghdād*, 3: 181–

b. Dāwar Abū al-ʿAwwām al-Qaṭṭān (d. *c.*160/776) was generally highly rated as a ḥadīth scholar.[56] But, like Abū Ḥanīfa, he was considered to be on very good terms with Ibrāhīm b. ʿAbd Allāh. Al-Fasawī informs us that Ibrāhīm befriended him when he rebelled in Basra.[57] He also issued a fierce religious edict at the time of Ibrāhīm's uprising permitting the rebellion.[58] This led people to declare him a heretic who advocated rebellion.[59] Similarly, there is the case of al-Ḥasan b. Ṣāliḥ (d. 169/785–6), a traditionist and traditionalist of good repute but whose doctrines concerning rebellion and the legitimacy of rulers placed him outside proto-Sunni traditionalist orthodoxy.[60]

5, esp. 185; Ibn ʿAsākir, *Tārīkh madīnat Dimashq*, 53: 4–16, esp. 10 (al-ʿAmrawī edn.); al-Mizzī, *Tahdhīb al-kamāl*, 25: 186–91, esp. 191; Ibn Ḥajar al-ʿAsqalānī, *Tahdhīb al-tahdhīb*, 3: 559–60 (Mu'assasat al-Risāla, edn.); al-Dhahabī, *Siyar*, 7: 343–4.

56 Khalīfa b. Khayyāṭ, *Kitāb al-Ṭabaqāt*, 221; al-Bukhārī, *al-Tārīkh al-kabīr*, 3.2: 425 (his name appears as Dāwūd); Yaḥyā b. Maʿīn, *al-Tārīkh*, 2: 437 (al-Dūrī's rescension) is not impressed with ʿImrān b. Dāwar's ḥadīth learning, and he does refer to his support for rebellion (*kāna yarā ra'y al-khawārij*); al-Marrūdhī, *Kitāb al-ʿIlal wa maʿrifat al-rijāl li Aḥmad b. Muḥammad b. Ḥanbal*, 107, 3908; ʿAbd Allāh b. Aḥmad b. Ḥanbal, *Kitāb al-ʿIlal wa maʿrifat al-rijāl ʿan Yaḥyā b. Maʿīn*, ed. Abū ʿAbd al-Hādī al-Jazā'irī (Beirut: Dār Ibn Ḥazm, 2004), 62–3, 101; ʿAlī b. al-Madīnī, *al-ʿIlal*, ed. Muḥammad Muṣṭafā al-Aʿẓamī, 2nd edn. (Beirut: al-Maktab al-Islāmī, 1980), 80 (where ʿImrān's view on a ḥadīth with implications for the doctrine of rebellion is noted); Ibn Abī Ḥātim, *al-Jarḥ*, 6: 297–8; Ibn ʿAdī, *al-Kāmil fī maʿrifat al-rijāl*, ed. Māzin b. Muḥammad al-Sarsāwī (Riyadh: Maktabat al-Rusdh, 2018), 7: 479–84; al-Dhahabī, *Siyar*, 7: 280, 4: 442, 5: 274. The index (25: 531) has his name as ʿImrān b. Dāwūd.

57 Al-Fasawī, *Kitāb al-Maʿrifa wa al-tārīkh*, 2: 258 (*wa kāna Ibrāhīm wallāhu ḥīna kharaja bi al-Baṣra al-ghazā*).

58 Al-Ājurrī, *Su'ālāt Abī ʿUbayd al-Ājurrī Abā Dāwūd Sulaymān b. al-Ashʿath al-Sijistānī fī maʿrifat al-rijāl wa jarḥihim wa taʿdīlihim*, ed. ʿAbd al-ʿAlīm ʿAbd al-ʿAẓīm al-Bastawī (Mecca: Maktabat Dār al-Istiqāma, 1997), 418–19 (where his weakness as a ḥadīth scholar seems tied to his involvement in Ibrāhīm's rebellion: *ḍaʿīf, aftā fī ayyām Ibrāhīm b. ʿAbd Allāh b. Ḥasan bi fatwā shadīda fīhā safk al-dimā'*); al-Dhahabī, *Mīzān al-iʿtidāl*, 3: 236.

59 Al-Fasawī, *Kitāb al-Maʿrifa wa al-tārīkh*, 2: 258 (*kāna ʿImrān ḥarūriyyan wa kāna yarā al-sayf ʿalā ahl al-qibla*); Al-Dhahabī, *Mīzān al-iʿtidāl*, 3: 237 (*kāna ḥarūriyyan yarā al-sayf*); Ibn Ḥajar al-ʿAsqalānī, *Tahdhīb al-tahdhīb*, 8: 131 (Hyderabad edn.).

60 Ibn Saʿd, *al-Ṭabaqāt al-kabīr*, 6: 260–1, esp. 261 (Leiden edn.) (his twin brother ʿAlī b. Ṣāliḥ); Khalīfa b. Khayyāṭ, *Kitāb al-Ṭabaqāt*, 168 (death dates for al-Ḥasan and ʿAlī); al-Bukhārī, *al-Tārīkh al-kabīr*, 1.2: 295 (no comment on his alleged deviances); Ibn Qutayba, *al-Maʿārif*, 509 (a brief biographical notice); al-Fasawī, *Kitāb al-Maʿrifa wa al-tārīkh*, 2: 805–6 (where al-Fasawī mentions, among other vices, his advocacy of rebellion (*al-khurūj ʿalayhim bi al-sayf*). There is also an interesting anecdote about his attitude to past caliphs, which other proto-Sunni traditionalists such as Wakīʿ b. al-Jarrāḥ did not find objectionable). For an overview see al-Dhahabī, *Siyar*, 7: 361–71, esp. 361, 363, 364, 365. In al-Dhahabī's assessment: 'I consider him one of the leaders of Islam, were it not for the fact that he became mired in heresy.' I am grateful to the editor of the *Siyar* for indicating where biographical notices on al-Ḥasan b. Ṣāliḥ can be found. Al-Dhahabī, *Tahdhīb tahdhīb al-kamāl fī asmā' al-rijāl*, ed. Ghunaym ʿAbbās Ghunaym and Majdī al-Sayyid Amīn (Cairo: al-Fārūq al-Ḥadīth li al-Ṭibāʿa wa al-Nashr, 2004), 2: 286–90; Ibn Ḥajar al-ʿAsqalānī, *Tahdhīb al-tahdhīb*, 2: 285–9 (Hyderabad edn.); Ibn Ḥajar al-ʿAsqalānī, *Taqrīb al-tahdhīb*, 1: 205.

By focusing on the mnemohistory of Abū Ḥanīfa, we have already seen that proto-Sunni traditionalists believed rebellion against rulers to go against a fundamental tenet of orthodoxy. In order to ensure that our picture reflects wider currents in proto-Sunni traditionalism during the ninth and tenth centuries, I should like to point out echoes of this doctrine of proto-Sunni traditionalist orthodoxy that can be heard in a number of works from this period.[61]

Consider the short epistle written by one of al-Shāfiʿī's leading students, Ismāʿīl b. Yaḥyā al-Muzanī (d. 264/877–8). Al-Muzanī's creedal work was, we are told, a response to a letter in which some scholars sought out his views concerning various doctrines and beliefs. Al-Muzanī obliged by composing a short creed. His *Sharḥ al-Sunna* discusses nineteen issues. Two of these have direct relevance for our discussion about proto-Sunni traditionalist attitudes to rulers and rebellion. First, al-Muzanī addresses the question of obeying the caliphs and governors and the prohibition against rebellion. He writes:[62]

> One must obey those in command with respect to that which is pleasing to God, mighty and majestic. And one must turn away from what is displeasing. One must not rebel in the face of their transgressions or oppression. One should repent to God, mighty and majestic, that He may make them appreciate their subjects.

Moreover, one of the issues he addresses is the question of performing communal rituals under the leadership of rulers. He contends that one must not avoid attending the Friday prayer, since praying behind the pious and wicked of this community is compulsory.[63] He adds that those performing the prayer are not culpable for any heretical innovation that rulers – I assume – might have incorporated into the religion.[64]

[61] This is a selective and not a comprehensive account of proto-Sunni traditionalist texts that speak against rebellion. Al-Khallāl, *al-Sunna*, ed. ʿAṭiyya al-Zahrānī (Riyadh: Dār al-Rāya, 1989), 1: 82–5, 97–126, esp. 130–44 (*bāb al-inkār ʿalā man kharaja ʿalā al-sulṭān*), where al-Khallāl cites the opinions of various ninth-century proto-Sunni traditionalists; al-Barbahārī, *Sharḥ Kitāb al-Sunna*, ed. ʿAbd al-Raḥmān b. Aḥmad al-Jumayzī (Riyadh: Maktabat Dār al-Minhāj, 2005), 57; al-Lālakāʾī, *Sharḥ uṣūl iʿtiqād ahl sunna wa al-jamāʿa*, ed. Kamāl al-Miṣrī (Alexandria: Maktabat Dār al-Baṣīra, n.d.), 1: 146–71.

[62] Ismāʿīl b. Yaḥyā al-Muzanī, *Sharḥ al-Sunna*, ed. Jamāl ʿAzzūn (Riyadh: Dār al-Minhāj, 2009), 85 (*ṭāʿatu al-aʾimma wa al-umarāʾ fīmā kāna ʿinda Allāh ʿazza wa jalla marḍiyyan wa ijtināb mā kāna [ʿinda Allāh] muskhiṭan wa tark al-khurūj ʿinda taʿaddīhim wa jawrihim, wa al-tawba ilā Allāh ʿazza wa jalla kaymā yaʿṭifa bihim ʿalā raʿiyyatihim*).

[63] Al-Muzanī, *Sharḥ al-Sunna*, 87 (*wa lā natruk ḥuḍūr al-jumuʿa, wa ṣalātahā maʿa barr hādhihi al-umma wa fājirihā lāzim*). It was because of the presence of rulers or governors that al-Ḥasan b. Ṣāliḥ did not perform the Friday prayer.

[64] Al-Muzanī, *Sharḥ al-Sunna*, 87 (*wa mā kāna min al-bidaʿ barīʾan*). The editor observes that one manuscript adds the following clause: if a ruler introduced a heresy, one should not pray behind him (*fa in ibtadaʿa ḍalālan fa lā ṣalāt khalfahu*).

Likewise, it is compulsory to fight and perform the greater pilgrimage with every ruler, be he just or oppressive.[65]

There is also the evidence from the proto-Sunni traditionalist community beginning with al-Khallāl and ending with al-Lālakā'ī. Abū Bakr al-Khallāl (d. 311/923) obsesses on the theme of political quietism and the impermissibility of rebellion.[66] Many of the traditions and sayings he mentions are attributed to his teacher, Abū Bakr al-Marrūdhī, whom we discussed in Chapter 3 of this study. They prohibit consistent rebellion against rulers. Al-Ḥasan b. Ṣāliḥ makes more than one appearance in this section, with al-Marrūdhī citing opinions of his teachers who objected to al-Ḥasan b. Ṣāliḥ's belief in the legitimacy of open rebellion.[67] Al-Khallāl speaks of historical episodes in Baghdad and during the reign of Hārūn al-Rashīd where rebellions broke out and scholars were asked whether they ought to join the rebels, and they were instructed firmly against it.[68] Al-Lālakā'ī's (d. 418/1027) discussion lacks the interest in historical episodes from the eighth and ninth centuries otherwise present in al-Khallāl's work, but he claims to have found the doctrine against rebellion stipulated in the creeds of proto-Sunni traditionalists such as Sufyān al-Thawrī, Aḥmad b. Ḥanbal, ʿAlī b. al-Madīnī, al-Bukhārī, Abū Zurʿa al-Rāzī, Abū Ḥātim al-Rāzī, and Sahl b. ʿAbd Allāh al-Tustarī.[69]

## 6.3 Orthodoxy and the State

Let us conclude now with some remarks about the formation of orthodoxy and heresy in the ninth and tenth centuries and how attitudes to the state might have influenced the religious communities invested in arguments of orthodoxy and heresy. The review of proto-Sunni traditionalist

[65] Al-Muzanī, *Sharḥ al-Sunna*, 87 (*wa al-jihād maʿ kulli imām ʿadl aw jā'ir wa al-ḥajj*).

[66] Jarrar, *Doctrinal Instruction* argues that *Sharḥ al-Sunna*, traditionally attributed to al-Barbahārī, was penned in the ninth century by Ghulām Khalīl. For Khalīl's statements on rebellion see Jarrar, *Doctrinal Instruction*, 158–9 (translation) = 267–70 (Arabic edn.).

[67] Al-Khallāl, *al-Sunna*, 1: 135–6.

[68] Al-Khallāl, *al-Sunna*, 1: 132–3, 137, 140 (where reactions of proto-Sunni traditionalists to the rebellion of Sahl b. Salāma are mentioned).

[69] Al-Lālakā'ī, *Sharḥ uṣūl iʿtiqād*, 1: 146 (citing the creed of Sufyān al-Thawrī: *wa al-ṣabr taḥta liwā' al-sulṭān jār am ʿadl*), 152 (citing the creed of Aḥmad b. Ḥanbal: *wa al-samʿ wa al-ṭāʿa li al-a'imma*), 153 (citing Aḥmad b. Ḥanbal again: *wa lā yaḥillu qitāl al-sulṭān wa lā al-khurūj ʿalayhi li aḥad min al-nās fa man faʿala dhālika fa huwa mubtadiʿ ʿalā ghayr al-sunna wa al-ṭarīq*), 158 (citing the creed of ʿAlī b. al-Madīnī: *wa lā yaḥillu qitāl al-sulṭān wa lā khurūj ʿalayhi li aḥad min al-nās fa man ʿamila dhālika fa huwa mubtadiʿ ʿalā ghayr al-sunna*), 164 (citing the creed of al-Bukhārī: *wa an lā yarā al-sayf ʿalā ummat Muḥammad ṣallā Allāhu ʿalayhi wa sallama*), 166 (citing the creed of Abū Zurʿa al-Rāzī: *wa lā narā al-khurūj ʿalā al-a'imma*), 170 (citing the creed of Abū Ḥātim al-Rāzī), 171 (citing the creed of Sahl b. ʿAbd Allāh al-Tustarī: *wa lā yakhruj ʿalā hādhihi al-umma bi al-sayf*).

attacks on Abū Ḥanīfa on account of his advocacy of rebellion has resulted in a greater awareness of the proto-Sunni traditionalist community and their conception of orthodoxy. We also looked beyond Abū Ḥanīfa to survey broader attacks on individuals who supported the idea of rebelling against legitimate rulers.

There is another important aspect of these attacks on Abū Ḥanīfa that warrants consideration. A prime motivation for proto-Sunni traditionalist discourses on Abū Ḥanīfa's 'heresy' concerning rebellion must have been to undermine the ʿAbbāsid state's reliance on Ḥanafī judges and to curtail the spread of Ḥanafism throughout the empire and its provinces. The circulation of a discourse of heresy that anchored Abū Ḥanīfa's heresy, and that of the movement that emerged after him, in his support for rebellion aimed to embarrass the ʿAbbāsid state and political elites into diminishing its employment of Ḥanafī scholars and judges.[70] The logic of their discourse was reasonable and powerful: how could the state facilitate and support proto-Ḥanafism when its eponymous founder not only doubted the legitimacy of the ʿAbbāsids but actively supported efforts to overthrow it? At the same time, proto-Sunni traditionalists were themselves well connected to rulers and political elites, found employment as judges, and were using their proximity to them to disseminate proto-Sunni traditionalism. I do not mean to suggest that any one of these three characteristics meant that scholars were agents of the state. The relationship was more complicated than that. Judges were intermediaries between the state and its subjects. Rulers recognised the need for religious scholars and wise counsel. Scholars understood that an efficient state and a stable society were prerequisites for the diffusion of religious orthodoxy and its norms.

The case of the Ṭāhirids and proto-Sunni traditionalism is a neat illustration of the symbiotic relationship that existed in the ninth century. On the one hand, when Ṭāhir b. al-Ḥusayn counselled his son ʿAbd Allāh b. Ṭāhir, he impressed upon him the importance of having religious scholars in close proximity.[71] This, he argued, would influence the way in which one's subjects would come to regard their rulers (*al-tawqīr li amrika*), it would augment their respect for the ruler's authority (*wa al-hayba li sulṭānika*), and it would enhance the justice of the ruler (*wa al-thiqa bi ʿadlika*).[72] Qadis, for example, are considered to be agents of

[70] On the employment of proto-Ḥanafī judges see Hinds, s.v. 'Miḥna', *EI*$^2$; Tsafrir, *The History of an Islamic School of Law*, 117–18; Melchert, 'How Ḥanafism Came to Originate in Kufa', 339–40; and Tillier, *Les cadis*, 177–86.

[71] Ibn Abī Ṭāhir Ṭayfūr, *Kitāb Baghdād*, 27, 30 (*mushāwarat al-fuqahāʾ*). On this epistle see Bosworth, 'An Early Arabic Mirror for Princes'.

[72] Ibn Abī Ṭāhir Ṭayfūr, *Kitāb Baghdād*, 27.

justice, truth, and order, not mere functionaries of the state.[73] In the other direction, proto-Sunni traditionalists such as Isḥāq b. Rāhawayh saw the Ṭāhirids as vehicles for promoting proto-Sunni traditionalism. Isḥāq b. Rāhawayh is described as being in the company of ʿAbd Allāh b. Ṭāhir on multiple occasions, and he seems to have used these opportunities to promote proto-Sunnī traditionalism as orthodoxy and distinguish it from proto-Ḥanafism. When, for example, ʿAbd Allāh b. Ṭāhir asked Isḥāq b. Rāhawayh about a certain issue, the latter responded: 'The orthodox doctrine (*al-sunna*) concerning this is such and such. This is the doctrine of those who follow proto-Sunni traditionalist orthodoxy (*wa ka dhākila yaqūl man salaka ṭarīq ahl al-sunna*). As for Abū Ḥanīfa and his followers, they oppose this (*wa ammā Abū Ḥanīfa wa aṣḥābuhu fa innahum qālū bi khilāf hādhā*).'[74] The rest of the report is illuminating: Ibrāhīm b. Ṣāliḥ was present during this conversation, and he objected to Isḥāq b. Rāhawayh's characterisation of the Ḥanafī position. Isḥāq b. Rāhawayh responded that he had memorised this Ḥanafī doctrine from the book composed by Ibrāhīm b. Ṣāliḥ's grandfather, with whom Ibn Rāhawayh had attended school. Ibrāhīm accused Ibn Rāhawayh of lying about his grandfather. The book was brought to the Ṭāhirid governor. Ibn Rāhawayh told him to turn to the eleventh folio and focus his attention on line nine. The governor did this and found the discussion of the legal problem. Needless to say, the governor was startled: 'You have memorised the legal discussions, I know, but I am amazed at this display of your prodigious memory.' Isḥāq replied, '[I memorised books] so that on a day such as this, God may manifest it against enemies [of mine] like Ibrāhīm.' We cannot be certain as to the authenticity of the details presented here. However, a few things seem very likely, based on the regularity of their depiction elsewhere in our medieval sources: first, that Isḥāq b. Rāhawayh was present in the company of ʿAbd Allāh b. Ṭāhir; second, that Isḥāq b. Rāhawayh sought to promote proto-Sunni traditionalism and attack proto-Ḥanafism under the Ṭāhirids; and third, that Isḥāq b. Rāhawayh, like many of his peers, memorised books.

Isḥāq b. Ḥanbal (d. 253/867) knew Isḥāq b. Rāhawayh as an intimate member of the Ṭāhirid court, and perhaps this was the disagreement between Aḥmad b. Ḥanbal and Isḥāq b. Rāhawayh hinted at in one

[73] Ibn Abī Ṭāhir Ṭayfūr, *Kitāb Baghdād*, 30–1.

[74] Al-Khaṭīb al-Baghdādī, *Tārīkh Baghdād*, 7: 372–3. Of course, 'proto-Sunni traditionalist orthodoxy' is not a literal translation for *ahl al-sunna*. This is why I've provided the original text in parenthesis. On Isḥāq b. Rāhawayh in conversation with ʿAbd Allāh b. Ṭāhir on a different occasion and discussing the former's prodigious memory, see al-Khaṭīb al-Baghdādī, *Tārīkh Baghdād*, 7: 373.

medieval source.[75] His students included both Ibn Qutayba and al-Bukhārī. Isḥāq b. Rāhawayh is purported to have shown ʿAbd Allāh b. Ṭāhir the *Kitāb al-Tārīkh* composed by al-Bukhārī.[76] There are a number of problems with evidence of this kind. It is preserved in later sources. It might be inspired by a desire to establish the early composition of al-Bukhārī's works. On the other hand, ʿAbd Allāh b. Ṭāhir's interests in proto-Sunni traditionalism are unusually prominent in a range of primary sources. I think there is some evidence to suggest, for example, that in the eastern provinces of the early Islamic empire during the ninth century proto-Sunni traditionalists had established good relations with the Ṭāhirids. Al-Khalīlī's *al-Irshād*, a key source for the religious history of Khurāsān, allows us to tease from it some meagre details about Ṭāhirids and proto-Sunnī traditionalism. We learn, for example, that one al-Ḥusayn b. al-Faḍl al-Bajalī arrived and settled in Nīshāpūr, having moved there from Iraq. Al-Khalīlī quotes al-Ḥākim al-Nīshāpūrī, who wrote that al-Bajalī was one among a group of scholars whom ʿAbd Allāh b. Ṭāhir had brought with him. These scholars were chosen from Iraq and transferred to Nīshāpūr.[77] Al-Ḥākim al-Nīshāpūrī's remark seems to indicate that this was a specific policy pursued by the Ṭāhirids and that al-Bajalī was one among many scholars now gathering around the Ṭāhirids. The Ṭāhirids were not an independent dynasty. They represented one of the empire's most important elite families. They were reliable provincial governors, but their authority had extended across the entire empire into Egypt and Baghdad. They were invested in the maintenance of ʿAbbāsid authority, and the ʿAbbāsids, in turn, invested in them.[78] The decisions Ṭāhirid governors made in Khurāsān and Transoxiana, especially the kind of religious culture they supported, were made independently of the ʿAbbāsids. In the light of this, I think it would be unreasonable to doubt the influence that a literate elite (the proto-Sunni traditionalist community) might have had on the political authorities of their day.

To conclude, what this may suggest is that we need to revise an interpretation of religion and politics in early Islam as old as Ibn

[75] Ibn Abī Yaʿlā, *Ṭabaqāt al-Ḥanābila*, 1: 112–13 (al-Fiqī edn.).

[76] Al-Khaṭīb al-Baghdādī, *Tārīkh Baghdād*, 2: 7; Ibn Ḥajar al-ʿAsqalānī, *Taghlīq al-taʿlīq*, 5: 405.

[77] Al-Khalīlī, *al-Irshād*, 2: 811–12 (Riyadh edn.). We have no reason to doubt al-Khalīlī's reliable transmission of al-Ḥākim's history, since an entry on this al-Bajalī survives in Khalīfa al-Nīshāpūrī, *Talkhīṣ tārīkh Nīshāpūr*, ed. Behmān Karīmī (Tehran: Kitābkhāneh-yi Ibn Sīnā, n.d.), 21, where the author notes: 'al-Ḥusayn b. Faḍl b. ʿUmayr b. al-Qāsim b. Kaysān al-Bajalī [not al-Ḥillī] Abū ʿAlī al-Kūfī, he was the imam of his age who came to Nīshāpūr with ʿAbd Allāh b. Ṭāhir. He took up residence in Nīshāpūr and died there. He is buried in the graveyard of al-Ḥusayn b. Muʿādh.'

[78] On the Ṭāhirids see Kennedy, *The Early Abbasid Caliphate*, 138–48; Kaabi, 'Les origines ṭāhirides'.

Khaldūn and as recent as Aḥmad Taymūr Pāshā – namely, that we might have to revisit our view of the spread of Ḥanafism as a product of ʿAbbāsid patronage.[79] The view that the ʿAbbāsids facilitated the spread of Ḥanafism rests on a number of accidents pertaining to the surviving corpus of primary sources.[80] The Ḥanafī biographical dictionaries are more copious and forthcoming concerning qadis. We know from specific examples that many proto-Sunni traditionalists served as qadis, but their biographical literature has not survived. This is the case for both proto-Ḥanbalism and proto-Shāfiʿism. This is not to say that Ḥanafism failed to benefit from the appointment of someone like Abū Yūsuf as Chief Judge.[81] But proto-Sunni traditionalists, too, appreciated what was advantageous in maintaining good relations with rulers and governors.

This chapter has attempted to document and explain why Abū Ḥanīfa's views on rebellion played such a dominant role in proto-Sunni traditionalist discourses of heresy against him. I have suggested that three historical developments in the middle of the ninth century contributed to charges of heresy against Abū Ḥanīfa on account of his doctrine of rebellion against rulers. First, the promotion of proto-Sunni traditionalism under al-Mutawakkil. Second, friendly relations between the Ṭāhirids and proto-Sunni traditionalists. Third, a desire among proto-Sunni traditionalists to undermine the ʿAbbāsid state's reliance on proto-Ḥanafī judges and to replace them with proto-Sunni traditionalist ones. The frequency with which Abū Hanīfa's involvement in rebellion pervaded discourses of heresy has to be seen as an attempt by proto-Sunni traditionalists to highlight the embarrassing contradiction that lay at the heart of perceived ʿAbbāsid patronage of Ḥanafism in the provinces of the empire. How could the ʿAbbāsids rely on a network of jurists, judges, and bureaucrats whose patron founder was so relentless in his efforts to support robust challenges to ʿAbbāsid authority?

[79] Aḥmad Taymūr Pāshā, *Naẓrat al-tārīkhiyya fī ḥudūth al-madhāhib al-fiqhiyya al-arbaʿa* (Beirut: Dār al-Qādirī, 1990), 51–3; Tsafrir, *The History of an Islamic School of Law*, 117–18.

[80] I shall take up this point in more detail in Chapter 10 below.

[81] See my discussion in Chapter 8 below.

# 7 Religion and Society

Part II of this monograph has been organised around the view that heresy and orthodoxy must be understood in the light of social, cultural, and political history. Chapters 3 and 4 have detailed the ways in which discourses of heresy were implicated in the society and social imaginaries of the ninth century. Chapter 6 argued that politics (and the state) were foundational to the discourses of heresy concerning Abū Ḥanīfa. I even suggested that it was the most odious aspect of Abū Ḥanīfa's legacy in the view of his proto-Sunni traditionalist critics and the one that contributed most to his reputation as a heretic among some proto-Sunni traditionalists. This chapter confronts those aspects of discourses of heresy that concerned Abū Ḥanīfa's jurisprudence, ḥadīth, theology, and piety. I will reiterate, one final time, my view that the discourses of heresy treated so far in this book belonged to the broader realm of religion. I conceive of religion in medieval Islam as a category within which were embedded questions of society and politics and not as a category defined solely by questions of ritual and dogma. Society and the state were no less important to discourses of heresy and orthodoxy than the nascent fields of Islamic learning in the eighth and ninth centuries placed here under the rubric of religion. Even my division of these dimensions of religion into distinct fields is somewhat anachronistic for the eighth century. There was no neat scholarly division of labour in the eighth century to distinguish expertise in jurisprudence from ḥadīth, theology, or modes of piety. I have separated them for purely organisational convenience.

This chapter distils a massive reservoir of discourses of heresy against Abū Ḥanīfa to document the capaciousness of proto-Sunni traditionalist discourses of heresy. It identifies the multifarious nature of criticisms of Abū Ḥanīfa. Proto-Sunni traditionalists assailed Abū Ḥanīfa on account of his jurisprudence (section 7.1), expertise in ḥadīth (7.2), theological doctrines (7.3), and his piety (7.4). These were, in the eyes of proto-Sunni traditionalists, a set of wide-ranging heresies, and the challenge presented by this scale of religious deviance prompted proto-Sunni traditionalists to cultivate a set of disciplinary mechanisms to regulate and enforce religious orthodoxy. This social dimension of marginalising heresy and regulating orthodoxy is the focus of the final section of this chapter (7.5).

## 7.1 Law

I outlined at the very beginning of this study that mnemohistory was particularly well suited to writing the social history of the formation of orthodoxy during the eighth–eleventh centuries. I explained that mnemohistory, much like this study, is not concerned with the life and career of Abū Ḥanīfa. The focus on discourses of heresy takes us to the moment in early Islamicate societies when textual communities begin to form on the heels of an explosion of the written word. In turn, the formation of these textual communities marks the beginning of discourses of heresy concerning Abū Ḥanīfa, and because of this the mnemohistory of Abū Ḥanīfa provides important insights into the development of discourses of heresy and their relevance to the formation of proto-Sunni orthodoxy. The fact that the literary record, by and large, dates to at least half a century after his death hampers the prospects of a comprehensive biography of Abū Ḥanīfa and an account of his legal doctrines. Historical criticism simply does not yield such desired results. Fortunately, this chapter is explicitly concerned with the ways in which his opponents interpreted his jurisprudence as evidence of his religious deviance and why jurisprudence formed an important component of discourses of heresy. Before turning to these heresiological discourses, I should like to explore briefly what can be known about the nature of Islamic law and jurisprudence in the time of Abū Ḥanīfa. This is necessary in so far as it provides a more concrete background to the jurisprudential dimensions of ninth-century discourses of heresy against Abū Ḥanīfa. It holds up a mirror against which we can better understand proto-Sunni traditionalist depictions of Abū Ḥanīfa's jurisprudence.

### *Jurisprudence in the Eighth Century*

That this is a question worth posing is because sources from the ninth century purport to preserve two 'texts' dating to the middle of the eighth century. I should like to examine the letters of Ibn al-Muqaffaʿ (d. *c.*139/756) to the caliph al-Manṣūr (r. 136–58/754–5) and ʿUbayd Allāh b. al-Ḥasan al-ʿAnbarī (d. 168/785) to the caliph al-Mahdī (r. 158/775–169/785).[1] They provide unrivalled social commentary on the world of law

[1] See Zaman, *Religion and Politics*, 82–5.

and jurisprudence in the middle of the eighth century and on the eve of discourses of heresy against Abū Ḥanīfa on account of his jurisprudence.

The first document is a letter authored by the Basran judge ʿUbayd Allāh b. al-Ḥasan al-ʿAnbarī to the caliph al-Mahdī. The letter is preserved in only one source, Muḥammad b. Khalaf Wakīʿ's (d. 306/917) ninth-century composition on the history of judges.[2] The document has been examined by a number of scholars to elucidate the relationship between scholars and caliphs.[3] To my knowledge, its authenticity has not been disputed.[4] Al-ʿAnbarī was involved intimately with political and administrative matters in the caliphate of al-Manṣūr and his son al-Mahdī.[5] He was appointed qadi and governor in charge of prayer over Basra by al-Manṣūr in 156/773 and removed a decade later.[6] Under al-Mahdī, al-ʿAnbarī retained his judgeship until 167/783–4. During his term as judge al-ʿAnbarī came into conflict with al-Mahdī a number of times.[7] His brief treatise deliberating on state administration (the military, judiciary, and taxes) betrays al-ʿAnbarī's professional experiences in the political life of the early ʿAbbāsids. Our concern here is with what al-ʿAnbarī's letter reveals about jurisprudence in the mid-eighth century.

Al-ʿAnbarī describes the role of judges and governors (*al-ḥukkām*) and how rulings (*al-aḥkām*) should be determined.

Judgment must be based on the book of God (*kitāb Allāh*). If such rulings are not found in the book of God, then they must be based on the Sunna of the messenger of God (*thumma bimā fī sunnat rasūl Allāh*). If such rulings are not found in the Sunna of the messenger of God, they must be based upon that which the imams–jurists have agreed (*mā ajmaʿa ʿalayhi al-aʾimma al-fuqahāʾ*). Finally, there is the

[2] Wakīʿ, *Akhbār al-quḍāt*, 2: 97–107. For a translation of the document into French see Tillier, 'Un traité politique', 155–67.

[3] Van Ess, 'La liberté'; van Ess, *Theologie und Gesellschaft*, 2: 167; Tillier, 'Un traité politique'; Zaman, *Religion and Politics*, 85–91; Crone and Hinds, *God's Caliph*, 93, 98, 103; Hallaq, *Origins and Evolution*, 185–6; Bligh-Abramski, 'The Judiciary (Qāḍīs)' 51, 70.

[4] See Tillier, 'Un traité politique', 145, where he writes: 'Les problèmes liés à l'édition de cet unicum ne permettent pas d'affirmer avec certitude que le texte est conforme, à la lettre près, à l'original du IIe/VIIIe siècle. Une référence aux quatre sources du droit (Coran, *sunna, iǧmāʿ et iǧtihād*) pourait même paraître anachronique. M. Q. Zaman, qui s'est interrogé le premier sur son authenticité, rapelle néanmoins que les fondements du droit musulman (*uṣūl*) commencent à être définis dans des écrits antérieurs.' To be clear, Zaman raises the question of the text's authenticity only to rule it out (see Zaman, *Religion and Politics*, 89). Tillier himself seems content with authenticity of the text to 159/775 as indicated in Wakīʿ's text (see Tillier, 'Un traité politique', 145: 'De fait, plusieurs indices laissent penser que l'épître a bien été écrite à l'époque indiquée par Wakīʿ').

[5] Wakīʿ, *Akhbār al-quḍāt*, 2: 91–123 (for the entry on al-ʿAnbarī), 91.

[6] Wakīʿ, *Akhbār al-quḍāt*, 2: 91. [7] Wakīʿ, *Akhbār al-quḍāt*, 2: 92–4, 117.

independent decision of the governor (*ijtihād al-ḥākim*), which he must exercise if the caliph has assigned him this responsibility, though in consultation with scholars (*fa innahu lā ya'lū idhā wallāhu al-imām dhālika ma'a mushāwarat ahl al-'ilm*).[8]

Al-'Anbarī's account of the process of Islamic law focuses on that dimension of it which relates to the state's administration of the early Islamic empire and its provinces. It must be admitted that al-'Anbarī seems less interested in the world of private jurisprudence in the first half of the eighth century. Perhaps for this reason he is silent on the role and relevance of *ra'y* to the elaboration of Islamic law. One could argue that al-'Anbarī hints at the importance of *ra'y* in his emphasis on the *ijtihād* of the governor, which he explains must be exercised in consultation with scholars and jurists (*ahl al-'ilm*).[9] Additionally, al-'Anbarī's remark about the importance of scholarly consensus may constitute another nod to the independent reasoning of jurists.[10] Still, what cannot be disputed is that al-'Anbarī believes that law and legal reasoning, to the extent possible, must be deduced on the basis of a hierarchy of scripture, Prophetic practice, and the consensus of jurists. As we shall see, discourses of heresy against Abū Ḥanīfa in the realm of jurisprudence echo a vision of law advocated by al-'Anbarī: a legal process wherein *ra'y* as a legal procedure is circumscribed. On account of his concern with the role of the state in implementing legal justice al-'Anbarī admittedly may not provide us with the most accurate portrait of Islamic law and legal reasoning in the eighth century; but, for now, his letter is one of the few eighth-century documents to which scholars can gain access. The other belongs to Ibn al-Muqaffa'.

Ibn al-Muqaffa''s treatise describes a society deeply affected by the vagaries of law and jurisprudence.[11] His view of jurists' law, however, is an unflattering one and is delivered as a blistering critique in one single paragraph:[12]

8 Wakī', *Akhbār al-quḍāt*, 2: 101. Tillier, 'Un traité politique', 160 translates *al-ḥākim*/*al-ḥukkām* as judge/judges ('juge/les juges'). In this context, I believe al-'Anbarī to be referring primarily to governors and only secondarily to judges (qadis).

9 Wakī', *Akhbār al-quḍāt*, 2: 101. 10 Wakī', *Akhbār al-quḍāt*, 2: 101.

11 Schacht was one of the first scholars to realise the potential of Ibn al-Muqaffa''s epistle as an early and external source for the history of Islamic legal reasoning in the eighth century. See Schacht, *The Origins of Muhammadan Jurisprudence*, 58–9, 95–6, 102–3, 137. The literature on Ibn al-Muqaffa' and his *Risāla fī al-ṣaḥāba* is vast, but I have limited myself to those sources treating the legal dimensions of the treatise. See Crone and Hinds, *God's Caliph*, 85–7; Zaman, *Religion and Politics*, 82–5; Goitein, 'A Turning Point', 149–67; van Ess, *Theologie und Gesellschaft*, 2: 22–36; Lowry, 'The First Islamic Legal Theory'; Lambton, *State and Government*, 53–4; and Pellat, *Ibn al-Muqaffa'* for a critical edition and translation.

12 Ibn al-Muqaffa', *al-Risāla fī al-ṣaḥāba*, in *Āthār Ibn al-Muqaffa'*, 316, though the critique of juristic reasoning (*ra'y*) and juristic analogical reasoning (*qiyās*) can be found at 316–18.

Among the matters which the Commander of the Faithful must consider, especially with respect to the situation in these two provinces and other provinces and regions, is the divergent nature of these contradictory rulings. In fact, its divergence has resulted in grave consequences relating to public violence (*al-dimāʾ*), sexual morality (*al-furūj*), and wealth and poverty (*al-amwāl*). In al-Ḥīrā, for example, public violence and sexual immorality is permitted, whilst the same things are prohibited in Kufa. Similar divergences can be observed in Kufa itself, where in one of its districts something is permissible which has been prohibited in another district. These rulings, notwithstanding their multiple variations, are executed against the Muslims in matters that lead to the spilling of their blood and violations against them, and it is pronounced by judges.

Ibn al-Muqaffaʿ is disturbed by the law's divergent, contradictory rulings, its different character from province to province, its extreme analogising (*qiyās*), the lack of consistent tradition (*sunna*), and its contribution to social disorder. He sees the jurists' law as arbitrary, unpredictable, and disorderly. Based on this he concludes that the ruler must impose his authority upon the jurists' law.[13] Our interest here is in the social commentary on Islamic law that Ibn al-Muqaffaʿ provides. Jurisprudence in the first half of the eighth century was a thriving enterprise that involved a number of mechanisms: juristic reasoning (*raʾy*), juristic analogising (*qiyās*), Prophetic or Companion practice (*sunna*), speculative inquiry (*naẓar*), and judicial decision making (*qaḍāʾ*). Ibn al-Muqaffaʿ recognises an environment in which jurists engaged in a variety of legal methods and thereby produced highly divergent results. He singles out the jurists' use of juristic reasoning (*raʾy*) and analogising (*qiyās*) as contributing to social and political chaos.

Taken together, the eighth-century testimonies of al-ʿAnbarī and Ibn al-Muqaffaʿ reflect an awareness of significant developments in Islamic legal reasoning. We should not make the mistake of reading their social commentary as historical fact, and this is especially the case with Ibn

[13] To be precise, Ibn al-Muqaffaʿ counsels the caliph to impose his own juristic authority (*raʾy*) with respect to legal cases. I see Ibn al-Muqaffaʿ's use of the term *raʾy* in this context as not incidental. The *raʾy* of the ruler or the governor referred to the scope of legal authority. Ibn al-Muqaffaʿ's argument seems to be that *raʾy* as practised by jurists lacks both a centralising authority and an executing function. The *raʾy* of the ruler (or the governor), on the other hand, comprises both. The term *raʾy* is referred to in some of the earliest documentary sources, but it is not *raʾy* as a juridical technique that is intended. See the discussion around P. Vindob. AP 5.379 in Sijpesteijn, 'The Archival Mind in Early Islamic Egypt', 172–5. However, it seems to me that the formulaic use of the term in early eighth-century documents, often official state correspondence, indicates that, even when employed in documents of this kind, *raʾy* conveyed something more considerable and authoritative than just one's opinion. For the phrase *in rāʾa al-amīr min al-raʾy* ... see Khan, 'Historical Development'. I would argue that the caliph's or the governor's *raʾy* was a legitimate and independent source of authority. Ibn al-Muqaffaʿ suggests as much in *Risāla fī al-ṣaḥāba*, in *Rasāʾil al-bulaghāʾ*, 126, 313, 318.

al-Muqaffaʿ, who was nothing if not a gifted rhetorician and astute political mind. Even if the terrain of Islamic law that they sketch, particularly that of Ibn al-Muqaffaʿ, may not be a flattering one, it is nevertheless one in which the jurisprudential methods that proto-Sunni traditionalists attacked Abū Ḥanīfa for are vaguely recognisable. Discourses of heresy with respect to Abū Ḥanīfa and his jurisprudence may feature much ninth-century back-projection, but at least some of the legal mechanisms for which Abū Ḥanīfa was pilloried can be dated to the middle of the eighth century. It is to these that we now turn.[14]

### *Speculative Jurisprudence (*Ra'y*)*

Modern scholars have identified the impact that diverging approaches to jurisprudence had on intensifying the rivalry between the partisans of ḥadīth (*ahl al-ḥadīth*) and the partisans of juristic reasoning (*ahl al-ra'y*).[15] In what follows, I should like to expand upon and provide earlier (and further) documentation for hostility to Abū Ḥanīfa on account of his jurisprudence.

Our first example demonstrates, once again, the overlapping nature of discourses of heresy against Abū Ḥanīfa. In the ninth century a steady stream of reports began to circulate establishing a connection between lowly social and ethnic status, the fall and decline of other religious communities, and the decisive role that juristic reasoning played in bringing about religious deviancy. Chapter 5 translated and analysed some of these reports, focusing on their ethnic and social dimensions. Here, I should like to show how, in order to interpret the trajectory of orthodoxy and heresy, proto-Sunni traditionalists also appealed to a cyclical view of history. These reports contrasting the history of Judaism with contemporary developments in the ninth century in Islam make it apparent that ninth-century religious scholars viewed their own history within explicitly inter-confessional paradigms. There were paradigms of religious heresy and deviance among the religions of late antiquity, and proto-Sunni traditionalists warned of the dangers of remaining oblivious to them:[16]

[14] *Ḥiyal*, for example, is absent from both Ibn al-Muqaffaʿ and al-ʿAnbarī's account of Islamic legal reasoning. We might wish to consider, therefore, whether proto-Sunni traditionalist criticisms of Abū Ḥanīfa's use of *ḥiyal* reflects late eighth-century proto-Ḥanafī developments. We shall return to this problem later in this chapter.

[15] The definitive account is given by Melchert, *The Formation of the Sunni Schools of Law*, 1–47. See also Melchert, 'Traditionist-Jurisprudents'; Goldziher, *The Ẓāhirīs*, 3–18; Hallaq, *Origins and Evolution*, 122–49.

[16] Al-Khaṭīb al-Baghdādī, *Tārīkh Baghdād*, 15: 543, where three slightly different iterations of this report can be found.

Abū al-Ḥasan ʿAlī b. Aḥmad b. Ibrāhīm al-Bazzāz < Abū ʿAlī al-Ḥasan b. Muḥammad b. ʿUthmān al-Fasawī < Yaʿqūb b. Sufyān < Muḥammad b. ʿAwf < Ismāʿīl b. ʿAyyāsh < Hishām b. ʿUrwa < Hishām's father said: 'The state of the Children of Israel remained upright until bastard foreigners descending from slaves (*abnā' sabāyā al-umam*) appeared among them and began to practise speculative jurisprudence. Consequently, they perished and caused others to perish.'

This is mentioned in al-Khaṭīb al-Baghdādī's history. Its provenance is much earlier, and the chain of transmission allows us to identify it with at least one ninth-century historical source: al-Fasawī's *Kitāb al-Maʿrifa wa al-tārīkh*.[17] In fact, variations of this tradition appear in other ninth-eleventh century sources, where on more than one occasion they purport to go back to the Prophet or a Companion. Among ninth-century proto-Sunni traditionalists we find that Ibn Abī Shayba, Ibn Māja (d. 273/887), and al-Dārimī (d. 255/869) include the report in their ḥadīth collections.[18] From the tenth century al-Dāraquṭnī (d. 385/995) and Ibn Baṭṭa al-ʿUkbarī (d. 387/997) refer to the tradition.[19] In the eleventh century the report attracted the attention of Abū Nuʿaym al-Iṣfahānī (d. 430/1038), al-Bayhaqī (d. 458/1066), and al-Khaṭīb al-Baghdādī.[20]

[17] Al-Fasawī, *Kitāb al-Maʿrifa wa al-tārīkh*, 2: 20–1.

[18] The earliest trace of this report can be found in Sayf b. ʿUmar, *Kitāb al-ridda wa al-futūḥ*, ed. Qāsim al-Sāmarrāʾī (Leiden: Brill, 1995), 18. See Ibn Abī Shayba, *al-Muṣannaf*, 21: 264; Ibn Māja, *Sunan, al-muqaddima, bāb ijtināb al-ra'y wa al-qiyās* 8, no. 56 (numbering after ʿAbd al-Bāqī's edition); al-Dārimī, *Kitāb al-Musnad al-Jāmiʿ [Sunan al-Dārimī]*, ed. Nabīl b. Hāshim b. ʿAbd Allāh al-Ghumarī (Beirut: Dār al-Bashā'ir al-Islāmiyya, 2013), *kitāb al-ʿilm* 2, *bāb al-tawarruʿ ʿan al-jawāb fīmā laysa fīhi kitāb wa lā sunna* 2, no. 130.

[19] Al-Dāraquṭnī, *Sunan*, ed. ʿĀdil Aḥmad ʿAbd al-Mawjūd and ʿAlī Muḥammad Muʿawwiḍ (Beirut: Dār al-Maʿrifa, 2001), 3: 379–80, *kitāb al-nawādir* 19, *bāb al-nawādir* 1, no. 12 and 13 = al-Dāraquṭnī, *Sunan al-Dāraquṭnī wa bi dhaylihi al-taʿlīq al-mughnī ʿalā al-Dāraquṭnī*, ed. Shuʿayb al-Arna'ūṭ (Beirut: Mu'assasat al-Risāla, 2004), 5: 257, with additional versions in the commentary; Ibn Baṭṭa al-ʿUkbarī, *al-Sharḥ wa al-ibāna ʿalā uṣūl al-sunna wa al-diyāna*, ed. Riḍā b. Naʿsān Muʿṭī (Medina: Maktabat al-ʿUlūm wa al-Ḥikam, 2002), 127 = Ibn Baṭṭa al-ʿUkbarī, *al-Sharḥ wa al-ibāna [al-ibāna al-ṣughrā]*, ed. ʿĀdil b. ʿAbd Allāh b. Saʿd al-Ghāmidī (Riyadh: Dār al-Amr al-Awwal, 2011), 24–5.

[20] Abū Nuʿaym al-Iṣfahānī, *Maʿrifat al-ṣaḥāba*, ed. ʿĀdil b. Yūsuf al-ʿAzzāzī (Riyadh: Dār al-Waṭan li al-Nashr, 1998), 1722 (under bāb al-ʿayn 'ʿAbd Allāh b. ʿAmr b. al-ʿĀṣ'); al-Bayhaqī, *Maʿrifat al-sunan wa al-āthār*, ed. ʿAbd al-Muʿṭī Amīn Qalʿajī (Aleppo: Dār al-Waʿy, 2012), 1: 182; al-Bayhaqī, *al-Madkhal ilā al-sunan al-kubrā*, ed. Muḥammad Ḍiyā' al-Raḥmān al-Aʿẓamī (Kuwait: Dār al-Khulafā' li al-Kitāb al-Islāmī, n.d.), 195, which appears in a chapter recollecting condemnations of speculative jurisprudence (*ra'y*); al-Khaṭīb al-Baghdādī, *Kitāb al-Faqīh wa al-mutafaqqih*, 1: 451 (under *dhikr al-aḥādīth al-wārida fī dhamm al-qiyās wa taḥrīmihi wa al-manʿ minhu*). For brief discussions of this report in the secondary sources see Kister, 'Ḥaddithū ʿan Banī Isrā'īla Wa-Lā Ḥaraja', 232, where Kister mentions the tradition by way of illustrating that early Muslims believed the Muslim community would undergo developments similar to those that the Jewish community had experienced; and El Shamsy, *The Canonization of Islamic Law*, 31.

The narrative is that the decline and fall of this religious community is reduced to the influence of foreigners, slaves, and female captives. It was they, as a social and ethnic group, who introduced juristic reasoning into Judaism, and now a similar process was threatening the early Islamic community. The rise of speculative jurisprudence marks the beginning of religious misguidance. Inquiries into the historical roots and causes of religious deviance are informed by an awareness of how previous monotheistic communities fell into heresies. This ancient form of historical explanation provides a template for the early Islamic community. The changing social and ethnic landscape of early Islamic society had produced serious anxieties, and this report reflects a miasma of fear about what effect such rapid changes might have on the religious integrity of the early Muslim community. Proto-Sunni traditionalists paid close attention to the social circumstances that produced religious deviants and heresies. They saw in these manifestations instances in which foreign, servile, and socially inferior origins gave birth to heresies in the central heartlands of the early Islamic empire. For proto-Sunni traditionalists this development signalled the beginning of a fateful turn in early Islam, which if it continued unchecked could result in the kind of irreparable damage that Judaism had suffered at the hands of foreigners descended from female slave captives, or so the argument went.

This correlative relationship between ethnicity and religious deviance in early Islam was widespread among proto-Sunni traditionalist textual communities, but there are indications that ninth-century proto-Sunni traditionalists tried to connect discourses of heresy concerning Abū Ḥanīfa and, in particular, his jurisprudence, to a broader interconfessional framework. ʿAbd Allāh b. Aḥmad b. Ḥanbal relates that Shuʿayb b. Ḥarb was instructed by Sufyān al-Thawrī to go to Abū Ḥanīfa to ask him about the waiting period for an *umm walad* (slave concubine who has given birth to her master's child) in the event that her master dies. Shuʿayb b. Ḥarb reports that he went to see Abū Ḥanīfa and posed this question to him. Abū Ḥanīfa responded that she did not have to observe a waiting period. Shuʿayb b. Ḥarb returned to Sufyān and told him of what had passed. Sufyān al-Thawrī responded by telling him that this was the precise jurisprudential opinion of the Jews.[21] Here, ʿAbd Allāh b. Aḥmad b. Ḥanbal suggests a deeper connection between Abū Ḥanīfa and the deviance of other religious communities. Deviant jurisprudential edicts are identical with jurisprudential positions taken by the

[21] ʿAbd Allāh b. Aḥmad b. Ḥanbal, *Kitāb al-Sunna*, 194. The *isnād* is Aḥmad b. Ibrāhīm al-Dawraqī < al-Ḥasan b. Mūsā al-Nasāʾī < ʿUbda/ʿAbda b. ʿAbd Allāh < Shuʿayb b. Ḥarb < Sufyān al-Thawrī.

Jewish community. The fact that Abū Ḥanīfa's legal opinions dovetail with those of the Jewish community is sufficient to bring Abū Ḥanīfa's religious credibility into grave disrepute. Some went even further than this. A scandalous rumour was circulated in tenth-century Wāsiṭ: someone had told someone else that he heard Ibn Abī Shayba say that he suspected Abū Ḥanīfa was a Jew.[22] Similar outlandish attempts to malign Ḥanafīs were originating, once more, from Wāsiṭ. Shādhdh b. Yaḥyā al-Wāsiṭī,[23] a companion of Yazīd b. Hārūn, reports that he heard Yazīd say: 'I have not seen anyone who resembled the Christians more than the followers of Abū Ḥanīfa.'[24] Proto-Sunni traditionalists in the ninth century were also circulating reports that the downfall of the Jews occurred at the hands of their reciters and their jurists, and that the same fate would befall the Muslims.[25]

The social and religious histories of late antique religions serve a parabolic purpose. Studying the causes for the decline and fall of late antique religious communities transforms an inter-confessional parable into an indictment of heresy and deviance, culminating in a paraenetic argument concerning the proximity between foreign peoples and the origins of heresy and religious deviance.[26] In the words of al-Fasawī: the people of heresy (*ahl al-ahwā'*) are equivalent to the Jews and Christians.[27] In some cases, the people of heresy were perceived to be more pernicious. Ibn Shaqīq was heard as having said: 'Indeed, we relate the doctrines of the Jews and Christians, but we cannot bring ourselves to relate the doctrines of the Jahmiyya.'[28]

22 Al-Khaṭīb al-Baghdādī, *Tārīkh Baghdād*, 15: 571.

23 Shādhdh b. Yaḥyā al-Wāsiṭī studied with Wakīʿ b. al-Jarrāḥ and Yazīd b. Hārūn, both of whom figure in reports praising and condemning Abū Ḥanīfa. On Shādhdh b. Yaḥyā al-Wāsiṭī see Ibn Abī Ḥātim, *al-Jarḥ*, 4: 392 (repr. Beirut: Dār al-Kutub al-ʿIlmiyya, n.d.); al-Mizzī, *Tahdhīb al-kamāl*, 12: 341–2. For the pointing of his name see Ibn Ḥajar al-ʿAsqalānī, *Tabṣīr al-muntabih*, 2: 764.

24 Al-Khaṭīb al-Baghdādī, *Tārīkh Baghdād*, 15: 566 (*mā ra'aytu qawm ashbah bi al-naṣārā min aṣḥāb Abī Ḥanīfa*).

25 Ibn Waḍḍāḥ, *Kitāb al-Bidaʿ*, 202 (*innamā halakat banī isrā'īl ʿalā yaday qurrā'ihim wa fuqahā'ihim wa sa tuhliku hādhihi al-umma ʿalā yaday qurrā'ihim wa fuqahā'ihim*).

26 In his (now lost) *Kitāb al-Sunna*, al-Fasawī gives a fascinating example of the curiosity that medieval Muslims displayed for inter-confessional accounts of religious deviance in Judaism. See al-Fasawī, *Kitāb al-Maʿrifa wa al-tārīkh*, 3: 493. The editor of al-Fasawī's history has gone to the trouble of collecting extracts from his *Kitāb al-Sunna* as they appear in later works. Much of al-Fasawī's *Kitāb al-Sunna* is reproduced by al-Lālakā'ī, 'Sharḥ uṣūl iʿtiqād ahl al-sunna wa al-jamāʿa', ed. Aḥmad b. Masʿūd b. Ḥamdān' (PhD thesis, Jāmiʿat Umm al-Qurā, 1990), 131 f. (and this particular report can be found in al-Lālakā'ī, *Sharḥ uṣūl iʿtiqād*, 142 (Ḥamdān edn.)).

27 Al-Fasawī, *Kitāb al-Maʿrifa wa al-tārīkh*, 3: 490; al-Lālakā'ī, *Sharḥ uṣūl iʿtiqād*, 131 (Ḥamdān edn.).

28 ʿAbd Allāh b. Aḥmad b. Ḥanbal, *Kitāb al-Sunna*, 174. The edited text reads: *anā la naḥkī kalām al-yahūd wa al-naṣārā wa lā nastaṭīʿ an naḥkiya kalām al-jahmiyya*. First, I would

If juristic reasoning was a mechanism for law making, some proto-Sunni traditionalists found it lacking some basic ingredients of the law – namely, consistency and predictability. For proto-Sunni traditionalists a law devised on the basis of a body of ḥadīth reports ensured both of these features. *Ra'y*, on the other hand, was a source of frivolous speculation, arbitrary legal opinion, flagrant contradictions, and legal absurdities. Sometimes Abū Ḥanīfa's detractors found gentle ways to express their dissatisfaction with the speculative nature of his jurisprudence. ʿAbd Allāh b. Aḥmad b. Ḥanbal's *Kitāb al-Sunna* describes a man contrasting Sufyān al-Thawrī's jurisprudence with Abū Ḥanīfa's: 'I found Sufyān to be more learned in legal problems that actually occurred, whilst Abū Ḥanīfa knew more about legal problems that had never occurred.'[29] Similarly, when Qays b. al-Rabīʿ was asked about Abū Ḥanīfa, his response is said to have mirrored this statement. 'Abū Ḥanīfa', he said, 'was the most learned person in legal problems that never occurred, yet he was the most ignorant person with respect to what had gone before.'[30] Both reports offer up a charientism: Abū Ḥanīfa was learned, but his knowledge had been wasted in impractical jurisprudential details and hypothetical legal scenarios. Sufyān al-Thawrī, on the other hand, put his learning to very good use. His jurisprudence was grounded in concrete realities and, as such, it offered real legal solutions to the everyday predicaments people confronted in their lives.

Criticisms of Abū Ḥanīfa were usually fiercer than this. We need look no further than the same book by ʿAbd Allāh b. Aḥmad b. Ḥanbal, who cites ʿUthmān al-Battī as having lamented that Abū Ḥanīfa arrived at the right answer only after having given the wrong one.[31] Abū Ḥanīfa was said to have counselled his student Abū Yūsuf not to transmit any of the opinions of his master because, 'By God, I don't know whether I am wrong or right.'[32] This relaxed attitude towards issuing legal opinions was a recurring concern for some proto-Sunni traditionalists. Sufyān b. ʿUyayna recounted his experience of being in the company of Abū

suppose *anā* should read *innā* because the latter corresponds to the consistent use of the first person plural. I would suppose two readings for *la naḥkī*. The first reads *la* as the inchoative particle (*lām al-ibtidāʾ*), whilst the second reads *lā* as the negative particle. In the latter case the translation would read: 'Indeed, we do not relate the doctrines of the Jews and Christians and, likewise, we cannot bring ourselves to relate the doctrines of the Jahmiyya.' As for the *lām*s, both readings seem plausible to me.

29 ʿAbd Allāh b. Aḥmad b. Ḥanbal, *Kitāb al-Sunna*, 223 (*fa ra'aytu Sufyān aʿlam bimā kāna, wa Abū Ḥanīfa aʿlam bimā lam yakun*).

30 For two versions of this report see al-Khaṭīb al-Baghdādī, *Tārīkh Baghdād*, 15: 558–9.

31 ʿAbd Allāh b. Aḥmad b. Ḥanbal, *Kitāb al-Sunna*, 191 (*waylun li Abī Ḥanīfa hādhā mā yukhṭīʾ marra fa yuṣīb*).

32 ʿAbd Allāh b. Aḥmad b. Ḥanbal, *Kitāb al-Sunna*, 226 (*lā tarwi ʿannī shay'an fa wa Allāhi mā adrī a mukhṭīʾ am muṣīb*).

Ḥanīfa when a man came to him and asked him a legal question concerning exchange transactions (*al-ṣarf*). Sufyān b. ʿUyayna heard Abū Ḥanīfa's incorrect response and interjected, 'This is wrong (*yā Abā Ḥanīfa hādhā khaṭaʾ*).' According to Sufyān b. ʿUyayna, this angered Abū Ḥanīfa (*fa ghaḍiba*) and he told the questioner to return home and act in accordance with the legal opinion he had issued, assuring the man that any sin that might accrue from the man's action would be on Abū Ḥanīfa's head (*wa mā kāna fīhā min ithm fa huwa fī ʿunuqī*).[33]

Some proto-Sunni traditionalists saw this kind of insouciance as stemming from the very nature of *raʾy*. As a speculative and arbitrary form of reasoning, it made light of matters of grave religious import. Sufyān b. ʿUyayna was reported to have complained about the utter brazenness encouraged by such forms of legal reasoning. When a man from Khurāsān came to Abū Ḥanīfa and said, 'I have come to you with a hundred thousand legal questions that I should like to ask you about,' Abū Ḥanīfa replied, 'Bring them here.' This outraged Sufyān b. ʿUyayna. 'I have never seen anyone more bold before God than Abū Ḥanīfa,' he is supposed to have remarked.[34]

It was not the number of questions that Abū Ḥanīfa was apparently willing to entertain that caused consternation among proto-Sunni traditionalists. They believed that such liberality in issuing legal opinions would implicate unsuspecting lay petitioners, such as the man from Khurāsān, even if Abū Ḥanīfa protested that it was his neck that was in the noose. Another Khurāsānian, Muḥammad b. Maymūn (also known as Abū Ḥamza al-Sukkarī), supposedly expressed his anxiety about disseminating Abū Ḥanīfa's legal opinions in the province of Khurāsān.[35]

> I went to Abū Ḥanīfa and asked him about some legal questions. I went away for some twenty years, then went to him, and lo, he had gone back on those legal opinions. All the while, I had issued these legal opinions to people. I told him this, and he said: 'We come to one opinion, then the next day we arrive at a different opinion, and we take it [the first one] back.' He [Abū Ḥamza] said: 'How remote you are. This is how you attend to your religion? What a wretched man you are.'

33 ʿAbd Allāh b. Aḥmad b. Ḥanbal, *Kitāb al-Sunna*, 216. *ʿUnuqī* literally translates as 'my neck', of course, but in this context 'on my head' is a smoother fit than, say, 'my neck in the noose'.

34 ʿAbd Allāh b. Aḥmad b. Ḥanbal, *Kitāb al-Sunna*, 215–16. This incident is also recorded by Melchert, *The Formation of the Sunni Schools of Law*, 12, though it is Sufyān b. ʿUyayna and not Sufyān al-Thawrī who is quoted as expressing his disbelief at Abū Ḥanīfa's response.

35 ʿAbd Allāh b. Aḥmad b. Ḥanbal, *Kitāb al-Sunna*, 220–1. See also Melchert, *The Formation of the Sunni Schools of Law*, 11.

Khurāsānians were not the only ones disturbed by their contribution to the spread of proto-Ḥanafism in their home province. Al-Naḍr b. Muḥammad recounted how once he was engaged in a dispute with Abū Ḥanīfa over some aspect of the law. A student from the province of Shām happened to be present. The man got up to leave and went to Abū Ḥanīfa to bid him farewell. As he was leaving, Abū Ḥanīfa asked him whether he intended to transmit what he had heard to the people of Shām. When the man confirmed that this indeed was his intention, Abū Ḥanīfa cautioned him that by doing so he would be causing great damage.[36] According to this report, Abū Ḥanīfa recognised that his legal discussions might be misconstrued as legal doctrines and reported as such in the provinces of the early Islamic empire. Indeed, proto-Ḥanafī accounts recognised some aspects of this portrayal of Abū Ḥanīfa's propensity for changing opinions. The following account is attributed to Abū Ḥanīfa's contemporary and student, Zufar b. Hudhayl (d. 158/774):[37]

> We were engaged in a legal discussion with Abū Ḥanīfa, and Abū Yūsuf and Muḥammad b. al-Ḥasan were present among us. We were writing notes based on the discussion. One day, Abū Ḥanīfa said to Abū Yūsuf: 'Woe to you, Abū Yaʿqūb! Do not write down everything you hear me say. After all, I arrive at a legal opinion one day and the next day I reject it. The day after that, I arrive at another legal opinion and, again, the next day I reject it.'

More proto-Ḥanafī accounts point to this attitude towards the rapidly changing nature of legal opinions. On another occasion, Abū Ḥanīfa is reported to have counselled Abū Yūsuf, 'Do not transmit anything from me because I do not know whether I am wrong or right.'[38] We hear frequently of Abū Ḥanīfa's insistence that his legal views were neither set in stone and nor indubitable. Someone once asked Abū Ḥanīfa whether his legal opinions and the views he set down in his notes were categorically true. 'I swear by God, I do not know,' replied Abū Ḥanīfa. 'Perhaps it is categorically false.' Given Abū Ḥanīfa's reputation among both friends and foes for quick wit, one cannot fail to appreciate his sardonic response. His answer seems to draw attention to the absurdity of the question and its very implication that one could be categorically certain as to the truth of one's legal opinions.[39]

Proto-Sunni traditionalists, however, had no interest in appreciating Abū Ḥanīfa's condign retort. In fact, for proto-Sunni traditionalists

[36] Al-Khaṭīb al-Baghdādī, *Tārīkh Baghdād*, 15: 553.
[37] Al-Khaṭīb al-Baghdādī, *Tārīkh Baghdād*, 15: 554.
[38] Al-Khaṭīb al-Baghdādī, *Tārīkh Baghdād*, 15: 554.
[39] Al-Khaṭīb al-Baghdādī, *Tārīkh Baghdād*, 15: 553–4 (*Yā Abā Ḥanīfa, hādhā alladhī tuftī wa alladhī waḍaʿta fī kutubika huwa al-ḥaqq alladhī lā shakka fīhi? Fa qāla: wa Allāhi mā adrī, laʿallahu al-bāṭil alladhī lā shakka fīhi*). I translate *kutub* as 'notes' and not 'books'.

circulating these accounts what this indicated was Abū Ḥanīfa's irresponsible and indifferent attitude to jurisprudence. In their view, jurisprudence practised in so casual a manner as this was ripe for inconsistencies and flagrant contradictions. ʿAbd Allāh b. Aḥmad b. Ḥanbal explains that this had a perplexing effect on Ḥafṣ b. Ghiyāth: 'I sat with Abū Ḥanīfa and he gave ten different answers in response to one legal issue. We did not know which answer we were to follow.'[40] Eventually, this form of jurisprudence turned out to be intolerable for Ḥafṣ b. Ghiyāth and, in fact, precipitated his conversion to the people of ḥadīth: 'I was sitting with Abū Ḥanīfa, and I heard him issue five different legal opinions in response to one legal question, and all this in the space of one day. When I saw this, I left him and adopted the way of jurisprudence based on the ḥadīth.'[41] Proto-Sunni traditionalists believed in a legal system that was cultivated in opposition to this image of Abū Ḥanīfa's jurisprudence – an image that they themselves took great pains to depict. The question of whether Ḥafṣ b. Ghiyāth's conversion really took place or not is irrelevant to the study of proto-Sunni traditionalist notions of religious deviance and the evolution of discourses of heresy and orthodoxy.[42] What such reports document is the way in which standards of proto-Sunni orthodoxy were described, depicted, and demarcated in the ninth century. Above all, they demonstrate that discourses of heresy were circulated in order to distinguish religious orthodoxy from heresy.

Proto-Sunni traditionalists also emphasised the frivolity of Abū Ḥanīfa's juristic reasoning. Aḥmad b. Ḥanbal reports that Raqaba b. Maṣqala (d. 129/746–7)[43] asked a man who passed by him, 'Where

[40] ʿAbd Allāh b. Aḥmad b. Ḥanbal, *Kitāb al-Sunna*, 220.

[41] ʿAbd Allāh b. Aḥmad b. Ḥanbal, *Kitāb al-Sunna*, 205; al-Fasawī, *Kitāb al-Maʿrifa wa al-tārīkh*, 2: 789; al-Khaṭīb al-Baghdādī, *Tārīkh Baghdād*, 15: 554.

[42] An indication of the difficulties involved in determining the precise religious orientation of eighth-century scholars can be found in the facts that Ḥafṣ b. Ghiyāth is claimed as a Ḥanafī in the earliest surviving Ḥanafī *ṭabaqāt* section (Ibn Abī al-ʿAwwām al-Saʿdī, *Faḍāʾil Abī Ḥanīfa*, 154–5) and that Ibn Manda (d. 395/1005) listed him as an exemplary representative of proto-Sunni traditionalism (*Shurūṭ al-aʾimma*, ed. ʿAbd al-Raḥmān b. ʿAbd al-Jabbār al-Faryawāʾī (Riyadh: Dār al-Muslim, 1995), 55.

[43] Raqaba b. Maṣqala was a Kufan scholar, and it is worth noting that he was opposed to the Murjiʾa. See Ibn Ḥajar al-ʿAsqalānī, *Tahdhīb al-tahdhīb*, 3: 286–7; Ibn Ḥajar al-ʿAsqalānī, *Taqrīb al-tahdhīb*, 1: 303 and cf. van Ess, *Theologie und Gesellschaft*, 2: 368–9, esp. n. 18. A curious coincidence is that Raqaba b. Maṣqala was notorious for his own chewing habits: al-Khaṭīb al-Baghdādī, *al-Taṭfīl wa ḥikāyāt al-ṭufayliyyīn wa akhbāruhum wa nawādir kalāmihim wa ashʿāruhum*, ed. Bassām ʿAbd al-Wahhāb al-Jābī (Beirut: Dār Ibn al-Ḥazm, 1999), 84–5. It was important enough for Ibn Ḥajar to record that Raqaba b. Maṣqala liked to joke, and this in a book, *Taqrīb al-tahdhīb*, rightly regarded for its ruthless parsimony with words (the twelve-volume *Tahdhīb al-tahdhīb*, consisting of 12,455 entries, does not mention this but the two-volume *Taqrīb al-tahdhīb*, treating 8,874 ḥadīth scholars, does); so I deemed it worthwhile to find out why Raqaba b. Maṣqala *kāna yamzaḥu*. The joking probably troubled Ibn Ḥajar because it displayed

are you coming from?' 'I was with Abū Ḥanīfa,' the man replied. 'I see you have returned from a man who will fill you with as much *ra'y* as you can chew, and all the while you will return to your people with nothing trustworthy.'[44] At least three other proto-Sunni traditionalists thought so, too.[45] Al-Fasawī transmits the report on the authority of al-Ḥumaydī;[46] Abū Zurʿa al-Dimashqī is the only source to identify the person returning from Abū Ḥanīfa's lesson, and it is none other than al-Qāsim b. Maʿn;[47] and al-ʿUqaylī records the incident.[48] Unsurprisingly, this incident did not go unreported in al-Khaṭīb al-Baghdādī's history.[49]

Raqaba b. Maṣqala seems to have been drawing attention to the propensity of *ra'y* to produce a form of legal expertise concerned with recondite matters that lacked any practical relevance to the communities that jurists were supposed to serve. Abū Zurʿa al-Dimashqī and ʿAbd Allāh b. Aḥmad b. Ḥanbal had access to reports in which Ibn ʿAwn expressed similar concerns about Abū Ḥanīfa's jurisprudence. ʿAbd Allāh b. ʿAwn (d. 151/768) was a contemporary of Abū Ḥanīfa.[50] His own background and career in some respects mirrored Abū Ḥanīfa's. His grandfather was from Khurāsān and became a *mawlā*, whilst his

a lack of seriousness. And unremitting seriousness, as Melchert has observed, was a 'salient feature of the piety of the hadith folk'. See Melchert, 'The Piety of the Hadith Folk', 427–8. Another curious fact is that Raqaba b. Maṣqala had a student, Muḥammad b. Maymūn, who transmitted a *nuskha* from him, yet was also a student of Abū Ḥanīfa and harboured Murji'ī sentiments. See van Ess, *Theologie und Gesellschaft*, 2: 551. For the *nuskha*, see al-Ḥākim al-Nīshāpūrī, *Maʿrifat ʿulūm al-ḥadīth*, ed. Aḥmad b. Fāris al-Sallūm (Beirut: Dār Ibn al-Ḥazm, 2003), 480 = *Kitāb Maʿrifat ʿulūm al-ḥadīth*, ed. Muʿaẓẓam Ḥusayn (Beirut: Dār al-Āfāq al-Jadīda, 1989), 164; for Muḥammad b. Maymūn's study with Abū Ḥanīfa see Ibn Abī al-Wafā', *al-Jawāhir al-muḍiyya*, 4: 39 (under 'Abū Ḥamza al-Sukkarī'); and for the former's Murji'ism (according to Abū Ḥātim al-Rāzī) see al-Khaṭīb al-Baghdādī, *Tārīkh Baghdād*, 7: 17 (under the *tarjama* of 'Ibrāhīm b. Ṭuhmān'), 4: 432–7 ('Muḥammad b. Maymūn's' *tarjama*), where there is no trace whatsoever of his connection to Abū Ḥanīfa, nor to Murji'ism.

44 Three different versions of this report are given in ʿAbd Allāh b. Aḥmad b. Ḥanbal, *Kitāb al-Sunna*, 191–2 (*kalām mā maḍaghta wa turājiʿu ahlaka bi ghayr thiqa*; *ji'ta min ʿindi rajul yumlīka min ra'y mā maḍaghta wa taqūmu bi ghayr thiqa*; *idhan yuʿṭīka ra'yan mā maḍaghta wa tarjiʿu bi ghayr thiqa*). Another variant can be found at ʿAbd Allāh b. Aḥmad b. Ḥanbal, *Kitāb al-Sunna*, 205 (*yumakkinuka min ra'y mā maḍaghta wa tarjiʿu ilā ahlika bi ghayr thiqa*).

45 It should not surprise us that all *isnād*s go through and begin with al-Ḥumaydī.

46 Al-Fasawī, *Kitāb al-Maʿrifa wa al-tārīkh*, 2: 779. The editor, Akram Ḍiyā' al-ʿUmarī, seems to have garbled the passage: Ru'ba should read Raqaba; *injafilū* should read *inḥafilū*.

47 Abū Zurʿa al-Dimashqī, *Tārīkh*, 2: 506.

48 Al-ʿUqaylī, *Kitāb al-Ḍuʿafā'*, 4: 1411. See also Ibn ʿAbd al-Barr, *Jāmiʿ bayān al-ʿilm wa faḍlihi*, ed. Abū al-Ashbāl al-Zuhayrī (Dammam: Dār Ibn al-Jawzī, 1994), 1074.

49 Al-Khaṭīb al-Baghdādī, *Tārīkh Baghdād*, 15: 576–7.

50 On Ibn ʿAwn see Judd, *Religious Scholars and the Umayyads*, 62–8; van Ess, *Theologie und Gesellschaft*, 2: 355–67.

grandmother was a captive in Khurāsān.[51] Our ninth-century sources, however, portray two men committed to opposing religious and political trends. Ibn ʿAwn both opposed Abū Ḥanīfa's style of jurisprudence and refused to grant an audience to the ʿAlid rebel Ibrāhīm b. ʿAbd Allāh.[52] Abū Ḥanīfa, on the other hand, spoke out in favour of Ibrāhīm's revolt. Like Raqaba b. Maṣqala, Ibn ʿAwn was perturbed by the arbitrary and speculative form of juristic reasoning being attributed to Abū Ḥanīfa. He is said to have had Abū Ḥanīfa in mind when he declared, 'News has reached me of a man in Kufa who answers legal questions concerning the most enigmatic issues.'[53]

There was no doubt among some proto-Sunni traditionalists as to Abū Ḥanīfa's learning and perspicacity. If anything, he was pilloried for being too clever or, alternatively, for a misapplication of his learning. Proto-Sunni traditionalists remembered him as a master of legal obscurities, wild legal speculation, and legal disputations. One former student recalled how he studied with Abū Ḥanīfa only to discover that Abū Ḥanīfa knew nothing about jurisprudence (*fiqh*) but certainly had a complete command of legal disputations (*al-khuṣūmāt*).[54] Labelling Abū Ḥanīfa as a master of *khuṣūmāt* had wider implications in the ninth century. In his treatise on heresies and heretics, Ibn al-Waḍḍāḥ contends that the *aṣḥāb al-khuṣūmāt* are the heretics (*ahl al-bidaʿ*).[55] Al-Dārimī, another potent force within the proto-Sunni traditionalist network, was also conscious of the existence of a group of scholars specialising in legal disputations. His *Musnad* contains a tradition warning people not to keep the company of the *aṣḥāb al-khuṣūmāt*.[56] In the tenth century al-ʿUqaylī produced a similar set of criticisms against Abū Ḥanīfa. He reports that both Sharīk b. ʿAbd Allāh and Abū Bakr b. ʿIyyāsh declared that Abū Ḥanīfa was a master of disputations, and he was not known for anything else.[57]

51 Khalīfa b. Khayyāṭ, *Tārīkh*, ed. Akram Ḍiyāʾ al-ʿUmarī (Riyadh: Dār al-Ṭayba, 1985), 128 (Ibn ʿAwn's grandfather), 167 (Ibn ʿAwn's Khurāsānī grandmother), 264 (Ibn ʿAwn's year of birth), 425 (Ibn ʿAwn's year of death).

52 Ibn Saʿd, *Ṭabaqāt al-kabīr* (Leiden edn.), 7.2: 24–30, 27.

53 ʿAbd Allāh b. Aḥmad b. Ḥanbal, *Kitāb al-Sunna*, 189 (*balaghanī anna bi al-Kūfa rajulan yujību fī al-muʿḍilāt, yaʿnī Abā Ḥanīfa.*). This report is also quoted (without naming Abū Ḥanīfa but in a section dedicated to condemning him) in Abū Zurʿa al-Dimashqī, *Tārīkh*, 2: 505.

54 ʿAbd Allāh b. Aḥmad b. Ḥanbal, *Kitāb al-Sunna*, 210 (*adraknā Abā Ḥanīfa wa mā yaʿrifu bi shayʾ min al-fiqh; mā yaʿrifu illā bi al-khuṣūmāt*).

55 Ibn Waḍḍāḥ, *Kitāb al-Bidaʿ*, 193.

56 Al-Dārimī, *Kitāb al-Musnad al-jāmiʿ [Sunan al-Dārimī]*, ed. Nabīl b. Hāshim b. ʿAbd Allāh al-Ghumarī (Beirut: Dār al-Bashāʾir al-Islāmiyya, 2013), *kitāb al-ʿilm* 2, *bāb fī karāhiyat akhdh al-raʾy* 8, no. 234.

57 Al-ʿUqaylī, *Kitāb al-Ḍuʿafāʾ*, 4: 1408.

Finally, al-Lālakā'ī (d. 418/1027) collected a group of reports declaring *khuṣūmāt* as the catalyst for destroying the faith.[58]

Whereas some proto-Sunnis marvelled at the kind of jurisprudence Abū Ḥanīfa and his followers became renowned for, proto-Sunni traditionalists were unreservedly dismayed by its cavalier approach to religious jurisprudence. Proto-Sunni traditionalists interpreted these developments as markers of heretics and deviant movements. For them, religious orthodoxy was dictated by canonised texts, not by one's casuistic reasoning; it was determined by judgements issued by epigones, not newfangled sophistry; and where these sources were silent, representatives of the people of orthodoxy were expected to admit this readily and avoid any pontification. Al-Fasawī, an agent of proto-Sunni traditionalist orthodoxy, said as much when he described religious knowledge as comprising three things: 'a speaking book, past precedent, and saying "I do not know."'[59] This proposition, so proto-Sunni traditionalists tell us, was once put to Abū Ḥanīfa. According to Yaḥyā b. Ādam, somebody asked Abū Ḥanīfa what he thought of the saying, 'I do not know is half of knowledge.' Abū Ḥanīfa's response was priceless. 'Let him say, "I do not know' twice, in order that he may complete his knowledge."'[60] If this was the actual response Abū Ḥanīfa issued, it was surely delivered with his characteristic style of satire. Once again, such light humour fell on deaf ears. Yaḥyā b. Ādam's response to Abū Ḥanīfa's remark illustrates this. He feels the need to clarify the meaning of the phrase. 'Saying "I do not know" is half of knowledge because knowledge consists only of saying "I know" and "I do not know." One of them is the half of the other.'[61] It was in this vein that proto-Sunni traditionalists such as al-Dārimī held up as exemplary the attitude of, for example, the jurist who, when asked about eight legal issues, answered four and refused to answer the remaining four.[62] Still, with this particular locution Yaḥyā b. Ādam was expressing a widely held belief among proto-Sunni traditionalists about the form that jurisprudence ought to take. A number of ninth-century sources underscore the necessity of avoiding speculation in the domain of law. Al-Shaʿbī was reported to have said: 'Saying "I do not know" is half of

[58] Al-Lālakā'ī, *Sharḥ uṣūl iʿtiqād*, 127–9 (Ḥamdān edn.).

[59] Al-Fasawī, *Kitāb al-maʿrifa wa al-tārīkh*, 3: 494 (apparently in a book he wrote condemning *ra'y* (*dhamm al-ra'y*)); and also found in al-Khaṭīb al-Baghdādī, *Kitāb al-Faqīh wa al-mutafaqqih*, 2: 172.

[60] Al-Khaṭīb al-Baghdādī, *Tārīkh Baghdād*, 15: 535 (*fa-l-yaqul marratayn 'lā adrī' ḥattā yastakmila al-ʿilm*).

[61] Al-Khaṭīb al-Baghdādī, *Tārīkh Baghdād*, 15: 534–5.

[62] Al-Dārimī, *Kitāb al-Musnad al-jāmiʿ [Sunan al-Dārimī]*, *kitāb al-ʿilm* 2, *bāb man hāba al-futyā wa kariha al-tanaṭṭuʿa wa al-tabadduʿa* 4, no. 140.

knowledge.'[63] Other ninth-century scholars identified the Companion Ibn ʿAbbās with this axiom.[64] Abū Zurʿā al-Dimashqī cites a version in which this aphorism is attributed to Saʿīd b. ʿAbd al-ʿAzīz.[65] Many proto-Sunni scholars associated this approach with Mālik b. Anas.[66] Ibn Abī Ḥātim related the story about Mālik b. Anas refusing to answer a questioner who had travelled for six months at the behest of the people of his home town.[67] Al-Dārimī was particularly aggressive against the style of jurisprudence attributed to Abū Ḥanīfa. His *Musnad* contains a chapter collecting harsh criticisms against those who rush to issue legal opinions. He told his readers that 'whoever issues legal opinions to people every time he is asked for one is certifiably mad (*inna alladhī yuftī al-nās fī kull mā yustaftā la majnūn*)'.[68] Somebody asked Saʿīd b. Jubayr why he never spoke about the legal rulings pertaining to divorce. He replied that this was his inveterate practice because he feared making permissible the impermissible and vice versa.[69] He also railed against the use of *ra'y*: 'Nothing was more loathsome to me than hearing the people who say, "What is your opinion?".'[70] Others were prohibited from sitting with people who would use such expressions.[71] The second book of al-Dārimī's *Musnad* is the Book of Knowledge (*Kitāb al-ʿIlm*). One section collects traditions from the Prophet, Companions, and Successors underscoring their dislike for issuing legal opinions (*bāb karāhiyat al-futyā* 3); another section describes the virtue of refusing to issue legal opinions and condemns those who delve into matters too deeply and the heretics (*bāb man hāba al-futyā wa kariha al-tanaṭṭuʿa wa al-tabadduʿa* 4); there are also chapters that warn of the dangers of issuing legal opinions (*bāb al-futyā wa mā fīhi min al-shidda* 4) and decry the employment of *ra'y* (*bāb fī karāhiyat akhdh al-ra'y* 8). Al-Dārimī is just one example of many proto-Sunni traditionalists whose ḥadīth compilations devoted special sections to sharp condemnations of the form of jurisprudence that Abū Ḥanīfa was associated with.

63 Al-Dārimī, *Kitāb al-Musnad al-jāmiʿ [Sunan al-Dārimī]*, *kitāb al-ʿilm* 2, *bāb* 6 [no title], no. 197; *bāb karāhiyat al-futyā* 3; *bāb man hāba al-futyā wa kariha al-tanaṭṭuʿa wa al-tabadduʿa* 4; *bāb al-futyā wa mā fīhi min al-shidda* 4; *bāb fī karāhiyat akhdh al-ra'y* 8.

64 Al-Balādhurī, *Ansāb al-ashrāf*, 3: 59 (al-ʿAẓm edn.).

65 Abū Zurʿa al-Dimashqī, *Tārīkh*, 1: 361.

66 Ibn ʿAbd al-Barr, *al-Intiqā'*, 74–5; al-Bayhaqī, *Manāqib al-Shāfiʿī*, 2: 151.

67 Ibn Abī Ḥātim, *al-Jarḥ [taqdima]*, 1: 18; See Melchert, *The Formation of the Sunni Schools of Law*, 12.

68 Al-Dārimī, *Kitāb al-Musnad al-jāmiʿ [Sunan al-Dārimī]*, *kitāb al-ʿilm* 2, *bāb* [no title] 6, no. 186.

69 Al-Dārimī, *Kitāb al-Musnad al-jāmiʿ [Sunan al-Dārimī]*, *kitāb al-ʿilm* 2, *bāb man hāba al-futyā wa kariha al-tanaṭṭuʿa wa al-tabadduʿa* 4, no. 144.

70 Al-Dārimī, *Kitāb al-Musnad al-jāmiʿ [Sunan al-Dārimī]*, *kitāb al-ʿilm* 2, *bāb taghayyur al-zamān wa mā yuḥdathu fīhi* 6, no. 210.

71 Al-Dārimī, *Kitāb al-Musnad al-jāmiʿ [Sunan al-Dārimī]*, *kitāb al-ʿilm* 2, *bāb taghayyur al-zamān wa mā yuḥdathu fīhi* 6, no. 211.

### *Legal Tricks (Ḥiyal)*

Discourses of heresy against Abū Ḥanīfa were not conjured out of nothing. As we observed in the case of *ra'y*, ninth-century discourses of heresy bore some similarity to earlier discontent with *ra'y*, particularly on account of the perception that it undermined a stable and consistent legal system, resulting in unpredictable implications for medieval Islamic societies. Proto-Sunni traditionalist antagonisms against Abū Ḥanīfa were rooted in wider controversies and developments in the ninth century. In this respect, proto-Sunni traditionalist condemnations of Abū Ḥanīfa's deployment of *ḥiyal* were no different. Proto-Sunni traditionalists exploited well-known legal and jurisprudential developments in an effort to undermine Abū Ḥanīfa's religious standing.

In the ninth century, the *ḥīla* was a recognisable and controversial legal mechanism identifiable not only in books and their titles but in the judgements of qadis and private jurists. *Ḥiyal* were legal devices that enabled certain objectives and desired results to be met, but only by subverting standard judicial norms, procedures, and forms of legal reasoning. Proto-Ḥanafīs believed *ḥiyal*, or *makhārij*, to be necessary in order to reach lawful resolutions in scenarios where one was likely to commit unlawful acts.[72] Proto-Ḥanafīs of the ninth and tenth centuries, for example, considered *makhārij* essential for 'avoiding sinful acts and transforming them into lawful ones'.[73] *Ḥiyal* were mechanisms by which one could escape committing prohibited acts and engage in licit acts (*farra al-qawm min al-ḥarām wa arādū al-dukhūl fī al-ḥalāl*).[74] Proto-Sunni traditionalists perceived the *ḥiyal* as allowing for this peculiar transformation of acts and the swift legal reclassification accompanying it, and they castigated proto-Ḥanafīs for facilitating such legal tricks. Where proto-Ḥanafīs believed they were attending to the spirit of the law, proto-Sunni traditionalists saw such manoeuvres as blatant transgressions of it.

Proto-Sunni traditionalists in the ninth century made reference to books dedicated to making such *ḥiyal* accessible to the Muslim

[72] See Schacht, 'Die arabische ḥijal-Literatur'; Schacht, *An Introduction to Islamic Law*, 78–85; Wichard, *Zwischen Markt und Moschee*, 78–85, esp. 81–8.

[73] For definitions, to the extent that they are provided, see al-Shaybānī, *Kitāb al-Ḥujja ʿalā ahl al-Madīna* (Hyderabad: Maṭbaʿat Dā'irat al-Maʿārif al-Sharqiyya, 1963), 2: 585–7; Horri, 'Reconsideration of Legal Devices', 318.

[74] Al-Shaybānī, *Kitāb al-Ḥujja ʿalā ahl al-Madīna*, 2: 584–5. This is al-Shaybānī's response upon being accused by his Medinan interlocutors of creating a means for usurious transactions (*dharīʿa ilā al-ribā*) because he allowed for payments in kind, but not in gold, in order to compensate for any weight differential in the value of gold being exchanged.

community. They were categorical in their opposition to these books, and they were the first to write against *ḥiyal*.[75] Ibn al-Mubārak was quoted as having said that whoever has a copy of *Kitāb al-Ḥiyal* and intends to act upon a judgement given in it is an unbeliever (*kāfir*), and, as such, his wife must separate from him and his greater pilgrimage (*ḥajj*) is invalid (*baṭala*).[76] According to one account, after having said this Ibn al-Mubārak was informed that *Kitāb Ḥiyal* opined that where a woman seeks to separate from her husband, she should apostatise from Islam in order to achieve this. Thereafter, she may return to Islam. Upon hearing this version of the book's contents, Ibn al-Mubārak is supposed to have said that the author of this book is an unbeliever (*kāfir*) and, as such, his marriage is invalid and his greater pilgrimage is to be considered void.[77] On another occasion, Ibn al-Mubārak is cited as having accused Abū Ḥanīfa of composing *Kitāb al-Ḥiyal*. 'Whoever examines *Kitāb al-Ḥiyal* of Abū Ḥanīfa has permitted what God has prohibited and prohibited what God has permitted,' Ibn al-Mubārak was alleged to have said.[78] A third and final statement concerning *Kitāb al-Ḥiyal* is attributed to Ibn al-Mubārak. When his client (*mawlā*) said to him, 'I do not believe that anyone but the devil has authored *Kitāb al-Ḥiyal*,' Ibn al-Mubārak is alleged to have responded that the author of *Kitāb al-Ḥiyal* was more pernicious than the devil.[79] Aḥmad b. Saʿīd al-Dārimī heard al-Naḍr b. Shumayl say that the *Kitāb al-Ḥiyal* covers such and such a legal issue, and it is all heresy (*kufr*).[80]

Despite ninth-century reports of proto-Sunni traditionalists reading books on *ḥiyal*, proto-Ḥanafīs rejected the ascription of some of these books to their masters. Writing in the eleventh century, al-Sarakhsī devoted a few pages to the uncertainty surrounding al-Shaybānī's authorship of *Kitāb al-Ḥiyal*. 'People differed', al-Sarakhsī explained, 'as to whether or not *Kitāb al-Ḥiyal* was one of the books authored by Muḥammad [al-Shaybānī].' Al-Jūzajānī, for instance, explicitly rejected the attribution of *Kitāb al-Ḥiyal* to his teacher, al-Shaybānī. He recognised that there was a book in circulation, and that it was being attributed to al-Shaybānī. He found this ascription totally unfounded, saying that it was absurd to believe that al-Shaybānī would have given any of his books

[75] Horri, *Die gesetzlichen Umgehungen*, 33–9.
[76] Ibn Ḥibbān, *Kitāb al-Majrūḥīn*, 3: 70–1 (Beirut edn.).
[77] Al-Khaṭīb al-Baghdādī, *Tārīkh Baghdād*, 15: 556.
[78] Al-Khaṭīb al-Baghdādī, *Tārīkh Baghdād*, 15: 556.
[79] Al-Khaṭīb al-Baghdādī, *Tārīkh Baghdād*, 15: 556 (*mā arā waḍaʿa Kitāb al-Ḥiyal illā shayṭān fa qāla Ibn al-Mubārak: alladhī waḍaʿa Kitāb al-Ḥiyal asharru min al-shayṭān*). Another version reads: *alladhī waḍaʿahu ʿindī ablasu min Iblīs*. See al-Khaṭīb al-Baghdādī, *Tārīkh Baghdād*, 15: 556.
[80] Al-Khaṭīb al-Baghdādī, *Tārīkh Baghdād*, 15: 556.

a title as inappropriate as this. How could he have done so knowing that ignorant critics would exploit this and cite it as evidence for their attacks on proto-Ḥanafism? According to al-Sarakhsī, the book was compiled by some copyists in Baghdad, and it was ascribed to al-Shaybānī in order to disgrace proto-Ḥanafīs.[81] Al-Jūzajānī's comments are insightful for our purposes. As one of al-Shaybānī's most influential students, al-Jūzajānī was well positioned to inform us of developments among proto-Ḥanafīs and their interlocutors. Like most proto-Ḥanafīs of the late eighth century he would have been privy to proto-Sunni traditionalist discourses of heresy. This was especially so in the light of the favour he found among proto-Sunni traditionalists, many of whom were particularly impressed by his refusal of the judgeship al-Ma'mūn offered to him and his, probably related, anathematisation of any person who believed the Quran was created.[82] For these very reasons, however, al-Jūzajānī's explicit rejection of al-Shaybānī's having authored such a book is instructive. It may reflect the beginnings of the traditionalisation of proto-Ḥanafism. Explicitly rejecting the authenticity of *Kitāb al-Ḥiyal* and its ascription to al-Shaybānī represented an important step towards proto-Sunni traditionalists softening in their hostility to Abū Ḥanīfa. His comment displays how conscious he was of proto-Sunni traditionalist criticisms of Abū Ḥanīfa and his disciples. He shows an awareness of proto-Sunni traditionalist tendencies to use the association between proto-Ḥanafīs and legal tricks (*ḥiyal*) to discredit them. It was inconceivable for him that proto-Ḥanafīs, aware of proto-Sunni traditionalist hostility, would have given a book a title as rebarbative as this. This, however, was not al-Sarakhsī's opinion. According to him and Abū Ḥafṣ al-Bukhārī – al-Shaybānī's other prominent student – the work did belong to al-Shaybānī's ouevre.[83]

Proto-Sunni traditionalists objected vehemently to the use of *ḥiyal*, which they saw as an activity practised by proto-Ḥanafīs. Discourses of heresy against Abū Ḥanīfa maintain that his (and his followers') method of jurisprudence up-ended religious and jurisprudential norms. The accusation that Abū Ḥanīfa and proto-Ḥanafīs transformed what God had decreed to be licit into the illicit, and vice versa, was espoused frequently by proto-Sunni traditionalists. Furthermore, when proto-Sunni traditionalists attacked Abū Ḥanīfa for issuing absurd legal rulings, they may have done so with proto-Ḥanafī proclivity to *ḥiyal* in mind. ʿAbd Allāh b. Aḥmad b. Ḥanbal rallied against Abū Ḥanīfa for supposedly permitting the consumption of pork, alcohol, and other prohibited

[81] Al-Sarakhsī, *Kitāb al-Mabsūṭ*, 30: 209. [82] Ibn Abī Ḥātim, *al-Jarḥ*, 4.1: 145.
[83] Al-Sarakhsī, *Kitāb al-Mabsūṭ*, 30: 209.

drinks.[84] He was aghast at Abū Ḥanīfa's edict that breaking musical instruments was a punishable crime.[85] Other proto-Sunni traditionalists claimed that Abū Ḥanīfa permitted adultery and usury and that his jurisprudence led to the shedding of blood with impunity.[86] Many were, of course, puzzled and startled by these allegations. When a sceptic demanded an explanation, he was told that Abū Ḥanīfa permitted usury because he did not object to deferred credit transactions that accrue additional charges (*nasī'a*); he permitted public violence (*al-dimā'*) since he ruled that if a man kills another man by striking him with a massive stone, the blood money must be paid by his male relatives, tribe, or social group (*al-ʿāqila*); he permitted adultery because he ruled that if a man and a woman have sexual intercourse in a house, whilst they are known to be parents, and both declare themselves that they are married to each other, no one should object to them. Upon hearing this detailed explanation the sceptic remarked that all of this amounted to invalidating God's laws (*al-sharā'iʿ*) and injunctions (*al-aḥkām*).[87]

### *Analogical Reasoning (*Qiyās*)*

Analogical reasoning (*qiyās*) was another legal mechanism that proto-Sunni traditionalists associated with Abū Ḥanīfa. They argued that proto-Ḥanafism's dependence on *qiyās* at the expense of other methods of legal reasoning signalled its religious deviance. One ninth-century source has al-Awzāʿī maintain that Abū Ḥanīfa was lacking in the very foundations of the law, so he embraced analogical reasoning.[88] *Qiyās* was seen not only as an illegitimate method, as practised by Abū Ḥanīfa and his followers, but proto-Sunni traditionalists saw in this technique the enactment of Satan's original sin. Satan, they argued, was the first person to invoke analogical reasoning by drawing an analogical argument between his creation from fire and Adam's from clay.[89]

Again, this study is not concerned with establishing whether proto-Sunni traditionalist attacks on proto-Ḥanafī uses of *qiyās* were accurate or not.[90] In the interests of providing some context, however, it is important to point out that proto-Sunni traditionalists themselves utilised forms

[84] Abd Allāh b. Aḥmad b. Ḥanbal, *Kitāb al-Sunna*, 206–7.
[85] Abd Allāh b. Aḥmad b. Ḥanbal, *Kitāb al-Sunna*, 206–7.
[86] Al-Khaṭīb al-Baghdādī, *Tārīkh Baghdād*, 15: 569.
[87] Al-Khaṭīb al-Baghdādī, *Tārīkh Baghdād*, 15: 569–70.
[88] ʿAbd Allāh b. Aḥmad b. Ḥanbal, *Kitāb al-Sunna*, 156.
[89] Al-Dārimī, *Kitāb al-Musnad al-jāmiʿ [Sunan al-Dārimī]*, *kitāb al-ʿilm* 2, *bāb taghayyur al-zamān wa mā yuḥdathu fīhi* 6, nos. 206, 207.
[90] Melchert, *The Formation of the Sunni Schools of Law*, 36–7; Lucas, 'Legal Principles', 303–7.

of analogical reasoning; but they chose their terms carefully and sometimes preferred to jettison *qiyās*, only to replace it with *tashbīh*. This can be observed in the legal responsa (*masā'il*) of Aḥmad b. Ḥanbal, who on a few occasions appears to employ a mode of analogical reasoning, which he signals with the words *ashbah* and *shabīh*, and in the writings of other proto-Sunni traditionalists.[91] The analogical reasoning of Abū Ḥanīfa and his followers, however, was believed to bring about legal rulings that contradicted Prophetic reports. Aḥmad b. Ḥanbal's son ʿAbd Allāh would cite reports to the effect that Abū Ḥanīfa permitted eating pork, drinking alcohol, and forbade the breaking of musical instruments.[92] It was this kind of logic that led one proto-Sunni traditionalist to suggest that highway robbery was better than the *qiyās* of Abū Ḥanīfa.[93] It was the lesser of two evils. Not all proto-Sunni traditionalists, however, were convinced by this caricature of Ḥanafī *qiyās*. At least some of them in the midst of their otherwise vituperative discourses of heresy against Abū Ḥanīfa cited a statement attributed to him that 'urinating in the mosque is better than some of their *qiyās*'.[94] That is to say, Abū Ḥanīfa was understood to be critical of some forms of *qiyās*.

What does seem clear is that in the ninth century proto-Ḥanafīs adopted a set of legal tools and techniques to elaborate the law that proto-Sunni traditionalists determined to be illegitimate. The legal strategies were so problematic because they produced results concerning legal matters that differed from the results reached by proto-Sunni traditionalists. But the latter were not content to view these legal developments simply as jurisprudential aberrations. The law was essential to the elaboration of the religion. If the legal strategies were unsound, then one's approach to the religion was unsound too. This is why proto-Sunni traditionalists of the ninth–tenth centuries argued that Abū Ḥanīfa harmed the religion through juristic strategies. Such people, proto-Sunni traditionalists alleged, sat precariously on the outer edges of orthodoxy.[95]

[91] Al-Kawsaj, *Masā'il al-Imām Aḥmad b. Ḥanbal wa Isḥāq b. Rāhawayh* (Medina: Maktabat al-Malik ʿAhd al-Waṭaniyya, 2004), 2894; Ṣāliḥ b. Aḥmad, *Masā'il al-Imām Aḥmad b. Ḥanbal*, ed. Ṭāriq b. ʿAwaḍ (Riyadh: Dār al-Waṭan, 1999), 142–3; al-Bukhārī, *Ṣaḥīḥ, kitāb al-iʿtiṣām bi al-kitāb wa al-sunna, bāb man shabbaha aṣlan maʿlūman bi aṣlin mubayyan qad bayyana Allāhu ḥukmahumā li yufhima al-sā'il*, 13. See Chapter 1 above, where I note al-Shāfiʿī's use of *tashbīh*.

[92] ʿAbd Allāh b. Aḥmad b. Ḥanbal, *Kitāb al-Sunna*, 206–7.

[93] ʿAbd Allāh b. Aḥmad b. Ḥanbal, *Kitāb al-Sunna*, 225.

[94] See Chapter 3 above.

[95] ʿAbd Allāh b. Aḥmad b. Ḥanbal, *Kitāb al-sunna*, 199 (two reports: *kāda bi al-dīn*); ʿAbd Allāh b. Aḥmad b. Ḥanbal, *Kitāb al-ʿIlal*, 2: 547, 3: 164 (Dār al-Khānī edn.); al-ʿUqaylī, *Kitāb al-Ḍuʿafā'*, 4: 1408 (al-Qalʿajī edn.); al-Khaṭīb al-Baghdādī, *Tārīkh Baghdād*, 15: 552.

## 7.2 Ḥadīth

The growth and circulation of traditions attributed to the Prophet Muḥammad was essential to the emergence of a proto-Sunni traditionalist community. These traditions consisted of two aspects: *isnād*s and *matn*s. The *isnād* contained a list of transmitters (traditionists), many of whom were also proto-Sunni traditionalists. The *matn* claimed to represent a saying or action of the Prophet Muḥammad or of his Companions. Proto-Sunni traditionalists devoted themselves to the task of studying, memorising, critiquing, and interpreting these traditions.

This spawned an entire range of written compositions by which proto-Sunni traditionalists were able to distinguish themselves and their craft. Books on transmitters were compiled that focused on detailing whom they studied with, whether they were reliable transmitters, and when they died (*tārīkh* and *rijāl* works). In order to facilitate the easy recognition of transmitters, works on transmitter nicknames flourished (*kutub al-kunā wa al-asmā'*). Specialists also began to detect flaws in the transmission of ḥadīth, both their *isnād*s and *matn*s (*kutub al-ʿilal*). Students wrote works in which they preserved transcripts of their conversations with teachers concerning specific transmitters (*kutub al-su'ālāt*). Others began to analyse and arrange traditions under legal headings to facilitate the study of legal jurisprudence and to augment the authority of ḥadīth in the realm of jurisprudence. Works devoted to establishing the authority of ḥadīth in law and theology began to emerge, too. And, in response to criticisms relating to the sheer number of ḥadīths and their contradictory nature, proto-Sunni traditionalists developed hermeneutical methods to reconcile them. All of these developments occurred in a very short span of time during the late eighth and ninth centuries.

Proto-Sunni traditionalists of the ninth and tenth centuries believed that Abū Ḥanīfa and his students had played no significant part in any of these transformative developments. In the earliest biographical dictionaries, which also showed a special interest in ḥadīth learning, it was Abū Ḥanīfa's poor standing as a ḥadīth transmitter that was highlighted. We saw this in Chapters 2 and 3 when we examined the entries on Abū Ḥanīfa in the works of Ibn Saʿd and al-Bukhārī, respectively. The rise of books dedicated to weak and unreliable ḥadīth transmitters had a decisive impact on Abū Ḥanīfa's reputation in the discipline of ḥadīth. Al-ʿUqaylī's collection of ninth-century criticisms of Abū Ḥanīfa's ḥadīth expertise included the exhortation that all of his ḥadīth should be dismissed;[96] that he was seriously deficient in ḥadīth;[97] we are told that one scholar, whenever he heard a ḥadīth that surprised him, would ask sarcastically whether it had been transmitted by Abū Ḥanīfa.[98] Ibn Shāhīn (d. 385/995–6?) included in his *al-Thiqāt* the view that Abū Ḥanīfa was too noble and pious to have lied with respect to transmitting ḥadīth.[99] Abū Ḥanīfa also made it into the author's other book on weak and untruthful transmitters, but even there Ibn Shāhīn dissents from many of his proto-Sunni traditionalist peers and fellow authors of books on ḥadīth transmitters by declaring that a group of scholars had declared Abū Ḥanīfa to be trustworthy.[100] Abū Aḥmad al-Ḥākim, a tenth-century Shāfiʿī judge from Khurāsān and a leading authority on the *Ṣaḥīḥ*s of al-Bukhārī and Muslim, also adopted a softer view of Abū Ḥanīfa's proficiency in ḥadīth. He provided a neutral biography of Abū Ḥanīfa, though he added at the end that most of his ḥadīth contained mistakes.[101] Al-Tirmidhī (d. 279/892) claimed that Abū Ḥanīfa had told his students as much: 'Most of the ḥadīth I relate to you are mistaken (*ʿāmmatu mā uḥaddithukum khaṭa'*).'[102] Muslim b. al-Ḥajjāj's book

[96] Al-ʿUqaylī, *Kitāb al-Ḍuʿafā'*, 4: 282, 285 (al-Qalʿajī edn.).

[97] Al-ʿUqaylī, *Kitāb al-Ḍuʿafā'*, 4: 285 (al-Qalʿajī edn.).

[98] Al-ʿUqaylī, *Kitāb al-Ḍuʿafā'*, 4: 283 (al-Qalʿajī edn.).

[99] Ibn Shāhīn, *Tārīkh asmā' al-thiqāt*, ed. Ṣubḥī al-Sāmarrā'ī (Kuwait: Dār al-Salafiyya, 1984), 241 (*wa Abū Yūsuf awthaqu min Abī Ḥanīfa fī al-ḥadīth wa kāna Abū Ḥanīfa anbala fī nafsihi min an yakdhiba, wa ism Abī Ḥanīfa al-Nuʿmān b. Thābit*) = ed. ʿAbd al-Muʿṭī Amīn Qalʿajī (Beirut: Dār al-Kutub al-ʿIlmiyya, 1986), 323–33 (*wa Abū Yūsuf awthaqu min Abī Ḥanīfa fī al-ḥadīth wa kāna Abū Ḥanīfa anbala fī nafsihi min an yakdhiba, wa ism Abī Ḥanīfa al-Nuʿmān b. Thābit*) = ed. ʿAbd al-Raḥīm Muḥammad Aḥmad al-Qashqarī (n.p.: n.d., 1989), 184 (*wa Abū Ḥanīfa: ismuhu al-Nuʿmān b. Thābit wa dhukira ʿan jamāʿa tawthīquhu*). The entry on Abū Ḥanīfa reads differently in one of these editions. These bold differences and inconsistencies are not recorded in the otherwise extremely useful and industrious study of Saʿdī Hāshimī, *Nuṣūṣ ṣāqiṭa min ṭabaʿāt asmā' al-thiqāt li Ibn Shāhīn* (Medina: Maktabat al-Dār, 1987). Although Hāshimī's study was published two years prior to the publication of al-Qashqarī's edition, it makes extensive use of the Marrakesh manuscript and presents a painstaking comparison between three editions of Ibn Shāhīn's book (one of which I have not seen: Ṣāliḥ b. ʿAbd al-Muḥaṭṭab, MA thesis, al-Jāmiʿa al-Imām Muḥammad b. Saʿūd, 1982) and the Marrakesh manuscript, listing any and every discrepancy between them. Somehow, the discrepancy regarding Abū Ḥanīfa's entry escaped him. Al-Qashqarī's edition is based on a single manuscript housed in Marrakesh. Unfortunately, this is the extent of his description of the manuscript. Hāshimī, *Nuṣūṣ ṣāqiṭa min ṭabaʿāt asmā' al-thiqāt li Ibn Shāhīn*, 41 provides more extensive details about this manuscript.

[100] Ibn Shāhīn, *Tārīkh*, 184–5 (al-Qashqarī edn.).

[101] Abū Aḥmad al-Ḥākim, *Kitāb al-Asāmī wa al-kunā*, 4: 175–7.

[102] Al-Tirmidhī, *ʿIlal al-Tirmidhī al-kabīr*, arranged by Abū Ṭālib al-Qāḍī [Maḥmūd b. ʿAlī (d. 585/1189)], ed. Ṣubḥī al-Sāmarrā'ī, Abū al-Maʿāṭī al-Nūrī, and Maḥmūd Muḥammad Khalīl al-Ṣaʿīdī (Beirut: ʿĀlam al-Kutub/Maktabat al-Nahḍa al-ʿArabiyya, 1989), 388. Al-Tirmidhī wrote two works on this subject: *al-ʿIlal al-kabīr* (*IK*) and *al-ʿIlal al-ṣaghīr* (*IṢ*).

on the subject of ḥadīth transmitters and their nicknames arrived at a similar conclusion: Abū Ḥanīfa was deficient in ḥadīth, and had very few sound ḥadīth.[103] Al-Nasā'ī's verdict was that Abū Ḥanīfa was weak in ḥadīth.[104] In his short book describing the standards of individual ḥadīth scholars, al-Jūzajānī described Abū Ḥanīfa as someone whose ḥadīth could not be relied upon.[105] In his *Sunan*, al-Dāraquṭnī called Abū Ḥanīfa weak (*ḍaʿīf*) in ḥadīth, and reportedly communicated the same point to Ḥamza al-Sahmī. Still, Abū Ḥanīfa found no place in al-Dāraquṭnī's history of weak ḥadīth scholars.[106]

It was not simply the fact that his name was featured regularly in these books; the entries on him became venues for authors to launch all kinds of attacks on Abū Ḥanīfa's character. Readers of and listeners to these works, therefore, would receive a fairly representative sample of wider proto-Sunni traditionalist discourses of heresy against Abū Ḥanīfa.

The same convention was applied to his students, but by no means with a broad brush. So, Yūsuf b. Khālid al-Samtī is described as being weak in ḥadīth, strong in *ra'y*.[107] We are told that Abū Yūsuf had learnt many ḥadīths from a range of Kufan ḥadīth scholars. His peers recognised him for his memorisation of ḥadīths. His proficiency as a ḥadīth scholar waned, however, after he became a dedicated student of Abū Ḥanīfa.[108] Al-Shaybānī is judged in a similar fashion: he studied ḥadīth and heard numerous traditions from ḥadīth scholars, but Abū Ḥanīfa and *ra'y* got the better of him. Henceforth, his peers disagreed about his expertise, although some continued to study ḥadīth and jurisprudence

There are internal references in the *IṢ* to a book, which I take to be the *IK* (. . . *qad bayyannā hādhā ʿalā wajhihi fī al-kitāb alladhī fīhi al-mawqūf wa mā kāna fīhi min dhikr al-ʿilal fī al-aḥādīth wa al-rijāl wa al-tārīkh* . . .). This has only survived in Abū Ṭālib's rearrangement. Sezgin believed that Ibn Rajab wrote a commentary on the *IK*, but Ḥamza Muṣṭafā has argued that the commentary is on the *IṢ*: see Sezgin, *GAS*, 1: 154–9, 159; al-Tirmidhī, *al-ʿIlal al-kabīr*, ed. Ḥamza Muṣṭafā (Amman: Maktabat al-Aqṣā, 1985), xx (editor's introduction); Akram Ḍiyā' al-ʿUmarī, *Turāth al-Tirmidhī al-ʿilmī* (Medina: Maktabat al-Dār, 1991), 52–4, where the treatment of these texts is brief and negligible; and Ibn Rajab, *Sharḥ ʿilal al-Tirmidhī*, ed. Ṣubḥī al-Sāmarrā'ī (Baghdad: Wizārat al-Awqāf al-ʿIrāqiyya, 1976) = ed. Nūr al-Dīn ʿItr (n.p: Dār al-Malāḥ, 1978) = ed. Hammād ʿAbd al-Raḥīm Saʿīd (Riyadh: Maktabat al-Rushd, 2001).

103 Muslim b. al-Ḥajjāj, *Kitāb al-Kunā wa al-asmā'*, ed. ʿAbd al-Raḥīm Muḥammad Aḥmad al-Qashqarī (Medina: Iḥyā' al-Turāth al-Islāmiyya, 1984), 276.

104 Al-Nasā'ī, *Kitāb al-Ḍuʿafā' wa al-matrūkīn*, 240 (*laysa bi al-quwwa fī al-ḥadīth*).

105 Al-Jūzajānī, *Aḥwāl al-rijāl*, 75.

106 Al-Dāraquṭnī, *Sunan*, 2: 107–8, 1: 223, 323 (al-Arna'ūṭ edn.); al-Sahmī, *Su'ālāt Ḥamza b. Yūsuf al-Sahmī li al-Dāraquṭnī*, 263, where we are informed that Abū Ḥanīfa's ḥadīth transmissions were unreliable since he never met a Companion.

107 Ibn Saʿd, *al-Ṭabaqāt al-kubrā*, 7.2: 47 (Leiden edn.).

108 Ibn Saʿd, *al-Ṭabaqāt al-kubrā*, 7.2: 73–4 (Leiden edn.).

under him.[109] However, other proto-Ḥanafīs fared better in Ibn Saʿd's view. Asad b. ʿAmr al-Bajalī had memorised numerous ḥadīths and he was believed to be a trustworthy transmitter of ḥadīths, despite having learnt jurisprudence from Abū Ḥanīfa.[110] Abū Yūsuf's son was characterised as someone who had studied ḥadīth and transmitted the jurisprudence of his father.[111] Al-Ḥusayn b. Ibrāhīm b. al-Ḥurr was described as having studied ḥadīth and gained expertise in *ra'y*. But he continued to teach both ḥadīth and jurisprudence in Baghdad to the end of his life. Ibn Saʿd had nothing damning to say about his knowledge of ḥadīth.[112] Bishr b. al-Walīd al-Kindī taught ḥadīth and issued legal rulings in Baghdad. He was on good terms with proto-Sunni traditionalists, it seems. He was imprisoned, after all, for refusing to declare the Quran to be created. It was only when he took a neutral position, refusing to declare the Quran either created or uncreated (*takallama bi al-waqf*) that the proto-Sunni traditionalist community renounced him.[113] Al-Muʿallā b. Manṣūr is even described as a master of ḥadīth (*ṣāḥib ḥadīth*), speculative jurisprudence (*ra'y*), and legal rulings (*fiqh*). Even though Ibn Saʿd rated him as truthful (*ṣadūq*), he acknowledged that proto-Sunni traditionalists remained ambivalent about his reputation: they would transmit his ḥadīth but not his speculative jurisprudence.[114]

I should emphasise though that this picture of ḥadīth learning among Abū Ḥanīfa and proto-Ḥanafīs cannot be taken to represent the opinions of proto-Sunni traditionalists at large. These same individuals, for example, receive more severe assessments in *rijāl* works from a later period. Al-ʿUqaylī's notice on Muʿallā b. Manṣūr consists of one damning judgement attributed to Aḥmad b. Ḥanbal, who declared proudly: 'I never wrote a single letter [let alone a ḥadīth] on his authority.'[115] ʿUqaylī has plenty of ammunition for Abū Yūsuf. He begins with the comparatively mild claim that Yaḥyā b. Maʿīn judged that Abū Yūsuf was not proficient in ḥadīth

[109] Ibn Saʿd, *al-Ṭabaqāt al-kubrā*, 7.2: 74 (Leiden edn.).
[110] Ibn Saʿd, *al-Ṭabaqāt al-kubrā*, 7.2: 74 (Leiden edn.) (*kāna ʿindahu ḥadīth kathīr wa huwa thiqa in shā'a Allāhu wa kāna qad ṣaḥiba Abā Ḥanīfa wa tafaqqaha*).
[111] Ibn Saʿd, *al-Ṭabaqāt al-kubrā*, 7.2: 78 (Leiden edn.).
[112] Ibn Saʿd, *al-Ṭabaqāt al-kubrā*, 7.2: 87–8 (Leiden edn.).
[113] Ibn Saʿd, *al-Ṭabaqāt al-kubrā*, 7.2: 93 (Leiden edn.). A similar fate was met by another proto-Ḥanafī, Muḥammad b. Shujāʿ al-Thaljī. Proto-Sunni traditionalists had a hard time incriminating him, but his alleged ambivalence concerning theological questions about the Quran made it all the easier. On this see Melchert, *The Formation of the Sunni Schools of Law*, 51–3.
[114] Ibn Saʿd, *al-Ṭabaqāt al-kubrā*, 7.2: 82 (Leiden edn.).
[115] Al-ʿUqaylī, *Kitāb al-Ḍuʿafā'*, 4: 1360–1 (Dār al-Ṣumayʿī edn.) = 4: 215–16 (al-Qalʿajī edn.).

and ends with an outrageous story of man who alleged that he saw Abū Yūsuf in a dream with a cross around his neck, gifted to him by a Jewish man.[116] For al-Bajalī, al-ʿUqaylī quotes the expertise of ʿAbd Allāh b. Aḥmad b. Ḥanbal. When the latter was asked whether al-Bajalī was a reliable ḥadīth scholar (*ṣadūq*), he replied: 'No one should relate anything on the authority of Abū Ḥanīfa's followers (*aṣḥāb Abī Ḥanīfa*).'[117] Al-ʿUqaylī was equally dismissive about Zufar b. Hudhayl. In the words of the authorities he cites, Zufar was a heretic who should be avoided at all cost.[118] Yūsuf b. Khālid al-Samtī receives a similar appraisal in al-ʿUqaylī's book on weak ḥadīth scholars. Yaḥyā b. Maʿīn's views on him are adduced by al-ʿUqaylī, and they are anything but flattering. He is described as an inveterate liar, a vile man, and an enemy of God, and no one who had an ounce of virtue related anything from him.[119]

Though there are substantial differences between Ibn Saʿd's *al-Ṭabaqāt al-kubrā* and al-ʿUqaylī's *Kitāb al-Ḍuʿafāʾ*, they share a tendency to dismiss Abū Ḥanīfa and his students' expertise in ḥadīth. Ibn Saʿd stands at the beginning of proto-Sunni traditionalist literature on ḥadīth learning, whereas al-ʿUqaylī represents its mature stage. Ibn Saʿd's interest in individuals is broad, and he sometimes neglects to mention their ḥadīth credentials. Al-ʿUqaylī is concerned with the vast swathes of ḥadīth scholars he believed possessed inadequate and deficient knowledge of the discipline. More pertinently, discourses of heresy against Abū Ḥanīfa were fully developed by al-ʿUqaylī's time, whereas they were still in their infancy when Ibn Saʿd was writing. Al-ʿUqaylī had more resources on which to draw when writing off Abū Ḥanīfa and his followers in the orthodox discipline of ḥadīth studies.

Though there was a growing consensus among proto-Sunni traditionalists that Abū Ḥanīfa was not a recognised ḥadīth expert, they did acknowledge that he was involved in the transmission of traditions. However, they deemed even these few traditions to reflect his lack of expertise as a ḥadīth transmitter. Even when discussing other traditionists, Abū Ḥanīfa's grasp of the science of ḥadīth was reckoned to be insufficient. Al-Jawraqānī's (d. 543/1148) book on false and sound ḥadīths twice cites ḥadīths containing Abū Ḥanīfa in the *isnād*s. He declares them to be false and states that Abū Ḥanīfa's ḥadīths are to be

[116] Al-ʿUqaylī, *Kitāb al-Ḍuʿafāʾ*, 4: 1544 and 4: 1548 (Dār al-Ṣumayʿī edn.).
[117] Al-ʿUqaylī, *Kitāb al-Ḍuʿafāʾ*, 1: 36–8 (Dār al-Ṣumayʿī edn.).
[118] Al-ʿUqaylī, *Kitāb al-Ḍuʿafāʾ*, 2: 456–7 (Dār al-Ṣumayʿī edn.).
[119] Al-ʿUqaylī, *Kitāb al-Ḍuʿafāʾ*, 4: 1555 (Dār al-Ṣumayʿī edn.).

renounced (*matrūk al-ḥadīth*).[120] Abū Ḥanīfa's traditions are discussed by al-Khalīlī in the course of a survey of the career of Abū ʿAbd al-Ḥusayn b. al-Walīd, a native of Nīshāpūr with impressive scholarly credentials. He had met and studied with Sufyān al-Thawrī, Shuʿba, and Mālik b. Anas.[121] In his entry on Abū al-Ḥusayn, al-Khalīlī seems concerned with preserving Abū al-Ḥusayn's good reputation. He cites a ḥadīth tradition in which Abū al-Ḥusayn transmits from Abū Ḥanīfa, who transmits from Suhayl b. Abī Ṣāliḥ, and then eventually back to the Prophet Muḥammad, who instructed that a person pray four *rakʿa*s after the Friday congregational prayer. Al-Khalīlī explains that there is an error in this tradition, and that the error returns to the person who transmits from al-Ḥusayn. He adds that Abū Ḥanīfa's transmissions from Suhayl are anomalous and unknown to specialists. Al-Khalīlī says he heard something similar from Abū ʿAlī ʿAbd al-Raḥmān b. Muḥammad al-Nīshāpūrī, who said:

> When I heard from Ibn ʿAbdān the ḥadīth of Abū Ḥanīfa from Suhayl, I returned to Basra. When I reached there, ʿAlī b. Muḥammad b. Mūsā, the servant of ʿUbayd, said to me: 'O Abū ʿAlī, have you heard from Ibn ʿAbdān the ḥadīth of Abū Ḥanīfa from Suhayl?' I said, 'Yes.' He smiled. He said: 'Abū al-ʿAbbās b. ʿUqda told me: "This error was committed by the person who related it from al-Ḥusayn b. al-Walīd. It must have been so, because al-Ḥusayn never met Abū Ḥanīfa. This would not have pleased him."'[122]

Here al-Khalīlī narrates how tenth-century ḥadīth scholars discussed among themselves traditions that contained Abū Ḥanīfa in the *isnād*. They were able to identify problems in these traditions by drawing attention to Abū Ḥanīfa's involvement, but they could do so without seeking to undermine his religious orthodoxy in its entirety, thereby exhibiting the variety among proto-Sunni traditionalists in their attitudes to Abū Ḥanīfa.

To a large degree, however, proto-Sunni traditionalists' attacks on Abū Ḥanīfa's ḥadīth learning were designed to raise serious and lingering doubts about his religious orthodoxy. Where some tenth- and eleventh-century scholars found sobering ways to discuss Abū Ḥanīfa's knowledge of ḥadīth, earlier proto-Sunni traditionalists insisted that he ignored and dismissed the authority of ḥadīths, and this in turn reflected his lack of regard for Prophetic authority. Indeed, this view became a hallmark of proto-Sunni traditionalist criticisms against Abū Ḥanīfa, and it occupied

[120] Al-Jawraqānī, *al-Abāṭīl wa al-manākīr wa al-ṣiḥāḥ wa al-mashāhīr*, ed. ʿAbd al-Raḥmān ʿAbd al-Jabbār al-Faryūwāʾī (Benares: Idārat al-Buḥūth al-Islāmiyya wa al-Daʿwa wa al-Iftāʾ, 1983), 2: 111, 170–1.

[121] Al-Bukhārī, *al-Tārīkh al-kabīr*, 2.1: 391.

[122] Al-Khalīlī, *al-Irshād*, 802–3 (Riyadh edn.).

many pages of a ninth-century manifesto of proto-Sunni traditionalist learning. One critic, referring to Abū Ḥanīfa and his followers, opined that 'their doctrine is to go against the traditions transmitted from the messenger of God'.[123] Another critic explained, 'It was not on account of Abū Ḥanīfa's juristic reasoning that we loathed him; after all, we all resort to juristic reasoning. Rather, we loathed him because when a ḥadīth from the messenger of God was mentioned to him, he would give an opinion contrary to it.'[124] Ḥammād b. Salama was thought to have made this very complaint, too: 'When faced with traditions and practices (*al-āthār wa al-sunan*), Abū Ḥanīfa would counter them with his juristic reasoning.'[125]

A general picture has emerged, then, of the proto-Sunni traditionalist community seeking to discredit Abū Ḥanīfa as a figure of orthodoxy by drawing attention to the paucity of his ḥadīth expertise. There were occasional proto-Sunni traditionalist exceptions to this broad consensus. We have highlighted some of these, and another important one whom we studied at the end of Chapter 3 was Yaḥyā b. Maʿīn, who deemed Abū Ḥanīfa to be a reliable and pious scholar. Still, the mainstream of proto-Sunni traditionalism had discredited Abū Ḥanīfa as a ḥadīth scholar. From the ninth century onwards ḥadīth became so critical to the orientation of proto-Sunnism that defenders of Abū Ḥanīfa had to do something out of the ordinary to respond to the hostile attacks upon their imam. As we shall see in Chapter 9 concerning the plethora of *masānīd* works composed for Abū Ḥanīfa, they did not disappoint. We should recognise that this important phenomenon had an impact on ḥadīth masters of the eleventh century such as al-Ḥākim al-Nīshāpūrī, who included Abū Ḥanīfa as one of the ḥadīth scholars of Kufa.[126] Al-Ḥākim even implies as much at the outset of the chapter when he writes: 'This category concerns those famous, trustworthy, leading scholars from the generation of Successors and their successors whose ḥadīth were collected for the purposes of memorisation, learning, and to gain blessings through them.'[127] For the great ḥadīth master al-Ḥākim, there was no doubt that Abū Ḥanīfa belonged to this category of ḥadīth specialists. This was nothing short of a sea change, then, from the days of ʿAbd Allāh b. Aḥmad b. Ḥanbal in the ninth century to al-Ḥākim in the eleventh.

[123] ʿAbd Allāh b. Aḥmad b. Ḥanbal, *Kitāb al-Sunna*, 204.

[124] ʿAbd Allāh b. Aḥmad b. Ḥanbal, *Kitāb al-Sunna*, 207 (*innā lā nanqumu ʿalā Abī Ḥanīfa al-ra'y, kullunā narā. Innamā nanqumu ʿalayhi annahu yudhkaru lahu al-ḥadīth ʿan rasūl Allāh fa yuftī bi khilāfihi*).

[125] ʿAbd Allāh b. Aḥmad b. Ḥanbal, *Kitāb al-Sunna*, 210.

[126] Al-Ḥākim al-Nīshāpūrī, *Maʿrifat ʿulūm al-ḥadīth*, 649 (Dār Ibn Ḥazm edn.).

[127] Al-Ḥākim al-Nīshāpūrī, *Maʿrifat ʿulūm al-ḥadīth*, 642 (Dār Ibn Ḥazm edn.).

## 7.3 Theology

The eighth and ninth centuries saw Muslims occupied with some fundamental theological questions.[128] How religious scholars responded to such questions had an immediate bearing on their status and association with the proto-Sunni community. It could be argued that there were two doctrinal controversies that animated theological perspectives on orthodoxy and heresy during these centuries. The first was the doctrine of Irjā', a theological epithet that could refer to a variety of 'heretical' doctrines, ranging from ideas about the status of sinners, disputes between the Companions of the Prophet Muḥammad, definitions of belief, and political quietism and rebellion. The second was the Miḥna, an attempt by the ʿAbbāsid caliph al-Ma'mūn to impose an empire-wide religious consensus that the Quran was the created word of God. We are concerned here with Irjā' and the Miḥna in so far as they were two theological developments that had a direct, adverse impact on Abū Ḥanīfa's status as a figure of orthodoxy among the proto-Sunni community.

The history of the Miḥna is well-charted territory in the field of Islamic history and theology. Al-Ma'mūn's attempt in 211/833 to impose the doctrine of the createdness of the Quran has been the subject of countless monographs and articles.[129] Our concern in the following pages is to explain how the Miḥna's association with Abū Ḥanīfa and his followers contributed to new discourses of heresy against Abū Ḥanīfa.[130] We can identify three factors that generated a unique relationship between the Miḥna and proto-Ḥanafism. The first and most obvious connection lies in the role that Ḥanafī judges played in spearheading the Miḥna. Not only were Ḥanafīs such as Bishr al-Marīsī prominent at the court of al-Ma'mūn and espousing the doctrine of the created Quran, but Ḥanafī judges such as Ibn Abī Du'ād were directing the Miḥna, and the Ḥanafī judges under his supervision were implementing the new imperial theology all across the empire.[131] A second link is the existence of Ḥanafī

[128] For a magisterial survey of early Muslim theology see van Ess, *Theologie und Gesellschaft*.

[129] Patton, *Ahmed ibn Hanbal and the Mihna*; Watt, *The Formative Period of Islamic Thought*, 280 ff.; Nawas, *Al-Ma'mūn*; Hinds, s.v. 'Miḥna', *EI*$^2$; van Ess, *Theologie und Gesellschaft*, 3: 446–508; Melchert, *The Formation of the Sunni Schools of Law*, 8 ff., 54–60; Zaman, *Religion and Politics*, 106–18; Turner, *Inquisition in Early Islam*; Hurvitz, 'Miḥna as Self-Defense'; Lucas, *Constructive Critics*, 192–202.

[130] See the excellent account given by Hinds, s.v. 'Miḥna', *EI*$^2$; and Melchert, 'Religious Policies of the Caliphs'.

[131] In Egypt, Ibn Abī Layth al-Aṣamm (see al-Kindī, *al-Wulāt wa kitāb al-quḍāt*, 452); in Baghdad, al-Ḥasan b. ʿAlī b. al-Jaʿd (see al-Khaṭīb al-Baghdādī, *Tārīkh Baghdād*, 7: 364) and ʿAbd Allāh b. Muḥammad al-Khalanjī (see al-Khaṭīb al-Baghdādī, *Tārīkh Baghdād*, 10: 73). On al-Ma'mūn's special interest in Ḥanafī jurisprudence see the profile of the caliph given by Ibn Taghrībirdī, *al-Nujūm al-ẓāhira fī mulūk Miṣr wa al-Qāhira* (Cairo: Maṭbaʿat Dār al-Kutub al-Miṣriyya, 1930), 2: 225.

scholars who professed the doctrine of the created Quran and submitted to it under interrogation or trial. Still, it is difficult to characterise proto-Ḥanafism in this period. For every Ḥanafī judge or scholar who espoused the doctrine of a created Quran and spearheaded trials and interrogations, we find Ḥanafī judges and scholars who were opposed to the theological doctrine and the Miḥna.[132] The third and final basis for attacks upon Abū Ḥanīfa on account of the doctrine of the created Quran pertained to the supposed personal doctrine of Abū Ḥanīfa. There is no early evidence to suggest that Abū Ḥanīfa held this doctrine. A significant attempt to ascribe this doctrine to Abū Ḥanīfa was made by his grandson, Ismāʿīl b. Ḥammād b. Abī Ḥanīfa (d. 212/827–8). Ismāʿīl b. Ḥammād was a judge on the eastern side of Baghdad in 194/809. He was then appointed to a judgeship in Raqqa, followed by an appointment in Basra in 210/825. He was one of the first Kufans to be quizzed about the doctrine of the created Quran and subsequently accede to it. We learn from an antagonist of Ismāʿīl b. Ḥammād, which is enough reason to call into question the report's veracity, that in the course of his interrogation he declared: 'The Quran is created, this is my religion, the religion of my father and of my grandfather [Abū Ḥanīfa].'[133]

The Miḥna instigated a controversy surrounding the createdness of the Quran, and these three levels of association between Abū Ḥanīfa (and Ḥanafism) and this emerging theological controversy undoubtedly contributed to discourses of heresy against Abū Ḥanīfa. Was this the main basis for the emergence of these discourses? It is unlikely. The discourse of heresy around him was much broader than this one doctrine. The entire tradition of *manāqib* works defending Abū Ḥanīfa against charges of heresy says relatively little about this doctrine. The Miḥna itself, as Zaman and Lucas have argued, was not as consequential to the scholarly community as has been supposed by scholars in the past. It could be argued that another theological controversy was more pertinent to the wave of heresiological discourses that engulfed Abū Ḥanīfa's mnemohistory.

Proto-Sunni traditionalists were unequivocal in charging Abū Ḥanīfa with heresy on account of Irjā'. The Murji'a were an amorphous segment of early Islamic society. They had no single leader; an array of doctrines

[132] See the discussion of this complicated picture of Ḥanafī jurists and scholars and their stance around the Miḥna controversy in Tsafrir, *The History of an Islamic School of Law*, 44–7 ('Thanks to this theological diversity the Hanafi school could supply most of the qadis of Baghdad for about a century and a half, both when qadis where [*sic*] required to admit the createdness of the Quran and when they were supposed to believe the contrary.').

[133] Ibn ʿAdī, *al-Kāmil fī al-ḍuʿafāʾ al-rijāl*, 1: 509 (Dār al-Kutub edn.); al-Khaṭīb al-Baghdādī, *Tārīkh Baghdād*, 7: 216–18.

were ascribed to them, which changed over time; and the label Irjā' denoted different doctrines from region to region.[134] It is possible, nevertheless, to identify three main strains of Murji'ism in the eighth–ninth centuries, all three of which were attributed to Abū Ḥanīfa and his followers.

The first was the doctrine of the created Quran, and in this respect the claim that Abū Ḥanīfa was a Murji'ī or Jahmī designated his alleged adherence to the doctrine of a created Quran. This collapsing of the Murji'a and Jahmiyya into one, and the amorphous character of the movement, is documented in *Kitāb al-Taḥrīsh*, which distinguishes between the Murji'a of Khurāsān and those of Kufa and Basra, explaining that the Murji'a of Khurāsān were the Jahmiyya, and that they were the leaders of the Murji'a.[135] How concerned Ḥanafīs were by this allegation of heresy is unclear, though our discussion of the Miḥna does suggest that it was not the central premise for discourses of heresy against Abū Ḥanīfa. Some Ḥanafī creeds written in the ninth–tenth centuries, such as al-Ṭaḥāwī's, refer to the controversy over the nature of the Quran and emphatically deny its createdness.[136]

Proto-Ḥanafīs were far more concerned with Irjā' as it pertained to the theological controversy over the nature of belief (*īmān*), though they rejected the label itself. A group of credal treatises circulated among students of Abū Ḥanīfa, sometimes attributed to Abū Ḥanīfa himself, responded to discourses of heresy. These texts reject the epithet of Murji'a, deny the allegation that they are heretical innovators (*ahl al-bidaʿ*), and instead posit their affiliation to *ahl al-ʿadl wa ahl al-sunna* (the people of justice and the Sunna).[137] These late eighth- and ninth-century texts show an awareness, therefore, among proto-Ḥanafīs of discourses of heresy. They use theological treatises to refute proto-Sunni traditionalist critics and seek to establish their own proto-Sunni credentials. The very existence of a debate over the term Sunni, being employed by proto-Sunni

[134] For much of the primary and secondary sources pertaining to Abū Ḥanīfa, Irjā', and the Quran see Melchert, *The Formation of the Sunni Schools of Law*, 54–60; van Ess, *Theologie und Gesellschaft*, 1: 179–214 (on Abū Ḥanīfa and Irjā'); Madelung, 'The Origins of the Controversy'.

[135] Ḍirār b. ʿAmr, *Kitāb al-Taḥrīsh*, 76–8. The association between Jahm b. Ṣafwān and Abū Ḥanīfa was discussed in Chapter 1 and is treated below in section 7.5. On the Jahmiyya and the doctrine of a created Quran see al-Khaṭīb al-Baghdādī, *Tārīkh Baghdād*, 15: 580; van Ess, *Theologie und Gesellschaft*, 2: 493–508, esp. 506–7.

[136] Al-Ṭaḥāwī, *al-ʿAqīda al-Ṭaḥāwiyya*, ed. Zuhayr al-Shāwīsh (Beirut: al-Maktab al-Islāmī, 1977), 5; Wensinck, *The Muslim Creed*, 127 [Abū Ḥanīfa (pseud.), *Waṣiyyat Abī Ḥanīfa*, art. 9], 189 [Abū Ḥanīfa (pseud.), *Fiqh al-akbar* II, art. 3].

[137] Abū Ḥanīfa (attr.), *al-ʿĀlim wa al-mutaʿallim*, ed. Muḥammad Zāhid al-Kawtharī (Cairo: Maṭbaʿat al-Anwār, 1948), 37–8 (*Risālat Abī Ḥanīfa ilā ʿUthmān al-Battī*). See also van Ess, 'Kritisches zum *Fiqh Akbar*', 336.

traditionalists against proto-Sunni followers of Abū Ḥanīfa and vice versa, is good evidence of the competing nature of proto-Sunni orthodoxy in the eighth–tenth centuries. Discourses of heresy were central to these competing claims over Sunni orthodoxy. Abū Ḥanīfa was attacked for establishing a low benchmark for belief and for excluding works (*ʿamal* or *farā'iḍ*) from the definition of belief. Both doctrines were considered heretical by proto-Sunni traditionalists. The cultural commentator al-Thaʿālibī (d. 429/1039) explained that the term *īmān murji'ī* had such wide usage that it simply denoted the idea that something does not increase or decrease. He explained that this idiomatic usage of the expression emerged because the Murji'a held that faith is only a statement and that it does not increase or decrease.[138] This contradicted the view of proto-Sunni traditionalists, who, in response to requests that they explain the doctrines of proto-Sunni majoritarian orthodoxy (*mā ʿalayhi ahl al-sunna*), posited that belief comprised of intention, speech, and works, all together.[139] The view of others, that belief comprised what is in one's heart and attestation by the tongue, whilst works were only expressions of God-consciousness and piety and not part of belief, was held to be untenable.[140] Despite eschewing the epithet Murji'a, followers of Abū Ḥanīfa upheld Murji'a doctrines in their theological treatises.[141]

The third implication of the charge of Irjā' against Abū Ḥanīfa was, as we saw in the previous chapter, that he supported rebellion against legitimate rulers. This was another discourse of heresy that Ḥanafī authors of the tenth century sought to refute.

When proto-Sunni traditionalists employed these labels against Abū Ḥanīfa, they were hoping to associate him and his followers with heretical groups and movements. Sometimes they were clear about which beliefs they were accusing Abū Ḥanīfa of holding, and sometimes they expressed ambivalence. On other occasions, Abū Ḥanīfa was charged with holding specific errant doctrines and beliefs.[142]

[138] Al-Thaʿālibī, *Thimār al-qulūb fī al-muḍāf wa al-mansūb*, ed. Muḥammad Abū al-Faḍl Ibrāhīm (Beirut: al-Maktaba al-ʿAṣriyya, 2003), 145 (*yuḍrabu bihi al-mathal limā lā yazīd wa lā yanquṣ li anna al-murji'a yaqūlūn: inna al-īmān qawl fard lā yazīd wa lā yanquṣ fa yushabbahu bi īmānihim mā yakūn bi hādhihi al-ṣifa*).

[139] Abū ʿUbayd al-Qāsim b. Sallām, *Kitāb al-Īmān*, 10 (*al-īmān bi al-niyya wa al-qawl wa al-ʿamal jamīʿan*). See also Madelung, 'Early Sunnī Doctrine'.

[140] Abū ʿUbayd al-Qāsim b. Sallām, *Kitāb al-Īmān*, 10 (*al-īmān bi al-qulūb wa al-alsina fa ammā al-aʿmāl fa innamā hiya taqwā wa birr wa laysat min al-īmān*).

[141] Abū Ḥanīfa, *al-ʿĀlim wa al-mutaʿallim*, 36–7 (*Risālat Abī Ḥanīfa ilā ʿUthmān al-Battī*).

[142] ʿAbd Allāh b. Aḥmad b. Ḥanbal, *Kitāb al-Sunna*, 194–5 (reports alleging Abū Ḥanīfa's deficient theology regarding the Prophet Muḥammad's birth and resting place). Note that later Ḥanafī works, including those attributed to Abū Ḥanīfa, adopted a different position: See Abū Muṭī al-Balkhī [attr. to Abū Muqātil al-Samarqandī], *Kitāb al-ʿĀlim wa al-mutaʿallim*, 8–32, 13 (on the nature of faith) and *Risāla ilā ʿUthmān al-Battī*, 34–38, 35

These theological issues posed a real problem for followers of Abū Ḥanīfa. They caused enough concern for them to compose works of theology and creed in an attempt to establish his Sunni credentials in the face of hostile opposition. In the realm of theology, the creed of al-Ṭaḥāwī perhaps played the most significant role in convincing other communities that Abū Ḥanīfa's theological opinions were inseparable from the emerging Sunni orthodoxy:[143]

The following is an exposition of the creed of majoritarian Sunni orthodoxy (*ahl al-sunna wa al-jamāʿa*) according to the school of the jurists of the community, Abū Ḥanīfa al-Nuʿmān b. Thābit al-Kūfī, Abū Yūsuf Yaʿqūb b. Ibrāhīm al-Anṣārī, and Abū ʿAbd Allāh Muḥammad b. al-Ḥasan al-Shaybānī, may God be pleased with them all. This is what they believe of the fundamental principles of religion and what they observe in serving the Lord of all worlds of beings.

Article 5 of the creed is explicit about the uncreated nature of the Quran, thereby undermining claims in the wake of the Miḥna that Abū Ḥanīfa and his followers stood outside Sunni orthodoxy on the question of the createdness of the Quran.[144] Article 20 renounces disputation about the Quran and emphasises the absence of conflict with other Sunnis on this issue.[145] But the most emphatic response to discourses of heresy against Abū Ḥanīfa in al-Ṭaḥāwī's creed pertains not to theological or doctrinal points, but rather to the matter of rebellion:[146]

We do not approve of the sword against any of the community of Muḥammad, God bless him and give him peace, except him against whom the sword is obligatory. We do not approve of rebelling against our imams and the administrators of our affairs, even if they act wrongfully, and we do not summon (others to rebel) against them and do not withdraw a hand from obeying them. We consider that obedience to them is obedience to God, as long as they do not instruct disobedience (to God), and we pray for soundness and pardon for them.

This credal point is a clear attempt to respond to a putative discourse of heresy around Abū Ḥanīfa's engagement with late Umayyad and early ʿAbbāsid uprisings. The creed's break with discourses of heresy is nowhere clearer than in the final article: 'We follow', writes al-Ṭaḥāwī, 'the majoritarian Sunni orthodoxy, and we avoid deviancy, disagreement, and

and 38 (denial of Irjāʾ), both texts in Abū Ḥanīfa (attr.), *al-ʿĀlim wa al-mutaʿallim*. On the attribution of these and other texts see Wensinck, *The Muslim Creed*, chs. 6, 7, and 8; Givony, 'The Murji'a and the Theological School of Abū Ḥanīfa', 117–21; Rudolph, *al-Māturīdī and the Development of Sunnī Theology*, 28 ff.; Schacht, 'An Early Murc'ite Treatise'.

143 Al-Ṭaḥāwī, *al-ʿAqīda al-Ṭaḥāwiyya*, 5.

144 Al-Ṭaḥāwī, *al-ʿAqīda al-Ṭaḥāwiyya*, 5. My numbering of the articles follows Watt, *Islamic Creeds*, 48–56. I have modified some of his translations.

145 Al-Ṭaḥāwī, *al-ʿAqīda al-Ṭaḥāwiyya*, 9.

146 Al-Ṭaḥāwī, *al-ʿAqīda al-Ṭaḥāwiyya*, 11.

sectarianism.'[147] We shall have occasion in Chapter 10 to say more about the role of theology and creed, including al-Ṭaḥāwī's, in the writings of Ḥanafīs seeking to represent majoritarian Sunni orthodoxy. For the present, I should like to note that these theological charges dominated discussions in tenth–eleventh-century heresiographical texts, and non-Ḥanafī works of theology were also categorical about Abū Ḥanīfa's sound, Sunni theological orthodoxy.[148]

Al-Ashʿarī (d. 324/935–6) counts Abū Ḥanīfa and his followers as one of the sects of the Murji'a.[149] In *al-Ibāna*, however, he cites contradictory material concerning Abū Ḥanīfa's theological views. In a number of places al-Ashʿarī cites reports describing Abū Ḥanīfa as a polytheist because he believed the Quran was created.[150] Al-Ashʿarī himself is entirely unmoved by such accusations. On one occasion, he declares: 'How utterly impossible for the great imam Abū Ḥanīfa to have held such a doctrine. It is a lie and falsehood, because Abū Ḥanīfa belongs to the very best of *ahl al-sunna*.'[151] After citing a report alleging that Abū Ḥanīfa was forced to repent from heresy but then started preaching that same heresy to others, al-Ashʿarī writes, 'What a pure lie against Abū Ḥanīfa.'[152] Abū Ḥanīfa then appears in a list of proto-Sunni traditionalist scholars who declared as heretics anyone espousing the doctrine of a created Quran.[153] ʿAbd al-Qāhir al-Baghdādī (d. 429/1037) adopts a similar tone to that of al-Ashʿarī. He regards Abū Ḥanīfa as one of the jurists of the Muslims.[154] He raises the issue of Abū

[147] Al-Ṭaḥāwī, *al-ʿAqīda al-Ṭaḥāwiyya*, 11.

[148] At the beginning of this study I signalled my scepticism regarding the utility of heresiographical sources to permit a detailed historical reconstruction of change over time in discourses of heresy and orthodoxy. I do not intend to repudiate this view here. As sources for the historical development of religious and political trends across the ninth and tenth centuries, creeds and heresiographical works are notoriously inscrutable. Credal formulations are characteristically laconic, whilst heresiographical works observe formulaic and schematic structures. The internal material of early creeds seldom exhibits allusions to historical persons, political circumstances, and contemporary events. Heresiographers make bolder claims to historical documentation, but their commitment to confessional legitimisation raises a different set of problems for historians. Furthermore, the discourses of heresy studied in Chapters 2 and 3 are done so on the basis of ninth–tenth-century sources, whereas the heresiographical sources date from the tenth–eleventh centuries. Put simply, the effort to reconstruct the vicissitudes of political, social, and religious history from heresiographical and doxographical works alone can be unrewarding. Nevertheless, it is important to present an overview of this material to gain a better understanding of how Abū Ḥanīfa was portrayed as an adherent of deviant theology.

[149] Al-Ashʿarī, *Maqālāt al-Islāmiyyīn*, ed. H. Ritter (Istanbul: Devlet Matbaasi, 1929–30), 138–9.

[150] Al-Ashʿarī, *al-Ibāna ʿan uṣūl al-diyāna*, ed. ʿAbbās Ṣabbāgh (Beirut: Dār al-Nafāʾis, 1994), 77–8.

[151] Al-Ashʿarī, *al-Ibāna*, 78. [152] Al-Ashʿarī, *al-Ibāna*, 78.

[153] Al-Ashʿarī, *al-Ibāna*, 82–3.

[154] ʿAbd al-Qāhir al-Baghdādī, *Kitāb al-Milal wa niḥal*, ed. Naṣrī Nādir (Beirut: Dār al-Machreq, 1982), 139–40, 100, 156.

Ḥanīfa more than once in his treatment of the Murji'a but dissociates him from any problematic Murji'ī doctrines.[155]

The primary focus of these heresiographical texts is on questions of doctrinal theology. In the main, they exculpate Abū Ḥanīfa from charges of deviance and heresy; and so they do not provide the full range of discourses of heresy found outside *firaq* works. The mnemohistory we see in these texts is, therefore, a partial one. But this is not their most serious shortcoming. *Firaq* texts furnish a view of medieval Sunni orthodoxy at the end of a long and arduous process. The approach taken in this study has been to examine a disparate pool of sources, both broader and earlier than the heresiographical literature, to understand the evolution of medieval Sunni orthodoxy as a process and not as a legal or theological category.

## 7.4 Piety

Piety was a fundamental virtue for the proto-Sunni community at large, and for the proto-Sunni traditionalist movement in particular. There was certainly a spectrum of pious expression, ranging from an unremitting seriousness to a less disciplined mode of piety, and as long as one remained within this one could avoid extreme censure.[156] Proto-Sunni traditionalists understood how central piety and the observance of religious norms were to the construction of orthodoxy. One way to ensure that Abū Ḥanīfa was jettisoned from a community of orthodoxy was to argue that his behaviour did not match up to the basic standards of orthodoxy.

Proto-Sunni traditionalists began with his lived example. They nurtured suspicions regarding Abū Ḥanīfa's religious orthodoxy by attacking his performance of the ritual prayer. We have already seen how his opponents had expressed their disapproval of the way in which Abū Ḥanīfa himself prayed and how he instructed his students to pray, which centred on the raising of the hands in prayer. Proto-Sunni traditionalists contended that the problem went deeper and complained that when they performed their prayers behind Abū Ḥanīfa something made them feel perturbed.[157] In fact, there was a general concern among proto-Sunni traditionalists about the decorum of Abū Ḥanīfa's prayer and piety, and they suggested that this spilled over into other aspects of his social life. Particular concerns were raised about his religious study-circles and the

155 ʿAbd al-Qāhir al-Baghdādī, *Kitāb al-Milal wa niḥal*, 140, 147 (Ḍirāriyya); ʿAbd al-Qāhir al-Baghdādī, *al-Farq bayn al-firaq*, 203.

156 See now the articles on piety gathered in Melchert, *Hadith, Piety, and Law*, 119–236.

157 Al-Khaṭīb al-Baghdādī, *Tārīkh Baghdād*, 15: 572–3.

way they were conducted. Onlookers observed that when Abū Ḥanīfa was presiding over lessons in the mosque there would be laughter and people would be raising their voices.[158] Others were affronted by more serious charges, namely, that Abū Ḥanīfa's lessons would go on without their being any praise for the Prophet Muḥammad.[159] Proto-Sunni traditionalists made these allegations because they wanted to sketch a portrait of a deviant and heretical figure. They saw Abū Ḥanīfa as a man who failed to live up to the acceptable standards of proto-Sunni traditionalists.

They even used his death as an occasion to publicise the consensus of the proto-Sunni traditionalist community concerning his religious orthodoxy. The death of a scholar was supposed to be a moment of sober reflection on their contributions, an opportunity to seek God's forgiveness on their behalf, and to wish them well in the hereafter. There was a different protocol, however, for people who were cast as deviants and heretics. In the case of Abū Ḥanīfa, proto-Sunni traditionalists purported to document the instant reactions of leading members of their textual community to the news that Abū Ḥanīfa had passed away. When Sufyān al-Thawrī heard the news of Abū Ḥanīfa's death, proto-Sunni traditionalists of the ninth century reported him as having exclaimed: 'Praise be to God who has relieved the Muslims of him [Abū Ḥanīfa]. He had been destroying systematically the foundations of Islam. No birth was more harmful (*ash'am*) to Islam than his.'[160] The same is reported on the authority of Mālik b. Anas: 'No one was born in Islam whose birth was more harmful to the Muslims than that of Abū Ḥanīfa.' The report continues:

> Mālik b. Anas would condemn speculative jurisprudence. He would say, 'We must adhere to the reports of the messenger of God, may God bless him and grant him peace, and the reports of his Companions. We cannot adhere to speculative jurisprudence, for it produces a situation whereby if someone comes along who is stronger in speculative jurisprudence, then one must adhere to him. We would have a situation whereby whenever someone comes along who displays a stronger grasp of speculative jurisprudence than you, you would be forced to follow him. The matter would continue in this [absurd] manner.'[161]

We find al-Fasawī's history again cited the following view: 'No one initiated more evil in Islam than Abū Ḥanīfa except so and so who was crucified.'[162] This particular expression of celebration at the death of Abū

[158] ʿAbd Allāh b. Aḥmad b. Ḥanbal, *Kitāb al-Sunna*, 216.
[159] ʿAbd Allāh b. Aḥmad b. Ḥanbal, *Kitāb al-Sunna*, 213–14.
[160] Al-Fasawī, *Kitāb al-Maʿrifa wa al-tārīkh*, 2: 785–6.
[161] Al-Fasawī, *Kitāb al-Maʿrifa wa al-tārīkh*, 2: 790.
[162] Al-Fasawī, *Kitāb al-Maʿrifa wa al-tārīkh*, 2: 783; al-Khaṭīb al-Baghdādī, *Tārīkh Baghdād*, 13: 396–7.

Ḥanīfa because it saw the elimination of a scholar whose heretical ideas had caused irreparable damage to the Muslim community is a regular feature in some of the most important ninth- and tenth-century texts written by proto-Sunni traditionalists.[163]

That proto-Sunni traditionalists were relentless in their pursuit of discourses of heresy against Abū Ḥanīfa can be discerned from the fact that they were not content to stop at his death. Even his funeral became a pretext for highlighting his remoteness from proto-Sunni traditionalist orthodoxy. Bishr b. Abī al-Azhar al-Nīshāpūrī told ʿAlī b. al-Madīnī about a dream he had seen of a funeral where the coffin was draped in white cloth and was encircled by priests. In the dream, Bishr asked, 'Whose funeral is this?' He was told: 'This is Abū Ḥanīfa's funeral.' Bishr told a leading proto-Ḥanafī, Abū Yūsuf, about this dream. Abū Yūsuf instructed him not to relate this dream to anyone.[164]

## 7.5 Sociology of Heresy

I have attempted in a number of places to emphasise the social dimensions of orthodoxy and discourses of heresy. In Chapters 2 and 3 I detailed the ways in which proto-Sunni traditionalists formed both a textual community and a social community of the learned. I documented the circulation of discourses of heresy in various social encounters and settings among proto-Sunni traditionalists. This provided an opportunity to draw attention to the promulgators of these discourses: the agents of proto-Sunni traditionalist orthodoxy. Chapters 4 (regionalism), 5 (ethnogenesis), and 6 (politics) studied the wider social sphere in which discourses of heresy flourished. In closing this chapter on religion I should like to argue that heresy was implicated not only in the social life of medieval Muslims but in the very attitudes towards social life and ways of living in communities and societies. Notions of orthodoxy and heresy in medieval Islam were accompanied by a set of moral social codes governing and restricting social interaction with heretics. There was a salient social dimension to discourses of heresy and conceptions of orthodox communities. When Max Weber wrote in his seminal essay, 'Prophecy has created a new social community, particularly where it became a soteriological religion of congregations,' he was merely scratching the surface concerning how groups organise the work of salvation in this world.[165] This section shall highlight the social

[163] Al-Fasawī, *Kitāb al-Maʿrifa wa al-tārīkh*, 2: 783; al-Khaṭīb al-Baghdādī, *Tārīkh Baghdād*, 4: 209.

[164] Al-Fasawī, *Kitāb al-Maʿrifa wa al-tārīkh*, 2: 784.

[165] Weber, *From Max Weber: Essays in Sociology*, 329.

mechanisms that proto-Sunni traditionalist communities used to regulate, isolate, mock, test, and marginalise those they considered to be deviants and heretics.

Strategies of exclusion are described in a number of theoretical anti-heresy treatises composed from the middle of the ninth century onwards. One could comb these texts to present a catalogue of social attitudes to heretics. However, anti-heresy treatises do not always speak of specific cases and circumstances, and the reader of these works runs the risk of reading theory and mistaking it for practice. It is more pertinent for our purposes to show how proto-Sunni traditionalists, in their own writings, used discourses of heresy to marginalise Abū Ḥanīfa and attempt to isolate his memory among societies and communities in the medieval Islamic world. A social history of heresy and orthodoxy has to go beyond theoretical disquisitions by placing the latter alongside specific instances and social strategies.

### *A Community of Heretics*

Proto-Sunni traditionalists conceived of heresy as a social phenomenon. The state's marginal role in the direct articulation and enforcement of religious orthodoxy, in addition to the absence of any ecclesiastical social structure or institution, meant that the task of regulating orthodoxy and heresy in the social life of Muslim communities rested with an informal network of learned communities.[166] One of these communities, the proto-Sunni traditionalists, developed a fairly consistent social vision of how orthodoxy could be articulated and maintained. It was a vision that focused on how heresy might be suppressed and marginalised. A close study of discourses of heresy targeted towards Abū Ḥanīfa reveals the extent to which sociological and anthropological concerns – how societies and individuals behave and interact – lay at the heart of proto-Sunni conceptions of orthodoxy and heresy.

Proto-Sunni traditionalists knew that Islam was a social religion, and their vision of heresy and heretics was informed explicitly by an awareness of this fact. They described heretics not as isolated and solitary individuals but rather as constituting a social community of heretics and deviants capable of, and indeed seeking to, disseminate their ideas across a wide spectrum of society. We have already observed, for instance, that when proto-Sunni traditionalists explained the spread of ideas they deemed to

[166] Occasionally, the state's qadis were called upon to regulate orthodoxy. The execution of Manṣūr al-Ḥallāj is the most well-known example. See Massignon, *The Passion of al-Hallaj*, 1: 277–8. See also Tillier, 'Qāḍīs and the Political Use', 57–9.

be deviant, such as *ra'y*, they did so by drawing attention to three religious scholars and their shared ethnic, genealogical, and social status, as well as their prominence in some of the key provinces of the early Islamic empire. Heresy as a social movement conveyed a more ominous image than the heresy of single individuals. It was important for proto-Sunni traditionalists to argue that different heresies were connected and that heresiarchs, far apart though they might be, constituted a network. This technique is noticeable, too, in proto-Sunni traditionalist attempts to suggest that Abū Ḥanīfa was a close associate of the heresiarch Jahm b. Ṣafwān. In his *al-Tārīkh al-awsaṭ* al-Bukhārī alludes to the kind of relationship the two men might have had. Al-Bukhārī writes:[167]

> I heard Ismāʿīl b. ʿUrʿura say that Abū Ḥanīfa said: 'The wife of Jahm [b. Ṣafwān] came to us here, and she educated our women (*addabat nisā'ana*).' I heard al-Dārimī say that Abū ʿĀṣim was asked: 'Was she intelligible (*kānat faṣīḥa*)?' He said: 'By God, certainly not. [She spoke] only with a stammering and defective speech (*lā wa Allāhi illā lathghā' laknā'*).'

Proto-Sunni traditionalists imagined a deep level of affinity between the two men. They saw this as a relationship that went beyond any doctrinal convergence of Abū Ḥanīfa and Jahm b. Ṣafwān's views. Abū Ḥanīfa is depicted as the informal head of a religious community who oversees the religious education of its womenfolk. He is portrayed as being comfortable with Jahm b. Ṣafwān's wife visiting and educating them. Jahm b. Ṣafwān's wife, it seems, had established a reputation for her religious views and interventions. When al-Asmaʿī, the philologist, heard that Jahm b. Ṣafwān's wife had described God and his throne as being confined entities (*maḥdūd*), he declared that this statement made her an unbeliever.[168]

This was not the only work of al-Bukhārī's to discuss Jahm b. Ṣafwān. In *Khalq afʿāl al-ʿibād wa al-radd ʿalā al-jahmiyya wa aṣḥāb al-taʿṭīl*, al-Bukhārī explains that he was privy to information that Jahm b. Ṣafwān abandoned the obligatory ritual prayer for forty days, and that this doubt stemmed from his discussions with the Sumaniyya – Buddhists from Khurāsān.[169] Proto-Sunni traditionalists believed that the friendship

[167] Al-Bukhārī, *al-Tārīkh al-awsaṭ*, 2: 37 (al-Luḥaydān edn.); al-Khaṭīb al-Baghdādī, *Tārīkh Baghdād*, 15: 514.

[168] Al-Dhahabī, *Mukhtaṣar al-ʿulūw li al-ʿalī al-ghaffār*, ed. Muḥammad Nāṣir al-Dīn al-Albānī (Damascus: al-Maktab al-Islāmī, 1981), 170–1.

[169] Al-Bukhārī, *Khalq afʿāl al-ʿibād* ( Mu'assasat al-Risāla edn.), 9(*qāla Ḍamra ʿan Ibn Shawdhab: taraka al-Jahm al-ṣalāt arbaʿīn yawman ʿalā wajh al-shakk fa khāṣamahu baʿḍ al-sumaniyya, fa shakka fa aqāma arbaʿīna yawm lā yuṣallī. Qāla Ḍamra: wa qad ra'āhu Ibn Shawdhab*). On Jahm and the Sumaniyya see al-Malaṭī, *Kitāb al-Tanbīh wa al-radd ʿalā ahl al-ahwā' wa al-bidaʿ*, ed. S. Dedering (Istanbul: Maṭbaʿat al-Dawla, 1936),

between Abū Ḥanīfa and Jahm b. Ṣafwān extended beyond just a concern for one another. Abū al-Akhnas al-Kinānī reported that he had it on the authority of a trustworthy man that he saw Abū Ḥanīfa holding the camel halter of the coffin carrying the women of Jahm b. Ṣafwān, which had been transported from Khurāsān. Abū Ḥanīfa led the camel and walked it through Kufa.[170] Proto-Sunni traditionalists insisted that there was a cross-fertilisation of ideas and teachings between Jahm b. Ṣafwān and Abū Ḥanīfa's community, which the latter seemingly welcomed. The spread of religious ideas did not always depend on formal instruction between (male) scholars and students. Concepts and beliefs travelled through personal networks and communities. Social relations were conduits for religious ideas. The controversy surrounding the status of *lafẓ al-Qur'ān* was, in the view of proto-Sunni traditionalists, another instance in which Abū Ḥanīfa and Jahm b. Ṣafwān were deemed to have shared heretical ideas.

One of the most ardent spokespersons of proto-Sunni traditionalism was cognisant of the convergence of ideas found in these two men. Ibn Qutayba's treatise *Ikhtilāf fī al-lafẓ wa al-radd ʿalā al-Jahmiyya wa al-mushabbiha* addresses a number of theological controversies and competing groups of his day. One of its sections is dedicated to clarifying the ontological status of the recital and pronunciation of the Quran. He begins this section by acknowledging the existence of contradictory reports circulating in his lifetime about the views of proto-Sunni traditionalists (*ahl al-ḥadīth*). He then turns to the question of the origins of this theological controversy. A decisive turning point, he argues, was the intervention of Jahm b. Ṣafwān and Abū Ḥanīfa. These two figures, he contends, were the first scholars who began to discuss such theological issues concerning the Quran. 'Prior to their intervention,' Ibn Qutayba states, 'such theological problems had not circulated among the people, they were unknown, and it was not from among the things that people discussed.'[171] What Ibn Qutayba presents here is a superficial connection between Jahm b. Ṣafwān and Abū Ḥanīfa. The burden of blame for this sharp and bitter theological controversy is assigned to two notable individuals, both of whom were placed outside the proto-Sunni traditionalist community.

Proto-Sunni traditionalists were relentless in their pursuit of the connections between Abū Ḥanīfa and Jahm b. Ṣafwān. For them, Abū

77 ff.; van Ess, *Theologie und Gesellschaft*, 2: 493–508, 503–4; Crone, 'al-Jāḥiẓ on *Aṣḥāb al-Jahālāt* and the Jahmiyya'; Crone, *The Iranian Reception of Islam*, ch 9.

170 Al-Khaṭīb al-Baghdādī, *Tārīkh Baghdād*, 15: 514.

171 Ibn Qutayba, *al-Ikhtilāf fī al-lafẓ wa al-radd ʿalā al-jahmiyya wa al-mushabbiha*, ed. Muḥammad Zāhid al-Kawtharī (Cairo: al-Maktaba al-Azhariyya li al-Turāth, 2001), 40–1 = ed. ʿUmar b. Maḥmūd b. ʿUmar (Riyadh: Dār al-Rāyya, 1991), 60–1.

Ḥanīfa and Jahm b. Ṣafwān were not simply arch-heresiarchs who knew each other and had some overlapping beliefs. The *Kitāb al-Sunna* of ʿAbd Allāh b. Aḥmad b. Ḥanbal alleges that Abū Yūsuf confirmed that Abū Ḥanīfa was a follower of Jahm b. Ṣafwān's doctrines. One report, set in the region of Jurjān, states that Abū Ḥanīfa died as a Jahmī.[172] This anecdote was preserved by ʿAbd Allāh b. Ḥanbal, but it also found a place in a local biographical dictionary of Jurjān.[173] Also originating from Jurjān was the claim that when asked about Abū Ḥanīfa, Abū Yūsuf responded brusquely, 'Why do you concern yourself with him, he died a Jahmī.'[174] In another report, when Abū Yūsuf was asked whether or not Abū Ḥanīfa followed the doctrines of Jahm b. Ṣafwān, he replied in the affirmative.[175] Abū Yūsuf was then asked to explain his relationship to Abū Ḥanīfa. 'He was a teacher,' Abū Yūsuf said, 'we accepted those of his teachings which were correct and we rejected whatever we considered to be abhorrent.'[176] There were also claims that Abū Ḥanīfa's adoption of Jahm b. Ṣafwān's doctrines was based on his reading of the latter's books, which were brought to Abū Ḥanīfa from Khurāsān. All of this points to a discernible discourse of heresy targeted towards Abū Ḥanīfa and his followers in Jurjān – one that was memorialised in the city's local histories.[177]

It bears reminding that the historicity of these reports is not the subject of this section, let alone this monograph. It is instructive enough for our purposes that ninth-century proto-Sunni traditionalists projected an image of a network of heretics forming a closely knit community. There is, however, a political dimension to reports attempting to connect Abū Ḥanīfa and Jahm b. Ṣafwān, and this is worth mentioning in so far as it might furnish some indications of how proto-Sunni traditionalists came to be convinced of a connection between these two individuals. What Abū Ḥanīfa and Jahm b. Ṣafwān shared was, in fact, an involvement in the life and career of al-Ḥārith b. Surayj, a subject discussed briefly in Chapter 6. There we analysed Abū Ḥanīfa's contribution to securing an amnesty for al-Ḥārith b. Surayj. What was not mentioned was that Jahm b. Ṣafwān

172 ʿAbd Allāh b. Aḥmad b. Ḥanbal, *Kitāb al-Sunna*, 181 ([chain of transmission:] I asked Abū Yūsuf when he was in Jurjān about Abū Ḥanīfa. He replied: 'What do you want with him? He died as a Jahmī.').

173 Al-Sahmī, *Tārīkh Jurjān*, 219. Abū Yūsuf's time in Jurjān is discussed elsewhere in al-Sahmī, *Tārīkh Jurjān*, 282, 372, 487.

174 Al-Khaṭīb al-Baghdādī, *Tārīkh Baghdād*, 15: 513.

175 ʿAbd Allāh b. Aḥmad b. Ḥanbal, *Kitāb al-Sunna*, 191 (*a kāna Abū Ḥanīfa yaqūl bi qawl Jahm? Fa qāla: naʿam*).

176 Al-Khaṭīb al-Baghdādī, *Tārīkh Baghdād*, 15: 512–13.

177 ʿAbd Allāh b. Aḥmad b. Ḥanbal, *Kitāb al-Sunna*, 183 (Aḥmad b. Ibrāhīm < Khālid b. Khidāsh < ʿAbd al-Malik b. Qarīb al-Asmaʿī < Ḥāzim al-Ṭafāwī: *Abū Ḥanīfa innamā kāna yaʿmal bi kutub Jahm*).

played a pivotal role in al-Ḥārith b. Surayj's career.[178] He served as al-Ḥārith b. al-Surayj's secretary.[179] In 128/745 Jahm b. Ṣafwān was appointed by al-Ḥārith b. Surayj to represent him in the arbitration settlement with the governor of Khurāsān, Naṣr b. Sayyār.[180] In the end, Jahm b. Ṣafwān died defending al-Ḥārith b. Surayj.[181]

Whatever the nature of their relationship, we can be sure that it was a complicated one. They were connected through their relationship with al-Ḥārith b. Surayj. Both Jahm b. Ṣafwān and Abū Ḥanīfa had students and disciples in Khurāsān, Balkh, and Ṭukhāristān who were known to have had Murji'ī sympathies. Murji'ī doctrines, in turn, were considered to have been an important ingredient of al-Ḥārith b. Surayj's revolt. Furthermore, both Jahm and Abū Ḥanīfa were renowned for their interventions in theological and doctrinal issues. Proto-Sunni traditionalists insisted on the social and intellectual proximity between them, although some proto-Ḥanafīs were adamantly opposed to such a suggestion. According to Abū Yūsuf, Abū Ḥanīfa condemned Jahm b. Ṣafwān and criticised his doctrines.[182] Abū Ḥanīfa himself was quoted as having called Jahm b. Ṣafwān an unbeliever (*kāfir*).[183] He was also reported to have decried the emergence in Khurāsān of Jahm b. Ṣafwān and Muqātil b. Sulaymān, describing them as the very worst of people.[184] The contradictory nature of these reports is very illuminating in that it points to the potency of the notion of a community of heretics in the eighth and ninth centuries. Proto-Sunni traditionalists were intent on documenting the close relations between Abū Ḥanīfa and Jahm because they believed religious deviance was not a solitary enterprise. It was the work of communities, networks, and parties sympathetic to each other's religious views. When proto-Ḥanafīs (and proto-Sunnis) of the ninth and tenth centuries categorically denied any affinity between Abū Ḥanīfa and Jahm b. Ṣafwān, they did so because they, too, appreciated the explanatory power that the argument from community carried.

### *Social Strategies of Exclusion*

The awareness among proto-Sunni traditionalists of heretics forming a coalition precipitated the growth of a number of strategies designed to marginalise deviants and heretics from the social life of medieval Islamic

[178] Al-Balādhurī, *Ansāb al-ashrāf [Tatimmat Ḥimyar b. Sabā']*, 25: 54, 57, 59.
[179] Al-Ṭabarī, *Tārīkh*, 2: 1918–19. [180] Al-Ṭabarī, *Tārīkh*, 2: 1919.
[181] Gardīzī, *Zayn al-akhbār*, 262.
[182] Al-Khaṭīb al-Baghdādī, *Tārīkh Baghdād*, 15: 514.
[183] Al-Khaṭīb al-Baghdādī, *Tārīkh Baghdād*, 15: 514–15.
[184] Al-Khaṭīb al-Baghdādī, *Tārīkh Baghdād*, 15: 514; Ibn Ḥajar al-ʿAsqalānī, *Tahdhīb al-tahdhīb*, 10: 281.

communities. Proto-Sunni traditionalists found in the language of disease a convenient and powerful metaphor for the deadly impact that heresy had on society. The work of Robert Moore has shown that the language of disease was an essential ingredient of heresy-making discourses.[185] Moore argued that the language of disease was more than simply a convenient metaphor for heresy. It provided a systematic model of heresy and how it worked grounded in then-current beliefs about disease. Ideas about heresy were rooted in the realities of social life. Heresies could spread like disease and infection, and their consequences were violent and fatal.[186] Remaining immune to the ideas and vicinity of heretics was at least as important as ensuring one's immunity from physical ailments.

Ibn Waḍḍāḥ's treatise on heresy invokes the metaphor on two occasions in the course of highlighting the dangers of mixing with the people of heresy. People were advised not to sit with a heretic because he could poison their hearts (*yumarriḍ qalbak*).[187] The way to protect one's religion was to withdraw from mixing with rulers and sitting with the people of heresy. Those who exposed themselves to the company of rulers (*al-sulṭān*) or heretics (*aṣḥāb al-ahwā'*) risked certain infection by the disease that plagued these two groups of people (*alṣaqu min al-jarab*).[188] It was literally 'more contagious than mange'. Even groups engaging in religious debate were seen as a threat to the social fabric of medieval life. One observer of a group of people debating among themselves rose up, dusted the dirt off his clothes, and departed. Before leaving, he described them as human parasites (*innamā antum jarab, innamā antum jarab*).[189]

Employing the language of disease to describe the work of heresy became a persistent feature of discourses of heresy against Abū Ḥanīfa. Al-Fasawī's history mentions a conversation between Kaʿb al-Aḥbār and Shamr, in which the latter communicates his desire to travel to Iraq (*arāda ʿUmar an ya'tiya al-ʿIrāq*). Kaʿb does not like the sound of this and responds with an ominous description of Iraq: 'There you will certainly find rebels against the truth and every kind of incurable disease (*inna bihā ʿuṣāt al-ḥaqq wa kullu dā' ʿuḍāl*).' Kaʿb and Shamr's conversation, it seems, was part of a wider discussion among a small group of people, for the report adds that 'someone asked Kaʿb what the incurable disease was'. 'Different heresies for which no cure exists (*fa qīla lahu: mā al-dā' al-ʿuḍāl? qāla: ahwā' mukhtalifa laysa lahā shifā'*),' Kaʿb added.[190] Here, Kaʿb employs the discourse of heresy and disease to dissuade

[185] Moore, 'Heresy as Disease'. [186] On this theme see Stearns, *Infectious Ideas*.
[187] Ibn Waḍḍāḥ, *Kitāb al-Bidaʿ*, 192. [188] Ibn Waḍḍāḥ, *Kitāb al-Bidaʿ*, 194.
[189] Ibn Waḍḍāḥ, *Kitāb al-Bidaʿ*, 196.
[190] Al-Fasawī, *Kitāb al-Maʿrifa wa al-tārīkh*, 2: 751; Muḥammad Zakariyyā' al-Kāndahlawī, *Awjaz al-Masālik ilā Muwaṭṭā' Mālik* (Damascus: Dār al-Qalam, 2003),

Shamr from going to Iraq, citing as factors the place's hosting of sedition, falsehood, and any number of heresies. We cannot be certain whether or not Shamr heeded Kaʿb's counsel about the unholiness of Kufa. But we must reckon with the likelihood that this type of exercise in persuasion had the potential to grow in a period in which regional divisions were beginning to mark differences in Islamic law, ritual, and political allegiances. The language of disease and heresy was weaponised in regional rivalries. As we saw in Chapter 4, al-Fasawī is determined to portray Kufa as a land of heresy and unbelief. Kufa is portrayed as a city where the devil resides, heretics flourish, and diseases proliferate. The city of Medina, meanwhile, is the one city where the plague shall never enter.[191] It is also the one city wherein the anti-Christ shall never enter.[192]

Kaʿb al-Aḥbār was not the only scholar to describe Kufa as a repository of incurable diseases. One of Medina's leading spokespersons, Mālik b. Anas, was reported to have been more specific than Kaʿb on the issue. 'The incurable disease', he said, 'was the destruction of the faith, and Abū Ḥanīfa was of the incurable diseases.'[193] Mālik b. Anas was also said to have expressed his disbelief at the fact that the people of Kufa were so hospitable to Abū Ḥanīfa and had not thrown him out of the city.[194] Other proto-Sunni traditionalists came to a similar conclusion about the ominous 'incurable disease':[195]

ʿAbd Allāh b. Aḥmad b. Ḥanbal > Muṭrif al-Yasārī al-Aṣamm > Mālik b. Anas said: 'The incurable disease is the destruction of faith. Abū Ḥanīfa is the incurable disease.'[196]

Ibn ʿAdī > Ibn Abī Dāwūd > al-Rabīʿ b. Sulaymān al-Jīzī > al-Ḥārith b. Miskīn > Ibn al-Qāsim > Mālik said: 'The incurable disease is the destruction of faith, and Abū Ḥanīfa is [one manifestation] of the incurable disease.'[197]

According to the historian of early Muslim judges Wakīʿ b. Jarrāḥ, this kind of discourse came to the knowledge of the caliph al-Ma'mūn. Wakīʿ

17: 355–61; Abū Bakr b. al-ʿArabī, *Kitāb al-Qabas fī sharḥ Muwaṭṭā' Mālik b. Anas*, ed. Muḥammad ʿAbd Allāh Wuld Karīm (Beirut: Dār al-Gharb al-Islāmī, 1992), 1: 1150.

191 Al-Samhūdī, *Wafā' al-wafā bi akhbār dār al-muṣṭafā*, ed. Muḥammad Muḥyī al-Dīn ʿAbd al-Ḥamīd (Beirut: Dār al-Kutub al-ʿIlmiyya, n.d.), 1: 61–7 = ed. Qāsim al-Sāmarrā'ī (London: Mu'assasat al-Furqān li al-Turāth al-Islāmī, 2001), 1: 144–52.

192 Al-Samhūdī, *Wafā' al-wafā*, 1: 144 ff. (al-Sāmarrā'ī edn.) in the chapter *fī ʿiṣmatihā min al-dajjāl wa al-ṭāʿūn*.

193 Abū Zurʿa al-Dimashqī, *Tārīkh*, 2: 507, 751; al-Bukhārī, *Kitāb Rafʿ al-yadayn*, 17–18.

194 ʿAbd Allāh b. Aḥmad b. Ḥanbal, *Kitāb al-Sunna*, 224; Ibn ʿAdī, *al-Kāmil fī al-ḍuʿafā' al-rijāl*, 7: 2473 (Dār al-Fikr edn.).

195 Abū al-Walīd al-Bājī, *al-Muntaqā sharḥ Muwaṭṭā'* (Cairo: Dār al-Saʿāda, 1914), 7: 299–300 states this as one possible interpretation of Abū Ḥanīfa and his followers (*Abū Ḥanīfa wa aṣḥābihi*) but then proceeds to dismiss it as unreliable.

196 ʿAbd Allāh b. Aḥmad b. Ḥanbal, *Kitāb al-Sunna*, 223.

197 Ibn ʿAdī, *al-Kāmil fī al-ḍuʿafā' al-rijāl*, 8: 236–7 (ʿAbd al-Mawjūd edn.).

mentions that a group of scholars were sitting when one of them mentioned the ḥadīth report that neither the plague nor the anti-Christ shall enter Medina. At this point, someone added, 'and neither the *ra'y* of Abū Ḥanīfa'. This was mentioned to the Ḥanafī judge Yaḥyā b. Aktham, who informed al-Ma'mūn about this. When a Ḥanafī judge was finally appointed to Medina, al-Ma'mūn said: 'It has happened, the legal doctrine (*qawl*) of Abū Ḥanīfa has entered Medina.'[198] Proto-Sunni traditionalists understood the weight of (mis-)attributing hostile remarks about Abū Ḥanīfa to Mālik b. Anas, and began to disseminate them among colleagues in the ninth century. References to Abū Ḥanīfa's legal doctrine not entering into Medina reflect later, ninth-century jurisprudential conflicts and seem to be a convenient addition to an otherwise widely reported idea about neither the plague nor the anti-Christ being present in Medina. Such discourses spread far and wide, even to the caliphal court, inspiring the ʿAbbāsid caliph to provide his own commentary of ninth-century polemics.

The resonance of the language of disease in heresiological discourses during the ninth–tenth centuries presents us with more than just another strategy for dismissing scholars as heretics and deviants. The written sources that perpetuate these kinds of heresiological discourses mirrored the development of another critical group of writings in the ninth century. Systematic works treating plagues and diseases were produced in the ninth century, detailing plagues and epidemics in the medieval Middle East. The acute and graphic descriptions of heretics and their beliefs seem to have occurred at a time when the Muslim community was beginning to confront and deal with these deadly scourges. The vivid and deadly consequences of such epidemics seem to acquire expression in the ways in which proto-Sunni traditionalists articulated their opposition to those they deemed to be heretics.[199]

Regulating orthodoxy and disciplining heresy through language was not always enough. More robust action was sometimes required. Proto-Sunni traditionalists developed a set of moral codes and social

198 Wakīʿ, *Akhbār al-quḍāt*, 1: 259–60.

199 On plagues and diseases from the seventh–ninth centuries see Conrad, 'The Plague in the Early Medieval Near East', 247–311; Conrad, 'Arabic Plague Chronologies and Treatises'; Conrad, 'A Ninth-Century Muslim Scholar's Discussion of Contagion'; Conrad, 'ʿUmar at Sargh'; Dols, *The Black Death in the Middle East*. For some primary source material on late seventh- and eighth-century plagues see John bar Penkāyē's description of the plague of 686 in northern Iraq in Mingana (ed. and trans.), *Sources syriaques*, 159–67; and Brock, 'North Mesopotamia in the Late Seventh Century'. The Zūqnīn chronicle discusses the plague of 743–5: see Anon., *The Chronicle of Zūqnīn*, 168–74. On a succession of earthquakes and plagues in 713 see Palmer, *The Seventh Century*, 45–6.

conventions designed to suppress the influence of ideas they perceived as deviant. The first and most important step was to exclude heretics and deviants from one's social environment. According to Sufyān al-Thawrī, being in the company of a heretic left a person susceptible to at least one of three calamities: he will become a trial for someone else; something will settle in his heart, which will cause him to commit an error, and subsequently God will consign him to the hellfire; or he will say to himself, 'By God, I have no regard for what they say, for I am confident about myself.' Sufyān al-Thawrī added, 'Whoever feels secure about God even for the blinking of an eye, God will deprive him of his religion.'[200] Ibn Waḍḍāḥ was concerned with more than simply the prospect of sitting down with the people of heresy. His treatise insists that if one happens to encounter a person of heresy on the street, then one ought to take a different route altogether.[201] Ibn Waḍḍāḥ also denounced the practice of debating with heretics.[202] His treatise recounts the practice of proto-Sunni traditionalists ostracising those known to interact or speak with heretics. One man reported that he happened to be walking with ʿAmr b. ʿUbayd, and Ibn ʿAwn saw the two of them together. Thereafter, Ibn ʿAwn refused to speak to the man for two months.[203] Al-Barbahārī was notoriously hostile towards heretics (*ahl al-bidaʿ*). Not only did he encourage Muslims to refuse to converse with them, he also urged that they should not hear the recital of the Quran from them.[204]

Others were forcibly removed or excluded from social and learned circles on account of their perceived heresies. Muḥammad b. al-Sā'ib was told to stay away on account of his being a Murji'ī.[205] A similar story is told about Ibrāhīm b. Yūsuf al-Balkhī, one of a small group of Mālik b. Anas's students from Balkh.[206] We learn in al-Khalīlī's *al-Irshād* how his plans to study with Mālik b. Anas were derailed by his fellow townsman, Qutayba b. Saʿīd al-Balkhī (d. 240/854).[207] When Ibrāhīm b. Yūsuf went to see Mālik b. Anas, Qutayba b. Saʿīd protested: 'This man holds the doctrine of the Iraqians concerning al-Irjā'.' Mālik b. Anas, or

[200] Ibn Waḍḍāḥ, *Kitāb al-Bidaʿ*, 192. [201] Ibn Waḍḍāḥ, *Kitāb al-Bidaʿ*, 193.

[202] Ibn Waḍḍāḥ, *Kitāb al-Bidaʿ*, 193. [203] Ibn Waḍḍāḥ, *Kitāb al-Bidaʿ*, 195.

[204] Al-Barbahārī, *Sharḥ Kitāb al-Sunna*, 124–5 (al-Jumayzī edn.) = ed. Khālid b. Qāsim al-Raddādī (Medina: Maktabat al-Ghurabā' al-Athriyya, 1993), 128. There are minor and major discrepancies between these editions. For now, al-Jumayzī's edition has the final word (14–18 for the catalogue of errors in previous editions); Ibn Abī Yaʿlā, *Ṭabaqāt al-Ḥanābila*, 2: 18–43, 39 (al-Fiqī edn.); Melchert, *The Formation of the Sunni Schools of Law*, 152. Ibn Abī Yaʿlā preserves an almost complete copy of al-Khallāl's work, but the entire text is available in the aforementioned editions of al-Barbahārī's work.

[205] Ibn Waḍḍāḥ, *Kitāb al-Bidaʿ*, 196.

[206] A number of such students are listed in al-Khalīlī, *al-Irshād*, 274–8 (Riyadh edn.) = 80–1 (Cairo edn.).

[207] See al-Khalīlī, *al-Irshād*, 935–8 (Riyadh edn.) = 445–7 (Cairo edn.).

possibly someone else who was present, grabbed him by the hand and showed him the way out. In so doing, Mālik b. Anas was perpetuating a practice of social exclusion that was the norm in proto-Sunni traditionalist circles. When Ibrāhīm b. Yūsuf al-Balkhī returned to his homeland, Balkh, Qutayba b. Saʿīd was on his case once again and had him banished from Balkh. Ibrāhīm b. Yūsuf was forced to live in exile in Baghlān.[208]

Proto-Sunni traditionalists such as Mālik b. Anas were intransigent when it came to marginalising those with heretical leanings. On a separate occasion, ʿUmar b. Maymūn came to Mālik b. Anas and began to ask him some questions. Mālik b. Anas responded angrily to ʿUmar b. Maymūn's line of questioning: 'This is the speech of the heretics,' he bellowed. Mālik b. Anas threw him out of the lesson, although he later forgave ʿUmar b. Maymūn for this transgression.[209] This strategy of social exclusion was not simply inflicted by proto-Sunni traditionalists upon heretics and deviants. It was understood as a social and moral convention beyond the proto-Sunni traditionalist community. Al-Fasawī's ninth-century *History* relates that a group of scholars and students were seated in a study circle with Ayyūb al-Sakhtiyānī. Ayyūb began to speak about the people of heresy, and maligned them. Suddenly, a man stood up and left the gathering. 'O Abū Bakr, this man is a heretic.' Ayyūb had had no idea about the man's heresy, and it perturbed him deeply that the man probably thought that Ayyūb's diatribe was directed towards him personally.[210] Marginalising and expelling deviants was a relentless but necessary activity, whether it be from one's town, one's study-circle, or one's home. Scholars and students sat together and articulated their concerns about heretics. Heretics were in their very midst. Discourses, diatribes, and forms of denunciation proved to be good and efficient ways of marginalising them. In his ninth-century credal work, al-Muzanī wrote of the necessity of

Holding back on hereticising the people of the *qibla* and dissociating oneself from their heretical innovations as long as they do not instigate a grave heretic error. Whoever does innovate a grave heretical error is outside the people of the *qibla* and becomes a heretic, having left the religion, and one becomes closer to God, almighty and majestic, by dissociating from such a person. His heresy is to be renounced (*yuhjaru*), scorned (*yuḥtaqaru*), and avoided; for it is more harmful and catching than a disease.[211]

[208] Al-Khalīlī, *al-Irshād*, 277–8 (Riyadh edn.) = 81 (Cairo edn.). Another version of the story is told by al-Khalīlī, *al-Irshād*, 937–8 (Riyadh edn.) = 446–7 (Cairo edn.) where we are told of his important standing among the followers of Abū Ḥanīfa.

[209] Al-Khalīlī, *al-Irshād*, 943–4 (Riyadh edn.) = 450 (Cairo edn.).

[210] Al-Fasawī, *Kitāb al-Maʿrifa wa al-tārīkh*, 2: 236 (*wa kunnā fī majlis Ayyūb fa dhakara ahl al-ahwāʾ, fa nāla minhum fa qāma rajul min al-majlis, fa qīla lahu: yā Abā Bakr, inna hādhā ʿalā hawāhu. Qāla: innā li Allāh, yaẓunnu innamā ʿarraḍnā lahu. Qāla: fa shaqqa dhālika ʿalayhi.*).

[211] Al-Muzanī, *Sharḥ al-Sunna*, 85.

Proto-Sunni traditionalists also believed in seeking clarification with respect to the doctrines of individuals. If they discovered particular scholars adhering to abhorrent doctrines, they recommended that such scholars keep their distance from them. ʿAbd Allāh b. Aḥmad b. Ḥanbal relates the following story from a man he considered to be reliable and trustworthy: Sufyān al-Thawrī was heard as having once said to Ḥammād b. Abī Sulaymān: 'Go and see that unbeliever, meaning Abū Ḥanīfa, and tell him: "If you believe that the Quran is created, stay well away from us."'[212]

If these were the social customs and norms for dealing with heretics, then we should see them reflected in discourses of heresy against Abū Ḥanīfa. Indeed, there seems to have been a concerted effort to implement the sociological and spatial dimensions of orthodoxy with respect to Abū Ḥanīfa. Abū ʿUbayd al-Qāsim b. Sallām said that he was sitting one day, with Aswad b. Sālim beside him. The people in the group were discussing a legal issue, to which he responded: 'Abū Ḥanīfa said such and such about this matter.' Aswad b. Sālim turned abruptly towards him and said: 'How dare you mention Abū Ḥanīfa's name in the mosque?' Abū ʿUbayd added that thenceforth Aswad b. Sālim never spoke to him until the day he died.[213] It was not simply in the mosque that some proto-Sunni traditionalists desisted from mentioning the name of Abū Ḥanīfa. Sharīk b. ʿAbd Allāh was reluctant even to mention his name. He deemed it a dishonour to one's lips.[214] Al-Ḥumaydī, as we saw in Chapter 3, refused to mention Abū Ḥanīfa's name even in the process of refuting him. He did this, apparently, because he disliked mentioning Abū Ḥanīfa's name in the sacred mosque of Mecca.[215] The influential ḥadīth scholar and historian Abū Zurʿa al-Dimashqī highlights the way in which social and spatial distance from those perceived as heretics was one way to inoculate oneself from their influence. Abū Zurʿa tells us that Ayyūb al-Sakhtiyānī was once in Mecca – teaching a class, presumably – when Abū Ḥanīfa happened to enter the study-circle. Upon learning of Abū Ḥanīfa's presence, Ayyūb brought an end to proceedings. 'Stand up,' he exclaimed to his students, 'otherwise he will infect us with his disease.'[216]

212 ʿAbd Allāh b. Aḥmad b. Ḥanbal, *Kitāb al-Sunna*, 184 (*ʿAbd Allāh b. ʿAwn b. al-Kharrāz Abū Muḥammad wa kāna thiqa < Shaykh min ahl al-Kūfa < Qīla li ʿAbd Allāh b. ʿAwn: huwa Abū al-Jahm, fa ka annahu aqarra annahu qāla: samiʿtu Sufyān al-Thawrī yaqūl: qāla lī Ḥammād b. Abī Sulaymān idhhab ilā al-kāfir yaʿnī Abā Ḥanīfa fa qul lahu: in kunta taqūl anna al-Qur'ān makhlūq, fa lā taqrubnā [or tuqarribnā].*).

213 ʿAbd Allāh b. Aḥmad b. Ḥanbal, *Kitāb al-Sunna*, 208 (*kuntu jālisan wa maʿanā Aswad b. Sālim fa dhakarū mas'ala fa qultu: inna Abā Ḥanīfa yaqūl kayta wa kayta. Fa iltafata ilayya fa qāla: tadhkuru Abā Ḥanīfa fī al-masjid? Fa lam yukallimnī ḥattā māta*).

214 ʿAbd Allāh b. Aḥmad b. Ḥanbal, *Kitāb al-Sunna*, 209.

215 Ibn Ḥibbān, *Kitāb al-Majrūḥīn*, 3: 70 (Beirut edn.).

216 Abū Zurʿā al-Dimashqī, *Tārīkh*, 2: 507. Ayyūb's remark seems to invoke an Arabic proverb: 'More contagious than the infection among the Arabs (*aʿda min al-jarab ʿinda*

Others vowed never to speak to Abū Ḥanīfa again upon claiming to hear his responses to some outlandish questions. 'I placed my sandals among some pebbles and asked Abū Ḥanīfa: "What do you say concerning a man who prays to these sandals until he dies, but he knows [who] God [is] with his heart?" "He is a believer," responded Abū Ḥanīfa. "I shall never to speak to you again,"' said the man.[217]

Proto-Sunni traditionalists found informal ways to regulate, discipline, and marginalise religious deviance. This did not necessitate their disappearance from the very fabric of social life. Religious scholars might have balked at the phenomenon of heresy, but they did find ways to deal with it. Even in a case so delicate as legal testimony, ninth-century jurists recognised the validity of a heretic's testimony (*shahādat ahl al-ahwā'*).[218]

### *Inquisitions*

Though I have emphasised the informal mechanisms that proto-Sunni traditionalists cultivated to regulate ideas and movements, I do not wish to suggest that formal disciplinary practices and institutions were entirely absent or foreign to early medieval Islamic societies. A deep suspicion of institutions and resistance to imperial interventions is, in my view, a hallmark of proto-Sunni communities from the ninth to tenth centuries. There was a recognition, however, that imperial authority did extend to certain significant realms of religious, political, and social life. To this extent, religious scholars welcomed (or tolerated) the latent political and imperial dimensions of particular religious rituals and obligations, such as the Friday prayer and sermon, payment of land, wealth, and charitable taxes, qadi and *maẓālim* courts, and the imperial Ḥajj procession. Recent scholarly attempts to demarcate secular authority (with caliphs) from religious power (with scholars) misread, in my view, what was a division of labour as an irrevocable divorce.[219]

*al-ʿarab*)'. See Lane, *An Arabic–English Lexicon*, 1.2: 403 (s.v. '*jarab*'). The editor of Abū Zurʿa's history has it has *yuʿdinā*. I am reading the *lā* as the *lām al-duʿā'* (or '*lā* of prohibition', as Wright has it), which is why I place the verb in the jussive. Another alternative may be to replace the ʿayn with a hamza, which would give us *yu'idnā* (to infect us). See Wright, *A Grammar of the Arabic Language*, 2: 36.

217 Al-Khaṭīb al-Baghdādī, *Tārīkh Baghdād*, 15: 510 (*waḍaʿtu naʿlī fī al-ḥaṣan thumma qultu li Abī Ḥanīfa: a ra'ayta rajulan ṣallā li hādhihi al-naʿl ḥattā māta illā annahu yaʿrifu bi qalbihi? Fa qāla: mu'min. Fa qultu: lā ukallimuka abadan.*).

218 Al-Ṭaḥāwī, *Mukhtaṣar ikhtilāf al-ʿulamā'*, ed. ʿAbd Allāh Nadhīr Aḥmad (Beirut: Dār al-Bashā'ir al-Islāmiyya, 1996), 3: 334–5.

219 For this reading see Lapidus, 'The Separation of State and Religion'; Crone and Hinds, *God's Caliph*, 93 ff. Crone and Hinds's narrative, which commits the methodological blunder of reading imperial propaganda (panegyric poetry, imperial coinage, and caliphal letters) as social fact, is given a new lease of life in Tor, 'God's Cleric'.

Inquisitions, too, belonged to this overlapping world of formal and informal measures designed to order and regulate orthodoxy; but not all inquisitions were manifestations of a single, uniform institution. A recent history of inquisitions in medieval Islam has overlooked this nuance. John Turner has seen the inquisition as a mechanism by which the caliph and, by extension, the state attempted to enforce and uphold orthodoxy. The examples Turner studies are exceptions in so far as they reflect the history of individuals believed to have held incorrect doctrines whilst simultaneously posing a (perceived) political threat to the authority of the caliph. Inquisitions were not always instantiations of caliphal or imperial efforts to enforce or uphold orthodoxy, and there is not yet enough documentation for the view that these in any way reveal an inquisitorial regime and society operating at the heart of medieval Islamic societies.[220]

Seeing the caliphs as shapers of religious orthodoxy and normativity is a result of what Peter Brown has described as 'institutionalised egotism' – the conviction that all power and political initiative should reside in the person or office of the emperor. Far away from the imperial gaze, however, regional and local communities pursued inquisitorial methods, with varying results;[221] and if they were outside the purview of the imperial machinery they were very much visible to proto-Sunni traditionalist communities of the ninth–tenth centuries. Proto-Sunni traditionalists were adamant that in the middle of the eighth century in Kufa Abū Ḥanīfa was the subject of a mild and haphazard inquisition that saw him repent from heresy twice. Sources both antagonistic and favourable towards Abū Ḥanīfa agree on this much, though the rest of the details are disputed. The *Kitāb al-ʿIlal* attributed to Aḥmad b. Ḥanbal preserves four different versions of this account:[222]

1. ʿAbd Allāh b. Aḥmad b. Ḥanbal < Aḥmad b. Ḥanbal < Mu'ammal said: I heard Sufyān al-Thawrī say: Abū Ḥanīfa was made to repent from heresy twice.
2. ʿAbd Allāh b. Aḥmad b. Ḥanbal < Aḥmad b. Ḥanbal said: I heard Sufyān b. ʿUyayna say: Abū Ḥanīfa was made to repent from heresy twice. One of Sufyān's companions, Abū Zayd (Ḥammād b. Dalīl), asked Sufyān, 'What was he made to repent from?' Sufyan replied: 'He

[220] One problem with Turner's (*Inquisition in Early Islam*) analysis of eighth-century heresy trials is that it depends on a twelfth-century source, Ibn ʿAsākir. Turner's analysis of heresy is therefore, strictly speaking, a study of twelfth-century perceptions of heresy and orthodoxy, normativity, and dissent.

[221] Though Chapter 8 discusses pourous boundaries between Sunnism and Shiʿism in the tenth century, a treatment of orthodoxy and heresy in Twelver Shiʿism or, for that matter, other religious movements, is well outside the scope of this monograph. For a recent contribution to mechanisms of regulation and discipline in Twelver Shiʿism see Hayes, *Agents of the Hidden Imam*, 198 ff.

[222] ʿAbd Allāh b. Aḥmad b. Ḥanbal, *Kitāb al-ʿIlal*, 2: 545, 548 (Dār al-Khānī edn.).

said something and his companions saw it appropriate to ask him to repent, and he did.’

3. ʿAbd Allāh b. Aḥmad b. Ḥanbal < Aḥmad b. Ḥanbal < Mu’ammal b. Ismāʿīl < Sufyān al-Thawrī < ʿAbbād b. Kathīr said: ʿAmr b. ʿUbayd said to me: ‘Ask Abū Ḥanīfa about a man who says: I know that the Kaʿba is a reality and that it is the house of God, but I do not know if it is the house in Mecca or the house in Khurāsān. Is such a person a believer?’ ‘He is a believer,’ replied Abū Ḥanīfa. ʿAmr b. ʿUbayd then asked me to ask Abū Ḥanīfa about a man who says, ‘I know that Muḥammad is a real person and that he is the messenger of God, but I do not know whether he is the person who lived in Medina or some other person.’ Is such a person a believer? ‘Yes, he is a believer,’ said Abū Ḥanīfa.
4. ʿAbd Allāh b. Aḥmad b. Ḥanbal said that my father said: ‘I think Abū Ḥanīfa was made to repent from heresy because he said the Quranic verse *subḥāna rabbika rabbi al-ʿizza ʿammā yaṣifūn* was created.’

The speculation concerning Abū Ḥanīfa’s alleged repentance from heresy was endless. Ibn Ḥibbān, for example, gave a very different account of the episode. He, too, had reason to believe that Abū Ḥanīfa was asked to repent from heresy twice. He had a report: ‘Zakariyyā’ b. Yaḥyā al-Sājī of Basra < Bundār and Muḥammad b. ʿAlī al-Muqaddamī < Muʿādh b. Muʿādh al-ʿAnbarī < Sufyān al-Thawrī said: Abū Ḥanīfa was made to repent from heresy twice.’ Ibn Ḥibbān was privy to a second account of this incident:

> Al-Ḥusayn b. Idrīs al-Anṣārī < Sufyān b. Wakīʿ < ʿUmar b. Ḥammād b. Abī Ḥanīfa < Ḥammād b. Abī Ḥanīfa said: I heard my father (Abū Ḥanīfa) say: ‘The Quran is created.’ This prompted Ibn Abī Layla to write to Abū Ḥanīfa, ‘Either you renounce this position or I shall take action against you.’ Abū Ḥanīfa said: ‘I renounce my view.’ When Abū Ḥanīfa returned to his house, I said to him: ‘O father, is the createdness of the Quran not your real belief?’ Abū Ḥanīfa replied, ‘Yes, my son, it is my view, and it is the view I stand by today, too. However, I had no choice other than to say it out of precautionary dissimulation (*taqiyya*).’[223]

Writers and scholars committed to establishing Abū Ḥanīfa’s religious orthodoxy were by no means oblivious to these reports. In fact, it is in some ways a remarkable testament to the nature of early Muslim writing that supporters of Abū Ḥanīfa did not attempt to conceal or suppress such scandalous reports. The earliest source I have discovered responding to reports about Abū Ḥanīfa’s repentance from heresy is, in fact, our earliest surviving *manāqib* work: Ibn Abī al-ʿAwwām al-Saʿdī’s (d. 335/947–8) *Faḍā’il Abī Ḥanīfa wa akhbāruhu wa manāqibuhu*. Ibn Abī al-ʿAwwām is

[223] Ibn Ḥibbān, *Kitāb al-Majrūḥīn*, 3: 64, 65 (Beirut edn.).

explicit in framing Abū Ḥanīfa's alleged repentance from heresy within the context of the provincial governor's efforts to install Abū Ḥanīfa as an official judge. Abū Ḥanīfa's refusal to serve in this position gave rise to speculation among the local population that Abū Ḥanīfa had been made to repent from heresy.[224] The subject of Abū Ḥanīfa's repentance from heresy appears a second time in Ibn Abī al-ʿAwwām al-Saʿdī's book. The second reference appears in a chapter devoted to examining discourses of heresy against Abū Ḥanīfa (*fī al-tashnīʿ ʿalayhi*). Abū Ḥanīfa, we are told, refused to swear oaths in God's name even with respect to things that were true. Some of Kufa's local officials sought to discredit him by making him announce in public that the Quran is created. Their plan was to make Abū Ḥanīfa swear an oath, knowing that Abū Ḥanīfa's principled refusal to swear oaths in God's name would create the impression that he held the Quran to be created. The governor seized Abū Ḥanīfa, and displayed him in front of a public audience, and said:

GOVERNOR: What are some of the people saying against you? What are they saying? They insist that you believe the Quran to be created.

ABŪ ḤANĪfa: I have heard no one say such a thing and nor have I heard anyone debate about it. In fact, it is something that makes the soul feel uneasy (*innahu la qawl taḍīqu lahu al-nafs*).

GOVERNOR: In that case, swear an oath [in God's name] to the effect that you have never expressed this doctrine.

ABŪ ḤANĪfa: God, exalted and almighty, is more knowledgeable than I as to the falseness of their claims (*huwa yaʿlamu tabāraka wa taʿālā minnī khilāf mā yaqūlūn*).

GOVERNOR: So swear an oath that you have never uttered it.

Once again, Abū Ḥanīfa refused to swear an oath. The governor then warned him that he would be forced to punish him if he refused a third time. Abū Ḥanīfa told the governor to do whatever he had to. The governor ordered Abū Ḥanīfa to be whipped, but when he witnessed the slenderness of his body and his old age (*naḥāfat jismihi wa shaybihi*) he asked Abū Ḥanīfa to repent. Abū Ḥanīfa insisted that he had never held such a doctrine and that it was not something that he had come to believe since. 'So repent,' said the governor. 'O God, accept our repentance,' Abū Ḥanīfa exclaimed. Then people began to say, 'Abū Ḥanīfa was made to repent from heresy, Abū Ḥanīfa was made to repent from heresy (*ustutība Abū Ḥanīfa ustutība Abū Ḥanīfa*).'[225]

In both accounts Ibn Abī al-ʿAwwām al-Saʿdī seeks to explain to readers that the infamous episode of Abū Ḥanīfa's inquisition and

[224] Ibn Abī al-ʿAwwām al-Saʿdī, *Faḍā'il Abī Ḥanīfa*, 66–7.
[225] Ibn Abī al-ʿAwwām al-Saʿdī, *Faḍā'il Abī Ḥanīfa*, 72–3.

repentance from heresy had been misinterpreted. There was, he suggests, no real heresy to speak of. Abū Ḥanīfa was subject to a vicious campaign by political authorities, and he used his quick wit and intelligence to avoid further persecution.

Another early *manāqib* work provides an alternative explanation for Abū Ḥanīfa's public repentance from heresy. In a work composed in the first half of the eleventh century, Abū al-Ḥusayn al-Qudūrī (d. 438/1037) states:[226]

> The truth of the matter concerning reports that Abū Ḥanīfa was made to repent from heresy twice is that his repenting from heresy was a show of great intelligence. This is because the Khawārij (*al-shurāt*) captured Abū Ḥanīfa when they entered Kufa, and they said to him: 'Repent from heresy.' They asked him to repent because it was their practice to hereticise anyone who opposed them. In response to this, Abū Ḥanīfa said: 'I repent to God from all heresy and unbelief.' They released Abū Ḥanīfa. However, someone said to one of the leaders of the Khawārij, 'He only repented from the heresy that he believes you to be committed to.' The Khawārij then demanded the return of Abū Ḥanīfa. They said to him, 'You repented from heresy, but you intended to repent from the heresy that you believe us to be steeped in.' Abū Ḥanīfa replied, 'Do you say this on the basis of evidence or speculation?' 'Of course, it is based on speculation,' replied the Khārijite. Abū Ḥanīfa said: 'God the exalted has said: "Certainly some forms of speculation are sinful." This, therefore, is a sin on your part and, according to your belief, every sin is heresy. You, too, must repent from heresy.' The Khārijite then said: 'I repent to God from all heresy and unbelief.' On the basis of the episode, people began to say: 'Abū Ḥanīfa was made to repent from heresy twice.' This is what they intend when they say, 'Abū Ḥanīfa repented from heresy twice.'

It is fascinating to see defenders of Abū Ḥanīfa not ignoring discourses of heresy against him. These authors do not challenge the veracity of the inquisition and repentance. From the ninth century onwards inquisitions and persecution at the hands of political authorities were a source of pride and credibility for medieval Sunnis.[227] Followers of Abū Ḥanīfa provide detailed accounts of the episode, which suggest that later proto-Sunni

[226] Al-Qudūrī, 'Manāqib al-Imām al-Aʿẓam', MS Arab 283, Houghton Library, Harvard University, fols. 1a–2a, at 1b. A critical edition of al-Qudūrī's *manāqib* work on the basis of five different manuscripts is being prepared by Talal Al-Azem and Ahmad Khan. For a similar account see Ibn Abī al-ʿAwwām al-Saʿdī, *Faḍāʾil Abī Ḥanīfa*, 90–1 (an account which our author tells us he wrote down in his collection of notes from his lessons with Aḥmad b. Ḥafṣ b. ʿAbd Allāh al-Sulamī. Aḥmad was the son of Ḥafṣ b. ʿAbd Allāh al-Sulamī. Ḥafṣ, the father, had been the qadi of Nīshāpūr.

[227] Consider the case of Abū al-ʿArab's *Kitāb al-Miḥan*, where the caliphs are depicted as assassinating and persecuting proto-Sunni scholars in a ruthless and routine fashion. Writing in Aghlabid North Africa, Abū al-ʿArab was far enough from the court of the ʿAbbāsid caliphs to make such bold claims without fear of ending up like his book's subjects.

traditionalists manipulated reports surrounding the inquisition and used it as a basis to charge Abū Ḥanīfa with heresy.

For proto-Sunni traditionalists, the precise circumstances surrounding Abū Ḥanīfa's inquisition were debatable. The fact that they could point to more than one reason why such an inquisition and demand for repentance from heresy might be warranted was further evidence of Abū Ḥanīfa's religious impropriety. What was not in dispute was that Abū Ḥanīfa was implicated by his contemporaries and social communities in statements of heresy, and these occasioned an official and recorded repentance. This was a narrative that other proto-Sunnis did not recognise. This incident marked a defining moment in the discourse of heresy against Abū Ḥanīfa. This was not because of its inquisitorial dimension. In fact, the incident itself was shorn of its original context, and proto-Sunni traditionalists promulgated as historical fact that Abū Ḥanīfa repented from heresy.[228]

Parts I and II of this monograph have described the formation of a discursive process among textualist communities of the eighth–eleventh centuries. A discourse around heresy was not merely floating in the air among intellectual elites. These textualist communities lived, studied, and taught in social contexts. They did not inhabit monasteries. Their ideas were promulgated in study-circles, but also during walks, visits, social congregations, and other casual and everyday settings. As such, processes of orthodoxy and heresy were anchored not only in texts but in social attitudes, practices, imaginaries, and lived contexts. The discourse around heresy and orthodoxy saw the emergence of competing and contrasting ideas about what constituted Sunni orthodoxy. As a living and lived religion, orthodoxy in Islam was constantly being refined, adjusted, and debated by communities. So, as dominant and powerful communities of proto-Sunni traditionalist orthodoxy may have been in the eighth–tenth centuries, they were neither static nor hermetically sealed. In fact, during the course of the tenth–eleventh centuries, this discrete though influential discourse of heresy against Abū Ḥanīfa was challenged. Major transformations were to take place that altered the character of medieval Sunni orthodoxy and gave way to a new and more lasting conception of medieval Sunnism.

[228] On a related note, some doubted the validity of repentance from heresy. Ibn Waḍḍāḥ's treatise presents a number of traditions declaring that a person of heresy only continues to evolve in a more sinister direction: Ibn Waḍḍāḥ, *Kitāb al-Bidaʿ*, 198.

## *Part III*

# Unmaking Heresy: Orthodoxy as History Writing

Parts I and II of this study have documented and analysed the growth of discourses of heresy against Abū Ḥanīfa in the ninth–eleventh centuries. We have shown the sheer variety, spread, and transmission of these discourses. In the face of this prominent and lively religious development, how can we explain the emergence in the tenth and eleventh centuries of Abū Ḥanīfa as a representative of medieval Sunni orthodoxy among a larger spectrum of the Muslim community? How did a school of legal orthodoxy form around his name in the midst of such disrepute, hostility, and open charges of heresy and deviance? How can we understand Abū Ḥanīfa's evolution from a heretic among a discrete coalition of proto-Sunni traditionalists between the late eighth and tenth centuries to a patron saint of medieval Sunnism by the eleventh century?[1]

Part III argues that the production of *manāqib* (biographies) and *masānīd* (collections of ḥadīth) works for Abū Ḥanīfa in the ninth–eleventh centuries was integral to his integration within medieval Sunnism. Without the invention and rapid production of these two genres of writing, it is difficult to imagine the subsequent apotheosis of Abū Ḥanīfa as an exemplar of medieval Sunni orthodoxy on such a wide scale as did occur, for these writings incorporated other major genres of texts within them, such as *ṭabaqāt* works. The processes by which Abū Ḥanīfa's perceived heresies were unmade and the mechanisms by which his religious orthodoxy was established constitute the focus of subsequent chapters. Chapter 8 introduces readers to a new tenth-century source and undertakes a detailed examination of this extremely valuable text. The main objective in doing so is to demonstrate that *manāqib* works were composed in response to discourses of heresy against Abū Ḥanīfa. These works were committed to transforming Abū Ḥanīfa's mnemohistory from

[1] Christopher Melchert has spoken of a predisposition to compromise from the ninth-century onwards (*The Formation of the Sunni Schools of Law*, 202–3). This section builds on his insight and argues that the compromise was not inevitable but rather that it was effected by a number of important religious and literary developments during the tenth–eleventh centuries.

one of heresy to one of orthodoxy. Nevertheless, a single source, however early and significant, is not enough. For this reason, this chapter also provides, for the first time, a detailed history of *Manāqib Abī Ḥanīfa* works from the ninth–eleventh centuries. Chapter 9 does something similar for *Musnad Abī Ḥanīfa* works. This genre of writing emerged at the same time as the *manāqib* genre, although it was more circumscribed in its focus. Where *manāqib* works sought to respond to the full range of proto-Sunni traditionalist discourses of heresy, *masānīd* works aimed to rehabilitate Abū Ḥanīfa's expertise in ḥadīth. Both the *manāqib* and *masānīd* genres have been neglected as sources for the history of medieval Islamic history and society. *Manāqib* works have been dismissed as works of pious hagiography, whilst *masānīd* works have been read with little attention to their social and historical context. Above all, the speed and scale of the production of *manāqib* and *masānīd* works was unprecedented. Together they constitute such a massive corpus of texts composed in the ninth–eleventh centuries that to ignore them as pious hagiographies or insignificant to the broader religious history of the period would be to dismiss entirely the significance given to them by the people and societies we study.

It is the aim of these chapters to show that these texts were alternative forms of historical writing about the past committed to fashioning a new consensus of what medieval Sunni orthodoxy ought to look like. In short, we shall study the genres, texts, authors, developments, and social and political pressures that contributed to such a fundamental and lasting reshaping of Abū Ḥanīfa's historical memory. We will come closer to understanding how and why this vision for medieval Sunni orthodoxy became a reality by the beginning of the eleventh century.

# 8 *Manāqib*: Narratives of Orthodoxy I

A considerable body of writing was produced between the late eighth and eleventh centuries by proto-Sunni traditionalists in order to document Abū Ḥanīfa's heresy and deviance and to place him outside the orbit of proto-Sunni orthodoxy. Proto-Sunni traditionalists and their followers maintained a fairly consistent view on the question of Abū Ḥanīfa's religious orthodoxy. Proto-Sunni traditionalist writings were beginning to dominate the religious landscape of medieval Islam, and their espousal of a proto-Sunnism that excluded and targeted Abū Ḥanīfa placed proto-Ḥanafīs in a difficult position. How do we explain the fact that by the eleventh century Abū Ḥanīfa's religious orthodoxy had gained wide acceptance among a broad coalition of Sunnis? In short, what happened in the tenth and eleventh centuries that effected a transformation in the memory (mnemohistory) of Abū Ḥanīfa and, thus, gave shape to a new conception of medieval Sunnism? This chapter argues against whiggish histories of Sunnism's development that posit a natural evolution or inevitable disposition towards a more accommodating trend in Sunni orthodoxy. I contend that one of the most decisive factors in shaping medieval Sunni orthodoxy was the rise and production of *Manāqib Abī Ḥanīfa* works. This genre provided a new forum for writing the history of religious orthodoxy, enabling a complete integration of Abū Ḥanīfa within Sunni orthodoxy.

Despite the commitment of proto-Sunnis to promulgating discourses of heresy against Abū Ḥanīfa, proto-Ḥanafism continued to operate in the medieval Islamicate world. Students of Abū Ḥanīfa had established jurisprudential traditions, with varying degrees of penetration, in Iraq, western Iran, the Jazīra, Shām, Egypt, the Maghrib, Khurāsān, and Transoxiana.[2] A number of factors contributed to proto-Ḥanafism's

[2] See Tsafrir, *The History of an Islamic School of Law*; and an important book review by Melchert, Review of Nurit Tsafrir; Melchert, *The Formation of the Sunni Schools of Law*, 32–8, 116–36; Melchert, 'How Ḥanafism Came to Originate in Kufa'; Melchert, 'The Early Ḥanafiyya and Kufa'; Melchert, 'The Spread of Ḥanafism'; Madelung, 'The Westward Migration of Ḥanafī Scholars'.

dissemination. State patronage had worked to the favour of proto-Ḥanafīs. Their jurisprudence seemed to equip jurists to deal with the kind of erratic and complex problems that local judges were expected to resolve. There was also a missionary dimension to proto-Ḥanafism, whose spread in remote and distant provinces in the Islamic world coincided with a rise in conversion to Islam. In many respects, these developments were not unique to proto-Ḥanafism. Other legal traditions, within and beyond the four schools of law, had experienced similar successes.[3] Not one of them, however, faced a situation in which their eponymous founder was attacked by a discrete but influential community of scholars as a heretic and deviant. In this respect, proto-Ḥanafism was the exception.

The challenge that confronted proto-Ḥanafīs was to counter the proliferation of discourses of heresy against their *madhhab*'s eponymous founder and to establish his religious orthodoxy. The evidence for this monograph's claim that the *Manāqib Abī Ḥanīfa* genre was the main instrument for integrating Abū Ḥanīfa into a new consensus of medieval Sunni orthodoxy in the tenth and eleventh centuries rests on two arguments. The first concerns dating and periodisation: the writing of *manāqib* works occurs in the late ninth to early tenth centuries, after the peak of discourses of heresy against Abū Ḥanīfa in the middle of the ninth century. Thereafter, the rise of *manāqib* works is concomitant with the waning of discourses of heresy against Abū Ḥanīfa and with the gradual acknowledgement by proto-Sunni traditionalists in

[3] The standard work for the spread of the Sunni schools of law is Melchert, *The Formation of the Sunni Schools of Law*, 68–86 (Shāfiʿism), 137–55 (Ḥanbalism), 156–77 (Mālikism), 178–90 (Ẓāhirism), 191–7 (Jarīrism). Apart from this, see also, on the spread of Shāfiʿism, Halm, *Die Ausbreitung*; El Shamsy, *The Canonization of Islamic Law*, 160–73; Hallaq, *Origins and Evolution*, 176–7. For the Mālikī school see Mansour, 'The Spread and the Domination'. Unfortunately, this thesis is replete with errors, fails to examine the primary sources with a critical eye, does not distinguish between early and late primary sources, shows a weakness for reading modern Arabophone and Anglophone scholarship as primary sources, regularly employs anachronisms, and its historical explanations are underwhelming. Miklos Muranyi's history of early Mālikī literature provides invaluable insights into the school's spread in North Africa, even if his findings do not furnish an accessible historical narrative of the school's regional history: Muranyi, *Die Rechtsbücher*; Muranyi, *Beiträge zur Geschichte*; Muranyi, *Materialien zur mālikitischen Rechtsliteratur*. The spread of the Ḥanbalī school has yet to be written: Hurvitz, *The Formation of Hanbalism* does not examine the school's spread in a systematic manner. The one study I have consulted that attempts a survey of the spread of Ḥanbalism is far from comprehensive and satisfactory; also, it is weak on the school's early spread: ʿAbd Allāh b. ʿAbd al-Ḥasan al-Turkī, *al-Madhhab al-Ḥanbalī: Dirāsa fī tārīkhihi wa simātihi wa ashhar aʿlāmihi wa mu'allafātihi* (Beirut: Mu'assasat al-Risāla, 2002), 227–90. A good overview of the school's history is provided by Laoust, *Le Hanbalisme sous les califat de Bagdad*. On legal traditions in Shām see Conrad, *Die quḍāt Dimašq*. For Ẓāhirism see Adang, 'The Beginnings of the Zahiri Madhhab'; Osman, *The Ẓāhirī Madhhab*, 48–89.

the tenth and eleventh centuries that he was a representative, par excellence, of medieval Sunni orthodoxy. The second argument pertains to the actual content of *manāqib* works: their organisation, themes, and content are concerned explicitly with responding to discourses of heresy against Abū Ḥanīfa – remarkably, *manāqib* works make no effort to conceal the fact that there was a significant body of writing devoted to attacking Abū Ḥanīfa and his religious orthodoxy. Ḥanafīs explicitly acknowledged and cited discourses of heresy against Abū Ḥanīfa. Both of these arguments can be established by examining a new source and subjecting it to close analysis for the first time in modern scholarship.

## 8.1 A New Tenth-Century Source

The published edition of *Faḍā'il Abī Ḥanīfa wa akhbāruhu wa manāqibuhu* ascribes the work to Abū al-Qāsim ʿAbd Allāh b. Muḥammad b. Aḥmad b. Yaḥyā b. al-Ḥārith b. Abī al-ʿAwwām al-Saʿdī (d. 335/946–7). To be precise, the *Faḍā'il Abī Ḥanīfa* is an eleventh-century redaction of a late ninth/early tenth-century composition. The book was composed originally by Qāḍī Ibn Abī al-ʿAwwām al-Saʿdī. The book was redacted by his grandson, Aḥmad b. Muḥammad b. ʿAbd Allāh b. Abī al-ʿAwwām (d. 450/1058–9). The book was transmitted by Qāḍī Ibn Abī al-ʿAwwām al-Saʿdī (the grandfather) to his son, who in turn transmitted the book to its final redactor (the grandson). This figure represents four alternative ways of understanding the text's transmission and composition:

*Ḥaddathanī Abī qāla* > *ḥaddathanī Abī qāla*:
Grandson: My father said > My father said:
Grandson > Father > Grandfather
Redactor > Transmitter > Author

Not much is known about Ibn Abī al-ʿAwwām al-Saʿdī's career. His list of teachers suggests that he was a prominent scholar of the tenth century. He studied under an influential group of Ḥanafī judges that included al-Ṭaḥāwī, al-Dūlābī, Jaʿfar b. Aʿyan, and Aḥmad b. Sahl al-Tirmidhī. He was also a student of the famous ḥadīth scholar and compiler of the *Sunan*, Aḥmad b. Shuʿayb al-Nasā'ī.[4] Later biographers described him as a qadi in Egypt, but this detail is missing in the surviving histories of judges in Egypt.[5] Muḥammad b. Yūsuf al-Ṣāliḥī (d. 942/1536) describes

[4] Ibn Ḥajar al-ʿAsqalānī, *Rafʿ al-iṣr ʿan quḍāt Miṣr*, ed. ʿAlī Muḥammad ʿUmar (Cairo: Maktabat al-Khānjī, 1998), 2: 71–5.

[5] Al-Dhahabī, *Tadhkirat al-ḥuffāẓ*, 2: 700 (s.v. 'al-Nasā'ī').

him as a qadi and one of the competent scholars of ḥadīth who authored a *manāqib* work for Abū Ḥanīfa.[6] We can say little more than this on the basis of the historical and biographical literature about our original author.[7]

His grandson, on the other hand, seems to have made quite a name for himself. Ibn Abī al-ʿAwwām followed his grandfather's footsteps and became a qadi in Egypt. He probably worked his way up gradually to become chief judge of Egypt (*qāḍī al-quḍāt*), since we learn that he was charged with overseeing shares of inheritance (*al-furūḍ*) around 389/999.[8] His attempt to progress to the judgeship got off to a false start when an attempt to have him appointed as a judge was rebuffed.[9] His career as a judge began in February 405/1015. He is described as Egypt's chief judge in April 416/1025.[10] He was an influential official responsible for introducing a number of innovations in judicial conventions, and his name turns up in several historical accounts alongside the Fāṭimid ruler al-Ḥākim bi-Amr Allāh (r. 386/996–411/1021).[11] Some biographers apparently had reasons to believe that high office went to Ibn Abī al-ʿAwwām's head (*ḥubb al-riyāsa ghalaba ʿalayhi*).[12] When the Fāṭimid caliphate passed on to Abū al-Ḥasan al-Ẓāhir, Ibn Abī al-ʿAwwām was reappointed to his position until just before his death in May 418/1027. His judicial career lasted twelve years and six months.[13]

A number of medieval Islamic historians knew of the grandfather's composition of *Faḍā'il Abī Ḥanīfa*. Ibn al-Ḥaṭṭāb al-Rāzī (d. 525/1130–1)

[6] Al-Ṣāliḥī, *ʿUqūd al-jumān fī manāqib al-Imām Abī Ḥanīfa al-Nuʿmān*, ed. Muḥammad Mullā ʿAbd al-Qādir al-Afghānī (Jeddah: Jāmiʿ al-Malik ʿAbd al-ʿAzīz, 1978), 69 (*min a'immat al-ḥadīth mimman ṣannafa fī manāqib al-Imām Abī Ḥanīfa ka Abī Jaʿfar al-Ṭaḥāwī wa al-qāḍī Abī al-Qāsim b. Abī al-ʿAwwām*); also ed. Abū al-Wafā' al-Afghānī (Hyderabad: Lajnat Iḥyā' al-Maʿārif al-Nuʿmāniyya, 1974).

[7] The following sources give the grandfather's name, but little beyond this: Ibn Abī al-Wafā', *al-Jawāhir al-muḍiyya*, 1: 282–4 (grandson), 2: 327 (grandfather); ʿAbd al-Qādir al-Tamīmī, *al-Ṭabaqāt al-saniyya*, 2: 94–7, 4: 202; al-Zaylaʿī, *Naṣb al-rāya li al-aḥādīth al-hidāya*, ed. Muḥammad ʿAwwāma (Beirut: Mu'assasat al-Rayān, 1997), 3: 140; Jalāl al-Dīn al-Suyūṭī, *Ḥusn al-muḥāḍara fī tārīkh Miṣr wa al-Qāhira*, ed. Muḥammad Abū al-Faḍl Ibrāhīm (Aleppo: Dār Iḥyā' al-Kutub al-ʿArabī ʿĪsā al-Bābī al-Ḥalabī, 1967; repr. n.p.: Dār Iḥyā' al-Kutub al-ʿArabiyya, 1968), 2:148 = *Ḥusn al-muḥāḍara fī akhbār Miṣr wa al-Qāhira*, ed. ʿAlī Muḥammad ʿUmar (Cairo: Maktabat al-Khānjī, 2007), 2: 130.

[8] Al-Kindī, *al-Wulāt wa kitāb al-quḍāt*, 596, 600, 605, 608, 610–12.

[9] Al-Kindī, *al-Wulāt wa kitāb al-quḍāt*, 604.

[10] Al-Kindī, *al-Wulāt wa kitāb al-quḍāt*, 299.

[11] Al-Kindī, *al-Wulāt wa kitāb al-quḍāt*, 612.

[12] Al-Kindī, *al-Wulāt wa kitāb al-quḍāt*, 611.

[13] Al-Kindī, *al-Wulāt wa kitāb al-quḍāt*, 496, 611 (twelve years and seven months), 612. Ibn Ḥajar al-ʿAsqalānī claims to have gathered this information from Ismāʿīl b. Mūsā al-Ḥabībī's *Akhbār quḍāt Miṣr* and Ibn Muyassar's *Tārīkh*. For a slightly more lucid account of the grandson's career see al-Maqrīzī, *Kitāb al-Muqaffā al-kabīr*, ed. Muḥammad al-Yaʿlāwī (Beirut: Dār al-Gharb al-Islāmī, 1991) 1: 603–6 (grandson).

reports that his father was reading the book in Egypt, probably in the eleventh century. A list of his father's teachers (*mashyakha*) and the books he read (*thabat*) was prepared by him and the ḥadīth master of Alexandria Abū Ṭāhir al-Silafī (d. 576/1180–1).[14] Both Ibn al-Ḥaṭṭāb and al-Silafī appear in the transmission history of the surviving manuscripts of *Faḍā'il Abī Ḥanīfa*.[15] Al-Silafī describes *Faḍā'il Abī Ḥanīfa* as having been authored by Ibn Abī al-ʿAwwām al-Saʿdī and transmitted by his son and grandson. He adds that the book consisted of five large parts (*ajzā' ḍikhām*).[16] Additionally, we know that a century later the book was circulating in North Africa, for al-Ḥāfiẓ al-Tujībī (d. 610/1213–14) mentions it in his catalogue of teachers and books studied under them (*barnāmaj*).[17]

The book was certainly being read and transmitted in the Middle Periods, but it was also part of a developing tradition of *manāqib* writing in the Islamicate world. When al-Dhahabī came to write his *manāqib* book on Abū Ḥanīfa and his followers in the fourteenth century, Ibn Abī al-ʿAwwām al-Saʿdī's work was an important source of information. On the occasions that al-Dhahabī quotes from the book, he introduces it as Qāḍī Ibn Abī al-ʿAwwām al-Saʿdī's one-volume *Faḍā'il Abī Ḥanīfa*.[18] Ibn Ḥajar al-ʿAsqalānī also attributed the work to the grandfather, but he provided a little more context to the work's authorship. He explained that the grandson, Ibn Abī al-ʿAwwām, transmitted an extensive amount of material (through his father) from his grandfather, Qāḍī Ibn Abī al-ʿAwwām al-Saʿdī; and this material gave him access to the narrations of Egypt's notable tenth-century scholars, men such as al-Ṭaḥāwī, al-Dūlābī, and Jaʿfar b. Aʿyan. Ibn Ḥajar states that Ibn Abī al-ʿAwwām had written a large book on the *Manāqib* of Abū Ḥanīfa and his followers (*lahu muṣannaf ḥāfil fī manāqib Abī Ḥanīfa wa aṣḥābihi*), but on the basis of Ibn Ḥajar's preceding explanation of where his grandson received his material from we can assume that Ibn Ḥajar was aware of the grandfather's original authorship.[19] Ibn Ḥajar al-ʿAsqalānī's grandson Yūsuf b.

[14] See the valuable introduction by the editor of the text in Ibn al-Ḥaṭṭāb al-Rāzī, *Mashyakhat al-shaykh al-ajall Abī ʿAbd Allāh Muḥammad b. Aḥmad b. Ibrāhīm al-Rāzī wa thabat masmūʿātihi*, ed. al-Sharīf Ḥātim b. ʿĀrif al-ʿAwnī (Riyadh: Dār al-Hijra, 1994), 30–53.

[15] Ibn Abī al-ʿAwwām al-Saʿdī, *Faḍā'il Abī Ḥanīfa*, 13–18 (editor's introduction).

[16] Ibn al-Ḥaṭṭāb al-Rāzī, *Mashyakhat al-Rāzī*, 243.

[17] Al-Ḥāfiẓ al-Tujībī, *Barnāmaj al-Ḥāfiẓ Abī ʿAbd Allāh Muḥammad b. ʿAbd al-Raḥmān al-Tujībī*, ed. al-Ḥasan Saʿīd (Rabat: Wizārat al-Awqāf wa al-Shu'ūn al-Islāmiyya, 2011), 140, 177, 186–7, 338.

[18] Al-Dhahabī, *Manāqib al-Imām Abī Ḥanīfa wa ṣāḥibayhi Abī Yūsuf wa Muḥammad b. al-Ḥasan*, ed. Muḥammad Zāhid al-Kawtharī and Abū al-Wafā' al-Afghānī (Hyderabad: Lajnat Iḥyā' al-Maʿārif al-Nuʿmāniyya, 1947), 16, 22.

[19] Ibn Ḥajar al-ʿAsqalānī, *Rafʿ al-iṣr*, 2: 71–5, where the next biographical notice summarises the career of Ibn Abī al-ʿAwwām al-Saʿdī's nephew.

Shāhīn was a prolific copyist of, and commentator on, his grandfather's works.[20] Yūsuf b. Shāhīn's autograph copy of his grandfather's work corroborates the latter's understanding of Ibn Abī al-ʿAwwām al-Saʿdī's authorship of the *manāqib* book.[21]

The dearth of information concerning Ibn Abī al-ʿAwwām is one reason for the lack of clarity we find in the later historical and biographical sources concerning the *Faḍā'il*'s authorship. The clearest evidence that the *Faḍā'il* had been composed originally by the grandfather in the tenth century and then transmitted by his son and grandson comes from the text itself and, in particular, in one decisive paragraph of the book:[22]

> My father < his father, God's mercy be upon him, said: it was mentioned to me by people utterly lacking in knowledge that Abū Ḥanīfa, God show him mercy, was not from among the generation of the Successors. So I decided to produce evidence by citing the death of every Companion who died after the birth of Abū Ḥanīfa. I had mentioned his birth in the first section (*al-juz' al-awwal*) of this book in the section on his merits (*faḍā'il*) and history (*akhbārihi*). I shall repeat some of that now in order to connect and contextualise it with the death dates of the Messenger of God's – God bless him and grant him peace – Companions.

In this passage we see that our original author, Ibn Abī al-ʿAwwām al-Saʿdī (the grandfather), refers directly to his authorship of the book. This is the only instance in the entire work where the author references and directs his readers to another section of his book, and from it we get a glimpse into the author's plan for the organisation of the book. Ibn Abī al-ʿAwwām al-Saʿdī authored and arranged his work into different parts

[20] On Yūsuf b. Shāhīn see al-Sakhāwī, *al-Ḍaw' al-lāmiʿ*, 10: 313–17; Raḍī al-Dīn Ibn Ḥanbalī, *Durr al-ḥabab fī tārīkh aʿyān Ḥalab*, ed. Maḥmūd Ḥamd al-Fākhūrī and Yaḥyā Zakariyyā' ʿAbbāra (Damascus: Wizārat al-Thaqāfa, 1972), 1: 53 (mentioned as having given the author of *Durr al-ḥabab* an *ijāza*), 731 (mentioned as having taught ḥadīth to al-Shiḥna), 2: 313 (mentions Ibn Shāhīn's father and grandfather in an entry on one of Ibn Shāhīn's students), 548 (mentioned as a teacher to the person in the entry); Najm al-Dīn al-Ghazzī, *al-Kawākib al-sā'ira bi-aʿyān al-mi'a al-ʿāshira* (Beirut: Dār al-Kutub al-ʿIlmiyya, 1997), 1: 219. The author mentions that ʿAbd al-Bāsiṭ b. Muḥammad b. al-Shiḥna heard ḥadīth from him (*samiʿa bihā [al-Qāhira] ʿalā al-Jamāl b. Shāhīn Sibṭ al-Ḥāfiẓ b. Ḥajar*); al-Shawkānī, *Badr al-ṭāliʿ bi-maḥāsin man baʿd al-qarn al-sābiʿ* (Cairo: Dār al-Kitāb al-Islāmī, n.d.), 2: 354–5. We are told that his name was Yūsuf b. Shāhīn al-Jamāl Abū al-Maḥāsin b. al-Amīr Abī Aḥmad al-ʿAlā'ī Quṭlūbughā al-Karkī al-Qāhirī al-Ḥanafī, but that he converted to Shāfiʿism: al-Ziriklī, *al-Aʿlām*, 3: 77 (3rd edn., 1969–70); al-Kattānī, *Fihris al-fahāris wa al-athbāt wa-muʿjam al-maʿājim wa al-mashyakhāt wa-musalsalāt*, ed. Iḥsān ʿAbbās (Beirut: Dār al-Gharb al-Islāmī, 1982), 1: 307, 2: 636, 913, and 1139–41.

[21] Yūsuf b. Shāhīn, 'al-Nujūm al-zāhira bi talkhīṣ Akhbār quḍāt Miṣr wa al-Qāhira', MS Arabe 2152, Bibliothèque nationale de France, 119 fols., 9a (Ibn Abī al-ʿAwwām was appointed qadi in 405/1014), 21a–21b, 73a (confirms departure of the grandson and his replacement by Qāsim b. ʿAbd al-ʿArs (?) Muḥammad b. al-Nuʿmān in the year 418/1027). On this manuscript see Vajda, 'Notices de manuscrits', 75.

[22] Ibn Abī al-ʿAwwām al-Saʿdī, *Faḍā'il Abī Ḥanīfa*, 222.

(*ajzāʾ*). As he states, the first part of the book does indeed open with reports concerning Abū Ḥanīfa's birth.

It contains three reports documenting his year of birth (80/699) and death (150/767) and how old he was when he passed away (seventy years). That *manāqib* works began by determining the birth and ancestry of their subjects is straightforward enough given that the genre was concerned with chronological coherence. The precise historical details about Abū Ḥanīfa's birth and ancestry, however, acquired greater social and religious significance in the ninth–tenth centuries. Ibn Abī al-ʿAwwām relates that Abū Ḥanīfa was born in the year 80, died in the year 150, and was seventy years old at the time of his death. Our author emphasises this point of chronology in the light of the discourses of heresy surrounding Abū Ḥanīfa in the centuries and decades prior to Ibn Abī al-ʿAwwām al-Saʿdī's composition of the *Faḍāʾil*. A second report confirms these basic chronological facts, whilst a third report is adduced to add that Abū Ḥanīfa died in the month of Shaʿbān in the year 150 during the caliphal reign of al-Manṣūr.

The passage cited above occurs near the middle of the book. Ibn Abī al-ʿAwwām al-Saʿdī informs his readers at this juncture of the book that they should expect some repetition of the material cited at the very beginning of the *Faḍāʾil*. His argument for Abū Ḥanīfa's belonging to the generation of the Successors rests on chronology and dating, and for this reason he must revisit material from the opening section. As promised, he supplements these three reports with an excursus listing those Companions who died after the year of Abū Ḥanīfa's birth. The first Companion he cites is Wāthila b. al-Asqaʿ. We learn that he died in the year 83, three years after Abū Ḥanīfa was born.[23] The next Companion is ʿUmar b. Abī Salama, one of the Prophet's stepsons by way of the latter's marriage to Umm Salama. He died in the year 83.[24] A third Companion, ʿAmr b. Ḥārith, died when Abū Ḥanīfa was five. Here, a report on ʿAmr suggests that ʿUmar b. Abī Salama died in the year 85, two years later than suggested by the report Ibn Abī al-ʿAwwām al-Saʿdī cites in his notice on him. The report adds that both Ḥārith and ʿUmar died in the same year (85) and were buried on the same day.[25] The final two reports provide clarification on the first companion Ibn Abī al-ʿAwwām al-Saʿdī mentions. In the notice on Wāthila b. al-Asqaʿ we are told he died in the year 83. The final two reports date his death two years later, in the year 85.[26] The next section groups three companions together: ʿAbd Allāh b. al-Ḥārith b. Juzʾ

[23] Ibn Abī al-ʿAwwām al-Saʿdī, *Faḍāʾil Abī Ḥanīfa*, 222.
[24] Ibn Abī al-ʿAwwām al-Saʿdī, *Faḍāʾil Abī Ḥanīfa*, 222.
[25] Ibn Abī al-ʿAwwām al-Saʿdī, *Faḍāʾil Abī Ḥanīfa*, 223.
[26] Ibn Abī al-ʿAwwām al-Saʿdī, *Faḍāʾil Abī Ḥanīfa*, 224.

al-Zabīdī, Ibn Abī Awfā, and Abū Umāma al-Bāhilī. Al-Zabīdī is recorded as having been the last Companion to die in Miṣr in the year 86; Ibn Abī Awfā, we are told, was the last companion to die in Kufa in the same year; and al-Bāhilī died aged ninety-one, also in the year 86.[27] Ibn Abī al-ʿAwwām al-Saʿdī is explicit about his intention to dip into the reservoir of historical information that he and his colleagues would have had at their disposal. He displays a voracious effort to make a case, based on chronological certainty, that would undermine any suspicions about Abū Ḥanīfa's status as a Successor. His *Faḍā'il* is dedicated to using history as a means to rehabilitate Abū Ḥanīfa's orthodoxy in the face of discourses of heresy against him.

It is possible to read a little more into Ibn Abī al-ʿAwwām al-Saʿdī's method. In the *Faḍā'il*, we read: '[Ibn Abī al-ʿAwwām al-Saʿdī]: Abū Maʿmar Muḥammad b. Aḥmad b. Khuzayma al-Baṣrī and Muḥammad b. Aḥmad b. Ḥammād < ʿAbbās al-Dūrī said: I heard Yaḥyā b. Maʿīn say: Wāthila b. al-Asqaʿ died in the year 83 at the age of one hundred and five.'[28] A number of Ibn Abī al-ʿAwwām al-Saʿdī's details are drawn from figures who were influential proto-Sunni traditionalists in the ninth century. As such, these figures, as my earlier chapters have explained, were actively engaged in transmitting heresiological discourses about Abū Ḥanīfa. Ibn Abī al-ʿAwwām al-Saʿdī's information about Wāthila b. al-Asqaʿ is based upon the testimony of Yaḥyā b. Maʿīn. Yaḥyā b. Maʿīn's *Tārīkh* contains a notice on Wāthila b. al-Asqaʿ and conveys this exact information: 'Wāthila b. al-Asqaʿ died in the year 83 at the age of one hundred and five.'[29] The second piece of evidence Ibn Abī al-ʿAwwām al-Saʿdī adduces for Wāthila's death date relies on the transmission of Abū Zurʿa al-Dimashqī. We encountered Abū Zurʿa in Chapter 3 as an important member of the proto-Sunni traditionalist network, where we also observed that his local history of Damascus provided a platform for discourses of heresy against Abū Ḥanīfa. Abū Zurʿa's *Tārīkh* contains the following notice on Wāthila b. al-Asqaʿ: 'Abū Zurʿa: Abū Zurʿa > Yazīd b. ʿAbd Rabbih > Ismāʿīl b. ʿIyyāsh said: Wāthila b. al-Asqaʿ died in the year 83.'[30]

Ibn Abī al-ʿAwwām's report is identical, notwithstanding one typographical error: 'Muḥammad b. Aḥmad b. Ḥammād > ʿAbd al-Raḥmān b. ʿAmr Abū Zurʿa al-Dimashqī said: Yazīd b. ʿAbd Rabbih > Ismāʿīl b.

[27] Ibn Abī al-ʿAwwām al-Saʿdī, *Faḍā'il Abī Ḥanīfa*, 224–5.

[28] Ibn Abī al-ʿAwwām al-Saʿdī, *Faḍā'il Abī Ḥanīfa*, 223.

[29] Yaḥyā b. Maʿīn, *Tārīkh Yaḥyā b. Maʿīn* [recension of Abū al-Faḍl al-ʿAbbāsī b. Muḥammad b. Ḥātim al-Dūrī al-Baghdādī], ed. ʿAbd Allāh Aḥmad Ḥasan (Beirut: Dār al-Qalam, n.d.), 1: 36. The same wording can be found in Yaḥyā b. Maʿīn's *Tārīkh*, 2: 627, as part of his *Yaḥyā b. Maʿīn wa kitābuhu al-tārīkh*, ed. Aḥmad Muḥammad Nūr Sayf (Mecca: n.p., 1979).

[30] Abū Zurʿa al-Dimashqī, *Tārīkh*, 1: 239.

ʿAbbās said: Wāthila b. al-Asqaʿ died in the year 83.'[31] Ibn Abī al-ʿAwwām lists another eleven companions who died after the birth of Abū Ḥanīfa:[32]

1. ʿUbayd Allāh b. al-ʿAbbās al-Muṭṭalib died in the year 87.
2. Al-Miqdām b. Maʿdīkarib died in Shām, aged ninety-one, in the year 87.
3. ʿUtba b. ʿAbd al-Sulamī died in the year 87 in Ḥimṣ.
4. ʿAbd Allāh b. Basr al-Māzinī died in year 88.
5. ʿAbd Allāh b. Thaʿlaba b. Ṣaʿīr al-Zuhrī died in the year 87, aged eighty-three. Second report says year 89, aged seventy-three.
6. Sahl b. Saʿd al-Sāʿidī died in Medina in year 91, aged 100.
7. Al-Sā'ib b. Yazīd al-Kindī was regarded as the last Companion of Medina. He died in the year 91, aged eighty-eight.
8. Anas b. Mālik. There are conflicting reports: year 90; year 91, aged ninety-nine; 93; 91; 91, aged ninety-nine; 91 or 92.
9. Abū Umāma b. Sahl b. Ḥanīf died in the year 100.
10. Abū Ṭufayl ʿĀmir b. Wāthila: Last Companion to die who saw the Prophet Muḥammad. Died in year 101, lived through eight years of the Prophet Muḥammad's life; born in the year 1.
11. ʿAbd al-Raḥmān b. ʿAbd al-Qārī died in year 81, aged 120.

Ibn Abī al-ʿAwwām's mining of historical data for death dates of Companions aims to respond to claims that Abū Ḥanīfa could not have heard traditions from Companions. The *manāqib* and *masānīd* works identify Abū Ḥanīfa as having been the only eponym to have seen or met a Companion, heard traditions from them, and transmitted these traditions. This was a veritable *coup de grâce* for followers of Abū Ḥanīfa,

[31] ʿAbbās for ʿIyyāsh: a very easy scribal error to make: Ibn Abī al-ʿAwwām al-Saʿdī, *Faḍā'il Abī Ḥanīfa*, 1: 285. Abū Zurʿa later reports an incident involving Yaḥyā b. al-Ḥārith, where he reports that he met Wāthila and asked him whether he performed the oath of allegiance to the Prophet with his hand. Wāthila confirmed this, and Yaḥyā proceeded to kiss his hand: Abū Zurʿa al-Dimashqī, *Tārīkh*, 1: 323. This report appears in a section that seems to recount incidents concerning Successors and Companions, wherein the latter had touched the body of the Prophet Muḥammad. Another report records a Successor's proud boast that he prayed funeral prayers with Wāthila. We have another report in which ʿAmr b. Muhājir recounts his prayer behind Wāthila (1: 324). Later on in the work Abū Zurʿa recounts the names of two more Successors who met Wāthila (1: 327). Abū Zurʿa would have been very well placed to supply this information on Wāthila. Ibn ʿAsākir frequently cites Abū Zurʿa's work, *Tasmiyat al-aṣāghir min aṣḥāb Wāthila b. al-Asqaʿ*. Ibn ʿAsākir mentions this in his *Tārīkh madīnat al-Dimashq*, 9: 217 (ʿAmr b. Muhājir b. Dīnār), 10: 369 (Muḥammad b. ʿAbd Allāh al-Shuʿaythī), 12: 197 (Yaḥyā b. al-Ḥārith al-Dhimārī), 12: 340 (Abū Muṣʿab), 7: 63 (ʿAbd al-Raḥmān b. Abī Qusaym al-Ḥajarī), 8: 39 (ʿAmr b. Ruwaym al-Lakhmī), 8: 80 (ʿAṭā' b. Maysara al-Khurāsānī), 10: 89 (Bishr b. Ḥayyān al-Khusanjī al-Balāṭī).

[32] Ibn Abī al-ʿAwwām al-Saʿdī, *Faḍā'il Abī Ḥanīfa*, 225–32.

and it was one that *manāqib* and *masānīd* works were keen to draw attention to, since it augmented Abū Ḥanīfa's orthodox credentials.

It is particularly significant that this passage offers the only bold statement of intent for the book's origins. We have Ibn Abī al-ʿAwwām expressing his awareness of discourses of heresy against Abū Ḥanīfa which originate, in this case, from the claim that he never met a Companion and thus did not qualify as a Successor. In formulating this attack, proto-Sunni traditionalists wished to eliminate Abū Ḥanīfa from a category that carried a certain amount of moral and orthodox probity. Ibn Abī al-ʿAwwām's intervention, which sets forth explicitly an explanation for some of the book's content, reflects the preoccupation of *manāqib* works with responding to discourses of heresy against Abū Ḥanīfa. This was their central social and religious function. A better appreciation of this is gained by examining Ibn Abī al-ʿAwwām al-Saʿdī's *Faḍāʾil* in more detail.

Following the section on the birth of Abū Ḥanīfa is a chapter concerning his social and ethnic background. In this section Ibn Abī al-ʿAwwām appears to have two main objectives. On the one hand, he is concerned with establishing a single narrative concerning Abū Ḥanīfa's ancestral origins that places Abū Ḥanīfa's father as a member of Kabul's aristocracy who became a prisoner of war. He was purchased by a lady from the tribe of Banī Taym Allāh b. Thaʿlaba who later freed him.[33] On the other hand, our author knows that proto-Sunni traditionalists used the uncertainty surrounding Abū Ḥanīfa's ancestral origins to undermine his religious orthodoxy. He mentions two instances to highlight the unreasonable nature of proto-Sunni traditionalist attacks on Abū Ḥanīfa's social background. One report describes the tension between al-Qāsim b. Maʿn and Sufyān al-Thawrī. The latter used to censure al-Qāsim b. Maʿn on account of his having studied with Abū Ḥanīfa (*qāla lī Sufyān al-Thawrī ghayra marra yuʿātibunī fī ityānī Abā Ḥanīfa*). They happened to meet each other one day, and al-Qāsim b. Maʿn demanded an explanation for Sufyān al-Thawrī's sharp hostility towards Abū Ḥanīfa: 'Why do you loathe him so much (*mā tanqimu ʿalā Abī Ḥanīfa*)?' Sufyān al-Thawrī was stymied (*fa sakata, lā yadrī mā yaqūl*). He had no credible defence, and instead found it puzzling that someone with al-Qāsim b. Maʿn's esteemed social origins, whose ancestor was the famed Companion ʿAbd Allāh b. Masʿūd, would frequent a man such as Abū Ḥanīfa, whose ancestors were clients (*rajul mithluka min wuld ʿAbd Allāh b. Masʿūd yakhtalifu ilā rajul min al-mawālī*).[34] Ibn Abī al-ʿAwwām

[33] Ibn Abī al-ʿAwwām al-Saʿdī, *Faḍāʾil Abī Ḥanīfa*, 40–1.
[34] Ibn Abī al-ʿAwwām al-Saʿdī, *Faḍāʾil Abī Ḥanīfa*, 41–2.

acknowledges the presence of proto-Sunni traditionalist hostility to and condemnation of Abū Ḥanīfa, but his aim is to convey just how unreasonable and petty it was. It was grounded in unreasonable social hierarchies and ethnic prejudices rather than religious principles.

Ibn Abī al-ʿAwwām al-Saʿdī is to keen to argue that others found such criticisms entirely inappropriate and bigoted. He relates Ṣāliḥ b. al-Ḥasan's analysis of the widespread proto-Sunni traditionalist criticisms of Abū Ḥanīfa. Ṣāliḥ b. al-Ḥasan believed that the Arabs were envious of Abū Ḥanīfa because someone of his standing did not emerge from among them. He recognised also that scholars whose ancestral origins were to be found among the *mawālī* were also scathing about Abū Ḥanīfa, but this too was to be explained on the grounds that, in one way, Abū Ḥanīfa did not claim to belong to them either. Ṣāliḥ b. al-Ḥasan ends this anecdote by relating the response he had heard Abū Ḥanīfa give to a man inquiring about his ancestral origins. 'I am from the community of Muḥammad, God bless him and grant him peace, and among those whom God, mighty and exalted, has granted His favour to by bestowing upon our ancestors Islam.'[35] *Manāqib* authors seeking to curtail the ethnic dimensions of discourses of heresy against Abū Ḥanīfa found comfort in the defence that one's greatest ancestry lay in a claim to the religion of Islam.

Proto-Sunni traditionalist attacks on Abū Ḥanīfa's religious credibility appear in different places throughout Ibn Abī al-ʿAwwām al-Saʿdī's *Faḍā'il* work. That they admitted the material of their interlocutors into *manāqib* works is surprising, even if the goal in doing so was to respond directly to their criticisms. Followers of Abū Ḥanīfa went even further than this, however. Ibn Abī al-ʿAwwām al-Saʿdī's *Faḍā'il* includes a chapter entitled 'Denunciations of Abū Ḥanīfa and the slander against him'.[36] This section concerns itself with a number of the gravest charges against Abū Ḥanīfa that we found in proto-Sunni traditionalist discourses of heresy between the ninth and tenth centuries. Proto-Sunni traditionalists disseminated the idea very widely in texts composed between the ninth and eleventh centuries that Abū Ḥanīfa had repented publicly from heresy on two occasions.

This charge against Abū Ḥanīfa had become so widespread that followers of Abū Ḥanīfa found themselves not so much doubting the existence of such incidences as giving an alternative explanation for them. One account given by Ibn Abī al-ʿAwwām explains that an abstruse, technical principle propelled the entire controversy. He says that the political authorities of Kufa arranged for the city's governor to question Abū

[35] Ibn Abī al-ʿAwwām al-Saʿdī, *Faḍā'il Abī Ḥanīfa*, 43–4.
[36] Ibn Abī al-ʿAwwām al-Saʿdī, *Faḍā'il Abī Ḥanīfa*, 72–80.

Ḥanīfa in public about his belief regarding the createdness of the Quran. When pressed to give an answer, Abū Ḥanīfa was non-committal in his responses. 'I have never heard anyone espouse this doctrine, nor have I known anyone to debate about it. In fact, it is the kind of speech that one finds disturbing (*innahu la qawl tuḍīqu lahu al-nafs*).' He was asked to swear an oath to this effect, but refused to do so. Ibn Abī al-ʿAwwām al-Saʿdī explains that this was because Abū Ḥanīfa, out of principle, would never swear an oath in God's name. The governor then threatened Abū Ḥanīfa that he would be flogged if he refused to swear an oath. In the light of Abū Ḥanīfa's persistent refusal to swear an oath, the governor began the process for flogging him, but when he noticed his body's slenderness and old age, he resorted to asking Abū Ḥanīfa to repent publicly. Abū Ḥanīfa was puzzled by this and told the governor that nothing that he had said or believed was in any way self-implicating. 'In that case, repent,' said the governor. So Abū Ḥanīfa said, 'O my Lord, accept our repentance.' This was the basis for people's saying, 'Abū Ḥanīfa was made to repent, Abū Ḥanīfa was made to repent.'[37]

It was the view of a number of important proto-Sunni traditionalists that Abū Ḥanīfa had repented from heresy on two occasions. News of this incident had clearly begun to circulate among Muslim communities. Ḥanafī authors such as Ibn Abī al-ʿAwwām contended that other proto-Sunnis and proto-Sunni traditionalists could not bring themselves to believe that Abū Ḥanīfa had been made to repent from heresy. But people wanted answers and so they sought clarification from leading scholars. One man plucked up the courage to ask ʿAbd Allāh b. al-Mubārak, 'Was Abū Ḥanīfa made to repent from heresy?' Ibn al-Mubārak was not moved to talk (*fa sakata*). The man posed the same question one month later. Ibn al-Mubārak relented: 'I seek refuge in God from the hostility of the readers (*al-qurrāʾ*), and I seek refuge in God from the hostility of those involved in government (*al-siyar*).'[38] Similarly, when ʿAbd al-Salām b. Ḥarb al-Malāʾī was asked whether Abū Ḥanīfa was forced to repent publicly from heresy, he expressed his outrage over the suggestion that Abū Ḥanīfa had any deviant beliefs that demanded a public repentance. 'God forgive you, my brother. I seek God's forgiveness from that. It was an attempt to slander him.'[39] Ibn Abī al-ʿAwwām al-Saʿdī reports Misʿar b. Kidām's thoughts on the entire episode: 'The people of government envied al-Nuʿmān b. Thābit on account of the latter's perspicacity (*fahm*) and learning (*ʿilm*). This was nothing but an attempt to slander him.'[40]

[37] Ibn Abī al-ʿAwwām al-Saʿdī, *Faḍāʾil Abī Ḥanīfa*, 72–3.
[38] Ibn Abī al-ʿAwwām al-Saʿdī, *Faḍāʾil Abī Ḥanīfa*, 73.
[39] Ibn Abī al-ʿAwwām al-Saʿdī, *Faḍāʾil Abī Ḥanīfa*, 73–4.
[40] Ibn Abī al-ʿAwwām al-Saʿdī, *Faḍāʾil Abī Ḥanīfa*, 74.

Again, whether Misʿar b. Kidām actually said this will interest historians of the eighth century who aim to use later texts to reconstruct the history of the eighth century. For our purposes, it shows how Ḥanafīs of the late ninth and tenth centuries interpreted attacks on their imam. Ibn Abī al-ʿAwwām does not stop here. He is absolutely committed to exonerating Abū Ḥanīfa from the charges directed towards the latter by proto-Sunni traditionalists, and so he draws our attention to other accounts sympathetic to Abū Ḥanīfa's ordeal. This was an account that Ibn Abī al-ʿAwwām al-Saʿdī (grandfather) found in his own book containing the traditions of al-Ḥasan b. Ḥammād Sajjāda (d. 241/855).[41] It relates the story of Abū Quṭun ʿAmr b. al-Haytham, who sets out for Kufa in search of religious scholars. He is guided in the direction of Abū Ḥanīfa and Sufyān al-Thawrī. In the course of a conversation with Sufyān al-Thawrī, al-Haytham decides to ask him something that has been on his mind:[42]

AL-HAYTHAM: I have heard the following statement attributed to you: 'Abū Ḥanīfa was made to repent from unbelief twice.' The unbelief that is mentioned here, does it imply the unbelief that constitutes the very opposite of belief?

AL-THAWRĪ: No one has asked me about this incident since the very day that I first spoke these words (*mā sa'alanī ʿan hādhihi al-mas'ala aḥad ghayruka mundhu kallamtu bihā*).

AL-HAYTHAM: He [al-Thawrī] then lowered his head and said the following:

AL-THAWRĪ: The answer is no. One day, Wāṣil al-Shārī entered Kufa. A group of people flocked to him and told him: 'Here in Kufa we have a man who does not declare as unbelievers people who commit sins (*lā yukaffir ahl al-maʿāṣī*).' The person they were referring to was Abū Ḥanīfa. Abū Ḥanīfa was then sent for and brought to Wāṣil.

WĀṢIL B. AL-SHĀRĪ: Old man, I have been informed that you do not declare sinners to be unbelievers. Is this so?

ABŪ ḤANĪFA: Yes, this is my position (*huwa madhhabī*).

WĀṢIL B. AL-SHĀRĪ: Holding such a position is itself unbelief (*inna hādhā kufr*). If you repent, we shall accept it from you. But if you refuse to repent, we shall kill you.

ABŪ ḤANĪFA: From what should I repent?

WĀṢIL B. AL-SHĀRĪ: Repent from what we have mentioned.

ABŪ ḤANĪFA: I repent from unbelief (*anā tā'ib min al-kufr*).

Abū Ḥanīfa then left. A group of the caliph al-Manṣūr's strongmen arrived and had Wāṣil banished from Kufa. After a short while, al-Manṣūr convened one of his sessions with the public. A group of people who had been present during proceedings between Wāṣil and Abū Ḥanīfa

[41] On al-Ḥasan b. Ḥammād Sajjāda see al-Dhahabī, *Siyar*, 11: 392–3.
[42] Ibn Abī al-ʿAwwām al-Saʿdī, *Faḍā'il Abī Ḥanīfa*, 74–5.

reported to the caliph that Abū Ḥanīfa had retracted his statement to Wāṣil. Once again, Abū Ḥanīfa was summoned:

AL-MANṢŪR: Old man, I have been informed that you have retracted the statement you gave earlier.
ABŪ ḤANĪFA: Which statement is that?
AL-MANṢŪR: That you do not declare sinners to be unbelievers.
ABŪ ḤANĪFA: Yes, this is my position.
AL-MANṢŪR: According to us, holding such a position constitutes unbelief. If you repent, we shall accept it from you. But if you refuse, we shall put you to death. The authorities do not have someone put to death from heresy or unbelief until they have been offered the chance to repent thrice (*wa al-shurāt lā yaqtulūna ḥattā yustatāba thalāth marrāt*).
ABŪ ḤANĪFA: From what should I repent?
AL-MANṢŪR: Repent from unbelief.
ABŪ ḤANĪFA: Then I repent from unbelief.

Al-Thawrī adds that this was the background to the unbelief from which Abū Ḥanīfa was made to repent.[43] Ibn Abī al-ʿAwwām al-Saʿdī acknowledges the sharp discourse of heresy against Abū Ḥanīfa and highlights the enmity Sufyān al-Thawrī displayed against Abū Ḥanīfa. However, Ibn Abī al-ʿAwwām al-Saʿdī seeks to draw attention to the misinterpretations of various controversial episodes that became the basis of this discourse of heresy. Therefore, these reports are valuable for our purposes because they document the development of narratives of orthodoxy and heresy in the centuries that concern us. Moreover, they reveal the extent to which authors of *manāqib* works were engaged intensely in shaping narratives of orthodoxy by confronting proto-Sunni traditionalist discourses of heresy head-on.

An important discourse of heresy against Abū Ḥanīfa that Ibn Abī al-ʿAwwām al-Saʿdī alludes to only in passing is the allegation that Abū Ḥanīfa permitted rebellion against the state (*yarā al-sayf*). He cites the disbelief and curt dismissal of al-Naḍr b. Muḥammad upon being asked whether Abū Ḥanīfa held this doctrine.[44] What this section in Ibn Abī al-ʿAwwām al-Saʿdī's *Faḍā'il* tells us is that there was an awareness and an acknowledgement that discourses of heresy against Abū Ḥanīfa were fairly widespread. Our author does not pretend that this material never existed. Rather, he cites it and shows the extent to which fierce opposition to Abū Ḥanīfa existed. This is because Abū Ḥanīfa's defenders saw these attacks as proof of his orthodoxy.

In one section of the *Faḍā'il*, Ibn Abī al-ʿAwwām al-Saʿdī gives numerous examples of this discourse of heresy and suggests that it was on the rise. He explains that once a son asked his father, 'Why do I see so many

[43] Ibn Abī al-ʿAwwām al-Saʿdī, *Faḍā'il Abī Ḥanīfa*, 74.
[44] Ibn Abī al-ʿAwwām al-Saʿdī, *Faḍā'il Abī Ḥanīfa*, 75.

people defaming Abū Ḥanīfa? They say [terrible] things about him and they have increased in number.' 'My dear son,' the father responded, 'everyone in Kufa had a tribe that protected its members. Abū Ḥanīfa was simply a man of the clients (*al-mawālī*). After a while, by God, no one remained except that he went to Abū Ḥanīfa and learnt from him. The only exception was Sharīk b. ʿAbd Allāh, who refused to do so, and his deficiency was well known up until the day he met his Lord.'[45] Crucially, what this account tells us is that Muslims, including Ibn Abī al-ʿAwwām, were sensitive to the fact that orthodoxy was a process. Discourses of heresy against Abū Ḥanīfa could be on the rise in a certain period, but that over time narratives of orthodoxy evolved. In addition, Ibn Abī al-ʿAwwām al-Saʿdī highlights instances wherein Abū Ḥanīfa's opponents described him as a heretic, unbeliever, and deviant.[46] Another report tells us that during the course of a conversation Abū Ḥanīfa's name was mentioned and it emerged that there were those who were extreme in their love for him and those whose animosity against him was extreme. One onlooker had more sympathy for Abū Ḥanīfa's admirers, for he described the state of those who heaped opprobrium on Abū Ḥanīfa as doing so 'out of envy, because they see in you [Abū Ḥanīfa] the virtues that God grants to His elect.'[47] Ibn Abī al-ʿAwwām al-Saʿdī understands this, but he shows that the basis for such opposition was often fickle, that it rested upon gross historical misunderstandings, and that it was subject to serious objections. He saw his *manāqib* work as the forum for documenting this complex and contested mnemohistory, so as to rehabilitate Abū Ḥanīfa as an exemplary figure of Sunni orthodoxy.

There was no doubt in Ibn Abī al-ʿAwwām's mind that proto-Sunni traditionalist opposition to Abū Ḥanīfa was real and substantial. He located the roots of this vehement hostility in the rising popularity of Abū Ḥanīfa in the eighth and ninth centuries. In his *Faḍā'il* he tries to suggest that it was personal animosity and prejudice that contributed to the growth of discourses of heresy. He quotes the words of al-Jāḥiẓ, 'People are of two types with respect to Abū Ḥanīfa: they are either envious or ignorant. The envious person is so because he has not been granted the like of which was granted to Abū Ḥanīfa. The ignorant person is so because he does not understand what Abū Ḥanīfa said.'[48]

[45] See Ibn Abī al-ʿAwwām al-Saʿdī, *Faḍā'il Abī Ḥanīfa*, 79.

[46] See Ibn Abī al-ʿAwwām al-Saʿdī, *Faḍā'il Abī Ḥanīfa*, 76, 78.

[47] See Ibn Abī al-ʿAwwām al-Saʿdī, *Faḍā'il Abī Ḥanīfa*, 78: *Ḥasadan an ra'ūka faḍḍalaka Allāh bimā fuḍḍilat bihi al-nujabā'*.

[48] See Ibn Abī al-ʿAwwām al-Saʿdī, *Faḍā'il Abī Ḥanīfa*, 78. I have not been able to locate this statement in al-Jāḥiẓ's works. The statement is attributed by other pre-modern

Ibn Abī al-ʿAwwām, like al-Jāḥiẓ before him, understood that Abū Ḥanīfa was a victim of his own success.

Ibn Abī al-ʿAwwām al-Saʿdī gives a number of examples to illustrate his argument. When, for example, Aḥmad b. Ḥanbal was asked why he insisted on attacking Abū Ḥanīfa so sharply he responded by saying that it was because of Abū Ḥanīfa's reliance on speculative jurisprudence (*al-ra'y*). This did not satisfy the questioner. 'Did not Mālik b. Anas rely on speculative jurisprudence?' he protested. Aḥmad b. Ḥanbal agreed. He added, though, that what made Abū Ḥanīfa's speculative jurisprudence so much more injurious was that it had endured in books. Aḥmad b. Ḥanbal's inquisitor found this answer unhelpful, too. 'Mālik b. Anas's speculative jurisprudence was also recorded in books,' he replied. 'That is true,' said Aḥmad b. Ḥanbal, 'but Abū Ḥanīfa relied on speculative jurisprudence more than Mālik b. Anas.' We can deduce from this that proto-Sunni traditionalists were being challenged on account of their dissemination of discourses of heresy against Abū Ḥanīfa. It was apparent to some that the grounds for proto-Sunni traditionalist condemnations of Abū Ḥanīfa as a heretic and deviant lacked credibility. There was certainly an increasing sentiment that Abū Ḥanīfa was being targeted unfairly, and that proto-Sunni traditionalists were playing the man and not his ideas. Another account in the *Faḍā'il*, for example, explains how Abū Ḥanīfa and his Kufan interlocutors, Ibn Shubruma and Ibn Abī Layla, gave identical responses to a legal question. They also provided similar reasoning for arriving at that particular answer. When it was put to them that Abū Ḥanīfa had given the same answer and provided similar legal reasoning, the two scholars supposedly retracted their position.[49] The point Ibn Abī al-ʿAwwām al-Saʿdī seems to want to convey is that, when it came to Abū Ḥanīfa and the Ḥanafīs in general, some proto-Sunni traditionalists exhibited double standards. They did so, evidently, because they deemed it necessary to draw a line between their religious conclusions and those ascribed to Abū Ḥanīfa.

We have seen that, for Ibn Abī al-ʿAwwām al-Saʿdī, demonstrating the orthodoxy of Abū Ḥanīfa could not be achieved without responding to specific discourses of heresy. It was necessary to cite them and explain them. In the process of doing so, Ibn Abī al-ʿAwwām al-Saʿdī even

writers to ʿAbd Allāh b. Dāwūd al-Khuraybī, whom al-Dhahabī (*Siyar*, 9: 348) believed was sympathetic to *ra'y*, in the following works: al-Khaṭīb al-Baghdādī, *Tārīkh Baghdād*, 13: 367; al-Dhahabī, *Siyar*, 6: 402; al-Mizzī, *Tahdhīb al-kamāl*, 29: 441; Ibn Ḥajar al-ʿAsqalānī, *Tahdhīb al-tahdhīb*, 10: 402; Murtaḍā al-Zabīdī, *ʿUqūd al-jawāhir al-munīfa fī adillat madhhab al-Imām Abī Ḥanīfa*, ed. Muḥammad al-ʿAzāzī (Beirut: Dār al-Kutub al-ʿIlmiyya, n.d.), 46.

[49] See Ibn Abī al-ʿAwwām al-Saʿdī, *Faḍā'il Abī Ḥanīfa*, 77.

reproduced some of this disparaging material, if only to deconstruct it or explain it away. It was also possible to undermine discourses of heresy against Abū Ḥanīfa and reinforce his orthodox credentials simply by emphasising the number of his followers and just how far and wide they had spread. Ibn Abī al-ʿAwwām achieved this in two ways. In the first place, the *Faḍā'il* contains chapters wherein religious scholars are seen to attest to Abū Ḥanīfa's orthodoxy. The first of these chapters appears immediately after two chapters that describe the torrent of heresiological discourses surrounding Abū Ḥanīfa's mnemohistory. Having analysed and responded to this critical material, our author considers this an opportune moment to furnish a catalogue of positive attestations to Abū Ḥanīfa's piety, learning, perspicacity, proficiency in ḥadīth, and unrivalled juristic knowledge.[50]

A second technique we can observe in the *Faḍā'il* for documenting Abū Ḥanīfa's orthodoxy is to incorporate into his *manāqib* work a genre of writing that was designed to convey the religious orthodoxy of legal eponyms, namely, *ṭabaqāt* works. *Ṭabaqāt* books were first composed in the late eighth century and became more prominent in the ninth and tenth centuries. They were essentially biographical dictionaries devoted to a particular social or religious group in which biographical notices, arranged by generation (*ṭabaqa*), were given for individuals.[51] These biographical dictionaries played a fundamental role in the formation of religious and social movements and helped to consolidate their collective identities. Their use in *manāqib* works from the ninth and tenth centuries, however, points to a more precise function. If the *manāqib* genre surrounding Abū Ḥanīfa in the ninth and tenth centuries sought to defend

[50] Ibn Abī al-ʿAwwām al-Saʿdī, *Faḍā'il Abī Ḥanīfa*, 80–92.

[51] Much has been written on the *ṭabaqāt* genre. See Makdisi, 'Ṭabaqāt-Biography'. A study that builds on Makdisi's insights and emphasises the relationship between authority and *ṭabaqāt* works is Jacques, *Authority, Conflict, and the Transmission of Diversity*. On orthodoxy and biographies see also Fierro, 'Why and How do Religious Scholars Write about Themselves?' For the view that the development of ḥadīth study prompted the rise of *ṭabaqāt* works see Loth, 'Ursprung und Bedeutung'; and Gibb, 'Islamic Biographical Literature'; a comprehensive overview of the genre across disciplines is provided by Hafsi, 'Recherches sur le genre Tabaqat'; Al-Qadi, 'Biographical Dictionaries'. See also Robinson, 'al-Muʿāfā b. ʿImrān'. Jokisch believes that *ṭabaqāt* works were modelled on Byzantine bishop lists. He tells us that 'Ibn Saʿd and possibly also the other early authors of *ṭabaqāt* works had direct or indirect knowledge of the Church History of Eusebius'. Readers of Jokisch's work will note that this seems to be his explanation for other developments in early Islam. He does not go to the effort of actually building a case for the relationship between *ṭabaqāt* works and Byzantine bishop lists, and, having read the relevant sections in Eusebius' *Ecclesiastical History*, I remain unconvinced. See Jokisch, *Islamic Imperial Law*, 435. One *ṭabaqāt* work not cited in the previous scholarship listed here was brought to our attention by Muranyi. For the ninth-century *Ṭabaqāt ahl al-Baṣra wa maʿrifat al-rijāl* see Muranyi, *Beiträge zur Geschichte*, 74–5 (Muranyi mistakenly gives al-ʿIjlī's death date as 975 instead of 875).

his orthodoxy against discourses of heresy, then the *ṭabaqāt* sections contained within *manāqib* works furnished an argument for orthodoxy that rested on perceived facts concerning the number of Abū Ḥanīfa's followers and the spread of his legal teachings across the early Islamic world. *Manāqib* and *ṭabaqāt* works came together, often in a single text such as Ibn Abī al-ʿAwwām al-Saʿdī's, to perform the work of orthodoxy.

The decision to bring these two distinct genres together seems to have been a conscious move. Ibn Abī al-ʿAwwām al-Saʿdī's *ṭabaqāt* section begins after the final detail concerning Abū Ḥanīfa's death has been recorded. Immediately following this is his historical account of scholars, jurists, and ḥadīth experts who studied jurisprudence or ḥadīth with him. A considerable amount of thinking seems to have gone into the organisation of the *ṭabaqāt* work. First, the *ṭabaqāt* section is arranged geographically. Second, each regional account begins with a list of names. After this, information is provided on each individual name and his relationship to Abū Ḥanīfa. The first part of the *ṭabaqāt* section treats Abū Ḥanīfa's followers in Kufa. A total of seventy names is provided in list form, and sixty-five of these scholars receive individual notices. According to this data, Abū Ḥanīfa's students and, thereby, his teachings were dominant in Kufa, Khurāsān, and Basra.[52]

It is important to point out that these notices differ from biographical notices that are common to the *ṭabaqāt* genre. Rather than providing some elementary details concerning the scholar's birth, education, teachers, students, and place and date of birth, Ibn Abī al-ʿAwwām cites reports that connect the scholar in question to Abū Ḥanīfa in some shape or form. For example, Ibn Abī al-ʿAwwām provides reports in which these scholars extol Abū Ḥanīfa, transmit legal opinions from him, report incidents about Abū Ḥanīfa, and narrate ḥadīths with a chain of transmission containing Abū Ḥanīfa. Ibn Abī al-ʿAwwām is drawing on the technique of *ṭabaqāt* works, but he is adapting it for the specific purposes of his *manāqib* book. In fact, his *ṭabaqāt* section on the followers of Abū Ḥanīfa ends where a new *ṭabaqāt* section begins, which has the explicit aim of

[52] Ibn Abī al-ʿAwwām al-Saʿdī's data on Kufa will reignite the debate concerning the importance of Kufa to the spread of proto-Ḥanafism. In a number of important studies Melchert has pointed out that a survey of a large pool of both Ḥanafī and non-Ḥanafī sources (*ṭabaqāt* and *masānīd* works) shows the dearth of Kufan Ḥanafīs: Melchert, 'How Ḥanafism Came to Originate in Kufa'; Melchert, 'The Early Ḥanafiyya and Kufa'. Melchert is certainly right to question modern scholarship's (Schacht and Tsafrir) reliance on the casual connection between Kufa and Ḥanafism, and he has marshalled more evidence than anyone else towards this research question. This new data from Ibn Abī al-ʿAwwām, however, suggests more strongly than any other primary source the dominance of Kufan Ḥanafism. This question is not directly relevant to this book, so, for now, I have avoided a closer analysis of Ibn Abī al-ʿAwwām al-Saʿdī's survey of Ḥanafism's regional distribution.

providing death dates for Companions of the Prophet to establish the plausibility of Abū Ḥanīfa's belonging to the generation of Successors. This second *ṭabaqāt* section resorts to the technique more common to *ṭabaqāt* works of recording death dates (see Table 8.1).

The *ṭabaqāt* model makes a third appearance in Ibn Abī al-ʿAwwām al-Saʿdī's *Faḍāʾil.* This section, however, was not composed by the original author of the work (the grandfather). It was authored by the author's grandson, and it was designed to supplement the *ṭabaqāt* section enumerating Abū Ḥanīfa's vast and expansive network of students. In what is only the second explicit statement of authorial intervention in the *Faḍāʾil,* the grandson states: 'I had uncovered a large number of people who transmitted reports from and studied with Abū Ḥanīfa but whose narrations from Abū Ḥanīfa my grandfather had failed to mention. They are as follows.'[53] Indeed, these names are omitted in the grandfather's *ṭabaqāt* section, which made no claims to being comprehensive. Whereas the earlier *ṭabaqāt* sections contain *isnād*s in which the grandson transmits (through his father) from the grandfather, this *ṭabaqāt* section does not refer to the father and grandfather in the *isnād*s. The grandson furnishes his own, non-family *isnād*s and even refers to his own written materials from which he derives information on students of Abū Ḥanīfa (see Table 8.2).[54]

The grandson also eschews the regional organisation of the *ṭabaqāt* favoured by his grandfather. He mentions thirteen scholars absent in his grandfather's account and provides evidence for their having studied with Abū Ḥanīfa. The fourth and final *ṭabaqāt* section returns to the grandfather's

Table 8.1 *Overview of* ṭabaqāt *section within Ibn Abī al-ʿAwwām al-Saʿdī's* Faḍāʾil Abī Ḥanīfa

| Region | Number of scholars | Reference |
|---|---|---|
| Kufa | 70 | *Faḍāʾil,* 143–84 |
| Medina | 5 | *Faḍāʾil,* 184–7 |
| Yemen | 7 | *Faḍāʾil,* 190–8 |
| Basra | 18 | *Faḍāʾil,* 194–204 |
| Yamāma | 2 | *Faḍāʾil,* 205 |
| Wāsiṭ | 6 | *Faḍāʾil,* 205–8 |
| Jazīra | 9 | *Faḍāʾil,* 208–9 |
| Shām and Miṣr | 7 | *Faḍāʾil,* 209–12 |
| Rayy and Khurāsān | 23 | *Faḍāʾil,* 212–22 |

53 Ibn Abī al-ʿAwwām al-Saʿdī, *Faḍāʾil Abī Ḥanīfa*, 234.
54 Ibn Abī al-ʿAwwām al-Saʿdī, *Faḍāʾil Abī Ḥanīfa*, 240–1.

Table 8.2 *The occurrence of* ṭabaqāt *sections within Ibn Abī al-ʿAwwām al-Saʿdī's* Faḍā'il Abī Ḥanīfa

| Author | *Ṭabaqāt* | Arrangement | Reference |
|---|---|---|---|
| Grandfather | Students of AH | Regional | *Faḍā'il*, 143–222 |
| Grandfather | Companions alive during AH's lifetime | Chronological | *Faḍā'il*, 222–33 |
| Grandson | Students of AH omitted by grandfather | Random | *Faḍā'il*, 234–42 |
| Grandfather | Biographies of major students of AH | Random | *Faḍā'il*, 242–375 |

composition and provides detailed biographies of three major students of Abū Ḥanīfa.[55]

In a landmark article, George Makdisi argued that the central motivation for writing *ṭabaqāt* works came from traditionalism. Makdisi is characteristically careful with the evidence, and he acknowledges that the current state of research shows that the earliest recorded *ṭabaqāt* work was authored by a tationalist scholar. For this reason, we cannot say that *ṭabaqāt* works originated with traditionalists. Nevertheless, Makdisi shows that the *ṭabaqāt* genre was developed by followers of the eponyms and that this development was integral to the formation of Sunni orthodoxy around the schools of law.[56] In a review essay, Melchert has presented some important modifications to Makdisi's hypothesis that traditionalists dominated the composition of *ṭabaqāt* works. The most significant one for our purposes is Melchert's point that deriving conclusions based upon titles of works overlooks the fact that *ṭabaqāt* works could appear within books that did not contain the word *ṭabaqāt* in the title.[57]

Building on Makdisi and Melchert's findings, I have argued that *manāqib* works were more important in establishing the orthodoxy of eponyms of legal schools than *ṭabaqāt* works.In this respect, my conclusions complement, extend, and modify Makdisi's hypothesis: 'The Traditionalists may or may not have created the *ṭabaqāt*; but there can be no doubt that they adopted it for a specific purpose. Their motivation was to identify the

[55] Ibn Abī al-ʿAwwām al-Saʿdī, *Faḍā'il Abī Ḥanīfa*, 242–375: Dāwūd al-Ṭāʾī (242–63), ʿAbd Allāh b. al-Mubārak (264–85), al-Qāsim b. Maʿn (285–90), Zufar b. Hudhayl (290–300), Abū Yūsuf (200–331), ʿAbd Allāh b. Dāwūd al-Khuraybī (332–41), Asad b. ʿAmr al-Bajalī (341–4), Yaḥyā b. Zakariyyā' b. Abī Zā'ida (344–6), Yūsuf b. Khālid al-Samtī (247–9), Muḥammad b. al-Ḥasan al-Shaybānī (349–75).

[56] Makdisi, 'Ṭabaqāt-Biography'.

[57] Melchert, 'George Makdisi and Wael B. Hallaq', 311–12.

scholars who had the legitimate authority to determine religious orthodoxy'.[58] Makdisi was right to highlight the consequences of the *ṭabaqāt* genre for the formation of religious movements. The data I have presented in this chapter, which was not available to Makdisi when he was writing, suggests that the opponents of traditionalism were equally, if not more, industrious and creative in their adoption of the *ṭabaqāt* genre to shape religious orthodoxy. Makdisi was also right, in a separate publication, to draw attention to the interdependence of different genres of historical writing and how, together, these forms of writing impacted in profound ways the development of religious movements.[59] Following this, whilst at the same time disagreeing with Makdisi's emphasis on the agency of traditionalism, I have tried to show the interdependence of genres of historical writing (*manāqib*, *masānīd*, and *ṭabaqāt*) and their collective contribution in the ninth–tenth centuries to unmaking heresy and shaping orthodoxy. This is abundantly clear in the case of Abū Ḥanīfa's mnemohistory.[60] It was the *manāqib* and *masānīd* genres, not

[58] Makdisi, 'Ṭabaqāt-Biography', 373 (the emphasis is Makdisi's); and see Makdisi, *Ibn ʿAqil et la résurgence*, 67–8.

[59] Makdisi, *Ibn ʿAqil et la résurgence*, 68.

[60] This is not the place to offer a comparative history of *manāqib* works. I am currently preparing a research article on the history of *manāqib* works for the eponyms of the four Sunni *madhhabs*. Abū Ḥanīfa stands out for the sheer number of *manāqib* works produced for him between the ninth and eleventh centuries and, I would venture to add, throughout Islamic history all the way up to the twentieth century. The earliest *manāqib* work for al-Shāfiʿī was authored by Dāwūd al-Ẓāhirī, followed shortly after by Zakariyyā' b. Yaḥyā al-Sājī (d. 307/919). On al-Sājī see al-ʿAbbādī, *Kitāb Ṭabaqāt al-fuqahā'*, 61–2; al-Dhahabī, *Siyar*, 14: 197–200. On al-Sājī's authorship of *Manāqib al-Shāfiʿī* see al-Sakhāwī, *al-Jawāhir wa al-durar fī tarjamat Shaykh al-Islām Ibn Ḥajar*, ed. Ibrāhīm Bājis ʿAbd al-Majīd (Beirut: Dār Ibn Ḥazm, 1999), 1258–9, who provides an authoritative though far from complete list of *manāqib* works for eponyms. Another list of *manāqib* works for al-Shāfiʿī is provided by al-Subkī, *Ṭabaqāt al-Shāfiʿiyya al-kubrā*, 1: 243–5. For excerpts of al-Sājī's *Manāqib* work see al-ʿAbbādī, *Kitāb Ṭabaqāt al-fuqahā'*, 8; al-Dhahabī, *Siyar*, 10: 23–4, 27, 28, 29, 31, 35, 59; Ibn Ḥajar al-ʿAsqalānī, *Iṣāba*, 11: 118–19, 661–2; Ibn Ḥajar al-ʿAsqalānī, *Tawālī al-ta'sīs*, 24, 40, 48, 53, 55, 61, 76, 79, 80, 81–2, 83, 84, 85, 88, 90, 91, 92, 97, 99, 114, 116, 122, 125, 129, 132–3, 147, 151, 181, 182; al-Bayhaqī, *Manāqib al-Shāfiʿī*, 1: 204, 460; ʿAbd Allāh al-Anṣārī, *Dhamm al-kalām wa ahlihi*, ed. ʿAbd al-Raḥmān b. ʿAbd al-ʿAzīz al-Shibl (Medina: Maktabat al-ʿUlūm wa al-Ḥikam, 1998), where al-Sājī is cited a number of times; but it is only in the following citations wherein I believe one can find remnants of his lost *Manāqib al-Shāfiʿī*: 3: 15, 26, 27, 170, 4: 638, 5: 169. I would understand the production of three *manāqib* works for al-Shāfiʿī in the ninth century as resembling the case of Abū Ḥanīfa. Al-Shāfiʿī faced some hostile opposition, but it paled in comparison with Abū Ḥanīfa. See Melchert, 'The Adversaries of Aḥmad Ibn Ḥanbal', 248–9. It seems that opposition to al-Shāfiʿī was forthcoming from other proto-Sunni circles, too. See the number of refutations of al-Shāfiʿī prior to Ibn al-Labbād's (d. 333/944) better-known refutation described in Muranyi, *Beiträge zur Geschichte*, 73 (Ibn Ṭālib al-Qāḍī (d. 275/888–9): *Radd ʿalā al-Shāfiʿī*; *al-Radd ʿalā man khālafa Mālik*; *al-Radd ʿalā al-mukhālifīn min al-Kūfiyyīn*, the latter probably directed against proto-Ḥanafites); 87–8 (Abū ʿUmar al-Azdī (d. 288/901): *Kitāb al-Radd ʿalā al-Shāfiʿī*; and the author of *Kitāb Faḍā'il Mālik b. Anas*); 92–5 (al-Kinānī (d. 289/902): *Kitāb al-Ḥujja fī al-radd ʿalā al-*

the *ṭabaqāt* genre, that was dedicated to building the case for Abū Ḥanīfa's status as a patron saint of Sunni orthodoxy. This is not to suggest that *ṭabaqāt* works were nugatory to the success of Abū Ḥanīfa's adoption as a pillar of Sunni orthodoxy. As I have shown, *manāqib* works of the late ninth and tenth centuries incorporated *ṭabaqāt* sections into these books. *Manāqib* works posited a vision of medieval Islamic society and portrayed their eponym as an exemplar of religious orthodoxy in society. The *ṭabaqāt* sections within these works were included to argue that the eponym's religious orthodoxy had obtained the consensus of the Muslim community in the past and the present and in almost every region of the medieval Islamicate world.

This discussion of the themes in a new medieval source has been the starting point for documenting a transition from the ninth century – during which Abū Ḥanīfa was depicted as a heretic and deviant scholar among a group of proto-Sunni traditionalists – to the tenth century, which saw the emergence and popularisation of a genre of writing that was dedicated to undermining discourses of heresy against Abū Ḥanīfa and establishing his credentials as an orthodox Sunni. We have chosen to focus on Ibn Abī al-ʿAwwām al-Saʿdī's wide-ranging and diverse composition, whose central social function was to facilitate the unmaking of Abū Ḥanīfa as a heretic and to root him firmly within a shifting consensus in medieval Sunnism. It is imperative to recognise, though, that Ibn Abī al-ʿAwwām al-Saʿdī was not unique in this respect. In fact, his efforts represent a wider trend in the tenth–eleventh centuries, and it is to documenting this historical development that we now turn.

## 8.2 A History of *Manāqib* Works

In the middle of the sixteenth century in Yemen an industrious Ḥanafī scholar decided that he would not let his frustration with provincial religious trends get the better of him. Sharaf al-Dīn al-Qartabī (*c.*974/1566) explained that he had embarked on a long and fruitless search for *manāqib* works centred around Abū Ḥanīfa.[61] It pained him immensely that biographies of Abū Ḥanīfa were so scarce in his native Yemen and its environs. Al-

*Shāfiʿī*); 155–7 (Ibn al-Ḥaddād al-Ghassānī (d. 302/915): *Kitāb al-Radd ʿalā al-Shāfiʿī*). Incidentally, Aḥmad b. Malūl al-Tanūkhī (d. 262/875–6) authored *Faḍāʾil al-Awzāʿī*: see Muranyi, *Beiträge zur Geschichte*, 67–8. There was a *manāqib* work for al-Bukhārī: al-Samʿānī, *al-Taḥbīr fī al-muʿjam al-kabīr*, 2: 69. For the relationship between *manāqib* works and social crises see below, pp. 312.

[61] See Kaḥḥāla, *Muʿjam al-muʾallifīn* (Beirut: Muʾassasat al-Risāla, 1993), 1: 812 (no. 6016). I understand there is a published version of al-Qartabī's *Manāqib* (ed. Khālid Nihād Muṣṭafā al-Aʿẓamī (Baghdad: Maktabat Amīr Baghdādī, 2001)), but no library in the United Kingdom houses it.

Qartabī was not simply venting about the state of religious learning and education in Yemen. He was a diligent researcher. He knew of al-Ṣaymarī's biography of Abū Ḥanīfa.[62] He had studied Ibn Abī al-Wafā's biographical dictionary of Ḥanafīs with a keen eye and discovered references to a number of *manāqib* works.[63] Al-Qartabī mentions al-Ṭaḥāwī's biography.[64] His wide reading of medieval Islamic literature meant that he was aware of *manāqib* works not commonly known in Ḥanafī circles. He mentions that al-Ḥākim al-Nīshāpūrī's monumental *Tārīkh Nīshāpūr* refers to an extensive *manāqib* work authored by Muḥammad b. Aḥmad b. Shuʿayb.[65] Al-Qartabī is also familiar with well-known *manāqib* works: he refers to al-Muwaffaq b. Aḥmad al-Makkī's work;[66] Ibn Abī al-Wafā's *Bustān*;[67] al-Zamakhsharī's *Shaqā'iq al-Nuʿmān*;[68] Sibṭ b. al-Jawzī and his *al-Instiṣār al-imām a'immat al-amṣār*, the existence of which he learnt from Ibn Wahbān's *Sharḥ Manẓūma*;[69] ʿAbd Allāh b. Muḥammad b. Yaʿqūb al-Ḥārithī's *Kashf al-āthār fī manāqib Abī Ḥanīfa*.[70] Al-Qartabī also described works by Ḥanafīs

[62] Al-Qartabī, 'Qalā'id ʿuqūd al-durar wa al-ʿuqyān fī manāqib Abī Ḥanīfa', MS. Or. 8224, British Museum, 3b. See al-Ṣaymarī, *Akhbār Abī Ḥanīfa*.

[63] Al-Qartabī, 'Qalā'id', 4b. See Ibn Abī al-Wafā, *al-Jawāhir al-muḍiyya*.

[64] Al-Qartabī, 'Qalā'id', 3b. See the discussion on pp. 291-300 below.

[65] Al-Qartabī, 'Qalā'id', 3b. Al-Ḥākim's *Tārīkh* has not survived *in toto*, and I have been unable to identify this work and its author. One 'Muḥammad b. Aḥmad al-Shuʿaythī' appears in an *isnād* extolling Abū Ḥanīfa: see Ibn Ḥajar al-ʿAsqalānī, *Lisān al-mīzān* (Beirut: Dār al-Bashā'ir al-Islāmiyya, 2002), 1: 613. Ibn Ḥajar's source for this tradition is al-Ḥākim's *Tārīkh*. This may or may not be the author to whom al-Qartabī is referring.

[66] Al-Qartabī, 'Qalā'id', 3b. See al-Makkī, *Manāqib Abī Ḥanīfa*.

[67] Al-Qartabī, 'Qalā'id', 3b. Ibn Abī al-Wafā' refers to this book as *al-Bustān fī manāqib imāminā al-Nuʿmān* and includes sections from it in the beginning of *al-Jawāhir al-muḍiyya*. See Ibn Abī al-Wafā, *al-Jawāhir al-muḍiyya*, 1: 49–63. Other references to this book appear in Ibn Quṭlūbughā, *Tāj al-tarājim*, 196; Ibn Ṭūlūn, 'al-Ghuraf al-ʿaliyya fī tarājim muta'akhkhirī al-Ḥanafiyya', MS Şehid Ali Paşa 1924, Süleymaniye Library, Istanbul, 141b. I have seen two other copies of Ibn Ṭūlūn's *al-Ghurar*: MS Taymūr Tārīkh 631, Dār al-Kutub, is incomplete, as it begins with the letter *alif* and ends with *ẓā'* (I thank Torsten Wollina for making me aware of the Taymūriyya manuscript); I was unable to identify the entry for Ibn Abī al-Wafā' in MS Or. 3046, British Museum (for a description of this manuscript see Rieu, *Supplement to the Catalogue of the Arabic Manuscripts*, 434–5).

[68] Al-Qartabī, 'Qalā'id', 3b. See Yāqūt al-Ḥamawī, *Muʿjam al-udabā'*, 6: 2687–91 (Dār al-Gharb al-Islāmī edn.) (the title of the work given is *Shaqā'iq al-Nuʿmān fī ḥaqā'iq al-Nuʿmān*); Ibn Quṭlūbughā, *Tāj al-tarājim*, 292; Kātib Çelebi, *Kashf al-ẓunūn*, ed. Şerefettin Yaltaka and Rifat Bilge (Istanbul: Maarif Matbaasi, 1951), 2: 1056, 1838.

[69] Al-Qartabī, 'Qalā'id', 4a. Sibṭ b. al-Jawzī, *al-Intiṣār wa al-tarjīḥ li al-madhhab al-ṣaḥīḥ*, ed. Muḥammad Zāhid al-Kawtharī (Cairo: Maṭbaʿat al-Anwār, 1941). I could not locate a reference to Sibṭ b. Jawzī's work in Ibn al-Shiḥna, 'Sharḥ manẓūmat Ibn Wahbān', MS 14866, Jāmiʿ Umm al-Qurā, Maktabat al-Malik ʿAbd Allāh b. ʿAbd al-ʿAzīz, 409 fols. (though Ibn Shiḥna's commentary contains one paragraph on the *Manāqib* of Abū Ḥanīfa, at 2a); al-Dhahabī, *al-ʿIbar fī khabar man ghabar*, ed. Ṣalāḥ al-Dīn al-Munajjid (Kuwait: Dā'irat al-Maṭbūʿāt wa al-Nashr, 1960), 5: 220 refers to Sibṭ b. al-Jawzī's authorship of a *manāqib* book on Abū Ḥanīfa.

[70] Al-Qartabī, 'Qalā'id', 4a. See my discussion on pp. 300-302 below of al-Subadhmūnī's work.

and non-Ḥanafis which contained *manāqib* sections devoted to Abū Ḥanīfa at the beginning and towards the end of their works: Abū al-Ḥusayn al-Qudūrī's *Manāqib* at the beginning of his *Sharḥ Mukhtaṣar* of al-Karkhī;[71] Muḥammad b. ʿAbd al-Raḥmān al-Ghaznawī;[72] Aḥmad b. Sulaymān b. Saʿīd at the end of his *Durar*;[73] Shams al-Dīn Yūsuf b. ʿUmar b. Yūsuf al-Ṣūfī al-Kamārūrī (d. 832/1429) in his *Jāmiʿ al-Muḍmarāt wa al-mushkilāt*;[74] Ibn ʿAbd al-Barr's *Intiqā'*;[75] Shams al-Dīn Yūsuf b. Abī Saʿīd b. Aḥmad al-Sijistānī in his *Munyat al-Muftī*;[76] Sharaf al-Dīn Ismāʿīl b. ʿĪsā al-Awghānī al-Makkī in his *Mukhtaṣar al-Musnad*;[77] Abū al-Bafā b. Abī al-Ḍibā' al-Qurashī al-Makkī in his *Mukhtaṣar al-Musnad*;[78] Abū ʿAbd Allāh Muḥammad b. Khusraw al-Balkhī in the beginning of his *Musnad*;[79] the author of *Safīnat al-ʿulūm*;[80] Abū Jaʿfar Aḥmad b. ʿAbd Allāh al-Qasam al-Sarmāw[r]ī al-Shīrāzī had a chapter in his *Tarjīḥ madhhab Abī Ḥanīfa*;[81] Abū al-ʿAbbās Aḥmad b. Muḥammad Maḥmūd al-Ghaznawī included a *manāqib* chapter in his *al-Muqaddima*;[82] ʿUthmān b. ʿAlī b. Muḥammad al-Shīrāzī's *al-Īḍāḥ li ʿulūm al-nikāḥ*;[83] Abū Isḥāq al-Shīrāzī al-Shāfiʿī in his *Ṭabaqāt*;[84] and Muḥyī al-Dīn al-Nawawī in *Tahdhīb al-asmā'*.[85] Al-Qartabī had done his homework to a very high standard, and one would not risk second guessing him when he adds that he could have mentioned many more works. However, al-Qartabī turns his attention to questions that readers might have posed to him:[86]

If you ask why, after mentioning all these works, I commit myself to writing a *Manāqib* work, I respond with this: all of these aforementioned works are either lost or not available in our lands, nor in the environs of Yemen. We have searched far and wide and for many years, but we have found no way to access them. The reason for this is that the detractors of Abū Ḥanīfa talk nonsense about him and

71 Al-Qartabī, 'Qalā'id', see pp. 259 above.
72 Al-Qartabī, 'Qalā'id', 4a.
73 Al-Qartabī, 'Qalā'id', 4a.
74 Al-Qartabī, 'Qalā'id', 4a. See al-Kādūrī, 'Jāmiʿ al-Muḍmarāt wa al-mushkilāt fī sharḥ Mukhtaṣar al-Qudūrī', MS 1409, Maktabat al-Malik ʿAbd al-ʿAzīz, 535 fols., 5b–6a (*faṣl fī faḍl al-fiqh wa dhikr al-fuqahā'*); al-Kādūrī, 'Jāmiʿ al-Muḍmarāt wa al-mushkilāt fī sharḥ Mukhtaṣar al-Qudūrī', MS 1697, Maktabat al-Malik ʿAbd al-ʿAzīz, 657 fols., 4b–6a (*faṣl fī faḍl al-fiqh wa dhikr al-fuqahā'*). MS Vollers 0356, Leipzig, Refaiya, does not contain the first two chapters of the book. On al-Kādūrī/Kamārūrī see al-Laknawī, *al-Fawā'id al-bahiyya fī tarājim al-Ḥanafiyya*, ed. Muḥammad Badr al-Dīn Abū Firās al-Niʿsānī (Cairo: Maṭbaʿat al-Saʿāda, 1906), 230= Cawnpore [Kanpur]: al-Maṭbaʿa al-Muṣṭafā li Muḥammad Muṣṭafā Khān, 1876) 96; Brockelmann, *GAL*, 1: 183 and supp. 1: 296, where he gives the author's name as al-Kādūzī; al-Ziriklī, *al-Aʿlām*, 8: 244 (15th edn.) (s.v. 'al-Ṣūfī'); Kātib Çelebi, *Kashf al-ẓunūn*, 1: 574, 2: 1713, 1: 455 (Maarif Matbaasi edn.); Kaḥḥāla, *Muʿjam al-mu'allifīn* (Beirut: Makabat al-Muthannā, 1957), 13: 320–1.
75 Al-Qartabī, 'Qalā'id', 4a; Ibn ʿAbd al-Barr, *al-Intiqā'*.
76 Al-Qartabī, 'Qalā'id', 4a.
77 Al-Qartabī, 'Qalā'id', 4a.
78 Al-Qartabī, 'Qalā'id', 4b.
79 Al-Qartabī, 'Qalā'id', 4b.
80 Al-Qartabī, 'Qalā'id', 4b.
81 Al-Qartabī, 'Qalā'id', 4b.
82 Al-Qartabī, 'Qalā'id', 4b.
83 Al-Qartabī, 'Qalā'id', 4b.
84 Al-Qartabī, 'Qalā'id', 4b.
85 Al-Qartabī, 'Qalā'id', 4b.
86 Al-Qartabī, 'Qalā'id', 5a.

seek to obliterate his memory. This is proven by the fact that the *Manāqib* book of al-Ṣaymarī was owned by someone who was opposed fanatically to Ḥanafīs. This man would never show the book to anyone. He never mentioned anything from the book to the day he died. Finally, I managed to purchase this book and I became its owner.

In al-Qartabī's assessment, the dearth of *Manāqib Abī Ḥanīfa* works was a consequence of the strength and purpose of Abū Ḥanīfa's detractors. The prevailing sense of hostility towards Abū Ḥanīfa and his followers, in addition to the predominance of the Shāfiʿī school in Yemen, had contributed to the censorship and suppression of *manāqib* works for Abū Ḥanīfa. Writing in sixteenth-century Yemen, more than six centuries after Abū Ḥanīfa's complete integration into medieval Sunni orthodoxy, al-Qartabī frames his *manāqib* work in the context of discourses of heresy against Abū Ḥanīfa. A history of the *Manāqib Abī Ḥanīfa* literature, one more complete than al-Qartabī's select bibliography, demonstrates that in the second half of the ninth and the tenth centuries a prolific *manāqib* genre arose out of similar concerns. It is to documenting this history that we now turn, first by listing *manāqib* works composed for Abū Ḥanīfa between the late ninth and early eleventh centuries; and, second, by examining particular works to understand the development of the genre across these centuries. As we can see from this list, *manāqib* works began to be composed in the immediate aftermath of ninth-century discourses of heresy against Abū Ḥanīfa.

1. Zakariyyā' b. Yaḥyā b. al-Ḥārith al-Nīshāpūrī (d. 298/910).
2. Abū al-ʿAbbās Aḥmad b. al-Ṣalt (d. 302/914).
3. Abū Jaʿfar al-Ṭaḥāwī (d. 321/933).
4. Ibn Kās al-Nakhaʿī (d. 324/935).
5. ʿAbd Allāh b. Muḥammad b. Yaʿqūb al-Ḥārithī al-Subadhmūnī (d. 340/952).
6. *Ibn ʿUqda (d. 333/944).
7. Ibn Abī al-ʿAwwām al-Saʿdī (d. 345/956).
8. Mukram b. Aḥmad al-Qāḍī (d. 345/956).
9. Muḥammad b. Aḥmad b. Shuʿayb b. Hārūn b. Mūsā (d. 357/968).
10. Abū Layth Naṣr b. Muḥammad b. Aḥmad al-Samarqandī (d. 373/983), *Tuḥfat al-anām fī manāqib al-a'imma al-arbaʿa al-aʿlām*.[87]
11. *Abū ʿAbd Allāh al-Marzubānī (d. 378/988).

[87] Arberry, *The Chester Beatty Library*, 6: 3936. This manuscript is attributed to Abū Layth, but it cannot have been written by him because fol. 1b cites Abū Isḥāq al-Shīrāzī (d. 476/1083) with respect to Abū Ḥanīfa's biography: Abū Layth Naṣr b. Muḥammad b. Aḥmad al-Samarqandī (attr.), 'Tuḥfat al-anām fī manāqib al- a'imma al-arbaʿa al-aʿlām', MS 3936, Chester Beatty Library, fols. 1–91a. I have read the manuscript once, and I have seen no name of the author. However, the author does refer to a work of his called *al-*

12. *Abū ʿAbd Allāh al-Dabīlī Muḥammad b. Wahbān (d. 385/995).
13. *Abū al-Mufaḍḍal al-Shaybānī (d. 387/997).
14. Ibn Dakhīl (d. 387–8/997–8).
15. Anonymous, *Maqām Abī Ḥanīfa ʿinda al-mulūk*.[88]
16. Abū al-Ḥusayn al-Qudūrī (d. 428/1037).
17. Maḥmūd b. Manṣūr b. Abī al-Faḍl (d. after 428/1037), *Faṣl ʿalā taqdīm madhhab Abī Ḥanīfa*.
18. Al-Ṣaymarī (d. 436/1045).

### *Beginnings: Ninth Century*

It is reasonable to assume from *isnād*s found in later works that individuals were transmitting and circulating reports to defend Abū Ḥanīfa in the ninth century. Figures such as Ḥammād b. Abī Ḥanīfa and Shujāʿ b. al-Thaljī are frequently cited in later *manāqib* works to this effect. The actual composition of *manāqib* works for Abū Ḥanīfa, however, first began in the late ninth century.

### *Nīshāpūr: Ninth Century*

Zakariyyāʾ b. Yaḥyā b. al-Ḥārith al-Nīshāpūrī (d. 298/910) should be considered as the first author of a *Manāqib Abī Ḥanīfa* work. Abū Yaḥyā al-Bazzār, as he was known to the Ḥanafī biographical tradition, was a native of Nīshāpūr. He had studied in Khurāsān, under the province's senior proto-Sunni scholars. Perhaps the most significant detail about his teachers is that one of them was Isḥāq b. Rāhawayh, a ninth-century proto-Sunni traditionalist who played a leading role in the diffusion of discourses of heresy against Abū Ḥanīfa.

Abū Yaḥyā al-Bazzār should be seen as a pivotal figure in Nīshāpūrī Ḥanafism during the ninth–tenth centuries. He seems to be a connecting link to many of Khurāsān's key Ḥanafī scholars. His teachers included Aḥmad b. Muḥammad b. Naṣr (d. 280/893–4), whom al-Ḥākim in his *Tārīkh Nīshāpūr* had described as the chief of the Ḥanafīs in his time (*shaykh ahl al-raʾy fī ʿaṣrihi wa raʾīsuhum*).[89] Another of Abū Yaḥyā al-Bazzār's eastern Ḥanafī teachers was Sahl b. ʿAmmār b. ʿAbd

*Ḥilya* on fols. 10b–11a, which he describes briefly. This fact, along with the emphasis on al-Shāfiʿī's *manāqib* in the manuscript, makes me conclude that the author of the manuscript is Sayf al-Dīn al-Qaffāl al-Shāshī (d. 507/1113–14): al-Shashī, *Ḥilyat al-ʿulamāʾ fī maʿrifat madhāhib al-fuqahāʾ*, ed. Yāsīn Aḥmad Ibrāhīm Darādika (Amman: Dār al-Bāz, 1988). This manuscript is listed as belonging to Sayf al-Dīn al-Shāshī's oeuvre in Brockelmann, *GAL*, 1: 489–90, supp. 1: 674.

[88] Sezgin, *GAS*, 1: 410. [89] Ibn Abī al-Wafāʾ, *al-Jawāhir al-muḍiyya*, 1: 320–1.

Allāh al-ʿAtakī (d. 267/880–1). He, too, was a native of Nīshāpūr, but his renown had spread to Khurāsān's other major cities. The local histories of Nīshāpūr and Herāt – al-Ḥākim's *Tārīkh Nīshāpūr* and *Muntakhab Tārīkh Herāt* – contained notices for him. He received appointments as a qadi in both Ṭūs and Herāt.[90] Al-Bazzār's students were also notable Ḥanafīs in Nīshāpūr. His nephew Aḥmad b. Muḥammad b. Sahl Abū al-Ḥasan b. Sahluwayh (d. 352/963) was described by al-Ḥākim as one of the leading Ḥanafīs of his time.[91] The extremely well-travelled and well-regarded Ḥanafī qadi Abū al-Ḥusayn Aḥmad b. Muḥammad b. ʿAbd Allāh had also studied with Abū Yaḥyā al-Bazzār in Nīshāpūr before going on to occupy judgeships in Mawṣil, Ramla, Mecca, Medina, and Nīshāpūr. Abū al-Ḥusayn had a sojourn in Baghdad, too, where he came to the attention of the caliph al-Muqtadir's (r. 295–320/908–32) vizier, ʿAlī b. ʿĪsā (d. 334/946). He died in Nīshāpūr in 351/962.[92] Another of Abū Yaḥyā al-Bazzār's students was Khadīja (d. 372/982–3?). She was the daughter of Nīshāpūr's Ḥanafī judge, Muḥammad b. Aḥmad Rajā' al-Jūzajānī (d. 285/898–9?).[93] Finally, there was Muḥammad b. ʿAbd Allāh b. Dīnār (d. 338/949), known as Abū ʿAbd Allāh al-Nīshāpūrī, and who was laid to rest beside Abū Ḥanīfa. He is particularly important for our purposes, because al-Ḥākim al-Nīshāpūrī informs us that this student transmitted the majority of Abū Yaḥyā al-Bazzār's books.[94] It is possible, therefore, that this student would have transmitted Abū Yaḥyā al-Bazzār's *Manāqib Abī Ḥanīfa*.

We know that Abū Yaḥyā al-Bazzār composed a *manāqib* work because al-Ḥākim al-Muwaffaq b. al-Makkī al-Khwārizmī (d. 568/1172) tells us about this book – and, indeed, cites it.[95] The fact that the first *manāqib* work defending Abū Ḥanīfa against discourses of heresy originated in Nīshāpūr corresponds to a number of ninth-century historical trends. Discourses of heresy against Abū Ḥanīfa were certainly a transregional phenomenon, but they were especially acute in the province of Khurāsān. Proto-Sunni traditionalists such as al-Bukhārī and Isḥāq b. Rāhawayh

[90] Ibn Abī al-Wafā', *al-Jawāhir al-muḍiyya*, 2: 239–40.

[91] Ibn Abī al-Wafā', *al-Jawāhir al-muḍiyya*, 1: 270–1.

[92] Ibn Abī al-Wafā', *al-Jawāhir al-muḍiyya*, 1: 285–8.

[93] Ibn Abī al-Wafā', *al-Jawāhir al-muḍiyya*, 3: 82, 4: 120.

[94] Ibn Abī al-Wafā', *al-Jawāhir al-muḍiyya*, 3: 188; al-Khaṭīb al-Baghdādī, *Tārīkh Baghdād*, 3: 474–6; al-Dhahabī, *Tārīkh al-Islām*, 25: 167; al-Dhahabī, *Siyar*, 15: 382–3; Ibn al-Jawzī, *al-Muntaẓam*, 14: 78; Ibn Taghrībirdī, *al-Nujūm al-zāhira fī mulūk Miṣr wa al-Qāhira* (n.p.: Wizārat al-Thaqāfa, 1963), 3: 300; al-Ṣafadī, *al-Wāfī bi al-wafāyāt*, 3: 316 (Dār al-Iḥyā' al-Turāth al-ʿArabī edn.); al-Yāfiʿī, *Mir'āt al-jinān*, ed. Khalīl al-Manṣūr (Beirut: Dār al-Kutub al-ʿIlmiyya, 1997), 2: 327 or 2: 246.

[95] Al-Muwaffaq al-Makkī, *Manāqib Abī Ḥanīfa*, 53. See also Kātib Çelebi, *Kashf al-ẓunūn*, 2: 1839 (Dār Iḥyā' edn.).

were at the forefront of condemnations of Abū Ḥanīfa. Isḥāq b. Rāhawayh, in particular, had gained a reputation in Khurāsān and beyond for his hostility to Abū Ḥanīfa and proto-Ḥanafīs. Abū Yaḥyā al-Bazzār had studied with Isḥāq b. Rāhawayh. He cannot have been aloof to Isḥāq b. Rāhawayh's condemnations of Abū Ḥanīfa. As a religious scholar from Nīshāpūr who had come under the tutelage of one of Abū Ḥanīfa's prominent detractors, Abū Yaḥyā al-Bazzār had good and compelling reasons to compose a *manāqib* work in order to respond to discourses of heresy against Abū Ḥanīfa and to establish his orthodox credentials.

### *Iraq: Ninth–Tenth Centuries*

A brief *manāqib* work is attributed to a second scholar active in the late ninth century. Abū al-ʿAbbās Aḥmad b. al-Ṣalt (d. 302/914) is credited with *Faṣl fī manāqib Abī Ḥanīfa*. Eerik Dickinson, who has studied the controversy surrounding Aḥmad b. al-Ṣalt, is of the opinion that he did not actually compose a *manāqib* work.[96] Instead, he is believed to have circulated numerous reports concerning the *manāqib* of Abū Ḥanīfa. These reports did enter a number of late ninth- and early tenth-century *manāqib* works to which better attestations exist.

There seems to be no obvious connection between the authors of the first and second *Manāqib Abī Ḥanīfa* works. Ibn Kās al-Nakhaʿī (d. 324/935) was a Kufan scholar, who spent most of his life in Baghdad. He had acquired a reputation as a leading representative of Ḥanafism, but this did not stop him being recognised as a reliable ḥadīth scholar. It seems he was in demand as a judge in the late ninth and early tenth centuries. He is supposed to have left Kufa towards the end of the ninth century and taken up judgeships in the province of Shām. At some point he took up residence in Baghdad, but was later on the move again, after being appointed judge in Ramla. After his term came to an end he returned to Baghdad. It was during a journey from Baghdad to Samarra that he drowned, soon after on the tenth day of Muḥarram.[97] In the midst of all these travels and appointments, Ibn Kās found time to compose *Kitāb al-Khiṣāl*, to which he attached a volume entitled *Faḍā'il al-Imām*.[98]

[96] Dickinson, 'Aḥmad b. al-Ṣalt', 413 n. 34.

[97] Al-Khaṭīb al-Baghdādī, *Tārīkh Baghdād*, 13: 540–1.

[98] See al-Sakhāwī, *al-Jawāhir*, 1255. On Ibn Kās see Ibn ʿAsākir, *Tārīkh madīnat Dimashq*, 43: 12 (al-ʿAmrawī edn.); al-Samʿānī, *al-Ansāb*, 5: 475–6 (Dār al-Jinān edn.); Ibn Kās's book caught the attention of a Mālikī peer, Abū Bakr al-Qurṭubī (d. 381/991–2), who responded with a *Kitāb al-Khiṣāl* for the Mālikī *madhhab*. See al-Ṣafadī, al-*Wāfī bi al-wafāyāt*, 5: 120 (Dār Iḥyā' al-Turāth al-ʿArabī edn.).

### *Egypt and al-Ṭaḥāwī's* Manāqib*: Ninth–Tenth Centuries*

Perhaps the most significant *manāqib* work of the tenth century was composed by the Egyptian scholar Abū Jaʿfar al-Ṭaḥāwī.[99] The late ninth and early tenth centuries were precarious times for Egyptian Ḥanafism. The rise of the Ṭūlūnids under Aḥmad b. Ṭūlūn (r. 254–70/868–84) and his sons witnessed the gradual waning of both Ḥanafism and Mālikism, giving way to greater dependence on Shāfiʿism.[100] Ibn Ṭūlūn's son, Abū Maʿadd ʿAdnān, was particularly proud of this shift in allegiance:[101]

God cast love for al-Shāfiʿī and his followers into my father's heart. Disturbances and clashes broke out between the Shāfiʿīs and Mālikīs in Egypt and my father always sided with the Shāfiʿīs. . . . I heard my father say on more than one occasion to anyone who came to him with news of disturbances among the Shāfiʿīs and Mālikīs, 'I am a Shāfiʿī.' He encouraged his deputies to side with the Shāfiʿīs, too. In this way, God empowered the Shāfiʿīs at the hands of my father and weakened the position of the Mālikīs.

During the first decade of Aḥmad b. Ṭūlūn's governorship Egyptian Ḥanafism had maintained its dominance under the protection of its erstwhile qadi, Bakkār b. Qutayba (d. 270/884).[102] Aḥmad b. Ṭūlūn had been successful in his attempts to obtain a considerable degree of independence from the ʿAbbāsid empire. He had secured both fiscal and administrative control over the province by removing the heads of the *dīwān* (chancery) and *barīd* (postal system).[103] Shāfiʿī scholars received judgeships, and students of al-Shāfiʿī such as al-Rabīʿ gained a pre-eminent status under the Ṭūlūnids.[104] The judiciary, however, remained in the hands al-Mutawakkil's appointee, Bakkār b. Qutayba. A political crisis provided Aḥmad b. Ṭūlūn with an opportunity to sideline Bakkār. The latter's refusal to sign a document declaring al-Muwaffaq's regency no longer legitimate gave Aḥmad b. Ṭūlūn the pretext he needed to

[99] Incidentally, al-Ṭaḥāwī himself became the subject of a *manāqib* work: al-Biqāʿī, 'Manāqib al-Imām al-Ṭaḥāwī', MS 12831, Maktabat al-Asad al-Ẓāhiriyya, 16 fols.

[100] On the schools of law in Egypt under the Ṭūlūnids see Melchert, *The Formation of the Sunni Schools of Law*, 119–22; El Shamsy, *The Canonization of Islamic Law*, 140–2; Tillier, 'The Qāḍīs of Fusṭāṭ-Miṣr'; and Hassan, *Les Tulunides*, 88.

[101] Ibn ʿAsākir, *Tārīkh madīnat Dimashq*, 40: 54 (al-ʿAmrawī edn.) (*fa alqā Allāh fī qalb Abī ḥubb al-Shāfiʿī wa ḥubb aṣḥābihi. Wa kānat takūn bi Miṣr khuṣūmāt wa fitan bayn al-shāfiʿiyyīn wa al-mālikiyyīn, fa kāna Abī abadan yamīlu ilā al-shāfiʿiyyīn. Qāla Abū Maʿadd: fa samiʿtu Abī ghayr marra yaqūl li man yarfaʿu ilayhi al-akhbār bi khuṣūma li al-shāfiʿiyyīn wa al-mālikiyyīn, anā Shāfiʿī. Wa yataqaddamu ilā khulafāʾihi an yamīlū ilā al-shāfiʿiyyīn ḥattā qawwā Allāh amr al-shāfiʿiyyīn ʿalā yaday Abī wa ḍuʿifa amr al-mālikiyyīn*). See also El Shamsy, *The Canonization of Islamic Law*, 141–2.

[102] For his life and career see al-Maqrīzī, *Kitāb al-Muqaffā al-kabīr*, 2: 442–53.

[103] Bianquis, 'Autonomous Egypt'.

[104] Ibn ʿAsākir, *Tārīkh madīnat Dimashq*, 40: 54–5 (al-ʿAmrawī edn.).

marginalise him. The Ḥanafī judge was arrested and unable to carry out his judicial duties.[105]

Al-Ṭaḥāwī would have been intimately familiar with these political intrigues, court politics, and their impact upon social attitudes to Abū Ḥanīfa and Ḥanafism in the late ninth and early tenth centuries. After all, he had been a student of Bakkār b. Qutayba.[106] And, in the wake of Bakkār b. Qutayba's death, he served as the secretary to Muḥammad ʿAbda b. Ḥarb al-ʿAbbādānī (d. 313/926–7) in the *maẓālim* courts.[107]

Moreover, he had undergone a fairly public transition from Shāfiʿīsm to Ḥanafism, which saw him part ways with the *madhhab* of his uncle, al-Muzanī, and establish himself as a pioneer of Ḥanafism's traditionalisation in the ninth and tenth centuries. This traditionalisation entailed, among other things – such as writing a traditionalist creed, analysed earlier in this monograph – establishing a greater degree of harmony between juristic reasoning and ḥadīth sources in order to demonstrate the scriptural basis for Ḥanafī jurisprudence.[108] The primary sources contain diverging accounts for the reasons behind al-Ṭaḥāwī's change in legal affiliation. There is the view that a stern reprimand from al-Muzanī served as the trigger for his conversion to Ḥanafism.[109] There is also the view that al-Ṭaḥāwī's conversion was on account of his having witnessed al-Muzanī's more than frequent study of proto-Ḥanafī books.[110] The dissenting opinion is given by Ibn Yūnus al-Ṣadafī, who claims to quote al-Ṭaḥāwī to the effect that the arrival in Egypt of the Ḥanafī Aḥmad b. Abī ʿImrān (d. 280/893) prompted

105 See al-Maqrīzī, *Kitāb al-Muqaffā al-kabīr*, 2: 444–9, where, as Melchert (*The Formation of the Sunni Schools of Law*, 121 n. 33) rightly notes, al-Maqrīzī insists that Bakkār b. Qutayba refused to legitimise Aḥmad b. Ṭūlūn's actions despite the fact that the document he provided named Bakkār b. Qutayba as a witness and signatory to it: Ibn Ḥajar al-ʿAsqalānī, *Rafʿ al-iṣr*, 98–197, 105 = *Rafʿ al-iṣr ʿan quḍāt Miṣr* in al-Kindī, *al-Wulāt wa kitāb al-quḍāt*, 501–614, 505–14, 512, 226 (al-Kindī's account of Bakkār b. Qutayba's dispute with Ibn Ṭūlūn); Ibn Khallikān, *Wafayāt al-aʿyān*, 1: 279; Ibn Abī al-Wafāʾ, *al-Jawāhir al-muḍiyya*, 1: 461; al-Dhahabī, *Siyar*, 12: 600–602.

106 Ibn Abī al-Wafāʾ, *al-Jawāhir al-muḍiyya*, 1: 165.

107 Ibn Ḥajar al-ʿAsqalānī, *Rafʿ al-iṣr ʿan quḍāt Miṣr* in al-Kindī, *al-Wulāt wa kitāb al-quḍāt*, 516; Ibn Abī al-Wafāʾ, *al-Jawāhir al-muḍiyya*, 1: 165; al-Dhahabī, *Tadhkirat al-ḥuffāẓ*, 3: 30; Ibn Ḥajar al-ʿAsqalānī, *Lisān al-mīzān*, 1: 274–82, 275 (Hyderabad edn.).

108 See Melchert, *The Formation of the Sunni Schools of Law*, 116–23; El Shamsy, *The Canonization of Islamic Law*, 205–7; Brunelle, 'From Text to Law', 281–2, where she describes al-Ṭaḥāwī's method as 'practical hermeneutics'.

109 Abū Isḥāq al-Shīrāzī, *Ṭabaqāt al-fuqahāʾ*, ed. Iḥsān ʿAbbās (Beirut: Dār al-Rāʾid al-ʿArabī, 1970), 142; al-Ṣaymarī, *Akhbār Abī Ḥanīfa*, 168. The relationship between al-Muzanī and al-Ṭaḥāwī has been discussed at length by Jacques, 'Contestation and Resolution'. See also the discussion of Saʿd al-Dīn Ünāl in al-Ṭaḥāwī, *Aḥkām al-Qurʾān al-Karīm*, ed. Saʿd al-Dīn Ünāl (Istanbul: ISAM, 1995), 16–19 (editor's introduction).

110 Al-Khalīlī, *al-Irshād*, 1: 431 (s.v. 'al-Muzanī') (Riyadh edn.); al-Yāfiʿī, *Mirʾāt al-jinān wa ʿibrat al-yaqẓān* (Hyderabad: Dāʾirat al-Maʿarif al-Niẓāmiyya, 1919), 2: 281; al-Ṣaymarī, *Akhbār Abī Ḥanīfa*, 168.

his embrace of Ḥanafism.[111] Al-Ṭaḥāwī's conversion from Shāfiʿīsm to Ḥanafism highlights the greater degree of competition and hostility that obtained among adherents of both *madhhab*s. According to Ibn Zūlāq (d. 386/996), when, for example, Bakkār b. Qutayba came to learn of al-Muzanī's criticisms of Abū Ḥanīfa contained in the former's *Mukhtaṣar*, Bakkār responded with a refutation of al-Shāfiʿī.[112]

It was in this milieu of charged exchanges, attempts to influence or control the judiciary, and the entangled webs of legal affiliations and family loyalties that al-Ṭaḥāwī decided to compose a *Manāqib Abī Ḥanīfa* work.[113] Al-Ṭaḥāwī's *Manāqib* work has not survived, but this does not mean that we cannot say anything about the content and context of al-Ṭaḥāwī's endeavour. It is thanks to the recent publication of a *manāqib* work dated to the tenth century – a work that is analysed in this study for the first time in modern scholarship – that we can now better understand the nature of al-Ṭaḥāwī's *Manāqib Abī Ḥanīfa*.

Ibn Abī al-ʿAwwām al-Saʿdī is a successor to the Egyptian tradition of *manāqib* writing around the person of Abū Ḥanīfa. His *Faḍā'il Abī Ḥanīfa* has been studied earlier in this chapter. Here, it is important to note that his work seems to preserve a significant proportion of al-Ṭaḥāwī's now lost *manāqib* work. Ibn Abī al-ʿAwwām al-Saʿdī's work consists of 900 reports; 20 per cent (183 reports) of the *Faḍā'il Abī Ḥanīfa* is narrated from al-Ṭaḥāwī. Ibn Abī al-ʿAwwām's *Faḍā'il Abī Ḥanīfa* is the earliest evidence for the fact that *manāqib* works devoted to Abū Ḥanīfa brought together two forms of historical writing: *manāqib* reports concerning an eponym and a *ṭabaqāt* section. The material attributed to al-Ṭaḥāwī appears in reports discussing the life and career of Abū Ḥanīfa, but al-Ṭaḥāwī is cited frequently in the *ṭabaqāt* section treating various students and disciples of Abū Ḥanīfa. In the light of this, we can assume that al-Ṭaḥāwī's *manāqib* work would have comprised both *manāqib* and *ṭabaqāt* sections.

We can also say something about al-Ṭaḥāwī's sources and what this might tell us about the circulation and dissemination of *manāqib* works and their content. It is the proportion of material that emerges from Egyptian qadis that is particularly striking. Three of al-Ṭaḥāwī's most frequent sources for reports about Abū Ḥanīfa and his followers are

[111] Ibn Yūnus al-Ṣadafī, *Tārīkh Ibn Yūnus*, 1: 21.

[112] Ibn Ḥajar al-ʿAsqalānī, *Rafʿ al-iṣr*, 105; al-Suyūṭī, *Ḥusn al-muḥāḍara*, 1: 433 (Cairo edn.) = 1: 463 (Aleppo edn.).

[113] Al-Ṣaymarī, *Akhbār Abī Ḥanīfa*, 37, 66; Ibn Abī al-Wafā', *al-Jawāhir al-muḍiyya*, 1: 277; Ibn Quṭlūbughā, *Tāj al-tarājim*, 100–102, at 101. Kātib Çelebi, *Kashf al-ẓunūn*, 2: 1836–7 (Matbaasi edn.). For information on al-Ṭaḥāwī's family (father, offspring, and grandchildren) see al-Samʿānī, *al-Ansāb*, 4: 53 (Dār al-Jinān edn.); and concerning his background and travels see Flügel, 'Die Classen'.

Aḥmad b. Abī ʿImrān, Bakkār b. Qutayba, and Abū Khāzim. All three men served as qadis in Egypt and taught al-Ṭaḥāwī.

Bakkār b. Qutayba was appointed qadi by al-Mutawakkil. His appointment began on Friday 10 September 860 and came to an end twenty-four years later in 884, and his judicial career was the subject of extensive commentary in medieval Arabic sources. Bakkār b. Qutayba was a ḥadīth scholar, too. Scholars such as Abū ʿAwāna and Ibn Khuzayma narrated traditions on his authority, and he was cited in some respected medieval ḥadīth collections.[114] He was reported to have written a number of works in the field of jurisprudence: *al-Shurūṭ*; *Kitāb al-Maḥāḍir wa al-sijillāt*; *Kitāb al-Wathā'iq wa al-ʿuhūd*; and a refutation of al-Shāfiʿī in response to criticisms of Abū Ḥanīfa in al-Muzanī's *Mukhtaṣar*, which the latter alleged were based exactly on al-Shāfiʿī's words.[115] Most of these books were particularly relevant to a qadi's career. All that has survived, however, of Bakkār b. Qutayba's oeuvre is a brief collection of his ḥadīth reports.[116] Before he came to Egypt, Bakkār b. Qutayba had lived and studied in Basra. It was there that he learnt jurisprudence from a leading Ḥanafī jurist and qadi, Hilāl b. Ra'y. Many of al-Ṭaḥāwī's *manāqib* reports from Bakkār b. Qutayba originate with Hilāl b. Ra'y.

One consequence of Bakkār b. Qutayba's involvement in Ṭūlūnid political machinations was that it created a vacancy within the judiciary. A qadi was needed, and the position was given to another of al-Ṭaḥāwī's teachers: the Ḥanafī judge Aḥmad b. Abī ʿImrān (d. 280/893).[117] Like his predecessor, Aḥmad b. Abī ʿImrān was in some respects an outsider – Ibn Yūnus included an entry for him in his ' History of outsiders who came to Egypt (*al-ghurabā' alladhīna qadimū Miṣr*)'.[118] He was originally from

[114] Al-Dhahabī, *Siyar*, 12: 599–605. For other biographical details see al-Kindī, *Kitāb al-Wulāt wa kitāb al-quḍāt*, 76, 477, 505; Ibn ʿAbd al-Ḥakam, *Futūḥ Miṣr* (London: n.p., 1858), 276; Ibn Ḥibbān, *Kitāb al-Thiqāt*, 8: 152 (Dā'irat al-Maʿārif edn.); Ibn Abī al-Wafā', *al-Jawāhir al-muḍiyya*, 1: 458–9; al-Suyūṭī, *Ḥusn al-muḥāḍara*, 1: 433 (Cairo edn.); Yūsuf b. Shāhīn, 'al-Nujūm al-ẓāhira', 26a–27b.

[115] Ibn Abī al-Wafā', *al-Jawāhir al-muḍiyya*, 1: 459.

[116] Bakkār b. Qutayba, 'Juz' fīhi min ḥadīth al-qāḍī Bakkār b. Qutayba al-Thaqafī', MS 124, fols. 1–7. The work was known to the following: Ibn Ḥajar al-ʿAsqalānī, *al-Majmaʿ al-mu'assas li al-muʿjam al-mufahras*, ed. Yūsuf ʿAbd al-Raḥmān al-Marʿashlī (Beirut: Dār al-Maʿrifa, n.d.); Muḥammad b. Sulaymān al-Rūdānī, *Ṣilat al-khalaf bi mawṣūl al-salaf*, ed. Muḥammad Ḥajī (Beirut: Dār al-Gharb al-Islāmī, 1988), 432; al-Ayyūbī, *Ḥaṣr al-shārid min asānīd Muḥammad ʿĀbid*, ed. Khalīl b. ʿUthmān and al-Jubūr al-Subayʿī (Riyadh: Maktabat al-Rushd, 2003), 1: 241–2; Kātib Çelebi, *Kashf al-ẓunūn*, 2: 596 (Flügel edn.).

[117] Al-Khaṭīb al-Baghdādī, *Tārīkh Baghdād*, 6: 348–9; Ibn Abī al-Wafā', *al-Jawāhir al-muḍiyya*, 1: 337–8; al-Suyūṭī, *Ḥusn al-muḥāḍara*, 1: 433 (Cairo edn.); al-ʿAbbādī, *Kitāb Ṭabaqāt al-fuqahā'*, 5; al-Shīrāzī, *Ṭabaqāt al-fuqahā'*, 140; Flügel, 'Die Classen', 292.

[118] Ibn Abī al-Wafā', *al-Jawāhir al-muḍiyya*, 1: 337 mentions seeing the entry in Ibn Yūnus's *Tārīkh* and the modern edition indeed preserves a notice on him: Ibn Yūnus al-Ṣadafī, *Tārīkh Ibn Yūnus*, 2: 27–8.

Baghdad and trained under one of its leading Ḥanafī scholars and judges, Muḥammad b. Samāʿa (d. 233/848). His arrival in Egypt seems to have been a significant development for Egyptian Ḥanafism, for it is one of the reasons given for al-Ṭaḥāwī's decision to switch his legal affiliation from Shāfiʿism to Ḥanafism.[119] It was probably in an official and bureaucratic capacity that Aḥmad b. Abī ʿImrān relocated to Egypt. We learn that he transferred to Egypt with another Ḥanafī scholar, Abū Ayyūb, who we know was employed in the state's administration as the official in charge of taxes (*ṣāḥib kharāj*).[120]

Al-Ṭaḥāwī's third important source for *manāqib* reports concerning Abū Ḥanīfa and his followers more generally was Abū Khāzim. Abū Khāzim's career began in Basra, where he studied with its leading jurisprudents. Like Bakkār b. Qutayba, Abū Khāzim learnt jurisprudence with Hilāl b. Ra'y. He was appointed chief judge of Damascus in 264/877–8 and retained this position until he transferred to Iraq. It was during these years that he served as judge in both Kufa and Karkh during the caliphal reigns of both al-Muʿtaḍid (r. 279–89/891–902) and al-Muktafī (r. 289–96/902–8); although, according to al-Ṭaḥāwī's biographers, al-Ṭaḥāwī met and studied jurisprudence and ḥadīth with Abū Khāzim in Shām in 268/862.[121] Wakīʿ tells us that Abū Khāzim succeeded Ibn Abī al-ʿAnbas as judge of Sharqiyya in Baghdad in 275/888 or 276/889, and that he saw out his last days as the judge of Kufa. He died in Baghdad in 292/905.[122]

The nature of al-Ṭaḥāwī's sources for *manāqib* reports about Abū Ḥanīfa betrays a number of salient points concerning the actors involved in using *manāqib* works to establish the orthodoxy of Abū Ḥanīfa. Al-Ṭaḥāwī's network of sources is drawn overwhelmingly from one professional class. In Egypt, and in other regions of the Islamic world, qadis were paramount to the production and dissemination of *manāqib* works

[119] Ibn Yūnus al-Ṣadafī, *Tārīkh Ibn Yūnus*, 1: 21.

[120] His full name was Aḥmad b. Muḥammad b. Shujāʿ. On the relocation of Aḥmad b. Abī ʿImrān and Abū Ayyūb together to Egypt see Ibn Abī al-Wafā', *al-Jawāhir al-muḍiyya*, 1: 338. On Abū Ayyūb's employment as *ṣāḥib kharāj* during the reign of Aḥmad b. Ṭūlūn see Ibn Taghrībirdī, *al-Nujūm al-zāhira*, 2: 311. Abū Ayyūb was also the author of panegyrics in praise of the ʿAbbāsid governor Ḥumayd b. ʿAbd al-Ḥamīd and his prominent family, for which see Khan, 'An Empire of Élites'; and al-Buḥturī, *Dīwān al-Buḥturī*, ed. Ḥasan Kāmil al-Ṣayrafī (Cairo: Dār al-Maʿārif, n.d.), 1: 491–2 (*qaṣīda* no. 206). Abū Ayyūb was also on the receiving end of panegyrics: al-Buḥturī, *Dīwān al-Buḥturī*, 1: 627–31 (*qaṣīda* no. 258).

[121] Ibn Abī al-Wafā', *al-Jawāhir al-muḍiyya*, 3: 26; Ibn Quṭlūbughā, *Tāj al-tarājim*, 101; Ibn ʿAsākir, *Tārīkh madīnat Dimashq*, 34: 78–87 (al-ʿAmrawī edn.); Ibn ʿImād, *Shadharāt al-dhahab*, 2: 210; Wakīʿ, *Akhbār al-quḍāt*, 3: 24; Flügel, 'Die Classen', 293–4.

[122] Al-Shīrāzī, *Ṭabaqāt al-fuqahā'*, 141; Ibn Abī al-Wafā', *al-Jawāhir al-muḍiyya*, 2: 366–8; Ibn Quṭlūbughā, *Tāj al-tarājim*, 182.

and reports in the ninth–eleventh centuries. The content of *manāqib* works was clearly fundamental to judges affiliated with Ḥanafism hailing from different parts of the early Islamic empire. Bakkār b. Qutayba and Abū Khāzim began their careers in Basra. Aḥmad b. Abī ʿImrān preserved material he had acquired from his native city, Baghdad, and from scholars such as Muḥammad b. Samāʿa. These scholars and judges learnt and transmitted material that was deemed necessary as a response to the growth of discourses of heresy against Abū Ḥanīfa, for *manāqib* works and their content provided a venue for consolidating Abū Ḥanīfa's credentials as an exemplar of orthodoxy. This material moved with them from Basra and Baghdad to Egypt, where it flourished and expanded among its network of judges. The successful reintegration of Abū Ḥanīfa within proto-Sunni orthodoxy in the tenth century cannot be appreciated without considering the persistent creativity and dedication of Ḥanafī judges and authors in developing the tradition of *manāqib* works. Judges functioned as intermediaries in medieval Islamicate societies.[123] They occupied positions of power and prestige in a way that allowed them to represent both the state and its subjects. On the one hand, they were an extension of the state's administrative apparatus. The rule of the qadi was a reflection of the state's duty to administer and dispense justice. He was to be appointed by caliphs and could be relieved of his duty by them alone. On the other hand, judges lived and worked in the provinces and not in the caliph's court. They had to represent the interests and respond to the quandaries of the empire's entire population: Zoroastrians, Christians, Jews, and Muslims. Survival in the provinces for judges meant accommodating the needs of two parties. They had to garner the admiration of the local population where their jurisdiction applied, all the while ensuring that they did not unsettle the state's interests in the provinces. Therefore, when judges transmitted and composed *manāqib* works defending the orthodoxy of Abū Ḥanīfa, they did so from a position of leadership and authority. This had important consequences for ensuring Abū Ḥanīfa's complete integration into medieval Sunni orthodoxy.

Writing as judges was not without its risks, however. Judges were required to strike a delicate balance between their professional loyalties and the kind of history writing they were producing when shaping the narrative of orthodoxy around Abū Ḥanīfa. This tension was particularly acute when it came to treating an aspect of Abū Ḥanīfa's mnemohistory that had generated discourses of heresy: his relationship with the state. Proto-Sunni traditionalists excoriated Abū Ḥanīfa and declared his

[123] Paul, *Herrscher, Gemeinwesen, Vermittler*, 243–6.

involvement with rebellions against the ʿAbbāsids to be heresy. No trace of the episodes with Zayd b. ʿAlī, Ibrāhīm b. ʿAbd Allāh, and al-Ḥārith b. Surayj is to be found in early *manāqib* works. In the same way that proto-Sunni traditionalists sought to emphasise the heresy of Abū Ḥanīfa's doctrines concerning rebellion against the state in order to undermine the wide-reaching dependence of the ʿAbbāsid state on Ḥanafī judges, defenders of Abū Ḥanīfa were determined to omit material of this kind that might create a divisive wedge between the empire's judiciary – so much of it populated by followers of Abū Ḥanīfa – and loyalty to the caliph. It was hardly in the interests of Ḥanafī members of the judiciary to add credibility to proto-Sunni traditionalist discourses of heresy by dwelling on Abū Ḥanīfa's support for uprisings against the ʿAbbāsids. The surest way to deal with this challenging fact was to ignore it altogether.[124]

However, we would be mistaken in assuming that these strategic literary decisions were motivated by an unwavering loyalty to the ʿAbbāsid state; or that the preservation of their careers was what compelled judges to avoid raising certain themes in *manāqib* works. Authors of *manāqib* works who were qadis were not mere agents of the state willing to expunge any and all embarrassing historical details and to treat history writing so flippantly, in order to satisfy their imperial employers. *Manāqib* works written by judges articulated a nuanced history of the relationship between scholars and the state. They recognised, for instance, the ethical and moral imperatives of steering clear of the caliph, his court, and state employment in general. Moreover, these authors also tried to explain to their readers the difficult and compromising nature of their employment. The longest report in Ibn Abī al-ʿAwwām al-Saʿdī's *Faḍā'il Abī Ḥanīfa* is a discussion around Muḥammad b. al-Ḥasan al-Shaybānī's proximity to the ruler. The narrative is one of the many reports that Ibn Abī al-ʿAwwām al-Saʿdī transmits from al-Ṭaḥāwī > Abū Khāzim Bakr al-ʿAmmī > Muḥammad b. Samāʿa:[125]

> The only reason for Muḥammad b. al-Ḥasan's association (*mukhālaṭa*) with the caliph was the following: Abū Yūsuf was consulted (*shūwira*) about whom to appoint as a judge in Raqqa. He told his seniors: 'I cannot give you the name of any man fit for the job except Muḥammad b. al-Ḥasan. But he lives in Kufa. If you want to appoint him, you must dispatch someone to bring him here.' They sent for him and had him brought to Raqqa (*fa baʿathū ilayhi fa ashkhaṣūhu*). When he arrived, he went to see Abū Yūsuf. Al-Shaybānī asked him: 'Explain to me why I was chosen for this office.' Abū Yūsuf replied: 'They asked me to recommend a candidate for the judgeship of Raqqa, so I proposed your name. In doing so, I had

[124] For a unique strategy adopted by one Ḥanafī judge, see my discussion below and in Chapter 10 of al-Surmārī's *al-Ibāna fī al-radd ʿalā mushanniʿīn ʿalā Abī Ḥanīfa*.

[125] Ibn Abī al-ʿAwwām al-Saʿdī, *Faḍā'il Abī Ḥanīfa*, 356–7.

a particular point in mind: God, mighty and exalted, has spread this knowledge of ours (*qad baththa ʿilmanā hādhā*) to Kufa, Basra, and the entire East. I desired for this to occur in this region; namely, that God, mighty and exalted, may extend our knowledge to this region and other areas in Shām through you.' 'Praise be to God,' exclaimed al-Shaybānī. 'All this time I harboured the delusion that it was on account of some greatness of mine that I had been selected for office. I was completely oblivious to this reason for my being selected.'

This is one of the rare insights into the inner intentions and motivations of qadis that we find in the primary sources. I do not propose that this citation preserves an original transcript of a conversation between al-Shaybānī and Abū Yūsuf.[126] It is enough for our purposes to acknowledge that members of the judiciary in the ninth and tenth centuries who were affiliated with Ḥanafism were circulating these reports. Judges such as Abū Khāzim and men such as al-Ṭaḥāwī who worked in the qadi's office transmitted this material, and probably found it at once edifying and empowering. Not only did it provide greater meaning to the excessive drudgery throughout the province's judicial system, it also connected Ḥanafī judges of the ninth and tenth centuries to an exemplary precedent reaching back to the foundational epigones of the Ḥanafī *madhhab*.

This was evidently an important tradition for Ḥanafī judges. But it did not translate into a dogmatism that they were unwilling to challenge themselves. *Faḍā'il Abī Ḥanīfa* recounts multiple anecdotes concerning the encounters of scholars with the state. It relates, for example, how Muḥammad b. Shujāʿ recognised that scrupulous piety was incompatible with employment in the judiciary. When he consulted ʿAbd Allāh b. Dāwūd al-Khuraybī as to whether he should take it upon himself to study Abū Ḥanīfa's legal teachings, al-Khuraybī responded to him sharply, 'Yes, do so. But only study with those among them who practise scrupulous piety.'[127] Muḥammad b. Shujāʿ interpreted this as an instruction not to study with those who sought judgeships.[128]

In Ibn Abī al-ʿAwwām's *Faḍā'il* we find reports from al-Ṭaḥāwī that place the judgeship in a slightly different light. With another qadi *isnād* from al-Ṭaḥāwī < Bakkār b. Qutayba we have Hilāl b. Ra'y giving us an eyewitness account, most probably as a youth, of Hārūn al-Rashīd's ritual performance of the pilgrimage at Mecca. Hilāl b. Ra'y follows the caliph's

[126] On the other hand, there is no reason to dismiss the report as a later fabrication. It is, indeed, plausible that this report gives an accurate account of how al-Shaybānī came to occupy the judgeship of Raqqa.

[127] Ibn Abī al-ʿAwwām al-Saʿdī, *Faḍā'il Abī Ḥanīfa*, 332 (*Qultu li ʿAbd Allāh b. Dāwūd al-Khuraybī: tarā an anẓura fī qawl Abī Ḥanīfa? Fa qāla lī shadīdan: Naʿam, wa lākin jālis ahl al-waraʿ minhum*).

[128] Ibn Abī al-ʿAwwām al-Saʿdī, *Faḍā'il Abī Ḥanīfa*, 332 (*Qāla Ibn Shujāʿ: yaʿnī man lā yurīd al-qaḍā*).

performance of the pilgrimage rites, noting along the way some of the mistakes that the caliph made. He describes how the caliph finally arrived at the Kaʿba, which was duly opened for him. He observed that the entire entourage of the caliph was standing, except the caliph and an elderly scholar. The caliph and the scholar were seated. Hilāl b. Ra'y continues:[129]

> I did not know who the man was (*wa lam adri man huwa*). So I said to some of my fellow companions, 'Who is this elderly man?' 'That is the caliph's judge, Asad b. ʿAmr,' they replied. It was at that point that I realised that after the office of the caliph the most exalted office was the judgeship (*lā martabata baʿda al-khilāfa ajallu min al-qaḍāʾ*).

From this small sample of al-Ṭaḥāwī narrations in Ibn Abī al-ʿAwwām al-Saʿdī's *Faḍāʾil* we can appreciate the complexity and conflict that judges were faced with in coming to terms with the nature of their employment. What emerges from this discussion of materials from al-Ṭaḥāwī's now lost *manāqib* work is that medieval scholars and judges did not disregard certain moral tensions, nor did they try to gloss over them. If anything, they used the texts that they wrote – in this case, *manāqib* works – to communicate to their audiences the difficulties that their social status presented.

A final point to consider in this survey of the sources al-Ṭaḥāwī's *Manāqib* most likely drew upon is his non-Ḥanafī sources. We discussed earlier his transition from the legal affiliation he inherited from his family to his adoption of the Ḥanafī *madhhab*. It was perhaps because of this that al-Ṭaḥāwī included reports extolling the orthodoxy of Abū Ḥanīfa and his followers which originated with members of the Shāfiʿī school. Al-Ṭaḥāwī adduces al-Shāfiʿī six times.[130] On two occasions he relies on an account transmitted to him by Yūnus b. ʿAbd al-Aʿlā (d. 264/877), an Egyptian student of al-Shāfiʿī whom some considered to be a teacher of Mālikī jurisprudence.[131] Al-Ṭaḥāwī's maternal uncle al-Muzanī is another source for al-Shāfiʿī's praise of Abū Ḥanīfa and his students.[132] Finally, al-Ṭaḥāwī's father makes an appearance in an *isnād* reaching back to al-Shāfiʿī.[133] It was important for al-Ṭaḥāwī that his readership understood that Abū Ḥanīfa's orthodox status was recognised by scholars outside the Ḥanafī tradition. Making this argument was essential to the broader embrace among Sunnis of Abū Ḥanīfa as an orthodox figure.

[129] Ibn Abī al-ʿAwwām al-Saʿdī, *Faḍāʾil Abī Ḥanīfa*, 343 and again, with some minor differences, at 162–3.
[130] Ibn Abī al-ʿAwwām al-Saʿdī, *Faḍāʾil Abī Ḥanīfa*, 87–8, 324–5, 348, 350 (x2), 366.
[131] Ibn Abī al-ʿAwwām al-Saʿdī, *Faḍāʾil Abī Ḥanīfa*, 324–5, 350.
[132] Ibn Abī al-ʿAwwām al-Saʿdī, *Faḍāʾil Abī Ḥanīfa*, 348.
[133] Ibn Abī al-ʿAwwām al-Saʿdī, *Faḍāʾil Abī Ḥanīfa*, 350.

Aside from what we can deduce as to al-Ṭaḥāwī's sources and the content of his *manāqib* work, there are also some indications as to how al-Ṭaḥāwī acquired his material. Much of it was related to him in person. In Ibn Abī al-ʿAwwām al-Saʿdī's notice on Asad b. ʿAmr al-Bajalī, we learn that al-Ṭaḥāwī also relied on written correspondence. Five of the ten reports about al-Bajalī return to al-Ṭaḥāwī. Four of these five indicate that al-Ṭaḥāwī's *Manāqib* drew upon written materials. In three instances Ibn Abī Thawr wrote to al-Ṭaḥāwī (*kataba ilayya*) to provide him with details concerning Abū Ḥanīfa and his followers.[134] In one instance, we are informed that ʿĪsā b. Rūḥ transferred his book or notes to al-Ṭaḥāwī (*nāwalanī*).[135] Clearly, these men had access to information integral to al-Ṭaḥāwī's broader aim of establishing Abū Ḥanīfa's religious orthodoxy. Ibn Abī Thawr furnished al-Ṭaḥāwī with reports from Ifrīqiya, by way of Asad b. al-Furāt, attesting to the scholarly prowess and literary production of Abū Ḥanīfa's students. Similarly, ʿĪsā b. Rūḥ was able to provide al-Ṭaḥāwī with details known in Ifrīqiya, once again through Asad b. al-Furāt, about Abū Ḥanīfa's legal opinions. The production of *Manāqib Abī Ḥanīfa* works owed themselves, in part, to a culture of knowledge sharing through both the oral and written medium.

### *Bukhārā: Tenth Century*

In Bukhārā another Ḥanafī scholar with experience of working with provincial state authorities was writing *manāqib* and *musnad* works for Abū Ḥanīfa. ʿAbd Allāh b. Muḥammad b. Yaʿqūb al-Ḥārithī al-Subadhmūnī (d. 340/952) composed *Kashf al-āthār fī manāqib Abī Ḥanīfa*.[136] He was born in 258/872, just as the reign of the Ṭāhirids

[134] Ibn Abī al-ʿAwwām al-Saʿdī, *Faḍā'il Abī Ḥanīfa*, 241–2. Ibn Abī al-Wafā', *al-Jawāhir al-muḍiyya*, 1: 387 cites one of these reports and attributes it to al-Ṭaḥāwī.

[135] Ibn Abī al-ʿAwwām al-Saʿdī, *Faḍā'il Abī Ḥanīfa*, 243.

[136] Al-Subadhmūnī, 'Kashf al-āthār fī manāqib Abī Ḥanīfa', MS 3105, no. 102, 326 fols. See Muḥammad Muṭīʿ al-Ḥāfiẓ and ʿAbd al-Raḥmān Farfūr, *al-Muntaqā min makhṭūṭāt maʿhad al-Bīrūnī li al-dirāsāt al-sharqiyya bi Ṭasqand* (Dubai: Markaz Jumʿat al-Mājid li al-Thaqāfa wa al-Turāth, 1995), 102. On al-Subadhmūnī see: al-Ziriklī, *al-Aʿlām*, 4: 120 (15th edn.); Kaḥḥāla, *Muʿjam al-mu'allifīn*, 6: 145 (Dār Iḥyā' al-Turāth al-ʿArabī edn.); Kātib Çelebi, *Kashf al-ẓunūn*, 2: 1485 (Dār Iḥyā' edn.); Ismāʿīl Pāshā al-Baghdādī, *Hadiyyat al-ʿārifīn*, 1: 445 (Dār Iḥyā' edn.). See al-Khaṭīb al-Baghdādī, *Tārīkh Baghdād*, 10: 126–7; al-Khalīlī, *al-Irshād*, 971–2 (s.v. 'al-Kalābādhī') (Riyadh edn.); al-Samʿānī, *al-Ansāb*, 1: 129 (Dār al-Jinān edn.) (s.v. 'al-Ustādh'), 3: 213 (Dār al-Jinān edn.) (s.v. 'al-Subadhmūnī'); Ibn Mākūla, *Ikmāl*, 3: 178; al-Dhahabī, *Tārīkh al-Islām*, 25 (years 331–50): 190–1 (s.v. 'year 340'); al-Dhahabī, *Mīzān al-iʿtidāl*, 2: 496–7; al-Dhahabī, *Tadhkirat al-ḥuffāẓ*, 3: 854; al-Dhahabī, *Siyar*, 15: 424; Ibn Quṭlūbughā, *Tāj al-tarājim*, 175–6 (where both his *manāqib* and *musnad* works are mentioned); Ibn Ḥajar al-ʿAsqalānī, *Lisān al-mīzān*, 4: 579–80 (Abū Ghudda edn.); Ibn Ḥajar al-ʿAsqalānī, *Taʿjīl al-manfaʿa bi zawā'id rijāl al-arbaʿa*, ed. Ikrām Allāh Imdād al-Ḥaqq

was coming to an end and the Sāmānids were rising to power in Transoxiana. He travelled to Khurāsān, Samarqand, Nasaf, Iraq, and the Ḥijāz.[137] He was a ḥadīth scholar and could count ḥadīth masters like Abū al-ʿAbbās b. ʿUqda and Abū ʿAbd Allāh Muḥammad b. Isḥāq b. Manda as his students. Despite this, al-Ḥākim was of the view that he possessed 'strange and unique traditions from reliable transmitters', and that, ultimately, the ḥadīth masters rejected him (*sakatū ʿanhu*). Similarly, al-Khaṭīb al-Baghdādī believed that he did not hold the status of being a proof.[138] Al-Subadhmūnī worked at the court of the Sāmānid amir, Ismāʿīl b. Aḥmad al-Sāmānī (r. 279/892–295/907). He was often summoned often to the amir's residence, where Ismāʿīl b. Aḥmad would ask him about certain things and al-Subadhmūni would answer him.[139] This earned him the nickname 'the Teacher' (*al-ustādh*), in addition to fame as 'the scholar of the realm of al-Sulṭān al-Saʿīd (Naṣr II r. 301/914–331/943)'.[140] He died on the evening of Friday the fifth of Shawwāl 340/952.

Al-Dhahabī had heard of but not seen a book of his entitled *Kitāb* [or *Kashf ʿan*] *Wahm al-ṭabaqa al-ẓalama Abā Ḥanīfa*, which one presumes from the title defended Abū Ḥanīfa against ninth-century proto-Sunni traditionalist discourses of heresy.[141] We can assume that, like most *manāqib* works, al-Subadhmūnī's included a section on Abū Ḥanīfa's followers. At least one report from al-Subadhmūnī on Abū Yūsuf turns

(Beirut: Dār al-Bashā'ir al-Islāmiyya, 2008), 1: 239–40; Ibn Ḥajar al-ʿAsqalānī, *Tabṣir al-muntabih*, 2: 801 (where al-Subadhmūnī is described as having transmitted ḥadīth to the Sāmānid ruler); Ibn Nāṣir al-Dīn, *Tawḍīḥ al-mushtabih fī ḍabṭ asmā' al-ruwāt wa ansābihim wa alqābihim wa kunāhum*, ed. Muḥammad Naʿīm al-ʿArqasūsī (Beirut: Mu'assasat al-Risāla, 1993), 1: 196, 7: 348; Ibn al-Athīr, *al-Lubāb* (Beirut: Dār Ṣādir, 1980), 1: 50 (s.v. 'al-Ustādh'), 2: 99–100 (s.v. 'al-Subadhmūnī'); Laknawī, *al-Fawā'id al-bahiyya* (Beirut: Dār al-Maʿrifa, 1906), 104–6; Ibn ʿImād, *Shadharāt al-dhahab*, 2: 357; Ibn Abī al-Wafā', *al-Jawāhir al-muḍiyya*, 2: 344–5; al-Samʿānī, *al-Muntakhab min muʿjam shuyūkh al-Samʿānī*, ed. Muwaffaq b. ʿAbd Allāh b. ʿAbd al-Qādir (Riyadh: Dār ʿĀlam al-Kutub, 1996), 3: 343–4, where al-Samʿānī recalls hearing the book from one of his teachers. I was unable to gain access to al-Subadhmūnī's manuscript, but I understand it is in the process of being edited by Laṭīf Raḥmān al-Bahrā'ichī al-Qāsimī and published by Maktabat al-Irshād in Istanbul.

137 Al-Nasafī, *al-Qand fī dhikr al-ʿulamā' Samarqand*, ed. Yūsuf al-Hādī (Tehran: Mīrāth-i Maktūb, 1999), 319–20.

138 Al-Samʿānī, *al-Ansāb*, 3: 213–14 (Dār al-Jinān edn.) (s.v. 'al-Subadhmūnī').

139 Ibn Ḥajar al-ʿAsqalānī, *Tabṣīr al-muntabih*, 2: 801.

140 Al-Samʿānī, *al-Ansāb*, 1: 129 (Dār al-Jinān edn.) (s.v. 'al-Ustādh'), 3: 213–14 (s.v. 'al-Subadhmūnī') = 1: 212, 7: 29–30 (Hyderabad edn.). See also Fu'ād Ṣāliḥ, *Muʿjam al-alqāb wa al-asmā' al-mustaʿāra fī tārīkh al-ʿarabī al-Islāmī* (Beirut: Dār al-ʿIlm li al-Malāyīn, 1990), 26.

141 Al-Dhahabī, *Siyar*, 15: 424–5 (s.v. 'al-Ustādh'); Ibn Nāṣir al-Dīn, *Tawḍīḥ al-mushtabih*, 7: 348 (s.v. 'al-Kalābādhī'). Reports from either his *Kashf al-āthār* or *Kitāb Wahm al-ṭabaqa al-ẓalama* appear in al-Muwaffaq al-Makkī, *Manāqib Abī Ḥanīfa* [printed with al-Kardarī, *Manāqib Abī Ḥanīfa*], 1: 123–4.

up in a later work.[142] There is good reason to believe that al-Subadhmūnī's *manāqib* work spread far and wide, for it entered the world of al-Tanūkhī and his *Nishwār al-muḥāḍara*. The notorious judge cites a *manāqib* report from al-Subadhmūnī in the *Nishwār*'s chapter on Abū Ḥanīfa.[143]

There was another *manāqib* work produced by a scholar from Bukhārā. His name was Aḥmad b. ʿAbd Allāh b. Abī al-Qāsim al-Surmārī, Abū Jaʿfar al-Qāḍī.[144] He belonged to the village of Surmārā, which was located in Bukhārā.[145] He was a judge, too. Frustratingly, we do not know when he lived. The sources that mention him provide no clues as to when he lived. We know that he wrote two books: *Ta'sīs al-naẓā'ir* and *al-Ibāna fī al-radd ʿalā mushtaniʿīn ʿalā al-Imām Abī Ḥanīfa*. On the basis of the pattern of *manāqib* works produced in Khurāsān and Transoxiana, along with the nature of the title of this *manāqib* work, I suspect that the author lived during the tenth–eleventh centuries. *Ta'sīs al-naẓā'ir* has not survived. A work with a similar title is attributed to both Abū Layth al-Samarqandī (d. 373/983) and Abū Zayd al-Dabūsī (d. 430/1038). My knowledge of Abū al-Qāsim al-Surmārī's authorship of this work comes from an unpublished manuscript, which mentions al-Surmārī as its author.[146] So we know he was writing before al-Marghīnānī (d. 593/1197).

A clearer picture of the book's textual history has now emerged thanks to Mehterhan Furkani's 2019 edition of al-Surmārī's *al-Ibāna fī al-radd ʿalā mushtaniʿīn ʿalā al-Imām Abī Ḥanīfa*.[147] Prior to his edition of the work, a basic description of the plan of the book was given by a number of authors, including Kāṭib Çelebī. The book consisted of six chapters. Chapter 1 presented the argument that the Ḥanafī *madhhab* was well suited to rulers and the management of state affairs. One wonders whether this, too, points to a pre-Saljūq historical context. The second chapter established the necessity of adhering to sound traditions (*āthār*). Chapter 3 discussed the importance of taking precautions in jurisprudence, and the fourth chapter followed on from this by warning about the

142 Al-Qāḍī ʿAbd al-Bāqī b. Muḥammad al-Anṣārī, *Aḥādīth al-shuyūkh al-thiqāt: al-shahīr bi al-mashyakha al-kubrā*, ed. al-Sharīf Ḥātim b. ʿĀrif al-ʿAwnī (Mecca: Dār al-ʿĀlam al-Fawā'id, 2001), 2: 878–9.

143 Al-Tanūkhī, *Nishwār al-muḥāḍara*, 7: 41.

144 Ibn Quṭlūbughā', *Tāj al-tarājim*, 113–14; ʿAbd al-Qādir al-Tamīmī, *al-Ṭabaqāt al-saniyya*, 1: 426–7 (the editor has al-Shayrabādī not al-Sarmārī); Ibn Abī al-Wafā', *al-Jawāhir al-muḍiyya*, 1: 183–4, 184 (two entries on same person).

145 Al-Samʿānī, *al-Ansāb*, 3: 247–8 (Dār al-Jinān edn.).

146 Al-Marghīnānī, 'Fuṣūl al-aḥkām fī uṣūl al-aḥkām [fuṣul al-ʿimādī]', MS 706, Jāmiʿat al-Malik Suʿūd, Riyadh, 290b.

147 Furkani, 'Taḥqīq al-Ibāna'.

dangers of not having a precautionary jurisprudential approach. The fifth chapter examined the legal rulings of other *madhhab*s that demanded censure. The final chapter responded to legal issues raised by opponents of the Ḥanafīs and which were used to slander Abū Ḥanīfa.[148] Thanks to Furkani's edition, we can say a little more about the text itself. Though we do not know about the author's precise date of death, we know for certain that he was writing between the tenth and eleventh centuries, for the book mentions tenth-century Ḥanafīs such as Abū al-ʿAbbās b. ʿUqda, whilst the text's transmitter, Abū Bakr Muḥammad b. ʿAbd al-Malik b. ʿAlī (d. 475/1082), heard the book from al-Surmārī.[149] The book's title is unique in the history of *manāqib* works, for it frames the book explicitly in response to attacks on Abū Ḥanīfa by 'slanderers', and he states at the very outset that his book aims to deal with the slanderous discourse around Abū Ḥanīfa.[150] The author's appeal to rulers and the state (*al-wulāt*) makes more explicit an emerging reality in the eastern provinces of the empire where provincial dynasties were emerging, with the Sāmānids and then the Ghaznavids. In these changing circumstances, religious scholars saw the state as a guarantor of religious stability.[151] The book also went on the offensive against other *madhhab*s, although there is nothing unusual about the final chapter, which would have gone into some detail about discourses of heresy against Abū Ḥanīfa, seeking to defend him against them.[152]

### *Iraq: Tenth Century*

*Manāqib* works began to emerge in Baghdad, too, in the tenth century. Mukram b. Aḥmad al-Bazzāz was a judge in his native city of Baghdad.[153] Nothing in his training or education suggests that he was a Ḥanafī. He was known to have studied under a group of ḥadīth scholars: Yaḥyā b. Abī Ṭālib (d. 275/889),[154] Muḥammad b. ʿĪsā al-Madā'inī (d. 274/887–8),[155] Muḥammad b. al-Ḥusayn al-Ḥunaynī (d. 277/890–1),[156] ʿAbd al-Karīm b.

[148] On the *manāqib* work see Kātib Çelebi, *Kashf al-ẓunūn*, 2: 1838–9 (Dār Iḥyā' edn.); ʿAbd al-Laṭīf b. Muḥammad Riyāḍī Zādah, *Asmā' al-kutub al-mutammim li kashf al-ẓunūn*, ed. Muḥammad al-Tūnjī (Cairo: Maktabat al-Khānjī, 1978), 25.

[149] Furkani, 'Taḥqīq al-Ibāna', 74. For this transmitter see also Ibn Abī al-Wafā', *al-Jawāhir al-muḍiyya*, 3: 238, a source not cited by Furkani.

[150] Furkani, 'Taḥqīq al-Ibāna', 89.

[151] Al-Sulamī, *Kitāb Ṭabaqāt al-ṣūfiyya*, ed. Johannes Pederson (Leiden: Brill, 1960), 217, quoting the ninth-century mystic Abū Bakr al-Warrāq (d. 280/893).

[152] This work shall be discussed in more detail in Chapter 10, when we examine the role of the state in discourses of heresy and orthodoxy around Abū Ḥanīfa.

[153] Al-Khaṭīb al-Baghdādī, *Tārīkh Baghdād*, 15: 295; al-Dhahabī, *Siyar*, 15: 517–18.

[154] Al-Dhahabī, *Siyar*, 12: 619–20. [155] Al-Dhahabī, *Siyar*, 13: 21–4.

[156] Al-Dhahabī, *Siyar*, 13: 243–4.

al-Haytham al-Dīr'āqūlī (d. 278/891),[157] and Muḥammad b. Ghālib (d. 283/896).[158] Among his students were men such as Ibn Manda, al-Ḥākim,[159] Abū al-Ḥasan b. Razqawayh (d. 412/1021–2),[160] and Ibn al-Faḍl al-Qaṭṭān (d. 415/1024).[161] Not one of the scholars he studied with, or those who studied under him, appear in Ḥanafī biographical dictionaries. The one exception might have been a student of Mukram b. Aḥmad, called Abū ʿAlī b. Shādhān (d. 425/1033–4).[162] Al-Khaṭīb al-Baghdādī knew this student intimately.[163] He writes in his *History* that 'the traditions I heard from him are more precious to me than those I have heard from anyone else'.[164] Naturally, al-Khaṭīb al-Baghdādī attended Abū ʿAlī b. Shādhān's funeral prayer.[165] He tells us that Abū ʿAlī b. Shādhān was an Ashʿarī who for a brief period adopted the Ḥanafī position (*ʿalā madhhab al-kūfiyyīn*) on *nabīdh*.[166] Furthermore, Ḥanafīs did claim him as one of their own.[167] If Abū ʿAlī b. Shādhān was a Ḥanafī, the association might have been short-lived.

Let us return to Mukram b. Aḥmad al-Bazzāz. What else do we know about his career and composition of a *manāqib* work for Abū Ḥanīfa? His scholarly links through teachers and students suggest no affiliation with Ḥanafism. We know that he was a ḥadīth scholar of good repute.[168] Al-Khaṭīb al-Baghdādī believed he was a reliable scholar (*thiqa*).[169] Traces of Mukram b. Aḥmad's *manāqib* work have survived in al-Ṣaymarī's *Akhbār Abī Ḥanīfa*. In fact, I have counted almost 250 references to Mukram b. Aḥmad.[170] Other works also cite Mukram b. Aḥmad with respect to *manāqib* reports for Abū Ḥanīfa.[171] Ḥadīth scholars such as al-Dāraquṭnī were

[157] Al-Dhahabī, *Siyar*, 13: 335–6, where we learn that he studied with Abū Bakr al-Ḥumaydī.
[158] Al-Dhahabī, *Siyar*, 13: 390–3.
[159] Al-Ḥākim, *al-Mustadrak ʿalā al-ṣaḥīḥayn* (Cairo: Dār al-Ḥaramayn, 1997), 4: 249, 590.
[160] Al-Dhahabī, *Siyar*, 17: 258–9 (a Shāfiʿī scholar).
[161] Al-Dhahabī, *Siyar*, 17: 331–2 (he heard al-Fasawī's *Kitāb al-Maʿrifa wa al-tārīkh* from ʿAbd Allāh b. Jaʿfar b. Durustuwayh).
[162] Al-Dhahabī, *Siyar*, 17: 415–18.
[163] I estimate that he is listed in the index over 680 times: al-Khaṭīb al-Baghdādī, *Tārīkh Baghdād*, 17: 218–21.
[164] Al-Khaṭīb al-Baghdādī, *Tārīkh Baghdād*, 8: 224.
[165] Al-Khaṭīb al-Baghdādī, *Tārīkh Baghdād*, 8: 224.
[166] Al-Khaṭīb al-Baghdādī, *Tārīkh Baghdād*, 8: 223.
[167] Ibn Abī al-Wafā', *al-Jawāhir al-muḍiyya*, 2: 38–9.
[168] Mukram b. Aḥmad had a good reputation as a ḥadīth scholar, no doubt aided by works such as his *Fawā'id*. Manuscripts of this work exist at Maktabat al-Ẓāhiriyya, 135, *Majmūʿa* 45, fols. 66–83 and Maktabat al-Ẓāhiriyya, 135, *Majmūʿa* 63, fols. 24–33. See Mu'assasat Āl al-Bayt, *al-Fahras al-shāmil li al-turāth al-ʿarabī al-islāmī al-makhṭūṭ: al-ḥadīth al-nabawī al-sharīf wa ʿulūmuhu wa rijāluhu* (Amman: Mu'assasat Āl al-Bayt, 1991), 1: 1203 and Sezgin, *GAS*, 1: 186–7.
[169] Al-Khaṭīb al-Baghdādī, *Tārīkh Baghdād*, 15: 295.
[170] Al-Ṣaymarī, *Akhbār Abī Ḥanīfa*, 16 ff.
[171] Al-Khaṭīb al-Baghdādī, *Tārīkh Baghdād*, 5: 342; al-Qāḍī ʿIyāḍ, *al-Ghunya: Fihrist shuyūkh al-Qāḍī ʿIyāḍ*, ed. Māhir Zuhayr Jarrār (Beirut: Dār al-Gharb al-Islāmī,

far from impressed with Mukram b. Aḥmad's *manāqib* work. He had seen Mukram b. Aḥmad's *Faḍā'il Abī Ḥanīfa* but declared it to consist of nothing but lies because of the regularity with which the work cited reports from Aḥmad b. al-Ṣalt.[172]

### *Nīshāpūr: Tenth Century*

East of Iraq, another Ḥanafī judge took some time away from his professional duties at the court to defend Abū Ḥanīfa as a figure of proto-Sunni orthodoxy. His name was Abū Aḥmad Muḥammad b. Aḥmad b. Shuʿayb b. Hārūn b. Mūsā al-Shuʿaybī. He had studied with scholars such as Abū ʿAbd Allāh al-Būshanjī, Abū Bakr Muḥammad b. Muḥammad b. Sulaymān al-Bāghandī, Ibrāhīm b. ʿAlī al-Dhuhlī, al-Ḥusayn b. Idrīs al-Anṣārī, Muḥammad b. ʿAbd al-Raḥmān al-Shāmī, Aḥmad b. Jaʿfar b. Naṣr al-Muzakkī, ʿAbd Allāh b. Maḥmūd al-Pazdawī, and Abū Bakr b. Dāwūd al-Sijistānī, among others. His students included the giant of ḥadīth learning in the tenth century, al-Ḥākim al-Nīshāpūrī. Al-Shuʿaybī died in 357/968.[173] One might presume that al-Shuʿaybī, as a judge, belonged to a learned family. Someone who appears to be his son attracted the notice of al-Ḥākim in his *History of Nīshāpūr*.[174] The Damascene scholar Ibn Nāṣir al-Dīn (d. 842/1438) knew of the son too, which should not surprise us since al-Shuʿaybī had studied with at least one scholar from Shām.[175] It seems as if al-Shuʿaybī worked his way up to a judgeship. In addition to being an expert in Quranic canonical readings, he was considered one of the most knowledgeable scholars in the science of writing documents (*shurūṭ*). He was charged with the task of monitoring merchant activity and assessing the probity of upright witnesses. This latter duty had been offered to him on multiple occasions, but he had refused to take it on. Al-Ḥākim al-Nīshāpūrī noted in his *History* that al-

1982), 79; ʿAbd al-Hādī al-Maqdisī, *Manāqib al-a'imma al-arbaʿa*, ed. Sulaymān Muslim Ḥarash (Riyadh: Dār al-Mu'ayyad, 1996), 75–6. See also Tsafrir, 'Semi-Ḥanafīs', 79.

172 Al-Khaṭīb al-Baghdādī, *Tārīkh Baghdād*, 5: 342.

173 Al-Samʿānī, *al-Ansāb*, 3: 435 (Dār al-Jinān edn.); Ibn al-Athīr, *al-Lubāb*, 2: 199 (Maktabat al-Muthannā edn.); Ibn Abī al-Wafā', *al-Jawāhir al-muḍiyya*, 3: 34; Ibn Quṭlūbughā, *Tāj al-tarājim*, 232; ʿAbd al-Qādir al-Tamīmī, *al-Ṭabaqāt al-saniyya*, 1: 255–6 (where he is mentioned in the context of one of his teachers, Ibrāhīm b. Muḥammad b. Ibrāhīm Abū Isḥaq al-Khidāmī al-Nīshāpūrī); Ismāʿīl Pāshā al-Baghdādī, *Hadiyyat al-ʿārifīn*, 2: 46 (Dār Iḥyā' edn.).

174 Al-Khalīfa al-Nīshāpūrī, *Talkhīṣ tārīkh Nīshāpūr*, 115.

175 Ibn Nāṣir al-Dīn, *Tawḍīḥ al-mushtabih*, 5: 342 (where he notes al-Shuʿaybī's son, Shayba, who died in 395/1004–5). Shayba had studied with ʿAbd Allāh Ibn al-Sharqī. Ibn al-Sharqī was a ḥadīth master from Khurāsān of immense standing: see al-Dhahabī, *Siyar*, 15: 37–9.

Shuʿaybī was the author of a book on asceticism (*zuhd*) and a *manāqib* work on Abū Ḥanīfa, which consisted of two fascicles (*ajzāʾ*). Al-Ḥākim regarded him as having a mastery over the Ḥanafī *madhhab* quite unlike some of his other fellow Ḥanafīs.[176] I have located at least one report that ought to have belonged to his *Faḍāʾil Abī Ḥanīfa*, which narrates Abū Ḥanīfa's astounding display of care for a drunkard neighbour who seemed to present an enormous nuisance for Abū Ḥanīfa, but who when imprisoned was released after Abū Ḥanīfa petitioned on his behalf. The story began in Nīshāpūr with al-Shuʿaybī, was transported by another native of Nīshāpūr, who told it to a well-known scholar from Bukhāra, who himself travelled to Damascus and circulated the story among its residents.[177] This captures well the extent to which *manāqib* works were integrated into different regions of the medieval Islamic world, and how 'Book Islam' was intimately connected to 'Lived and Experienced Islam'.

### *Eleventh Century*

The final specimen of *manāqib* works for Abū Ḥanīfa I should like to highlight is an unpublished manuscript.[178] MS 4216 is a short treatise entitled 'Faṣl ʿalā taqdīm Abī Ḥanīfa fī al-jumla ʿalā sāʾir fuqahāʾ al-amṣār'. An author is identified in the middle of the manuscript as Maḥmūd b. Manṣūr b. Abī al-Faḍl in the context of his explaining the purpose of a section in which he provides a typology of jurists in the Ḥanafī *madhhab*.[179] I have not been able to identify this author. At this moment I can only offer a tentative sketch based on this manuscript and the collection (*majmūʿ*) in which it is found. As for the manuscript itself, our author presents a periodisation of the Ḥanafī *madhhab*, which begins with Abū Ḥanīfa's students and ends with the third generation of jurists, giving the name of Abū al-Ḥusayn al-Qudūrī as the last jurist.[180] This leaves us with a *terminus post quem* of 428/1037. This manuscript is coupled with a second treatise, 'Kitāb al-ʿĀlim wa al-Mutaʿallim'. The beginning of this second treatise contains a record of transmission. The

[176] Al-Samʿānī, *al-Ansāb*, 3: 435 (Dār al-Jinān edn.).

[177] Al-Khaṭīb al-Baghdādī, *Tārīkh Baghdād*, 15: 497.

[178] I should add that there are some *manāqib* works I can say little about. For example, al-Samʿānī (*al-Ansāb*, 1: 381 (Maktabat Ibn Taymiyya edn.)) tells us of a *Manāqib Abī Ḥanīfa* work authored by one Abū Jaʿfar al-Zajjāj circulating in the tenth century in Marw. Another *manāqib* work authored by one Abū al-Ḥasan al-Dīnavarī was edited in 2020: Kütük 'Ebu'l-Hasen ed-Dîneverî'nin Menâkibu Ebî Hanîfe'.

[179] Maḥmūd b. Manṣūr b. Abī al-Faḍl, 'Faṣl ʿalā taqdīm madhhab Abī Ḥanīfa', MS 4216, Chester Beatty Library, 38b. On typologies of jurists in the Ḥanafī *madhhab* see now Al-Azem, *Rule-Formulation*, 93–101.

[180] Maḥmūd b. Manṣūr b. Abī al-Faḍl, 'Faṣl ʿalā taqdīm madhhab Abī Ḥanīfa', 39a.

name of the redactor is not given, but the teacher who transmitted the text to him is: 'The shaykh, the imam, the scholar, the scrupulous ascetic, the authority, the chief of the school, Majd al-Dīn ʿAbd al-Raḥmān b. ʿAmr b. Aḥmad b. Hibat Allāh b. Abī Jarāda'.[181] The text was transmitted to Ibn Abī Jarāda by the teacher at Abū Ḥanīfa's shrine in Baghdad on Friday evening, 30 June 1245.[182] If we assume that the copyist of 'Kitāb al-ʿĀlim wa al-Mutaʿallim' is the author of 'Faṣl ʿalā taqdīm madhhab Abī Ḥanīfa', and the scripts and hands in the treatises in the manuscript seem identical, then we might suggest that the author is a student of Ibn Abī Jarāda. The final indication of dating is a reference to one ʿAlī b. Mūsā al-Qummī (d. 305/917–18), who we are informed wrote *Kitāb al-Radd ʿalā aṣḥāb al-Shāfiʿī*.[183] This must be the famous tenth-century Ḥanafī scholar from Nīshāpūr, who had studied jurisprudence under Muḥammad b. Shujāʿ al-Thaljī.[184]

In this work, too, our author openly recognises discourses of heresy transmitted by proto-Sunni traditionalists.[185] He writes: 'As for those who spoke against Abū Ḥanīfa during his lifetime, they did so out of spite because Abū Ḥanīfa had surpassed them in knowledge and they found this unbearable.'[186] Our author gives the example of Sufyān al-Thawrī. He explains that Sufyān al-Thawrī delivered a *mea culpa* on his deathbed and repented from his contribution to discourses of heresy against Abū Ḥanīfa. Nevertheless, our author details some of these discourses of heresy. One pertains to a book that was discovered under Sufyān al-Thawrī's pillow after he passed away in which he related a tradition from Abū Ḥanīfa and then accused him of forgery (*dallasahu*).[187] The author even admits that Sufyān al-Thawrī accused Abū Ḥanīfa of being forced to repent from heresy twice. He makes no effort to attack the credibility of such reports.

181 Abū Ḥanīfa (attr.), 'Kitāb al-ʿĀlim wa al-mutaʿallim', MS 4216, Chester Beatty Library, 1a.

182 Abū Ḥanīfa (attr.), 'Kitāb al-ʿĀlim wa al-mutaʿallim', 1a.

183 Maḥmūd b. Manṣūr b. Abī al-Faḍl, 'Faṣl ʿalā taqdīm madhhab Abī Ḥanīfa' 39b.

184 Ibn al-Nadīm, *Kitāb al-Fihrist*, 2: 32 (A. F. Sayyid edn.); Ibn Abī al-Wafā', *al-Jawāhir al-muḍiyya*, 1: 380; Ibn Quṭlūbughā, *Tāj al-tarājim*, 31; al-Dhahabī, *Siyar*, 14: 236–7.

185 Arberry, *The Chester Beatty Library*, 5: 68. Sezgin, *GAS*, 1: 411. Sezgin suggests that the author may correspond to one Maḥmūd b. Manṣūr b. Manṣūr. For this person, Sezgin refers readers to Yāqūt al-Ḥamawī, *Kitāb Muʿjam al-buldān*, 3: 535. I found no such person cited there. The next page (3: 536 refers to one Manṣūr b. Manṣūr al-Rūdhābādhī). I also checked more recent editions of the work, and the indices list no one resembling this name.

186 Maḥmūd b. Manṣūr b. Abī al-Faḍl, 'Faṣl ʿalā taqdīm madhhab Abī Ḥanīfa', 36a: (*fa ammā man takallama fī Abī Ḥanīfa min ahl ʿaṣrihi fa li al-munāfasa li annahu taqammahum fī al-ʿilm fa shaqqa ʿalayhim*).

187 Maḥmūd b. Manṣūr b. Abī al-Faḍl, 'Faṣl ʿalā taqdīm madhhab Abī Ḥanīfa', 36a. Alternatively, *dallasahu* might imply that Sufyān transmitted the tradition but concealed his embarrassing source.

Instead, he explains that the incident in which a public repentance from heresy was extracted from Abū Ḥanīfa was a case in which he had outwitted (*yulāḥinu*) his inquisitors.[188] The last word, however, is given to Abū Ḥanīfa's admirers, as our author devotes the remaining pages to those who praised him.[189]

## 8.3 Conclusion

Let us summarise some of the key patterns that have emerged from our study of the *manāqib* genre. Perhaps the most central aspect of the production of *manāqib* works for Abū Ḥanīfa is their timing. They were first composed in the aftermath of ninth-century discourses of heresy against Abū Ḥanīfa, and their proliferation marks the beginning of a shift in conceptions of medieval Sunni orthodoxy.

The geographical spread of these works is also significant. It is no coincidence, for example, that the first *manāqib* works of the late ninth to early tenth centuries were written in regions where discourses of heresy against Abū Ḥanīfa were especially strong. In Chapters 2 and 3 of this study I emphasised the transregional dimension of proto-Sunni traditionalist discourses of heresy. In the light of this, it is not surprising that the task of establishing Abū Ḥanīfa as a patron saint of medieval Sunnism required authors of *manāqib* works in major centres of the medieval Islamic world: Iraq, Transoxiana, Khurāsān, and Egypt. Any adjustments to the evolving orthodoxy of medieval Sunnism demanded a consenting community directing these changes from different provinces.

A third pattern we have identified pertains to the professional occupations of our *manāqib* authors. Al-Ṭaḥāwī, Ibn Abī al-ʿAwwām, al-Subadhmūnī, al-Surmārī, Mukram b. Aḥmad, and al-Shuʿaybī were all judges and had relationships of some kind with local rulers. There has been a tendency in modern scholarship to see judges as nugatory to the development of Islam as a religion, but this chapter suggests that qadis, as authors, were instrumental in bringing about major transformations in the evolution of medieval Sunnism.

A fourth discernible trend in the composition of *manāqib* works for Abū Ḥanīfa is the diverse sectarian backgrounds of their authors. Though the overwhelming majority of *manāqib* authors were associated with Ḥanafism, in Ibn ʿUqda and Abū al-Mufaḍḍal al-Shaybānī we have two authors who occupied an ambivalent place in medieval Sunnī and Shiʿite memory. Since these works have not survived, we cannot determine their

[188] Maḥmūd b. Manṣūr b. Abī al-Faḍl, 'Faṣl ʿalā taqdīm madhhab Abī Ḥanīfa', 36a.
[189] Maḥmūd b. Manṣūr b. Abī al-Faḍl, 'Faṣl ʿalā taqdīm madhhab Abī Ḥanīfa', 36b.

precise nature. On the one hand, medieval Shiʿite works attempt to portray Abū Ḥanīfa in a positive light in order to claim that his achievements were due to his proto-Shiʿi teachers.[190] On the other hand, there existed a more belligerent strain within medieval Shiʿi works that attacked Abū Ḥanīfa.[191] In any case, this is an interesting phenomenon that we shall encounter again in the next chapter when we turn to the history of *masānīd* works for Abū Ḥanīfa.

A final point I wish to emphasise is something that was implicit in my treatment of Ibn Abī al-ʿAwwām al-Saʿdī and al-Ṭaḥāwī's *manāqib* works but deserves to be reiterated, and that is the extent to which *manāqib* works reflect a broader nexus between the law, the *madhhab*s, social norms, and lived Islam. The schools of law, through the medium of *manāqib* works and biographical dictionaries, became schools of orthodoxy in medieval Sunnism.[192] This meant that *manāqib* works were essential to the consolidation of orthodox identities.[193] They helped to fashion an orthodox school identity that would prove integral to the community of masters, professors, teachers, students, judges, and others that made up the classical guild school. At the same time, the production of *manāqib* works reflects the *madhhab*s' wider social remit. *Manāqib* works provide insights into the kind of social world that the law, broadly conceived, attempted to nourish. *Manāqib* works were a form of composite historical writing in which the features of history, biographical dictionary, and biography were all integrated. These constitutive elements of *manāqib* works all served to accentuate different aspects of the lives of medieval Muslims. The form of writing one finds in *manāqib* works sought to create a society and not simply describe a past one.[194] This is why it spoke to everyday concerns. *Manāqib* works, after all, were performed

[190] Qazwīnī al-Rāzī, *Kitāb al-Naqż: maʿrūf bih baʿż-i mathālib al-navāṣib fī naqż baʿż fażāʾiḥ al-ravāfiż*, ed. Jalāl al-Dīn Muḥaddith (Tehran: Anjuman-i Āthār-i Millī, 1980), 159–60, 236, 455.

[191] Al-Shaykh al-Mufīd, 'Kitāb Faḍāʾiḥ Abī Ḥanīfa', Majmūʿa MS no. 2, Marʿashī Library, Qum. See also al-Majlisī, *Biḥār al-anwār* (Tehran: Dār al-Kutub al-Islāmiyya, 1956), 10: 202–4, 212–14, 216, 220–2.

[192] I should emphasise, again, that this study examines one aspect of the formation of Sunni orthodoxy. Other aspects, such as Sunni–Shiʿi relations, gender, politics, and so on, deserve independent treatment. On Sunni–Shiʿi relations and the question of orthodoxy see Stewart, *Islamic Legal Orthodoxy*; and Dann, 'Contested Boundaries'.

[193] Ahmed's *What Is Islam?*, 453 ff., a sweeping critique of the legal discourse of *fiqh*, fails to apply his sensitive and brilliant analyses of poetry and ethical treatises to works of law.

[194] This relationship between historical writing, its reception among readers or listeners, and its subsequent impact on shaping the present and future is described by Koselleck, *The Practice of Conceptual History*, 111: 'Historical times can be identified if we direct our view to where time itself occurs or is subjectively enacted in humans as historical beings: in the relationship between past and future, which always constitutes an elusive present. The compulsion to coordinate past and future so as to be able to live at all is inherent in any human being. Put more concretely, on the one hand, every human being and every human community has a space of experience out of which one acts in which past things

in everyday, lived, experienced, and public settings, such as when they were taught and performed beside the shrine of Abū Ḥanīfa. Early Muslims did not conceive of time in one single fashion. They knew of historical epochs. Narratives about the sequential progression of time – from accounts of creation, antediluvian period, and prognostications about the future (eschatology) – represented one conception of time. The division of history into generational epochs (*ṭabaqāt*) was another form of periodisation. But perhaps the conception of time most germane to medieval Muslims was the lifespan of the human. It was this conception of time and its organisation that became the central preoccupation of *manāqib* works. Authors began with Abū Ḥanīfa's birth, gave an overview of the life of his ancestors, provided some details about his childhood, outlined his educational trajectory, deliberated upon features of his adult life, and culminated with the final years of his life. This was a schema of time that was immediate to all potential readers and listeners. Furthermore, narratives of ritual purity, education, asceticism, economic scarcity, hardships, enemies, suffering, and political pressure and persecution were entirely consistent with the life that most people experienced. In this respect, *manāqib* works were a far cry from the world of country leisures, delights, coquettes, and flamboyance described by works of *Fürstenspiegel*. Societies needed heroes, and durable ones at that. The lifespan of dynasties and the durability of their legacies paled in comparison to those of the eponyms. *Manāqib* works served to define a catholic community whose goal became not just salvation and piety but the cultivation of virtue in a testing social world. The social and moral consistency of a select group of great Sunni heroes was woven into narratives to which ordinary members of society could relate. The world of princes was never going to resonate with most people, and, in any case, princes and rulers came and went by the hundreds and were mere drops in the ocean. *Manāqib* works were another way of establishing the fact that the Abū Ḥanīfas of the world were like gold dust. They were exemplars of orthodoxy and virtue.

It might be that this fact has not been appreciated because little attention has been paid to these works and that, when scholars have written about them, they have understood them to be literary artefacts of Muslim hagiography.[195] The use of hagiography to describe *manāqib* works for the eponymous founders of the *madhhab*s has been both unfortunate and misleading. The problem of hagiography is the problem of *fabula*, and it was an ideological project of the nineteenth century engineered by the Bollandists that sought to distinguish hagiography (miraculous events)

are present or can be remembered, and, on the other, one always acts with reference to specific horizons of expectation.'

195 Pellat, s.v. '*Manakib*', $EI^2$.

from *historia*.[196] Such miraculous events are absent, almost in their entirety, from *manāqib* works for eponyms. So, reading these works carefully requires confronting certain errors of classification and preconceptions regarding genres of history and hagiography. Additionally, it demands a recognition of tendentious treatments of medieval Islamic scholarship, texts, and scholars. Nietzsche's cynical reading of European morality as 'nothing but a series of disguises for the will to power',[197] inflected with Weberian notions of authority and power, has produced scholarship on medieval Islamic religious societies that sometimes struggles to move beyond the platitudes about legitimacy, power, and authority.[198] Medieval moral and ethical traditions are seen as veils for deeper motives such as the exercise of power, the extension of authority, and the establishment of legitimacy. This reading of medieval religious traditions makes unintelligible the deeper, explicit currents that move these texts, their authors, and their readers. It was the cultivation of virtues (and movements that could channel them) among moral communities in a difficult and unsettling world that *manāqib* works sought. They posited a social vision, a society, and the bonds and loyalties that would make life within it worthwhile and facilitate the passage to the life that they believed existed beyond it, and it was a path that our authors believed had been trodden by the likes of Abū Ḥanīfa. We historians need not believe in this or any other vision sketched by medieval religious communities, but we nevertheless must try to make sense of its appeal among the people we study.[199]

[196] For a sympathetic account see Delahaye, *The Work of the Bollandists*, esp. ch. 6 and ch. 8. For the Bollandist method see de Gaffier, 'L'Hagiographe et son public'. A number of important studies have been published in the field of medieval history and literature seeking to challenge the utility of a history–hagiography binary. I have consulted a number of studies, such as Lifshitz, 'Beyond Positivism and Genre'. Heffernan, *Sacred Biography*, 15–71, is another important intervention, which reads 'hagiographical' texts as sacred biography. Heffernan's discussion, especially his historiographical introduction, ignores the contributions of Bollandists. Still, I have benefited from Heffernan's insights into medieval texts and their relationship to history writing. I also benefited from reading two books that focus on medieval Christian hagiography: Kreiner, *The Social Life of Hagiography*; and Krueger, *Writing and Holiness*, esp. 189–97.

[197] Macintyre, *After Virtue*, 299. See also Ricoeur on the 'masters of suspicion' in Ricoeur, *Freud and Philosophy*, 32 ff.; and Felski, *The Limits of Critique*, ch. 1.

[198] There are many examples, but some that come to mind are Safi, *The Politics of Knowledge*, xxiii–xxviii, xxxi (for examples of such programmatic statements); Crone, *Slaves on Horses*, 62–3, 88; Crone, *Pre-Industrial Societies*, 133–9 (the account is general and not specific to pre-modern Islam); Dabashi, *Authority in Islam*, where the author reads early Islamic history through a strictly Weberian and sociological lens.

[199] I do not mean to dismiss other ways of reading these texts. There are many lines of inquiry we must pursue when analysing these sources, some of which I hope to explore in the future.

The main aim of this chapter has been to draw attention to the fact that the late ninth century witnessed the beginning of a concentrated effort to contest ninth-century discourses of heresy against Abū Ḥanīfa, to unmake him as a heretic, and to establish him as a paragon of medieval Sunni orthodoxy. I have argued here that the *manāqib* genre was instrumental to this effort. This led me to undertake a detailed study of *manāqib* works written for Abū Ḥanīfa. In one respect, this represents a significant advance in our understanding and appreciation of a literary genre that has been either neglected or described as mere hagiography. I have rooted the development of this genre in a specific historical context. To this extent, our history of the *manāqib* genre has endeavoured to introduce new data and to study new or previously unexamined texts and scholars. What we should understand in these two phases marked by distinct literary phenomena – ninth-century discourses of heresy and shaping a new vision of medieval Sunni orthodoxy through *manāqib* works in the ninth–eleventh centuries – is that they reflect what Victor Turner has called a 'social drama' in which contesting religious movements were confronted with a choice between reconciliation and permanent cleavage.[200]

Discourses of heresy, gone unchallenged, might have resulted in permanent cleavage, but the decision to compose *manāqib* works helped to avoid this and instead fostered medieval Sunnism's great convergence. Discourses of heresy did not disappear, and attempts to rehabilitate them continued in the course of the medieval and early modern periods. We can hear the survival of these social and religious tensions in texts from this period. However, they were challenged consistently by *manāqib* authors, many of whom were Ḥanafīs but others who were not.[201] Permanent cleavage was no longer a viable option after the eleventh century. There was nothing inevitable about the compromise that gave way to a medieval Sunni orthodoxy in which four eponyms acquired the status of orthodox patron saints. The decision to compose *manāqib* works was a decisive one, and it was to have lasting consequences for the evolution of Sunni orthodoxy up until the modern day. In short, *manāqib* works acquired a key role in shaping the religious orientation of medieval Sunni orthodoxy.

200 Turner, 'Social Dramas and Stories about Them'.

201 Ibn ʿAbd al-Barr's (d. 463/1070) *al-Intiqāʾ* was a decisive work in this respect. I have counted and gathered notes on close to fifty *manāqib* works for Abū Ḥanīfa written after the eleventh century, but they are not immediately relevant to the period in question.

# 9 *Masānīd*: Narratives of Orthodoxy II

Works dedicated to reshaping conceptions of medieval Sunni orthodoxy were, as I argued in the previous chapter, composite in their nature. *Manāqib* works aimed to respond to a wide-ranging set of themes raised in the ninth–tenth centuries by proto-Sunni traditionalists to brand Abū Ḥanīfa as a heretic. A comprehensive defence of Abū Ḥanīfa required, therefore, authors of *manāqib* works to employ forms of argumentation that leaned on techniques familiar to historical writing, biographical dictionaries, and ḥadīth scholars.

*Masānīd* works mirrored this strategic diversity, too. Nevertheless, *musnad* books for Abū Ḥanīfa were devoted to defending him against one substantial charge: that he lacked sufficient expertise in a staple discipline of medieval proto-Sunni orthodoxy, ḥadīth. In this chapter I will provide a brief history of *masānīd* works.[1] This is necessary because, I argue, the genre was instrumental in establishing Abū Ḥanīfa as a pillar of medieval Sunni orthodoxy. After providing a historical overview of the development of this genre in the ninth–eleventh centuries with respect to Abū Ḥanīfa, I shall present two specimens from the genre. The first seeks to highlight the porous boundaries between *manāqib* and *masānīd* works, showing that they were both engaged in the task of defending Abū Ḥanīfa against charges of heresy and consolidating his orthodoxy identity. The second example points to an equally significant feature of *musnad* works for Abū Ḥanīfa – one that we also observed in our history of *manāqib* works – whereby proto-Sunni traditionalists as well as Ḥanafīs began to defend Abū Ḥanīfa and compose *musnad* works for him in an effort to document his orthodoxy.

[1] On *musnad* works for Abū Ḥanīfa see Melchert, 'Traditionist-Jurisprudents', 396 n. 50. A new twenty-volume history of *musnads* published in 2020, which I have not seen, has been produced by the prodigious scholar Latīf Raḥmān al-Bahrā'ichī, *Mawsūʿat al-ḥadīthiyya li-marwīyāt al-Imām Abī Ḥanīfa* (Istanbul: Dār al-Bayrūtī, 2020).

## 9.1 History of *Masānīd* Works

We saw in Chapter 7 that proto-Sunni traditionalists claimed a monopoly over the discipline of ḥadīth studies, which they extolled as a premier proto-Sunni discipline. They used this expertise to produce discourses of heresy against Abū Ḥanīfa by claiming that he showed little respect for the authority of ḥadīth, that he was an unreliable ḥadīth transmitter, and that he lacked expertise in its study. This was a serious charge, and there were no signs in the ninth or tenth centuries that such criticisms were letting up. Those movements seeking to promote Abū Ḥanīfa's proto-Sunni orthodoxy could not simply ignore them either, because by the ninth and tenth centuries the authority of ḥadīth in religious matters was now widely accepted by most medieval groups. Something had to be done.

A potent and ingenious solution was found in a genre of writing that had been the exclusive purview of proto-Sunni traditionalists of the ninth century. It was a leading proto-Sunni traditionalist of the tenth century who took it upon himself to document the first writers in the genre.[2] Ibn ʿAdī identified Yaḥyā b. ʿAbd al-Ḥamīd al-Ḥimmānī (d. 228/842–3) as the first author of a *musnad* work in Kufa;[3] in Basra, it was Musaddad b. Musarhad al-Baṣrī (d. 228/842–3);[4] in Egypt it was Asad b. Mūsā al-Umawī (d. 212/827);[5] and another candidate was Mūsā b. Qurra al-Zabīdī (d. 203/818).[6] According to al-Ḥākim al-Nīshāpūrī, the first scholars to write *musnad* works were ʿUbayd Allāh b. Mūsā al-ʿAbsī (d. 213/828)[7] and Abū Dāwūd al-Ṭayālisī (d. 203–4/818).[8] Other *musnad* authors of the ninth century included Isḥāq b. Rāhawayh,[9] ʿUthmān b. Saʿīd al-Dārimī,[10] and al-Ḥumaydī.[11]

[2] Ibn ʿAdī, *al-Kāmil*, 7: 2694–5, though for a more complete list of candidates seemingly culled from earlier sources see al-Suyūṭī, *Tadrīb al-rāwī fī sharḥ taqrīb al-Nawawī*, ed. Abū Qutayba Naẓar Muḥammad al-Fārayābī (Cairo: Maktabat al-Kawthar, 1994), 2: 599; and al-Kattānī, *al-Risāla al-mustaṭrafa*, 61–76; Kātib Çelebi, *Kashf al-ẓunūn*, 2: 1678–85 (Dār Iḥyā' edn.).

[3] Al-Kattānī, *al-Risāla al-mustaṭrafa*, 62. It seems al-Ḥimmānī made the claim himself, too: see al-Suyūṭī, *Tadrīb al-rāwī*, 2: 599. Al-Ḥimmānī's proto-Sunni credentials were questioned: see al-Dhahabī, *Siyar*, 10: 527–40. Since I am not making any specific arguments surrounding these individuals, I have used al-Dhahabī rather than earlier sources to acquire a basic overview of their careers.

[4] Al-Kattānī, *al-Risāla al-mustaṭrafa*, 62; al-Suyūṭī, *Tadrīb al-rāwī*, 2: 599; al-Dhahabī, *Siyar*, 10: 591–5.

[5] Al-Kattānī, *al-Risāla al-mustaṭrafa*, 61–2; al-Suyūṭī, *Tadrīb al-rāwī*, 2: 599; al-Dhahabī, *Siyar*, 10: 162–4.

[6] Al-Dhahabī, *Siyar*, 9: 346.

[7] Al-Kattānī, *al-Risāla al-mustaṭrafa*, 61; al-Suyūṭī, *Tadrīb al-rāwī*, 2: 599.

[8] Al-Suyūṭī, *Tadrīb al-rāwī*, 2: 599; al-Kattānī, *al-Risāla al-mustaṭrafa*, 61; al-Ishbīlī, *Fihrist*, 141; al-Sakhāwī, *Fatḥ al-Mughīth*, 1: 85.

[9] Al-Kattānī, *al-Risāla al-mustaṭrafa*, 65.

[10] Al-Kattānī, *al-Risāla al-mustaṭrafa*, 64.

[11] Al-Kattānī, *al-Risāla al-mustaṭrafa*, 67.

Our aim here is not to produce a complete list of authors, but rather to evidence the monopoly that proto-Sunni traditionists and traditionalists had over the *musnad* genre.[12] In the ninth century, defenders of Abū Ḥanīfa turned to this popular genre among proto-Sunni traditionalists and began to compile ḥadīths that they claimed Abū Ḥanīfa had learnt and transmitted. This decision was motivated by attempts to silence Abū Ḥanīfa's ninth- and tenth-century critics. These critics, we should remember, had Abū Ḥanīfa as their primary target. They were keenly aware, though, that their criticisms of him were meant to undermine the religious orthodoxy of Ḥanafīs of the ninth and tenth centuries. Authors of *musnad* works for Abū Ḥanīfa were hoping to establish him as a ḥadīth master par excellence; but they were also trying to make a point about themselves and the school's larger legacy – namely, that Ḥanafism was engaged in the same orthodox discipline of ḥadīth studies. Here is a list of *musnad* works for Abū Ḥanīfa composed during the eighth–eleventh centuries:

1. Ḥammād b. Abī Ḥanīfa (d. 176/792–3), *Musnad.*[13]
2. Abū Yūsuf (d. 182/798), *Nuskhat Abī Yūsuf.*[14]
3. Muḥammad b. al-Ḥasan al-Shaybānī (d. 189/805), *Nuskhat Muḥammad.*[15]
4. Al-Ḥasan b. Ziyād al-Lu'lu'ī (d. 204/819–20), *Musnad.*[16]
5. Abū Bakr Aḥmad b. Muḥammad b. Khālid al-Kalāʿī (*fl.* 300/912), *Musnad.*[17]
6. *Ibn ʿUqda (d. 333/944), *Akhbār Abī Ḥanīfa wa musnaduhu.*[18]
7. Ibn Abī al-ʿAwwām al-Saʿdī (d. 335/946), *Musnad.*[19]
8. **ʿUmar b. al-Ḥasan al-Ushnānī (d. 339/951), *Musnad.*[20]

[12] A Moroccan historian of the early twentieth century has produced a comprehensive survey of the genre, listing a total of forty-four works composed during the ninth century: see al-Kattānī, *al-Risāla al-mustaṭrafa*, 61–70.

[13] Al-Khwārizmī, *Jāmiʿ masānīd al-Imām al-Aʿẓam* (Hyderabad: Maṭbaʿat Majlis Dā'irat al-Maʿārif, 1914), 1: 5, 75–6.

[14] Al-Khwārizmī, *Jāmiʿ masānīd*, 1: 5, 75; Sezgin, *GAS*, 1: 414.

[15] Al-Khwārizmī, *Jāmiʿ masānīd*, 1: 5, 75, 76–7.

[16] Al-Khwārizmī, *Jāmiʿ masānīd*, 1: 5, 73–4.

[17] Al-Khwārizmī, *Jāmiʿ masānīd*, 1: 5; Murtaḍā al-Zabīdī, *ʿUqūd al-jawāhir*, 84; Abū al-Wafā' al-Afghānī in Abū Yūsuf, *Kitāb al-Āthār*, ed. Abū al-Wafā' al-Afghānī (Hyderabad: Lajnat Iḥyā' al-Maʿārif al-Nuʿmāniyya, n.d.), 4 (editor's introduction).

[18] Āghā Buzurg al-Ṭiḥrānī, *al-Dharīʿa ilā taṣānīf al-shīʿa* (Beirut: Dār al-Aḍwā, 1983), 1: 316. See also al-Najāshī, *Rijāl al-Najāshī*, ed. Muḥammad Jawād Nāʿīnī (Beirut: n.k., 1988), 1: 240 = ed. Mūsā al-Shabīrī al-Zanjānī (Qum: Mu'assasat al-Nashr al-Islāmī, 1998), 94–5; al-Ṭūsī, *Rijāl al-Ṭūsī*, 409; al-Ṭūsī, *Fihrist al-Ṭūsī*, ed. Muḥammad Ṣādiq Āl Baḥr al-ʿUlūm (Najaf: n.p., 1960), 57 = Sharīf al-Riḍā edn., 28–9; Ibn Shahrāshūb, *Maʿālim al-ʿulamā'*, 17.

[19] Al-Khwārizmī, *Jāmiʿ masānīd*, 1: 5, 77.

[20] Al-Khwārizmī, *Jāmiʿ masānīd*, 1: 5, 73–4. In Ibn al-Ushnānī we have a Sunni traditionalist (*aṣḥāb al-ḥadīth*) who authored a *musnad* work for Abū Ḥanīfa. For al-Dāraquṭnī's assessment of him see al-Ḥākim al-Nīshāpūrī, *Su'ālāt al-Ḥākim al-Nīshāpūrī li Dāraquṭnī*,

9. ʿAbd Allāh b. Muḥammad b. Yaʿqūb al-Ḥārithī al-Subadhmūnī (d. 340/952), *Musnad.*[21]
10. ***Ibn Ḥibbān al-Bustī (d. 354/965), *Kitāb ʿIlal mā istanada ilayhi Abū Ḥanīfa.*[22]
11. ***Abū Aḥmad ʿAbd Allāh b. ʿAdī al-Qaṭṭān (d. 360/970–1), *Musnad.*[23]
12. Muḥammad b. Isḥāq al-Kalābādhī (d. *c.*380/990), *Sharḥ musnad Abī Ḥanīfa.*[24]
13. Abū al-Qāsim Ṭalḥa b. Muḥammad b. Jaʿfar al-Shāhid (d. 380/990–1), *Musnad.*[25]
14. Abū Bakr Muḥammad b. Ibrāhīm b. ʿAlī b. ʿĀṣim b. al-Muqrī al-Iṣfahānī (d. 381/991–2), *Musnad.*[26]
15. *Abū al-Mufaḍḍal al-Shaybānī (d. 387/997), *Akhbār Abī Ḥanīfa wa musnaduhu.*[27]
16. **Abū ʿAlī Muḥammad b. Isḥāq b. Muḥammad b. Manda (d. 395/1005), *Musnad.*[28]
17. Abū al-Ḥusayn Muḥammad b. al-Muẓaffar b. Mūsā b. ʿĪsā b. Muḥammad (d. *c.*400/1009–10), *Musnad.*[29]
18. **Abū Nuʿaym al-Iṣfahānī (d. 430/1038), *Musnad.*[30]
19. Abū Bakr Muḥammad b. ʿAbd al-Bāqī b. Muḥammad al-Anṣārī (*fl.* fifth/eleventh century).[31]

162–4. See also al-Khaṭīb al-Baghdādī, *Tārīkh Baghdād*, 13: 90–3; al-Samʿānī, *al-Ansāb*, 1: 180 (Dār al-Jinān edn.); al-Dhahabī, *Siyar*, 15: 406.

[21] Al-Khwārizmī, *Jāmiʿ masānīd*, 1: 4, 69–70; Ibn Abī al-Wafā', *al-Jawāhir al-muḍiyya*, 2: 344–5; Ibn Quṭlūbughā, *Tāj al-tarājim*, 175–6; Sezgin, *GAS*, 1: 415.

[22] Yāqūt al-Ḥamawī, *Kitāb Muʿjam al-buldān*, 1: 616.

[23] Al-Khwārizmī, *Jāmiʿ masānīd*, 1: 4, 72–3; Kātib Çelebi, *Kashf al-ẓunūn*, 2: 1681 (Dār Iḥyā' edn.).

[24] al-Ḥibshī, *Jāmiʿ al-shurūḥ*, 3: 1700–1701; Mu'assasat Āl al-Bayt, *Al-Fihras al-shāmil li al-turāth al-ʿarabī al-islāmī al-makhṭūṭ: al-ḥadīth al-nabawī al-sharīf wa ʿulūmuhu wa rijāluhu* (Amman: Mu'assasat Āl al-Bayt, 1991), 1008 (extant in manuscript).

[25] Al-Khwārizmī, *Jāmiʿ masānīd*, 1: 4, 70–1. His affiliations are unclear. He seems to have been yet another Sunni traditionalist author of a *musnad*, who also happened to study under Ibn al-Ushnānī. He was the representative of the official court witnesses, and his proximity to judges helped him to write a history of them (*Akhbār al-quḍāt*). Then there are strong indications of his Muʿtazilī beliefs: see al-Khaṭīb al-Baghdādī, *Tārīkh Baghdād*, 10: 480–1; al-Dhahabī, *Siyar*, 16: 396–7.

[26] Al-Khwārizmī, *Jāmiʿ masānīd*, 1: 5; al-Ḥibshī, *Jāmiʿ al-shurūḥ*, 3: 1701; Ziriklī, *al-Aʿlām*, 5: 295 (15th edn.); al-Dhahabī, *Siyar*, 16: 398; Ibn ʿImād, *Shadharāt al-dhahab*, 3: 101; al-Sakhāwī, *al-Iʿlān*, 220, 378; al-Kattānī, *Fihris al-fahāris*, 2: 972; Sezgin, *GAS*, 1: 415.

[27] Al-Ṭihrānī, *al-Dharīʿa ilā taṣānīf al-shīʿa*, 1: 316.

[28] Brockelmann, *GAL*, supp. 1: 286; Sezgin, *GAS*, 1: 415. I have not seen the Berlin manuscript, but there is a suggestion that Ibn Manda represents another Sunni traditionalist aiming to consolidate Abū Ḥanīfa's orthodoxy: see al-Khwārizmī, *Jāmiʿ masānīd*, 1: 129.

[29] Al-Khwārizmī, *Jāmiʿ masānīd*, 1: 4, 71–2.

[30] Al-Khwārizmī, *Jāmiʿ masānīd*, 1: 4, 71–2; Sezgin, *GAS*, 1: 415.

[31] Al-Khwārizmī, *Jāmiʿ masānīd*, 1: 4–5, 72.

20. Abū ʿAbd Allāh Muḥammad b. Khusraw al-Balkhī (d. 522–3/1128–9), *Musnad*.[32]
21. Anonymous, *Jazāʾ al-aʿmāl*.[33]

It is difficult to say anything about the late eighth- and early ninth-century *musnad* works, and without having compared them to the extant works attributed to Abū Yūsuf and al-Shaybānī, I shall let them pass without comment. My interest here is in the production of *musnad* works during the ninth–eleventh centuries. A large body of material had been produced by proto-Sunni traditionalists in the ninth century to discredit Abū Ḥanīfa's learning in the discipline of ḥadīth. As the ninth century went on it was becoming clear that patron saints of medieval Sunni orthodoxy were required to have a good grasp of ḥadīth. During the very century that proto-Sunni traditionalists were attacking Abū Ḥanīfa's orthodoxy and were themselves writing *musnad* works, other proto-Sunni scholars began to compile works that contained the ḥadīths that Abū Ḥanīfa had memorised and learnt. Who was writing these *musnads*?

Surprisingly, only a handful of Ḥanafīs were involved in writing such works (three from the tenth–eleventh centuries who appear in Ḥanafī biographical dictionaries). They began to see the potential in the *musnad* genre to curtail criticisms of Abū Ḥanīfa's ḥadīth expertise. There was the added pressure to respond to proto-Sunni traditionalist objections to a jurisprudence supposedly practised by the Ḥanafīs that was deemed to be anchored in speculation and not ḥadīth. The sight of numerous *musnad* works in the name of their eponymous founder would serve as evidence of Ḥanafism's ḥadīth pedigree.

Interestingly, Ḥanafīs were not the only scholarly community involved in producing *musnad* works for Abū Ḥanīfa. The first phenomenon that we have, indicated by an asterisk next to the names of Abū al-Mufaḍḍal al-Shaybānī and Ibn ʿUqda, is that of non-Sunni authors writing *musnad* works. I have identified two such examples. Abū al-Mufaḍḍal al-Shaybānī was a Kufan scholar who had studied in Shām and Egypt before settling in Baghdad. He had studied under numerous scholars but he was known to have been a close student of al-Ṭabarī. There was, however, a cloud of suspicion that had gathered around him on account of his tendency to transmit strange traditions (*gharāʾib*) and traditions perceived as bolstering Shiʿism. There was a growing consensus among Sunni traditionalists that he had pretensions to being a Sunni scholar but failed to meet their standards.[34]

[32] Al-Khwārizmī, *Jāmiʿ masānīd*, 1: 5, 74.
[33] Al-Nasafī, *al-Qand fī dhikr al-ʿulamāʾ Samarqand*, 144; al-Samʿānī, *al-Ansāb*, 5: 538 (Dār al-Jinān edn.).
[34] Al-Khaṭīb al-Baghdādī, *Tārīkh Baghdād*, 3: 499–501; al-Sahmī, *Suʾālāt Ḥamza b. Yūsuf al-Sahmī li al-Dāraquṭnī*, 274–5.

It seems as if the Shiʿi community saw him in a similar light. Al-Najāshī puts it slightly differently: 'In the beginning of his career he was reliable, but he got things messed up towards the end of it.' Al-Najāshī does give us a list of his works, which certainly betrays a sympathy for Shiʿism, Zaydism, and Ḥanafism. Based on other precedents, I am assuming that the *Akhbār Abī Ḥanīfa* ascribed to Abū al-Mufaḍḍal al-Shaybānī would have included a *musnad*, too.[35] Our second author whose relationship to medieval Sunnism was ambivalent was Ibn ʿUqda. He was known as a Sunni ḥadīth scholar, but historians gave him mixed reviews. He had an impressive array of Sunnī teachers and students, yet he managed to give some the impression that he was a Zaydī, and others cast aspersions on his reliability as a ḥadīth scholar.[36] In medieval Shiʿi biographical dictionaries he is classed as a Zaydī of the Jārūdī branch and as someone who was revered among that religious community. Like Abū al-Mufaḍḍal al-Shaybānī, Ibn ʿUqda's list of works speaks to a diverse heritage. For our immediate purposes, it is his authorship of *Akhbār Abī Ḥanīfa wa musnaduhu* that stands out.[37]

Why were scholars such as Abū al-Mufaḍḍal al-Shaybānī and Ibn ʿUqda interested in writing *musnad* works for Abū Ḥanīfa? Their works have not survived, so we can do no more than hazard some guesses. One possibility is that we are still dealing in the middle of the tenth century with eclectic identities, such that some students and scholars could move between Shiʿi and Zaydī identities and Sunni ones. In this case, scholars moving along such a spectrum saw it as perfectly natural to compose *musnad* works for Abū Ḥanīfa. On the other hand, as was highlighted in Chapter 8, there were Shiʿi scholars who wrote about Abū Ḥanīfa from a slightly negative perspective, or sought to highlight his dependence on Shiʿi imams. In this case, these *musnad* authors might have been interested in drawing attention to traditions that Abū Ḥanīfa transmitted from these imams. Here, the Zaydīs too might have wanted to show connections between Abū Ḥanīfa and Zayd b. ʿAlī that went beyond support for the latter's rebellion.

Then there is the authorship of *musnad* works for Abū Ḥanīfa by proto-Sunni traditionalists. The consolidation of Abū Ḥanīfa's orthodox Sunni

[35] Al-Najāshī, *Rijāl al-Najāshī*, 396 (al-Zanjānī edn.).

[36] Al-Khaṭīb al-Baghdādī, *Tārīkh Baghdād*, 6: 147–59. See also ʿAbd al-Rashīd al-Nuʿmānī, *Naẓarāt ʿalā kutub al-thalāth fī al-ḥadīth*, ed. Muḥammad ʿUmar ʿUthmān al-Nadwī (n.p.: Iḥyāʾ al-Maʿārif al-Islāmiyya, 2016), 32–44(for an account of *musnad* works for Abū Ḥanīfa), 34 (on Ibn ʿUqda). ʿAbd al-Rashīd al-Nuʿmānī was one of the great Ḥanafī scholars of ḥadīth in India and Pakistan, and his *Makānat al-Imām Abī Ḥanīfa fī al-ḥadīth* has become a classic in modern times.

[37] Al-Najāshī, *Rijāl al-Najāshī*, 1: 240 (Nāʾīnī edn.) = 94–5 (al-Zanjānī edn.); al-Ṭūsī, *Rijāl al-Ṭūsī*, 409; al-Ṭūsī, *Fihrist al-Ṭūsī*, 57 (Āl Baḥr al-ʿUlūm edn.) = al-Sharīf al-Riḍā edn.), 28–9; Ibn Shahrāshūb, *Maʿālim al-ʿulamāʾ*, 17.

identity was aided in great measure by the appearance of *musnad* works for him composed by proto-Sunni traditionalists of the late tenth and early eleventh centuries. In the list above, two asterisks appear next to Ibn al-Ushnānī, al-Kalābādhī, Ibn Manda, and Abū Nuʿaym. Three of these four were Sunni traditionalists and one was possibly a Ḥanafī. Let us begin with the latter. Al-Kalābādhī is the author of two works, his landmark manual of Sufism and a less well-known work on traditions with mystical themes.[38] These books contain no clues as to his legal affiliation, but he has been claimed as a Ḥanafī by more than one Ḥanafī biographical dictionary.[39]

As for Ibn al-Ushnānī, he signals a crucial moment in the history of unmaking Abū Ḥanīfa as a heretic and establishing his orthodox Sunni identity. Ibn al-Ushnānī belonged to a learned family.[40] His father had studied under proto-Sunni traditionalists such as Ibn ʿAwn and Yaḥyā b. Maʿīn. The father had at least three sons: about ʿUmar we know next to nothing; Muḥammad had studied with ninth-century ḥadīth scholars, one of whom was ʿAlī b. Sahl b. al-Mughīra al-Bazzāz (d. 271/884);[41] another brother was a judge, Abū al-Ḥusayn.[42] Ibn al-Ushnānī himself was considered to be an outstanding Sunni traditionalist (*ṣāḥib al-ḥadīth mujawwidan*). Those who related traditions from him included the Sunni traditionalist Abū al-ʿAbbās Ibn ʿUqda mentioned earlier and Abū Ḥafṣ b. Shāhīn (d. 385/996). Ibn al-Ushnānī was a judge in Shām, but he was remembered as having served as the judge of Baghdad for three days under the caliph al-Muqtadir. He had also held a position as a *ḥisba* officer. But it was as a ḥadīth scholar that he was best known.[43] There is nothing to indicate that he was a Ḥanafī, and the descriptions we have of his learning point to a Sunni traditionalist orientation. His role as

[38] Al-Kalābādhī, *Baḥr al-fawāʾid al-mashhūr bi maʿānī al-akhbār*, ed. Wajīh Kamāl al-Dīn Zakī (Cairo: Dār al-Salām, 2008); al-Kalābādhī, *al-Taʿarruf li madhhab ahl al-taṣawwuf*, ed. ʿAbd al-Ḥalīm Maḥmūd (Cairo: Maktabat al-Thaqāfa al-Ḥīniyya, n.d.). See also Sezgin, *GAS*, 1: 668–9.

[39] Ibn Abī al-Wafāʾ, *al-Jawāhir al-muḍiyya*, 4: 105–6; Ibn Quṭlūbughā, *Tāj al-tarājim*, 333; al-Laknawī, *al-Fawāʾid al-bahiyya*, 161, 234 (Dār al-Maʿrifa edn.). There is also the possibility that al-Kalābādhī has been confused with ʿAbd Allāh b. Muḥammad b. Yaʿqūb al-Ḥārithī al-Subadhmūnī (no. 9 in our list), whose name was also al-Kalābādhī.

[40] Al-Samʿānī, *al-Ansāb*, 1: 170–1 (Dār al-Jinān edn.).

[41] Al-Dhahabī, *Siyar*, 13: 159–60.

[42] A work of his has survived: Ibn al-Ushnānī, *Juzʾ al-Qāḍī al-Ushnānī in Majmūʿat ajzāʾ ḥadīthiyya*, ed. Mashhūr b. Ḥasan Āl Salmān Abū ʿUbayda (Beirut: Dār Ibn Ḥazm, 2001), 307–28. This same brother also wrote *maqtal* works on Ḥusayn b. ʿAlī and Zayd b. ʿAlī, which makes one wonder yet again about the fluid identities of Sunni traditionalists and, perhaps, Ibn al-Ushnānī himself.

[43] Al-Khaṭīb al-Baghdādī, *Tārīkh Baghdād*, 13: 90–3; al-Samʿānī, *al-Ansāb*, 1: 170–1 (Dār al-Jinān edn.); al-Dhahabī, *Siyar*, 15: 406–7.

a teacher to Ibn Shāhīn may be significant, since we have identified Ibn Shāhīn as an exceptional Sunni traditionalist ḥadīth critic who adopted a more accommodating tone towards Abū Ḥanīfa.

We have a similar case in the person of Abū Nuʿaym al-Iṣfahānī. A ḥadīth master from Iṣfahān, Abū Nuʿaym was an Ashʿarī Shāfiʿī scholar who produced a number of monumental works on Ṣūfism, ḥadīth, local history, and traditionists.[44] His *Musnad Abī Ḥanīfa* is an intriguing work. It documents very clearly a new phase in tenth-century Sunnism in which there was a conscious attempt to portray Abū Ḥanīfa as a man of orthodoxy. It opens with eleven reports of a biographical nature. Three of these portray Abū Ḥanīfa as a persecuted martyr–patron saint who supported the family of the Prophet Muḥammad.[45] This is followed by a chapter with seventeen reports extolling his piety, asserting his juristic skill, exhibiting his unwavering commitment to ḥadīth, and absolving him of any doctrinal deviance.[46] Then there is a brief section on Companions of the Prophet Muḥammad whom Abū Ḥanīfa saw. This was one argument defenders of Abū Ḥanīfa could employ against his proto-Sunni traditionalist critics. Abū Ḥanīfa had seen some Companions and, according to some Ḥanafīs, had heard traditions from them. This privilege escaped al-Shāfiʿī, Mālik b. Anas, and Aḥmad b. Ḥanbal, all of whom were born too late. Abū Nuʿaym takes a moderate position on the contentious issue of how many Companions Abū Ḥanīfa saw and heard traditions from, and concludes that he saw two Companions and probably heard something from them.[47] At the same time, the work includes a few unflattering views of Abū Ḥanīfa.[48] The overwhelming majority of the text is concerned with documenting 325 traditions Abū Ḥanīfa related from other ḥadīth scholars. Abū Nuʿaym singles out 266 shaykhs from whom Abū Ḥanīfa heard traditions: 259 are identified and 7 remain unknown to him. Abū Nuʿaym's other works might be suggestive of a certain animosity towards Abū Ḥanīfa. He is the only one of the four Sunni eponyms who does not receive a notice in Abū Nuʿaym's *Ḥilyat al-awliyāʾ*. He also finds a place in Abū Nuʿaym's book on weak traditionists. It is bad enough that he makes it into this book, but Abū Nuʿaym's entry goes on to say that Abū Ḥanīfa believed that the Quran was created and that he was made to repent from his disgraceful views on more than one occasion. Abū Nuʿaym ends the entry by saying that Abū Ḥanīfa made numerous

[44] Al-Dhahabī, *Siyar*, 17: 453–64.
[45] Abū Nuʿaym al-Iṣfahānī, *Musnad al-Imām Abī Ḥanīfa*, 18–19.
[46] Abū Nuʿaym al-Iṣfahānī, *Musnad al-Imām Abī Ḥanīfa*, 20–3.
[47] Abū Nuʿaym al-Iṣfahānī, *Musnad al-Imām Abī Ḥanīfa*, 24.
[48] Abū Nuʿaym al-Iṣfahānī, *Musnad al-Imām Abī Ḥanīfa*, 19 (Abū Ḥanīfa invented his genealogy), 20 (Abū Ḥanīfa concerned himself with obscure issues).

mistakes (*kathīr al-khaṭa' wa al-awhām*).[49] He concludes his book with this summary statement:[50]

> The people I have named in this chapter I have done so on account of their transmitting rejected *(al-manākīr)*, forged (*al-mawḍūʿāt*), and false narrations (*al-abāṭīl*). I have spoken about their weakness (*duʿf*). Their case is not concealed to the scholars of this discipline. The light of their traditions is lost, and instead darkness is found in most of their traditions. ... In my opinion, one cannot transmit narrations from most of these people. Their ḥadīth cannot be adduced as proofs. They can only be written down for consideration (*al-iʿtibār*) and for general awareness (*al-maʿrifa*).

I would characterise Abū Nuʿaym's *musnad* as one that indicates the new conciliatory approach towards Abū Ḥanīfa that facilitated the disappearance of discourses of heresy and enabled his integration into the new Sunni orthodoxy of the tenth and eleventh centuries. At the same time, however, Abū Nuʿaym's works also reflect the anxieties that Sunni traditionalists still felt about the legacy of discourses of heresy in the ninth–tenth centuries, on the one hand, and the contemporary climate of Sunnism during the tenth–eleventh centuries that was unmaking these heresiological discourses, on the other.

Ibn Manda also poses a slight predicament. He was a renowned Sunni traditionalist of the tenth century. Modern scholars have described him as the author/redactor of a *musnad* for Abū Ḥanīfa.[51] This does not give an entirely accurate picture of Ibn Manda's *musnad* and his views on Abū Ḥanīfa and Ḥanafism. I have not seen the manuscript in Berlin. I am aware that Ibn Manda is the transmitter of al-Subadhmūnī's *musnad* for Abū Ḥanīfa.[52] I suspect, therefore, that this led Sezgin to attribute the *musnad* to Ibn Manda. So, we know Ibn Manda as a transmitter of a *musnad* work for Abū Ḥanīfa, which he heard from a tenth-century Ḥanafī scholar. This Ḥanafī scholar, al-Subadhmūnī, was known as one of Ibn Manda's teachers.[53] However, there is a tiny detail contained within a barely legible manuscript that complicates this story of Ibn Manda as a Sunni traditionalist writing a *musnad* to rehabilitate Abū Ḥanīfa. *Majmūʿa* 62 of the Ẓāhiriyya manuscript library includes fragments from two works authored by Ibn Manda.[54] One is

[49] Abū Nuʿaym, *Kitāb al-Ḍuʿafā'*, ed. Fārūq Ḥamāda (Casablanca: Dār al-Thaqāfa, 1984), 154. Other proto-Ḥanafīs make it into the book: the Kufan judge, Nūḥ b. Darrāj (151); the judge of Marw, Nūḥ b. Abī Maryam (151); and Yūsuf b. Khālid al-Samtī (164).

[50] Abū Nuʿaym, *Kitāb al-Ḍuʿafā'*, 167–70.

[51] Sezgin, *GAS*, 1: 415.

[52] Al-Ḥārithī al-Subadhmūnī, *Musnad Abī Ḥanīfa* (Beirut: Dār al-Kutub al-ʿIlmiyya, 2008), 19.

[53] Al-Samʿānī, *al-Ansāb* (al-Bārūdī edn.), 3: 213.

[54] Muḥammad Nāṣir al-Dīn al-Albānī, *Fihris makhṭūṭāt dār al-kutub al-ẓāhiriyya: al-muntakhab min makhṭūṭāt al-ḥadīth* (Riyadh: Maktabat al-Maʿārif, 2001), 170.

Ibn Manda's *Kitāb al-Tawḥīd*, and its fragment found in the manuscript contains an exposition of Sunni creed concerning the uncreated nature of the Quran and its pronunciation. The second fragment appears to contain a critique of Abū Ḥanīfa under the title 'The view of leading ḥadīth critics and their testimony against him and exposing his shortcomings'.[55] Much of the manuscript is illegible, but in one line we have Ibn Manda quoting someone who said that Abū Ḥanīfa died as someone who was misguided and misguided others (*ḍāll muḍill*).[56] The short treatise begins with a Quranic theme. Ibn Manda cites Quran 2.143, 'And so too have We made you a select nation of faith, nobly upright in equity, that you might be witnesses over all men, and the Messenger alone be witness over you.' which was a verse used often when medieval scholars sought to establish consensus (*ijmāʿ*).[57] Ibn Manda then fills the page with a long list of scholars, which I presume from the context he gives consists of the names of ḥadīth scholars who attacked the religious credibility of Abū Ḥanīfa in an effort to establish a scholarly consensus regarding his shortcomings.[58] It is quite possible, then, that scholars such as Ibn Manda did not write or transmit a *musnad* in order to defend Abū Ḥanīfa.

Though these *musnad*s signal a new direction in the history of Sunni orthodoxy and provide a more detailed picture of how it was taking shape in the tenth century, other Sunni traditionalists were disturbed by these developments. We can sense, in fact, a crisis among Sunni traditionalists. Men such as Ibn ʿAdī and Ibn Ḥibbān took to writing explicitly against the growing phenomenon of *musnad*s for Abū Ḥanīfa. Ibn ʿAdī, a staunch proponent of discourses of heresy against Abū Ḥanīfa, wrote a critique of Abū Ḥanīfa's *musnad*s. He closes his entry on Abū Ḥanīfa in *al-Kāmil* with a number of ḥadīths Abū Ḥanīfa is said to have transmitted, and he then identifies problems with them. According to Ibn ʿAdī, one problem concerns Abū Ḥanīfa's informants. He claimed to transmit ḥadīth on the authority of transmitters who were not known by other traditionists to have transmitted them.[59] Ibn ʿAdī accuses Abū Ḥanīfa of making additions to the content of traditions. Not one of the other traditionists who transmitted the tradition narrated the phrase Abū Ḥanīfa is said to have

[55] Ibn Manda, 'Nubdha fī naqd Abī Ḥanīfa [Qawl al-thiqāt al-mutaqaddimīn wa shahādātuhim ʿalayhi wa al-kashf ʿan masāwīhi]', Makabat al-Ẓāhiriyya, *Majmūʿa* 62, fol. 141a.

[56] Ibn Manda, 'Nubdha fī naqd Abī Ḥanīfa', fol. 141a.

[57] Al-Jaṣṣāṣ, *al-Fuṣūl fī al-uṣūl*, ed. Muḥammad Tāmir (Beirut: Dār al-Kutub al-ʿIlmiyya, 2000), 2: 154.Translation from Nuh Ha Mim Keller, *The Quran Beheld: An English Translation from the Arabic* (Istanbul: Stanchion Press, 2022), 22.

[58] Ibn Manda, 'Nubdha fī naqd Abī Ḥanīfa', fol. 141b.

[59] Ibn ʿAdī, *al-Kāmil*, 8: 243, 245 (Dār al-Kutub edn. = Riyadh: Maktabat al-Rushd, 2018, 10: 131, 133).

added.[60] He points out other irregularities in Abū Ḥanīfa's traditions. He compares Abū Ḥanīfa's habit in this regard with another traditionist. Though both of them were weak, Ibn ʿAdī says, at least the other knew the ḥadīth with more precision.[61] Ibn ʿAdī tries to come to a fair judgement with respect to Abū Ḥanīfa's *musnad*s. His assessment is that some of Abū Ḥanīfa's ḥadīths are accurate. The vast majority of the traditions he transmitted contain inaccuracies (*ghalaṭ*), distortions (*taṣāḥīf*), and additions (*ziyādāt*) in both their chains of transmission (*asānīd*) and content (*mutūn*). There are also distortions with respect to the names of traditionists (*al-rijāl*). Ibn ʿAdī believes that this is the case with respect to almost all of Abū Ḥanīfa's transmissions. In fact, no more than seven to ten of his ḥadīths can be considered sound.[62] This should not surprise people, Ibn ʿAdī writes, 'because Abū Ḥanīfa was not among the scholars of ḥadīth. It is only natural, after all, that an individual whose situation is as we have described, cannot be relied upon with respect to ḥadīth.'[63]

Ibn Ḥibbān must have put forward similar criticisms of *musnad* works composed for Abū Ḥanīfa. A small part of his literary career was devoted to combating the rise of *manāqib* and *musnad* works for Abū Ḥanīfa. We know that he wrote a book entitled 'The defects of Abū Ḥanīfa transmissions' and another on 'The defects of praiseworthy and blameworthy reports about Abū Ḥanīfa'.[64] Al-Khaṭīb al-Baghdādī, himself a notorious critic of Abū Ḥanīfa, provided a recommended reading list he had received from his teacher of beneficial ḥadīth works written by Ibn Ḥibbān, which included both of these works.[65] Though these works have not survived, Ibn Ḥibbān's major works have, and they give us an insight into his attempts to resist Sunnism's new consensus forming around Abū Ḥanīfa. His *al-Thiqāt* and *Mashāhīr ʿulamāʾ al-amṣār* we can deal with very quickly. The books on reliable ḥadīth scholars and famous scholars in the Islamic world contain no entry for Abū Ḥanīfa. Conversely, Ibn Ḥibbān's history of weak and rejected ḥadīth transmitters has much to say about Abū Ḥanīfa. The notice begins with a broad evaluation of Abū Ḥanīfa and it betrays Ibn Ḥibbān's special interest in Abū Ḥanīfa's ḥadīth transmissions. Ibn Ḥibbān tells us that Abū

[60] Ibn ʿAdī, *al-Kāmil*, 8: 243–4 (*zāda Abū Ḥanīfa hādhā fī al-matn*) 245 (Dār al-Kutub edn. = Riyadh edn., 10: 131–2).
[61] Ibn ʿAdī, *al-Kāmil*, 8: 245 (Dār al-Kutub edn. = Riyadh edn., 10: 132).
[62] Ibn ʿAdī, *al-Kāmil*, 8: 246 (*lam yaṣiḥḥa lahu fī jamīʿ mā yarwīhi illā biḍʿa ʿashar ḥadīthan*) (Dār al-Kutub edn. = Riyadh edn., 10: 133-4).
[63] Ibn ʿAdī, *al-Kāmil*, 8: 246 (Dār al-Kutub edn. = Riyadh edn., 10: 134).
[64] *Kitāb ʿIlal mā asnada Abū Ḥanīfa* and *Kitāb ʿIlal manāqib Abī Ḥanīfa wa mathālibihi*. See Yāqūt al-Ḥamawī, *Muʿjam al-buldān* (Beirut: Dār Ṣādir, 1977), 1: 417; al-Suyūṭī, *al-Baḥr alladhī zakhara fī sharḥ Alfiyat al-Suyūṭī fī al-ḥadīth* (Medina: Maktabat al-Ghurabāʾ al-Athariyya, 1999), 3: 888; al-Ḥibshī, *Jāmiʿ al-shurūḥ*, 3: 1701; Ismāʿīl Pāshā al-Baghdādī, *Hadiyyat al-ʿārifīn*, 2: 45 (Dār Iḥyāʾ edn.).
[65] Al-Khaṭīb al-Baghdādī, *al-Jāmiʿ li al-akhlāq al-rāwī wa ādāb al-sāmiʿ*, 2: 302–3.

Ḥanīfa transmitted 130 ḥadīths with *isnāds*. Ibn Ḥibbān wrote with supreme confidence that there are no other ḥadīths from him in the entire world other than these 130. Of these 130 ḥadīths, Ibn Ḥibbān believed that Abū Ḥanīfa had committed errors in 120 by way of either mixing up the *isnāds* or changing the *matn*. He concludes that in situations when someone's errors significantly outweigh their positive results, their traditions cannot be relied upon. This seems like a précis of Ibn Ḥibbān's now lost book on the defects of Abū Ḥanīfa's ḥadīths. For Ibn Ḥibbān this was not the only reason for Abū Ḥanīfa to be denounced. He continues in the next sentence: 'There is another reason why one cannot use him as a proof and that is because he invited people to [the heresy of] Irjā', and there is a total consensus among every single one of our imams that one may not rely upon somebody as a proof if he calls others to heresy (*al-bida'*).'[66]

This chapter has documented the efforts of proto-Sunni and Ḥanafī scholars between the ninth and eleventh centuries in rehabilitating Abū Ḥanīfa as a Sunni scholar of unimpeachable orthodox credentials. In this and the previous chapter I have argued that the *manāqib* and *masānīd* genres were indispensable mechanisms through which the history and memory of Abū Ḥanīfa was reshaped. *Musnad* works, as we have seen, were integral to the early ḥadīth community. It was members of this community who were responsible for the spread of discourses of heresy against Abū Ḥanīfa. This consanguinity between discourses of heresy and the *musnad* genre was fundamental to the decision of defenders of Abū Ḥanīfa to compose *musnad* works to refute Abū Ḥanīfa's reliability as a ḥadīth transmitter. As such, it was a masterstroke. *Musnad* works now established Abū Ḥanīfa's mastery of ḥadīth. I drew attention to the *manāqib* genre not only because of its importance for the broader cultural memory of the *madhhabs* among medieval Islamic societies, but also on account of its attempt to respond to some of the gravest charges made against Abū Ḥanīfa. When we consider the very pervasiveness of discourses of heresy against Abū Ḥanīfa in the ninth century, he comes across as an arch-heretic in the writings of proto-Sunni traditionalists. If we think about why, then, he did not become a heresiarch, we should keep in mind that discourses of heresy against him existed in circumstantial reports, anecdotes, statements, utterances, and books. As long as this remained the evidential basis for discourses of heresy, even if they were etched into the textual record of the ninth–tenth centuries, discourses of heresy were also going to be susceptible to the kind of textual tsunami and revolution that carried forward the defence of Abū Ḥanīfa in the form of *manāqib* and *masānīd* works. Furthermore, authors of *manāqib* and

[66] Ibn Ḥibbān, *Kitāb al-Majrūḥīn*, 2: 405–6 (Riyadh edn.).

*masānīd* works were able to turn discourses of heresy to their advantage. No saint, they argued, could acquire such orthodox standing without attracting the scorn of his contemporaries.

Yet, we have also seen that though the genre exemplifies a concerted effort to rehabilitate Abū Ḥanīfa's religious orthodoxy, these same works elucidate the tensions that had emerged in the tenth–eleventh centuries with respect to the changing nature of Sunni orthodoxy and Abū Ḥanīfa's place within it. Sunnis of the tenth–eleventh centuries were recognising that change was afoot. Most, it seems, engineered and encouraged it. Others were reluctant to commit to the new consensus. It is to these diverse responses that we now turn.

*Part IV*

# The Formation of Classical Sunnism

# 10 Consensus and Heresy

As we draw to the denouement of this study, let us briefly recall its earlier phases. At the beginning of this book I presented material from the late eighth–tenth centuries that highlighted the formation of proto-Sunni traditionalist orthodoxy and the movement's commitment to the idea of Abū Ḥanīfa's heresy. We then explored some of the thematic strands that made up medieval conceptions of orthodoxy and heresy. As well established as the idea of Abū Ḥanīfa's heresy was in the eighth–tenth centuries, fundamental changes to this were introduced through the production of new genres in the tenth and eleventh centuries. The *manāqib* and *masānīd* genres were crucial in transforming Abū Ḥanīfa's mnemohistory from one of heresy to orthodoxy. This chapter is designed to bring our long story, which began in the late eighth century with proto-Sunni traditionalist discourses of heresy, to a close by considering three tenth-century attempts to define Sunnism in the wake of Abū Ḥanīfa's rehabilitation. The first example looks at the reaction of the state, the second examines efforts by Sunni traditionalists to revive discourses of heresy against Abū Ḥanīfa through the argument of consensus, and the third gives an insight into how Ḥanafīs, in the light of Abū Ḥanīfa's reintegration into orthodoxy, could now claim to represent medieval Sunni orthodoxy on the grounds of communal consensus.

## 10.1 The State

Wider social and political developments in the tenth century give us indications of a medieval Sunnism whose character was changing; one in which, as Makdisi has shown, the schools of law had become markers of Sunni orthodoxy and their eponyms paragons of orthodoxy.[1] The political manifestations of this new consensus can be traced to 381/991, which saw the unremarkable occasion of an ʿAbbāsid caliph's deposition at the hands of a Būyid amir. The new balance of power under the Būyids had given Bahāʾ al-Dawla the prerogative to terminate al-Ṭāʾiʿ's (r. 363–81/974–91) caliphal

[1] On the nature of the medieval 'state' see Hallaq, *The Impossible State*, ch. 2.

reign. On Thursday 21 Shawwāl at a ceremony in the caliphal palace, Bahā' al-Dawla gave his oath of allegiance to the new caliph, al-Qādir (r. 381–422/991–1031). Al-Qādir, in turn, gave his oath of fidelity to Bahā' al-Dawla.[2]

Al-Qādir's reign as caliph witnessed a number of significant religious developments. The intellectual landscape of tenth-century Baghdad was increasingly dominated by Shiʿism, Ḥanbalism, and Muʿtazilism. Al-Qādir's overtures to Baghdadi Ḥanbalism had seen him adopt antagonistic measures against Shiʿi communities and Muʿtazilī scholars. He clamped down on the practice of cursing Muʿāwiya and Yazīd in mosques and dismissed Shiʿi preachers. He introduced new measures to enforce public morality in Baghdad. Religious scholars were required to publicly renounce Muʿtazilī doctrines. It was many of these developments that Makdisi had in mind when he made the case for the decidedly traditionalist character of al-Qādir's religious policies.[3] The Qādirī creed, in particular, came to characterise the religious orientation of traditionalist Sunnism in the eleventh century.

Traditionalist Sunnism certainly received the endorsement of the caliphal office, but towards the end of the caliph's reign we can detect a move towards a more accommodating view of Sunnism. Information about this different direction in caliphal religious policy seems to have been scarce. The one source who reports it, Yāqūt al-Ḥamawī (d. 626/1229), was privy to its details only because he chanced upon some writings belonging to his acquaintances in Basra. Yāqūt writes:[4]

> I read the following in a work belonging to some people in Basra: al-Qādir bi Allāh commissioned four of the leading Muslim scholars during his reign who belonged to the four *madhhab*s to do the following: each of these four scholars should compose (*yuṣannif*) for the caliph a legal digest (*mukhtaṣar*) of his *madhhab*. Accordingly, al-Māwardī authored *Kitāb al-Iqnāʿ*. Abū al-Ḥusayn al-Qudūrī wrote his famous *Mukhtaṣar* for the *madhhab* of Abū Ḥanīfa. The Mālikī judge Abū Muḥammad ʿAbd al-Wahhāb b. Muḥammad b. Naṣr wrote a *Mukhtaṣar*. And a legal digest was produced for the *madhhab* of Aḥmad b. Ḥanbal, though I do not know the name of its author.

It seems that these four scholars were asked to submit their *mukhtaṣar*s and subsequently were summoned to the caliphal residence. Al-Yāqūt's source continues:[5]

> These four works were presented to the caliph. The caliph's servant then went to the supreme judge (*aqḍā al-quḍāt*) al-Māwardī and said to him: 'The

[2] Ibn al-Jawzī, *al-Muntaẓam*, 14: 348–9.
[3] Makdisi, 'The Sunni Revival', esp. 156, 164; Ibn al-Jawzī, *al-Muntaẓam*, 14: 353 ff.
[4] Yāqūt al-Ḥamawī, *Muʿjam al-udabā'*, 5: 1956 (Dār al-Gharb al-Islāmī edn.).
[5] Yāqūt al-Ḥamawī, *Muʿjam al-udabā'*, 5: 1956 (Dār al-Gharb al-Islāmī edn.).

Commander of the Faithful says to you: "May God preserve for you your religion just as you have preserved for us our religion."'

Al-Qādir's decision to commission the writing of four legal digests representing only four legal schools cannot be explained by the traditionalist doctrines usually associated with his reign. Baghdadi Ḥanbalism might have dominated the outlook of the caliphal office, but it is important to point out that this strain of traditionalism did not seek to challenge the legitimacy of Ḥanafism, Mālikism, and Shāfiʿīsm. When, for example, al-Ṣaymarī was recognised as an official legal witness it was any supposed fealty to Muʿtazilism that he was pressed to renounce, not his Ḥanafism.[6] In an important study of caliphal religious policy in the ʿAbbāsid period, Melchert has reminded us that caliphs tended to follow dominant religious developments, not set them.[7] Al-Qādir's decision to anchor Sunni orthodoxy in four legal schools should be read in the same manner. We should consider his religious policies and measures not as progenitors of new religious trends but rather as late endorsements of prevailing religious developments and consensuses. A consensus that Sunni orthodoxy converged around four legal *madhhab*s preceded al-Qādir's reign, and the *manāqib* and *masānīd* genre that grew around the persons of Abū Ḥanīfa, Mālik b. Anas, al-Shāfiʿī, and Aḥmad b. Ḥanbal played no small part in the consolidation of this consensus. Interestingly, ʿAbd al-Qāhir al-Baghdādī tells us:[8]

God almighty has singled out the *ahl al-sunna* by making them alone the locus of [orthodox] legal views. In the lands of the Muslims, the legal view of a qadarī, jahmī, najjārī, khārijī, rāfiḍī, and jismī are not accepted; unless one of their muftis hides behind an affiliation to the *madhhab* of al-Shāfiʿī or Abū Ḥanīfa, whilst concealing their heresy.

Some Ḥanafīs made more concerted efforts than others to appeal to the state's role in endorsing religious trends. The previously discussed *al-Ibāna fī al-radd ʿalā al-mushanniʿīn ʿalā Abī Ḥanīfa* by al-Qāḍī al-Surmārī in the tenth–eleventh centuries devotes the first chapter to criticising those who claim that the *madhhab* of Abū Ḥanīfa is ill-suited to governance and that it was founded to undermine government and rule (*al-imāra wa al-imāma*). Our author proceeds to sketch a portrait of positive relations between Abū Ḥanīfa and the ʿAbbāsids.[9] At the same time, in chapters 2, 3, and 4 al-Surmārī is at pains to depict a Ḥanafism that is principled, organised

[6] Ibn al-Jawzī, *al-Muntaẓam*, 15: 176.
[7] Melchert, 'Religious Policies of the Caliphs', 342.
[8] ʿAbd al-Qāhir al-Baghdādī, *Kitāb al-Milal wa niḥal*, 158.
[9] Furkani, 'Taḥqīq al-Ibāna', 91–3.

around scriptural sources, and more scrupulous in its moral reasoning than the other *madhhabs*. Al-Surmārī's treatise is unique in so far as it recognises proto-Sunni traditionalist attacks on Abū Ḥanīfa and politics, but contends that Abū Ḥanafī's legal opinions were more suitable for government and that Ḥanafism was the most prudent *madhhab* for administering state and society. Al-Surmārī's work belonged to a new emerging consensus, alongside al-Qādir's advocacy of four Sunni *madhhabs*, that represented an official endorsement and recognition of one of medieval Sunnism's defining moments: when it became synonymous with the orthodoxy of four eponymous founders. To understand the emergence of this new consensus and subsequent dissatisfaction with it we must consider the conceptual history of consensus as a social and not purely legal doctrine in proto-Sunnism.

## 10.2 Resisting the New Orthodoxy

ʿAbd Allāh b. ʿAdī b. ʿAbd Allāh b. Muḥammad b. Mubārak, better known to modern scholars as Ibn ʿAdī, was born in Jurjān in 277/890.[10] His religious education probably began with his father, who had been a student of one of the leading ḥadīth scholars of Rayy in the ninth century, Abū Zurʿa al-Rāzī.[11] Religious education, particularly the study of ḥadīth, began at a very early age, and Ibn ʿAdī was no exception. In his *al-Kāmil*, for instance, he informs us of an oral dictation session (*imlaʾ*) during the ḥadīth lessons of one Muḥammad b. ʿUbayda al-Maṣṣīṣī in Jurjān in 288/901, which he attended as an eleven-year-old.[12] By the time he was twenty he had left his homeland of Jurjān, and headed towards Shām and Egypt. In an entry on Abū al-Qāsim al-Baghawī, Ibn ʿAdī tells us about his time in Iraq and his inquiries into al-Baghawī's reputation among its local scholars.[13] He says that he was in Egypt in 299/911–12 and again in 304/916–17, and on both occasions he wrote down traditions from one Jaʿfar b. Aḥmad b. ʿAlī b. Bayān b. Zayd b. Siyāba.[14] Elsewhere in *al-Kāmil* Ibn ʿAdī provides details about his travels to Baghdad,[15] Basra,[16] Kufa,[17]

[10] For an indispensable guide to Ibn ʿAdī's life and career see Zuhayr ʿUthmān ʿAlī Nūr, *Ibn ʿAdī wa manhajuhu fī kitāb al-kāmil fī ḍuʿafāʾ al-rijāl* (Riyadh: Maktabat al-Rushd, 1997).
[11] Ibn ʿAdī, *al-Kāmil*, 1: 141 (Dār al-Fikr edn.).
[12] Ibn ʿAdī, *al-Kāmil*, 7: 2720 (Dār al-Fikr edn.).
[13] Ibn ʿAdī, *al-Kāmil*, 4: 1578–9 (Dār al-Fikr edn.).
[14] Ibn ʿAdī, *al-Kāmil*, 2: 578 (Dār al-Fikr edn.).
[15] Ibn ʿAdī, *al-Kāmil*, 4: 1557 (Dār al-Fikr edn.), where he heard a fantastic story about a woman who only ever spoke the words of the Quran.
[16] Ibn ʿAdī, *al-Kāmil*, 4: 1607.
[17] Ibn ʿAdī, *al-Kāmil*, 5: 1891. He states that this was in 298/910–11.

Mecca,[18] Bukhārā,[19] Sarakhs,[20] Marw,[21] Nīshāpūr,[22] and many others regions of the medieval Islamic world.

It was during these travels that Ibn ʿAdī came into contact with a number of very significant ḥadīth scholars and teachers. In Egypt he heard traditions from al-Nasāʾī, Ibn Khuzayma, al-Baghawī, Abū Yaʿlā al-Mawṣilī, and Muḥammad b. ʿUthmān b. Abī Shayba. Ibn ʿAdī became an important teacher in his own right. His intellectual legacy was felt deeply in his home town of Jurjān, and it was one of his students, Ḥamza b. Yūsuf al-Sahmī, who ensured that Ibn ʿAdī's reputation was recorded in his local history of the scholars of Jurjān.[23]

We have no information about Ibn ʿAdī's relationship with the political authorities of his day. In some ways, his stable and successful career stood in contrast to the political uncertainties experienced by the ʿAbbāsids in the ninth and tenth centuries. Ibn ʿAdī had lived through the reigns of a total of ten ʿAbbāsid caliphs. As a young student he would have begun his career during the reign of Hārūn al-Rashīd (r. 279/786–289/809) and it would have ended with al-Ṭāʾiʿ li-Allāh. Ibn ʿAdī also would have been aware of Jurjān's precarious position as a site of frequent contestations over suzerainty between various provincial rulers and dynasties. In 872 a rebellion against ʿAbbāsid rule was raised by the ʿAlid Ḥasan b. Zayd, and this successful venture extended Zaydī rule over Jurjān and the Caspian provinces. The rise of the Sāmānids resulted in a successful march against Muḥammad b. Zayd, the ʿAlid ruler of Ṭabaristān and Jurjān. The founder of the Ziyārid dynasty, Mardāwīj b. Ziyār (d. 323/935), had set his sights on Jurjān, too, in the early 930s.[24]

Despite these massive changes, or perhaps precisely because of them, Ibn ʿAdī was keenly aware of the world around him. The religious transformation that saw proto-Sunni traditionalism, with its discourse of heresy against Abū Ḥanīfa, evolve into a medieval Sunni orthodoxy that had embraced him wholeheartedly was one change too many. His *al-Kāmil fī al-ḍuʿafāʾ* exemplifies his stubborn resistance to the new Sunnism. The book is replete with enmity towards Abū Ḥanīfa and his followers. It seeks to resurrect discourses of heresy from the ninth–tenth centuries for a new readership. A number of familiar reports appear in the entry on Abū Ḥanīfa. We have the claim that Abū Ḥanīfa was forced to repent from

[18] Ibn ʿAdī, *al-Kāmil*, 4: 1562. In a tradition praising Mecca as a place where no usurious person resides, no person who spills blood, and no public slander exists.

[19] Ibn ʿAdī, *al-Kāmil*, 4: 1514 (Dār al-Fikr edn.).

[20] Ibn ʿAdī, *al-Kāmil*, 1: 229 (Dār al-Fikr edn.).

[21] Ibn ʿAdī, *al-Kāmil*, 7: 2563 (Dār al-Fikr edn.).

[22] Ibn ʿAdī, *al-Kāmil*, 4: 1568 (Dār al-Fikr edn.).

[23] Al-Sahmī, *Tārīkh Jurjān*, 266–8.

[24] Bosworth, 'On the Chronology of the Ziyārids'. On the scholars of Jurjān see Brown, *The Canonization*, 128–31; see also Savant, *The New Muslims of Post-Conquest Iran*, 111–15.

heresy.[25] He is described as a Murji'ī missionary, and this is one reason why a scholar refused to transmit anything from him: 'I sell meat with the bones,' he said, implying that doctrinal deviance could not be separated from a man's transmitting traditions.[26] Ibn ʿAdī recalls the celebratory words of Sufyān al-Thawrī when he learned of Abū Ḥanīfa's passing: 'Praise be to God. He was destroying Islam systematically. No one was born in Islam more harmful than him.'[27] Abū Ḥanīfa is described as a devil who opposed the reports of the Prophet Muḥammad with his speculative jurisprudence.[28] His ḥadīth learning is described in the most unflattering fashion.[29] Finally, we have the claim that a group of ninth-century proto-Sunni traditionalists refused to accept the legal testimony of Abū Ḥanīfa and his followers.[30] There is one passage, however, that provides an important insight into Ibn ʿAdī's attempt to push back against the growing consensus of Abū Ḥanīfa's orthodoxy by urgently reminding his audience of an older, well-established consensus among proto-Sunni traditionalists. He writes:[31]

> There is a consensus of the scholars as to the fall of Abū Ḥanīfa. We know this because the leading authority of Basra, Ayyūb al-Sakhtiyānī, had aspersed him; the leading authority of Kufa, al-Thawrī, had aspersed him; the leading authority of the Ḥijāz, Mālik, had aspersed him; the leading authority of Miṣr, al-Layth b. Saʿd, had aspersed him; the leading authority of Shām, al-Awzāʿī, had aspersed him; and the leading authority of Khurāsān, ʿAbd Allāh b. al-Mubārak, had aspersed him. That is to say, we have here the consensus of the scholars in all of the regions.

In another place, Ibn ʿAdī expresses the very same sentiment: 'There is not a scholar who is well respected except that he has denounced Abū Ḥanīfa.'[32] There is no need here to revisit the discourses of heresy that Ibn ʿAdī has in mind. Readers of Chapters 2 and 3 of this study will

[25] Ibn ʿAdī, *al-Kāmil*, 8: 239 (Dār al-Kutub edn. = Riyadh edn., 10: 125).
[26] Ibn ʿAdī, *al-Kāmil*, 8: 239 (Dār al-Kutub edn. = Riyadh edn., 10: 125).
[27] Ibn ʿAdī, *al-Kāmil*, 8: 239 (Dār al-Kutub edn. = Riyadh edn., 10: 126).
[28] Ibn ʿAdī, *al-Kāmil*, 8: 239 (Dār al-Kutub edn. = Riyadh edn., 10: 125).
[29] Ibn ʿAdī, *al-Kāmil*, 8: 236 (Dār al-Kutub edn. = Riyadh edn., 10: 121 (*lā yuktab ḥadīthuhu, muḍṭarib al-ḥadīth, wāhī al-ḥadīth*), 237 = 122-3 (*fī al-ḥadīth yatīm, laysa ṣāḥib al-ḥadīth, laysa bi al-qawī*), 238 = 123 (*matrūk al-ḥadīth*).
[30] Ibn ʿAdī, *al-Kāmil*, 8: 239 (Dār al-Kutub edn. = Riyadh edn., 10: 124–5).
[31] Ibn ʿAdī, *al-Kāmil*, 8: 241 (Dār al-Kutub edn. = Riyadh edn., 10: 129) (*samiʿtu Ibn Abī b. Dāwūd yaqūl: al-waqīʿa fī Abī Ḥanīfa, ijmāʿuhu min al-ʿulamāʾ li anna imām al-Baṣra Ayyūb al-Sakhtiyānī wa qad takallama fīhi; wa imām al-Kūfa al-Thawrī wa qad takallama fīhi; wa imām al-Ḥijāz Mālik wa qad takallama fīhi; wa imām Miṣr al-Layth b. Saʿd wa qad takallama fīhi; wa imām al-Shām al-Awzāʿī wa qad takallama fīhi; wa imām Khurāsān ʿAbd Allāh b. al-Mubārak wa qad takallama fīhi. Ijmāʿ min al-ʿulamāʾ fī jamīʿ al-āfāq aw kamā qāla*).
[32] Ibn ʿAdī, *al-Kāmil*, 8: 238 (Dār al-Kutub edn. = Riyadh edn., 10: 123) (*lam yakun bayn al-mashriq wa al-maghrib faqīhan yudhkar bi khayr illā ʿāba Abā Ḥanīfa wa majlisahu*).

recognise that Ibn ʿAdī's argument, and the evidence he adduces, is not imagined. Ibn ʿAdī is giving a summary account of what he has gleaned from a disparate discourse of heresy that was widespread during the ninth–tenth centuries.

What I wish to emphasise here is that, for Ibn ʿAdī, consensus is operating as a social and religious doctrine outside the sphere of jurisprudence proper. *Ijmāʿ* is not invoked for a particular interpretation of Islamic law or legal practice. Ibn ʿAdī marshals *ijmāʿ* as a social doctrine to undermine and diminish the religious orthodoxy of an individual scholar and what he has come to represent in the tenth century. It is a consensus, he claims, that has the support of leading proto-Sunni traditionalist scholars of the ninth century. Ibn ʿAdī lays special emphasis on the regional breadth of this consensus. It is clear that his conception of orthodoxy is neither local nor regional. He conceives of orthodoxy – understood as the consensus of proto-Sunni traditionalist scholars and their denunciation of Abū Ḥanīfa – as a transregional phenomenon.

A fascinating parallel can be found in the work of Ibn Ḥibbān. In the notice on Abū Ḥanīfa in *Kitāb al-Majrūḥīn*, Ibn Ḥibbān writes:[33]

> Among every single one of our imams, I know of no disagreement between them concerning him [Abū Ḥanīfa]: the leaders of the Muslims and those of scrupulous piety in the religion, in all of the regions and provinces [of the Islamic world], one after another, they all have declared him to be unreliable and have vilified him. We have included examples of these statements in our book entitled 'The Warning about the Falsification'. There is no need, then, to repeat all of this in our present book. Instead, I shall simply cite here a summary from which readers will be able to deduce for themselves everything else that lies behind it.

Ibn ʿAdī and Ibn Ḥibbān were contemporaries. Though they wrote on similar subjects, they lived slightly different lives.[34] Ibn Ḥibbān was born in Sijistān, but his professional commitments took him to Khurāsān and Transoxiana. In Khurāsān he studied Shāfiʿī jurisprudence under Ibn Khuzayma and taught in Nīshāpūr at a Khānqah. He was qadi of Samarqand and Nasā.[35] Yet, he arrived at the same conclusion about

[33] Ibn Ḥibbān, *Kitāb al-Majrūḥīn*, 3: 64 (Beirut edn.) = 2: 406 (Riyadh edn.) (*ʿinda aʾimmatinā lā aʿlamu baynahum fīhi khilāfan ʿalā anna aʾimmata al-muslimīn wa ahl al-waraʿ fī al-dīn fī jamīʿ al-amṣār wa sāʾir al-aqṭār jaraḥūhu wa aṭlaqū ʿalayhi al-qadḥ illā wāḥid baʿda al-wāḥid. Qad dhakarnā mā ruwiya fīhi min dhālika fī kitāb al-tanbīh ʿalā al-tamwīh, fa aghnā dhālika ʿan takrārihā fī hādhā al-kitāb ghayra annī adhkur minhā jumalan mā yustadallu bihā ʿalā mā warāʾuhā*).

[34] On comparisons between Ibn ʿAdī's *al-Kāmil* and Ibn Ḥibbān's *Kitāb al-Majrūḥīn* see Nūr, *Ibn ʿAdī wa manhajuhu*, 1: 259–68.

[35] Al-Subkī, *Ṭabaqāt al-Shāfiʿiyya al-kubrā*, 3: 131–5 (where one also learns that Ibn Ḥibbān was forced into exile from Sijistān on a charge of heresy); al-Dhahabī, *Siyar*, 16: 92–104.

Abū Ḥanīfa as did Ibn ʿAdī. They both believed that, in spite of the efforts of medieval Sunnis (Ḥanafīs and non-Ḥanafīs) to rehabilitate Abū Ḥanīfa as an orthodox Sunni using the *manāqib* and *masānīd* genres, the consensus of ninth-century discourses of heresy against him had to be re-established. In fact, so complete was the new character of medieval Sunni orthodoxy with Abū Ḥanīfa at its heart that at least one transmitter or scribe of Ibn Ḥibbān's *Kitāb al-Majrūḥīn* could not bring himself to include Ibn Ḥibbān's vilification of Abū Ḥanīfa and other Ḥanafīs in the final manuscript.[36] MS 1 retains passages condemning Abū Ḥanīfa and his followers, whilst MS 2 omits them. The entire entry on Abū Ḥanīfa, a scathing and captious account of Abū Ḥanīfa, is absent in MS 2.[37] Ibn Ḥibbān begins his entry on al-Shaybānī by drawing a direct relationship between him and Abū Ḥanīfa. MS 1 describes him as an upholder of speculative reasoning (*ṣāḥib ra'y*) and as someone who studied under Abū Ḥanīfa for a short period of time (*ṣaḥiba al-Nuʿmān wa huwa Abū Ḥanīfa ayyāman yasīra*). This entire passage referring to al-Shaybānī as a practitioner of speculative jurisprudence and his association with Abū Ḥanīfa is absent from MS 2. There are other omissions. As is conventional in such works, Ibn Ḥibbān lists the scholars from whom al-Shaybānī narrated traditions. MS 1 states that al-Shaybānī narrated from al-Nuʿmān b. Thābit and Yaʿqūb b. Ibrāhīm and that he heard from Yaʿqūb on the authority of Abū Ḥanīfa more than what he is frequently judged to have heard. MS 2 states none of this. The entry opens by stating that al-Shaybānī narrated traditions on the authority of Yaʿqūb b. Ibrāhīm and the people of Kufa, adding that many people narrated traditions on his authority. MS 2 does add a slight criticism from Ibn Ḥibbān to the effect that any traditions unique to al-Shaybānī are unreliable. This wording is absent from MS 1, although Ibn Ḥibbān's criticism of al-Shaybānī's expertise in ḥadīth is articulated in more severe language:

He was bright, but he had no expertise in ḥadīth. He would relate ḥadīth on the authority of trustworthy transmitters (*al-thiqāt*), but he would get them wrong (*yahimu fīhā*). When this became excessive and shameless, it became necessary to abandon him as an authority due to the sheer number of errors he committed,

[36] There is more than one edition of this work: *Kitāb al-Majrūḥīn min al-muḥaddithīn wa al-ḍuʿafā' wa al-matrūkīn*, ed. Muḥammad Ibrāhīm Zāyid (Beirut: Dār al-Maʿrifa, 1996); ed. ʿAzīz Bayg al-Qādirī (Hyderabad: al-Maṭbaʿa al-ʿAzīziyya, 1970–7; reprinted); *Kitāb al-Majrūḥīn min al-muḥaddithīn*, ed. Ḥamdī ʿAbd al-Majīd al-Salafī (Riyadh: Dār al-Ṣumayʿī, 2000). Al-Salafī alleges that the two previous editions (Aleppo/Beirut and Hyderabad) contain grievous errors, with entire passages and entries omitted. His edition is based on MS 496 (MS 2), Aya Sophia. Muḥammad Ibrāhīm Zāyid's edition is based on MS 195998 (MS 1), Dār al-Kutub al-Miṣriyya.

[37] Ibn Ḥibbān, *Kitāb al-Majrūḥīn*, 3: 61 (MS 1 – Beirut edn.) = 2: 405 (MS 2 – Riyadh edn.).

which likely had something to do with the fact that he was an avid propagandist for his school's doctrines (*fa lammā faḥusha dhālika minhu istaḥaqqa tarkuhu min ajl kathrat khaṭī'a li annahu kāna dāʿiya ilā madhhabihim*).

This entire passage is absent from MS 2. There are other important criticisms of al-Shaybānī in the preliminary part of the entry in MS 1 that are absent from MS 2. MS 1 adds that al-Shaybānī was a propagandist for the Murji'a, whom he defines elsewhere as heretics. The statement that al-Shaybānī was the first person to write refutations against the people of Medina is also missing from MS 2. So too is the remark made by Ibn Ḥibbān that al-Shaybānī was committed to aiding and supporting Abū Ḥanīfa. The only other detail shared in the opening reports of both entries is the fact that al-Shaybānī died in the same year as al-Kasā'ī in Rayy as he was en route to Khurāsān in the entourage of Hārūn al-Rashīd. MS 2 also abridges a judgement from Yaḥyā b. Maʿīn concerning al-Shaybānī and, by extension, Abū Ḥanīfa: 'al-Ḍaḥḥāk b. Hārūn < Muḥammad b. Aḥmad al-Aṣfarī: I heard Yaḥyā b. Maʿīn say: Muḥammad b. al-Ḥasan al-Shaybānī was a liar (*kadhdhāb*) and close associate (*ṣāḥib*) of Abū Ḥanīfa.' The part about al-Shaybānī being a close associate of Abū Ḥanīfa is absent from MS 2.[38] This is all to say that even the manuscript evidence indicates that some elements of the new medieval Sunni orthodoxy resorted to omitting earlier discourses of heresy that no longer belonged in the new consensus.[39]

Al-ʿUqaylī's work is the final example of dissent from the new medieval orthodoxy I should like to highlight. His *Kitāb al-Ḍuʿafā'* belongs to the same genre as the works of Ibn Ḥibbān and Ibn ʿAdī, which we looked at briefly above. Al-ʿUqaylī puts on display a small but biting exhibitition of ninth-century proto-Sunni traditionalist discourses of heresy against Abū Ḥanīfa. His views on rebellion are presented as heresy.[40] The claim that Abū Ḥanīfa was forced to repent from heresy twice is included.[41] There is more venom directed towards Abū Ḥanīfa in the thirty-seven reports against him contained in al-ʿUqaylī's work.[42]

[38] Ibn Ḥibbān, *Kitāb al-Majrūḥīn*, 2: 275–6 (MS 1 – Beirut edn.) = 2: 287 (MS 2 – Riyadh edn.).

[39] This technique was not at odds with medieval philological methods. Al-Rāmahurmuzī's manual of ḥadīth learning speaks about philological techniques and copying practices. He mentions erasure (*al-ḥakk*) and adds that erasing passages amounted to an accusation (*tuhma*) – I presume, against the material itself. See al-Rāmahurmuzī, *al-Muḥaddith al-fāṣil*, 606. For other types of erasure among ḥadīth scholars see Melchert, 'The Destruction of Books by Traditionists', 219, 220, 226.

[40] Al-ʿUqaylī, *Kitāb al-Ḍuʿafā'*, 4: 1409, 1410 (Dār al-Ṣumayʿī edn.).

[41] Al-ʿUqaylī, *Kitāb al-Ḍuʿafā'*, 4: 1409 (Dār al-Ṣumayʿī edn.).

[42] Al-ʿUqaylī, *Kitāb al-Ḍuʿafā'*, 4: 1407–12 (Dār al-Ṣumayʿī edn.).

Ibn ʿAdī, al-ʿUqaylī, and Ibn Ḥibbān shared more than just a commitment to establish Abū Ḥanīfa as someone outside medieval Sunni orthodoxy. These three scholars were important figures at the heart of a tenth-century movement devoted to looking back on the eighth and ninth centuries and determining the religious credibility and orthodoxy of figures from that period. Many of the numerous figures they deemed unreliable had fallen by the wayside. Abū Ḥanīfa, in this sense, was exceptional. Here was a figure who, despite the acrimony surrounding his mnemohistory, had been revived as a figure of medieval Sunni orthodoxy. The desperate attempts of Ibn ʿAdī, al-ʿUqaylī, and Ibn Ḥibbān to revive the ninth–tenth-century discourses of heresy against him must be seen as a last-ditch effort to turn back the clock of orthodoxy. Discourses of heresy did not disappear, and attempts to rehabilitate them continued in the course of the medieval and early modern periods. We can hear the survival of these social and religious tensions in texts from this period. Between the eleventh and twelfth centuries a number of very significant historical sources exhibit a central concern with the fallout from ninth-century discourses of heresy. Al-Khaṭīb al-Baghdādī's entry on Abū Ḥanīfa is the longest entry in the entire *Tārīkh Baghdād*, and it represents a comprehensive attempt to rehabilitate ninth-century discourses of heresy against Abū Ḥanīfa. At the same time, it also contains a *manāqib* section, albeit an extremely brief one, which was quoted frequently by Ḥanafī and non-Ḥanafī admirers of Abū Ḥanīfa.[43] The lesson to be learnt for such dissenting voices was that, far from being an antiquarian doctrine lodged in ancient texts, Sunni orthodoxy was a living tradition, and its orthodoxy required constant supervision by an evolving scholarly consensus.

## 10.3 Ḥanafism as Majoritarian Orthodoxy

The rehabilitation of Abū Ḥanīfa is also evidenced by the new confidence palpable among Ḥanafī scholarly communities who in the tenth century began to assert a universal consensus (*al-sawād al-aʿẓam*) that they represented majoritarian orthodoxy (*ahl al-sunna wa al-jamāʿa*), and that this empowered them to define heresy. During the mid-ninth–tenth centuries a number of prominent Ḥanafī scholars turned to the genre of heresiography and doxography to assert Abū Ḥanīfa's fidelity to certain theological postulates.[44] Al-Ṭaḥāwī's traditionalist creed, for example, claimed to

[43] Al-Khaṭīb al-Baghdādī, *Tārīkh Baghdād*, 15: 444–586 (entire entry on Abū Ḥanīfa), 459–63 (*manāqib* section). On medieval (and modern) refutations of al-Khaṭīb al-Baghdādī's diatribe against Abū Ḥanīfa, see Khan, 'Islamic Tradition in an Age of Print', 62–3.

[44] On these genres see Rudolph, *Al-Māturīdī and the Development of Sunnī Theology*, 23–124; Lewinstein, 'Notes on Eastern Ḥanafite Heresiography'; Bernand, 'Le Kitāb al-Radd ʿalā ahl al-bidaʿ wa al-ahwā''.

represent the doctrines of Abū Ḥanīfa and his followers in the name of *ahl al-sunna wa al-jamāʿa* (majoritarian orthodoxy). This traditionalist creed dovetailed neatly with al-Ṭaḥāwī's traditionalisation of Ḥanafī jurisprudence, as well as his important *manāqib* work. As we have seen, works of theology and heresiography by figures such as al-Ashʿārī and al-Baghdādī also made the case for, not against, Abū Ḥanīfa's orthodoxy. Whilst the heresiographical sources do not allow us to reconstruct the precise changes that Abū Ḥanīfa's reputation underwent in the ninth–eleventh centuries, they nevertheless highlight the attempt to cultivate a tradition of Ḥanafī heresiographical works which placed Abū Ḥanīfa at the head of a programme of theological Sunni orthodoxy. That is to say, defenders of Abū Ḥanīfa turned to the genre of heresiography, supplementing the production of *manāqib* and *masānīd* works, in order to establish Abū Ḥanīfa as an exemplar of Sunni orthodoxy.

The peculiar nature of one particular tenth-century work helps to underline some of the difficulties that such sources pose to historians, but it also provides a more promising perspective on the scraps of historical information that such sources might yet yield. The *al-Sawād al-aʿẓam* has caught the attention of a number of historians interested in the religious history of eastern Iran between the ninth and tenth centuries.[45] Despite this interest from historians, no comprehensive study of the work has been published. In particular, there is no clear consensus regarding the function of the work. The *al-Sawād al-aʿẓam* is commonly described as the official catechism of the Sāmānid dynasty. The only evidence that we have for the circumstances surrounding its composition comes not from the original Arabic treatise, but from a later Persian version.[46]

The redactor of the Persian work informs us that a group of Ḥanafī jurists and theologians were perturbed by the appearance of heresies and innovations, which threatened to undermine the traditional form of Sunni orthodoxy (*ṭarīq-i sunnat va jamāʿat*) that reigned supreme in Transoxiana.[47] These concerns were relayed to the amir of Khurāsān, Ismāʿīl b. Aḥmad (r. 279–95/892–907). The amir instructed a certain ʿAbd Allāh b. Abī

[45] Van Ess, *Der Eine und das Andere*, 1: 448–53; Rudolph, *Al-Māturīdī*, 97–121; al-Tanchî, 'Abû Mansûr al-Mâturîdî'; Ritter, 'Philologika. III. Muhammedansiche Häresiographien'; ʿAbd-Allāh, 'The Doctrines of the Māṭurīdite School'; Madelung, 'The Early Murji'a', 32–9; Ḥabībī, 'Yek kitāb gum shud qadīm nathr-i fārsī paydā shud'; Pākatchī, 'Abū al-Qāsim Ḥakīm Samarqandī'; Dānishpazūh, 'Dū risāla dar bāra-yi ihdā'ī-yi haftād u dū gurūh'.

[46] The Arabic version of *al-Sawād al-Aʿẓam* is almost impossible to access. To my knowledge, only two universities in the western world house copies of the published text (UCLA and Chicago). Instead, I have relied on the English translation of the Arabic version. A week before submitting this book for publication, I managed to access the original Arabic version: al-Samarqandī, *Kitāb al-Sawād al-aʿẓam* (Cairo: Būlāq, 1837).

[47] Al-Samarqandī, *Tarjumeh-yi al-sawād al-aʿẓam*, ed. ʿAbd al-Ḥayy Ḥabībī (Tehran: Bunyād-i Farhang-Īrān, 1969), 18.

Jaʿfar and some other jurists to establish the correct orthodox doctrine which the region's ancestors had observed for centuries (*madhhab-i rast va ṭarīq-i sunnat va jamāʿat ānkeh pidarān-i mā bar ān būdeh and*). ʿAbd Allāh b. Abī Jaʿfar and his fellow jurists turned to Abū al-Qāsim Samarqandī (d. 342/953) and said to him:

Guide us as to the correct path of Sunni orthodoxy, which the Messenger, upon him be peace, was on. This creed was presented to the amir of Khurāsān. He approved of it and declared that the creed represented the correct doctrines of Sunni orthodoxy (*rāh-i rāst-i sunnat va jamāʿat īn ast*). In order to make the creed available to both scholars and the wider public, and in order for the Muslim population to distance themselves from heresies, the amir of Khurāsān (Nūḥ b. Manṣūr, though not mentioned by name here) instructed that the work be translated into Persian.[48]

In these passages, the only explanation of the creed's origins, we have a clear indication that it was the local Ḥanafī scholars of Transoxiana who sought the political intervention of the Sāmānid rulers in order to impose some degree of theological and legal uniformity upon the Muslim communities of Transoxiana. There is nothing unoriginal in the claim that local Ḥanafī scholars were responding to the threat of heresies. Raising the spectre of threats from heretics was a staple technique of heresiographers and doxographers. However, we do know that Transoxiana in the ninth century was the scene of a number of hostile and competing religious trends in law, theology, and mysticism. The Ḥanafī communities of Transoxiana and Khurāsān, in particular, had experienced mixed fortunes under the Ṭāhirids and Ṣaffārids. This is all to suggest that there are good grounds for asserting that the Ḥanafī scholars were anxious to claim the primacy of their doctrines and practices in the region by appealing to the Sāmānid amir. Already, this undermines the idea that the creed was the official catechism of the Sāmānids. The redactor of the Persian *al-Sawād al-aʿẓam* states that the translation was commissioned by Nūḥ b. Manṣūr (r. 366–87/976–97), but no single individual is credited with having executed this task. It is possible to infer from this (and from the circumstances surrounding the Persian adaption of al-Ṭabarī's *Tafsīr*) that a group of scholars was appointed to translate al-Ḥakīm al-Samarqandī's creed. In the Persian *al-Sawād al-aʿẓam* we read that Nūḥ b. Manṣūr's central objective behind commissioning the work was

[48] Al-Samarqandī, *Tarjumeh-yi al-sawād al-aʿẓam*, 19. Some scholars dispute the attribution of the work to al-Ḥakīm al-Samarqandī and ascribe it instead to Abū Ḥafṣ al-Kabīr (d. 216/831). See Akram Muḥammad Ismāʿīl's forthcoming edition of the text (Amman: Dār al-Nūr).

also concerned with making the doctrines and practices of Sunnism, as promulgated by eastern Ḥanafism, available to a wider audience.[49]

Locating the Persian *al-Sawād al-aʿẓam* within the broader context and enterprise of Sāmānid patronage of religious learning provides a clearer view of the function of al-Ḥakīm al-Samarqandī's creed. We see a concentrated effort to make available to the Persian-speaking communities of Khurāsān and Transoxiana the religious heritage of ninth-century Islamic learning and scholarship. At the same time, this heritage was not simply imposed upon these regions. Rather, these texts were adapted to suit specific local and regional circumstances. Al-Samarqandī's creed represents an attempt to establish eastern Ḥanafism as the normative practice and creed of greater Khurāsān under the Sāmānids.

The Persian *al-Sawād al-aʿẓam* can be considered only a partial translation and adaptation of the original Arabic work. The substance of *al-Sawād al-aʿẓam* consists of a detailed exposition of sixty-two points of doctrine and ritual. All but one of these are presented in the Persian *al-Sawād al-aʿẓam*, even if the latter frequently departs from the Arabic original. More importantly, the Persian *al-Sawād al-aʿẓam* contains a lengthy introduction, not found in the Arabic original, furnishing a more elaborate insight into the functions of the creed. More than anything, the introduction displays a heightened sense of threat from the spectre of heresy. Readers are regularly cautioned, from the outset, to guard their religion carefully because of the rapid diffusion of heresies among the populace.[50] In the light of the prevalence in society of these heresies and heretics, the author of the Persian *al-Sawād al-aʿẓam* advances a policy of isolation and exclusion as the only way to retain one's affiliation with the way of truth and majoritarian Sunnism of Transoxiana.[51] As we shall see, this majoritarian Sunnism is, in fact, conceived of as being exclusive and narrow. Our Persian author continues his exhortation and counsels his readers to 'beware of heretics (*havādārān va bidʿat*). Do not sit with them, and do not keep their company; that way, you ensure that you do not perform the ritual prayer led by them. After all, the very residence of heretics is hell.' Our Persian redactor continues with

[49] Al-Samarqandī, *Tarjumeh-yi al-sawād al-aʿẓam*, 19 (*pas Amīr-i Khurāsān bi farmūd: keh īn kitāb-rā bi-pārsī gardānīd tā chunānkeh khāṣṣ-rā buvad ʿāmm-rā nīz buvad va manfaʿat kunad va madhhab-rā nīkū bi-dānand va az havā va bidʿat dūr bāshand*).

[50] Al-Samarqandī, *Tarjumeh-yi al-sawād al-aʿẓam*, 21 (*va dīn-i khūd-rā nigāh dār az ān jihat keh havā dar miyān-i khalq basyār shudeh ast va amānathā bar-khāsteh va hark az bar havāhā-yi khwīsh mashghūl gashteh*).

[51] Al-Samarqandī, *Tarjumeh-yi al-sawād al-aʿẓam*, 21 (*pas bāyad keh nishast va khāst, khwīsh-rā bi ahl-i ḥaqq dārī va khūd rā az ahl-i bidʿat dūr dārī va ṭarīq-i ahl-i sunnat va jamāʿat nigāh dārī*).

these urgent appeals for readers and listeners to steer well clear of heretics.[52] Just prior to the section where the Persian adaptation of the Arabic *al-Sawād al-aʿẓam* begins, we are presented with another explanation of the book's composition in Persian:[53]

I have composed this work in Persian because the amir of Khurāsān, Nūḥ b. Manṣūr, gathered all of the scholars of Transoxiana to discover and establish the correct path, in line with the way of the messenger of God, may God bless him and grant him peace, and the Companions and Rightly Guided Caliphs, may God be pleased with them all.

At this point, the author provides a definition of Sunni orthodoxy:[54]

That correct path is majoritarian Sunnism, which is the belief of the scholars of majoritarian Sunnism. This is also the school of the foremost imam, the master of the jurists, the lord of religion and knowledge, and the king of kings in jurisprudence, Abū Ḥanīfa Nuʿmān b. Thābit b. Ṭāwus b, Hurmuz b. Kisrā Malik Baghdad; he was on this very path, as were all of his followers, and all the representatives of majoritarian Sunnism are on this path.

The Persian *al-Sawād al-aʿẓam* informs us of the Sāmānid amir's objective of making the creed widely known throughout Khurāsān and Transoxiana. There seems to be a conscious effort in the Persian *al-Sawād al-aʿẓam* to make the work accessible to a broader readership. There are appeals throughout the introduction for readers to study the book closely. Learning the book is declared to be obligatory. The Persian *al-Sawād al-aʿẓam* describes the book's function to be like 'a sacred periapt (*taʿvīdh sāzī*), which people must read with their children and families (*mar farzandān va ahl-rā bi-yāmūzī*), because the salvation of you, your family, and your children depends on learning this book'.[55] Those who ignore the book are described as wretched.[56] Most severely, those who oppose the book are heretics.[57] Not only is it clear from these passages that the Persian *al-Sawād al-aʿẓam* was intended for a wide readership, but the intensity with which it rallies against heresy and

[52] Al-Samarqandī, *Tarjumeh-yi al-sawād al-aʿẓam*, 22–3.

[53] Al-Samarqandī, *Tarjumeh-yi al-sawād al-aʿẓam*, 22.

[54] Al-Samarqandī, *Tarjumeh-yi al-sawād al-aʿẓam*, 22–3 (*va ān madhhab-i sunnat va jamāʿat ast va madhhab-i ʿulamā-yi keh ahl-i sunnat va jamāʿat and va ān madhhab-i imām-i imāmān va sayyid-i fuqahā' va kadkhudāy-yi dīn va ʿilm va shāhanshāh-i fiqh … ke īn bar īn madhhab būd va hameh aṣḥāb-i ān bar īn madhhab būdand va hameh ahl-i sunnat va jamāʿat bar īn madhhab būd*).

[55] Al-Samarqandī, *Tarjumeh-yi al-sawād al-aʿẓam*, 24 (*zīrā keh rastagārī-yi tū va ahl va farzandān-i tu bih āmukhtan-i īn kitāb buvad*).

[56] Al-Samarqandī, *Tarjumeh-yi al-sawād al-aʿẓam*, 24 (*pas amūkhtan-i īn kitāb farīḍeh ast va rūy gardānīdan az īn kitāb shiqāvat ast*).

[57] Al-Samarqandī, *Tarjumeh-yi al-sawād al-aʿẓam*, 24 (*khilāf kardan mar īn kitāb-rā bidʿat ast*).

strictly defines Sunni orthodoxy within the confines of *al-Sawād al-aʿẓam* is striking.

The main substance of *al-Sawād al-aʿẓam*, present in both the Arabic and Persian versions, consists of detailed commentary on sixty-one (sixty-two in the Persian version) points of doctrine. These discussions and doctrinal issues are not always confined to theological matters. Matters of ritual performance, political thought, and asceticism and mysticism receive attention, too. Despite this eclectic range of themes, scholarly discussions surrounding *al-Sawād al-aʿẓam* have sought singular explanations of the creed's historical context and function. The predominant view is that *al-Sawād al-aʿẓam* should be understood as an eastern Ḥanafī polemic against the Karrāmiyya. There are two main reasons for this interpretation. The first concerns the background tension between eastern Ḥanafism and the Karrāmiyya in the ninth and tenth centuries. Despite a number of affinities in jurisprudence between eastern Ḥanafīs and Muḥammad b. Karrām (d. 255/869) and his followers, Ḥanafī theologians increasingly became hostile to Ibn Karrām's anthropomorphic theology. On the basis of perceived hostilities between the Karrāmiyya and the Ḥanafiyya, scholars have read certain passages in the *al-Sawād al-aʿẓam* as support for the creed's anti-Karrāmiyya orientation. Articles 45, 46, and 48 make explicit reference to the Karrāmiyya. Article 45 stipulates that belief in God's oneness must reside in the heart and be confessed with the tongue. Anyone who does not subscribe to this tenet is described as a heretic. Those who hold the view that faith is in the heart apart from the tongue are labelled Jahmiyya and others who declare that faith is utterance of the tongue without knowledge in the heart are described as Murji'a and Karrāmiyya. Both positions are deemed heretical. Article 46 condemns anthropomorphic interpretations of God, and here the author invokes a familiar accusation against the Karrāmiyya of their likening God to anything or asserting that He possesses a member. Article 48 intervenes in the debates about the obligation of earning a living. The Karrāmiyya are labelled as heretics because they do not regard earning to be a duty.

*Al-Sawād al-aʿẓam* had ambitions to be more than just an anti-Karrāmī creed. It can be argued that the creed reflects attempts by Ḥanafīs to respond to discourses of heresy against Abū Ḥanīfa. On the one hand, this meant undermining proto-Sunni traditionalist conceptions of orthodoxy. Article 53, for example, takes up the issue of the *witr* prayer. It contends that the *witr* prayer consists of three *rakʿa*s and one *taslīma*, and that whoever says otherwise is considered a heretic. This was a direct attack on proto-Sunni traditionalists, who advocated that *witr* prayer was one *rakʿa*. Although proto-Sunni traditionalists are not mentioned explicitly in this article of the creed, one might be tempted to argue that the fact that this article cites more Prophetic traditions, fifteen to be precise, than anywhere else in the creed betrays the identity of their opponents, for whom argument by tradition was considered decisive. On the other hand, it required articulating a narrow conception of orthodoxy that gave pride of place to Abū Ḥanīfa and his followers. In order to do this, *al-Sawād al-aʿẓam* takes up a number of themes common to ninth-century discourses of heresy against Abū Ḥanīfa and seeks to establish an orthodox narrative around them. Articles 1, 10, 44, 49, and 58 all concern debates surrounding the nature of faith: article 1 states that one must not have any doubt with respect to one's faith; article 10 declares that faith is a gift; article 44 states that faith involves two members of the body, the heart and the tongue; article 49 distinguishes between faith and action; and article 58 establishes that faith does not increase or decrease. Articles 11 and 12 pertain to debates about the created nature of deeds and of the Quran. Deeds, we are told, are created. As for the Quran, it is uncreated. But *al-Sawād al-aʿẓam* points to the difficulty involved in arriving at this conclusion, for it reports that Abū Yūsuf said that he debated with Abū Ḥanīfa for six months concerning the Quran, and they agreed that whoever says the Quran is created is an unbeliever. Finally, article 7 argues against proto-Sunni traditionalist orthodoxy by permitting rebellion against Muslims with a just cause.

What *al-Sawād al-aʿẓam* suggests, therefore, is that the rehabilitation of Abū Ḥanīfa as a figure of Sunni orthodoxy enabled Ḥanafī communities in Transoxiana to claim to represent majoritarian Sunni orthodoxy. Theirs was a narrow, regional conception of orthodoxy at the helm of which stood Abū Ḥanīfa and his followers. A century earlier they had been described by proto-Sunni traditionalists as heretics and deviants. By the tenth century they had found the confidence to depict themselves and Abū Ḥanīfa as vanguards of medieval Sunni orthodoxy.

Staying in the eastern regions of the Islamic world, another text from this period gives us an insight into how and when discourses of heresy against Abū Ḥanīfa were invoked and, in particular, how the *manāqib* genre was key to diminishing any tensions arising from them.[58] The text in question is

[58] On Ḥanafī and Shāfiʿī rivalry in Khurāsān see Bulliet, *The Patricians of Nishapur*, 28–46. Al-Ghazālī, *al-Mankhūl*, 471, 500, 504. Shams al-Dīn Muḥammad b. Muḥammad b. ʿAbd Allāh al-Sattār al-ʿImādī al-Kardarī al-Barānīqī (d. 642/1244) penned a *manāqib* work in response (although there were rumours that it was a Muʿtazilī author and not al-Ghazālī himself who had authored the treatise): al-Kardarī, 'Kitāb al-Radd ʿalā Abī Ḥāmid al-Ghazālī', MS Vollers 0351, Universitätbibliothek Leipzig, fols. 21a–25b; al-Kardarī, 'Kitāb al-Radd wa al-intiṣār li Abī Ḥanīfa imām fuqahā' al-amṣār', MS

a Persian history of the Saljūqs, *Rāḥat al-ṣudūr va āyat al-surūr dar tārīkh āl-saljūq*.[59] The author of the history, al-Rāwandī, was born in the mid- to late twelfth century. Under the tutelage of his maternal uncle, Tāj al-Dīn al-Rāwandī, he gained favour with the Saljūq sultans and, in particular, with Sultan Tughril (r. 571–90/1175–94). With the dynasty's demise, al-Rāwandī took the wise decision to reorient his career towards the Saljūq sultans of Anatolia. The *Rāḥat al-ṣudūr* was composed between 599/1202 and 601/1204, and was dedicated to the ruling sultan, Rukn al-Dīn Sulaymān (d. 601/1204) and then to his successor, Ghiyāth al-Dīn Kaykhusraq (d. 644/1246).[60] Abū Ḥanīfa receives profuse praise in the *Rāḥat al-ṣudūr*,[61] but I should like to draw attention to a small *manāqib* section in the work (*madḥ-i imām al-aʿẓam*). The section begins with some lines of poetry in which we see al-Rāwandī's playful and ambiguous interest in diminishing hostilities between Ḥanafis and Shāfiʿīs:[62]

> *Dīnī li aṣḥāb al-nabī al-Muṣṭafā,*
> *Innī kafartu bi rabbī in law aftarī.*
> *Yā rabbī in ghalabat dhunūbī ṭāʿatī,*
> *Fa Abū Ḥanīfa Shāfiʿī fī al-maḥshari.*

> My religion is that of the Companions of the Prophet, al-Muṣṭafā,
> I have disbelieved in my lord if I slander [them].
> My lord, if my sins outweigh my obedience to you,
> Then [I take refuge in being with] Abū Ḥanīfa and al-Shāfiʿī in the Assembly [or: Abū Ḥanīfa as my intercessor in the Assembly].

Then, when al-Rāwandī lists the leaders of the religion and the foremost experts of the sacred law, Abū Ḥanīfa and al-Shāfiʿī head up the list. They are followed by Abū Yūsuf, al-Shaybānī, al-Thawrī, Mālik b. Anas, Zufar

194, Dār al-Kutub al-Miṣriyya, fols. 46–55. In one of his final works al-Ghazālī wrote a glowing tribute to Abū Ḥanīfa: al-Ghazālī, *Iḥyāʾ ʿulūm al-dīn* (Jeddah: Dār al-Minhāj, 2011), 1: 106–8. On al-Kardarī see Ibn Abī al-Wafāʾ, *al-Jawāhir al-muḍiyya*, 3: 228–30; Ibn Quṭlūbughā, *Tāj al-tarājim*, 267–8; al-Kaffawī, 'Katāʾib aʿlām al-akhyār min fuqahāʾ madhhab al-Nuʿmān al-mukhtār', MS 1381 Feyzullah, fols. 242b–243b, no. 418; al-Laknawī, *al-Fawāʾid al-bahiyya*, 176–7 (Cairo edn.). For the refutation see al-Laknawī, *al-Fawāʾid al-bahiyya*, 50–1 (Cairo edn.); Littman, *A List of Arabic Manuscripts*, 82; Brockelmann, *GAL*, 1: 474; supp. 1: 654; Madelung, 'The Spread of Māturīdism', 126–7; Bouges, *Essai de Chronologie*, 8; Badawī, *Muʾallafāt al-Ghazālī*, 6–8.

59 Browne, 'Manuscript History of the Seljūqs'. On this work see also Meisami, 'History as Literature', 27; Meisami, 'The Past in Service of the Present', 272.

60 Al-Rāwandī, *Rāḥat al-ṣudūr va āyat al-surūr dar tārīkh āl-saljūq*, ed. Muḥammad Iqbāl (Leiden: Brill, 1921).

61 Al-Rāwandī, *Rāḥat al-ṣudūr*, 14.

62 Al-Rāwandī, *Rāḥat al-ṣudūr*, 14 (the meaning could be: Then [I take refuge in being with] Abū Ḥanīfa as my intercessor in the Assembly).

b. Hudhayl, and Aḥmad b. Ḥanbal.[63] His preference for Ḥanafis is transparent given that half of these scholars were considered Ḥanafis in his time. He warns his readers and listeners that 'whoever uttered words of abuse or reproach against any one of them was a terribly ill-fated person, because all of them were on the truth, all their paths led to God, and the religion of them all was based upon the commandments of the prophet Muḥammad'.[64]

What al-Rāwandī was trying to explain to his readers was that medieval Sunni orthodoxy was anchored in the legacies and institutions that were spawned by these men, their followers, and their schools. By his time, medieval Sunnism was (in theory and, most of the time, in practice) an accommodating tradition: 'Abū Ḥanīfa was the right eye and al-Shāfiʿī the left eye . . . two *madhhab*s sharing one truth, one piece of wood but of two different shades.'[65] He continues in the *Rāḥat al-ṣudūr*:[66]

> It is not extreme fanaticism when the follower of the *madhhab* of the greatest imam, Abū Ḥanīfa the Kufan, says that the path of Abū Ḥanīfa has greater spiritual illumination and is closer to God. Similarly, it is not extreme fanaticism when the follower of the esteemed imam al-Shāfiʿī al-Muṭṭalibī holds fast to the belief that the path of al-Shāfiʿī is easier and more honest. However, anyone who says about either Abū Ḥanīfa or al-Shāfiʿī that they were not on the truth, that person is, with all certainty, an unbeliever and someone whose religion is in turmoil.

Al-Rāwandī himself was clearly partisan to the *madhhab* of Abū Ḥanīfa, and his work gives many examples of the kind of unproblematic commitment to a *madhhab* he defends in this passage above. One example of this is his remark that

> Abū Ḥanīfa was the light of the umma. At that time, when the stars – 'my companions are like the stars' – had set in the dust of the West, a light from the lamp of Kufa was ignited such that with its light Iraq, Khurāsān, Rūm, and Turkistān were lighted; that the light of my umma is Abū Ḥanīfa – this is my religion, and this is my *madhhab*.[67]

[63] Al-Rāwandī, *Rāḥat al-ṣudūr*, 13–14.

[64] Al-Rāwandī, *Rāḥat al-ṣudūr*, 13 (*va sakht bad bakht kesī būd keh zabān-i ṭaʿn dar yekī az īshān darāz kunad, az ānke hameh bar ḥaqq and rāh-i hameh bi khudā ast va dīn-i jumleh sharʿ-i Muṣṭafā ast*).

[65] Al-Rāwandī, *Rāḥat al-ṣudūr*, 17 (*Abū Ḥanīfa chashme rāst, Shāfiʿī chashme chap . . . madhhab-i dū, ḥaqq yek, ābnūs yek, rang dū*).

[66] Al-Rāwandī, *Rāḥat al-ṣudūr*, 13 (*taʿaṣṣub az īn nabāyad kī ān kesī keh madhhab-i imām aʿẓam Abū Ḥanīfa kūfī dārad guyad rāhe-yi Abū Ḥanīfa rūshantar va bi khudā nazdīktar ast, va ānke madhhab-i imām muʿaẓẓām Shāfiʿī muṭṭalibī dārad iʿtiqād bandad ke rāhe-yi Shāfiʿī sahaltar va amīntar ast. Ammā ānkeh guyad Abū Ḥanīfa yā Shāfiʿī nah bar ḥaqq būdand kāfir yaqīn va bad-i dīn bāshad*).

[67] Al-Rāwandī, *Rāḥat al-ṣudūr*, 14 (*Abū Ḥanīfa sirāj-i ummat būd. Dar ān vaqt keh sitārgān – aṣḥābī ka al-nujūm' – dar maghrib khāk-i afūl kardand, chirāghī az mishkāt-i Kūfa bar*

One of the poems in this *manāqib* section reads:[68]

*Nīstī islām agar fatā va-yi Nu'mān nīstī,*
*Kīstī muftī agar Nu 'mān nabū deh rah'numā.*

There is no Islam, if there are no edicts of Nuʿmān,
Who can be a mufti, if Nuʿmān was not a guide.

In making these remarks, al-Rāwandī was defending the right to express such fidelity. He recognised that *madhhab* affiliation conveyed a deep and penetrating commitment to the eponymous founder. What troubled him was that this loyalty had the potential to result in animosity against other eponymous founders, especially with the knowledge of earlier proto-Sunni traditionalist discourses of heresy. It was, in the end, the vision of orthodoxy espoused by *manāqib* and *musnad* authors of the ninth–eleventh centuries, the convictions of scholars such as Ibn ʿAbd al-Barr and al-Rāwandī's vision and not the one advanced by al-Khaṭīb al-Baghdādī's captious account in his *Tārīkh Baghdād*, that prevailed. For someone like al-Rāwandī, this was never in doubt. He told his readers a story of a class Abū Ḥanīfa supervised at the Kaʿba, where Abū Ḥanīfa reportedly prayed: 'God, if my *ijtihād* is correct and my *madhhab* is true, make it victorious since it is for your sake, God, that I assert the sacred law of Muṣṭafā.' Al-Rāwandī tells us that at this point a voice from the Kaʿba declared: 'Thou hast uttered the truth; thy doctrine shall not wane so long as the sword abides in the hands of the Turks.'[69] This is a fantastical story, and its immediate context was the Saljūq sultans of the east. Al-Rāwandī reminds his readers that in Arabia, Persia, Rūm, and Rūs, the sword is indeed in the hands of the Turks and fear of their sword is implanted firmly in all hearts. Furthermore, this section of *Rāḥat al-ṣudūr* closes with our author listing examples of Saljūq sultans who provided patronage and support to the Ḥanafī *madhhab* and favoured Ḥanafī institutions over Shāfiʿī ones. Beyond this immediate historical context, al-Rāwandī's employment of the heavenly voice device (*ḥawātif*) conveys an integral point about the evolution of Sunni orthodoxy and its conception among medieval Muslims. A return to an earlier phase of proto-Sunni

*afrūkhtan keh bi nūr-i ū 'Irāq va Khurāsān va Rūm va Turkistān rūshan shud keh sirāj-i ummatī Abū Ḥanīfa, dīn-i man īn ast, va madhhab-i man chinīn ast).*

68 Al-Rāwandī, *Rāḥat al-ṣudūr*, 14.

69 Al-Rāwandī, *Rāḥat al-ṣudūr*, 14 (*keh chūn Imām Aʿẓam Abū Ḥanīfa Kūfī bi ḥajjat al-vidāʿ būd ḥalaqa dar kaʿba bi-garaft va guft khudāvand agar ijtihād durust ast va madhhab-i man ḥaqq ast nuṣratish kun keh az bi-rāy-i tū khudā taqrīr-i sharʿ-i Muṣṭafā kardam. Ḥātifī az khāneh-yi kaʿba āvāz dād va guft: ḥaqq qulta; lā zāla madhhabuka mā dāma al-sayf fī yad al-atrāk*).

traditionalist orthodoxy was no longer viable. A new orthodoxy had been consecrated, and it was (and still is today) one that outlasted the Turks. What was once a consensus concerning Abū Ḥanīfa's heresy among proto-Sunni traditionalists had been transformed into a more lasting consensus among a broader Muslim community of the tenth–eleventh centuries. This was a consensus about orthodoxy that now proved to be unshakeable.

# 11 Conclusion

This monograph has aimed to address both general and specific problems in our understanding of medieval Islamic history. There are a number of gaps and weaknesses, though, that I hope future scholarship will be better placed to deal with. One obvious weakness in this study is the absence of any serious examination of the texts and manuscripts attributed to Abū Ḥanīfa. The question of whether Abū Ḥanīfa actually composed any works is not a simple one; eighth- and ninth-century authors did not remember him as an author. His detractors did not cite specific books or passages in the course of their diatribes against him. His students, followers, and admirers neither cited nor pointed to his books to defend him against his critics until the eleventh century.[1] In line with one of the finest researchers and philologists of Islamicate learning, Murtaḍā al-Zabīdī, where medieval sources do refer to *kutub Abī Ḥanīfa*, one possibility is that the authors intended notebooks or dictation to his students.[2]

The absence of such books probably helped to stem discourses of heresy against Abū Ḥanīfa. (As I have pointed out already, the absence of such texts made the work of proto-Sunni traditionalists who sought to frame him as a heretic so much harder.) ʿAmr b. Dīnār said that he went to visit Wahb b. Munabbih at his house in Ṣanʿāʾ and, during a conversation over walnuts, ʿAmr b. Dīnār said to Wahb b. Munabbih: 'How I wish you had not written a book on the subject of predestination (*wadadtu annaka lam takun katabta fī al-qadar kitāban*).' Wahb b. Munabbih felt the same way: 'By God, how I would have wished that, too.'[3] After all, there was no written record to point to Abū Ḥanīfa's heresy, and in fact the written record that did exist later on in

[1] ʿAbd al-Qāhir al-Baghdādī, *Uṣūl al-dīn* (Istanbul: Maṭbaʿat al-Dawla, 1928), 308.

[2] Al-Zabīdī, *Itḥāf al-sāda al-muttaqīn* (Beirut: Dār al-Fikr, n.d.), 2: 14. See also Nuʿmānī, 'Imām Abū Ḥanīfa kī taṣānīf se Imām Mālik kā istifādah [On Imam Mālik's Benefiting from the Books of imam Abū Ḥanīfa]', in *Uṣūl-i ḥadīth kī baʿḍ ahamm mabāḥith [Some Important Researches in the Science of Ḥadīth]* (Karachi: al-Raḥīm Akīdamī, n.d.), 58–64.

[3] Al-Fasawī, *Kitāb al-Maʿrifa wa al-tārīkh*, 2: 281.

the form of texts emerging from the master's students established his orthodox credentials.

I was unable to examine the eleventh century in more detail and, in particular, the emergence of the new and more accommodating medieval Sunnism. This, too, I leave to historians of the Ghaznavids and Saljūqs. There are certain paradoxes and contradictions that warrant closer investigation. The fact that this discourse of heresy against Abū Ḥanīfa existed during a time when the Ḥanafī school continued to spread is perhaps the most glaring paradox. But here I would tend to agree with Shahab Ahmed's suggestion that contradictions of this kind were crucial to the formation of meaning making in medieval Islamic societies.[4] Another subject that has been raised in this book is that of porous boundaries between Sunnism and Shiʿism. The question of ambiguous confessional loyalties certainly requires further research; and whilst this study has been an account of orthodoxy and heresy in the history of proto-Sunnism and medieval Sunnism, I hope it might serve as a model for understanding the dynamics of orthodoxy and heresy among other religious movements in medieval Islam. On other questions, my explanations simply do not satisfy me. I am sure other readers may feel the same way, but I leave it up to them to form their own opinions and close now with a summary of this study's main contributions.

***

Part I provided a history of invective against Abū Ḥanīfa during the ninth–eleventh centuries. I described this invective as a discourse of heresy because of its wide, regular, and recurring circulation among a discrete yet influential network of proto-Sunni traditionalists. All of these scholars and writers were major figures in the growth and development of religious writing in the formative period of medieval Islam. These discourses of heresy were disseminated, therefore, by and among a textual community. This did not mean that such discourses were shorn of their oral dimensions. Discourses of heresy were recorded and memorialised in texts; but they continued to circulate as anecdotal and oral materials. The oral and the written existed side by side.

Taking into consideration the oral and textual dimensions of these discourses permitted us to detail the lives, connections, and shared beliefs of proto-Sunni traditionalists. Discourses of heresy against Abū Ḥanīfa illuminated the deep and penetrating loyalties that bound together religious scholars in the ninth–eleventh centuries. Our history of proto-Sunni traditionalism documented new insights about figures familiar to

[4] Ahmed, *What Is Islam?*, 405 (though I find Ahmed's evidence and argumentation in ch. 6 unconvincing).

Islamicists. It went further, though, by highlighting the formidable contributions made by figures who remain unstudied in modern scholarship. We were able to compose a broader history of the proto-Sunni traditionalist community that recognised an empire-wide network of religious scholars dedicated to a particular version of proto-Sunni orthodoxy. Their commitment to constructing a discourse of heresy against Abū Ḥanīfa that excluded him was instrumental to the very process of the formation of orthodoxy. It was in the process of framing and combating the heresy of the proximate other that proto-Sunni traditionalists were able to embolden their own group identity and fashion orthodoxy. Emphasising this diverse and messy process has meant pushing back against essentialising narratives about Sunnism's development.[5]

Part II of this study contextualised the data amassed in Part I. It used this data to argue that modern scholarship in Islamic Studies and within the field of Religious Studies more broadly has adopted too narrow an understanding of heresy and orthodoxy. Discourses of heresy against Abū Ḥanīfa demonstrate that notions of orthodoxy and heresy were not limited to the realm of belief (*doxa*) and practice (*praxis*). Heresiological discourses against Abū Ḥanīfa were rooted in wider social phenomena, attitudes, ideas, mentalités, and social and political trends in medieval Islam. Chapter 4 examined how one ninth-century historian perceived and depicted the religious deviance of Abū Ḥanīfa. We learnt that, for al-Fasawī, Abū Ḥanīfa's heresy was an extension of prevailing attitudes and mentalités about the holy and unholy nature of regions and cities in the medieval Islamic world. Al-Fasawī saw Kufa as the devil's first place of residence after his exile. This foundational event set the stage for Iraq's dark and ignoble history in the eyes of al-Fasawī and others. The region was a breeding ground for religious heresies and political chaos. Al-Fasawī's extensive section assailing Abū Ḥanīfa is prefaced with material of this kind depicting Iraq as an unholy region. This broader social and cultural history concerning particular regions helped to situate Abū Ḥanīfa's religious deviance for proto-Sunni traditionalist scholars.

In Chapter 5 we analysed another social dimension of medieval Islamicate societies that was employed in discourses of heresy against Abū Ḥanīfa. We demonstrated that ethnogenesis played a crucial role in accentuating the discourse of difference that separated orthodoxy from heresy. The chapter pointed to the ways in which ethnogenesis, religious conversion, and language were interwoven into discourses of heresy

[5] There can be no harm in re-stating Smith's formulation of the proximate other: 'The radically "other" is merely "other"; the proximate "other" is problematic, and hence, of supreme interest.' See Smith, 'What a Difference a Difference Makes'.

against Abū Ḥanīfa. Proto-Sunni traditionalists exploited these themes in order to bring Abū Ḥanīfa's ancestry, genealogy, and social status into disrepute. Proto-Sunni traditionalists presented his social, ethnic, and religious background as a necessary precursor to his religious deviance. These factors were instrumental and not incidental to what they conceived of as the heresy of Abū Ḥanīfa.

Chapter 6 showed that politics and the role of the state were fundamental to discourses of heresy against Abū Ḥanīfa. It maintained that his association with ʿAlid revolts, in addition to other rebellions, in the eighth century was one of the cornerstones of proto-Sunni traditionalist discourses of heresy against him. His alleged support for Zayd b. ʿAlī's rebellion, backing for Ibrāhīm b. ʿAbd Allāh's revolt, and intervention during the uprising of al-Ḥārith b. Surayj all contributed to a near-consensus among proto-Sunni traditionalists that Abū Ḥanīfa advocated rebellion against Muslim rulers. It was further argued that proto-Sunni traditionalist discourses of heresy were overwhelmingly concerned with this aspect of Abū Ḥanīfa's mnemohistory. We suggested that this preoccupation with Abū Ḥanīfa's involvement with rebellions owed itself to two factors. First, political quietism had become a core and indisputable doctrine of proto-Sunni traditionalist orthodoxy by the middle of the ninth century. Rebellion against rulers constituted heresy. This doctrine extended to scholars supporting rebellions. There was a second factor that energised proto-Sunni traditionalist attacks on Abū Ḥanīfa on account of his involvement in political upheavals during the late Umayyad and early ʿAbbāsid periods. The first half of the ninth century witnessed a rise in the appointment of proto-Ḥanafī judges. Local and provincial courts all over the early Islamic empire were being populated by proto-Ḥanafī qadis. The appointment of judges became a very sensitive issue for both local scholars and communities. Judges were crucial intermediaries between the state and provincial subjects. The social status of judges as brokers of justice afforded them a degree of social prestige. Proto-Sunni traditionalists had been observing this phenomenon in different provinces of the empire. They recognised the implications of judges, aligned to an eponymous founder whom they regarded as a heretic, being scattered across the empire and administering religious law to society at large. In the eyes of many proto-Sunni traditionalists the judiciary was becoming a vehicle for proto-Ḥanafism's wide dissemination across the empire. One way to disrupt the ʿAbbāsid empire's reliance on proto-Ḥanafī judges was to emphasise and indeed publicise Abū Ḥanīfa's support for rebellions against caliphs and the state, and to insist that he was a heretic. By communicating this fact far and wide, proto-Sunni traditionalists would place the ʿAbbāsids in the awkward position of appointing proto-Ḥanafī judges to represent the legal authority of the medieval state when their eponymous founder had been at the forefront of past attempts to overthrow the caliphal administration and when his orthodoxy, so they argued, had been in doubt. The focus on Abū Ḥanīfa's politics served to undergird proto-Sunni traditionalist orthodoxy whilst at the same time undermining proto-Ḥanafī claims to religious orthodoxy.

The distinct treatment of 'religion' in Chapter 7 represented little more than a capitulation to the organisational demands of a lengthy monograph. The division of discourses of heresy into separate realms of politics, society, and religion is a compartmentalisation that this book rails against. We historians have imposed the model of fragmentation that obtains in the twenty-first century and have begun to see and analyse medieval Islamicate societies on the basis of it. This study has insisted on the necessity of seeing discourses of heresy and orthodoxy as the product of a broad and integrated conception of religion and religious life, one in which the social and the political often lacked any clear lines of demarcation. It should be understood, then, that I have been compelled to organise this study in a way in which religion, society, and politics appear only superficially to be treated in a distinct manner.[6] Chapter 7 proceeded to analyse discourses of heresy that pertained to Abū Ḥanīfa's jurisprudence, theology, expertise in ḥadīth, and personal piety. Its aim was to amplify the fears and threats that proto-Sunni traditionalist orthodoxy perceived from those they described as heretics: to give readers and specialists a comprehensive view of how proto-Sunni traditionalists constructed a discourse of heresy in the ninth–eleventh centuries. The final section of the chapter emphasised that discourses of orthodoxy and heresy emerged alongside a developed sociology of heresy. Heresy was to be marginalised and orthodoxy was to be promoted by means of regulating societies, places of communal worship, communities, and individuals. In this sense, discourses of heresy and orthodoxy can hardly be understood as merely floating in the air or being confined to closed texts. The growth and importance of such organic and non-institutional mechanisms for disciplining society cannot be appreciated without recognising the muted role of the state in discourses of heresy and orthodoxy. Under the Saljūqs, institutions were integrated within the sphere of religious learning. How

[6] For recent attempts to posit a clearer distinction between the secular and the religious in pre-modern Islam see Abbasi, 'Did Premodern Muslims Distinguish the Religious and Secular?', where the author's deployment of *dīnī–dunyāwī* does not, in my estimation, map neatly onto the secular–religious categories in the modern world. A more thorough and theoretically robust interrogation of these categories can be found in Ahmed, *What Is Islam?*, 176–245.

the proto-Sunnism of the ninth and eleventh centuries that was so suspicious of institutions and institutionalisation was transformed under the Saljūqs into a Sunnism integrated so seamlessly into institutionalisation is a fascinating question which historians of the twelfth century must address.

Where Parts I and II of this book examined the construction of discourses of heresy and the dominance of proto-Sunni traditionalist visions of orthodoxy, Part III revealed the dramatic evolution and failings of proto-Sunni traditionalism. The concerted efforts of proto-Sunni traditionalists in the ninth–eleventh centuries to establish Abū Ḥanīfa as being outside the realm of orthodoxy were met with a new kind of resistance. This response to proto-Sunni traditionalism is essential, I have argued, to understanding the emergence of medieval Sunnism. Part III contended that two neglected but prolific genres of historical writing were indispensable to explaining this historical transformation in proto-Sunnism: How it was that discourses of heresy against Abū Ḥanīfa were committed to portraying him as a heretic and deviant in the ninth–eleventh centuries; and how over the course of the tenth–eleventh centuries Abū Ḥanīfa was considered by members of the Shāfiʿī, Ḥanbalī, Mālikī, and other proto-Sunni movements as a pillar of Sunni orthodoxy. The production and unprecedented proliferation of *manāqib* and *masānīd* works – the former dismissed as mere hagiography and the latter barely utilised by modern scholars – are crucial documents for marking the evolution of medieval Sunnism. The apotheosis of Abū Ḥanīfa as a figure of unimpeachable Sunni orthodoxy alongside Mālik b. Anas, al-Shāfiʿī, and Aḥmad b. Ḥanbal cannot be understood without a scholarly appreciation for what *manāqib* and *masānīd* works sought to do. The new consensus regarding Abū Ḥanīfa's orthodoxy was not merely a convenient rationalisation of orthodoxy as it was beginning to take shape. We must recognise *manāqib* and *masānīd* works as agents of these changes. I hope to show elsewhere how the emergence of the *manāqib* literature, in particular, around these four eponyms constituted a defining feature of medieval Sunnism's identity and memory, but I believe its contribution to the transformation of Abū Ḥanīfa's mnemohistory has been established by this study. Chapter 8 proposed that hagiography is a misleading description of and category in which to place *manāqib* works that revolve around the eponyms of the legal schools. The *manāqib* literature represented a form of biographical and historical writing. It contained narratives that framed a society and posited a social vision. They advocated a social world that consisted of living by particular types of loyalties, devotional practices, pedagogical norms, and moral codes. Authority, heresy, and orthodoxy were defined and delineated by authors of these books, who chose to craft these visions around one figure. Though *manāqib* works were dedicated to orthodox masters of the past, their defining orientation was towards the present and the future. Their authors saw history as the history of a few great men. But they believed that the future could be effected and affected by many men (and women)[7] who emulated such epigones and who embodied the social vision that authors of *manāqib* works sought to articulate. *Manāqib* works were commentaries on a basic but essential credo of medieval Islamicate societies: What has been may be again.

The concluding part of this study examined attempts in the post-formative period of Islamic history to unsettle medieval Sunnism's new consensus concerning Abū Ḥanīfa's flawless orthodoxy. Religious scholars such as Ibn ʿAdī and Ibn Ḥibbān tried to resurrect discourses of heresy against Abū Ḥanīfa from the ninth–tenth centuries by documenting what they described as the consensus of proto-Sunni traditionalist orthodoxy. But this consensus had vanished. It had been replaced by a new one. And there was no disputing it now. This was a lesson that traditionalist Salafis of the twentieth century learned, too, as they arrived at the realisation that Abū Ḥanīfa was too big to fail.[8] It seems to me that someone like Muḥammad Zāhid al-Kawtharī, a twentieth-century scholar whose oeuvre was dedicated to defending Abū Ḥanīfa, understood and appreciated the fact that Sunnism was a cumulative force. His robust and relentless defence of Abū Ḥanīfa had little to do with what both his detractors and admirers described as his *taʿaṣṣub* (extreme partisanship) for Ḥanafism. What al-Kawtharī was defending was a historical process that took some four centuries to reach maturation. He considered short-sighted and ahistorical the view of numerous contemporaries who looked back on the historical past and reduced the dynamic history of orthodoxy in medieval Sunnism to the narrow *belle époque* of Salafism. This study has argued that the formation of medieval Sunni orthodoxy was the work of medieval scholarly and textual communities and the social, cultural, political, and intellectual contexts that they participated

[7] For an uncommon example see al-Sulamī, *Dhikr al-niswa al-mutaʿabbidāt al-ṣūfiyyāt*, ed. Maḥmūd Muḥammad al-Ṭanāḥī (Cairo: Maktabat al-Khānjī, 1993); and Melchert's finding that 'there is no room here to say that collections of renunciant sayings name surprisingly many saintly women, or that the tradition systematically suppressed reports of saintly women from disbelief in female saintliness. On the contrary, saintly women were part of the prevailing ideology, at least of the renunciant tradition as represented by the male-authored literature. Pious Muslim men expected to hear of pious Muslim women. Whether women would have transmitted different sorts of reports if they had written books can only be guessed at': Melchert, 'Before Ṣūfiyyāt', 139.

[8] See Maḥmūd Shukrī al-Alūsī, *Tajrīd al-sinān fī al-dhabb ʿan Abī Ḥanīfa al-Nuʿmān ʿalayhi al-raḥma wa al-riḍwān*, ed. Iyād b. ʿAbd al-Laṭīf b. Ibrāhīm al-Qaysī (Damascus: Dār al-Nawādir, 2017).

in for over four centuries. Medieval Sunni orthodoxy took time to take shape, and among its most decisive characteristics was its recognition of the unimpeachable orthodoxy of four legal schools and their eponymous founders.[9] But this grand consensus was possible only through a series of failures, successes, conflicts, and compromises between different strains of proto-Sunnism. It was this consensus that al-Kawtharī believed was the cornerstone of Sunnism and its homeostatic stability throughout Islamic history. For him, few developments personified the quintessence of consensus than Abū Ḥanīfa's consecration as a paragon of Sunni orthodoxy. The danger that al-Kawtharī recognised was that any attempts, however bold or subtle, to unsettle this consensus would mark the beginning of the end of Sunnism. This was the stark yet understandable frame of reference within which al-Kawtharī understood debates concerning the heresy and orthodoxy of Abū Ḥanīfa.[10]

Let me now turn to some of the broader arguments this monograph has made, and its implications, if any, for the study of medieval Islamic history and Islamicate societies. I have tried to offer some alternative ways of understanding the history of orthodoxy and heresy in Islam – ways that describe more accurately how our subjects themselves, over centuries, understood and participated in such efforts. Proposing this alternative history has required, at least on my part, rethinking certain approaches found in modern treatments of heresy and orthodoxy in Islam. On one spectrum, we have the influential framework of Durkheim, whose definition of religion states that 'religious phenomena fall into two basic categories: beliefs and rites'. This definition of the work that religion does in society has helped to confine the study of orthodoxy and heresy to the realm of heresiography (*doxa* and *praxis*). Specialists in Islamic Studies, such as van Ess, Wilson, and Knysh, have been particularly susceptible to this approach, seeing in theology and heresiography the most complete representation of orthodoxy and heresy. This approach has found a much wider audience through comparative accounts of history and orthodoxy in Islam, such as those given by Henderson and Ames, which offer sweeping conclusions based on a limited corpus of Islamic theological works in translation. Our study has examined works of theology and theological debates as one resource for the study of orthodoxy and heresy; but, similar to Fierro's work on heresy in Andalus and the Islamic west, it has sought to go beyond the genre of heresiography to exhibit a more dynamic and diverse set of

[9] The reader should not assume that I am claiming that medieval Sunnism did not evolve after the eleventh century. When I speak of the maturation of classical Sunnism, I am speaking of its consensus – an unshakeable one from the eleventh century onwards – concerning the orthodoxy of the legal eponyms.

[10] Khan, 'Islamic Tradition in an Age of Print', 77–8.

processes visible across the corpus of medieval Muslim writings and social experiences.[11] The work of texts and textualist communities, as one late scholar has reminded us, is to create experiences. This insight, to my mind, enables us to move beyond the binary of Historical (Book) Islam versus Lived Islam.[12] If we understand that texts (written, performed, or memorised) form experiences – that women, men, children, rulers, and scholars begin to live through their engagement with these texts – we can appreciate how Lived Islam did not necessarily operate above and beyond a historical, source-based corpus. Societies lived these texts in the sense that they used them to create and explore. Society was possessed, as Ahmed explains, of the sensibilities and modalities of these texts. No experience is ever the same (*lā takrār fī al-tajallī*), according to a medieval maxim employed in a different context, and so each reading and engagement with texts and textualist communities paves the way for different encounters. And the rise of new genres, such as *manāqib*, *masānid*, *ṭabaqāt*, and doxographical works gave rise to an alternative conception of Sunni orthodoxy.[13] Another implication of the Durkheimian model has been a focus on institutions and power.[14] Durkheim insisted that 'in history we do not find religion without Church'.[15] The absence of such an institution in Islam has resulted in vertical, state-centric histories of orthodoxy and heresy in Islam. Ames's comparative history of medieval heresies reflects this very well. The story she provides is one of triumph and repression, exhibited by the Umayyad caliphs, the Miḥna of the ʿAbbāsids, Saljūq viziers, and, finally, Mamlūk

[11] Fierro, 'Heresy in al-Andalus'.

[12] Reinhart, *Lived Islam*, 1–10. Reinhart's fascinating book does, in my view, begin by positing an unfortunate, straightforward dichotomy between Lived Islam and Book Islam: Reinhart, *Lived Islam*, 32–6 ('Lived Religion is an approach that studies the religiosity of those who don't write books, though it studies also the religiosity of clerics that isn't expressed in their books'). Lived Islam, in contrast to Book Islam, is thus characterised as 'irremediably heterogeneous, unstable, dynamic, creative, and enriching'. There is no reason why these very attributes could not be ascribed to Book Islam. Ahmed, in his sweeping critique of Islamic legal studies, has presented a similar and, in my view, misleading caricature of Book Islam; though in the same work Ahmed shows through an exceptionally sensitive reading of epics that Book Islam and Lived Islam need not be construed as binaries: Ahmed, *What Is Islam?*, 303–43 ('Fictional texts construct and communicate Islam through the exercise of the creative and explorative imagination. A society that lives these texts is necessarily a society possessed of the sensibilities and values of the modalities of fiction').

[13] On the relationship between texts and experiences see Ahmed, *What Is Islam?*, 310–43.

[14] Henderson, *The Construction of Orthodoxy and Heresy*, 108 ff.; Ames, *Medieval Heresies*, 93 ff.

[15] Durkheim, *The Elementary Forms of Religious Life*, 41, 42, 44 ('Religion is inseparable from the idea of Church'). It should be noted that Durkheim took a broader view of institutions. By 'Church' he meant a society or moral community whose members were united, and this phenomenon could exist 'without any official directing body'. See Durkheim, *The Elementary Forms of Religious Life*, 41. This resonates with the Weberian notion of a church as an 'association aspect of community organization for religious ends'. See Parsons, *The Structure of Social Action*, 1: 435.

rulers.[16] Van Ess and Wilson, meanwhile, have concluded that the lack of any central institutional authorities (churches and councils) in early and medieval Islamicate societies meant that orthodoxy did not and could not have existed. I have argued that, though institutions were not entirely absent, they were not a prerequisite for the construction of heresy and orthodoxy. We have looked at the formation of diverse communities, forming loose networks, agreeing and disagreeing with one another. They espoused moral, religious, and social codes and conventions. They sought to persuade, shape, and direct the course of orthodoxy. They managed to regulate and discipline outside state and institutional apparatuses.[17] But the discourse of heresy and orthodoxy reflected the nature of Islam, which was a living and lived religion and not a dead tradition. For this important reason, orthodoxy was constantly being refined, adjusted, and debated by communities. Communities of proto-Sunni traditionalist orthodoxy may have been dominant and powerful in the eighth–tenth centuries, but they were neither static nor hermetically sealed. As we saw, during the course of the tenth–eleventh centuries this discrete though influential discourse of heresy against Abū Ḥanīfa was challenged. Major transformations took place that altered the character of medieval Sunni orthodoxy and gave way to a new and more lasting conception of medieval Sunnism.

The central preoccupation of this book has been with orthodoxy and heresy in medieval Islam, not the life and times of Abū Ḥanīfa. Orthodoxy and heresy are categories that have unsettled many scholars in our field. In large part, the study of heresy and orthodoxy in Islam has been undertaken by non-Islamicists whose inability to engage with primary sources, except by way of translations, has resulted in trite narratives about medieval Islam. Specialists have written articles and essays counselling scholars on the dangers of these categories. Some historians working with chronicles have seen heresy and the regulation of orthodoxy through the lens of the state, which has led them to posit that heresy and orthodoxy were functions of the state. Islamicists have even suggested jettisoning these terms altogether. A more thorough critique of orthodoxy and heresy has been made very recently by the leading scholar of medieval Islamic theology. Josef van Ess's tome surveying the history of Islam's heresiographical literature – it reviews practically every single work of heresiography in Islamic history – contains countless statements repeating his central claim that heresy did not exist in medieval Islam because it lacked any centralising authority, institution, or church to impose doctrines or

[16] Ames, *Medieval Heresies*, 86–93 (Umayyads to ʿAbbāsids), 167 ff. (ʿAbbāsids to Mamlūks).

[17] Durkheim himself recognised this function. See Nisbet, *The Sociological Tradition*, 89, 150; Durkheim, *Moral Education*, 23 ff.

practices.[18] This study has reached a very different conclusion. I have argued (not against van Ess per se) that religious communities in medieval Islam cultivated their own techniques, strategies, and mechanisms for establishing the preponderance of doctrines, practices, attitudes, and beliefs. This was the work of orthodoxy; and it was best achieved by constructing discourses of heresy. My work has sought to undermine the view that orthodoxy and heresy are terms ill-suited to medieval Islam because it lacked the kind of institutional structure that existed in medieval Christianity and Judaism for regulating beliefs, practices, and ideas. Proto-Sunni traditionalists in the ninth century were curious, and were aware of confessional accounts of religious deviance in Judaism and Christianity. This awareness evolved into a conscious effort to read the trajectory of orthodoxy and heresy in medieval Islam against religious developments in Christianity and Judaism. To jettison concepts such as orthodoxy and heresy altogether and to insist on their incommensurability with medieval Islam requires ignoring the fact that proto-Sunni traditionalists in the ninth century interwove religious narratives about orthodoxy and heresy in Christianity and Judaism into their own communal discourses of heresy. Inspired by the work of scholars such as Alain Le Boulluec in the field of medieval religious history, I have argued that the history of orthodoxy and heresy in medieval Islam can be written by examining their discursive formation. These heresiological discourses have been shown to exist in a diverse range of genres and sources,

[18] Van Ess, *Der Eine und das Andere*, 1: 1303, 1315. In these passages van Ess argues that orthodoxy was an urban phenomenon but even then was not orthodoxy proper because Islam lacked a church. He writes that there was no church to regulate or discipline religion. But, as our monograph has shown, one does not need institutions to regulate or discipline religion. At one point van Ess states that the word 'orthodoxy' is useful only in so far as it operates as a metaphor. But he adds quickly that orthodoxy represents the view of the ruling elite. He also contends that orthodoxy was a local phenomenon, which approaches the view of Walter Bauer's history of orthodoxy and heresy in early Christian history (Bauer, *Rechtgläubigkeit und Ketzerei im ältesten Christentum*). *Pace* van Ess, I have tried to show how discourses of heresy were not restricted to specific locales and regions. They circulated in texts and among communities all over the provinces of the early Islamic empire. He also proposes that Islam was not a religious orthodoxy but a network of power. This sounds convincing, but it also approximates the ambiguity of some writing that reduces various phenomena to the work of power, without actually defining or explaining power (see the critique in Ahmed, *What Is Islam?*, 270 ff.). Van Ess knows the heresiographical genre better than any other Islamicist, especially this one. I am willing to concede, therefore, that his interpretation may be viable with respect only to the heresiographical genre. His conclusions stem from an unremitting focus on one genre, which he defines as a literary genre. Our study, on the other hand, eschews this approach of studying orthodoxy and heresy through works of heresiography only. I argue that understanding the evolution of orthodoxy and heresy should not be based on a single genre, especially a literary one dedicated systematically to classifying movements as orthodox and heretical.

including historians, litterateurs, jurists, and ḥadīth scholars. Some of these discourses have also survived in the form of records of intimate conversations, witty asides, and constant gossiping. Some historians may dismiss this material as anecdotal. But it is probably in the unrefined, untutored, and unscripted material that we are likely to find traces of the most personal beliefs and convictions held by members of medieval societies. *L'histoire est anecdotal.*[19]

It is worth repeating towards the end of this study that the use of terms such as heretic and orthodox has not been dogmatic, theological, or legal. *I have studied orthodoxy and heresy as processes and shifting strategies of denunciation and consensus making.* My immersion in these texts and sources does not seek to furnish an epistemology of heresy or orthodoxy, or a positivistic elucidation of doctrine and theology.[20] Rather, I have conceived of heresy and orthodoxy as representing impulses by medieval religious communities to construct notions of religious deviance and to denounce them. Proto-Sunni traditionalists aimed to establish clear differences between their conception of orthodoxy and that of the proximate other, and they then converted this difference into a programme of exclusion by constructing discourses of heresy. My readings of these sources, as well as my analytical interpretations of them, originate from the understanding that there are no neutral texts. This lack of neutrality has often been viewed as undermining the scholar's craft. This study has argued that the very lack of neutrality represented by the evidence of past societies is their greatest strength for the historian. The reading of personal and conflicting distant voices helps the historian to listen in on the tensions that characterised medieval societies, appreciate precisely what was at stake for them, and understand how they were resolved. This can be achieved when one recognises the changing nature of the balance of power implicit in such texts – depicting heresy and articulating claims to orthodoxy – and integrates this into a study of how these relationships reflect broader social and religious developments.[21]

This study has not attempted a comparative history of heresy and orthodoxy in medieval religious history. It has sometimes read in a tertiary manner episodes in the story of orthodoxy and heresy in medieval Islam against or alongside developments in late antique societies and medieval Christianity. For example, I have insisted that the absence of episcopal power, the lack of official imperial institutions, councils, and churches, and the marginal role that caliphs played in the religious

[19] Veyne, *Comment on écrit l'histoire*, 23.
[20] It would be a grave misreading of this monograph, for example, to posit theological claims on its basis, especially against Abū Ḥanīfa.
[21] Ginzburg, 'The Inquisitor as Anthropologist', 161.

development of Islam in the ninth–eleventh centuries did not render orthodoxy and heresy missing from medieval Islam. Yet, the absence of these dimensions ensured that orthodoxy and heresy took on a different character in medieval Islam than they did in some manifestations of medieval Christianity. Sometimes this had profound consequences. Persecution was by no means absent in medieval Islamicate societies. But a persecuting society, targeting members of the same confession, can hardly be discerned as a general pattern of medieval Islamic history. Similarly, the absence of powerful institutions for imposing orthodoxy and suppressing heresy in medieval Islam fostered the necessity for resolving tensions through the power of persuasion. More often than not, religious scholars knew that they had to resort to the written word to articulate their opposition or to resolve their differences.

When I first began researching this monograph, I assumed on the basis of my reading into the history of orthodoxy and heresy in medieval religious history that the story of orthodoxy and heresy in medieval Islam would mirror that found in medieval religious communities conceived more widely. There were a number of axioms common to the secondary literature that I was expecting to find in my study of medieval Islam: there is, for example, the idea that the transformation of old heresies into new orthodoxies results in the suppression of memories and narratives about this complicated trajectory. Similarly, there is the view that religious communities are committed to concealing or whitewashing earlier conflicts and tensions. I was expecting to find something similar in my study of discourses of heresy against Abū Ḥanīfa: a concerted effort to conceal the dramatic evolution of Abū Ḥanīfa from a heretic (among some influential proto-Sunnis) to a saint of orthodoxy (among the broad coalition of medieval Sunnis); and a determination to create a smokescreen so that this embarrassing fact would remain obscure and even undetectable. However, I found very little evidence of medieval scholarly communities glossing over or suppressing earlier contestations. This is one important aspect where prevailing assumptions in the fields of Memory Studies and Religious Studies can be less instructive for specific investigations into the history of medieval Islam, or where the study of Islam calls into question such prevailing assumptions. The notion of orthodoxy demanding the oblivion of earlier, turbulent aspects of the early Islamic community's history has been generally absent in this study. Discourses of heresy against Abū Ḥanīfa were a constant feature of religious writing even after the great convergence of medieval Sunnism, which witnessed his elevation as one of a few patron saints of medieval Sunni orthodoxy. In fact, defenders of Abū Ḥanīfa regularly and almost without fail cited from and included sections on these condemnations of

Abū Ḥanīfa by proto-Sunni traditionalists. They were explicit about these discourses of heresy, for they saw in such vehement criticism and slander the very mark of Abū Ḥanīfa's religious orthodoxy. Seldom did supporters of Abū Ḥanīfa turn a blind eye to discourses of heresy. The corpus of medieval religious writing, therefore, is far more forthcoming with respect to evolutions and transformations within the history of medieval Sunnism than our field sometimes assumes. The medieval Muslims studied in this monograph were not committed *de nier ce qui est, et d'expliquer ce qui n'est pas* (to deny what is and explain what is not).

This study has argued that the formation of proto-Sunni orthodoxy was an evolving process. Not only did it undergo a number of iterations, but it was characterised by internal contradictions and divisions. The failures of proto-Sunnism were as relevant to the formation of medieval Sunnism as were its successes. Medieval Sunnism was a product of constant tensions. These required negotiations. In order to appreciate the historical achievement of classical Sunnism, examining proto-Sunnism's most contentious times is integral to making sense of its most agreeable times. In this sense, to study the formation of orthodoxy and heresy in medieval Islam is to come to terms with a truism that 'traditions, when vital, embody continuities of conflict'.[22]

We might even dispense with Macintyre and reach further back in history, closer to the period studied in this work. One might suggest that the study of orthodoxy and heresy by modern scholars and by medieval Muslims differs more in style than in substance. Writing in the thirteenth century, Ibn Ṭumlūs reflected upon the erratic evolution of Sunni orthodoxy in the Islamic world. The evolution of orthodoxy and heresy was apparent to him, he observed, in studying the cases of Baqī b. Makhlad in the ninth century and al-Ghazālī in the twelfth. Baqī b. Makhlad had been declared a heretic in al-Andalus on account of his identifying with the *ahl al-ḥadīth* and was summoned to a heresy trial. The introduction of al-Ghazālī's books into al-Andalus led to charges of heresy against him and the burning of his books. Ibn Ṭumlūs tells us that, with time, the heresy trials and the book burning were forgotten:[23]

> When they realised that it was the truth bestowed upon them by God, they became convinced of the unbelief and heresy of its opponents. … What they had once considered reprehensible became good. What they believed to be unbelief and heresy became right belief and the true religion (*lammā kānū yaʿtaqidūn fīhi annahu al-ḥaqq wa annahu min ʿindi Allāh iʿtaqadū fī mukhālifīhi al-kufr wa al-zandaqa … fa*

[22] Macintyre, *After Virtue*, 257.

[23] Ibn Ṭumlūs, *Kitāb al-Madkhal li ṣināʿat al-manṭiq [Introducción al arte de la lógica por Abentomlús de Alcira]* ed. and trans. M. Asín Palacios (Madrid: Centro de Estudios Historicus, 1916), 9–11; Fierro, 'Heresy in al-Andalus', 904.

*ʿāda mā kāna munkaran ʿindahum maʿrūfan wa mā iʿtaqadūhu kufran wa zandaqa īmānan wa dīnan ḥaqqan*).

Ibn Ṭumlūs's pithy reflection on the transformation of orthodoxy and heresy in medieval Islam holds as true for religious developments in al-Andalus as it does for the history of discourses of orthodoxy and heresy concerning Abū Ḥanīfa: orthodoxy was real and not a fiction of an imagined community, but it was nevertheless a complex process of consensus making.

In a study that began with Abū Ḥanīfa's detractors, it seems fitting that the last word be given to a card-carrying tenth-century Ḥanafī. Al-Muqaddasī (d. 380/991) was an astute observer of the entire Islamic world. He made it his life's mission to catalogue the diversity in the social world he was familiar with. He interrupts his description of Iraq with a digression, seeking to justify his affiliation with the Ḥanafī *madhhab*. Al-Muqaddasī was aware that in his day and age discourses of heresy were still floating around, so he decided to pre-empt Abū Ḥanīfa's critics. He writes:[24]

> If someone were to object and say: 'Abū Ḥanīfa has been vilified (*maṭʿūn ʿalayhi*),' it should be said to him: 'Know that all men may be placed in three classes: a class of people for which there is complete consensus as to their uprightness; a class of people for which there is an overwhelming consensus as to their [religious] corruption; and a class of people who have been praised by some and reproached by others. The last class is the best of the three. . . . Even though there is a group of ignorant people who rebuke him, there are many people of virtue who support and praise him. Moreover, look at the spiritual opening that God granted his heart (*mā fataḥa Allāh ʿalā qalbihi*), such that he was able to interpret the Sharīʿa so that the rest of mankind did not have to concern themselves with this. . . . The like of Abū Ḥanīfa will not be seen.'

Al-Muqaddasī was deeply aware of discourses of heresy against his imam, but he also recognised that a new consensus concerning heresy and orthodoxy had emerged by his time. Speaking about the religious milieu of Jurjān, al-Muqaddasī writes:[25]

> If someone were to say: 'Did you not say that no heretics resided in Biyār, but now you speak of the presence there of the Karrāmiyya?' I would say the following to them: 'The Karrāmiyya are a people of asceticism and devotion, and they rely on Abū Ḥanīfa as their authority. Now, anyone who appeals to the authority of Abū Ḥanīfa, Mālik b. Anas, al-Shāfiʿī, or proto-Sunni traditionalists (*a'immat al-ḥadīth*) who does not go to extremes, does not display excessive love for Muʿāwiya, does not liken God or ascribe to Him attributes of created beings,

[24] Al-Muqaddasī, *Aḥsan al-taqāsīm*, 127–8.
[25] Al-Muqaddasī, *Aḥsan al-taqāsīm*, 365–6.

then such a person is not a heretic. I am determined not to let my tongue speak against the umma of Muḥammad, God bless him and grant him peace, and nor shall I testify against them as to their deviance as long as I can find a reason to avoid this. . . . So may God grant mercy to any worshipper who reflects upon this anecdote and adheres to one of the four *madhāhib*, for they comprise the vast majority of people; [and may God grant mercy to the person who] restrains his tongue from tearing apart the Muslims and going to extremes in the religion.'

It seems to me that both Ibn Ṭumlūs and al-Muqaddasī understood heresy and orthodoxy as processes, appreciated the authority of majoritarian forms of orthodoxy, and recognised its constant regulation and supervision by a textualist community. Perhaps medieval scholars were no less cognisant than modern academics of the changes that marked their societies. They simply saw no need to dwell on them for almost four hundred pages.

# Bibliography

## Primary Sources in Manuscript


Abū Ḥafṣ al-Nīshāpūrī. 'Rawnaq al-majālis', MS Berlin 8855.

Abū Layth Naṣr b. Muḥammad b. Aḥmad al-Samarqandī (attr.). 'Tuḥfat al-anām fī manāqib al-a'imma al-arbaʿa al-aʿlām', MS 3936, Chester Beatty Library, fols. 1–91a.

Abū Zurʿa al-Dimashqī. 'Al-Fawā'id al-muʿallala', MS Feyzullah 2169, Millet Kütüphanesi.

Bakkār b. Qutayba. 'Juz' fīhi min ḥadīth al-qāḍī Bakkār b. Qutayba al-Thaqafī', MS 124, fols. 1–7.

al-Biqāʿī. 'Manāqib al-Imām al-Ṭaḥāwī', MS 12831, Maktabat al-Asad al-Ẓāhiriyya, 16 fols.

Ibn Manda. 'Nubdha fī naqd Abī Ḥanīfa [Qawl al-thiqāt al-mutaqaddimīn wa shahādātuhum ʿalayhi wa al-kashf ʿan masāwīhi], Makabat al-Ẓāhiriyya, *Majmūʿa* 62.

'Tasmiyat al-mashāyikh alladhīna yarwī ʿanhum al-Imām Abū ʿAbd Allāh Muḥammad b. Ismāʿīl al-Bukhārī fī kitābihi al-jāmiʿ al-ṣaḥīḥ alladhī ṣannafahu', MS 1530, Idārat al-Makhṭūṭāt wa al-Maktabāt al-Islāmiyya bi Wizārat al-Awqāf al-Kuwaytiyya, fols. 1–23.

Ibn al-Shiḥna. 'Sharḥ manẓūmat Ibn Wahbān', MS 14866, Jāmiʿat Umm al-Qurā, Maktabat al-Malik ʿAbd Allāh b. ʿAbd al-ʿAzīz, 409 fols.

Ibn Ṭūlūn. 'Al-Ghuraf al-ʿaliyya fī tarājim muta'akhkhirī al-Ḥanafiyya', MS Şehid Ali Paşa 1924, Süleymaniye Library, Istanbul = MS Taymūr Tārīkh 631, Dār al-Kutub = MS Or. 3046, British Museum.

Al-Kādūrī. 'Jāmiʿ al-Muḍmarāt wa al-mushkilāt fī sharḥ Mukhtaṣar al-Qudūrī', MS 1409, Maktabat al-Malik ʿAbd al-ʿAzīz, 535 fols. = MS 1697, Maktabat al-Malik ʿAbd al-ʿAzīz, 657 fols.

Al-Kaffawī. 'Katā'ib aʿlām al-akhyār min fuqahā' madhhab al-Nuʿmān al-mukhtār', MS 1381 Feyzullah.

Al-Kardarī. 'Kitāb al-Radd ʿalā Abī Ḥāmid al-Ghazālī', MS Vollers 0351, Universitätbibliothek Leipzig, fols. 21a–25b = 'Kitāb al-Radd wa al-intiṣār li Abī Ḥanīfa imām fuqahā' al-amṣār', MS 194, Dār al-Kutub al-Miṣriyya, fols. 46–55.

Maḥmūd b. Manṣūr b. Abī al-Faḍl. 'Faṣl ʿalā taqdīm madhhab Abī Ḥanīfa'; Abū Ḥanīfa (attr.), 'Kitāb al-ʿĀlim wa al-mutaʿallim', MS 4216, Chester Beatty Library.

Al-Marghīnānī. 'Fuṣūl al-aḥkām fī uṣūl al-aḥkām [fuṣul al-ʿimādī]', MS 706, Jāmiʿat al-Malik Saʿūd, Riyadh.
Al-Qartabī. 'Qalā'id ʿuqūd al-durar wa al-ʿuqyān fī manāqib Abī Ḥanīfa', MS Or. 8224, British Museum.
Al-Qudūrī. 'Manāqib al-Imām al-Aʿẓam', MS Arab 283, Houghton Library, Harvard University.
Al-Shaykh al-Mufīd. 'Kitāb Faḍā'iḥ Abī Ḥanīfa', Majmūʿa MS no. 2, Marʿashī Library, Qum.
Al-Subadhmūnī. 'Kashf al-āthār fī manāqib Abī Ḥanīfa', MS 3105, no. 102, 326 fols.
Yūsuf b. Shāhīn. 'Al-Nujūm al-zāhira bi talkhīṣ Akhbār quḍāt Miṣr wa al-Qāhira, MS Arabe 2152, Bibliothèque nationale de France, 119 fols.
Al-Zandawasītī. 'Rawḍat al-ʿulamā' wa bahjat al-fuḍalā'', MS Syria, Maktabat ʿUyūn al-Sūd, MS 707 = 'Rawḍat al-ʿulamā' wa nuzhat al-fuḍalā'', MS Dublin, Chester Beatty, MS 6820.

## Primary Sources

Al-ʿAbbādī. *Kitāb Ṭabaqāt al-fuqahā' al-Shāfiʿiyya*, ed. Gösta Vitestam (Leiden: Brill, 1964).
ʿAbd Allāh al-Anṣārī. *Dhamm al-kalām wa ahlihi*, ed. ʿAbd al-Raḥmān b. ʿAbd al-ʿAzīz al-Shibl (Medina: Maktabat al-ʿUlūm wa al-Ḥikam, 1998).
ʿAbd Allāh b. Aḥmad b. Ḥanbal. *Kitāb al-ʿIlal wa maʿrifat al-rijāl ʿan Yaḥyā b. Maʿīn*, ed. Abū ʿAbd al-Hādī al-Jazā'irī (Beirut: Dār Ibn Ḥazm, 2004) = ed. Waṣī Allāh b. Muḥammad ʿAbbās (Riyadh: Dār al-Khānī, 2001).
*Kitāb al-Sunna*, ed. Muḥammad Saʿīd b. Sālim al-Qaḥṭānī (Riyadh: Dār ʿĀlam al-Kutub, 1996).
*Masā'il al-Imām Aḥmad b. Ḥanbal riwāyat ibnihi ʿAbd Allāh b. Aḥmad*, ed. Zuhayr al-Shāwīsh (Damascus: al-Maktab al-Islāmī, 1981).
ʿAbd al-Qādir al-Tamīmī. *Al-Ṭabaqāt al-saniyya fī tarājim al-Ḥanafiyya*, ed. ʿAbd al-Fattāḥ Muḥammad Ḥulw (Riyadh: Dār al-Rifāʿī, 1983).
Abū Aḥmad al-Ḥākim. *Kitāb al-Asāmī wa al-kunā*, ed. Yūsuf b. Muḥammad al-Dakhīl (Medina: Maktabat al-Ghurabā' al-Athariyya, 1994).
Abū al-ʿArab al-Tamīmī. *Kitāb al-Miḥan*, ed. Yaḥyā al-Jabbūrī (Beirut: Dār al-Gharb al-Islāmī, 2006).
Abū ʿAwāna. *Musnad Abī ʿAwāna*, ed. Ayman b. ʿĀrif al-Dimashqī (Beirut: Dār al-Maʿārif, 1998).
Abū Bakr b. al-ʿArabī. *Kitāb al-Qabas fī sharḥ Muwaṭṭā' Mālik b. Anas*, ed. Muḥammad ʿAbd Allāh Wuld Karīm (Beirut: Dār al-Gharb al-Islāmī, 1992).
Abū Bakr al-Ismāʿīlī. *Kitāb al-Muʿjam fī asāmī shuyūkh Abī Bakr al-Ismāʿīlī*, ed. Ziyād Muḥammad Manṣūr (Medina: Maktabat al-ʿUlūm wa al-Ḥikam, 1990).
Abū Ḥanīfa (attr.). *Al-ʿĀlim wa al-mutaʿallim*, ed. Muḥammad Zāhid al-Kawtharī (Cairo: Maṭbaʿat al-Anwār, 1948).
Abū al-Ḥasan ʿAlī b. Muḥammad al-Rabaʿī. *Faḍā'il al-Shām wa al-Dimashq*, ed. Salāḥ al-Dīn al-Munajjid (Damascus: al-Majmaʿ al-ʿIlmī al-ʿArabī, 1950).

Abū Ḥayyān al-Andalūsī. *Tafsīr baḥr al-muḥīṭ* (Beirut: Dār al-Kutub al-ʿIlmiyya, 1993).
Abū Isḥāq al-Shīrāzī. *Ṭabaqāt al-fuqahāʾ*, ed. Iḥsān ʿAbbās (Beirut: Dār al-Rāʾid al-ʿArabī, 1970).
Abū al-Muẓaffar al-Isfarāʾīnī. *Al-Tabṣīr fī al-dīn*, ed. Muḥammad Zāhid al-Kawtharī (Cairo: al-Maktaba al-Azhariyya li al-Turāth, 1940).
Abū Nuʿaym al-Iṣfahānī. *Ḥilyat al-awliyāʾ* (Cairo: Maktabat al-Khānjī, 1996; repr. Beirut: Dār al-Fikr, n.d.) = *Ḥilyat al-awliyāʾ wa ṭabaqāt al-aṣfiyāʾ* (Cairo: Maktabat al-Khānjī/Maṭbaʿat al-Saʿāda, 1932–8).
*Kitāb Dhikr akhbār Iṣfahān*, ed. Sven Dedering (Leiden: Brill, 1931).
*Kitāb al-Ḍuʿafāʾ*, ed. Fārūq Ḥamāda (Casablanca: Dār al-Thaqāfa, 1984).
*Maʿrifat al-ṣaḥāba*, ed. ʿĀdil b. Yūsuf al-ʿAzzāzī (Riyadh: Dār al-Waṭan li al-Nashr, 1998).
*Musnad al-Imām Abī Ḥanīfa*, ed. Naẓar Muḥammad al-Fāryābī (Riyadh: Maktabat al-Kawthar, 1994).
Abū Shāma al-Maqdisī. *Mukhtaṣar al-muʾammal fī al-radd ilā al-amr al-awwal*, ed. Ṣalāḥ al-Dīn Maqbūl Aḥmad (Kuwait: Maktabat al-Ṣaḥwa al-Islāmiyya, n.d.).
Abū al-Shaykh. *Ṭabaqāt al-muḥaddithīn bi Iṣfahān wa al-wāridīn ʿalayhā*, ed. ʿAbd al-Ghafūr ʿAbd al-Ḥaqq Ḥusayn al-Balūshī (Beirut: Muʾassasat al-Risāla, 1996).
Abū Ṭālib Yaḥyā b. al-Ḥusayn al-Hārūnī. *Al-Ifāda fī tārīkh al-aʾimma al-sāda*, ed. Muḥammad Kāẓim Raḥmatī (Tehran: Mīrāth-i Maktūb, 2008).
Abū ʿUbayd al-Qāsim b. Sallām. *Kitāb al-Amwāl*, ed. Muḥammad Ḥāmid al-Fiqī (Cairo: n.p., 1975).
*Kitāb al-Īmān*, ed. Muḥammad Nāṣir al-Dīn al-Albānī (Riyadh: Maktabat al-Maʿārif, 2000).
Abū Yaʿlā al-Mawṣilī. *Musnad Abī Yaʿlā al-Mawṣilī*, ed. Ḥusayn Salīm Asad (Beirut: Dār al-Maʾmūn li al-Turāth, 1987).
Abū Yūsuf (attr.). *Ikhtilāf Abī Ḥanīfa wa Ibn Abī Laylā*, ed. Abū al-Wafāʾ al-Afghānī (Hyderabad: Dāʾirat al-Maʿārif al-ʿUthmāniyya, 1938–9).
*Kitāb al-Āthār*, ed. Abū al-Wafāʾ al-Afghānī (Hyderabad: Lajnat Iḥyāʾ al-Maʿārif al-Nuʿmāniyya, n.d.).
*Kitāb al-Kharāj* (Beirut: Dār al-Maʿrifa, 1979).
Abū Zurʿa al-Dimashqī. *Tārīkh*, ed. Shukr Allāh b. Niʿmat Allāh al-Qūjānī (Damascus: Majmaʿ al-Lugha al-ʿArabiyya, 1990).
Aḥmad b. Ḥanbal. *Al-Musnad li Aḥmad b. Ḥanbal*, ed. Muḥammad Aḥmad Shākir (Cairo: Dār al-Ḥadīth, 1995).
Aḥmad b. Ḥanbal (attr.). *Kitāb al-Radd ʿalā al-jahmiyya wa al-zanādiqa*, ed. Daghīs b. Shubayb al-ʿAjmī (Kuwait: Gharās, 2005) = ed. Ṣabrī Salāma Shahīn (Riyadh: Dār al-Thibāt li al-Nashr wa al-Tawzīʿ, 2002) = ed. Muḥammad Ḥasan Rāshid (Cairo: al-Maṭbaʿa al-Salafiyya, 1973) = ed. ʿAbd al-Raḥmān ʿUmayra (Riyadh: Dār al-Liwāʾ, 1982) = ed. Muḥammad Fahr Shafqa (Ḥamā: Maktabat Ibn al-Haytham, 1967) = ed. Qiwām al-Dīn, 'Imam Ahmed'in bir eseri: İslâmın en kadim iki mezhebinin münakaşası', *Darülfünun İlâhiyat Fâkültesi Mecmuası*, 2: 5/6 (1927), 278–327.
Al-Ājurrī. *Suʾālāt Abī ʿUbayd al-Ājurrī Abā Dāwūd Sulaymān b. al-Ashʿath al-Sijistānī fī maʿrifat al-rijāl wa jarḥihim wa taʿdīlihim*, ed. ʿAbd al-ʿAlīm ʿAbd al-ʿAẓīm al-Bastawī (Mecca: Maktabat Dār al-Istiqāma, 1997).

ʿAlī b. al-Madīnī. *Al-ʿIlal*, ed. Muḥammad Muṣṭafā al-Aʿẓamī, 2nd edn. (Beirut: al-Maktab al-Islāmī, 1980).
Al-ʿAlmawī. *Al-Muʿīd fī adab al-mufīd wa al-mustafīd*, ed. Aḥmad ʿUbayd (Damascus: al-Maktaba al-ʿArabiyya, 1930).
Anon. *The Chronicle of Zūqnīn, Parts III and IV, AD 488–775*, trans. A. Harrak (Toronto: Pontifical Institute of Mediaeval Studies, 1999).
Anon. *Tārīkh-i Sīstān* (Tehran: Kitābkhāna-i Zawwār, n.d.).
Al-Anṣārī, al-Qāḍī ʿAbd al-Bāqī b. Muḥammad. *Aḥādīth al-shuyūkh al-thiqāt: al-shahīr bi al-mashyakha al-kubrā*, ed. al-Sharīf Ḥātim b. ʿĀrif al-ʿAwnī (Mecca: Dār al-ʿĀlam al-Fawā'id, 2001).
Al-Ashʿarī. *Al-Ibāna ʿan uṣūl al-diyāna*, ed. ʿAbbās Ṣabbāgh (Beirut: Dār al-Nafā'is, 1994).
*Maqālāt al-Islāmiyyīn*, ed. H. Ritter (Istanbul: Devlet Matbaasi, 1929–30).
Al-Asnawī. *Ṭabaqāt al-Shāfiʿiyya*, ed. ʿAbd Allāh al-Jubūrī (Riyadh: Dār al-ʿUlūm, 1981).
Al-ʿAynī. *ʿUmdat al-qārī fī sharḥ Ṣaḥīḥ al-Bukhārī* (Beirut: Idārat al-Ṭibāʿa al-Munīriyya/Dār al-Kutub al-ʿIlmiyya, 2001) = *ʿUmdat al-qārī sharḥ Ṣaḥīḥ al-Bukhārī* (Beirut: Dār al-Fikr, n.d.).
Al-Ayyūbī. *Ḥaṣr al-shārid min asānīd Muḥammad ʿĀbid*, ed. Khalīl b. ʿUthmān and al-Jubūr al-Subayʿī (Riyadh: Maktabat al-Rushd, 2003).
Al-Azdī. *Tārīkh Mawṣil*, ed. ʿAlī Ḥabība (Cairo: Lajnat Iḥyā' al-Turāth al-Islāmī, 1967).
Al-Baghdādī, ʿAbd al-Qāhir. *Al-Farq bayn al-firaq*, ed. Muḥammad Muḥyī al-Dīn ʿAbd al-Ḥamīd (Beirut: al-Maktaba al-ʿAṣriyya, 1995).
*Kitāb al-Milal wa niḥal*, ed. Naṣrī Nādir (Beirut: Dār al-Machreq, 1982).
*Uṣūl al-dīn* (Istanbul: Maṭbaʿat al-Dawla, 1928).
Al-Bājī, Abū al-Walīd. *Al-Muntaqā sharḥ Muwaṭṭā'* (Cairo: Dār al-Saʿāda, 1914).
Al-Bakrī. *Muʿjam mā istaʿjama min al-asmā' al-bilād wa al-mawāḍiʿ*, ed. Muṣṭafā al-Saqqā (Beirut: Dār al-Kutub al-ʿIlmiyya, n.d.).
Al-Balādhurī. *Ansāb al-ashrāf*, ed. W. Madelung (Berlin and Beirut: Klaus Schwarz, 2003) = ed. Maḥmūd al-Firdaws al-ʿAẓm (Damascus: Dār al-Yaqẓa al-ʿArabiyya, 1999) = ed. Suhayl Zakkār (Beirut: Dār al-Fikr, 1996) = *Ansāb al-ashrāf [Tatimmat Ḥimyar b. Sabā'] = Anonyme arabische Chronik [Ansāb al-ashrāf]*, ed. W. Ahlwardt (Greifswald: Selbstverlag, 1883).
Al-Barbahārī. *Sharḥ Kitāb al-Sunna*, ed. ʿAbd al-Raḥmān b. Aḥmad al-Jumayzī (Riyadh: Maktabat Dār al-Minhāj, 2005) = ed. Khālid b. Qāsim al-Raddādī (Medina: Maktabat al-Ghurabā' al-Athriyya, 1993) = ed. Muḥammad b. Saʿīd al-Qaḥṭānī (Dammām: Dār Ibn al-Qayyim, 1988).
Al-Bardhaʿī. *Kitāb al-Ḍuʿafā' wa al-kadhdhābīn wa al-matrūkīn min aṣḥāb al-ḥadīth* in *Abū Zurʿa al-Rāzī wa juhūduhu fī al-sunna al-nabawiyya maʿa taḥqīq kitābihi al-Ḍuʿafā' wa ajwibatihi ʿalā as'ilat al-Bardhaʿī*, ed. Saʿdī al-Hāshimī (Medina: n.p., 1989).
Al-Bayhaqī. *Dalā'il al-nubūwa wa maʿrifat aḥwāl ṣāḥib al-sharīʿa*, ed. ʿAbd al-Muʿṭī Qalʿajī (Beirut: Dār al-Kutub al-ʿIlmiyya, 1988).
*Al-Madkhal ilā al-sunan al-kubrā*, ed. Muḥammad Ḍiyā' al-Raḥmān al-Aʿẓamī (Kuwait: Dār al-Khulafā' li al-Kitāb al-Islāmī, n.d.).
*Manāqib al-Shāfiʿī*, ed. Aḥmad Ṣaqr (Cairo: Dār al-Turāth, 1970).

*Ma'rifat al-sunan wa al-āthār*, ed. 'Abd al-Mu'ṭī Amīn Qal'ajī (Aleppo: Dār al-Wa'y, 2012).

Bayhaqī, Abū al-Faḍl. *Tārīkh-i Bayhaqī*, ed. 'Alī Akbar Fayyāḍ (Mashhad: Mu'assasah-i Chāp va Intishārāt-i Dānishgah-i Firdaws, 1963).

Al-Bīrūnī. *Al-Āthār al-bāqiya 'an al-qurūn al-khāliya [Chronologie Orientalischer Völker]*, ed. Eduard Sachau (Leipzig: Otto Harrassowitz, 1923).

Al-Buḥturī. *Dīwān al-Buḥturī*, ed. Ḥasan Kāmil al-Ṣayrafī (Cairo: Dār al-Ma'ārif, n.d.).

Al-Bukhārī. *Al-Ḍu'afā' al-ṣaghīr*, ed. Abū 'Abd Allāh Aḥmad b. Ibrāhīm b. Abī al-'Aynayn (n.p.: Maktabat Ibn 'Abbās, 2005).

. *Al-Jāmi' al-ṣaḥīḥ*.

*Khalq af'āl al-'ibād wa radd 'alā al-jahmiyya wa aṣḥāb al-ta'ṭīl* (Beirut: Mu'assasat al-Risāla, 1990) = ed. 'Abd al-Raḥmān 'Amīra (Riyadh: Dār 'Ukāẓ, n.d.).

*Kitāb al-Adab al-mufrad*, ed. Samīr b. Amīn al-Zuhayrī (Riyadh: Maktabat al-Ma'ārif li al-Nashr wa al-Tawzī', 1998).

*Kitāb al-Ḍu'afā' al-ṣaghīr [wa yalīhi Kitāb al-Ḍu'afā' wa al-matrūkīn li al-Nasā'ī]*, ed. Maḥmūd Ibrāhīm Zāyid (Beirut: Dār al-Ma'rifa, 1986) = ed. Maḥmūd Ibrāhīm Zāyid (Aleppo: Dār al-Wa'y, 1976) = *Majmū' fī al-ḍu'afā' wa al-matrūkīn*, ed. 'Abd al-'Azīz 'Izz al-Dīn Sayrawān (Beirut: Dār al-Qalam, 1985).

*Kitāb al-Kunā juz' min al-Tārīkh al-kabīr* (Hyderabad: Dā'irat al-Ma'ārif al-'Uthmāniyya, 1978).

*Kitāb Raf' al-yadayn fī al-ṣalāt*, ed. Badī' al-Dīn al-Rāshidī (Beirut: Dār Ibn Ḥazm, 1996).

*Al-Tārīkh al-awsaṭ*, ed. Muḥammad Ibrāhīm al-Luḥaydān (Riyadh: Dār al-Ṣumay'ī, 1998) = *al-Tārīkh al-awsaṭ [Kitāb al-Mukhtaṣar]*, ed. Taysīr b. Sa'd Abū Ḥaymad (Riyadh: Dār al-Rushd, 2005).

*Al-Tārīkh al-awsaṭ* [published twice under the mistaken title al-Tārīkh al-ṣaghīr] (Hyderabad: Maṭba'at Dā'irat al-Ma'ārif al-'Uthmāniyya, n.d.) = ed. Maḥmūd Ibrāhīm Zāyid, 2 vols. (Beirut: Dār al-Ma'rifa, 1986).

*Al-Tārīkh al-kabīr* (Hyderabad: Maṭba'at Jam'iyyat Dā'irat al-Ma'ārif al-'Uthmāniyya, 1958) = ed. Hāshim al-Nadwī et al. (Hyderabad: Maṭba'at Jam'iyyat Dā'irat al-Ma'ārif al-'Uthmāniyya, 1941–63).

Al-Dāraquṭnī. *Al-Mu'talif wa al-mukhtalif*, ed. Muwaffaq b. 'Abd Allāh b. 'Abd al-Qādir (Beirut: Dār al-Gharb al-Islāmī, 1986).

*Sunan al-Dāraquṭnī wa bi dhaylihi al-ta'līq al-mughnī 'alā al-Dāraquṭnī*, ed. Shu'ayb al-Arnā'ūṭ (Beirut: Mu'assasat al-Risāla, 2004) = *Sunan*, ed. 'Ādil Aḥmad 'Abd al-Mawjūd and 'Alī Muḥammad Mu'awwiḍ (Beirut: Dār al-Ma'rifa, 2001).

Al-Dārimī. *Kitāb al-Musnad al-jāmi' [Sunan al-Dārimī]*, ed. Nabīl b. Hāshim b. 'Abd Allāh al-Ghumarī (Beirut: Dār al-Bashā'ir al-Islāmiyya, 2013).

Al-Dārimī, 'Uthmān b. Sa'īd. *Tārīkh ['an Yaḥyā b. Ma'īn]*, ed. Aḥmad Muḥammad Nūr Sayf (Damascus: Dār al-Ma'mūn li al-Turāth, 1980).

Al-Dawlābī. *Al-Kunā wa al-asmā'* (Beirut: Dār al-Kutub al-'Ilmiyya, 1999).

Al-Dhahabī. *Al-'Ibar fī khabar man ghabar*, ed. Ṣalāḥ al-Dīn al-Munajjid (Kuwait: Dā'irat al-Maṭbū'āt wa al-Nashr, 1960).

*Juz' fīhi tarjamat al-Bukhārī*, ed. Ibrāhīm b. Manṣūr al-Hāshimī (Beirut: Mu'assasat al-Rayyān, 2002).

*Kitāb Tadhkirat al-ḥuffāẓ*, ed. ʿAbd al-Raḥmān b. Yaḥyā al-Muʿallimī (Hyderabad: Dā'irat al-Maʿārif al-ʿUthmāniyya, 1954).
*Manāqib al-Imām Abī Ḥanīfa wa ṣāḥibayhi Abī Yūsuf wa Muḥammad b. al-Ḥasan*, ed. Muḥammad Zāhid al-Kawtharī and Abū al-Wafā' al-Afghānī (Hyderabad: Lajnat Iḥyā' al-Maʿārif al-Nuʿmāniyya, 1947).
*Mīzān al-iʿtidāl fī naqd al-rijāl*, ed. ʿAlī Muḥammad al-Bijāwī (Beirut: Dār al-Maʿrifa, 1963).
*Mukhtaṣar al-ʿulūw li al-ʿalī al-ghaffār*, ed. Muḥammad Nāṣir al-Dīn al-Albānī (Damascus: al-Maktab al-Islāmī, 1981).
*Al-Mūqiẓa fī ʿilm muṣṭalaḥ al-ḥadīth*, ed. ʿAbd al-Fattāḥ Abū Ghudda (Aleppo: Maktab al-Maṭbūʿāt al-Islāmiyya, 1984–5).
*Siyar aʿlām al-nubalā'*, ed. Shuʿayb al-Arnā'ūṭ et al. (Beirut: Mu'assasat al-Risāla, 1996).
*Tahdhīb siyar aʿlām al-nubalā'*, ed. Shuʿayb al-Arnā'ūṭ (Beirut: Mu'assasat al-Risāla, 1991).
*Tahdhīb tahdhīb al-kamāl fī asmā' al-rijāl*, ed. Ghunaym ʿAbbās Ghunaym and Majdī al-Sayyid Amīn (Cairo: al-Fārūq al-Ḥadīth li al-Ṭibāʿa wa al-Nashr, 2004).
*Tarājim al-a'imma al-kibār aṣḥāb al-sunan wa al-āthār*, ed. Fahmī Saʿd (Beirut: ʿĀlam al-Kutub, 1993).
*Tārīkh al-Islām wa wafayāt al-mashāhīr wa al-aʿlām*, ed. ʿUmar ʿAbd al-Salām Tadmurī (Beirut: Dār al-Kitāb al-ʿArabī, 1987–2000).
*Tarjamat al-imām Aḥmad min Tārīkh al-Islām li al-Ḥāfiẓ al-Dhahabī* (Aleppo: Dār al-Waʿy, n.d.).
Al-Dīnawarī. *Al-Akhbār al-ṭiwāl* (Leiden: Brill, 1888).
Ḍirār b. ʿAmr. *Kitāb al-Taḥrīsh*, ed. Hüseyin Hansu and Mehmet Kaskin (Istanbul: Shirkat Dār al-Irshād; Beirut: Dār Ibn Ḥazm, 2014).
Al-Fākihī. *Akhbār Makka fī qadīm al-dahr wa ḥadīthihi*, ed. ʿAbd al-Malik ʿAbd Allāh b. Duhaysh (Beirut: Dār Khiḍr, 1994).
Al-Fasawī. *Kitāb al-Maʿrifa wa al-tārīkh*, 3rd edn., ed. Akram Ḍiyā' al-ʿUmarī (Medina: Maktabat al-Dār, 1989).
*Mashyakhat Yaʿqūb b. Sufyān al-Fasawī*, ed. Muḥammad b. ʿAbd Allāh al-Sarrīʿ (Riyadh: Dār al-ʿĀṣima, 2010).
Gardīzī, Abū Saʿīd. *Zayn al-akhbār*, ed. ʿAbd al-Ḥayy Ḥabībī (Tehran: Dunyā-yi Kitāb, 1944).
Al-Ghassānī, Abū al-Ḥasan Muḥammad b. al-Fayḍ. *Akhbār wa ḥikāyāt*, ed. Ibrāhīm Ṣāliḥ (Damascus: Dār al-Bashā'ir, 1994).
Al-Ghazālī. *Iḥyā' ʿulūm al-dīn* (Jeddah: Dār al-Minhāj, 2011).
*Al-Mankhūl min taʿlīqāt al-uṣūl*, ed. Muḥammad Ḥasan Ḥītū (Damascus: n.p., 1970).
Al-Ḥāfiẓ al-Tujībī. *Barnāmaj al-Ḥāfiẓ Abī ʿAbd Allāh Muḥammad b. ʿAbd al-Raḥmān al-Tujībī*, ed. al-Ḥasan Saʿīd (Rabat: Wizārat al-Awqāf wa al-Shu'ūn al-Islāmiyya, 2011).
Al-Ḥākim al-Nīshāpūrī. *Maʿrifat ʿulūm al-ḥadīth*, ed. Aḥmad b. Fāris al-Sallūm (Beirut: Dār Ibn al-Ḥazm, 2003) = ed. Muʿaẓẓam Ḥusayn (Beirut: Dār al-Āfāq al-Jadīda, 1989).
*Al-Mustadrak ʿalā al-ṣaḥīḥayn* (Cairo: Dār al-Ḥaramayn, 1997).

*Su'ālāt al-Ḥākim al-Nīshāpūrī li Dāraquṭnī fī al-jarḥ wa al-ta'dīl*, ed. Muwaffaq b. 'Abd Allāh b. 'Abd al-Qādir (Riyadh: Maktabat al-Ma'ārif, 1984).
*Tārīkh Nīshāpūr*, ed. Muḥammad Riḍā Shafī'ī Kadkanī (Tehran: Āgāh, 1996).
Al-Ḥakīm al-Tirmidhī. *Nawādir al-uṣūl fī ma'rifat al-aḥādīth al-rasūl*, ed. Ismā'īl Ibrāhīm 'Awaḍ (Cairo: Maktabat al-Imām al-Bukhārī, 2008).
Ḥanbal b. Isḥāq. *Dhikr miḥnat al-imām Aḥmad b. Ḥanbal*, ed. Muḥammad Naghsh (Cairo: Dār al-Nashr al-Thaqāfa, 1983).
Al-Ḥumaydī. *Musnad*, ed. Ḥabīb al-Raḥmān al-A'ẓamī (Karachi: al-Majlis al-'Ilmī, 1963; repr. Beirut: 'Ālam al-Kutub, 1988) = ed. Ḥusayn Salīm Asad (Damascus: Dār al-Saqqā, 1996).
*Uṣūl al-sunna*, ed. Mish'al Muḥammad al-Ḥaddādī (Kuwait: Dār Ibn al-Athīr, 1997).
Ibn 'Abd al-Barr. *Al-Intiqā' fī faḍā'il al-a'imma al-fuqahā'*, ed. 'Abd al-Fattāḥ Abū Ghudda (Beirut: Dār al-Bashā'ir al-Islāmiyya, 1997).
*Jāmi' bayān al-'ilm wa faḍlihi*, ed. Abū al-Ashbāl al-Zuhayrī (Dammam: Dār Ibn al-Jawzī, 1994).
Ibn 'Abd al-Ḥakam. *Futūḥ Miṣr* (London: n.p., 1858).
Ibn Abī 'Āṣim. *Kitāb al-Sunna*, ed. Bāsim b. Fayṣal al-Jawābara (Riyadh: Dār al-Ṣumay'ī, 1998).
Ibn Abī al-'Awwām al-Sa'dī. *Faḍā'il Abī Ḥanīfa wa akhbārihi wa manāqibihi*, ed. Laṭīf al-Raḥmān al-Bahrā'ijī al-Qāsimī (Mecca: al-Maktaba al-Imdādiyya, 2010).
Ibn Abī al-Dunyā. *Makā'id al-shayṭān* (Cairo: Maktabat al-Qur'ān, 1991).
Ibn Abī Ḥātim al-Rāzī. *Ādāb al-Shāfi'ī wa manāqibuhu*, ed. 'Abd al-Ghanī 'Abd al-Khāliq (Cairo: Maktabat al- Khānjī, 1993).
*Al-Jarḥ wa al-ta'dīl*, ed. 'Abd al-Rāḥmān b. Yaḥyā al-Mu'allimī (Hyderabad: Maṭba'at Dā'irat al-Ma'ārif al-'Uthmāniyya, 1953; repr. Beirut: Dār al-Kutub al-'Ilmiyya, n.d.).
*Kitāb al-'Ilal*, ed. Sa'īd b. 'Abd Allāh al-Ḥumayd and Khālid b. 'Abd al-Raḥmān al-Juraysī (Riyadh: Maktabat al-Malik Fahd al-Waṭaniyya, 2006).
*al-Taqdima fī ma'rifa li al-kitāb al-jarḥ wa al-ta'dīl*, ed. 'Abd al-Raḥmān b. Yaḥyā al-Yamānī (Hyderabad: Maṭba'at Jam'iyyat Dā'irat al-Ma'ārif al-'Uthmāniyya, 1952–3).
Ibn Abī Shayba. *Kitāb al-Adab*, ed. Muḥammad Riḍā al-Qahwajī (Beirut: Dār al-Bashā'ir al-Islāmiyya, 1999).
*Kitāb al-Īmān*, ed. Muḥammad Nāṣir al-Dīn al-Albānī (Damascus: al-Maktab al-Islamī, 1983).
*Al-Muṣannaf*, ed. Muḥammad 'Awwāma (Jeddah: Dār al-Qibla li al-Thaqāfa al-Islāmiyya, 2006) = (Hyderabad: al-Maṭba'a al-'Azīziyya, 1966).
Ibn Abī Ṭāhir Ṭayfūr. *Kitāb Baghdād*, ed. Muḥammad Zāhid al-Kawtharī (Cairo: 'Izzat al-'Aṭṭār al-Ḥusaynī, 1949).
Ibn Abī al-Wafā'. *Al-Jawāhir al-muḍiyya fī ṭabaqāt al-Ḥanafiyya*, ed. Abd al-Fattāḥ Muḥammad Ḥulw (Cairo: Hajr li al-Ṭibā'a wa al-Nashr, 1993).
Ibn Abī Ya'lā. *Ṭabaqāt al-Ḥanābila*, ed. Muḥammad Ḥāmid al-Fiqī (Cairo: Maṭba'at al-Sunna al-Muḥammadiyya, 1952) = ed. 'Abd al-Raḥmān b. Sulaymān al-'Uthaymīn (Riyadh: al-Mamlaka al-'Arabiyya al-Sa'ūdiyya,

al-Amāna al-ʿĀmma li al-Iḥtifāl bi Murūr Miʾat ʿAm ʿalā Taʾsīs al-Mamlaka, 1999).

Ibn ʿAdī. *Asāmī man rawā ʿanhum Muḥammad b. Ismāʿīl al-Bukhārī min mashāyikhihi alladhīna dhakarahum fī jāmiʿihi al-ṣaḥīḥ*, ed. Badr b. Muḥammad al-ʿAmmāsh (Medina: Dār al-Bukhārī, 1994–5) = ed. ʿĀmir Ḥasan Ṣabrī (Beirut: Dār al-Bashāʾir al-Islāmiyya, 1994).

*Al-Kāmil fī ḍuʿafāʾ al-rijāl*, ed. ʿĀdil Aḥmad ʿAbd al-Mawjūd and ʿAlī Muḥammad Muʿawwiḍ (Beirut: Dār al-Kutub al-ʿIlmiyya, 1997) = ed. al-Ghazzāwī and Suhayl Zakkār (Beirut: Dār al-Fikr, 1988) = Riyadh: Maktabat al-Rushd, 2018.

*Al-Kāmil fī maʿrifat al-rijāl*, ed. Māzin b. Muḥammad al-Sarsāwī (Riyadh: Maktabat al-Rusdh, 2018).

Ibn al-Anbārī. *Kitāb al-Inṣāf fī masāʾil al-khilāf bayn al-naḥwiyyīn al-baṣriyyīn wa al-kūfiyyīn*, ed. Gotthold Weil (Leiden: Brill, 1913).

Ibn ʿAsākir. *Al-Muʿjam al-mushtamil ʿalā dhikr asmāʾ al-shuyūkh al-aʾimma al-nabal*, ed. Sukayna al-Shihābī (Damascus: Dār al-Fikr, 1981).

*Tārīkh madīnat Dimashq*, ed. ʿUmar b. Gharāma al-ʿAmrawī (Beirut: Dār al-Fikr, 1996) = ed. ʿAbd al-Bāqī b. Aḥmad and ʿAbd al-Raḥmān b. Qaḥṭān (Beirut: Dār al-Fikr, 1996).

Ibn al-Aʿtham al-Kūfī. *Kitāb al-Futūḥ*, ed. Suhayl Zakkār (Damascus: Dār al-Fikr, 1992) = ed. Muḥammad ʿAbd al-Muʿīd Khān et al. (Hyderabad: Dāʾirat al-Maʿārif al-ʿUthmāniyya, 1968–75).

Ibn al-Athīr. *Al-Kāmil fī al-tārīkh*, ed. Abū al-Fidāʾ ʿAbd al-Qāḍī (Beirut: Dār al-Kutub al-ʿIlmiyya, 1987) = Beirut: Dār Ṣādir, 1966.

*Al-Lubāb fī tahdhīb al-ansāb* (Baghdad: Maktabat al-Muthannā, n.d.) = Beirut: Dār Ṣādir, 1980.

Ibn ʿAṭiyya. *Al-Muḥarrar al-wajīz fī tafsīr al-kitāb al-ʿazīz*, ed. ʿAbd al-Salām ʿAbd al-Shāfī Muḥammad (Beirut: Dār al-Kutub al-ʿIlmiyya, 2001).

Ibn Bashkuwāl. *Al-Ṣila fī tārīkh aʾimmat al-Andalus wa ʿulamāʾihim wa muḥaddithīhim wa fuqahāʾihim wa udabāʾihim*, ed. Bashshār ʿAwwād Maʿrūf (Beirut: Dār al-Gharb al-Islāmī, 2010).

Ibn Baṭṭa al-ʿUkbarī. *Al-Sharḥ wa al-ibāna [al-ibāna al-ṣughrā]*, ed. ʿĀdil b. ʿAbd Allāh b. Saʿd al-Ghāmidī (Riyadh: Dār al-Amr al-Awwal, 2011) = *Al-Sharḥ wa al-ibāna ʿalā uṣūl al-sunna wa al-diyāna*, ed. Riḍā b. Naʿsān Muʿṭī (Medina: Maktabat al-ʿUlūm wa al-Ḥikam, 2002).

Ibn Baṭṭāl. *Sharḥ Ṣaḥīḥ al-Bukhārī*, ed. Abū Tamīm Yāsir b. Ibrāhīm (Riyadh: Maktabat al-Rushd, 2000).

Ibn al-Faqīh. *Kitāb al-Buldān*, ed. M. J. de Goeje (Leiden: Brill, 1885).

Ibn Funduq. *Tārīkh-i Bayhaq*, ed. Aḥmad Bahmanyār (Tehran: Kitābfurūshī Furūghī dar Chāpkhāneh-yi Islāmiyya, 1938).

Ibn Ḥajar al-ʿAsqalānī. *Fatḥ al-bārī bi sharḥ ṣaḥīḥ al-Bukhārī*, ed. ʿAbd al-Qādir Shaybat al-Ḥamd (Riyadh: Maktabat al-Malik Fahd al-Waṭaniyya Athnāʾ al-Nashr, 2001) = ed. Naẓar al-Faryābī (Riyadh: Dār al-Ṭayba, 2005) = ed. ʿAbd al-ʿAzīz b. Bāz (Beirut: Dār al-Maʿrifa, 1970; repr. Beirut: Dār al-Kutub al-Salafiyya, n.d.).

*Hady [sic] al-sārī: muqaddimat Fatḥ al-Bārī*, ed. Muḥammad Fuʾād ʿAbd al-Bāqī and Muḥibb al-Dīn al-Khaṭīb (Beirut: Dār al-Maʿrifa, 1959).

*Intiqāḍ al-iʿtirāḍ fī al-radd ʿalā al-ʿAynī fī sharḥ al-Bukhārī*, ed. Ḥamdī b. ʿAbd al-Majīd al-Salafī and Ṣubḥī b. Jāsim al-Sāmarrāʾī (Riyadh: Maktabat al-Rushd, n.d.).

*Al-Iṣāba fī tamyīz al-ṣaḥāba*, ed. ʿAbd Allāh b. ʿAbd al-Muḥsin al-Turkī and ʿAbd al-Samad Ḥasan Yamāma (Cairo: Dār al-Ḥijr, 2008).

*Lisān al-mīzān*, ed. ʿAbd al-Fattāḥ Abū Ghudda (Beirut: Maktabat al-Maṭbūʿāt al-Islāmī, 2002) = Beirut: Dār al-Bashāʾir al-Islāmiyya, 2002 = Hyderabad: Dāʾirat al-Maʿārif al-Niẓāmiyya, 1911–13.

*Al-Majmaʿ al-muʾassas li al-muʿjam al-mufahras*, ed. Yūsuf ʿAbd al-Raḥmān al-Marʿaslī (Beirut: Dār al-Maʿrifa, n.d.).

*Rafʿ al-iṣr ʿan quḍāt Miṣr*, ed. ʿAlī Muḥammad ʿUmar (Cairo: Maktabat al-Khānjī, 1998).

*Tabṣīr al-muntabih bi taḥrīr al-Mushtabih*, ed. ʿAlī Muḥammad al-Bajāwī and Muḥammad ʿAlī al-Najjār (Beirut: al-Maktaba al-ʿIlmiyya, n.d.).

*Taghlīq al-taʿlīq ʿalā Ṣaḥīḥ al-Bukhārī*, ed. Saʿīd ʿAbd al-Raḥmān Mūsā al-Qazafī (Beirut: al-Maktab al-Islāmī, 1985).

*Tahdhīb al-tahdhīb*, ed. Ibrāhīm al-Zaybaq and ʿĀdil Murshid (Beirut: Muʾassasat al-Risāla, n.d.) = Beirut: Muʾassasat al-Risāla, 1995 = Hyderabad: Dāʾirat al-Maʿārif al-Niẓāmiyya, 1907 and 1909.

*Taʿjīl al-manfaʿa bi zawāʾid rijāl al-arbaʿa*, ed. Ikrām Allāh Imdād al-Ḥaqq (Beirut: Dār al-Bashāʾir al-Islāmiyya, 2008).

*Taqrīb al-tahdhīb*, ed. Muṣṭafā ʿAbd al-Qādir ʿAṭāʾ (Beirut: Dār al-Kutub al-ʿIlmiyya, 1993) = ed. ʿĀdil Murshid and Ibrāhīm al-Zaybaq (Beirut: Muʾassasat al-Risāla, 1995).

*Tawālī al-taʾsīs li maʿālī Muḥammad b. Idrīs*, ed. Abū al-Fidāʾ ʿAbd Allāh al-Qāḍī (Beirut: Dār al-Kutub al-ʿIlmiyya, 1986).

Ibn al-Ḥaṭṭāb al-Rāzī. *Mashyakhat al-shaykh al-ajall Abī ʿAbd Allāh Muḥammad b. Aḥmad b. Ibrāhīm al-Rāzī wa thabat masmūʿātihi*, ed. al-Sharīf Ḥātim b. ʿĀrif al-ʿAwnī (Riyadh: Dār al-Hijra, 1994).

Ibn Ḥazm. *Jamharat ansāb al-ʿarab*, ed. ʿAbd al-Salām Hārūn (Cairo: Dār al-Maʿārif, 1962) =ed. Évariste Lévi-Provençal (Cairo: Dār al-Maʿārif, 1948).

Ibn Ḥibbān. *Kitāb al-Majrūḥīn min al-muḥaddithīn wa al-ḍuʿafāʾ wa al-matrūkīn*, ed. Maḥmūd Ibrāhīm Zāyid (Beirut: Dār al-Maʿrifa, 1992) = ed. ʿAzīz Bayg al-Qādirī (Hyderabad: al-Maṭbaʿa al-ʿAzīziyya, 1970–7 = *Kitāb al-Majrūḥīn min al-muḥaddithīn*, ed. Ḥamdī ʿAbd al-Majīd al-Salafī (Riyadh: Dār al-Ṣumayʿī, 2009).

*Kitāb al-Thiqāt* (Hyderabad: Dāʾirat al-Maʿārif al-ʿUthmāniyya, 1973) = *Kitāb al-Thiqāt*, ed. ʿAzīz Bayg al-Qādirī (Hyderabad: al-Maṭbaʿa al-ʿAzīziyya, 1970–7).

Ibn Hubayra. *Ikhtilāf al-aʾimma wa al-umam*, ed. al-Sayyid Yūsuf Aḥmad (Beirut: Dār al-Kutub al-ʿIlmiyya, 2002).

Ibn ʿImād. *Shadharāt al-dhahab fī akhbār man dhahab*, ed. ʿAbd al-Qādir al-Arnāʾūṭ and Maḥmūd al-Arnāʾūṭ (Beirut: Dār Ibn Kathīr, 1986–9).

Ibn Jamāʿa. *Tadkhirat al-sāmiʿ wa al-mutakallim fī adab al-ʿālim wa al-mutaʿallim*, ed. Muḥammad b. Mahdī al-ʿAjmī, 4th edn. (Beirut: Dār al-Bashāʾir al-Islāmiyya, 2012).

Ibn al-Jawzī. *Kitāb al-Ḍuʿafāʾ wa al-matrūkīn* (Beirut: Dār al-Kutub al-ʿIlmiyya, 1986).

*Manāqib al-Imām Aḥmad b. Ḥanbal*, ed. Muḥammad Amīn Khānjī (Cairo: Maktabat al-Khānjī, 1931) = ed. ʿAlī Muḥammad ʿUmar (Cairo: Maktabat al-Khānjī, 2009) = ed. ʿAbd al-Muḥsin al-Turkī (Giza: Dār Hajr, 1988).

*Al-Muntaẓam fī tārīkh al-mulūk wa al-umam*, ed. Muḥammad ʿAbd al-Qādir ʿAṭāʾ and Muṣṭafā ʿAbd al-Qādir ʿAṭāʾ (Beirut: Dār al-Kutub al-ʿIlmiyya, 1992).

*Talqīḥ fuhūm ahl al-athar fī ʿuyūn al-tārīkh wa al-siyar* (Cairo: Maktabat al-Ādāb, 1975).

Ibn al-Jazarī. *Ghāyat al-nihāya fī ṭabaqāt al-qurrāʾ*, ed. Gotthelf Bergsträßer (Cairo: Maktabat al-Khānjī, 1932–3; repr. Beirut: Dār al-Kutub al-ʿIlmiyya, 2006).

Ibn al-Junayd. *Suʾālāt Ibn al-Junayd li Yaḥyā b. Maʿīn*, ed. Aḥmad Muḥammad Nūr Sayf (Medina: Maktabat al-Dār, 1988).

Ibn al-Kalbī. *Jamharat al-nasab*, ed. Nājī Ḥasan (Beirut: ʿĀlam al-Kutub, 1986) = *Ǧamharat an-nasab: Das genealogische Werk des Hišām ibn Muḥammad al-Kalbī*, ed. Werner Caskel (Leiden: Brill, 1966).

Ibn Kathīr. *Al-Bāʿith al-ḥathīth: Sharḥ ikhtiṣār ʿulūm al-ḥadīth li al-Ḥāfiẓ Ibn Kathīr*, ed. and commentary Aḥmad Muḥammad Shākir (Beirut: Dār al-Kutub al-ʿIlmiyya, n.d.).

*Al-Bidāya wa al-nihāya* (Damascus: Dār Ibn Kathīr, 2010).

*Jāmiʿ al-masānīd wa al-sunan al-hādī li aqwam sunan*, ed. ʿAbd al-Muʿṭī Amīn Qalʿajī (Beirut: Dār al-Fikr, 1994).

Ibn Khalfūn. *Al-Muʿlim bi shuyūkh al-Bukhārī wa Muslim*, ed. Abū ʿAbd al-Raḥmān ʿĀdil b. Saʿd (Beirut: Dār al-Kutub al-ʿIlmiyya, 2000).

Ibn Khallikān. *Wafāyāt al-aʿyān wa anbāʾ abnāʾ al-zamān*, ed. Iḥsān ʿAbbās (Beirut: Dār al-Ṣādir, 1978).

Ibn Khayr al-Ishbīlī. *Fihrist*, ed. Bashshār ʿAwwād Maʿrūf and Maḥmūd Bashshār ʿAwwād (Beirut: Dār al-Gharb al-Islāmī, 2009).

Ibn Khurradādhbih. *Kitāb al-Masālik wa al-mamālik*, ed. M. J. de Goeje (Leiden: Brill, 1889).

Ibn Mākūlā. *Ikmāl fī rafʿ al-irtiyāb ʿan al-muʾtalif wa al-mukhtalif fī al-asmāʾ wa al-kunā wa al-ansāb*, ed. ʿAbd al-Raḥmān b. Yaḥyā al-Muʿallimī al-Yamānī (Hyderabad: Dāʾirat al-Maʿārif al-ʿUthmāniyya, 1962–7).

Ibn Manda. *Fatḥ al-bāb fī al-kunā wa al-alqāb*, ed. Abū Qutayba Naẓar Muḥammad al-Fārayābī (Riyadh: Maktabat al-Kawthar, 1996).

*Kitāb al-Īmān*, ed. ʿAlī b. Muḥammad b. Nāṣir al-Faqīhī (Beirut: Muʾassasat al-Risāla, 1985).

*Shurūṭ al-aʾimma*, ed. ʿAbd al-Raḥmān b. ʿAbd al-Jabbār al-Farīwāʾī (Riyadh: Dār al-Muslim, 1995).

Ibn Manẓūr. *Lisān al-ʿArab* (Beirut: Dār Ṣādir, n.d.) = *Lisān al-ʿArab* (Cairo: Dār al-Maʿārif, n.d.).

*Mukhtaṣar Tārīkh Dimashq li Ibn ʿAsākir*, ed. Sukayna al-Shihābī (Damascus: Dār al-Fikr, 1989).

Ibn Mufliḥ. *Al-Ādāb al-sharʿiyya*, ed. Shuʿayb al-Arnāʾūṭ and ʿUmar al-Qayyām (Beirut: Muʾassasat al-Risāla, 1999).

*Maṣā'ib al-insān min makā'id al-shayṭān* (Cairo: Maktabat al-Khānjī, 1943).
Ibn al-Mulaqqin. *Al-Tawḍīḥ li sharḥ al-Jāmi' al-Ṣaḥīḥ*, ed. Khālid al-Ribāṭ (Qatar: Wizārat al-Awqāf wa al-Shu'ūn al-Islāmiyya, 2008).
Ibn al-Muqaffa'. *Āthār Ibn al-Muqaffa'*, ed. Muḥammad Kurd 'Alī (Beirut: Dār al-Kutub al-'Ilmiyya, 1989).
*Rasā'il al-bulaghā'*, ed. Muḥammad Kurd 'Alī (Cairo: Dār al-Kutub al-'Arabiyya al-Kubrā, 1913).
Ibn al-Nadīm. *Kitāb al-Fihrist*, ed. Ayman Fu'ād al-Sayyid (London: Mu'assasat al-Furqān li al-Turāth al-Islāmī, 2009; 2nd edn. 2014) = ed. Gustav Flügel (Leipzig: F. C. W. Vogel, 1872) = ed. Riḍā Tajaddud (Tehran: Maṭba'āt Dānishgāh, 1971).
Ibn Nāṣir al-Dīn. *Tawḍīḥ al-mushtabih fī ḍabṭ asmā' al-ruwāt wa ansābihim wa alqābihim wa kunāhum*, ed. Muḥammad Na'īm al-'Arqasūsī (Beirut: Mu'assasat al-Risāla, 1993).
Ibn Nuqṭa. *Al-Taqyīd li ma'rifat al-ruwāt wa al-sunan wa al-masānīd* (Hyderabad: Dā'irat al-Ma'ārif al-'Uthmāniyya, 1983).
Ibn al-Qaysarānī. *Al-Jam' bayna kitābay Abī Naṣr al-Kalābādhī wa Abī Bakr al-Iṣfahānī fī rijāl al-Bukhārī wa Muslim* (Hyderabad: Maṭba'at Majlis Dā'irat al-Ma'ārif al-Niẓāmiyya, 1905; repr. Beirut: Dār al-Kutub al-'Ilmiyya, 1984).
Ibn Qayyim al-Jawziyya. *Ḥādī al-arwāḥ ilā bilād al-afrāḥ*, ed. Zā'id b. Aḥmad al-Nushayrī (Beirut: Dār 'Ālam al-Fawā'id, 2007).
Ibn Qūlūwayh. *Kāmil al-ziyārāt* (Qum: Nashr al-Faqāha, 2009).
Ibn Qutayba. *Faḍl al-'arab wa al-tanbīh 'alā 'ulūmihā*, ed. Walīd Maḥmūd Khāliṣ (Abu Dhabi: al-Majma' al-Thaqafī, 1998).
*Al-Ikhtilāf fī al-lafẓ wa al-radd 'alā al-jahmiyya wa al-mushabbiha*, ed. Muḥammad Zāhid al Kawtharī (Cairo: al-Maktaba al-Azhariyya li al-Turāth, 2001) = ed. 'Umar b. Maḥmūd b. 'Umar (Riyadh: Dār al-Rāyya, 1991).
*Kitāb Adab al-kātib [Ibn Kutaiba's Adab al-kātib]*, ed. Max Grünert (Leiden: Brill, 1900).
*Kitāb al-Ma'ārif*, ed. Tharwat 'Ukāsha (Cairo: Dār al-Ma'ārif, 1969).
*Kitāb Ta'wīl mukhtalif al-ḥadīth*, ed. Abū al-Muẓaffar Sa'īd b. Muḥammad al-Sinnārī (Cairo: Dār al-Ḥadīth, 2006) = ed. Muḥammad Zuhrī Najjār (Cairo: Maktabat al-Kulliyyāt al-Azhariyya, 1973) = ed. Muḥammad 'Abd al-Raḥīm (Beirut: Dār al-Fikr, 1995) = ed. F. Zakī al-Kurdī (Cairo: Maṭba'at Kurdistān al-'Ilmiyya, 1908) = trans. G. Lecomte as *Le Traité des divergences du ḥadīt d'Ibn Qutayba (mort en 276/889)* (Damascus: Presses de l'ifpo, 1962).
*'Uyūn al-akhbār* (Beirut: Dār al-Kitāb al-'Arabī, 1925).
Ibn Quṭlūbughā. *Tāj al-tarājim*, ed. Muḥammad Khayr Ramaḍān Yūsuf (Beirut: Dār al-Qalam, 1992).
Ibn Rajab al-Ḥanbalī. 'Al-Radd 'alā man ittaba'a ghayr al-madhāhib al-arba'a', in Ṭal'at Fu'ād al-Ḥulwānī (ed.), *Majmū' rasā'il al-ḥāfiẓ Ibn Rajab al-Ḥanbalī* (Cairo: al-Fārūq al-Ḥadītha, 2002).
*Sharḥ 'ilal al-Tirmidhī*, ed. Ṣubḥī al-Sāmarrā'ī (Baghdad: Wizārat al-Awqāf al-'Irāqiyya, 1976) = ed. Nūr al-Dīn 'Itr (n.p.: Dār al-Malāḥ, 1978) = ed. Hammād 'Abd al-Raḥīm Sa'īd (Riyadh: Maktabat al-Rushd, 2001).

Ibn al-Rūmī. *Dīwān Ibn al-Rūmī*, ed. Ḥuṣayn Naṣṣār (Cairo: Dār al-Kutub al-Wathā'iq al-Qawmiyya, 2003).

Ibn Rushd. *Bidāyat al-mujtahid wa nihāyat al-muqtaṣid*, ed. ʿAlī Muḥammad Muʿawwaḍ and ʿĀdil Aḥmad ʿAbd al-Mawjūd (Beirut: Dār al-Kutub al-ʿIlmiyya, 1996) = ed. Muḥammad Ṣubḥī Ḥasan Ḥallāq (Cairo: Maktabat Ibn Taymiyya, 1994).

Ibn Saʿd. *Ṭabaqāt al-kubrā* (Beirut: Dār al-Ṣādir, 1957–68) = *Kitāb al-Ṭabaqāt al-kabīr [Biographien]*, ed. E. Sachau et al. (Leiden: Brill, 1904–40).

*Al-Ṭabaqāt al-ṣaghīr*, ed. Bashshār ʿAwwād Maʿrūf and Muḥammad Zāhid Jawl (Beirut: Dār al-Gharb al-Islāmī, 2009).

Ibn al-Ṣalāḥ al-Shahrazūrī. *ʿUlūm al-ḥadīth*, ed. Nūr al-Dīn ʿItr (Beirut: Dār al-Fikr, 1986).

Ibn Shāhīn. *Tārīkh asmā' al-thiqāt*, ed. ʿAbd al-Raḥīm Muḥammad Aḥmad al-Qashqarī (n.p.: n.p., 1989) = ed. Ṣubḥī al-Sāmarrā'ī (Kuwait: Dār al-Salafiyya, 1984) = ed. ʿAbd al-Muʿṭī Amīn Qalʿajī (Beirut: Dār al-Kutub al-ʿIlmiyya, 1986).

Ibn Shahrāshūb. *Maʿālim al-ʿulamā'*, ed. al-Sayyid Muḥammad Ṣādiq Āl Baḥr al-ʿUlūm (Beirut: Dār al-Aḍwā', n.d.).

Ibn Taghrībirdī. *Al-Nujūm al-zāhira fī mulūk Miṣr wa al-Qāhira* (Cairo: Maṭbaʿat Dār al-Kutub al-Miṣriyya, 1930) = (n.p.: Wizārat al-Thaqāfa, 1963).

Ibn Ṭumlūs. *Kitāb al-Madkhal li ṣināʿat al-manṭiq [Introducción al arte de la lógica por Abentomlús de Alcira]* ed. and trans. M. Asín Palacios (Madrid: Centro de Estudios Historicus, 1916).

Ibn al-Ushnānī. *Juz' al-Qāḍī al-Ushnānī in Majmūʿat ajzā' ḥadīthiyya*, ed. Mashhūr b. Ḥasan Āl Salmān Abū ʿUbayda (Beirut: Dār Ibn Ḥazm, 2001).

Ibn Waḍḍāḥ. *Kitāb al-Bidaʿ [Tratado contra las innovaciones]*, ed. M. Isabel Fierro (Madrid: Consejo Superior de Investigaciones Cientificas, 1988).

Ibn Yūnus al-Ṣadafī. *Tārīkh Ibn Yūnus al-Ṣadafī [Tārīkh al-Miṣriyyīn and Tārīkh al-Ghurabā']*, ed. ʿAbd al-Fattāḥ Fatḥī ʿAbd al-Fattāḥ (Beirut: Dār al-Kutub al-ʿIlmiyya, 2000).

Al-ʿIjlī. *Tārīkh al-thiqāt*, ed. ʿAbd al-Muʿṭī al-Qalʿajī (Beirut: Dār al-Kutub al-ʿIlmiyya, 1984).

Al-ʿIrāqī. *Sharḥ al-tabṣira wa al-tadhkira*, ed. ʿAbd al-Laṭīf al-Hāmīm and Māhir Yāsīn al-Faḥl (Beirut: Dār al-Kutub al-ʿIlmiyya, 2002) = *Sharḥ alfiyat al-ʿIrāqī*, ed. Muḥammad b. al-Ḥusayn al-ʿIrāqī al-Ḥusaynī (Beirut: Dār al-Kutub al-ʿIlmiyya, n.d.).

Al-Iṣfahānī, Abū al-Faraj. *Kitāb al-Aghānī* (Beirut: Dār al-Iḥyā' al-Turāth al-ʿArabī, 1994) = *Kitāb al-Aghānī*, ed. Iḥsān ʿAbbās (Beirut: Dār Ṣādir, 2002).

*Maqātil al-ṭālibiyyīn*, ed. al-Sayyid Aḥmad Ṣaqr (Qum: Intishārāt al-Sharīf al-Riḍā, 1996).

Ismāʿīl Ḥaqqī al-Būrsawī. *Rūḥ al-bayān fī tafsīr al-Qur'ān* (Istanbul: al-Maṭbaʿa al-ʿUthmāniyya, n.d.).

Ismāʿīl Pāshā al-Baghdādī. *Hadiyyat al-ʿārifin* (Istanbul: n.p., 1955) = (Beirut: Dār Iḥyā' al-Turāth al-ʿArabī, 1955).

Ismāʿīl b. Yaḥyā al-Muzanī. *Sharḥ al-Sunna*, ed. Jamāl ʿAzzūn (Riyadh: Dār al-Minhāj, 2009).

Al-Iṣṭakhrī, Abū Isḥāq al-Fārisī. *Kitāb al-Masālik wa al-mamālik*, ed. M. J. de Goeje (Leiden: Brill, 1870).
Al-Jāḥiẓ. *Kitāb al-Ḥayawān*, ed. ʿAbd al-Salām Muḥammad Hārūn (Beirut: Dār al-Kitāb al-ʿArabī, 1966).
*Thalāth rasā'il [Tria Opuscula Auctore]*, ed. G. van Vloten (Leiden: Brill, 1903).
Al-Jahshiyārī. *Kitāb al-Wuzarā' wa al-kuttāb*, ed. Muṣṭafā Saqqā et al. (Cairo: Maktabat al-Bābī al-Ḥalabī, 1938).
Al-Jaṣṣāṣ. *Aḥkām al-Qur'ān*, ed. Muḥammad al-Ṣādiq al-Qamḥāwī (Beirut: Dār Iḥyā' al-Turāth al-ʿArabī, 1996).
*Al-Fuṣūl fī al-uṣūl*, ed. Muḥammad Tāmir (Beirut: Dār al-Kutub al-ʿIlmiyya, 2000).
Al-Jawraqānī. *Al-Abāṭīl wa al-manākīr wa al-ṣiḥāḥ wa al-mashāhīr*, ed. ʿAbd al-Raḥmān ʿAbd al-Jabbār al-Faryūwā'ī (Benares: Idārat al-Buḥūth al-Islāmiyya wa al-Daʿwa wa al-Iftā', 1983).
Al-Jūzajānī. *Aḥwāl al-rijāl*, ed. ʿAbd al-ʿAlīm ʿAbd al-ʿAẓīm al-Bastawī (n.p. [Pakistan]: Ḥadīth Academy, n.d.).
Al-Kalābādhī. *Rijāl Ṣaḥīḥ Bukhārī*, ed. ʿAbd Allāh al-Laythī (Beirut: Dār al-Maʿrifa, 1987).
Al-Kalābādhī. *Baḥr al-fawā'id al-mashhūr bi maʿānī al-akhbār*, ed. Wajīh Kamāl al-Dīn Zakī (Cairo: Dār al-Salām, 2008).
*al-Taʿarruf li madhhab ahl al-taṣawwuf*, ed. ʿAbd al-Ḥalīm Maḥmūd (Cairo: Maktabat al-Thaqāfa al-Ḥīniyya, n.d.).
Kātib Çelebi. *Kashf al-ẓunūn* (Beirut: Dār Iḥyā' al-Turāth al-ʿArabī, n.d.) = ed. Şerefettin Yaltaka and Rifat Bilge (Istanbul: Maarif Matbaasi, 1951) = Kâtip Çelebi, *Lexicon bibliographicum et encyclopaedicum [Kashf al-ẓunūn ʿan asāmī al-kutub wa al-funūn]*, ed. and trans. Gustav Flügel (Leipzig: Oriental Translation Fund of Great Britain and Ireland, 1835–58).
Al-Kattānī. *Fihris al-fahāris wa al-athbāt wa-muʿjam al-maʿājim wa al-mashyakhāt wa-musalsalāt*, ed. Iḥsān ʿAbbās (Beirut: Dār al-Gharb al-Islāmī, 1982).
*Al-Risāla al-mustaṭrafa li bayān mashhūr kutub al-sunna al-masharrafa* (Beirut: Dār al-Bashā'ir al-Islāmiyya, 1993).
Al-Kawsaj. *Masā'il al-Imām Aḥmad b. Ḥanbal wa Isḥāq b. Rāhawayh* (Medina: Maktabat al-Malik ʿAhd al-Waṭaniyya, 2004).
Khalīfa b. Khayyāṭ. *Kitāb al-Ṭabaqāt*, ed. Akram Ḍiyā' al-ʿUmarī (Baghdad: Baghdad University and Maṭbaʿat al-ʿĀnī, 1967).
*Tārīkh*, ed. Akram Ḍiyā' al-ʿUmarī (Riyadh: Dār al-Ṭayba, 1985).
Al-Khalīfa al-Nīshāpūrī. *Talkhīṣ tārīkh Nīshāpūr*, ed. Behmān Karīmī (Tehran: Kitābkhāneh-yi Ibn Sīnā, n.d.).
Al-Khalīlī. *Al-Irshād fī maʿrifat ʿulamā' al-ḥadīth*, ed. Muḥammad Saʿīd ʿUmar Idrīs (Riyadh: Maktabat al-Rushd, 1989) = ed. Walīd Mutawallī Muḥammad (Cairo: al-Fārūq al-Ḥadītha li al-Ṭibāʿa wa al-Nashr, 2010).
Al-Khallāl. *Al-Sunna*, ed. ʿAṭiyya al-Zahrānī (Riyadh: Dār al-Rāya, 1989).
*Ṭabaqāt aṣḥab al-Imām Aḥmad b. Ḥanbal* (Riyadh: Markaz al-Malik Fayṣal li al-Buḥūth wa al-Dirāsāt al-Islāmiyya, 2019).
al-Khaṭīb al-Baghdādī. *Al-Jāmiʿ li al-akhlāq al-rāwī wa ādāb al-sāmiʿ*, ed. Maḥmūd al-Ṭaḥḥān (Riyadh: Maktabat al-Maʿārif, 1983).

*Al-Kifāya fī ʿilm al-riwāya* (Hyderabad: Dā'irat al-Maʿārif al-ʿUthmāniyya, 1938).
*Kitāb al-Faqīh wa al-mutafaqqih*, ed. Abū ʿAbd al-Raḥmān and ʿĀdil b. Yūsuf al-ʿAzzāzī (Riyadh: Dār Ibn al-Jawzī, 1996).
*Kitāb Sharaf aṣḥāb al-ḥadīth*, ed. Muḥammad Saʿīd Khaṭīb Ughlī (Ankara: Jāmiʿat Anqara, 1969).
*Al-Muttafiq wa al-muftariq*, ed. Muḥammad Ṣādiq (Damascus: Dār al-Qādirī, 1997).
*Tārīkh Baghdād*, ed. Bashshār ʿAwwād Maʿrūf (Beirut: Dār al-Gharb al-Islāmī, 2001).
*Al-Taṭfīl wa ḥikāyāt al-ṭufayliyyīn wa akhbāruhum wa nawādir kalāmihim wa ashʿāruhum*, ed. Bassām ʿAbd al-Wahhāb al-Jābī (Beirut: Dār Ibn al-Ḥazm, 1999).
Al-Khaṭṭābī. *Aʿlām al-ḥadīth fī sharḥ Ṣaḥīḥ al-Bukhārī*, ed. Muḥammad b. Saʿd b. ʿAbd al-Raḥmān al-Saʿūd (Mecca: Jāmiʿat Umm al-Qurā, 1988) = *Aʿlām al-sunan*, ed. Yūsuf al-Kattānī (Rabat: n.p., 1988).
Al-Khwārizmī. *Jāmiʿ masānīd al-Imām al-Aʿẓam* (Hyderabad: Maṭbaʿat Majlis Dā'irat al-Maʿārif, 1914).
Al-Kinānī, ʿAbd al-ʿAzīz. *Kitāb al-Ḥayda* (Giza: Maktabat al-Nawʿiyya al-Islāmiyya li al-Iḥyā' al-Turāth al-Islāmī, n.d.).
Al-Kindī. *Kitāb al-Wulāt wa kitāb al-quḍāt [The Governors and Judges of Egypt]*, ed. Rhuvon Guest (Leiden: Brill, 1912).
Al-Laknawī. *Aḥkām al-nafā'is fī adā' al-adkhār bi lisān al-fāris*, in *Majmūʿat al-rasā'il al-Laknawī*, ed. Naʿīm Ashrāf Nūr Aḥmad (Karachi: Idārat al-Qur'ān wa al-ʿUlūm al-Islāmiyya, 1998–9).
*Al-Fawā'id al-bahiyya fī tarājim al-Ḥanafiyya*, ed. Muḥammad Badr al-Dīn Abū Firās al-Niʿsānī (Cairo: Maṭbaʿat al-Saʿāda, 1906) = Cawnpore [Kanpur]: al-Maṭbaʿa al-Muṣṭafā li Muḥammad Muṣṭafā Khān, 1876 = Beirut: Dār al-Maʿrifa, 1906.
al-Laknawī, ʿAbd al-ʿAlī. *Fawātīḥ al-raḥamūt sharḥ musallam al-thubūt fī uṣūl al-fiqh*, ed. ʿAbd Allāh Maḥmūd Muḥammad ʿUmar (Beirut: Dār al-Kutub al-ʿIlmiyya, 2002).
Al-Lālakā'ī. *Sharḥ uṣūl iʿtiqād ahl al-sunna wa al-jamāʿa*, ed. Aḥmad b. Masʿūd b. Ḥamdān (Riyadh: Dār al-Ṭayba, 2003) = 'Sharḥ uṣūl iʿtiqād ahl al-sunna wa al-jamāʿa', ed. Aḥmad b. Masʿūd b. Ḥamdān (PhD thesis, Jāmiʿat Umm al-Qurā, 1990) = *Sharḥ uṣūl iʿtiqād ahl sunna wa al-jamāʿa*, ed. Kamāl al-Miṣrī (Alexandria: Maktabat Dār al-Baṣīra, n.d.).
Al-Majlisī. *Biḥār al-anwār* (Tehran: Dār al-Kutub al-Islāmiyya, 1956).
Al-Malaṭī. *Kitāb al-Tanbīh wa al-radd ʿalā ahl al-ahwā' wa al-bidaʿ*, ed. S. Dedering (Istanbul: Maṭbaʿat al-Dawla, 1936).
Mālik b. Anas. *Al-Muwaṭṭa' bi riwāyat Yaḥyā b. Yaḥyā al-Laythī.*
Al-Malik al-Muʿaẓẓam Abū Muẓaffar ʿĪsā b. Abī Bakr. *Al-Sahm al-muṣīb fī kabid al-Khaṭīb* (Cairo: Maṭbaʿat al-Saʿāda, 1932).
Al-Maqdisī, ʿAbd al-Hādī. *Manāqib al-a'imma al-arbaʿa*, ed. Sulaymān Muslim Ḥarash (Riyadh: Dār al-Mu'ayyad, 1996).
Al-Maqrīzī. *Kitāb al-Muqaffā al-kabīr*, ed. Muḥammad al-Yaʿlāwī (Beirut: Dār al-Gharb al-Islāmī, 1991).

al-Marrūdhī, Abū Bakr. *Akhbār al-shuyūkh wa akhlāquhum*. ed. ʿĀmir Ḥasan Ṣabrī (Beirut: Dār al-Bashā'ir al-Islāmiyya, 2005).

*Kitāb al-ʿIlal wa maʿrifat al-rijāl li Aḥmad b. Muḥammad b. Ḥanbal: riwāyat al-Marrūdhī*, ed. Waṣī Allāh b. Muḥammad ʿAbbās (Bombay: al-Dār al-Salafiyya, 1988; repr. Cairo: Dār al-Imām Aḥmad, 2006).

*Masā'il al-Imām Aḥmad al-fiqhiyya bi riwāyat al-Marrūdhī min al-nikāḥ ḥattā nihāyat al-qaḍā' wa al-shahādāt*, ed. ʿAbd al-Muḥsin b. Muḥammad al-Maʿyūf (Mecca: Jāmiʿat Umm al-Qurā, 2011) = ed. ʿAbd al-Raḥmān b. ʿAlī al-Ṭarīqī (Mecca: Jāmiʿ Umm al-Qurā, 2011) = ed. ʿAbd al-Raḥmān b. ʿAlī al-Ṭarīqī in *Majallat al-Jāmiʿa al-Islāmiyya bi al-Madīna al-Munawwara*, 1; *Majalla Jāmiʿat al-Malik Saʿūd li al-ʿUlūm al-Tarbawiya wa al-Dirāsāt al-Islāmiyya*, 2, 20 (2008); *Majallat Jāmiʿat Umm al-Qurā li ʿUlūm al-Sharīʿa wa al-Lugha wa Ādābihā*, 33 (2005).

*al-Waraʿ*, ed. Muḥammad al-Saʿīd Basyūnī Zaghlūl (Beirut: Dār al-Kitāb al-ʿArabī, 1988) = ed. Zaynab Ibrāhīm al-Qārūṭ (Beirut: Dār al-Kutub al-ʿIlmiyya, 1983) = ed. Samīr al-Amīn al-Zuhayrī (Riyadh: Dār al-Ṣumayʿī, 1997).

Al-Marwazī, Muḥammad b. Naṣr. *Ikhtilāf al-fuqahā'*, ed. Muḥammad Ṭāhir Ḥakīm (Riyadh: Maktaba Aḍwā' al-Salaf, 2000).

*Kitāb al-Sunna*, ed. ʿAbd Allāh b. Muḥammad al-Buṣīrī (Riyadh: Dār al-ʿĀṣima, 2001).

Al-Masʿūdī. *Kitāb al-Tanbīh wa al-ishrāf*, ed. M. J. de Goeje (Leiden: Brill, 1894).

*Murūj al-dhahab wa maʿādin al-jawhar*, ed. Kamāl Ḥasan Marʿī (Beirut: al-Maktaba al-ʿAṣriyya, 2005) = *Les prairies d'or. Texte et traduction par C. Barbier de Meynard et Pavet de Courteille [Murūj al-dhahab]* (Paris: Société Asiatique, 1861–77).

Al-Māturīdī, Abū al-Manṣūr. *Ta'wīlāt al-Qur'ān*, ed. Ahmed Vanlioğlu and Bekir Topaloğlu (Istanbul: Dār al-Mīzān, 2005).

Al-Māwardī. *Adab al-qāḍī*, ed. Muḥyī Hilāl al-Sarḥān (Baghdad: Maṭbaʿat al-Irshād, 1971).

*Al-Aḥkām al-ṣulṭāniyya wa al-wilāyāt al-dīniyya*, ed. Aḥmad Mubārak al-Baghdādī (Kuwait: Maktaba Dār Ibn Qutayba, 1989).

Al-Mizzī. *Tahdhīb al-kamāl fī asmā' al-rijāl*, ed. Bashshār ʿAwwād Maʿrūf (Beirut: Mu'assasat al-Risāla, 1996).

Mu'assasat Āl al-Bayt. *Al-Fihras al-shāmil li al-turāth al-ʿarabī al-islāmī al-makhṭūṭ : al-ḥadīth al-nabawī al-sharīf wa ʿulūmuhu wa rijāluhu* (Amman: Mu'assasat Āl al-Bayt, 1991).

Mughalṭāy b. Qalīj, *Ikmāl Tahdhīb al-kamāl fī asmā' al-rijāl*, ed. ʿĀdil b. Muḥammad and Usāma b. Ibrāhīm (Cairo: al-Fārūq al-Ḥadītha li al-Ṭibāʿa wa al-Nashr, 2001).

*Sharḥ Sunan Ibn Māja*, ed. Kāmil ʿUwayḍa (Mecca: Nizār Muṣṭafā al-Bāz, 1999).

Muḥammad b. Abī Bakr al-Rāzī. *Mukhtār al-ṣiḥāḥ* (Beirut: Maktabat Lubnān, 1986).

Muḥammad b. Sulaymān al-Rūdānī. *Ṣilat al-khalaf bi mawṣūl al-salaf*, ed. Muḥammad Ḥajī (Beirut: Dār al-Gharb al-Islāmī, 1988).

Muḥammad Zakariyyā' al-Kāndahlawī. *Awjaz al-Masālik ilā Muwaṭṭā' Mālik* (Damascus: Dār al-Qalam, 2003).

Mujāhid b. Jabr (attr.). *Tafsīr Mujāhid*, ed. Muḥammad ʿAbd al-Islām Abū al-Nayl (Cairo: Dār al-Fikr al-Islāmī al-Ḥadītha, 1989).

Al-Muqaddasī. *Aḥsan al-taqāsīm fī maʿrifat al-aqālīm*, 2nd edn., ed. M. J. de Goeje (Leiden: Brill, 1906).

(pseudo?-) Muqātil b. Sulaymān al-Balkhī. *Tafsīr Muqātil b. Sulaymān*, ed. ʿAbd Allāh Maḥmūd Shiḥāta (Beirut: Mu'assasat al-Tārīkh al-ʿArabī, 2002).

Muslim b. al-Ḥajjāj. *Kitāb al-Kunā wa al-asmā'*, ed. ʿAbd al-Raḥīm Muḥammad Aḥmad al-Qashqarī (Medina: Iḥyā' al-Turāth al-Islāmiyya, 1984).

.*Al-Ṣaḥīḥ*.

Al-Muṭahhar b. Ṭāhir al-Maqdīsī. *Kitāb al-Bad' wa al-tārīkh*, ed. M. C. Huart (Paris: Ernest Leroux, 1907).

Al-Muwaffaq al-Makkī. *Manāqib Abī Ḥanīfa* [printed with al-Kardarī, *Manāqib Abī Ḥanīfa*] (Hyderabad: Maṭbaʿat Dā'irat al-Maʿārif al-ʿUthmāniyya, 1894).

Al-Nābulusī. *Ikhtiṣār Ṭabaqāt al-Ḥanābila*, ed. Aḥmad ʿUbayd (Damascus: al-Maktaba al-ʿArabiyya, 1930).

Al-Najāshī. *Rijāl al-Najāshī*, ed. Mūsā al-Shabīrī al-Zanjānī (Qum: Mu'assasat al-Nashr al-Islāmī, 1998) = ed. Muḥammad Jawād Nāʿīnī (Beirut: n.p., 1988).

Najm al-Dīn al-Ghazzī. *Al-Kawākib al-sā'ira bi-aʿyān al-mi'a al-ʿāshira* (Beirut: Dār al-Kutub al-ʿIlmiyya, 1997).

Al-Narshakhī. *Tārīkh-i Bukhārā*, ed. Mudarris Riẓavī (Tehran: n.p., 1984) = ed. Mudarris Riẓavī (Tehran: Intishārāt-i Tūs, 1967) = *The History of Bukhara*, trans. Richard N. Frye (Cambridge, MA: Medieval Academy of America, 1954).

Al-Nasafī. *al-Qand fī dhikr al-ʿulamā' Samarqand*, ed. Yūsuf al-Hādī (Tehran: Mīrāth-i Maktūb, 1999).

Al-Nasā'ī. *Kitāb al-Ḍuʿafā' wa al-matrūkīn* [published with *Kitāb al-Ḍuʿafā' al-ṣaghīr*], ed. Maḥmūd Ibrāhīm Zāyid (Beirut: Dār al-Maʿrifa, 1986).

Al-Nawawī. *Kitāb tahdhīb al-asmā'*, ed. F. Wustenfeld (Göttingen: London Society for the Publication of Oriental Texts, 1842–7).

*Sharḥ al-Nawawī ʿalā Muslim* (Cairo: al-Maṭbaʿa al-Miṣriyya bi al-Azhar, 1929).

al-Nuʿmānī, ʿAbd al-Rashīd. *Naẓarāt ʿalā kutub al-thalāth fī al-ḥadīth*, ed. Muḥammad ʿUmar ʿUthmān al-Nadwī (n.p.: Iḥyā' al-Maʿārif al-Islāmiyya, 2016).

Qāḍī Ibn Shuhba. *Ṭabaqāṭ al-shāfiʿiyya* (Hyderabad: Dā'irat al-Maʿārif al-ʿUthmāniyya, 1978).

Al-Qāḍī ʿIyāḍ. *Al-Ghunya: Fihrist shuyūkh al-Qāḍī ʿIyāḍ*, ed. Māhir Zuhayr Jarrār (Beirut: Dār al-Gharb al-Islāmī, 1982).

Al-Qāḍī al-Nuʿmān. *Ikhtilāf uṣūl al-madhāhib*, ed. S. T. Lockandwalla (Simla: Indian Institute for Advanced Study, 1972).

al-Qartabī. *Manāqib*, ed. Khālid Nihād Muṣṭafā al-Aʿẓamī (Baghdad: Maktabat Amīr Baghdādī, 2001).

Al-Qazwīnī. Zakariyyā' b. Muḥammad b. Maḥmūd. *Āthār al-bilād wa akhbār al-ʿibād* (Beirut: Dār Ṣādir, n.d.).

Qazwīnī al-Rāzī. *Kitāb al-Naqẓ: maʿrūf bih baʿẓ-i mathālib al-navāṣib fī naqẓ baʿẓ faẓā'iḥ al-ravāfiẓ*, ed. Jalāl al-Dīn Muḥaddith (Tehran: Anujman-i Āthār-i Millī, 1980).

Al-Qummī. *Maqālāt wa al-firaq*, ed. Muḥammad Jawād Mashkūr (Tehran: Maṭbaʿat Ḥaydarī, 1923).

Qummī, Ḥasan b. Muḥammad. *Tārīkh-i Qum*, ed. Muḥammad Riḍā Anṣārī Qummī (Qum: Kitābkhāneh-yi Buzurg-i Hazrat-i Āyat Allāh al-ʿUẓmā Marʿashī Najafī, 2006).

Raḍī al-Dīn Ibn Ḥanbalī. *Durr al-ḥabab fī tārīkh aʿyān Ḥalab*, ed. Maḥmūd Ḥamd al-Fākhūrī and Yaḥyā Zakariyyāʾ ʿAbbāra (Damascus: Wizārat al-Thaqāfa, 1972).

Al-Rāmahurmuzī. *Al-Muḥaddith al-fāṣil bayn al-rāwī wa al-wāʿī*, ed. Muḥammad ʿAjāj al-Khaṭīb (Beirut: Dār al-Fikr, 1971).

Al-Rāwandī. *Rāḥat al-ṣudūr va āyat al-surūr dar tārīkh āl-saljūq*, ed. Muḥammad Iqbāl (Leiden: Brill, 1921).

Al-Rāzī, Fakhr al-Dīn. *Manāqib al-Imām al-Shāfiʿī*, ed. Aḥmad Saqqā (Cairo: Maktabat al-Kulliyyāt al-Azhariyya, 1986).

*Al-Tafsīr al-kabīr* (Beirut: Dār al-Fikr, 1981).

Saʿdī, *Ghazalīyāt-i Saʿdī*, ed. Kāẓim Bargnaysī (Tehran: Fikr-i Ruẓ, 2002).

Al-Ṣafadī. *Kitāb al-Wāfī bi al-wafayāt*, ed. Aḥmad al-Arnāʾūṭ and Turkī Muṣṭafā (Beirut: Dār Iḥyāʾ al-Turāth al-ʿArabī, 2000) = *Kitāb al-Wāfī bi al-wafāyāt*, ed. H. Ritter et al. (Leipzig, Istanbul, and Beirut: German Oriental Institute, 1962–97).

Al-Sahmī, Ḥamza b. Yūsuf. *Suʾālāt Ḥamza b. Yūsuf al-Sahmī li al-Dāraquṭnī wa ghayrihi min al-mashāyikh fī al-jarḥ wa al-taʿdīl*, ed. Muwaffaq b. ʿAbd Allāh b. ʿAbd al-Qādir (Riyadh: Maktabat al-Maʿārif, 1984).

*Tārīkh Jurjān aw kitāb maʿrifat ʿulamāʾ ahl Jurjān*, ed. ʿAbd al-Raḥmān al-Muʿallimī (Hyderabad: Dāʾirat al-Maʿārif al-ʿUthmāniyya, n.d.; repr. Beirut: ʿĀlam al-Kutub, 1987) = Beirut: ʿĀlam al-Kutub, 1981.

Al-Sakhāwī. *Al-Ḍawʾ al-lāmiʿ li ahl al-qarn al-tāsiʿ* (Beirut: Dār al-Jīl, 1992).

*Fatḥ al-mughīth bi sharḥ alfiyat al-ḥadīth* (Riyadh: Maktabat Dār al-Minhāj, 2005).

*Al-Iʿlān bi al-tawbīkh li man dhamma ahl al-tārīkh*, ed. Franz Rosenthal (Beirut: Muʾassasat al-Risāla, 1986).

*Al-Jawāhir wa al-durar fī tarjamat Shaykh al-Islām Ibn Ḥajar*, ed. Ibrāhīm Bājis ʿAbd al-Majīd (Beirut: Dār Ibn Ḥazm, 1999).

Ṣāliḥ b. Aḥmad. *Masāʾil al-Imām Aḥmad b. Ḥanbal*, ed. Ṭāriq b. ʿAwaḍ (Riyadh: Dār al-Waṭan, 1999).

*Sīrat al-Imām Aḥmad b. Ḥanbal*, ed. Fuʾād ʿAbd al-Munʿim Aḥmad (Riyadh: Dār al-Salaf, 1995).

Al-Ṣāliḥī. *ʿUqūd al-jumān fī manāqib al-Imām Abī Ḥanīfa al-Nuʿmān*, ed. Muḥammad Mullā ʿAbd al-Qādir al-Afghānī (Jeddah: Jāmiʿ al-Malik ʿAbd al-ʿAzīz, 1978) = ed. Abū al-Wafāʾ al-Afghānī (Hyderabad: Lajnat Iḥyāʾ al-Maʿārif al-Nuʿmāniyya, 1974).

Al-Samʿānī. *al-Ansāb*, ed. ʿAbd al-Raḥmān al-Muʿallimī al-Yamānī (Hyderabad: Dāʾirat al-Maʿārif al-ʿUthmāniyya, 1979; repr. Cairo: Maktabat Ibn Taymiyya, 1981–4) =ed. ʿAbd Allāh ʿUmar al-Bārūdī (Beirut: Dār al-Jinān, 1988).

*Al-Muntakhab min muʿjam shuyūkh al-Samʿānī*, ed. Muwaffaq b. ʿAbd Allāh b. ʿAbd al-Qādir (Riyadh: Dār ʿĀlam al-Kutub, 1996).

*Al-Taḥbīr fī mu'jam al-kabīr*, ed. Munīra Nājī Sālim (Baghdad: al-Irshād Press, 1975).

Al-Samarqandī. *Kitāb al-Sawād al-a'ẓam* (Cairo: Būlāq, 1837).

*Tarjumeh-yi al-sawād al-a'ẓam*, ed. 'Abd al-Ḥayy Ḥabībī (Tehran: Bunyād-i Farhang-Īrān, 1969).

Al-Samhūdī. *Wafā' al-wafā bi akhbār dār al-muṣṭafā*, ed. Muḥammad Muḥyī al-Dīn 'Abd al-Ḥamīd (Beirut: Dār al-Kutub al-'Ilmiyya, n.d.) = ed. Qāsim al-Sāmmarā'ī (London: Mu'assasat al-Furqān li al-Turāth al-Islāmī, 2001).

Al-Ṣan'ānī, 'Abd al-Razzāq. *Al-Muṣannaf*, ed. Ḥabīb al-Raḥmān al-A'ẓamī (n.p. [South Africa]: al-Majlis al-'Ilmī, 1970).

Al-Ṣan'ānī, 'Alī b. Ismā'īl al-Mu'ayyad. *Kitāb Ra'b al-ṣad'* (Beirut: Dār al-Nafā'is, 1990).

Al-Sarakhsī. *Kitāb al-Mabsūṭ* (Beirut: Dār al-Ma'rifa, 1989; repr. Cairo: Dār al-Sa'āda, 1906–13).

*Al-Muḥarrar fī uṣūl al-fiqh*, ed. Abū 'Abd al-Raḥmān Ṣalāḥ b. Muḥammad b. 'Uwayḍa (Beirut: Dār al-Kutub al-'Ilmiyya, 1996).

*Tamhīd al-fuṣūl fī al-uṣūl*, ed. 'Abd Allāh b. Sulaymān b. 'Āmir al-Sayyid (Mecca: Umm al-Qurā University, 2011).

*Uṣūl al-Sarakhsī*, ed. Rafīq al-'Ajam (Beirut: Dār al-Ma'rifa, 1997) = ed. Abū al-Wafā' al-Afghānī (Hyderabad: Lajnat Iḥyā' al-Ma'ārif al-Nu'māniyya, 1953–4).

Sayf b. 'Umar. *Kitāb al-ridda wa al-futūḥ*, ed. Qāsim al-Sāmarrā'ī (Leiden: Brill, 1995).

Al-Ṣaymarī. *Akhbār Abī Ḥanīfa wa aṣḥābihi*, ed. Abū al-Wafā' al-Afghānī (Beirut: 'Alam al-Kutub, 1985).

Sayyid Murtaḍā Ibn Dā'ī. *Tabṣirat al-'awāmm fī ma'rifat maqālāt al-anām*, ed. 'Abbās Iqbāl, 2nd edn. (Tehran: Maṭba'ah-yi Majlis, 1964).

al-Shāfi'ī. *Kitāb al-Umm*, ed. Rif'at Fawzī 'Abd al-Muṭṭalib (Mansoura: Dār al-Wafā', 2001) = *Kitāb al-Umm* (Bulaq: al-Maṭba'a al-Kubrā al-Amīriyya, 1907).

Al-Shashī. *Ḥilyat al-'ulamā' fī ma'rifat madhāhib al-fuqahā'*, ed. Yāsīn Aḥmad Ibrāhīm Darādika (Amman: Dār al-Bāz, 1988).

Al-Shawkānī. *Badr al-ṭāli' bi-maḥāsin man ba'd al-qarn al-sābi'* (Cairo: Dār al-Kitāb al-Islāmī, n.d.).

Al-Shaybānī. *Al-Aṣl*, ed. Mehmet Boynukalin (Qatar: Wizārat al-Awqāf and Beirut: Dār Ibn Ḥazm, 2012) = ed. Abū al-Wafā' al-Afghānī (Hyderabad: Majlis Dā'irat al-Ma'ārif al-'Uthmāniyya, 1966; repr. Beirut: 'Ālam al-Kutub, 1990).

*Al-Jāmi' al-ṣaghīr* [published with the commentary of al-Laknawī, *al-Nāfi' al-Kabīr*] (Karachi: Idārat al-Qur'ān wa al-'Ulūm al-Islāmiyya, 1990).

*Kitāb al-Ḥujja 'alā ahl al-Madīna* (Hyderabad: Maṭba'at Dā'irat al-Ma'ārif al-Sharqiyya, 1963).

Al-Shaykh al-Mufīd. *Al-Irshād fī ma'rifat ḥujaj Allāh 'alā al-'ibād* (Beirut: Mu'assasat Āl al-Bayt li Iḥyā' al-Turāth, 1995).

Sibṭ b. al-Jawzī. *Al-Intiṣār wa al-tarjīḥ li al-madhhab al-ṣaḥīḥ*, ed. Muḥammad Zāhid al-Kawtharī (Cairo: Maṭba'at al-Anwār, 1941).

Al-Subadhmūnī, al-Ḥārithī. *Musnad Abī Ḥanīfa* (Beirut: Dār al-Kutub al-ʿIlmiyya, 2008).

Al-Subkī, Tāj al-Dīn. *Ṭabaqāt al-Shāfiʿiyya al-kubrā*, ed. Maḥmūd Muḥammad al-Ṭanāḥī and ʿAbd al-Fattāḥ Muḥammad al-Ḥulw (Aleppo: ʿĪsā al-Bābī al-Ḥalabī, 1964) = (Cairo: ʿĪsā al-Bābī al-Ḥalabī, 1964–76; repr. Cairo: Dār Iḥyāʾ al-Kutub al-ʿArabiyya, 1992).

Al-Sughdī. *Al-Nutaf fī al-fatāwā*, ed. Ṣalāḥ al-Dīn al-Nāhī (Baghdad: al-Maktaba al-Waṭaniyya, 1976).

Al-Sulamī. *Dhikr al-niswa al-mutaʿabbidāt al-ṣūfiyyāt*, ed. Maḥmūd Muḥammad al-Ṭanāḥī (Cairo: Maktabat al-Khānjī, 1993).

*Kitāb Ṭabaqāt al-ṣūfiyya*, ed. Johannes Pederson (Leiden: Brill, 1960).

Al-Suyūṭī, Jalāl al-Dīn. *Al-Baḥr alladhī zakhara fī sharḥ Alfiyyat al-Suyūṭī fī al-ḥadīth* (Medina: Maktabat al-Ghurabāʾ al-Athariyya, 1999).

*Ḥusn al-muḥāḍara fī akhbār Miṣr wa al-Qāhira*, ed. ʿAlī Muḥammad ʿUmar (Cairo: Maktabat al-Khānjī, 2007) = *Ḥusn al-muḥāḍara fī tārīkh Miṣr wa al-Qāhira, ed. Muḥammad Abū al-Faḍl Ibrāhīm*, ed. Muḥammad Abū al-Faḍl Ibrāhīm (Aleppo: Dār Iḥyāʾ al-Kutub al-ʿArabī ʿĪsā al-Bābī al-Ḥalabī, 1967; repr. n.p.: Dār Iḥyāʾ al-Kutub al-ʿArabiyya, 1968).

*Khaṣāʾis al-kubrā aw kifāyat al-ṭālib al-labīb fī khaṣāʾiṣ al-ḥabīb*, ed. Muḥammad Khalīl Hirās (ʿAbdūn: Dār al-Kutub al-Ḥadītha, 1967).

*Al-Muzhir fī ʿulūm al-lugha wa anwāʿihā* (Cairo: Dār Iḥyāʾ al-Kutub al-ʿArabiyya, 1958).

*Tadrīb al-rāwī fī sharḥ taqrīb al-Nawawī*, ed. Abū Qutayba Naẓar Muḥammad al-Fārayābī (Cairo: Maktabat al-Kawthar, 1994).

Al-Ṭabarānī. *Al-Muʿjam al-kabīr*, ed. Ḥamdī ʿAbd al-Majīd al-Silāfī (Cairo: Maktabat Ibn Taymiyya, 1983).

Al-Ṭabarī. *Tafsīr al-Ṭabarī: jāmiʿ al-bayān ʿan taʾwīl āy al-Qurʾān*, ed. Maḥmūd Muḥammad Shākir and Aḥmad Muḥammad Shākir (Cairo: Dār al-Maʿārif, 1954).

*Tārīkh al-rusul wa al-mulūk*, ed. M. J. de Goeje et al. (Leiden: Brill, 1879–1901).

*Tarjama-i tafsīr-i Ṭabarī*, ed. Ḥabīb Yaghmāʾī (Tehran: Dānishgāh-i Ṭihrān, 1960).

al-Tahānawī, Ẓafar Aḥmad al-ʿUthmānī. *Muqaddimat iʿlāʾ al-sunan: Abū Ḥanīfa wa aṣḥābuhu al-muḥaddithūn* (Karachi: Idārat al-Qurʾān wa al-ʿUlūm al-Islāmiyya, 1984).

Al-Ṭaḥāwī. *Aḥkām al-Qurʾān al-karīm*, ed. Saʿd al-Dīn Awnāl (Istanbul: Markaz al-Buḥūth al-Islāmiyya, 1998) = ed. Saʿd al-Dīn Ünāl (Istanbul: ISAM, 1995).

*Al-ʿAqīda al-Ṭaḥāwiyya*, ed. Zuhayr al-Shāwīsh (Beirut: al-Maktab al-Islāmī, 1977).

*Mukhtaṣar ikhtilāf al-ʿulamāʾ*, ed. ʿAbd Allāh Nadhīr Aḥmad (Beirut: Dār al-Bashāʾir al-Islāmiyya, 1996).

*Sharḥ mushkil al-āthār*, ed. Shuʿayb al-Arnaʾūṭ (Beirut: Muʾassasat al-Risāla, 1994).

Al-Tanūkhī. *Nishwār al-muḥāḍara wa akhbār al-mudhākara*, ed. ʿAbūd al-Shālijī (Beirut: Dār Ṣādir, 1995 [1973]) = *The Table-Talk of a Mesopotamian Judge*, trans. D. S. Margoliouth (London: Royal Asiatic Society, 1922).

Taymūr Pāshā, Aḥmad *Naẓrat al-tārīkhiyya fī ḥudūth al-madhāhib al-fiqhiyya al-arbaʿa* (Beirut: Dār al-Qādirī, 1990).

Al-Thaʿālibī. *Thimār al-qulūb fī al-muḍāf wa al-mansūb*, ed. Muḥammad Abū al-Faḍl Ibrāhīm (Beirut: al-Maktaba al-ʿAṣriyya, 2003).

Al-Tirmidhī. *Al-ʿIlal al-kabīr*, ed. Ḥamza Muṣṭafā (Amman: Maktabat al-Aqṣā, 1985)

*ʿIlal al-Tirmidhī al-kabīr*, arranged by Abū Ṭālib al-Qāḍī [Maḥmud b. ʿAlī (d. 585/1189)], ed. Ṣubḥī al-Sāmarrāʾī, Abū al-Maʿāṭī al-Nūrī, and Maḥmūd Muḥammad Khalīl al-Ṣaʿīdī (Beirut: ʿĀlam al-Kutub/Maktabat al-Nahḍa al-ʿArabiyya, 1989).

Al-Ṭūsī. *Fihrist al-Ṭūsī*, ed. Muḥammad Ṣādiq Āl Baḥr al-ʿUlūm (Najaf: n.p., 1960) = *al-Fihrist* (Qum: Sharīf al-Riḍā, n.d.).

*Kitāb al-Amālī*, ed. Baharād Jaʿfarī and ʿAlī Akbar Ghaffārī (Tehran: Dār al-Kutub al-Islāmiyya, 1961).

*Rijāl al-Ṭūsī*, ed. Jawād al-Qayyūmī al-Iṣfahānī (Qum: Muʾassasat al-Nashr al-Islāmī, n.d.).

Al-Tustarī. *Qāmūs al-rijāl* (Qum: Muʾassasat al-Nashr al-Islāmī, 2009).

Al-ʿUqaylī. *Kitāb al-Ḍuʿafāʾ*, ed. Ismāʿīl al-Salafī (Riyadh: Dār al-Ṣumayʿī, 2000) = *Kitāb al-Ḍuʿafāʾ al-kabīr*, ed. ʿAbd al-Muʿṭī Amīn Qalʿajī (Beirut: Dār al-Kutub al-ʿIlmiyya, 1984) = ed. Bashshār ʿAwwād Maʿrūf and Muḥammad Bashshār Maʿrūf (Tunis: Dār al-Gharb al-Islāmī, 2015).

Al-Wāʾiẓ, ʿAbd Allāh b. ʿUmar and ʿAbd Allāh b. Muḥammad b. al-Qāsim al-Ḥusaynī. *Faḍāʾil-i Balkh*, ed. ʿAbd al-Ḥayy Ḥabībī (Tehran: Intishārāt-i Bunyād-i Farhang-i Irān, 1971).

Wakīʿ. *Akhbār al-quḍāt*, ed. ʿAbd al-ʿAzīz Muṣṭafā al-Marāghī (Cairo: Maṭbaʿat al-Saʿāda, 1947–50; repr. Beirut: ʿĀlam al-Kutub, n.d.).

Wakīʿ b. al-Jarrāḥ. *Kitāb al-Zuhd*, ed. ʿAbd al-Raḥmān ʿAbd al-Jabbār al-Farīwāʾī (Riyadh: Dā al-Ṣumayʿī, 1994).

*Nuskhat Wakīʿ b. al-Jarrāḥ*, ed. Fahd al-Ḥammūdī (Beirut: al-Shabaka al-ʿArabiyya, 2014).

Al-Yāfiʿī. *Mirʾāt al-jinān*, ed. Khalīl al-Manṣūr (Beirut: Dār al-Kutub al-ʿIlmiyya, 1997) = *Mirʾāt al-jinān wa ʿibrat al-yaqẓān* (Hyderabad: Dāʾirat al-Maʿarif al-Niẓāmiyya, 1919).

Yaḥyā b. Maʿīn. *Maʿrifat al-rijāl*, ed. Muḥammad Kāmil al-Qaṣṣār (Damascus: Majmaʿ al-Lugha al-ʿArabiyya, 1985).

*Tārīkh Yaḥyā b. Maʿīn* [recension of Abū al-Faḍl al-ʿAbbāsī b. Muḥammad b. Ḥātim al-Dūrī al-Baghdādī], ed. ʿAbd Allāh Aḥmad Ḥasan (Beirut: Dār al-Qalam, n.d.) = *al-Tārīkh* (al-Dūrī's recension), ed. Aḥmad Muḥammad Nūr Sayf (Mecca: Markaz al-Baḥth al-ʿIlmī wa Iḥyāʾ al-Turāth al-Islāmī, 1979) = ed. Aḥmad Muḥammad Nūr Sayf (Medina: Maktaba al-Mukarrama, 1979).

*Yaḥyā b. Maʿīn wa kitābuhu al-tārīkh*, ed. Aḥmad Muḥammad Nūr Sayf (Mecca: n.p., 1979).

Al-Yaʿqūbī. *Kitāb al-Buldān*, ed. M. J. de Goeje (Leiden: Brill, 1892).

Yāqūt al-Ḥamawī. *Kitāb al-Muqtaḍab min kitāb Jamharat al-nasab*, ed. Nājī Ḥasan (Beirut: al-Dār al-ʿArabiyya li al-Mawsūʿāt, 1987).

*Muʿjam al-buldān* (Beirut: Dār Ṣādir, 1977).

*Mu'jam al-udabā': Irshād al-arīb ilā ma'rifat al-adīb*, ed. Iḥsān 'Abbās (Beirut: Dār al-Gharb al-Islāmī, 1993) = *Mu'jam al-udabā'* (Beirut: Dār Iḥyā' al-Turāth al-'Arabī, 1988) = *Jacut's Geographisches Wörterbuch: aus den Handschriften zu Berlin (Kitāb Mu'jam al-buldān)*, ed. Ferdinand Wüstenfeld (Leipzig: In Commission bei F. A. Brockhaus, 1886–73) = *The irshād al-arīb ilā ma'rifat al-adīb: or Dictionary of Learned Men of Yāqūt*, ed. D. S. Margoliouth, 2nd edn. (London: Luzac, 1923–31).

al-Zabīdī, Murtaḍā. *Itḥāf al-sāda al-muttaqīn* (Beirut: Dār al-Fikr, n.d.).

*'Uqūd al-jawāhir al-munīfa fī adillat madhhab al-Imām Abī Ḥanīfa*, ed. Muḥammad al-'Azāzī (Beirut: Dār al-Kutub al-'Ilmiyya, n.d.).

Al-Zajjājī. *Majālis al-'ulamā'*, ed. 'Abd al-Salām Hārūn (Cairo: Maktabat al-Khānjī, 1999).

Al-Zayla'ī. *Naṣb al-rāya li al-aḥādīth al-hidāya*, ed. Muḥammad 'Awwāma (Beirut: Mu'assasat al-Rayān, 1997).

Al-Zubayr b. Bakkār. *Jamharat nasab quraysh wa akhbārihā*, ed. Maḥmūd Muḥammad Shākir (Cairo: Maktabat Dār al-'Urūba, 1962).

## Secondary Sources

Abbasi, Rushain. 'Did Premodern Muslims Distinguish the Religious and Secular? The *Dīn–Dunyā* Binary in Medieval Islamic Thought', *Journal of Islamic Studies*, 31: 2 (2020), 185–225.

Abbott, Andrew. *Chaos of Disciplines* (Chicago: University of Chicago Press, 2001).

Abbott, Nabia. *The Qurrah Papyri from Aphrodito in the Oriental Institute* (Chicago: University of Chicago Press, 1938).

'Abd-Allāh, Farouq 'Omar. 'The Doctrines of the Māṭurīdite School with Special Reference to *As-Sawād al-A'ẓam* of al-Ḥakīm al-Samarqandī', PhD thesis, University of Edinburgh, 1974.

'Abd Allāh bt. Maḥrūs al-'Asālī. *Fihris Muṣannafāt al-imām ... al-Bukhārī ... al-mashhūra fīmā 'adā 'al-Ṣaḥīḥ*, arr. Muḥammad b. Ḥamza b. Sa'd (Riyadh: Dār al-'Āṣima, 1988).

'Abd al-Laṭīf b. Muḥammad Riyāḍī Zādah. *Asmā' al-kutub al-mutammim li kashf al-ẓunūn*, ed. Muḥammad al-Tūnjī (Cairo: Maktabat al-Khānjī, 1978).

Abdul-Jabbar, Ghassan. *Bukharī* (London: I. B. Tauris, 2007).

Abou El Fadl, Khaled. *Rebellion and Violence in Islamic Law* (Cambridge: Cambridge University Press, 2001).

Adang, Camilla. 'The Beginnings of the Zahiri Madhhab in al-Andalus', in P. Bearman, R. Peters, and F. E. Vogel (eds.), *The Islamic School of Law: Evolution, Devolution, and Progress* (Cambridge, MA: Harvard University Press, 2005), 117–25, 241–4.

Ahlwardt, W. *Die Handschriften-Verzeichnisse der Königlichen Bibliothek zu Berlin* (Berlin: A. Asher & Co., 1895).

Ahmed, Shahab. *Before Orthodoxy: The Satanic Verses in Early Islam* (Cambridge, MA: Harvard University Press, 2017).

*What Is Islam? The Importance of Being Islamic* (Princeton: Princeton University Press, 2016).

Al-Albānī, Muḥammad Nāṣir al-Dīn. *Fihris makhṭūṭāt dār al-kutub al-ẓāhiriyya: al-muntakhab min makhṭūṭāt al-ḥadīth* (Riyadh: Maktabat al-Maʿārif, 2001).

Ali, Kecia. *Imam Shafiʿi: Scholar and Saint* (Oxford: Oneworld, 2011).

AlSayyad, Nezar. *Cities and Caliphs: On the Genesis of Arab Muslim Urbanism* (New York: Greenwood Press, 1991).

Ames, Christine Caldwell. *Medieval Heresies: Christianity, Judaism, and Islam* (Cambridge: Cambridge University Press, 2015).

Amory, P. *People and Identity in Ostrogothic Italy, 489–554* (Cambridge: Cambridge University Press, 1997).

Andersson, Tobias. *Early Sunnī Historiography: A Study of the* Tārīkh *of Khalīfa b. Khayyāṭ* (Leiden: Brill, 2019).

Anthony, S. W. *The Caliph and the Heretic: Ibn Saba' and the Origins of Shīʿism* (Leiden: Brill, 2012).

Antrim, Zayde. *Routes and Realms: The Power of Place in the Early Islamic World* (Oxford: Oxford University Press, 2012).

Arberry, A. J. *The Chester Beatty Library: A Handlist of the Arabic Manuscripts*, volume 5: *MSS. 4001–4500* (Dublin: Hodges, Figgis & Co. Ltd., 1962).

*The Chester Beatty Library: A Handlist of the Arabic Manuscripts*, volume 6: *MSS. 3751–4000* (Dublin: Hodges, Figgis & Co. Ltd., 1959).

Armstrong, John. *Nations before Nationalism* (Chapel Hill: University of North Carolina Press, 1982).

Asad, Talal. *The Idea of an Anthropology of Islam* (Washington, DC: Center for Contemporary Arab Studies, Georgetown University, 1986).

Assmann, Jan. *Moses the Egyptian: The Memory of Egypt in Western Monotheism* (Cambridge, MA: Harvard University Press, 1997).

*Religion and Cultural Memory* (Stanford: Stanford University Press, 2006).

Auerbach, Erich. *Mimesis: The Representation of Reality in Western Literature*, trans. Willard R. Trak (Princeton: Princeton University Press, 1974).

Al-ʿAwnī, al-Sharīf Ḥātim. *Sharḥ Mūqiẓa li al-Dhahabī* (Dammām: Dār Ibn al-Jawzī, 2006).

Azad, Arezou. *Sacred Landscape in Medieval Afghanistan: Revisiting the* Faḍā'il-i Balkh (Oxford: Oxford University Press, 2013).

Al-Azami, M. Mustafa. *On Schacht's 'Origins of Muhammad Jurisprudence'* (Cambridge: Islamic Texts Society, 1996).

Al-Azem, Talal. *Rule-Formulation and Binding Precedent in the Madhhab-Law Tradition: Ibn Quṭlūbughā's Commentary on the Compendium of Qudūrī* (Leiden: Brill, 2017).

Al-Azmeh, Aziz. *The Arabs and Islam in Late Antiquity: A Critique of Approaches to Arabic Sources* (Berlin: Gerlach Press, 2014).

Badawī, A. *Mu'allafāt al-Ghazālī*, 2nd edn. (Kuwait: Wikālat al-Maṭbūʿāt, 1977).

al-Bātilī, Aḥmad ʿAbd Allāh. *Al-Imām al-Khaṭṭābī: al-muḥaddith al-faqīh wa al-adīb al-shāʿir* (Damascus: Dār al-Qalam, 1996).

Bauer, Walter. *Rechtgläubigkeit und Ketzerei im ältesten Christentum* (Tübingen: Mohr, 1964); trans. Robert Kraft and Gerhard Krodel as *Orthodoxy and Heresy in Earliest Christianity* (Philadelphia: Fortress Press, 1971).

Bautsch, Kelley. *A Study of the Geography of I Enoch 17–19 'No One Has Seen What I Have Seen'* (Leiden: Brill, 2003).

Bayless, Martha. *Sin and Filth in Medieval Culture: The Devil in the Latrine* (New York: Routledge, 2012).

Beck, E. 'Iblis und Mensch, Satan und Adam: Der Werdegang einer koranischen Erzählung', *Le Muséon*, 89 (1976), 195–244.

Beeston, A. F. L. 'Background Topics', in A. F. L. Beeston, T. M. Johnstone, R. B. Serjeant, and G. R. Smith (eds.), *Arabic Literature to the End of the Umayyad Period* (Cambridge: Cambridge University Press, 1983), 1–26.

Bellah, Robert N. and Hans Joas (eds.). *The Axial Age and Its Consequences* (Cambridge, MA: Belknap Press of Harvard University Press, 2012).

Bellamy, J. 'Sources of Ibn Abī 'l-Dunyā's *Kitāb Maqtal Amīr al-Mu'minīn 'Alī*', *JAOS*, 1 (1984), 3–19.

Berger, Peter and Thomas Luckmann. *The Social Construction of Reality: A Treatise in the Sociology of Knowledge* (London: Penguin, 1991).

Bernand, M. 'Le Kitāb al-Radd 'alā ahl al-bida' wa al-ahwā'', *Annales Islamogiques*, 16 (1980), 40–126.

Berzon, Todd S. *Classifying Christians: Ethnography, Heresiology, and the Limits of Knowledge in Late Antiquity* (Oakland: University of California Press, 2016).

Bianquis, Thierry. 'Autonomous Egypt from Ibn Ṭūlūn to Kāfūr, 868–969', in *The Cambridge History of Egypt*, volume 1: *Islamic Egypt, 640–1517*, ed. C. F. Petry (Cambridge: Cambridge University Press, 1998), 86–119.

*Damas et la Syrie sous la domination fatimide (359–468/969–1076). Essai d'interprétation de chroniques arabes médiévales* (Damascus: Institut français de Damas, 1986).

Blankinship, Khalid Y. *The End of the Jihād State: The Reign of Hishām ibn 'Abd al-Malik and the Collapse of the Umayyads* (New York: State University of New York Press, 1994).

Blecher, J. 'Revision in the Manuscript Age: New Evidence of Early Versions of Ibn Ḥajar's *Fatḥ al-bārī*', *JNES*, 76: 1 (2017), 39–51.

'In the Shade of the *Ṣaḥīḥ*: Politics, Culture and Innovation in an Islamic Commentary Tradition', PhD thesis, Princeton University, 2012.

Bligh-Abramski, I. 'The Judiciary (Qāḍīs) as a Governmental-Administrative Tool in Early Islam', *JESHO*, 35 (1992), 40–71.

Bloch, Marc. 'Collective Memory, Custom, and Tradition: About a Recent Book', in Jeffrey K. Olick, Vered Vinitzky-Seroussi, and Daniel Levy (eds.), *The Collective Memory Reader* (Oxford: Oxford University Press, 2011), 150–5.

Bloom, Jonathan M. *Paper before Print: The History and Impact of Paper in the Islamic World* (New Haven and London: Yale University Press, 2001).

Bonner, Michael. *Aristocratic Violence and Holy War: Studies in the Jihad and the Arab–Byzantine Frontier* (New Haven: American Oriental Society, 1996).

Borrut, Antoine. *Entre mémoire et pouvoir. L'espace syrien sous les derniers Omeyyades et les premiers Abbasides (v. 72–193/692–809)* (Leiden: Brill, 2011).

Borrut, Antoine and Fred M. Donner (eds.), *Christians and Others in the Umayyad State* (Chicago: Oriental Institute of the University of Chicago, 2016).

Borst, Arno. *Der Turmbau von Babel: Geschichte der Meinungen über Ursprung und Vielfalt der Sprachen und Völker* (Stuttgart: Hiersemann, 1957–63).

Bosworth, Edmund C. 'On the Chronology of the Ziyārids in Gurjān and Ṭabaristān', *Der Islam*, 40 (1964), 25–34.

'An Early Arabic Mirror for Princes: Ṭāhir Dhū l-Yamīnain's Epistle to His Son ʿAbdallāh (206/821)', *JNES*, 29: 1 (1970), 25–41.

'The Rise of the Karāmiyyah in Khurasan', *Muslim World*, 50 (1960), 6–14.

'Sistan and Its Local Histories', *Iranian Studies*, 33: 1/2 (2000), 31–43.

Bouges, M. *Essai de chronologie des ouevres de al-Ghazālī* (Beirut: Institut de lettres orientales de Beyrouth, 1959).

Bourdieu, Pierre. *Distinction: A Social Critique of the Judgement of Taste*, trans. Richard Nice (Cambridge, MA: Harvard University Press, 1984).

*Outline of a Theory of Practice*, trans. Richard Nice (Cambridge: Cambridge University Press, 1977).

Boyarin, D. *Border Lines: The Partition of Judaeo-Christianity* (Philadelphia: University of Pennsylvania Press, 2010).

Brock, S. P. 'North Mesopotamia in the Late Seventh Century: Book XV of John Bār Penkāyē's Rīš Mellē', *JSAI*, 9 (1987), 51–75.

Brockelmann, Carl. *Geschichte der Arabischen Litteratur* (Leiden: Brill, 1943).

Brown, Daniel W. *A New Introduction to Islam* (Oxford: Wiley Blackwell, 2003).

Brown, Jonathan A. C. *The Canonization of al-Bukhārī and Muslim: The Formation and Function of the Sunnī Ḥadīth Canon* (Leiden: Brill, 2007).

Brown, Peter. *Augustine of Hippo: A Biography* (London: Faber & Faber, 1976).

*Power and Persuasion in Late Antiquity: Towards a Christian Empire* (London: University of Wisconsin Press, 1992).

*Society and the Holy in Late Antiquity* (London: Faber & Faber, 1982).

*Through the Eye of a Needle: Wealth, the Fall of Rome, and the Making of Christianity in the West, 350–550 AD* (Princeton: Princeton University Press, 2012).

Browne, E. 'An Account of a Rare, If Not Unique, Manuscript History of the Seljūqs Contained in the Schefer Collection Lately Acquired by the Bibliotheque Nationale in Paris', *JRAS*, 34: 3 (1902), 567–610.

Brunelle, Carolyn Anne. 'From Text to Law: Islamic Legal Theory and the Practical Hermeneutics of Abū Jaʿfar Aḥmad al-Ṭaḥāwī (d. 321/933)', PhD thesis, University of Pennsylvania, 2016.

Buell, Denise Kimber. *Why This New Race: Ethnic Reasoning in Early Christianity* (New York: Columbia University Press, 2005).

Bujnūrdī, Kaẓem Musavi (ed.). *Dā'irat al-Maʿārif-i Buzurg-i Islāmī* (Tehran: Markazi-i Dā'irat al-Maʿārif-i Buzurg-i Islāmī, 1989–).

Bulliet, Richard. 'The Age Structure of Medieval Islamic Education', *Studia Islamica*, 57 (1983), 105–17.

'City Histories in Medieval Iran', *Iranian Studies*, 3 (1968), 104–9.

*Islam: The View from the Edge* (New York: Columbia University Press, 1994).

*The Patricians of Nishapur: A Study in Medieval Islamic Social History* (Cambridge, MA: Harvard University Press, 1972).

Burke, Peter. *History and Social Theory* (Cambridge: Polity Press, 2005).
'Reflections on the Historical Revolution in France: The Annales School and British Social History', *Review*, 1 (1978), 147–64.
Calder, Norman. 'The Limits of Islamic Orthodoxy', in Farhad Daftary (ed.), *Intellectual Traditions in Islam* (London: I. B. Tauris, 2000), 66–86.
*Studies in Early Muslim Jurisprudence* (Oxford: Clarendon Press, 1993).
Chabbi, J. 'Remarques sur le développement historique des mouvements ascétiques et mystiques au Khurasan: IIIe/IXe siècle–IVe/Xe siècle', *Studia Islamica*, 46 (1977), 5–72.
Clanchy, M. T. *From Memory to Written Record: England 1066–1307*, 2nd edn. (Oxford: Blackwell, 1993).
Cobb, Paul. 'Virtual Sacrality: Making Muslim Syria Sacred before the Crusades', *Medieval Encounters*, 8: 1 (2002), 35–55.
'Review of Nezar AlSayyad, *Cities and Caliphs: On the Genesis of Arab Muslim Urbanism*', *Journal of Near Eastern Studies*, 54: 3 (1995), 224–6.
*White Banners: Contention in ʿAbbasid Syria, 750–880* (New York: State University of New York Press, 2001).
Conrad, Gerhard. *Abū 'l-Ḥusain al-Rāzī (-347/958) und seine Schriften: Untersuchungen zur frühen Damaszener Geschichtsschreibung* (Stuttgart: Kommissionsverlag Franz Steiner, 1991).
'Das *Kitāb al-Ṭabaqāt* des Abū Zurʿa al-Dimašqī (-281 H.): Anmerkungen zu einem unbekannten frühen riǧāl-Werk', *Die Welt des Orients*, 20: 21 (1989/1990), 167–226.
*Die quḍāt Dimašq und der maḏhab al-Awzāʿī: Materialien zur syrischen Rechtsgeschichte* (Beirut: Franz Steiner Verlag Stuttgart, 1994).
Conrad, Lawrence. 'Arabic Plague Chronologies and Treatises: Social and Historical Factors in the Formation of a Literary Genre', *Studia Islamica*, 54 (1981), 51–95.
'Ibn Aʿtham and his History', *al-ʿUṣūr al-Wusṭā*, 23 (2015), 87–125.
'A Ninth-Century Muslim Scholar's Discussion of Contagion', in Lawrence Conrad and Dominik Wujastyk (eds.), *Contagion: Perspectives from Pre-Modern Societies* (Burlington, VT: Ashgate, 2000), 163–77.
'The Plague in the Early Medieval Near East', PhD thesis, Princeton University, 1981.
'ʿUmar at Sargh: The Evolution of an Umayyad Tradition on Flight from the Plague', in Stefan Leder (ed.), *Story-Telling in the Framework of Non-fictional Arabic Literature* (Wiesbaden: Harrassowitz, 1998), 488–528.
Cook, M. *Commanding Right and Forbidding Wrong in Islamic Thought* (Cambridge: Cambridge University Press, 2004).
'Early Muslim Dietary Law', *JSAI*, 7 (1986), 218–77.
*Early Muslim Dogma: A Source-Critical Study* (Cambridge: Cambridge University Press, 1981).
'Ibn Qutayba and the Monkeys', *Studia Islamica*, 89 (1999), 43–74.
'The Opponents of the Writing of Tradition in Early Islam', *Arabica*, 44: 4 (1997), 437–530.
Cooperson, Michael. '"Arabs" and "Iranian": The Uses of Ethnicity in the Early Abbasid Period', in B. Sadeghi, A. Ahmed, A. Silverstein, and R. Hoyland

(eds.), *Islamic Cultures, Islamic Contexts: Essays in Honor of Professor Patricia Crone* (Leiden: Brill, 2015), 364–87.

'Ibn Saʿd', in Michael Cooperson and Shawkat M. Toorawa (eds.), *Arabic Literary Culture, 500–925* (Detroit: Thomson Gale, 2005), 193–204.

Crone, Patricia. 'The Book of Watchers in the Qur'an', in H. Ben-Shammai, S. Shaked, and S. Stroumsa (eds.), *Exchange and Transmission across Cultural Boundaries: Philosophy, Mysticism and Science in the Mediterranean World* (Jerusalem: Israel Academy of Sciences and Humanities, 2013), 16–51.

'Al-Jāḥiẓ on Aṣḥāb al-Jahālāt and the Jahmiyya', in Rotraud Hansberger, M. Afifi al-Akiti, and Charles Burnett (eds.), *Medieval Arabic Thought: Essays in Honour of Fritz Zimmermann* (London: Warburg Institute, 2012), 27–39.

*The Iranian Reception of Islam: The Non-Traditionalist Strands: Collected Studies in Three Volumes*. Volume 2 (Leiden: Brill, 2016).

'Mawālī and the Prophet's Family: An Early Shīʿite View', in Monique Bernards and John Nawas (eds.), *Patronate and Patronage in Early and Classical Islam* (Leiden: Brill, 2005), 167–94.

*Medieval Islamic Political Thought* (Edinburgh: Edinburgh University Press, 2005).

*The Nativist Prophets of Early Islamic Iran: Rural Revolt and Local Zoroastrianism* (Cambridge: Cambridge University Press, 2012).

*Pre-Industrial Societies: Anatomy of the Pre-Modern World* (Oxford: Oneworld, 2003 [1989]).

*Roman, Provincial and Islamic Law: The Origins of the Islamic Patronate* (Cambridge: Cambridge University Press, 1987).

'The Significance of Wooden Weapons in al-Mukhtār's Revolt and the ʿAbbāsid Revolution', in Ian Richard Netton (ed.), *Studies in Honour of Clifford Edmund Bosworth*, volume 1: *Hunter of the East: Arabic and Semitic Studies* (Leiden: Brill, 2000), 174–87.

*Slaves on Horses: The Evolution of the Islamic Polity* (Cambridge: Cambridge University Press, 1980).

Crone, Patricia and M. Hinds. *God's Caliph: Religious Authority in the First Centuries of Islam* (Cambridge: Cambridge University Press, 1986).

Crone, Patricia and F. W. Zimmermann. *The Epistle of Sālim Ibn Dhakwān* (Oxford: Oxford University Press, 2001).

Curiel, Raoul and Philippe Gignoux. 'Un poids arabo-sasanide', *Studia Iranica*, 5: 2 (1976), 165–9.

Dabashi, H. *Authority in Islam: From the Rise of Muhammad to the Establishment of the Umayyads* (New Brunswick: Transaction Publishers, 1989).

Dahhan, Sami. 'The Origins and Development of the Local Histories of Syria', in B. Lewis and P. M. Holt (eds.), *Historians of the Middle East* (London: Oxford University Press, 1962), 108–17.

Dānishpazūh, Muḥammad Taqī. 'Dū risāla dar bāra-yi ihdā'ī-yi haftād u dū gurūh', *Nashriyya-yi Dānishgada-yi Adabiyyāt-i Tabrīz*, 18 (1966), 247–59.

Dann, Michael. 'Contested Boundaries: The Reception of Shi'ite Narrators in the Sunni Hadith Tradition', PhD thesis, Princeton University, 2015.

Darnton, Richard. 'Intellectual and Cultural History', in M. Kammen (ed.), *The Past before Us: Contemporary Historical Writing in the United States* (Ithaca: Cornell University Press, 1980), 327–54.

de Certeau, Michael. *The Writing of History*, trans. Tom Conley (New York: Columbia University Press, 1998).

de Gaffier, Baudouin. 'L'Hagiographe et son public au XI siècle', in *Miscellanea historica in honorem Leonis van der Essen* (Paris: Éditions universitaires, 1947), 135–66.

Delahaye, Hipplolyte. *The Work of the Bollandists through Three Centuries, 1615–1915* (Princeton: Princeton University Press, 1922).

de Menasce, Jean. 'Une légende indo-iranienne dans l'angélogie judéo-musulmane: à propos de Hārut et Mārut', *Études Asiatiques*, 1 (1947), 10–18.

de Wet, Chris L. *Preaching Bondage: John Chrysostom and the Discourse of Slavery in Early Christianity* (Oakland: University of California Press, 2015).

Dickinson, Eerik. 'Aḥmad b. al-Ṣalt and his Biography of Abū Ḥanīfa', *JAOS*, 116: 3 (1996), 406–17.

*The Development of Early Sunnite Ḥadīth Criticism: The* Taqdima *of Ibn Abī Ḥātim al-Rāzī (240/854–327/938)* (Leiden: Brill, 2001).

Dixon, ʿAbd al-Ameer. *The Umayyad Caliphate, 65–86/684–705: A Political Study* (London: Luzac, 1971).

Djaït, Hichem. *Al-Kūfa. Naissance de la ville islamique* (Paris: G. P. Maisonneuve et Larose, 1986).

Dols, Michael. *The Black Death in the Middle East* (Princeton: Princeton University Press, 1977).

*Majnūn: The Madman in Medieval Islamic Society*, ed. Diana E. Immisch (Oxford: Clarendon Press, 1992).

Donner, Fred M. *The Early Islamic Conquests* (Princeton: Princeton University Press, 1981).

Douglas, Mary. *Mary Douglas: A Very Personal Method: Anthropological Writings Drawn from Life*, ed. Richard Fardon (London: Sage, 2013).

Doyle, Arthur Conan. *Sherlock Holmes: The Complete Illustrated Short Stories* (London: Chancellor Press, 1985).

Drechsler, Andreas. *Die Geschichte der Stadt Qom im Mittelalter (650–1350): Politische und wirtschaftliche Aspekte* (Berlin: Klaus Schwartz, 1999).

Durkheim, Émile. *The Elementary Forms of Religious Life*, trans. Karen E. Fields (New York: Free Press/Simon & Schuster, 1995).

*Moral Education: A Study in the Theory and Application of the Sociology of Education*, trans. E. K. Wilson and H. Schnurer (New York: Free Press of Glencoe/Crowell-Collier, 1961).

Eichler, P. *Die Dschinn, Teufel und Engel im Koran* (Leipzig: Klein, 1928).

'Debates on Prayer in Second/Eighth-Century Islam: Some Remarks on Sijpesteijn's Papyrus', *JNES*, 75: 2 (2016), 335–7.

'From Tradition to Law: The Origins and Early Development of the Shāfiʿī School of Law in Ninth-Century Egypt', PhD thesis, Harvard University, 2009.

'Al-Shāfiʿī's Written Corpus: A Source-Critical Study', *JAOS*, 132 (2012), 199–220.

Elad, Amikam. 'The Ethnic Composition of the Abbasid Revolution: A Reevaluation of Some Recent Research', *JSAI*, 24 (2000), 246–326.

'Mawālī in the Composition of al-Ma'mūn's Army: A Non-Arab Takeover?', in Monique Bernards and John Nawas (eds.), *Patronate and Patronage in Early and Classical Islam* (Leiden: Brill, 2005), 278–325.

*Medieval Jerusalem and Islamic Worship: Holy Places, Ceremonies, Pilgrimage* (Leiden: Brill, 1995).

*The Rebellion of Muhammad al-Nafs al-Zakiyya in 145/762: Ṭālibīs and Early ʿAbbāsīs in Conflict* (Leiden: Brill, 2016).

El-Hibri, Tayeb. *Parable and Politics in Early Islamic History* (New York: Columbia University Press, 2010).

Eliade, Mircea. *The Sacred and the Profane: The Nature of Religion. The Significance of Religious Myth, Symbolism, and Ritual within Life and Culture*, trans. Willard R. Trask (New York: Harcourt, Brace & World, Inc., 1959).

El Omari, Racha. '*Kitāb al-Ḥayda*: The Historical Significance of an Apocryphal Text', in Felicitas Opwis and David Reisman (eds.), *Islamic Philosophy, Science, Culture, and Religion* (Leiden: Brill, 2012), 419–52.

El Shamsy, Ahmed. *The Canonization of Islamic Law: A Social and Intellectual History* (Cambridge: Cambridge University Press, 2013).

Enderwitz, Suzanne. *Gesselschaftlicher Rang und ethnische Legitimation: Der arabische Schriftseller Abū ʿUthmān al-Ǧāḥiẓ (gest. 868) über die Afrikaner, Perser, und Araber in der islamischen Gesellschaft* (Freiburg: Klaus Schwartz, 1979).

Felski, Rita. *The Limits of Critique* (Chicago: University of Chicago Press, 2015).

Fentress, James J. and C. Wickham. *Social Memory: New Perspectives on the Past* (Oxford: Blackwell, 1992).

Fierro, Maribel. *ʿAbd al-Rahman III: The First Cordoban Caliph* (Oxford: Oneworld, 2005).

'Accusations of Zandaqa in al-Andalus', *Quaderni di Studi Arabi*, 5–6 (1987–8), 251–8.

'Heresy in al-Andalus', in Salma Khadra Jayyusi (ed.), *The Legacy of Muslim Spain* (Leiden: Brill, 1992), 2: 895–908.

*La heterodoxia en al-Andalus durante el periodo omeya* (Madrid: Instituto Hispano-Árabe de Cultura, 1987).

'Religious Dissension in al-Andalus: Ways of Exclusion and Inclusion', *al-Qanṭara*, 22: 2 (2001), 463–87.

'Why and How Do Religious Scholars Write about Themselves? The Case of the Islamic West in the Fourth/Tenth Century', *Mélanges de l'Université Saint-Joseph*, 58 (2005), 403–23.

Fishbein, Michael. 'The Life of al-Mukhtār b. Abī ʿUbayd in Some Early Arabic Historians', PhD thesis, University of California, Los Angeles, 1988.

Flügel, Gustav. 'Die Classen der hanefitischen Rechtsgelehrten', in *Abhandlungen der philologisch-historischen Classe der Königlich Sächsischen Gesellschaft der Wissenschaften* (Leipzig: n.p., 1861), 267–358.

Forsyth, Neil. *The Old Enemy: Satan and the Combat Myth* (Princeton: Princeton University Press, 1987).

Foucault, M. *The Archaeology of Knowledge* (Oxford and New York: Routledge, 2002).
*Essential Works of Foucault, 1954–1984, Volume 1: Ethics, Subjectivity of Truth* (New York: New Press, 1997).
*Essential Works of Foucault, 1954–1984, Volume 2: Aesthetics, Method, and Epistemology* (New York: New Press, 1998).
Friedman, Yaron. '"Kufa Is Better": The Sanctity of Kufa in Early Islam and Shīʿism in Particular', *Le Muséon*, 126 (2013), 203–37.
Frye, Richard. 'City Chronicles of Central Asia and Khurasan: *Ta'rix-i Nīsāpūr*', in *Zeki Velidi Togan'a Armağan. Symbolae in Honorem Z. V. Togan* (Istanbul: Maarif Basimevi, 1950–5), 405–20; repr. in Richard N. Frye, *Islamic Iran and Central Asia* (London: Variorum Reprints, 1979), 405–20.
Fück, J. W. 'Die Rolle des Traditionalismus im Islam', *ZDMG*, 90 (1939), 1–32.
Furkani, Mehterhan. 'Taḥqīq al-Ibāna fī al-radd ʿalā al-mushanniʿīn ʿalā Abī Ḥanīfa', *Islam Arastirmalari Dergisi*, 43 (2019), 73–81
Geiger, Abraham. *Judaism and Islam: A Prize Essay* (Madras: MDCSPCK Press, 1898).
Gernet, Louis. *Le génie grec dans la religion* (Paris: Éditions Albin Michel, 1970).
Gibb, H. A. R. 'Islamic Biographical Literature', in B. Lewis and P. M. Holt (eds.), *Historians of the Middle East* (London: Oxford University Press, 1962), 54–8.
'The Social Significance of the Shuubiya', in *Studies on the Civilization of Islam* (Boston: Beacon Press, 1962), 62–73.
Gignoux, Philippe. 'Pour une origine iranienne du bi'smillah', in Philippe Gignoux (ed.), *Pad nām i Yazdān. Études d'épigraphie, de numismatique et d'histoire de l'Iran ancient* (Paris: Klincksieck, 1979), 159–63.
Gillet, Andrew. 'Ethnogenesis: A Contested Model of Early Medieval Europe', *History Compass*, 4: 2 (2006), 241–60.
Gilliot, C. 'Muqātil, grand exégète, traditionniste et théologien maudit', *Journal Asiatique*, 279 (1991), 39–92.
Gimaret, D. *Une lecture muʿtazilite du Coran. Le* Tafsīr *d'Abū ʿAlī al-Djubbāʾī (m. 303/915) partiellement reconstitué à partir de ses citateurs* (Louvain and Paris: Peeters, 1994).
Ginzberg, L. *Legends of the Jews* (Philadelphia: Jewish Publication Society, 2003).
Ginzburg, Carlo. 'The Inquisitor as Anthropologist', in *Clues, Myths and the Historical Method* (Baltimore: Johns Hopkins University Press, 1989), 156–74.
'Microhistory: Two or Three Things That I Know About', *Critical Inquiry*, 20: 1 (1993), 10–35.
Givony, Joseph. 'The Murji'a and the Theological School of Abū Ḥanīfa: A Historical and Ideological Study', PhD thesis, University of Edinburgh, 1977.
Glassen, E. *Der mittlere Weg: Studien zur Religionspolitik und Religiosität der späteren Abbasiden-Zeit* (Weisbaden: Steiner, 1981).
Goitein, S. D. 'A Turning Point in the History of the Islamic State', in *Studies in Islamic History and Institutions*, volume 5 (Leiden: Brill, 2010), 149–67.

Goldziher, Ignaz. *Abhandlungen zur arabischen Philologie* (Leiden: Brill, 1896).
'Die Ginnen der Dichter', *ZDMG*, 45 (1891), 685–90.
*Muslim Studies*, ed. S. M. Stern, trans. C. R Barber and S. M. Stern (London: Allen & Unwin, 1967).
*Vorlesungen uber den Islam*, 2nd edn. (Heidelberg: Carl Winter, 1925); trans. Andras and Ruth Hamori as *Introduction to Islamic Theology and Law* (Princeton: Princeton University Press, 1981).
*Die Ẓāhiriten: Ihr Lehrsystem und ihre Geschichte. Beitrag zur Geschichte der muhammedanischen Theologie* (Leipzig: Otto Schulze, 1884); trans. W. Behn as *The Ẓāhirīs: Their Doctrine and their History. A Contribution to the History of Islamic Theology* (Leiden: Brill, 1971).
Goody, Jack. *The Domestication of the Savage Mind* (Cambridge: Cambridge University Press, 1977).
Goody, Jack and Ian Watt. 'The Consequences of Literacy', *Comparative Studies in Society and History*, 5: 3 (1963), 304–45.
Gordon, Matthew S. 'The Khāqānid Families of the Early ʿAbbāsid Period', *JAOS*, 121: 2 (2001), 236–55.
Görke, A. and G. Schoeler. 'Reconstructing the Earliest *Sīra* Texts: The Hiğra in the Corpus of ʿUrwa b. al-Zubayr', *Der Islam*, 82 (2005), 209–20.
Graham, William A. 'Traditionalism in Islam: An Essay in Interpretation', *Journal of Interdisciplinary History*, 23: 3 (1993), 495–522.
Günther, Sebastian. *Quellenuntersuchungen zu den 'Maqātil aṭ-Ṭālibiyyīn' des Abū 'l-Farağ al-Iṣfahānī (gest. 356/967)* (Hildesheim: Georg Olms, 1991).
Guzman, M. 'Ethnic Groups and Social Classes in Muslim Spain', *Islamic Studies*, 30: 1/2 (1991), 37–66.
Haas, V. *Magie und Mythen in Babylonien: Von Dämonen, Hexen und Beschwörungspriestern* (Gifkendorf: Merlin, 1986).
Ḥabībī, ʿAbd al-Ḥayy. 'Yek kitāb gum shud qadīm nathr-i fārsī paydā shud: tarjumeh-yi fārsī al-sawād al-aʿẓam va rafʿ-i ishtibāhāt-i wārideh dar bāreh-yi īn kitāb', *Yaghmā*, 181 (1923), 193–200.
Al-Ḥāfiẓ, Muḥammad Muṭīʿ and ʿAbd al-Raḥmān Farfūr. *Al-Muntaqā min makhṭūṭāt maʿhad al-Bīrūnī li al-dirāsāt al-sharqiyya bi Ṭasqand* (Dubai: Markaz Jumʿat al-Mājid li al-Thaqāfa wa al-Turāth, 1995).
Hafsi, Ibrahim. 'Recherches sur le genre Tabaqat dans la littérature arabe', *Arabica*, 23 (1976), 227–65 and *Arabica*, 24 (1977), 1–41, 150–86.
Haider, Najam. *The Origins of the Shīʿa: Identity, Ritual, and Scared Space in Eighth-Century Kūfa* (Cambridge: Cambridge University Press, 2011).
Halbwachs, Maurice. *On Collective Memory*, ed. and trans. Lewis Coser (Chicago: University of Chicago Press, 1993 [1952]).
*La topographie légendaire des évangiles en terre sainte. Étude de mémoire collective* (Paris: Presses Universitaires de France, 1971).
Hallaq, Wael. *The Impossible State: Islam, Politics, and Modernity's Moral Predicament* (New York: Columbia University Press, 2012).
*The Origins and Evolution of Islamic Law* (Cambridge: Cambridge University Press, 2004).
'Was al-Shāfiʿī the Master Architect of Islamic Jurisprudence?', *IJMES*, 25: 4 (1993), 587–605.

Halm, Heinz. *Die Ausbreitung der šāfiʿitischen Rechtsschule von den Anfängen bis zum 8./14. Jahrhundert* (Wiesbaden: L. Reichert, 1972).

Ḥamdān, ʿĀdil. *Silsilat taʿlīqātī ʿalā taḥqīqāt kutub al-sunna: Kitāb al-Sunna* (n.p.: Dār al-Naṣīḥa, n.d.).

Hanne, E. *Putting the Caliph in His Place: Power, Authority, and the Late Abbasid Caliphate* (Madison, NJ: Farleigh Dickinson University Press, 2007).

Hartog, François. *The Mirror of Herodotus: The Representation of the Other in the Writing of History*, trans. Janet Lloyd (Berkeley and Los Angeles: University of California Press, 1988).

Hāshimī, Saʿdī. *Abū Zurʿa al-Rāzī wa juhūduhu fī al-sunna al-nabawiyya maʿa taḥqīq kitābihi al-Ḍuʿafāʾ wa ajwibatihi ʿalā asʾilat al-Bardhaʿī* (Medina: al-Maktaba al-ʿArabiyya al-Suʿūdiyya al-Jāmiʿa al-Islāmiyya, n.d.).

*Nuṣūṣ ṣāqiṭa min ṭabaʿāt asmāʾ al-thiqāt li Ibn Shāhīn* (Medina: Maktabat al-Dār, 1987).

Hassan, Zaki Mohamed. *Les Tulunides* (Paris: Établissements Busson, 1933).

Hatoum, Afaf. 'An Eleventh Century Karrāmī Text: Abū Ḥafṣ al-Nīsābūrī's "Raunaq al-Majālis"', PhD thesis, Columbia University, 1991.

Hawting, Gerald. 'The Case of Jaʿd b. Dirham and the Punishment of Heretics in the Early Caliphate', in Christian Lange and Maribel Fierro (eds.), *Public Violence in Islamic Societies* (Edinburgh: Edinburgh University Press, 2009), 27–41.

Hayes, Edmund. *Agents of the Hidden Imam: Forging Twelver Shiʿism, 850–950 CE* (Cambridge: Cambridge University Press, 2022).

Heffernan, Thomas J. *Sacred Biography: Saints and their Biographers in the Middle Ages* (Oxford: Oxford University Press, 1988).

Henderson, John B. *The Construction of Orthodoxy and Heresy: Neo-Confucian, Islamic, Jewish, and Early Christian Patterns* (Albany: State University of New York Press, 1998).

Al-Ḥibshī, ʿAbd Allāh Muḥammad. *Jāmiʿ al-shurūḥ wa al-ḥawāshī: muʿjam shāmil li al-asmāʾ al-kutub al-mashrūḥa fī al-turāth al-Islāmī wa bayān shurūḥihā* (Abu Dhabi: al-Majmaʿ al-Thaqāfī, 2004).

Hinds, Martin. 'Kufan Political Alignments and Their Background in the Mid-Seventh Century AD', *IJMES*, 2 (1971), 346–67.

Hobsbawm, Eric. 'Comment', *Review*, 1 (1978), 162.

Hodge, Caroline Johnson. *If Sons, Then Heirs: A Study of Kinship and Ethnicity in the Letters of Paul* (Oxford: Oxford University Press, 2007).

Hodgson, Marshall G. S. *The Venture of Islam: Conscience and History in a World Civilization* (Chicago: University of Chicago Press, 1961).

Horri, Satoe. *Die gesetzlichen Umgehungen im islamischen Recht (Ḥiyal): Unter besonderer Berücksichtigung der Ǧannat al-aḥkām wa-ǧunnat al-ḥuṣṣām des Ḥanafīten Saʿīd b. ʿAlī as-Samarqandī (gest. 12. Jhdt.)* (Berlin: Klaus Schwarz, 2001).

'Reconsideration of Legal Devices (Ḥiyal) in Islamic Jurisprudence: The Ḥanafīs and their "Exits" (Makhārij)', *ILS*, 9: 3 (2002), 312–57.

Hoyland, Robert. *Arabia and the Arabs: From the Bronze Age to the Coming of Islam* (London: Routledge, 2001).

*In God's Path: The Arab Conquests and the Creation of an Islamic Empire* (Oxford: Oxford University Press, 2015).

Hurvitz, Nimrod. *The Formation of Hanbalism: Piety into Power* (London: RoutledgeCurzon, 2002).

'Miḥna as Self-Defense', *Studia Islamica*, 92 (2001), 93–111.

Husaini, Ishaq Musa. *The Life and Works of Ibn Qutayba* (Beirut: Beirut Academic Press, 1950).

Hutton, Patrick. 'The History of Mentalities: The New Map of Cultural History', *History and Theory*, 20 (1981), 413–23.

Jacques, K. *Authority, Conflict, and the Transmission of Diversity in Medieval Islamic Law* (Leiden: Brill, 2006).

'The Contestation and Resolution of Inter and Intra-School Conflicts through Biography', in Zulfikar Hirji (ed.), *Diversity and Pluralism in Islam: Historical and Contemporary Discourses amongst Muslims* (London: I. B. Tauris, 2010), 107–33.

János, J. 'The Four Sources of Law in Zoroastrian and Islamic Jurisprudence', *ILS*, 12: 3 (2005), 291–332.

Jarrar, Maher. *Doctrinal Instruction in Early Islam: The Book of the Explanation of the Sunna by Ghulām Khalīl (d. 275/888)* (Leiden: Brill, 2020).

Jaspers, Karl. *The Origin and Goal of History* (New Haven: Yale University Press, 1953).

Johansen, Baber. 'Casuistry: Between Legal Concept and Social Praxis', *ILS*, 2 (1995), 135–56.

Johnson, Aaron P. *Ethnicity and Argument in Eusebius'* Praeparatio Evangelica (Oxford: Oxford University Press, 2005).

Jokisch, B. *Islamic Imperial Law: Hārūn al-Rashīd's Codification Project* (Berlin: Walter de Gruyter, 2007).

Jones, A. H. M. *The Later Roman Empire 284–602: A Social, Economic, and Administrative Survey* (Oxford: Oxford University Press, 1964).

Judd, Steven C. 'Competitive Hagiography in Biographies of al-Awzāʿī and Sufyān al-Thawrī', *JAOS*, 122: 1 (2002), 25–37.

*Religious Scholars and the Umayyads: Piety-Minded Supporters of the Marwānid Caliphate* (London: Routledge, 2014).

'The Third Fitna: Orthodoxy, Heresy, and Coercion in Late Umayyad History', PhD thesis, University of Michigan, 1997.

Jung, Leo. *Fallen Angels in Jewish, Christian, and Mohammedan Literature* (Eugene, OR: Wipf & Stock, 2007 [1926]).

Juynboll, G. H. A. *Encyclopedia of Canonical Ḥadīth* (Leiden: Brill, 2007).

'An Excursus on the Ahl as-Sunna in Connection with Van Ess, *Theologie und Gesellschaft*, Vol. IV', *Der Islam*, 75 (1998), 318–30.

*Muslim Tradition: Studies in Chronology, Provenance and Authorship of Early Ḥadīth* (Cambridge: Cambridge University Press, 1983).

'Nāfiʿ, the Mawlā of Ibn ʿUmar, and His Position in Muslim Ḥadīth Literature', *Der Islam*, 70 (1993), 207–44.

'Some New Ideas on the Development of Sunna as a Technical Term in Early Islam', *JSAI*, 10 (1987), 97–118.

Kaabi, M. 'Les origines ṭāhirides dans la daʿwa ʿabbaside', *Arabica*, 19: 2 (1972), 145–64.

Kaḥḥāla, ʿUmar Riḍā. *Muʿjam al-mu'allifīn* (Beirut: Dār Iḥyā' al-Turāth al-ʿArabī, n.d.) = (Beirut: Makabat al-Muthannā, 1957) = (Beirut: Mu'assasat al-Risāla, 1993).

Karabela, Mehmet Kadri. 'The Development of Dialectic and Argumentation Theory in Post-Classical Islamic Intellectual History', PhD thesis, McGill University, 2010.

Karev, Yuri. *Samarqand et le Sughd à l'époque ʿabbāsside. Histoire politique et sociale* (Paris: Studia Iranica, 2015).

Katz, M. *Prayer in Islamic Thought and Practice* (Cambridge: Cambridge University Press, 2013).

'The Study of Islamic Ritual and the Meaning of Wuḍū'', *Der Islam*, 82: 1 (2005), 106–45.

Kennedy, Hugh. *The Armies of the Caliphs: Military and Society in the Early Islamic State* (Oxford and New York: Routledge, 2001).

*The Early Abbasid Caliphate: A Political History* (London: Croom Helm, 1986).

'Military Pay and the Economy of the Early Islamic State', *Historical Research*, 75: 188 (2002), 155–69.

*The Prophet and the Age of the Caliphates* (Harlow: Pearson Longman, 2004).

Khalek, Nancy. *Damascus after the Muslim Conquest: Text and Image in Early Islam* (Oxford: Oxford University Press, 2011).

Khalidi, Tarif. *Arabic Historical Thought in the Classical Period* (Cambridge: Cambridge University Press, 1994).

Khan, Ahmad. 'Before Shurūḥ: Reading Ḥadīth Works in Khurāsān, Ninth–Tenth Centuries', forthcoming.

'An Empire of Élites: Mobility in the Early Islamic Empire', in Hannah Lena-Hagemann and Stefan Heidemann (eds.), *Transregional and Regional Elites: Connecting the Early Islamic Empire* (Berlin: De Gruyter, 2020), 147–169.

'Ḥadīth Commentary and Philology in the Tenth-Century', forthcoming.

'Islamic Tradition in an Age of Print: Editing, Printing and Publishing the Classical Heritage', in Elisabeth Kendall and Ahmad Khan (eds.), *Reclaiming Islamic Tradition: Modern Interpretations of the Classical Heritage* (Edinburgh: Edinburgh University Press, 2016), 52–100.

Khan, Geoffrey. *Arabic Documents from Early Islamic Khurasan* (London: Nour Foundation, 2007).

'The Historical Development of the Structure of Medieval Arabic Petitions', *BSOAS*, 53: 1 (1990), 8–11.

Kilpatrick, Hilary. *Making the Great Book of Songs: Compilation and the Author's Craft in Abū l-Faraj al-Iṣbahānī's* Kitāb al-Aghānī (London: Routledge Curzon, 2003).

Kinberg, Leah. 'Interaction between This World and the Afterworld in Early Islamic Tradition', *Oriens*, 29: 30 (1986), 285–308.

Kirschner, Robert. 'The Vocation of Holiness in Late Antiquity', *Vigiliae Christianae*, 38 (1984), 105–24.

Kister, M. J. 'A Comment on the Antiquity of Traditions Praising Jerusalem', *Jerusalem Cathedra*, 1 (1981), 185–6.

'Ḥaddithū ʿan Banī Isrā'īla wa-lā Haraja: A Study of an Early Tradition', *Israel Oriental Studies*, 2 (1972), 215–39.

. . . Lā taqra'ū l-qur'āna ʿalā l-muṣḥafiyyīn wa-lā taḥmilū l-ʿilma ʿani l-ṣaḥafiyyīn . . .: Some Notes on the Transmission of Ḥadīth', *JSAI*, 22 (1998), 127–62.

'Sanctity Joint and Divided: On Holy Places in the Islamic Tradition', *JSAI*, 20 (1996), 18–65.

Knysh, Alexander. 'Orthodoxy and Heresy in Medieval Islam: An Essay in Reassessment', *Muslim World*, 83 (1993), 48–67.

Koselleck, Reinhart. *The Practice of Conceptual History: Timing History, Spacing Concepts*, trans. Todd Samuel Presner et al. (Stanford: Stanford University Press, 2002).

Kreiner, Jamie. *The Social Life of Hagiography in the Merovingian Kingdom* (Cambridge: Cambridge University Press, 2014).

Krueger, Derek. *Writing and Holiness: The Practice of Authorship in the Early Christian East* (Philadelphia: University of Pennsylvania Press, 2004).

Kvanvig, Helge S. *Primeval History: Babylonian, Biblical, and Enochic: An Intertextual Reading* (Leiden: Brill, 2011).

*Roots of Apocalyptic: The Mesopotamian Background of the Enoch Figure and of the Son of Man* (Neukirchen: Neurkirchener Verlag, 1988).

Ladurie, Emmanuel Le Roy. *Montaillou: Cathars and Catholics in a French Village, 1294–1324* (London: Penguin, 1980).

Lambton, Ann K. S. 'An Account of the Tārīkhi Qumm', *BSOAS*, 12: 3/4 (1948), 586–96.

'Persian Local Histories: The Tradition behind Them and the Assumptions of their Authors', in Biancamaria Scarcia Amoretti and Lucia Rostagano (eds.), *Yād-Nāma in Memoria Di Allesandro Bausani* (Rome: Bardi, 1991), 227–38.

*State and Government in Medieval Islam: An Introduction to the Study of Islamic Political Theory: The Jurists* (Oxford: Oxford University Press, 1981).

Lane, Edward William. *An Arabic–English Lexicon*, ed. Stanley Lane Poole (Lahore: Suhail Academy, 2003).

Lange, Christian. *Justice, Punishment and the Medieval Muslim Imagination* (Cambridge: Cambridge University Press, 2008).

Langer, Ruth. *Cursing the Christians? A History of the Birkat HaMinim* (Oxford: Oxford University Press, 2012).

Laoust, Henri. *Le Hanbalisme sous les califat de Bagdad (241/855–656/1258)* (Paris: P. Geuthner, 1959).

*La profession de foi d'Ibn Baṭṭa* (Damascus: Institut français de Damas, 1958).

*Les schismes dans l'Islam. Introduction à une étude de la religion musulmane* (Paris: Payot, 1965).

Lapidus, Ira. M. 'The Separation of State and Religion in the Development of Early Islamic Society', *IJMES*, 6: 4 (1975), 363–85.

Laporte, Dominique. *History of Shit*, trans. Nadia Benabid and Rudolphe el-Khoury (Cambridge, MA: MIT Press, 2000).

Le Boulluec, Alain. *La notion d'hérésie dans la littérature grecque IIe-IIIe siècles* (Paris: Etudes Augustiniennes, 1985–6).

Lecomte, G. *Ibn Qutayba (m. 276/889), l'homme, son oeuvre, ses idées* (Damascus: Institut français de Damas, 1965).

Lefebvre, Henri. *Introduction to Modernity* (London: Verso, 1995).

Le Goff, J. 'Mentalities: A New Field for the Historian', *International Social Science Council Information*, 13 (1974), 64–86.

Lepore, Jill. 'Historians Who Love Too Much: Reflections on Microhistory and Biography', *Journal of American History*, 88: 1 (2001), 129–44.

Lewinstein, Keith. 'The Azāriqa in Islamic Heresiography', *BSOAS*, 54: 2 (1991), 251–681.

'Making and Unmaking a Sect: The Heresiographers and the Ṣufriyya', *Studia Islamica*, 76 (1992), 75–96.

'Notes on Eastern Ḥanafite Heresiography', *JAOS*, 114 (1994), 583–98.

Lewis, Bernard. 'Some Observations on the Significance of Heresy in the History of Islam', *Studia Islamica*, 1 (1953), 43–63.

Lieu, Judith M. *Christian Identity in the Jewish and Graeco-Roman World* (Oxford: Oxford University Press, 2004).

Lifshitz, F. 'Beyond Positivism and Genre: "Hagiographical" Texts as Historical Narrative', *Viator*, 25 (1994), 95–113.

Lindstedt, Ilkka. 'al-Madā'inī's *Kitāb al-Dawla* and the Death of Ibrāhīm al-Imām', in I. Lindstedt et al. (eds.), *Case Studies in Transmission* (Münster: Ugarit-Verlag, 2014), 118–23.

'Sources for the Biography of the Historian Ibn Aʿtham al-Kūfī', in Jakko Hämeen-Anttila, Petteri Koskikallio, and Ilkka Lindstedt (eds.), *Proceedings of Union Européenne des Arabisants et Islamisants 27, Helsinki, June 2nd–6th 2014* (Leuven: Peeters, 2017), 299–309.

Littman, A. *A List of Arabic Manuscripts in Princeton University Library* (Princeton: Otto Harrassowitz, 1904).

Littmann, Enno. 'Ḥārut and Mārut', in *Festschrift Friedrich Carl Andreas: Zur Vollendung des siebzigsten Lebensjahres am 14. April 1916 dargebracht von Freunden und Schülern* (Leipzig: Otto Harrassowitz, 1916), 70–87.

Livne-Kafri, O. 'The Early Shīʿa and Jerusalem', *Arabica*, 48 (2001), 112–20.

Loth, Otto. *Das Classebuch des Ibn Saʿd: Einleitende Untersuchungen über Authentie und Inhalt nach den Handschriftlichen überresten* (Leipzig: Druck von G. Kreysing, 1869).

'Die Ursprung und Bedeutung der Tabaqat', *ZDMG*, 23 (1869), 593–614.

Lowry, Joseph E. 'Does Shāfiʿī Have a Theory of "Four Sources" of Law?', in Bernard G. Weiss (ed.), *Studies in Islamic Legal Theory* (Leiden: Brill, 2002), 23–50.

*Early Islamic Legal Theory: The* Risāla *of Muḥammad ibn Idrīs al-Shāfiʿī* (Leiden: Brill, 2007).

'The First Islamic Legal Theory: Ibn al-Muqaffaʿ on Interpretation, Authority, and the Structure of the Law', *JAOS*, 128: 1 (2008), 25–40.

'The Legal Hermeneutics of al-Shāfiʿī and Ibn Qutayba: A Reconsideration', *ILS*, 11 (2004), 1–41.

Lucas, Scott C. *Constructive Critics, Hadith Literature, and the Articulation of Sunni Islam: The Legacy of the Generation of Ibn Saʿd, Ibn Maʿin, and Ibn Hanbal* (Leiden: Brill, 2004).

'The Legal Principles of Muḥammad b. Ismāʿīl al-Bukhārī and Their Relationship to Classical Salafi Islam', *ILS*, 13: 3 (2006), 289–324.

'Where Are the Legal Ḥadīth? A Study of the *Muṣannaf* of Ibn Abī Shayba', *ILS*, 15 (2008), 283–314.

MacCormack, Sabine. 'Loca Sancta: The Organisation of Sacred Topography in Late Antiquity', in Robert Ousterhout (ed.), *The Blessings of Pilgrimage* (Urbana: University of Illinois Press, 1990), 7–40.

Macintyre, Alasdair. *After Virtue: A Study in Moral Theory*, 3rd edn. (London: Bloomsbury, 2007).

Macuch, M. 'Die sasanidische fromme Stiftung und der islamische waqf: Eine Gegenuberstellung', in A. Meier, J. Pahlitzsch, and L. Reinfandt (eds.), *Islamische Stiftungen zwischen juristischer Norm und sozialer Praxis* (Berlin: Akademie Verlag, 2009), 19–38.

'Die sasanidische Stiftung "für die Seele": Vorbild für den islamischen waqf?', in P. Vavroušek (ed.), *Iranian and Indo-European Studies: Memorial Volume of Otakar Klíma* (Prague: Enigma, 1994), 163–80.

Madelung, Wilferd. 'Apocalyptic Prophecies in Ḥimṣ in the Umayyad Age', *Journal of Semitic Studies*, 31 (1986), 141–85.

'The Early Murji'a in Khurāsān and Transoxania and the Spread of Ḥanafism', *Der Islam*, 59 (1982), 32–9.

'Early Sunnī Doctrine concerning Faith as Reflected in the Kitāb al-Īmān of Abū ʿUbayd al-Qāsim b. Sallām (d. 244/839)', *Studia Islamica*, 32 (1970), 233–54.

*Der Imam al-Qāsim ibn Ibrāhīm und die Glaubenslehre der Zaiditen* (Berlin: Walter de Gruyter, 1965).

'The Origins of the Controversy concerning the Creation of the Koran', in J. M. Barral (ed.), *Orientalia Hispanica: sive studia F. M. Pareja octogenario dicata* (Leiden: Brill, 1974), 504–25.

*Religious Trends in Early Islamic Iran* (Albany: State University of New York Press, 1988).

'The Spread of Māturīdism and the Turks', in *Actas, IV Congresso de Estudos Arabes e Islâmicos, Coimbra-Lisboa, 1 a 8 de setembro de 1968* (Leiden: Brill, 1971), 109–68.

'The Westward Migration of Ḥanafī Scholars from Central Asia in the 11th to 13th Centuries', *Ankara Üniversitesi Ilâjouat Falültesi Dergisi*, 43: 2 (2002), 41–55.

Maghen, Ze'ev. 'Close Encounters: Some Preliminary Observations on the Transmission of Impurity in Early Sunnī Jurisprudence', *ILS*, 6: 3 (1999), 348–92.

'First Blood: Purity, Edibility and the Independence of Islamic Jurisprudence', *Der Islam*, 81 (2004), 49–95.

Maier, H. O. 'The Topography of Heresy and Dissent in Late Fourth Century Rome', *Historia*, 44 (1995), 232–49.

Makdisi, G. 'Ashʿarī and the Ashʿarites in Islamic Religious History I', *Studia Islamica*, 17 (1962), 37–80.

*Ibn ʿAqīl: Religion and Culture in Classical Islam* (Edinburgh: Edinburgh University Press, 1997).

*Ibn ʿAqīl et la résurgence de l'Islam traditionaliste au XIe siècle (Ve siècle de l'Hégire)* (Damascus: Institut français de Damas, 1963).

'Ibn Taimīya's Autograph Manuscript on Istiḥsān: Materials for the Study of Islamic Legal Thought', in G. Makdisi (ed.), *Arabic and Islamic Studies in Honor of Hamilton A. R. Gibb* (Leiden: Brill, 1965), 446–79.

'Remarks on Traditionalism in Islamic Religious History', in Carl Leiden (ed.), *The Conflict of Traditionalism and Modernism in the Muslim Middle East* (Austin: University of Texas Press, 1966), 77–87.

'The Significance of the Sunni Schools of Law in Islamic Religious History', *IJMES*, 10: 1 (1979), 1–8.

'The Sunni Revival', in D. S. Richards (ed.), *Islamic Civilisation 950–1150* (Oxford: B. Cassirer, 1973), 155–68.

'Ṭabaqāt-Biography: Law and Orthodoxy in Classical Islam', *Islamic Studies* (Islamabad), 32 (1993), 371–96.

Makdisi, J. 'Legal Logic and Equity in Islamic Law', *American Journal of Comparative Law*, 33 (1985), 63–92.

'A Reality Check on Istihsan as a Method of Islamic Legal Reasoning', *UCLA Journal of Islamic and Near Eastern Law*, 99 (2003), 99–127.

Mannheim, Karl. *Ideology and Utopia: An Introduction to the Sociology of Knowledge* (London: Routledge & Kegan Paul, 1960).

Mansour, Mansour. 'The Spread and the Domination of the Maliki School of Law in North and West Africa, Eighth–Fourteenth Century', PhD thesis, University of Illinois at Chicago Circle, 1981.

Markus, R. A. 'How on Earth Could Places Become Holy? Origins of the Christian Idea of Holy Places', *Journal of Early Christian Studies*, 2 (1994), 257–71.

Marsham, Andrew. 'Public Execution in the Umayyad Period: Early Islamic Punitive Practice and Its Late Antique Context', *Journal of Arabic and Islamic Studies*, 11 (2011), 101–36.

Massignon, L. *Essai sur les origines du lexique technique de la mystique musulmane*, 2nd edn. (Paris: J. Vrin, 1954).

*The Passion of al-Hallaj*, trans. Herbert Mason (Princeton: Princeton University Press, 1982).

McCants, William F. *Founding Gods, Inventing Nations: Conquest and Culture Myths from Antiquity to Islam* (Princeton: Princeton University Press, 2012).

McKitterick, Rosamund. *Charlemagne: The Formation of a European Identity* (Cambridge: Cambridge University Press, 2008).

*Perceptions of the Past in the Early Middle Ages* (Notre Dame: University of Notre Dame Press, 2006).

Meisami, Julie Scott. 'History as Literature', *Iranian Studies*, 33 (2000), 15–30.

'The Past in Service of the Present: Two Views of History in Medieval Persian', *Poetics Today*, 14: 2 (1993), 247–75.

*Persian Historiography to the End of the Twelfth Century* (Edinburgh: Edinburgh University Press, 1999).

Melchert, C. 'The Adversaries of Aḥmad Ibn Ḥanbal', *Arabica*, 44: 2 (1997), 234–53.

*Ahmad ibn Hanbal* (Oxford: Oneworld, 2006).

'Before Ṣūfiyyāt: Female Muslim Renunciants in the 8th and 9th Centuries CE', *Journal of Sufi Studies*, 5 (2016), 115–39.

'Bukhārī and Early Hadith Criticism', *JAOS*, 121: 1 (2001), 7–19.
'Bukhārī and his *Ṣaḥīḥ*', *Le Muséon*, 123: 3–4 (2010), 424–54.
'The Destruction of Books by Traditionists', *al-Qanṭara*, 35: 1 (2014), 213–31.
'The Early Ḥanafiyya and Kufa', *Journal of Abbasid Studies*, 1 (2014), 23–45.
*The Formation of the Sunni Schools of Law, 9th–10th Centuries CE* (Leiden: Brill, 1997).
'George Makdisi and Wael B. Hallaq', *Arabica*, 44: 2 (1997), 308–16.
*Hadith, Piety, and Law: Selected Studies* (Atlanta: Lockwood Press, 2015).
'How Ḥanafism Came to Originate in Kufa and Traditionalism in Medina', *ILS*, 6: 3 (1999), 318–47.
'The Meaning of "Qāla al-Shāfiʿī" in Ninth-Century Sources', in James E. Montgomery (ed.), *ʿAbbāsid Studies* (Leuven: Peeters, 2004), 277–302.
'The Piety of the Hadith Folk', *IJMES*, 34: 9 (2002), 425–39.
'Religious Policies of the Caliphs from al-Mutawakkil to al-Muqtadir, AH 232–295/AD 847–908', *ILS*, 3: 3 (1996), 316–42.
'Review of Nurit Tsafrir, *The History of an Islamic School of Law: The Early Spread of Hanafism* (Cambridge, Massachusetts: Islamic Legal Studies Program, Harvard Law School, 2004)', *JNES*, 67: 3 (2008), 228–30.
'Sectaries in the Six Books: Evidence for Their Exclusion from the Sunni Community', *The Muslim World*, 82: 3–4 (1992), 287–95.
'The Spread of Ḥanafism to Khurasan and Transoxiana', in A. C. S. Peacock and D. G. Tor (eds.), *Medieval Central Asia and the Persianate World: Iranian Tradition and Islamic Civilisation* (London: I. B. Tauris, 2015), 13–30.
'Sufis and Competing Movements in Nishapur', *Iran*, 39 (2001), 237–47.
'Traditionist-Jurisprudents and the Framing of Islamic Law', *ILS*, 8 (2001), 383–406.
Melville, Charles. 'The Caspian Provinces: A World Apart Three Local Histories of Mazandaran', *Iranian Studies*, 33: 1/2 (2000), 45–91.
'Persian Local Histories: Views from the Wings', *Iranian Studies*, 33: 1/2 (2000), 7–14.
Meri, Josef W. *The Cult of Saints among Muslims and Jews in Medieval Syria* (Oxford: Oxford University Press, 2002).
Miller, Isabel. 'Local History in Ninth/Fifteenth Century Yazd', *Iran*, 27 (1989), 75–9.
Mingana, A. (ed. and trans.). *Sources syriaques* (Leipzig: Otto Harrassowitz, 1907–8).
Mochiri, Melick Iradj. 'A Pahlavi Forerunner of the Umayyad Reform Coinage', *JRAS*, 2 (1981), 168–72.
Montgomery, James E. *Al-Jāḥiẓ: In Praise of Books* (Edinburgh: Edinburgh University Press, 2013).
Moore, Michael Edward. *A Sacred Kingdom: Bishops and the Rise of Frankish Kingship, 300–850* (Washington, DC: Catholic University of America Press, 2011).
Moore, R. I. 'Heresy as Disease', in W. Lourdaux and D. Verhelst (eds.), *The Concept of Heresy in the Middle Ages* (Leuven: Leuven University Press, 1983), 1–11.

Morgan, David. *Medieval Persia 1040–1797* (New York: Routledge, 2013).
Morony, Michael G. *Iraq after the Muslim Conquest* (Princeton: Princeton University Press, 1984; repr. Piscataway, NJ: Gorgias Press, 2005).
'Religious Communities in Late Sasanian and Early Muslim Iraq', *JESHO*, 17: 2 (1974), 113–35.
Morrison, Susan Signe. *Excrement in the Late Middle Ages: Sacred Filth and Chaucer's Fecopoetics* (New York: Palgrave Macmillan, 2008).
Mosca, Gaetono. *The Ruling Class* (New York: McGraw-Hill, 1939).
Mottahedeh, Roy. P. 'The Shuʿūbiyyah Controversy and the Social History of Early Islamic Iran', *IJMES*, 7: 2 (1976), 161–82.
Motzki, H. 'Quo vadis Ḥadīth-Forschung? Eine kritische Untersuchung von G. H. A. Juynboll: "Nāfiʿ, the Mawlā of Ibn ʿUmar, and his Position in Muslim Ḥadīth Literature"', *Der Islam*, 73 (1996), 40–80, 193–231.
Mu'assasat Āl al-Bayt. *Al-Fahras al-shāmil li al-turāth al-ʿarabī al-islāmī al-makhṭūṭ: al-ḥadīth al-nabawī al-sharīf wa ʿulūmuhu wa rijāluhu* (Amman: Mu'assasat Āl al-Bayt, 1991).
Mubārak, Zakī. *Iṣlāḥ ashnaʿ khaṭa' fī tārīkh al-tashrīʿ al-islāmī* (Cairo: al-Maktaba al-Tijāriyya al-Kubrā, 1934).
Munt, Harry. *The Holy City of Medina: Sacred Space in Early Islamic Arabia* (Cambridge: Cambridge University Press, 2014).
Muranyi, Miklos. *Beiträge zur Geschichte der Ḥadīt und Rechtsgelehrsamkeit der Mālikiyya in Nordafrika bis zum 5. Jh. d. H.: Bio-bibliographische Notizen aus der Moscheebibliothek von Qairawān* (Wiesbaden: Harrassowitz, 1997).
'Das *Kitāb al-Siyar* von Abū Isḥāq al-Fazārī: Das Manuskript der Qarawiyyīn Bibliothek zu Fās', *JSAI*, 6 (1985), 63–97.
*Materialien zur mālikitischen Rechtsliteratur* (Wiesbaden: Harrassowitz, 1984).
*Die Rechtsbücher des Qairawaners Saḥnūn b. Saʿīd: Enstehungsgeschichte und Werküberlieferung* (Stuttgart: Franz Steiner, 1999).
Nawas, John. 'The Appellation Ṣāḥib Sunna in Classical Islam: How Sunnism Came to Be', *ILS*, 23 (2016), 1–22.
'The Birth of an Elite: Mawālī and Arab ʿUlamā'', *JSAI*, 31 (2006), 74–91.
'The Contribution of the Mawālī to the Six Sunnite Canonical Ḥadīth Collections', in Sebastian Günther (ed.), *Ideas, Images, and Methods of Portrayal: Insights into Classical Arabic Literature and Islam* (Leiden: Brill, 2005), 141–52.
*Al-Ma'mūn, the Inquisition, and the Quest for Caliphal Authority* (Atlanta: Lockwood Press, 2015).
'A Profile of the Mawālī Ulama', in Monique Bernards and John Nawas (eds.), *Patronate and Patronage in Early and Classical Islam* (Leiden: Brill, 2005), 454–80.
Newman, Andrew J. *The Formative Period of Twelver Shīʿism: Ḥadīth as Discourse between Qum and Baghdad* (London and New York: Routledge, 2000).
Nisbet, R. *Émile Durkheim* (New Jersey: Prentice-Hall, 1965).
*The Sociological Tradition* (London: Heinemann, 1970).
Noble, Thomas F. X. 'Topography, Celebration, and Power: The Making of a Papal Rome in the Eighth and Ninth Centuries', in M. de Jong, F. Theuws,

and C. van Rhijn (eds.), *Topographies of Power in the Middle Ages* (Leiden: Brill, 2001), 45–91.

Nora, Pierre. 'Between Memory and History: Les Lieux de Mémoire', *Representations*, 26 (1989), 7–24.

'Comment écrire l'histoire de France?', in Pierre Nora (ed.), *Les lieux de mémoire, III: Les France, 1: Conflits et partages* (Paris: Gallimard, 1992), 11–32.

Nuʿmānī, ʿAbd al-Rashīd. 'Imām Abū Ḥanīfa kī taṣānīf se Imām Mālik kā istidādah [On Imam Mālik's Benefiting from the Books of Imam Abū Ḥanīfa]', in *Uṣūl-i ḥadīth kī baʿḍ ahamm mabāḥith [Some Important Researches in the Science of Ḥadīth]* (Karachi: al-Raḥīm Akīdamī, n.d.), 58–64.

Nūr, Zuhayr ʿUthmān ʿAlī. *Ibn ʿAdī wa manhajuhu fī kitāb al-kāmil fī ḍuʿafāʾ al-rijāl* (Riyadh: Maktabat al-Rushd, 1997).

Orlov, Andrei A. *Divine Scapegoats: Demonic Mimesis in Early Jewish Mysticism* (Albany: State University of New York Press, 2015).

Osman, Amr. *The Ẓāhirī Madhhab (3rd/9th–10th/16th Century): A Textualist Theory of Islamic Law* (Leiden: Brill, 2014).

Pagels, Elaine. *The Origin of Satan* (New York: Random House, 1995).

Pākatchī, Aḥmad. 'Abū al-Qāsim Ḥakīm Samarqandī', in Kaẓem Musavi Bujnūrdī (ed.), *Dāʾirat al-Maʿārif-i Buzurg-i Islāmī* (Tehran: Markazi-i Dāʾirat al-Maʿārif-i Buzurg-i Islāmī, 1989–), 6: 158–62.

Palmer, A. *The Seventh Century in the West-Syrian Chronicles* (Liverpool: Liverpool University Press, 1993).

Pareto, Vilfredo. *The Rise and Fall of Elites: An Application of Theoretical Sociology* (Totowa, NJ: Bedminister Press, 1968).

Parsons, Talcott. *The Structure of Social Action: A Study in Social Theory with Special Reference to a Group of Recent European Writers* (London: Collier Macmillan, 1968).

Patton, Walter M. *Ahmed ibn Hanbal and the Mihna* (Leiden: Brill, 1897).

Paul, Jürgen. *Herrscher, Gemeinwesen, Vermittler: Ostiran und Transoxanien in vormongolischer Zeit* (Stuttgart: Franz Steiner, 1996).

'The Histories of Herat', *Iranian Studies*, 33: 1/2 (2000), 93–115.

'The Histories of Isfahan: Mafarrukhi's *Kitāb Maḥāsin Iṣfahān*', *Iranian Studies*, 33: 1/2 (2000), 117–32.

'The Histories of Samarqand', *Studia Iranica*, 22 (1993), 69–92.

'Where Did the Dihqāns Go?', *Eurasian Studies*, 11 (2013), 1–34.

Pedersen, Johannes. *The Arabic Book*, trans. Geoffrey French (Princeton: Princeton University Press, 1984).

Pellat, Charles. *Ibn al-Muqaffaʿ (mort vers 140/757). 'Conseilleur' du calife* (Paris: G. P. Maisonneuve et Larose, 1976).

*Le milieu basrien et la formation de Gāhiz* (Paris: Maisonneuve, 1953).

Pohl, Walter. 'Conceptions of Ethnicity in Early Medieval Studies', in L. R. Little and B. Rosenwein (eds.), *Debating the Middle Ages: Issues and Readings* (Malden, MA: Blackwell, 1998), 15–24.

'Introduction: Strategies of Distinction', in Walter Pohl and Helmut Reimitz (eds.), *Strategies of Distinction: The Construction of Ethnic Communities, 300–800* (Leiden: Brill, 1998), 1–16.

Pohl, Walter and Helmut Reimitz (eds.). *Strategies of Distinction: The Construction of Ethnic Communities, 300–800* (Leiden: Brill, 1998).

Popovic, Alexandre. *The Revolt of African Slaves in Iraq in the 3rd/9th Century*, trans. Léon King (Princeton: Markus Wiener, 1999).

Pourshariati, Parvaneh. 'The *Akhbār al-ṭiwāl* of Abū Ḥanīfa Dīnawarī: A Shuʿūbī Treatise on Late Antique Iran', in Rika Gyselen (ed.), *Sources for the History of Sasanian and Post-Sasanian Iran* (Leuven: Peeters, 2010), 201–89.

'Local Histories of Khurasan and the Pattern of Arab Settlement', *Studia Iranica*, 27 (1998), 41–81.

'Local Historiography in Early Medieval Iran and the *Tārīkh-i Bayhaq*', *Iranian Studies*, 33: 1/2 (2000), 133–64.

Al-Qadi, Wadad. 'Biographical Dictionaries: Inner Structure and Cultural Significance', in George N. Atiyeh (ed.), *The Book in the Islamic World: The Written Word and Communication in the Middle East* (Albany: State University of New York Press, 1995), 93–122.

'Population Census and Land Surveys under the Umayyads (41–132/661–759)', *Der Islam*, 83: 2 (2008), 341–416.

Radtke, Bernd. 'Towards a Typology of Abbasid Universal Chronicles', *Occasional Papers of the School of Abbasid Studies*, 3 (1991), 1–18.

*Weltgeschichte und Weltbeschreibung im mittelalterlichen Islam* (Beirut and Stuttgart: Franz Steiner, 1992).

Reed, Annette Yoshiko. 'Heavenly Ascent, Angelic Descent, and the Transmission of Knowledge in 1 Enoch 6–16', in Raʿanan S. Boustan and Annette Yoshiko Reed (eds.), *Heavenly Realms and Earthly Realities in Late Antique Religions* (Cambridge: Cambridge University Press, 2004), 47–66.

'The Trickery of the Fallen Angels and the Demonic Mimesis of the Divine: Aetiology, Demonology, and Polemics in the Writings of Justin Martyr', *Journal of Early Christian Studies*, 12: 2 (2004), 141–71.

Reid, Megan H. *Law and Piety in Medieval Islam* (Cambridge: Cambridge University Press, 2013).

Reinhart, Kevin. 'Impurity/No Danger', *History of Religions*, 30: 1 (1990), 1–24.

*Lived Islam: Colloquial Religion in a Cosmopolitan Tradition* (Cambridge: Cambridge University Press, 2020).

Rekaya, M. 'Le Khurram-dīn et les mouvements khurramites sous les ʿAbbāsides', *Studia Islamica*, 60 (1984), 5–57.

Retsö, Jan. *The Arabs in Antiquity: Their History from the Assyrians to the Umayyads* (London: RoutledgeCurzon, 2003).

Ricoeur, Paul. *Freud and Philosophy: An Essay in Interpretation*, trans. Denis Savage (New Haven and London: Yale University Press, 1970).

*Memory, History, Forgetting*, trans. Kathleen Blamey and David Pellauer (Chicago: University of Chicago Press, 2004).

Rieu, C. *Supplement to the Catalogue of the Arabic Manuscripts in the British Museum* (London: British Museum, 1894).

Rippin, Andrew. *Muslims: Their Religious Beliefs and Practices* (New York: Routledge, 2005).

Ritter, Helmut. 'Philologika. III. Muhammedansiche Häresiographien', *Der Islam*, 18 (1929), 34–55.

Robinson, Chase F. *Empire and Elites after the Muslim Conquest: The Transformation of Northern Mesopotamia* (Cambridge: Cambridge University Press, 2000)

*Islamic Historiography* (Cambridge: Cambridge University Press, 2003).

'Al-Muʿāfā b. ʿImrān and the Beginnings of the Ṭabaqāt Literature', *JAOS*, 116: 1 (1996), 114–20.

Rosenthal, Franz. *A History of Muslim Historiography* (Leiden: Brill, 1968).

'"Of Making Many Books There Is No End": The Classical Muslim View', in George N. Atiyeh (ed.), *The Book in the Islamic World: The Written Word and Communication in the Middle East* (Albany: State University of New York Press, 1995), 33–56.

Rothstein, Gustav. *Dynastie der Laḥmiden in al-Ḥīra: Ein Versuch zur arabische–persischen Geschichte zur Zeit der Sasaniden* (Berlin: Reuther & Reichard, 1899).

Rotter, G. 'Abū Zurʿa al-Dimashqī und das Problem der frühen arabischen Geschichtsschreibung in Syrien', *Welt des Orient*, 6 (1971), 80–104.

*Die Umayyaden und der zweite Bürgerkrieg (680–692)* (Wiesbaden: Franz Steiner, 1982).

Rubin, Milka. 'The Language of Creation or the Primordial Language: A Case of Cultural Polemics in Antiquity', *Journal of Jewish Studies*, 49 (1998), 306–33.

Rubin, Uri. *Between Bible and Qur'an: The Children of Israel and the Islamic Self-Image* (Princeton: Darwin Press, 1999).

Rudolph, Ulrich. *Al-Māturīdī and the Development of Sunnī Theology in Samarqand*, trans. Rodrigo Adem (Leiden: Brill, 2014).

Russell, Jeffrey Burton. *Satan: The Early Christian Tradition* (New York: Cornell University Press, 1981).

Sadeghi, B. 'The Authenticity of Two 2nd/8th-Century Legal Texts: The *Kitāb al-Āthār* and *al-Muwaṭṭa'* of Muḥammad b. al-Ḥasan al-Shaybānī', *ILS*, 17: 3 (2010), 291–319.

*The Logic of Law Making in Islam: Women and Prayer in the Legal Tradition* (Cambridge: Cambridge University Press, 2013).

Sadighi, G. H. *Les mouvements religieux iraniens au IIe et au IIIe siècle de l'hégire* (Paris: Les Presses Modernes, 1938) = *Junbishhā-yi dīnī-yi īrānī dar qarnhā-yi duvvum va sivvum-i hijrī* (Tehran: n.p., 1996).

Safi, Omid. *The Politics of Knowledge in Premodern Islam: Negotiating Ideology and Religious Inquiry* (Chapel Hill: University of North Carolina Press, 2006).

Ṣāliḥ, Fu'ād. *Muʿjam al-alqāb wa al-asmā' al-mustaʿāra fī tārīkh al-ʿarabī al-Islāmī* (Beirut: Dār al-ʿIlm li al-Malāyīn, 1990).

Al-Sarhan, Saud. 'Early Muslim Traditionalism: A Critical Study of the Works and Political Theology of Aḥmad Ibn Ḥanbal', PhD thesis, University of Exeter, 2011.

Al-Ṣarrāf. 'al-Ḥīra fī al-qarnayn al-awwal wa al-thānī al-hijrayn: dirāsa tārīkhiyya', Master's thesis, University of Kufa, 2007.

Savant, Sarah Bowen. *The New Muslims of Post-Conquest Iran: Tradition, Memory, and Conversion* (Cambridge: Cambridge University Press, 2013).

Savant, Sarah and Helena de Felipe. *Genealogy and Knowledge in Muslim Societies: Understanding the Past* (Edinburgh: Edinburgh University Press, 2014).

Schacht, Joseph. 'Die arabische ḥijal-Literatur: Ein Beitranf zur Erforschung der islāmischen Rechtpraxis', *Der Islam*, 15 (1926), 211–32.

'An Early Murc'ite Treatise: The *Kitāb al-ʿĀlim wa al-Mutaʿallim*', *Oriens*, 17 (1964), 96–117.

*An Introduction to Islamic Law* (Oxford: Clarendon Press, 1982).

*The Origins of Muhammadan Jurisprudence* (Oxford: Clarendon Press, 1950).

Schäfer, Peter. 'In Heaven as It Is in Hell: The Cosmology of Seder Rabbah di-Bereshit', in Raʿanan S. Boustan and Annette Yoshiko Reed (eds.), *Heavenly Realms and Earthly Realities in Late Antique Religions* (Cambridge: Cambridge University Press, 2004), 233–74.

Schoeler, G. *The Genesis of Literature in Islam: From the Aural to the Read*, trans. Shawkat M. Toorawa (Edinburgh: Edinburgh University Press, 2009).

*The Oral and the Written in Early Islam*, trans. Uwe Vagelpohl (London: Routledge, 2006).

Sellheim, R. *Der zweite Bürgerkrieg im Islam (680–692): Das Ende der mekkanisch-medinensischen Vorherrschaft* (Wiesbaden: Franz Steiner, 1970).

Selove, Emily. 'Who Invented the Microcosm?', in Monique Bernards (ed.), *ʿAbbasid Studies IV: Occasional Papers of the School of ʿAbbāsid Studies* (Exeter: E. J. W. Gibb Memorial Trust, 2013), 76–97.

Sezgin, F. *Buhârî'nin Kaynakları: Hakkinda araṣtirmalar ryasani* (Istanbul: Ibrahim Hotoz Basimevi, 1956).

*Geschichte des arabischen Schrifttums* (Leiden: Brill, 1967).

Sezgin, U. *Abū Mihnaf: Ein Beitrag zur Historiographie der umaiyadischen Zeit* (Leiden: Brill, 1971).

Shaked, Shaul. 'Mihr the Judge', *JSAI*, 2 (1980), 1–30.

Shaltūt, F. M. 'Ta'rīkh al-Madīna al-munawwara ta'līf ʿUmar b. Shabba al-Numayrī', in A. ʿAbd Allāh, R. Mortel, and S. al-Ṣaqqār (eds.), *Studies in the History of Arabia*, volume 1: *Sources for the History of Arabia* (Riyadh: University of Riyadh Press, 1979), 3–8.

Sharon, Moshe. *Black Banners from the East II. Revolt: The Social and Military Aspects of the ʿAbbāsid Revolution* (Jerusalem: Max Schloessinger Memorial Fund, Hebrew University, 1990).

Sherman, P. M. *Babel's Tower Translated: Genesis 11 and Ancient Jewish Interpretation* (Leiden: Brill, 2013).

Shimamoto, Takamitsu. 'Some Reflections on the Origin of Qom: Myth and History', *Orient*, 27 (1991), 95–113.

Shukrī al-Alūsī, Maḥmūd. *Tajrīd al-sinān fī al-dhabb ʿan Abī Ḥanīfa al-Nuʿmān ʿalayhi al-raḥma wa al-riḍwān*, ed. Iyād b. ʿAbd al-Laṭīf b. Ibrāhīm al-Qaysī (Damascus: Dār al-Nawādir, 2017).

Sijpesteijn, Petra M. 'The Archival Mind in Early Islamic Egypt: Two Arabic Papyri', in Petra M. Sijpesteijn et al. (eds.), *From al-Andalus to Khurasan: Documents from the Medieval Muslim World* (Leiden: Brill, 2007), 163–86.

'A Ḥadīth Fragment on Papyrus', *Der Islam*, 92: 2 (2015), 321–31.

Silverstein, Adam J. 'The Medieval Islamic Worldview: Arabic Geography in Its Historical Context', in Kurt A. Raaflaub and Richard J. A. Talbert (eds.), *Geography and Ethnography: Perceptions of the World in Pre-Modern Societies* (Oxford: Wiley-Blackwell, 2010), 273–90.

Sizgorich, Thomas. *Violence and Belief in Late Antiquity: Militant Devotion in Christianity and Islam* (Philadelphia: University of Pennsylvania Press, 2009).

Smith, Anthony D. 'Chosen Peoples: Why Ethnic Groups Survive', *Ethnic and Racial Studies*, 15: 3 (1992), 436–56.

Smith, Jonathan Z. *To Take Place: Toward Theory in Ritual* (Chicago: University of Chicago Press, 1987).

'What a Difference a Difference Makes', in *Relating Religion: Essays in the Study of Religion* (Chicago: University of Chicago Press, 2004), 251–302.

Sourdel, Dominique. *Le vizirat ʿabbāside de 749 à 936 (132 à 324 de l'hégire)* (Damascus: Institut français de Damas, 1959–60).

Springberg-Hinsen, Monika. *Die Zeit vor dem Islam in arabischen Universalgeschichten des 9. bis 12. Jahrhunderts* (Würzburg: Echter, 1989).

Spuler, B. *Iran in früh-islamischer Zeit: Politik, Kultur, Verwaltung und öffentliches Leben zwischen der arabischen und der seldschukischen Eroberung 633 bis 1055* (Wiesbaden: Franz Steiner, 1952).

Stearns, Justin K. *Infectious Ideas: Contagion in Premodern Islamic and Christian Thought in the Western Mediterranean* (Baltimore: Johns Hopkins University Press, 2011).

Stewart, Devin J. *Islamic Legal Orthodoxy: Twelver Shiite Responses to the Sunni Legal System* (Salt Lake City: University of Utah Press, 1998).

Stock, Brian. *The Implications of Literacy: Written Language and Models of Interpretation in the Eleventh and Twelfth Centuries* (Princeton: Princeton University Press, 1983).

Stroumsa, Guy. *Barbarian Philosophy: The Religious Revolution of Early Christianity* (Tübingen: Mohr [Siebeck], 1999).

'Barbarians or Heretics? Jews and Arabs in the Mind of Byzantium (Fourth to Eighth Centuries)', in Robert Bonfil, Oded Irshai, Guy Stroumsa, and Rina Talgam (eds.), *Jews in Byzantium: Dialectics of Minority and Majority Cultures* (Leiden: Brill, 2012), 761–77.

Al-Ṣuwayyān, Aḥmad b. ʿAbd al-Raḥmān. *Al-Imām ʿAbd Allāh b. al-Zubayr al-Ḥumaydī wa kitābuhu al-musnad* (Riyadh: Dār al-Miʿrāj al-Dawlīya li al-Nashr, 1996).

Szombathy, Zoltán. 'Genealogy in Medieval Muslim Societies', *Studia Islamica*, 95 (2002), 5–35.

Tafazzoli, Ahmad. *Sasanian Society: I. Warriors II. Scribes III. Dehqāns* (New York: Bibliotheca Persica Press, 2000).

Tamm, Marek (ed.). *Afterlife of Events: Perspectives on Mnemohistory* (Basingstoke: Palgrave Macmillan, 2015).

Al-Tanchî, Muḥammad b. Tavît. 'Abû Mansûr al-Mâturîdî', *Ankara Ilahiyat Fakültesi Dergisi*, 4 (1955), 1–12.

Thomas, Keith. *Religion and the Decline of Magic: Studies in Popular Beliefs in Sixteenth and Seventeenth Century England* (New York: Charles Scribner's Sons, 1971).

al-Ṭihrānī, Āghā Buzurg. *Al-Dharīʿa ilā taṣānīf al-shīʿa* (Beirut: Dār al-Aḍwā, 1983).

Tillier, Mathieu. *Les cadis d'Iraq et l'état abbaside (132/750–334/945)* (Damascus: Institut français du Proche-Orient, 2009).

*L'invention du cadi. La justice des musulmans, des Juifs et des chrétiens aux premiers siècles de l'Islam* (Paris: Publications de la Sorbonne, 2017).

'The Qāḍīs of Fusṭāṭ-Miṣr under the Ṭūlūnids and the Ikhshīds: The Judiciary and Egyptian Autonomy', *JAOS*, 131 (2011), 207–22.

'Qāḍīs and the Political Use of the Maẓālim Jurisdiction under the ʿAbbāsids', in Christian Lange and Maribel Fierro (eds.), *Public Violence in Islamic Societies* (Edinburgh: Edinburgh University Press, 2009), 42–66.

'Un traité politique du IIe/VIIIe siècle. L'épître de ʿUbayd Allāh b. al-Ḥasan al-ʿAnbarī au calife al-Mahdī', *Annales Islamogiques*, 40 (2006), 139–70.

Tokatly, Vardit. 'The *Aʿlām al-ḥadīth* of al-Khaṭṭābī: A Commentary on al-Bukhārī's *Ṣaḥīḥ* or a Polemical Treatise?', *Studia Islamica*, 92 (2001), 53–91.

Toorawa, Shawkat M. *Ibn Abī Ṭāhir Ṭayfūr and Arabic Writerly Culture* (London: RoutledgeCurzon, 2005).

Tor, D. G. 'God's Cleric: Fuḍayl b. ʿIyāḍ and the Transition from Caliphal to Prophetic Sunna', in Behnam Sadeghi, Asad Q. Ahmed, Adam Silverstein, and Robert Hoyland (eds.), *Islamic Cultures, Islamic Contexts: Essays in Honor of Professor Patricia Crone* (Leiden: Brill, 2014), 195–228.

*Violent Order: Religious Warfare, Chivalry, and the ʿAyyār Phenomenon in the Medieval Islamic World*. Istanbuler Texte und Studien 11 (Würzburg: Ergon Verlag Würzburg in Komission, 2007).

Toral-Niehoff, Isabel. *Al-Ḥīra: Eine arabische Kulturmetropole im spätantiken Kontext* (Leiden: Brill, 2013).

'The ʿIbād of al-Ḥīra: An Arab Christian Community', in Angelika Neuwirth, Nicolai Sinai, and Michael Marx (eds.), *The Qur'ān in Context: Historical and Literary Investigations into the Qur'ānic Milieu* (Leiden: Brill, 2012), 323–48.

Tottoli, Roberto. *Biblical Prophets in the Qur'ān and Muslim Literature* (London and New York: Routledge, 2002).

Troeltsch, Ernst. *Gesammelte Schriften I. Band: Die Soziallehren der christlichen Kirchen und Gruppen* (Tübingen: Mohr, 1923) = *The Social Teachings of the Christian Churches* (New York: Macmillan, 1960).

Tsafrir, Nurit. *The History of an Islamic School of Law: The Early Spread of Hanafism* (Cambridge, MA: Islamic Legal Studies Program, Harvard Law School, 2004).

'Semi-Ḥanafīs and Ḥanafī Biographical Sources', *Studia Islamica*, 84 (1996), 67–85.

Tucker, W. F. *Mahdis and Millenarians: Shīʿite Extremists in Early Muslim Iraq* (Cambridge: Cambridge University Press, 2008).

al-Turkī, ʿAbd Allāh b. ʿAbd al-Ḥasan. *al-Madhhab al-Ḥanbalī: Dirāsa fī tārīkhihi wa simātihi wa ashhar aʿlāmihi wa mu'allafātihi* (Beirut: Mu'assasat al-Risāla, 2002).

Turner, John P. 'The Enigmatic Reign of al-Wāthiq (r. 227/842–232/847)', in Monique Bernards (ed.), *'Abbāsid Studies IV: Occasional Papers of the School of 'Abbāsid Studies* (Exeter: Gibb Memorial Trust, 2013), 218–31.

*Inquisition in Early Islam: The Competition for Political and Religious Authority in the Abbasid Empire* (New York: I. B. Tauris, 2013).

Turner, Victor. 'Social Dramas and Stories about Them', *Critical Inquiry*, 7: 1 (1980), 141–68.

Al-'Umarī, Akram Ḍiyā'. *Mawārid al-Khaṭīb al-Baghdādī fī Tārīkh Baghdād*, 2nd edn. (Riyadh: Dār Ṭayba, 1985; Damascus: Dār al-Qalam, 1975).

*Turāth al-Tirmidhī al-'ilmī* (Medina: Maktabat al-Dār, 1991).

Urban, Elizabeth. *Conquered Populations in Early Islam: Non-Arabs, Slaves, and the Sons of Slave Mothers* (Edinburgh: Edinburgh University Press, 2020).

'The Early Islamic Mawālī: A Window onto Processes of Construction and Social Change', PhD thesis, University of Chicago, 2012.

Vajda, Georges. 'Notices de manuscrits Arabe', unpublished typescript, Bibliothèque nationale de France, 1940–69.

van Arendonk, C. *De Opkomst van het zaidietische Imamaat in Yemen* (Leiden: Brill, 1919) = *Les débuts de l'imāmat zaidite au Yemen*, trans. J. Ryckmans (Leiden: Brill, 1960).

van Ess, Josef. *Der Eine und das Andere: Beobachtungen an islamischen häresiographischen Texten* (Berlin and New York: De Gruyter, 2011).

*Kleine Schriften* (Leiden: Brill, 2017).

'Kritisches zum *Fiqh Akbar*', *Revue des Études Islamiques*, 56 (1986), 327–38.

'La liberté du judge dans le milieu basrien du VIIIe siècle', in D. Sourdel et al. (eds.), *La notion de liberté au Moyen Âge: Islam, Byzance, Occident* (Paris: Les belles-lettres, 1985).

*Theologie und Gesellschaft im 2. und 3. Jahrhundert Hidschra: Eine Geschichte des religiosen Denkens im fruhen Islam* (Berlin: Walter de Gruyter, 1991–7).

*Ungenützte Texte zur Karrāmīya: Eine Materialsammlung, Sitzungsberichte der heidelberger Akademie der Wissenschaften, Philosophisch-historische Klasse, Jahrgang 1980–6. Abhandlung* (Heidelberg: Carl Winter, 1980).

van Gelder, Geert Jan. 'Kufa vs. Basra: The Literary Debate', *Asiatischen Studien*, 50 (1996), 339–62.

Versteegh, Kees. 'Grammar and Exegesis: The Origins of Kufan Grammar and the *Tafsīr Muqātil*', *Der Islam*, 67 (1990), 206–42.

Veyne, Paul. *Comment on écrit l'histoire. Essai d'épistémologie* (Paris: Seuil, 1971).

Vishanoff, David R. *The Formation of Islamic Hermeneutics: How Sunni Legal Theorists Imagined a Revealed Law* (New Haven: American Oriental Society, 2011).

von Gelder, H. D. *Muhtar de valsche Profeet* (Leiden: Brill, 1888).

von Grunebaum, Gustave E. *Medieval Islam: A Study in Cultural Orientation* (Chicago: University of Chicago Press, 1953).

von Martin, Alfred. *The Sociology of the Renaissance*, ed. Karl Mannheim (London: Kegan Paul, 1944).

Waines, D. *An Introduction to Islam* (Cambridge: Cambridge University Press, 2003).

Walker, P. W. L. *Holy City, Holy Places? Christian Attitudes to Jerusalem and the Holy Land in the Fourth Century* (Oxford: Clarendon Press, 1990).

Wansbrough, J. *The Sectarian Milieu: Content and Composition of Islamic Salvation History* (New York: Prometheus Books, 2006).

Watt, W. Montgomery. *The Formative Period of Islamic Thought* (Oxford: Oneworld, 1998).

*Islamic Creeds: A Selection* (Edinburgh: Edinburgh University Press, 1994).

Webb, P. *Imagining the Arabs: Arab Identity and the Rise of Islam* (Edinburgh: Edinburgh University Press, 2016).

Weber, Max. *From Max Weber: Essays in Sociology*, ed. and trans. H. H. Gerth and C. Wright Mills (New York: Oxford University Press, 1946).

Weinberger, James. 'The Authorship of Two Twelfth Century Transoxanian Biographical Dictionaries', *Arabica*, 33 (1986), 369–82.

Weiss, Bernard G. *The Spirit of Islamic Law* (Athens: University of Georgia Press, 1998).

Wellhausen, Julius. *Religio-Political Factions in Early Islam*, ed. R. C. Ostle, trans. R. C. Ostle and S. M. Walzer (New York: American Elsevier, 1975) = *Die religiös-politischen Oppositionsparteien im alten Islam* (Berlin: Weidmann, 1901).

Wensinck, A. J. *The Muslim Creed: Its Genesis and Historical Development* (Oxford: Routledge, 1932).

Wichard, Johannes Christian. *Zwischen Markt und Moschee: Wirtschaftliche Bedürfnisse und religiöse Anforderungen im frühen islamischen Vertragsrecht* (Paderborn: Ferdinand Schöningh, 1995).

Wilken, R. L. *The Land Called Holy* (New Haven: Yale University Press, 1992).

Wilson, M. Brett. 'The Failure of Nomenclature: The Concept of "Orthodoxy" in the Study of Islam', *Comparative Islamic Studies*, 3: 2 (2007), 169–94.

Witztum, J. 'The Syriac Milieu of the Quran: The Recasting of Biblical Narratives', PhD thesis, Princeton University, 2011.

Wolfensohn, Israel. *Kaʿb al-Aḥbār und seine Stellung im Ḥadīth und in der islamischen Legendliteratur* (Gelnhausen: F. W. Kalbfleisch, 1933).

Wright, William *A Grammar of the Arabic Language* (Cambridge: Cambridge University Press, 1933).

Yahia, M. *Šāfiʿī et les deux sources de la loi islamique* (Turnhout: Brepols, 2009).

Yarbrough, Luke B. *Friends of the Emir: Non-Muslim State Officials in Premodern Islamic Thought* (Cambridge: Cambridge University Press, 2019).

Young, G. M. *Last Essays* (London: R. Hart-Davis, 1950).

Young, Walter Edward. *The Dialectical Forge: Juridical Disputation and the Evolution of Islamic Law* (Cham: Springer, 2017).

Zadeh, Travis. 'The *Fātiḥa* of Salmān al-Fārisī and the Modern Controversy over Translating the Qur'an', in S. R. Burge (ed.), *The Meaning of the Word: Lexicology and Qur'anic Exegesis* (Oxford: Institute of Ismaili Studies/ University of Oxford Press, 2015), 375–420.

*The Vernacular Qur'an: Translation and the Rise of Persian Exegesis* (Oxford: Institute of Ismaili Studies/Oxford University Press, 2012).

Zakeri, Mohsen. *Sāsānid Soldiers in Early Muslim Society: The Origins of the ʿAyyārān and Futuwwa* (Wiesbaden: Harrassowitz, 1995).

Zaman, Muhammad Qasim. 'The Nature of Muḥammad al-Nafs al-Zakiyya's Mahdiship: A Study of Some Reports in Iṣbahānī's *Maqātil*', *Hamdard Islamicus*, 13 (1990), 65–9.

*Religion and Politics under the Early ʿAbbāsids: The Emergence of the Proto-Sunnī Elite* (Leiden: Brill, 1997).

Zayd, Naṣr Abū. *Al-Imām al-Shāfiʿī wa ta'sīs al-īdiyūlūgiyya al-wasaṭiyya* (Cairo: Sīnā, 1992).

Ziriklī, Khayr al-Dīn. *Al-Aʿlām: qāmūs tarājim li ashhar al-rijāl wa al-nisā' min al-ʿArab wa al-mustaʿribīn wa al-mustashriqīn* (Beirut: Dār al-ʿIlm li al-Malāyīn, 1979; 15th edn. Beirut: Dār al-ʿIlm li al-Malāyīn, 2002).

al-Zuraqī, ʿĀdil b. ʿAbd al-Shukr. *Tārīkh al-Bukhārī* (Riyadh: Dār al-Ṭuwayq, 2002).

Zysow, Aron. *The Economy of Certainty: An Introduction to the Typology of Islamic Legal Theory* (Atlanta: Lockwood Press, 2013).

'Two Unrecognised Karrāmī Texts', *JAOS*, 108 (1988), 577–87.

# Index


'Abbāsid caliphate. *See also individual caliphs*
caliphs, 209, 255–6, 296, 297, 333
Ḥanafism, spread of, 204–5
Ibn Sa'd serving, 32
rebellions, 149, 189, 197, 202, 297, 333
'Abd Allāh (son of Ibn Abī Shayba), 91
'Abd Allāh b. Abī Ja'far, 340
'Abd Allāh b. Aḥmad b. Ḥanbal
on Abū Yūsuf, 80
on affliction by Abū Ḥanīfa, 87
on Aḥmad b. Ḥanbal, 94, 96, 98
biographical details of, 89–91
ethno-racial reasoning by, 163, 164
implicating students of Abū Ḥanīfa, 80
on Jahmiyya, 247
*Kitāb al-'Ilal wa ma'rifat al-rijāl*, 164
*Kitāb al-Sunna*, 87, 92, 94–8, 97, 215–16, 247
legal arguments against Abū Ḥanīfa
analogical reasoning, 227
ḥadīth, 232
*ḥiyal* (legal tricks), 225
speculative jurisprudence, 96, 99, 213, 215–16, 218
on Murji'a, 95, 97
on Quran, createdness of, 95, 97, 103, 257
on rebellion, 97
on repenting from heresy, 97
on social exclusion, 254
Yaḥyā b. Ma'īn and, 90
'Abd Allāh b. al-Ḥasan, 185
'Abd Allāh b. Basr al-Māzinī, 271
'Abd Allāh b. Dāwūd al-Khuraybī, 278
'Abd Allāh b. al-Ḥārith b. Juz' al-Zab īdī, 270
'Abd Allāh b. Maḥmūd al-Pazdawī, 305
'Abd Allāh b. Marwān b. Mu'āwiya al-Faz ārī, 188
'Abd Allāh b. Mas'ūd, 131, 272
'Abd Allāh b. Mu'āwiya, 150
'Abd Allāh b. Muḥammad b. Ya'qūb al-Ḥārithī, 285
'Abd Allāh b. Muḥammad al-Khalanjī, 235
'Abd Allāh b. Qafal, 157
'Abd Allāh al-Ṣādiq, 189
'Abd Allāh b. Ṭāhir, 49, 202–4
'Abd Allāh b. Tha'laba b. Ṣa'īr al-Zuhr ī, 271
'Abd al-Karīm b. al-Haytham al-Dīr'āqūlī, 304
'Abd al-Malik b. Marwān, 150
'Abd al-Qāhir al-Baghdādī, 331
'Abd Rabbih b. Rāshid, 128
'Abd al-Raḥmān, 107
'Abd al-Raḥmān b. 'Abd al-Qārī, 271
'Abd al-Raḥmān b. Mahdī, 50–2
'Abd al-Rashīd al-Nu'mānī, 318
'Abd al-Razzāq al-Ṣan'ānī, 143
'Abd al-Salām b. Ḥarb al- Malā'ī, 274
'Abda b. Sulaymān al-Marwazī, 79
Abū al-'Abbās Aḥmad b. Muḥammad Maḥmūd al-Ghaznawī, 286
Abū al-'Abbās al-Saffāḥ, 128
Abū al-'Abbās b. 'Uqda, 233, 301, 303
Abū 'Abd Allāh al-Būshanjī, 305
Abū 'Abd Allāh Muḥammad b. Khusraw al-Balkhī, 286
Abū 'Abd Allāh al-Nīshāpūrī, 289
Abū 'Abd al-Ḥusayn b. al-Walīd, 233
Abū Aḥmad al-Ḥākim, 169, 229
Abū al-Akhnas al-Kinānī, 246
Abū 'Alī 'Abd al-Raḥmān b. Muḥammad al-Nīshāpūrī, 233
Abū 'Alī b. Shādhān, 304
Abū al-'Arab, 259
Abū 'Awāna, 294
Abū 'Awāna al-Isfarā'īnī, 98
Abū Ayyūb, 295
Abū al-Bafā b. Abī al-Ḍibā' al-Qurashī al-Makkī, 286
Abū Bakr (caliph), 185
Abū Bakr al-Ḥudhalī, 128

Abū Bakr b. ʿIyyāsh, 220
Abū Bakr al-Marrūdhī, 50–2, 98, 201
Abū Bakr Muḥammad b. ʿAbd al-Malik b. ʿAlī, 303
Abū Bakr Muḥammad b. Muḥammad b. Sulaymān al-Bāghandī, 305
Abū Dāwūd al-Sijistānī, 86, 305
Abū Dāwūd al-Ṭayālisī, 314
Abū al-Faraj al-Iṣfahānī, 127–8, 168, 186, 191
Abū Ḥafṣ al-Kabīr, 180, 340
Abū Ḥamza al-Sukkarī, 216, 219
Abū Ḥanīfa. *See also* Ḥanafism; *madhhabs* (schools of law); proto-Ḥanafism
  absence of texts from, 349
  death of, 64, 68, 77, 192, 242–3, 269–72, 334
  as exemplar of Sunni orthodoxy. *see* Sunni orthodoxy
  as founder of *madhhab*, 3
  heresy, discourses of heresy on. *See* heresy, discourses of
  satire, use of, 221
  scholarship on, 17
  shrine of, 310
Abū al-Ḥasan ʿAlī, 49
Abū al-Ḥasan ʿAlī b. al-ʿAbbās b. al-Walīd al-Maqāniʿī, 188
Abū al-Ḥasan al-Ẓāhir, 266
Abū Hāshim al-Rummānī, 186
Abū al-Ḥusayn, 319
Abū al-Ḥusayn Aḥmad b. Muḥammad b. ʿAbd Allāh, 289
Abū al-Ḥusayn al-Qudūrī, 259, 286, 330
Abū Isḥāq al-Fazārī, 190–3, 194–8
Abū Isḥāq al-Shīrāzī al-Shāfiʿī, 286
Abū Jaʿfar Aḥmad b. ʿAbd Allāh al-Qasam al-Sarmāw[r]ī al-Shīrāzī, 286
Abū Jaʿfar Muḥammad b. ʿUthmān b. Abī Shayba, 34
Abū Khaythama, 32
Abū Khāzim, 294, 295, 296, 298
Abū Layth al-Samarqandī, 302
Abū Maʿadd ʿAdnān, 291
Abū al-Manṣūr al-Māturīdī, 179
Abū al-Mufaḍḍal al-Shaybānī, 317
Abū Muḥammad ʿAbd al-Wahhāb b. Muḥammad b. Naṣr, 330
Abū Muḥammad ʿUthmān b. ʿAffān al-Sijz ī, 122
Abū Naṣr Aḥmad al-Kalābādhī, 43
Abū Nuʿaym, 46, 105
Abū Nuʿaym al-Iṣfahānī, 212, 320–1
Abū al-Qāsim Samarqandī, 339–44
Abū Quṭun ʿAmr b. al-Haytham, 275
Abū Ṭālib Yaḥyā b. al-Ḥusayn al-Hārūnī, 187, 192
Abū Tamīla Yaḥyā b. Wāḍiḥ al-Anṣārī, 51
Abū Thawr, 46
Abū Ṭufayl ʿĀmir b. Wāthila, 271
Abū ʿUbayd al-Qāsim b. Sallām, 94, 254
Abū ʿUdhba, 148
Abū Umāma al-Bāhilī, 270
Abū Umāma b. Sahl b. Ḥanīf, 271
Abū Yaḥyā al-Bazzār, 288–90
Abū Yaʿlā al-Mawṣilī, 333
Abū Yūsuf
  ʿAbd Allāh b. Aḥmad b. Ḥanbal on, 80
  al-Bukhārī on, 64, 198
  on dream about Abū Ḥanīfa's funeral, 243
  elites, proximity to, 65, 196–8
  al-Fasawī on, 79–81
  al-Fazārī and, 65, 196–8
  ḥadīth proficiency, 230, 231
  al-Ḥārithī al-Subadhmūnī on, 301
  at Hārūn al-Rashīd's court, 65, 196–8
  Ibn Saʿd on, 33–4
  Ibn Shabbuwayh on, 88
  implicating Abū Ḥanīfa, 79–81
  on *istiḥsān*, 29
  on Jahmiyya, 247, 248
  on jurisprudence, 215, 217
  *Kitāb al-Kharāj*, 29
  Murji'a and, 73, 80
  on Quran, createdness of, 344
  al-Rāwandī on, 345
  religious authority of, 345
  on ritual prayer, 178, 181
  al-Shaybānī and, 297–8, 308
  al-Ṭaḥāwī on, 239
Abū Zayd (Ḥammād b. Dalīl), 256
Abū Zayd al-Dabūsī, 302
Abū Zurʿa al-Dimashqī
  Aḥmad b. Ḥanbal and, 84, 103, 105
  al-Bardhaʿī and, 100
  al-Fasawī and, 82–4
  *al-Fawāʾid al-muʿallala*, 84
  al-Ḥumaydī and, 85
  on Murji'a, 85
  on orthodoxy, 85
  on Quran, createdness of, 89
  on repenting from heresy, 89
  on social exclusion, 254
  on speculative jurisprudence, 77, 219, 222
  *Tārīkh*, 83, 84–5, 88–9, 270
  on Wāthila b. al-Asqaʿ, 270
Abū Zurʿa al-Rāzī, 46, 52, 100–5, 332
Adam, 143, 226

Ādam b. Abī Iyā, 171
administration, state, 168, 177, 208–9, 291, 296
adultery, 226
*ahl al-ḥadīth*. *See* proto-Sunni traditionalism
*ahl al-ra'y*. *See* proto-Ḥanafism
*ahl al-sunna*. *See* proto-Sunni traditionalism
Aḥmad b. Abī ʿImrān, 292, 294, 296
Aḥmad b. Dawraqī, 32
Aḥmad b. Ḥanbal. *See also* Ḥanbalism
ʿAbd Allāh b. Aḥmad b. Ḥanbal on, 94, 96, 98
Abū Zurʿa al-Dimashqī and, 84, 103, 105
analogical reasoning, use of, 227
al-Bukhārī and, 58, 68
Companions, has not met, 320
elites, proximity to, 69
as founder of *madhhab*, 3
ḥadīth proficiency, 231
al-Ḥumaydī and, 48, 112
Ḥusn (wife of), 90
Ibn Shabbuwayh and, 86
Isḥāq b. Rāhawayh and, 49, 53, 203
*Kitāb al-ʿIlal*, 256–7
al-Rāwandī on, 346
Rayḥāna (wife of), 90
on rebellion against the state, 95
on repenting from heresy, 256–7
Ṣāliḥ (son of), 90
social exclusion by, 105
sons serving as qadis, 90
on speculative jurisprudence, 218, 278
on state employment, 70
Yaḥyā b. Maʿīn and, 75
Aḥmad b. Ibrāhīm, 101
Aḥmad b. Ibrāhīm al-Dawraqī, 94
Aḥmad b. Jaʿfar b. Naṣr al-Muzakkī, 305
Aḥmad b. Khalīl, 79
Aḥmad b. Muḥammad b. Naṣr, 288
Aḥmad b. Muḥammad b. Sahl Abū al-Ḥasan b. Sahluwayh, 289
Aḥmad b. Naṣr al-Khuzāʿī, 95
Aḥmad b. al-Ṣalt, 290, 305
Aḥmad b. Shuʿayb al-Nasā'ī, 265
Aḥmad b. Sulaymān b. Saʿīd, 286
Aḥmad b. Ṭūlūn, 291–2
Aḥmad b. Yaḥyā, 188
Ahmed, Shahab, 350, 357
al-Aḥnaf b. Qays, 125–8
ʿĀ'isha bt. al-Faḍl, 90
*ʿajam*, 160, 167–9, 172
al-Ajlaḥ, 190
*Akhbār Abī Ḥanīfa* (Abū al-Mufaḍḍal al-Shaybānī (attr.)), 318
*Akhbār Abī Ḥanīfa* (al-Ṣaymarī), 304
*Akhbār al-shuyūkh wa akhlāquhum* (al-Marrūdhī), 98
ʿAlī b. Abī Ṭālib (caliph), 131, 147, 149, 161, 163
ʿAlī b. ʿĪsā, 289
ʿAlī b. al-Madīnī, 187, 243
ʿAlī b. Muḥammad b. Mūsā, 233
ʿAlī b. Mūsā al-Qummī, 307
ʿAlī b. Sahl b. al-Mughīra al-Bazzāz, 319
ʿAlid families, 185, 333
almsgiving (*zakāt*), 59
al-Aʿmash, 142
Ames, Christine Caldwell, 356, 357
ʿAmr b. ʿAbd al-Ghaffār b. ʿUmar, 187
ʿAmr b. Dīnār, 349
ʿAmr b. Ḥārith, 269
ʿAmr b. Muhājir, 271
ʿAmr b. ʿUbayd, 73, 252, 257
*amṣār*, 159
analogical reasoning (*qiyās*)
ʿAbd Allāh b. Aḥmad b. Ḥanbal on, 227
Aḥmad b. Ḥanbal, used by, 227
Ibn al-Muqaffaʿ on, 210
Isḥāq b. Rāhawayh on, 55
*istiḥsān* and, 29, 30
proto-Ḥanafism and, 226–7
as religious deviance, 226–7
al-Shāfiʿī on, 31
Wakīʿ b. al-Jarrāh on, 77–8
Anas b. Mālik, 271
anathematisers, 12
Anbār, 161
al-ʿAnbarī, ʿUbayd Allāh b. al-Ḥasan, 207–9
ancestry, 88, 268, 272–3, 281
al-Andalus, 362
anecdotes, 110
angels, 141–2
*Ansāb al-ashrāf* (al-Balādhurī), 186
antediluvian narratives, 131, 141–5
anthropomorphic theology, 343
anti-Christs, 64, 68, 175, 250, 251
anti-heresy treatises, 244
Antrim, Zayde, 120
Arabic language
Abū Ḥanīfa's proficiency in, 182
Quran and, 154, 176–82
state administration, used for, 168
Arabs, 155–6, 164, 167–9, 273
Asad b. ʿAmr, 299
Asad b. ʿAmr al-Bajalī, 231, 300
Asad b. al-Furāt, 300
Asad b. Mūsā al-Umawī, 314
al-Aʿshā Hamdān, 125–8

*aṣḥāb al-ḥadīth* (traditionalists), 14, 72
*aṣḥāb al-kalām*, 73
al-Ashʿarī, 8, 240, 339
al-Aṣmaʿī, 196
Assmann, Jan, 5, 21. *See also* mnemohistory
Aswad b. Sālim, 254
ʿAṭāʾ b. Muslim, 186
*āthār* (reports). *See* Prophetic ḥadīth
Auerbach, Erich, 130
authority
  of Prophetic ḥadīth, 28, 30, 36, 74, 172–4, 228, 233, 242, 314
  of qadis, 208, 296, 353
  of rulers, 202, 208–9, 210, 255–6, 311
authority, religious
  of ʿAbd Allāh b. Aḥmad b. Ḥanbal, 96
  of Abū Yūsuf, 345
  curses and, 145
  al-Fazārī on, 195
  Ibn Abī Ḥātim on, 106–7
  of Mālik b. Anas, 107–8, 345
  perceived absence of, in Islam, 7, 19, 357, 358, 360
  of al-Shaybānī, 345
  of Sufyān al-Thawrī, 106, 345
al-Awzāʿī, 74, 84, 88, 194, 226, 334
Ayyūb al-Sakhtiyānī, 78, 253, 254

*bāb al-firya* (slander), 163
Babel, 131–3
Babylon (Bābil), 141–2, 161
*baʿḍ al-nās* ('some people'), 45, 46, 58–9
al-Baghawī, Abū al-Qāsim, 332, 333
Baghdad
  al-Bukhārī in, 62, 68
  al-Fasawī on, 123
  Ibn Abī Shayba in, 34
  *madhhab*s in, 330–1
  *manāqib* works from, 296, 303
Bahāʾ al-Dawla, 330
al-Bajalī, al-Ḥusayn b. al-Faḍl, 204, 232
Bakkār b. Qutayba, 291, 293, 294, 296
al-Balādhurī, 186
Balkh, 190, 252
Banī Taym Allāh b. Thaʿlaba, 158
Banū Qafal, 157–8
Banū Rabīʿa Taym Allāh Najd, 157
Baqī b. Makhlad, 362
al-Barbahārī, 252
al-Bardhaʿī, 100, 102–5
Basra, 125–9, 143, 185, 280, 296, 314
Bauer, Walter, 9–10
al-Bayhaqī, 212
Baysān, 143
belief, nature of (*īmān*), 237
belief, realm of (*doxa*), 12, 117, 351, 356
Bellamy, James, 186
biographical dictionaries. *See also manāqib* (biographies); *masānīd* (collections of ḥadīth); *ṭabaqāt* works (biographical dictionaries)
  on genealogy, 157–9, 160
  Ḥanafī, 175, 205
  on Isḥāq b. Rāhawayh, 54
  *ṭabaqāt* works, 279–84, **281**, **282**, 293
  *Tārīkh Baghdād*, 24–5, 157–8, 165–6, 182, 219, 338
  on Wakīʿ b. al-Jarrāh, 78
biographies. *See manāqib* (biographies)
Bishr b. Abī al-Azhar al-Nīshāpūrī, 243
Bishr al-Ḥāfī, 86
Bishr al-Marīsī, 235
Bishr b. al-Walīd al-Kindī, 231
black clothing, 197
Bollandists, 310
book production, 109
Boyarin, Daniel, 12
Brown, Jonathan, 8, 17
Brown, Peter, 8, 112, 145, 256
Bukhārā, 68, 88, 169, 179, 300–3
al-Bukhārī, 43–6, 56, 58–61
  Abū Yūsuf and, 64, 198
  Aḥmad b. Ḥanbal and, 58, 68
  in Baghdad, 62, 68
  biographical details of, 121–2
  on ethnogenesis, 167
  al-Ḥumaydī and, 39–41, 47, 81, 219
  Ibn al-Mubārak and, 80
  Ibn Qutayba and, 71
  on Ibn Shabbuwayh, 85
  Isḥāq b. Rāhawayh and, 48, 112
  on Jahmiyya, 245–6
  *Khalq afʿāl al-ʿibād wa al-radd ʿalā al-jahmiyya wa aṣḥāb al-taʿṭīl*, 245
  in Khurāsān, 62, 68, 171, 174
  *Kitāb al-Ḍuʿafāʾ al-ṣaghīr*, 67
  *Kitāb al-Tārīkh*, 204
  on Kufa, 134–6
  Mālik b. Anas and, 58, 88
  on Murjiʾa, 63
  on orthodoxy, 172
  proto-Ḥanafīs and, 62
  *Rafʿ al-yadayn fī al-ṣalāt*, 173, 175
  on rebellion, 194, 199
  on repenting from heresy, 81
  on ritual prayer, 171–4
  *Ṣaḥīḥ*, 43–5, 49, 85, 204
  al-Sarrāj and, 58
  on scholars, 67
  al-Shāfiʿī and, 47

al-Shaybānī and, 225
'some people' (*ba'ḍ al-nās*), 45, 46, 58–9
Sufyān al-Thawrī and, 66
*al-Tārīkh al-awsaṭ*, 64–7, 195, 245
*al-Tārīkh al-kabīr*, 50, 63–4
on Wakī' b. al-Jarrāh, 62, 173
Busāq, 138, 139
Būyid dynasty, 329

Calder, Norman, 7, 72
caliphs, 209, 255–6, 296, 297, 333. *See also* 'Abbāsid caliphate; *individual caliphs*
Carlyle, Thomas, 16
cattle, 135, 136
charity, 36, 197
chosen people, 154–6
Christianity, 123, 154, 158, 214, 359, 360
cities, unholy. *See* regionalism
civil war (First Fitna), 148
coins, 177
collective memory. *See* mnemohistory
Companions, 36, 230, 242, 268, 269–72, 281, 320. *See also* Prophetic ḥadīth
comparative research, 6
consensus (*ijmā'*)
proto-Sunni traditionalist response to, 334–7, 355–6
Quran 2.143, 322
Sunni orthodoxy, 329, 332, 338, 348
conversion, 51, 174–7, 264, 292, 299
converts, 159–60, 168, 169, 273
Cook, M., 71
credal treatises, 237, 238–40, 253, 340–1
Crone, Patricia, 171
curses, 145–51

al-Ḍaḥḥāk b. Qays, 150
Damascus, 129, 306
al-Dāraquṭnī, 86, 212, 230, 304
al-Dārimī, 212, 220, 221, 222, 224, 245, 314
Dāwūd al-Ẓāhirī, 283
death
of Abū Ḥanīfa, 64, 68, 77, 192, 242–3, 269–72, 334
of scholars, 242
of Sufyān al-Thawrī, 307
deeds, 344
defecation, 138, 141
destinarianism, 95
devil. *See also* Iblīs; Satan
defecation, 138, 141
al-Fasawī on, 134, 138, 143–4, 148–51
horns of, 144, 146–7
in Kufa, 138–45, 148, 149, 250, 351
lack of scholarship on, 139
as social actor, 138, 139–45, 148, 149
al-Dhahabī, 44, 56, 85, 169, 199, 267, 301
Dharr b. 'Abd Allāh, 85
Dībāja (Muḥammad b. Ja'far b. Muḥammad b. 'Alī), 189
Dickinson, Eerik, 8, 17, 100, 290
Dīnawār, 70
al-Dīnawārī, 168
Ḍirār b. 'Amr, 92, 165, 237
discourse, definition of, 11, 20. *See also* heresy, discourses of
disease used as metaphor for heresy, 248–51, 253, 254
disenchantment, 117
distribution of good and evil, 130–1, 138
divine election, 154–6
divine providence, 130
*dīwān* (chancery), 177
doxography, 338
al-Dūlābī, 265, 267
al-Dūrī, 75
Durkheim, É., 356

Egypt, 291–300, 314, 333
El Shamsy, Ahmed, 27, 31
elegies (*marthiya*), 50
El-Hibri, Tayeb, 148
Eliade, Mircea, 124
elites, political, 34, 65, 69, 196, 202, 204
elites, religious, 111
epidemics, 64, 250, 251
epithets, 85
eponyms. *See also* Abū Ḥanīfa; Aḥmad b. Ḥanbal; *madhhabs* (schools of law); Mālik b. Anas; al-Shāfi'ī
Abū Nu'aym al-Iṣfahānī on, 320
Companions and, 271
in general, 3, 4, 16, 25
*madhhab*s and, 16, 347
*manāqib* works and, 310, 312
al-Rāwandī on, 347
erasure (*al-ḥakk*), 337
ethnicity. *See also* genealogy
Arab identity and, 154–7, 167–9, 273
ethnogenesis, 153–4, 156, 162, 167, 351
ethno-racial reasoning
'Abd Allāh b. Aḥmad b. Ḥanbal, 163, 164
*'ajam*, 160, 167–9, 172
in general, 153–4, 162
influence on society, 156
Iraq, against people from, 162
by al-Khaṭīb al-Baghdādī, 157–8

ethnicity (cont.)
muwalladūn (acculturated Arabs), 164–6, 212
nabaṭī, 162–4
scholars, used to discredit, 164, 169
in general, 153–4, 156
Islam and, 154
military life, influence on, 156
Persians, 155, 167–9, 177
Shuʿūbism, 167–9
ethnography, 162
ethnos (Arabness), 154–6
Eusebius of Caesarea, 124
Eve, 143
executions, 185, 189

Faḍāʾil Abī Ḥanīfa (Ibn Abī al-ʿAwwām al-Saʿdī)
on ancestry, 272–3
authorship of, 265–9, 281–2
on judgeships, 297–9
proto-Ḥanafism, spread of, 175
on rebellion, 276
on repenting from heresy, 257–9, 273–6
responding to heresy, 257–9, 272, 273, 276–9
on Successors, 268–72
ṭabaqāt in, 279–82, **281**, **282**
al-Ṭaḥāwī and, 293, 300
Faḍāʾil Abī Ḥanīfa (al-Shuʿaybī), 306
Faḍāʾil al-Imām (Ibn Kās), 290
al-Faḍl b. Mūsā al-Sīnānī, 49, 52
faith, nature of, 95, 344
Fārs, 121
Fasā, 121
al-Fasawī
on Abū Ḥanīfa's death, 77, 242
on Abū Yūsuf, 79–81
Abū Zurʿa al-Dimashqī and, 82–4
on Baghdad, 123
biographical details of, 169–71
al-Ḥumaydī and, 58, 67, 68
Ibn al-Mubārak and, 62, 66, 172
Kitāb al-Sunna, 41
Mashyakha, 41, 123
on Murjiʾa, 79
on other religions, 214
on rebellion, 65
regionalism
Basra, 125–7, 128
curses, 145–8
devil, 134, 138, 143–4, 148–51
disease used as metaphor for heresy, 249
distribution of good and evil, 130, 138
in general, 120
Iraq, 76, 138, 142–4, 145–7, 148–9, 249
Kufa, 118–19, 123, 124, 125–9, 131–3, 134, 138, 143, 145, 147, 249, 351
scholarship and, 122–4
Shām, 129, 138, 139, 148
on repenting from heresy, 68
on social exclusion, 253
on speculative jurisprudence, 78, 212, 214, 219, 221
travels, 121–3
Faṣl ʿalā taqdīm Abī Ḥanīfa (Maḥmūd b. Manṣūr b. Abī al-Faḍl), 306–8
Faṣl fī manāqib Abī Ḥa (Aḥmad b. al-Ṣalt), 290
fātiḥa, 181
al-Fawāʾid al-muʿallala (Abū Zurʿa al-Dimashqī), 84
Fierro, Maribel, 8, 356
al-Firabrī, 62
firaq genre. See heresiography
First Fitna, 148
foreignness, 162
Foucault, Michel, 11, 20
freedmen, 159
Friday prayer, 200
Fuḍayl b. Zubayr al-Rassān, 187
funeral of Abū Ḥanīfa, 243
Furkani, Mehterhan, 302

Gedächtnisgeschichte. See mnemohistory
genealogies, 155, 161
genealogy. See also ethnicity
biographical dictionaries, 157–9, 160
falsifying, 160–2
Ibn Ḥibbān on, 157
importance of, in medieval society, 157
al-Khaṭīb al-Baghdādī on, 157–9, 160
scholars, used to discredit, 157
servile origins, 157–9, 160–2
Shuʿūbism and, 168
genres
hagiography, 311
heresiography. See heresiography
impacting development of religious movements, 283
jurisprudential, 28–32, 35
Gernet, Louis, 112
al-Ghassānī, Abū Mushir, 84
Ghaylān al-Dimashqī, 72
al-Ghazālī, 344, 362
Ghiyāth al-Dīn Kaykhusraq, 345
al-Ghulām al-Thaqafī, 148

Ghunjār, 169, 170–1
gifts, 59
Ginzburg, Carlo, 22, 23
Goldziher, Ignaz, 17
governors, 209
greater pilgrimage (*ḥajj*), 67, 193, 201, 224, 298
Gunther, Sebastian, 186

ḥadīth
 ʿAbd Allāh b. Aḥmad b. Ḥanbal on, 232
 Abū Yūsuf's proficiency in, 230, 231
 Aḥmad b. Ḥanbal, 231
 authority of, 228, 314
 Ḥanafism and, 317
 heresy, discourses of, 33, 36, 172, 228–34, 314, 322, 334
 al-Ḥumaydī, 41, 44, 58
 Ibn Abī Shayba, 34
 Ibn Ḥibbān on, 336
 of intention, 58, 59
 *masānīd*. *See masānīd* (collections of ḥadīth)
 Prophetic ḥadīth. *See* Prophetic ḥadīth
 proto-Ḥanafism, 216–18
 proto-Sunni traditionalism, 228–34, 314
 proto-Sunnism, 234
 al-Shaybānī's proficiency in, 230
 speculative jurisprudence and, 214–22
 study of, 121–3, 332
al-Ḥāfiẓ al-Tujībī, 267
Ḥafṣ b. Ghiyāth, 218
hagiography, 310–12
*ḥajj* (greater pilgrimage), 67, 193, 201, 224, 298
al-Ḥajjāj (governor of Babel), 142, 149
Ḥajjāj b. Yūsuf al-Thaqafī, 150
al-Ḥākim bi-Amr Allāh, 266
al-Ḥākim al-Nīshāpūrī, 56, 204, 234, 285, 288, 301, 305, 314
*al-ḥakk* (erasure), 337
Hallaq, Wael, 8
Ḥammād b. Abī Ḥanīfa, 288
Ḥammād b. Abī Sulaymān, 73, 85, 254
Ḥammād b. Salama, 234
Ḥanafism. *See also madhhabs* (schools of law); proto-Ḥanafism
 ʿAbbāsid caliphate and, 204–5
 in Egypt, 291–3, 295
 ḥadīth and, 317
 Karrāmiyya and, 343
 in Khurāsān, 340–2
 *madhhab*s and, 345–8
 as majoritarian orthodoxy, 338
 *masānīd*, 315, 317
 in Nīshāpūr, 288–9
 al-Qādir and, 331–2
 qadis, 202, 205, 251, 291, 296, 298
 al-Rāwandī on, 345–8
 al-Samarqandī on, 340–1, 344
 al-Ṭaḥāwī and, 292, 295, 299
 textual communities and, 300
 traditionalisation, 292, 339
 in Transoxiana, 340–1, 344
Ḥanbal b. Isḥāq, 69
Ḥanbalism, 330, 331
al-Ḥārithī al-Subadhmūnī, 300, 319, 321
al-Ḥārith b. Surayj, 160, 190, 247–8, 297
Hārūn al-Rashīd (caliph), 65, 196–8, 298
Hārūt (angel), 141–2
al-Ḥasan b. ʿAlī b. al-Jaʿd, 312
al-Ḥasan b. Ḥammād Sajjāda, 275
al-Ḥasan b. Ṣāliḥ, 199, 201
Ḥasan b. Zayd, 333
al-Ḥasan family land endowments, 185
Hegesippus, 10
Henderson, John B., 356
Herāt, 289
heresiography
 Abū Ḥanīfa as exemplar of Sunni orthodoxy in, 338
 discourses of heresy and, 241
 historiography and, 8, 13–14, 113, 117, 240, 356, 358, 359
heresiologists, 10, 12
heresy. *See also* orthodoxy
 defining of, against orthodoxy, 52, 91, 93
 discourses of. *See* heresy, discourses of
 historiography and, 113–15, 361
 regulation of, 3, 20, 52, 104–5, 244, 256
 repenting from. *See* repenting from heresy
 scholarship on, modern, 7–17
 sociology of. *See* heresy, sociology of
heresy, discourses of
 ancestry, 88, 268, 272
 anti-Christ, 64, 68
 Arabic language proficiency, 182
 conciliatory approach to, 320–1
 confessional impurity, 158
 danger to Islam, Abū Ḥanīfa as, 65, 96
 death of Abū Ḥanīfa, 64, 68, 96, 195, 242–3, 334
 disease used as metaphor for, 249–51, 253, 254
 ethnicity. *See* ethnicity
 genealogy, 157–9, 160–2
 in general, 25–6, 350
 ḥadīth, 33, 36, 172, 228–34, 314, 322, 334

heresy, discourses of (cont.)
harmful birth of Abū Ḥanīfa, 89, 96, 242–3, 334
heresiography and, 241
Jahmiyya, 245–8
Judaism and, 78, 166, 213, 359
legal arguments. *See* analogical reasoning (*qiyās*); jurisprudence; speculative jurisprudence (*ra'y*)
*manāqib* works, leading to lack of, 286
*masānīd*, 314–17, 320–1, 322
Miḥna, 235–7
Muḥammad, failure to praise, 242
Murji'a. *See* Murji'a (movement)
piety, 241–3
proximate 'other', 61–3, 351, 360
Quran, createdness of. *See* Quran, createdness of
rebellion. *See* rebellion, discourses of heresy
refusing to swear oaths, 258–9
repenting from heresy. *See* repenting from heresy
ritual prayer, 171–4, 178–81, 241
scholars and, 79
social exclusion. *See* social exclusion
society, in all aspects of, 12, 113–15, 117, 118, 206, 353, 360
students implicating Abū Ḥanīfa, 79–81
Successors, not from generation of, 88, 268, 272
theological arguments, 235–41
transregional phenomenon, 81, 83, 289, 335
'true believers' and ignorance, 47–8, 81, 255, 257
heresy, sociology of
disease used as metaphor for heresy, 248–51, 253, 254
in general, 243, 353
network of heresiarchs, 244–8
proto-Sunni traditionalist view of, 244–8
social exclusion. *See* social exclusion
heretics, 127–8, 134, 138, 249, 252–5
Ḥijāz, 39, 47, 68. *See also* Mecca; Medina
Hilāl b. Ra'y, 294, 295, 298
*Ḥilyat al-awliyā'* (Abū Nu'aym), 320
Ḥīra, 132
Hishām (caliph), 185, 189
Hishām al-Burayd, 186
Hishām b. 'Urwa, 39, 165
historical documents. *See* primary sources
historiography
devil, lack of study on, 139
heresiography and, 8, 13–14, 113, 117, 240, 356, 358, 359
of medieval local historians, 119
model of fragmentation, 353
orthodoxy/heresy and, 113–15, 361
primary sources. *See* primary sources
Zaydī, 186
*ḥiyal* (legal tricks), 44, 58, 59, 211, 223–6
holy places, 123–4, 129
horns of the devil, 144, 146–7
al-Ḥumaydī
Abū Zur'a al-Dimashqī and, 85
Aḥmad b. Ḥanbal and, 48, 112
al-Bukhārī and, 43–6, 58, 67, 68
disciplinary dimension, 52
al-Fasawī and, 39, 47, 81, 219
ḥadīth, 41, 44, 58
Ibn Abī Ḥātim on, 46, 47
Ibn Ḥibbān on, 46
Isḥāq b. Rāhawayh and, 52–4
al-Khalīlī on, 195
in Mecca, 39, 45, 81, 254
*Musnad*, 40, 42–3, 44, 314
*Refutation against al-Nu'mān*, 46, 47
on rituals, 67
al-Shāfi'ī and, 58
social exclusion by, 45, 254
on speculative jurisprudence, 219
statement on Proto-sunni traditionalism, 48, 112
on 'true believers' and ignorance, 47–8, 81, 255, 257
al-Ḥusayn b. Ibrāhīm b. al-Ḥurr, 231
al-Ḥusayn b. Idrīs al-Anṣārī, 305
al-Ḥusayn b. Muḥammad, 150
al-Ḥusayn b. al-Qāsim al-Ibrāhīm, 187
al-Ḥusayn family land endowments, 185
Ḥusn (wife of Aḥmad b. Ḥanbal), 90

*al-Ibāna* (al-Ash'arī), 240
*al-Ibāna* (al-Surmārī), 302, 331
Iblīs, 139, 140, 143
Ibn 'Abbās, 222
Ibn 'Abd al-Barr, 54, 286, 312, 347
Ibn 'Abdān, 233
Ibn Abī al-'Anbas, 295
Ibn Abī 'Āṣim, 93, 245
Ibn Abī Awfā, 270
Ibn Abī al-'Awwām
on ancestry, 269, 270–3
authorship of *Faḍā'il Abī Ḥanīfa*, 265, 267–9, 281–2
as qadi, 265–6
responding to heresy, 275, 279
on Sufyān al-Thawrī, 272, 275–6

*ṭabaqāt* section of, 280, 281–2
Ibn Abī al-ʿAwwām al-Saʿdī, 267
authorship of *Faḍā'il Abī Ḥanīfa*, 267, 268
biographical details of, 265–6
*Faḍā'il Abī Ḥanīfa. See Faḍā'il Abī Ḥanīfa* (Ibn Abī al-ʿAwwām al-Saʿdī)
responding to heresy, 275, 276–7, 278
*ṭabaqāt* section of, 280
al-Ṭaḥāwī and, 265
Ibn Abī Du'ād, 235
Ibn Abī Dunyā, 140
Ibn Abī Ḥātim
accommodating towards Abū Ḥanīfa, 105–9
on authority, religious, 106–7
on al-Ḥumaydī, 46, 47
on Ibn Saʿd, 32
on Ibn Shabbuwayh, 86
on Isḥāq b. Rāhawayh, 50, 53, 101
on Mālik b. Anas, 107–8
on speculative jurisprudence, 222
on Sufyān al-Thawrī, 106
*Taqdima, Kitāb al-Jarḥ wa al-taʿdīl*, 100, 106
Ibn Abī Ḥātim al-Rāzī, 32, 99, 100, 194
Ibn Abī Jarāda, 307
Ibn Abī Layla, 257, 278
Ibn Abī Layth al-Aṣamm, 235
Ibn Abī Shayba, 34–7, 85, 90, 94, 178, 212
Ibn Abī Ṭāhir Ṭayfūr, 32
Ibn Abī Thawr, 300
Ibn Abī al-Wafā', 285
Ibn ʿAdī, 43, 314, 322–3, 332–6, 338, 355
Ibn ʿAsākir, 271
Ibn Ashʿath, 150, 160
Ibn ʿAwn, 219, 252, 319
Ibn ʿAyyāsh, 128
Ibn Baṭṭa al-ʿUkbarī, 212
Ibn Baṭṭāl, 61
Ibn al-Faḍl al-Qaṭṭān, 304
Ibn al-Faqīh, 128
Ibn Ḥajar, 62, 218
Ibn Ḥajar al-ʿAsqalānī, 44, 169, 267–8
Ibn al-Ḥaṭṭāb al-Rāzī, 266
Ibn Ḥibbān
on genealogy, 157
on al-Ḥumaydī, 46
on Karrāmīs, 175
al-Khaṭīb al-Baghdādī and, 323
in Khurāsān, 335
*Kitāb al-Majrūḥīn*, 335–7
*masānīd*, reaction to, 323–4
on medieval Sunni orthodoxy, 335–7, 338, 355
on Murji'a, 324, 337
refuses to speak Abū Ḥanīfa's name, 45
on repenting from heresy, 257
on al-Shaybānī, 336–7
on Yaḥyā b. Maʿīn, 337
Ibn Hubayra, 76
Ibn al-Junayd, 75
Ibn Karrām, 175, 176, 343
Ibn Kās al-Nakhaʿī, 290
Ibn Khallikān, 49
Ibn Khuzayma, 294, 333, 335
Ibn Māja, 212
Ibn Manda, 218, 301, 316, 321–2
Ibn Manẓūr, 126, 162, 164
Ibn al-Mubārak
al-Bukhārī and, 62, 66, 172
denouncing Abū Ḥanīfa, 51, 334
al-Fasawī and, 80
Hārūn al-Rashīd on, 196
Isḥāq b. Rāhawayh and, 49, 51
on *Kitāb al-Ḥiyal*, 99, 224
praising Abū Ḥanīfa, 87–8
on rebellion, 188
on repenting from heresy, 274
on Sufyān al-Thawrī, 66
Ibn al-Mufliḥ, 140
Ibn al-Muqaffaʿ, 209–11
Ibn al-Nadīm, 50
Ibn Nāṣir al-Dīn, 305
Ibn al-Qaysarānī, 43
Ibn Qutayba, 39, 54–6, 69–75, 76, 168, 246
Ibn Saʿd, 32–4, 37, 39, 228, 231, 232
Ibn Shabbuwayh, 85–9, 90, 94
Ibn Shāhīn, 229, 319
Ibn Shaqīq, 214
Ibn al-Sharqī, ʿAbd Allāh, 305
Ibn Shubruma, 278
Ibn Ṭumlūs, 362–3, 364
Ibn ʿUmar, 128, 173
Ibn ʿUqda, 308, 318, 319
Ibn al-Ushnānī, 315, 319
Ibn ʿUyayna, 164
Ibn Waḍḍāḥ, 163–4, 220, 249, 252, 260
Ibn Wahbān, 285
Ibn Yūnus, 294
Ibn Yūnus al-Ṣadafī, 292
Ibn Zūlāq, 293
Ibrāhīm b. ʿAbd Allāh, 150, 186, 197, 199, 220, 297
Ibrāhīm b. Abī Bakr, 34
Ibrāhīm b. ʿAlī al-Dhuhlī, 305
Ibrāhīm b. Arūma, 103, 104
Ibrāhīm b. Muḥammad al-Fazārī, 65
Ibrāhīm al-Nakhaʿī, 72
Ibrāhīm b. Saʿd, 148

Ibrāhīm b. Ṣāliḥ, 203
Ibrāhīm b. Yūsuf al-Balkhī, 252
*al-Ifāda* (Abū Ṭālib al-Hārūnī), 192
Ifrīqiya, 300
*ijmāʿ*. *See* consensus (*ijmāʿ*)
*ijtihad* (independent legal reasoning), 31
*Ikhtilāf fī al-lafẓ wa al-radd ʿalā al-Jahmiyya wa al-mushabbiha* (Ibn Qutayba), 246
*īmān* (belief, nature of), 237
ʿImrān b. Dāwar Abū al-ʿAwwām al-Qaṭṭān, 199
inquisitions, 255–60. *See also* Miḥna; repenting from heresy
institutionalised egotism, 8, 256
institutions
 Durkheim on, 357
 in Islam, perceived absence of, 7, 19, 357, 358, 360
 Saljūq dynasty, 353
interdisciplinary research, 6
*iqāma* (final call to prayer), 57
Iraq. *See also* Baghdad; Kufa
 curse against, 145–7
 devil in, 138, 142–4, 145–7, 148–9
 ethno-racial reasoning against people from, 162
 al-Fasawī on, 76, 138, 142–4, 145–7, 148–9, 249
 *manāqib* works from, 290, 303–5
 political upheaval in, 148–9, 150–1
 as unholy region, 76, 135–7, 138, 249, 351
Irenaeus, 10
Irjāʼ. *See* Murjiʼa (movement)
*al-Irshād fī maʿrifat ʿulamāʼ al-ḥadīth* (al-Khalīlī), 69, 195, 204, 252
ʿĪsā b. Abān, 45
ʿĪsā b. Rūḥ, 300
Isḥāq b. Ḥanbal, 203
Isḥāq b. Rāhawayh
 Abū Zurʿa al-Rāzī and, 101–2
 Aḥmad b. Ḥanbal and, 49, 53, 203
 on analogical reasoning, 55
 al-Bazzār and, 288, 289
 al-Bukhārī and, 48–56, 68, 204
 in general, 38
 al-Ḥumaydī and, 48, 112
 Ibn Abī Ḥātim and, 50, 53, 101
 Ibn al-Mubārak and, 49, 51
 Ibn Qutayba and, 54–6, 71–2, 74
 on Khurāsān, 52, 289
 *masānīd* works by, 314
 name of, 49
 on orthodoxy, 98
 as Persian scholar, 168
 al-Shāfiʿī and, 52–4
 on speculative jurisprudence, 51, 53, 55, 87
 Ṭāhirid dynasty and, 203–4
 Wakīʿ b. al-Jarrāh and, 49
Isḥāq b. Ṭulayq, 177
Islam. *See also madhhabs* (schools of law); proto-Ḥanafism; proto-Sunni traditionalism; Quran; Shiʿism; Sunnism
 Abū Ḥanīfa as danger to, 65, 96
 Arabic language, revealed in, 154
 ethnicity and, 154
 institutional structures, absence of, 7, 19, 357, 358, 360
 as lived religion, 260, 358
 rationality of, 144
 scholarship on, modern, 20
 *shahāda* (testification of Islam), 177
Ismāʿīl b. Aḥmad, 339
Ismāʿīl b. Aḥmad al-Sāmānī, 301
Ismāʿīl b. Ḥammād b. Abī Ḥanīfa, 161, 236
Ismāʿīl b. Ibrāhīm b. Mughīra, 169
Ismāʿīl b. Mūsā al-Ḥabībī, 266
Ismāʿīl b. ʿUrʿura, 245
Ismāʿīl b. Yaḥyā al-Muzanī, 60, 200–1, 253, 292, 294, 299
*isnād*s (lists of transmitters), 186–9, 228, 233, 281, 324
*istiḥsān* (juristic technique), 28–32
Iyās b. Muʿāwiya, 29

Jābir, 103
Jaʿfar b. Aḥmad b. ʿAlī b. Bayān b. Zayd b. Siyāba, 332
Jaʿfar b. Aʿyan, 265, 267
Jaʿfar al-Ṣādiq, 189
al-Jāḥiẓ, 109, 110, 156, 169, 277
Jahm b. Ṣafwān, 190, 245–8
Jahmiyya. *See also* Murjiʼa (movement); Quran, createdness of
 ʿAbd Allāh b. Aḥmad b. Ḥanbal on, 95, 97, 247
 Abū Ḥanīfa and, 80, 102, 237, 247
 Abū Yūsuf on, 80
 Murjiʼa and, 237, 343
 other religions as preferable to, 214
 al-Samarqandī on, 343
al-Jahshiyārī, 177
al-Jamal, 192
Jārūdī branch of Zaydism, 318
al-Jawraqānī, 232
Jerusalem, 124
Jones, A.H.M., 14
Judaism, 78, 166, 211–14, 359

judges. *See* qadis
jurisprudence
  Abū Ḥanīfa's lack of knowledge on, 220
  analogical reasoning. *See* analogical reasoning (*qiyās*)
  dialectic, jurisprudential, 28–32, 35
  in general, 208–11
  *ḥiyal* (legal tricks), 44, 58, 59, 211, 223–6
  'I do not know', 221–2
  Ibn al-Muqaffaʿ on, 210
  *istiḥsān*, 28–32
  judicial decision making (*qaḍāʾ*), 210
  jurists, 193, 209
  from Kufa, 210
  lawmaking, 214–18
  legal disputations (*al-khuṣūmāt*), 220
  proto-Ḥanafism, 216–18, 223, 224–5, 226–7
  proto-Sunni traditionalism, 217, 221–2, 223–7
  retracting earlier opinions, 74, 215–18
  al-Shāfiʿī on, 27–9, 30–2, 35, 37
  speculative. *See* speculative jurisprudence (*raʾy*)
  of Sufyān al-Thawrī, 213, 215
juristic reasoning. *See* speculative jurisprudence (*raʾy*)
Jurjān, 185, 247, 332–3
Justin, 10
al-Jūzajānī, 224, 230

Kaʿb al-Aḥbār, 137, 249
Kaʿba, 47, 81, 93, 257, 299, 347
*kāfir* (unbeliever), 224, 248
al-Kalābādhī, 319
*al-Kāmil fī al-ḍuʿafāʾ* (Ibn ʿAdī), 333
al-Karābisī, 27
al-Karkhī, 286
Karrāmiyya, 175, 343, 363
*Kashf al-āthār fī manāqib Abī Ḥanīfa* (al-Ḥārithī al-Subadhmūnī), 300
Kāṭib Çelebī, 302
al-Kawtharī, Muḥammad Zāhid, 355–6
Khadīja, 289
Khālid b. ʿAmr, 190
Khālid al-Qasrī, 82, 185
Khālid b. Ziyād, 190
al-Khalīlī, 69, 194, 204, 233, 252
al-Khallāl, 201
*Khalq afʿāl al-ʿibād wa al-radd ʿalā al-jahmiyya wa aṣḥāb al-taʿṭīl* ((al-Bukhārī), 245
Khārijites, 82
al-Khaṭīb al-Baghdādī
  Abū ʿAlī b. Shādhān and, 304
  on Abū Ḥanīfa's weak grasp of Arabic, 182
  on genealogy, 157–9, 160
  on al-Ḥārithī al-Subadhmūnī, 301
  Ibn Ḥibbān and, 323
  *manāqib*, use of, 338, 339
  on Mukram b. Aḥmad, 304
  on speculative jurisprudence, 212, 219
  *Tārīkh Baghdād*, 24–5, 157–8, 165–6, 182, 219, 338
al-Khaṭṭābī, 59, 135
Khawārij, 125, 259
Khurāsān
  Abū Yaḥyā al-Bazzār in, 288
  al-Bukhārī on, 62, 68, 171, 174
  discourses of heresy from, 289
  Ḥanafism in, 340–2
  Ibn Ḥibbān in, 335
  Isḥāq b. Rāhawayh on, 52, 289
  *mawālī* soldiers from, 168
  Murjiʾa in, 192
  proto-Ḥanafism in, 174–8, 216, 280
  rebellions in, 171, 190
al-Khuraybī, ʿAbd Allāh b. Dāwūd, 298
*al-khuṣūmāt* (legal disputations), 220
*Kitāb al-Adab* (Ibn Abī Shayba), 178
*Kitāb al-Aghānī* (Abū al-Faraj al-Iṣfahānī), 127
*Kitāb al-Ḍuʿafāʾ* (al-ʿUqaylī), 337
*Kitāb al-Ḍuʿafāʾ al-ṣaghīr* (al-Bukhārī), 67
*Kitāb al-Ḥayawān* (al-Jāḥiẓ), 110
*Kitāb al-Ḥiyal* (book on legal tricks), 99, 224–5
*Kitāb Ibṭāl al-istiḥsān* (al-Shāfiʿī), 28, 30
*Kitāb al-ʿIlal* (Aḥmad b. Ḥanbal (attr.)), 256–7
*Kitāb al-ʿIlal wa maʿrifat al-rijāl* (ʿAbd Allāh b. Aḥmad b. Ḥanbal), 164
*Kitāb al-ʿIlm* (al-Dārimī), 222
*Kitāb al-Kharāj* (Abū Yūsuf (attr.)), 29
*Kitāb al-Khiṣāl* (Ibn Kās), 290
*Kitāb al-Maʿārif* (Ibn Qutayba), 70, 72–3
*Kitāb al-Majrūḥīn* (Ibn Ḥibbān), 335–7
*Kitāb al-Maʿrifa wa al-tārīkh* (al-Fasawī). *See* al-Fasawī
*Kitāb al-Siyar* (al-Fazārī), 195
*Kitāb al-Sunna* (ʿAbd Allāh b. Aḥmad b. Ḥanbal), 87, 92, 94–8, *97*, 215–16, 247
*Kitāb al-Sunna* (al-Fasawī), 41
*Kitāb al-Sunna* (Ibn Abī ʿĀṣim), 93
*Kitāb al-Sunna* (Muḥammad b. Naṣr al-Marwazī), 94
*Kitāb al-Taḥrīsh* (Ḍirār b. ʿAmr), 92, 165, 237

*Kitāb al-Tārīkh* (al-Bukhārī), 204
*Kitāb al-Tawḥīd* (Ibn Manda), 322
*Kitāb al-Umm* (al-Shāfiʿī), 27–8, 30, 163
*Kitāb Wahm al-ṭabaqa al-ẓalama Abā Ḥanīfa* (al-Subadhmūnī), 301
*Kitāb al-Waraʿ* (Abū Bakr al-Marr ūdhī), 50–2
Knysh, Alexander, 7, 8, 356
Kufa
  Abū Ḥanīfa repenting from heresy in, 81, 275
  Basra, rivalry with, 125–9
  al-Bukhārī on, 134–6
  devil in, 138–45, 148, 149, 250, 351
  disease, as repository of, 250–1
  false prophets from, 128
  foreign ethnicities in, 132
  jurisprudence from, 210
  *masānīd* from, 314
  Murji'a in, 192
  proto-Ḥanafism in, 280
  rebellions, 148–51, 185, 191
  al-Shāfiʿī on, 28
  al-Shaybānī in, 298
  as unholy region, 131–3, 134, 138

*lā ba's bi dhālika* (not a problem), 36
al-Lālakā'ī, 201, 221
language
  Abū Ḥanīfa's proficiency of Arabic, 182
  Arabic, 154, 168, 176–82
  groups, spoken by, 46
  liturgical, 176, 178–81
  Pahlavi, 177
  Persian, 176, 178–82
  Quran and, 154, 176–82
  al-Shaybānī on, 178, 181
  state administration, used for, 168
al-Layth b. Saʿd, 334
Le Boulluec, Alain, 10–11, 13, 359
legal arguments against Abū Ḥanīfa. *See* jurisprudence
legal disputations (*al-khuṣūmāt*), 220
Lewis, Bernard, 8
libel, 163
liturgical language, 176, 178–81
local histories, 119, 129, 133
local orthodoxies, 52, 81
Lucas, Scott, 8, 17, 36, 236

*al-Mabsūṭ* (al-Sarakhsī), 180
al-Madā'in, 185
Madelung, Wilferd, 8, 17
*madhhabs* (schools of law). *See also* Ḥanafism; Ḥanbalism; eponyms; Mālikism; Shāfiʿism
  eponymous founders and, 16, 347
  Ḥanafism and, 345–8
  *manāqib* works and, 264, 302, 309
  al-Muqaddasī on, 363–4
  al-Qādir and, 329–32
  al-Rāwandī on, 345–8
  Sunni orthodoxy, importance for, 16, 356, 363–4
  *ṭabaqāt* developed by followers of, 282
magic, 141
al-Mahdī (caliph), 207–8
Maḥmūd b. Manṣūr b. Abī al-Faḍl, 306–8
*Majmūʿa* 62 (manuscript), 321
*Makā'id al-shayṭān* (Ibn Abī Dunyā), 140
Makdisi, George, 8, 282–3, 329
*makhārij*, 223. *See also* *ḥiyal* (legal tricks)
Mālik b. Anas
  on Abū Ḥanīfa's death, 242
  al-Bukhārī on, 58, 88
  Companions, has not met, 320
  denouncing Abū Ḥanīfa, 334
  as founder of *madhhab*, 3
  on heresy coming from al-Mashriq, 136
  Ibn Abī Ḥātim on, 107–8
  on Kufa as repository for diseases, 250–1
  *Muwaṭṭa'*, 136
  al-Rāwandī on, 345
  religious authority of, 107–8, 345
  al-Shāfiʿī and, 107
  al-Shaybānī on, 107–8
  social exclusion by, 252–3
  on speculative jurisprudence, 222, 242, 278
Mālikism, 291, 331
*mamlūk* (slave captives), 157, 158
al-Ma'mūn (caliph), 32, 189, 225, 235, 250
Ma'mūn b. Aḥmad al-Sulamī, 175
*manāqib* (biographies). *See also* biographical dictionaries; *masānīd* (collections of ḥadīth); *ṭabaqāt* works (biographical dictionaries)
  from Baghdad, 296, 303
  from Bukhārā, 300–3
  chronology in, 269, 310
  on Companions, 271
  from Egypt, 291–300
  eponyms and, 310, 312
  in general, 261–2, 263–5, 308–12, 354–5
  geographical spread of, 308
  heresy, discourses of, influence on, 286
  history of, 284–8
  from Iraq, 290, 303–5

by al-Khaṭīb al-Baghdādī, 338, 339
*madhhab*s and, 264, 302, 309
on Miḥna, 236
from Nīshāpūr, 288–90, 305–6
qadis and, 293–9, 308
by al-Rāwandī, 344–8
on rebellion, 296
responding to heresy, 257–60, 265, 270, 272, 273, 276–9, 307–8
sectarian backgrounds of authors, 308
on al-Shāfiʿī, 283
social aspect of, 309–10
*ṭabaqāt* works and, 279
by al-Ṭaḥāwī, 285, 291, 292–5, 299–300
textual communities and, 306
timing of, 264, 308
*Manāqib Abī Ḥanīfa* (al-Bazzār), 289
*Manāqib Abī Ḥanīfa* (al-Ṭaḥāwī), 293–5, 299–300
Mannheim, Karl, 46
al-Manṣūr (caliph), 150, 190, 192, 195, 197, 275–6
Manṣūr al-Ḥallāj, 244
*Maqātil al-ṭālibiyyīn* (Abū al-Faraj al-Iṣfahānī), 186, 191
Mardāwīj b. Ziyār, 333
al-Marghīnānī, 302
marginalisation, 248
marriage, 53
*marthiya* (elegies), 50
Mārūt (angel), 141–2
Marw, 49, 50, 190
Marwān b. Muʿāwiya, 189, 198
*Masā'il* (Abū Ḥafṣ al-Kabīr), 180
*Masā'il* (legal questions and answers), 84, 90
*masānīd* (collections of ḥadīth)
by Ḥanafis, 315, 317
heresy, discourses of, 234, 314–17, 320–1, 322
by al-Ḥumaydī, 40, 42–3, 44, 314
by Ibn Ḥibbān, 323–4
by Isḥāq b. Rāhawayh, 314
from Kufa, 314
list of *musnad* works, 315–17
by non-Sunni authors, 317–18
orthodoxy in, narratives of, 262, 283, 313, 317, 324, 331, 354–5
by proto-Sunni traditionalists, 314–17, 318–25
on speculative jurisprudence, 317
textual communities and, 324
al-Mashriq, 134–7. *See also* Iraq
*Mashyakha* (al-Fasawī), 41, 123
al-Maṣṣīṣa, 195
*matn* (content of report), 228
*mawālī* (converts), 159–60, 168, 169, 273
al-Māwardī, 330
Mawṣil, 185
Mecca
al-Ḥumaydī in, 39, 45, 81, 254
Kaʿba, 47, 81, 93, 257, 299, 347
local orthodoxy in, 81
pilgrimage, 67, 193, 201, 224, 298
'true believers' and ignorance, 47–8, 81, 255, 257
Medina, 47, 64, 81, 250, 251, 257, 337
Melchert, Christopher, 8, 17, 36, 282, 331
memorising books, 203
memory studies. *See* mnemohistory
mentalités. *See* society, medieval
Mesopotamia, 141
microhistory, 22
Miḥna, 32, 95, 235–6. *See also* inquisitions; repenting from heresy
military life, 156
al-Miqdām b. Maʿdīkarib, 271
miraculous events, 310
Misʿar b. Kidām, 73, 191, 274
Miṣr, 123, 139, 143
mnemohistory, 5, 21–2, 207, 277
Moore, Robert, 249
Mottahedeh, Roy P., 169
al-Muʿallā b. Manṣūr, 103, 105, 231
Muʿāwiya, 149
Muḥammad, Prophet. *See also* Companions
ignorance of location of resting place, 47, 81, 257
praising, Abū Ḥanīfa's lack of, 242
Prophetic ḥadīth. *See* Prophetic ḥadīth
on Shām, 129
on tribulation, 134–7, 146–7
Muḥammad (son of Ibn al-Ushnānī), 319
Muḥammad ʿAbda b. Ḥarb al-ʿAbbādānī, 292
Muḥammad b. ʿAbd Allāh b. Dīnā, 289
Muḥammad b. ʿAbd al-Raḥmān al-Ghaznawī, 286
Muḥammad b. ʿAbd al-Raḥmān al-Shāmī, 305
Muḥammad b. Abī Ḥātim, 62
Muḥammad b. Abī Ḥātim al-Warrāq, 170
Muḥammad b. Aḥmad b. Shuʿayb, 285
Muḥammad b. Aḥmad Rajā' al-Jūzajānī, 289
Muḥammad al-Bāqir, 185
Muḥammad b. al-Ḥusayn al-Ḥunaynī, 303
Muḥammad b. ʿĪsā al-Madā'inī, 303
Muḥammad b. Jaʿfar b. Muḥammad, 188

Muḥammad b. Jaʿfar b. Muḥammad b. ʿAlī (Dībāja), 189
Muḥammad b. Khalaf Wakī, 208
Muḥammad b. Maslama Abū Hishām al-Makhzūmī, 64
Muḥammad b. Maymūn, 216, 219
Muḥammad b. Muqātil, 101
Muḥammad al-Nafs al-Zakiyya, 150, 191
Muḥammad b. Naṣr al-Marwazī, 94
Muḥammad b. Rāshid al-Makḥūlī, 198
Muḥammad b. al-Sā'ib, 252
Muḥammad b. Samāʿa, 295, 296
Muḥammad b. Shujāʿ al-Thaljī, 231, 298, 307
Muḥammad b. ʿUbayda al-Maṣṣīṣī, 332
Muḥammad b. ʿUmar al-Wāqidī, 32
Muḥammad b. ʿUthmān b. Abī Shayba, 333
Muḥammad b. Zayd, 333
Muḥyī al-Dīn al-Nawawī, 286
Mujāhid b. Jabr, 141–2
al-Mukhtār, 125, 126, 150, 159
*Mukhtaṣar* (Abū al-Ḥusayn al-Qudūrī), 330
*Mukhtaṣar* (al-Muzanī), 60, 293, 294
Mukram b. Aḥmad, 303, 304–5
al-Muktafī (caliph), 295
al-Muqaddasī, 127, 363–4
Muqātil b. Sulaymān, 248
al-Muqtadir (caliph), 289, 319
Murji'a (movement). *See also* Jahmiyya; Quran, createdness of
  ʿAbd Allāh b. Aḥmad b. Ḥanbal on, 95, 97
  Abū Yūsuf and, 73, 80
  Abū Zurʿa al-Dimashqī on, 85
  al-Ashʿarī on, 240
  al-Bukhārī on, 63
  faith as utterance of the tongue, 343
  al-Fasawī on, 79
  in general, 235, 236–8
  Ibn ʿAdī on, 334
  Ibn Ḥibbān on, 324, 337
  Ibn Qutayba on, 73
  Ibn Shabbuwayh on, 87
  Jahmiyya and, 237, 343
  in Khurāsān, 192
  in Kufa, 192
  proto-Ḥanafism and, 237–8
  on rebellion, 191, 248
  al-Shaybānī as follower of, 73, 337
  social exclusion of followers of, 252
  Wakīʿ b. al-Jarrāh on, 77
Murtaḍā al-Zabīdī, 349
Mūsā b. Qurra al-Zabīdī, 314
Musaddad b. Musarhad al-Baṣrī, 314
*Muṣannaf* (Ibn Abī Shayba), 34–7
Muslim b. al-Ḥajjāj, 229
*Musnad* (al-Dārimī), 220, 222
*Musnad* (al-Ḥumaydī), 40, 42–3, 44, 314
*Musnad Abī Ḥanīfa* (Abū Nuʿaym), 320–1
al-Muʿtaḍid (caliph), 150, 295
Muṭarrif b. ʿAbd Allāh, 40
al-Mutawakkil (caliph), 34, 69, 95, 294
Muʿtazilism, 92, 330, 331
al-Muwaffaq (caliph), 90, 291
al-Muwaffaq b. al-Makkī, 285, 289
*muwalladūn* (acculturated Arabs), 164–6, 212
*Muwaṭṭa'* (Mālik b. Anas), 136

*nabaṭī* (pejorative term), 162–4
al-Naḍr b. Muḥammad, 217, 276
al-Naḍr b. Shumayl, 224
al-Najāshī, 318
Najd, 136
al-Narsakhī, 178
Nasā, 161
al-Nasā'ī, 230, 333
Naṣr b. Sayyār, 190, 248
al-Nawawī, 60
*naẓar* (speculative inquiry), 210
Nietzsche, Friedrich, 311
Nīshāpūr, 56–7, 204, 288–90, 305–6
*notion d'hérésie, La* (Le Boulluec), 10–11
Nūḥ b. Abī Maryam, 321
Nūḥ b. Darrāj, 321
Nūḥ b. Manṣūr, 340, 342

oral communication, 110
original sin, 226
orthodoxy. *See also* heresy
  Abū Zurʿa al-Dimashqī on, 85
  al-Bukhārī on, 172
  defining of, against heresy, 52, 91, 93
  disciplinary dimension of, 52
  of eponymous founders, 3, 4, 16, 25
  formation of, 52, 154, 260, 358, 362–3
  Ḥanafism as majoritarian, 338
  historiography and, 113–15, 361
  Ibn Qutayba on, 76
  Ibn Shabbuwayh on, 87, 89
  Isḥāq b. Rāhawayh on, 98
  in Islam, perceived absence of, 7, 19, 357, 358, 360
  local orthodoxies, 52, 81
  *manāqib* works shaping, 263
  piety and, 241
  as process, 277, 362
  proto-Sunni, 6, 237–8

proto-Sunni traditionalism and. *See* proto-Sunni traditionalism, orthodoxy
qadis and, 89, 244
regulation of, 3, 20, 52, 104–5, 244, 251
religious jurisprudence and, 221–2, 227
scholarship on, 7–17
Sunni. *See* Sunni orthodoxy
Wakīʿ b. al-Jarrāh on, 172
orthodoxy, narratives of
on ancestry, 268–73, 281
in general, 261–2
in *manāqib* works. *See manāqib* (biographies)
in *masānīd*, 262, 283, 313, 317, 324, 331, 354–5
al-Muqaddasī on, 363–4
process, seeing orthodoxy as, 277, 363–4
on rebellion, 344
on refusing to swear oaths, 274
on repenting from heresy, 273–6, 307
responding to heresy in, 257–60, 265, 270, 272, 273, 276–9, 307–8, 361
*al-Sawād al-aʿẓam*, 343
on Successors, 268–72, 281
*ṭabaqāt* and, 279
transregional spread of, 308
orthopraxy, 7, 117, 172, 174, 356
'other', proximate, 61–3, 351, 360

Pahlavi language, 177
paper, introduction of, 109
Persian language, 176, 178–82
Persians, 155, 167–9, 177, 340–3
philology, 337
piety, 66, 241–3
pilgrimage (*ḥajj*), 67, 193, 201, 224, 298
plague, 64, 250, 251
political elites, 34, 65, 69, 196, 202, 204
practice, realm of (*praxis*), 12, 117, 351, 356
prayer, 57, 171–6, 178–81, 200, 241, 343
predestination, 349
primary sources. *See also* textual communities
absence of Abū Ḥanīfa's texts, 349
heresiography and, 7, 13–14
lack of neutrality of, 17, 20–1, 22–4, 25–6, 204, 360
quantity of, 11
survival of written work, 41
Prophet. *See* Muḥammad, Prophet
Prophetic ḥadīth
ʿAbd Allāh b. Aḥmad b. Ḥanbal on, 96
analogical reasoning and, 227
al-Awzāʿī on, 74
al-Bukhārī on, 172–4
in general, 228, 233
Ibn Abī Shayba on, 36
Ibn Qutayba on, 74
al-Khalīlī on, 233
legal authority of, 28, 30, 36, 74, 172–4, 233, 242
Mālik b. Anas on, 242
al-Shāfiʿī on, 28, 30
prosopography, 33, 64, 123–4
proto-Ḥanafism. *See also* Ḥanafism; Sunni orthodoxy
ʿAbbāsids and, 202
Abū Zurʿa al-Rāzī and, 100, 102
in general, 15
ḥadīth, 216–18
Ibn Qutayba on, 72–5
*istiḥsān* and, 29
Jahmiyya and, 248
jurisprudence, 216–18, 223, 224–5, 226–7
al-Khaṭṭābī on, 60
in Khurāsān, 174–8, 216, 280
in Kufa, 280
Miḥna, 235
Murji'a and, 237–8
as proximate 'other', 62
qadis, 202, 235, 263–4, 352–3
spread of, 175
states and, 202, 264
*ṭabaqāt* works by, 282
Wakīʿ b. al-Jarrāh and, 78
proto-Ḥanbalism, 175
proto-Shāfiʿism, 175
proto-Sunni traditionalism
accommodating towards Abū Ḥanīfa, 25, 106
Christianity and, 359
as community, 41, 67, 91
consensus (*ijmāʿ*), 334–7, 355–6
discourses of heresy. *See* heresy, discourses of
dissensus on Abū Ḥanīfa, 75–6, 78
elites, proximity to, 34, 65, 69, 196, 202–4
ethno-racial reasoning by, 154
in general, 14–16, 350
ḥadīth, 228–34, 314
heresy as a social phenomenon, 244–8
al-Ḥumaydī's statement on, 48, 112
Judaism and, 78, 166, 211–14, 359
jurisprudence, 217, 221–2, 223–7
*masānīd* by, 314–17, 318–25
al-Mutawakkil and, 34, 69
piety, 241–3

proto-Sunni traditionalism (cont.)
  proximate 'other', 61–3, 351, 360
  publicly opposing deviants, 91, 96
  Qādirī creed, 330
  qadis, serving as, 70, 205
  quietism, 93, 191, 193, 201, 352
  rebellion, 184, 190–2, 193–201, 202
  *ṭabaqāt* works by, 282–3
  Ṭāhirid dynasty and, 202–4
  as textual community, 81, 82, 83, 111–12, 242
  transregional phenomenon, 81, 83, 289, 335
proto-Sunni traditionalism, orthodoxy
  Abū Zur'a al-Dimashqī on, 85
  defining of, against heresy, 52, 91, 93
  disciplinary dimension of, 52
  discursive formation of, 11, 38–9, 46
  Ibn 'Adī on, 335
  Ibn Shabbuwayh on, 85
  piety and, 241
  regulation of, 52, 104–5, 244, 251
  religious jurisprudence and, 221–2, 227
proto-Sunnism
  Abū Ḥanīfa, embracing of, 25
  in general, 14
  heresy, discourses of, 108
  orthodoxy, 6, 237–8
  piety, 241
  as proximate 'other', 62
  spread of, 175
proximate 'other', 61–3, 351, 360
purity laws, 141

al-Qadi, Wadad, 33
al-Qādir (caliph), 4, 330–1
qadis
  Aḥmad b. Ḥanbal's sons serving as, 90
  al-'Anbarī on, 208
  authority of, 208, 296, 353
  Ḥanafī, 205, 251, 291
  Ibn Abī al-'Awwām as, 265–6
  Ibn Shabbuwayh on, 89
  intermediary function of, 296, 352–3
  *manāqib* works, 293–9, 308
  orthodoxy, 89, 244
  proto-Ḥanafī, 202, 235, 264, 352–3
  proto-Sunni traditionalist, 70, 205
  rebellion and, 202, 296, 352–3
al-Qartabī, Sharaf al-Dīn, 284–7
Qāsim b. Abī Shayba, 34
al-Qāsim b. Ma'n, 219, 272
Qays b. al-Rabī', 215
al-Qazwīnī, 142
*qiyās*. *See* analogical reasoning (*qiyās*)
quietism, 93, 191, 192, 193, 201, 352
al-Qūjānī, 84
Quran
  2.143, 322
  Arabic language, 154, 176–82
  establishing consensus and, 322
  *istiḥsān* and, 30
  theological controversy over, 246
Quran, createdness of. *See also* Jahmiyya; Miḥna; Murji'a (movement)
  'Abd Allāh b. Aḥmad b. Ḥanbal on, 95, 97, 103, 257
  Abū Yūsuf on, 344
  Abū Zur'a al-Dimashqī on, 89
  al-Ash'arī on, 240
  Bishr b. al-Walīd al-Kindī on, 231
  Miḥna, 32, 95, 235–6
  al-Samarqandī on, 344
  al-Shaybānī on, 225
  social exclusion and, 254
  al-Ṭaḥāwī on, 239
Quraysh, 44
Qutayba b. Sa'īd al-Balkhī, 252

al-Rabī', 291
Rabī'at al-Ra'y, 72, 165–6
*Raf' al-yadayn fī al-ṣalāt* (al-Bukhārī), 173, 175
*Rāḥat al-ṣudūr* (al-Rāwandī), 344–8
raising of hands during prayer, 171, 173, 241
Raqaba b. Maṣqala, 218–19
Raqqa, 297
rationalists (*aṣḥāb al-ra'y*). *See* proto-Ḥanafism
al-Rāwandī, 344–8
*ra'y*. *See* speculative jurisprudence (*ra'y*)
Rayḥāna (second wife of Aḥmad b. Ḥanbal), 90
Rayy, 46, 52, 68, 100, 175, 185
rebellion
  'Abbāsid caliphate and, 149, 189, 197, 202, 297, 333
  in *Faḍā'il Abī Ḥanīfa*, 276
  Ibn al-Mubārak on, 188
  in Khurāsān, 171, 190
  in Kufa, 148–51, 185, 191
  *manāqib* works on, 296
  al-Mukhtār, 125, 150, 159
  Murji'a and, 191, 248
  orthodoxy, narratives of, 344
  qadis and, 202, 296, 352–3
  scholars' lack of support for, 185
  al-Ṭaḥāwī on, 239–40
  Zayd b. 'Alī, 150, 185–90, 297

rebellion, discourses of heresy
'Abd Allāh b. Aḥmad b. Ḥanbal on, 97
Aḥmad b. Ḥanbal on, 95
al-Bukhārī on, 65
al-Fasawī on, 194, 199
in general, 184, 352–3
al-Ḥārith b. Surayj, 190, 247–8, 297
Ibrāhīm b. 'Abd Allāh, 186, 190–3, 197, 199, 220, 297
quietism, 191, 193–201, 352
state, against, 95, 186, 238–40, 276, 296
al-'Uqaylī on, 337
Zayd b. 'Alī, 185–90
reception history. *See* mnemohistory
*Rechtgläubigkeit und Ketzerei im ältesten Christentum* (Bauer), 9
*Refutation against al-Nu'mān* (al-Ḥumaydī), 46, 47
regional orthodoxies, 52, 81
regionalism
Basra, 125–7, 128
curses and, 145–8
devil and, 134, 138, 143–4, 148–51
disease used as metaphor for heresy, 249
distribution of good and evil, 130, 138
in general, 120, 134, 151
Iraq, 76, 138, 142–4, 145–7, 148–9, 249
Kufa, 118–19, 123, 124, 125–9, 131–3, 134, 138, 143, 145, 147, 249, 351
scholarship and, 122–4
Shām, 129, 138, 139, 148
Reinhart, Kevin, 357
religions in Islamic world, 3
religious deviance, 93, 164, 166. *See also* heresy, discourses of; Jahmiyya; Murji'a (movement)
religious elites, 111
repenting from heresy. *See also* inquisitions; Miḥna
'Abd Allāh b. Aḥmad b. Ḥanbal on, 97
Abū Zur'a al-Dimashqī on, 89
Aḥmad b. Ḥanbal on, 256–7
al-Ash'arī on, 240
al-Bukhārī on, 68
in *Faḍā'il Abī Ḥanīfa*, 257–9, 273–6
al-Fasawī on, 81
Ibn 'Adī on, 333
Ibn Ḥibbān on, 257
Ibn al-Mubārak on, 274
in Kufa, 81, 275
orthodoxy, narratives of, 273–6, 307
state's role in inquisitions, 256–60
Sufyān al-Thawrī on, 81, 256, 275–6
al-'Uqaylī on, 337
reports (*āthār*). *See* Prophetic ḥadīth
revelatory sources. *See* Prophetic ḥadīth
*Risāla* (al-Shāfi'ī), 53
ritual cleansing (*wuḍū'*), 55
ritual and practice (orthopraxy), 7, 117, 172, 356
ritual prayer, 171–6, 178–81, 241, 343
Robinson, Chase, 27
Rome, 123
Rukn al-Dīn Sulaymān, 345
rule determination, 31
al-Ruṣāfa, 34

sacred places, 123–4, 129
Sa'd b. Abī Waqqāṣ, 149
*ṣadaqāt* (land endowments), 185
al-Saffāḥ (caliph), 150
Ṣaffārid dynasty, 340
*Ṣaḥīḥ* (al-Bukhārī), 43–5, 49, 58–61, 85, 204
Sahl b. 'Ammār b. 'Abd Allāh al-'Atakī, 289
Sahl b. Sa'd al-Sā'idī, 271
al-Sahmī, 230, 333
al-Sā'ib b. Yazīd al-Kindī, 271
Sa'īd b. 'Abd al-'Azīz, 222
Sa'īd b. Jubayr, 222
Sa'īd b. Sālim80
*sakatū 'an* (denouncing by scholars), 63
al-Sakhtiyānī, 334
Salafism, 355
Salama b. Kuhayl, 186
salaries of military personnel, 156
Ṣāliḥ b. Aḥmad, 50, 90
Ṣāliḥ b. al-Ḥasan, 273
al-Ṣāliḥī, 265
Saljūq dynasty, 345, 353
Salmān al-Fārisī, 181
al-Sam'ānī, 49
Sāmānid dynasty, 301, 333, 339–41
al-Sarakhsī, 179, 180, 224
al-Sarrāj, Abū al-'Abbās, 56–7
Satan, 226
satire, 221
Savant, Sarah Bowen, 155–6
Sawād, 185
*al-Sawād al-a'ẓam* (al-Samarqandī), 339–44
Sayf al-Dīn al-Qaffāl al-Shāshī, 288
al-Ṣaymarī, 285, 287, 304, 331
scholars
al-Bukhārī on, 67
death of, 242
ethno-racial reasoning towards, 164, 169
genealogy, discrediting by means of, 157
heresy and, 79
jurisprudence and, 209

scholars (cont.)
rebellion, lack of support for, 185
regionalism and, 123
*sakatū ʿan* (denouncing by), 63
Ṭāhirid dynasty and, 204
Zaydi, 187–9
schools of law. *See madhhab*s (schools of law)
sedition, 149
Sezgin, F., 321
al-Shaʿbī, 125–8, 221
Shādhdh b. Yaḥyā al-Wāsiṭī, 214
al-Shāfiʿī
on Abū Ḥanīfa's weak grasp of Arabic, 182
Bakkār b. Qutayba on, 294
al-Bukhārī on, 58
Companions, has not met, 320
as founder of *madhhab*, 3
al-Ḥumaydī and, 47
Isḥāq b. Rāhawayh and, 48–56, 68, 204
al-Khaṭṭābī on, 60
*Kitāb Ibṭāl al-istiḥsān*, 28, 30
*Kitāb al-Umm*, 27–8, 30, 163
on Kufa, 28
legal arguments against Abū Ḥanīfa, 27–9, 30–2, 35, 37
on Mālik b. Anas, 107
*manāqib* works on, 283
*Risāla*, 53
'some people' (*baʿḍ al-nās*), 45
speculative jurisprudence of, 75
al-Ṭaḥāwī on, 299
Yaḥyā b. Maʿīn on, 75
Shāfiʿism, 291–3, 331, 345–6. *See also madhhab*s (schools of law)
*shahāda* (testification of Islam), 177
al-Shahrastānī, 8
Shām, 84, 129, 138, 139, 148, 149, 217
Shamr, 249
Shams al-Dīn Yūsuf b. Abī Saʿīd b. Aḥmad al-Sijistānī, 286
Shams al-Dīn Yūsuf b. ʿUmar b. Yūsuf al-Ṣūfī al-Kamārūrī, 286
Sharaf al-Dīn Ismāʿīl b. ʿĪsā al-Awghānī al-Makkī, 286
*Sharḥ al-Sunna* (al-Muzanī), 200–1
Sharīk b. ʿAbd Allāh, 81, 220, 254, 277
al-Shaybānī
Abū Yūsuf and, 297–8, 308
authorship of *Kitāb al-Ḥiyal*, 224–5
al-Bukhārī and, 225
denouncing Abū Ḥanīfa, 64
ḥadīth scholarship, 230
on *ḥiyal* (legal tricks), 223
Ibn Ḥibbān on, 336–7
in Kufa, 298
on language used for prayer, 178, 181
on Mālik b. Anas, 107–8
Murji'a and, 73, 337
qadi in Raqqa, asked to be, 297–8
on Quran, createdness of, 225
al-Rāwandī on, 345
religious authority of, 345
'some people' (*baʿḍ al-nās*), 45
al-Ṭaḥāwī on, 239
Shaykh al-Islām (epithet), 85
Shiʿism, 188, 309, 317, 330, 350
shrine of Abū Ḥanīfa, 310
Shuʿayb b. Ḥarb, 213
al-Shuʿaybī, 305
Shujāʿ b. al-Thaljī, 288
Shuʿūbism, 167–9
al-Sibawayh, 168
Sibṭ b. al-Jawzī, 285
al-Silafī, Abū Ṭāhir, 267
*sīra/maghāzī* literature, 26
slander (*bāb al-firya*), 163
slave captives (*mamlūk*), 157, 158
slave-concubines (*umm walad*), 213
slaves, 125
Smith, Anthony D., 154–6
Smith, Jonathan Z., 62, 124, 153
social exclusion
ʿAbd Allāh b. Aḥmad b. Ḥanbal, 254
Abū Zurʿa al-Dimashqī, 254
Aḥmad b. Ḥanbal, 105
al-Fasawī, 253
in general, 251–5
Mālik b. Anas, 252–3
Murji'a and, 252
Quran, createdness of, and, 254
*al-Sawād al-aʿẓam* on, 341
speculative jurisprudence and, 222
Sufyān al-Thawrī, 88, 252, 254, 272
society, medieval
antediluvian past, 144
curses, 151
devil, influence of, 139–45
discourses of heresy in all aspects of life, 12, 113–15, 117, 118, 206, 353, 360
ethnography, 162
ethno-racial reasoning, 167
formation of meaning making in, 350
genealogy, importance of, 157
imperial authority over, 255
regions, importance of, 130, 145
regulation of, 6–9
religious heterogeneity, 3, 92
ritual prayer, 174–8

texts creating experiences in, 357
time, concept of, 310
Solomon, 141
'some people' (*ba'ḍ al-nās*), 45, 46, 58–9
speculative inquiry (*naẓar*), 210
speculative jurisprudence (*ra'y*)
'Abd Allāh b. Aḥmad b. Ḥanbal on, 96, 99, 213, 215–16, 218
Abū Zur'a al-Dimashqī on, 77, 219, 222
Aḥmad b. Ḥanbal on, 218, 278
al-'Anbarī on, 209
al-Fasawī on, 78, 212, 214, 219, 221
al-Ḥumaydī on, 219
Ibn Abī Ḥātim on, 222
Ibn 'Adī on, 334
Ibn al-Muqaffa' on, 210
Ibn Qutayba on, 73
Ibn Sa'd on, 33, 37
Ibn Shabbuwayh on, 87
Isḥāq b. Rāhawayh on, 51, 53, 55, 87
Judaism linked to, 78, 166, 211–14
al-Khaṭīb al-Baghdādī on, 212, 219
Mālik b. Anas on, 222, 242, 278
*masānīd* responding to criticism about, 317
*muwalladūn* and, 164–6, 212
Prophetic ḥadīth and. *See* Prophetic ḥadīth
al-Shāfi'ī on, 75
social exclusion and, 222
Wakī' b. al-Jarrāh on, 77–8
Yaḥyā b. Ma'īn on, 75–6
state employment, 70, 90, 168, 297
states
administration of, 168, 177, 208–9, 291, 296
employment by, 70, 90, 168, 297
fragmentation of political power of, 120
Ḥanafism and, 329–32
inquisitions, 255
proto-Ḥanafism and, 202, 264
qadis and, 202
rebellion against, 95, 186, 238–40, 276, 296
regulation of heresy and orthodoxy by, 353, 358
Stewart, Devin, 8
Stock, Brian, 27
stoning, 35
al-Subkī, 60
Successors. *See also* Prophetic ḥadīth
Abū Ḥanīfa's ancestry and, 88, 268, 272
in *Faḍā'il Abī Ḥanīfa*, 268–72
in Ibn Qutayba's book, 72
ritual prayer, 172
Sufyān al-Thawrī
on Abū Ḥanīfa repenting from heresy, 81, 256, 275–6
on Abū Ḥanīfa's death, 68, 242, 334
al-Bukhārī on, 66
death of, 307
denouncing Abū Ḥanīfa, 334
Ibn Abī al-'Awwām on, 272, 275–6
Ibn Abī Ḥātim on, 106
Ibn 'Adī on, 334
Ibn al-Mubārak on, 66
jurisprudence and, 213, 215
al-Rāwandī on, 345
religious authority of, 106, 345
repenting from discourses of heresy against Abū Ḥanīfa, 307
social exclusion by, 88, 252, 254, 272
Sufyān b. 'Uyayna, 39, 42, 49, 195, 215–16, 256
al-Sughdī, 179, 180
Suhayl b. Abī Ṣāliḥ, 233
al-Sulṭān al-Sa'īd (Naṣr II), 301
Sumaniyya (Buddhists), 245
*Sunan* (al-Dāraquṭnī), 230
Sunni orthodoxy
Abū Ḥanīfa as exemplar of, 239–40, 261, 277, 284, 296, 310, 318–20, 324–5, 339, 354
consensus. *See* consensus (*ijmā'*)
definition of, Nūḥ b. Manṣūr's, 342
Ibn 'Adī on, 333
*madhhabs* and, 3–5, 14, 16
*manāqib* works establishing, 282–4, 309, 312
*masānīd* and, 318–20, 321, 322, 324–5
Qādirī creed, 331
resistance to, 333–8
*al-Sawād al-a'ẓam* on, 339–44
*ṭabaqāt* works and, 282–4
Sunnism
formation of, 6, 111
legacy of, 3
orthodoxy. *See* Sunni orthodoxy
porous boundaries of, 318, 350
proto-Sunnism. *See* proto-Sunnism
terminology of, **16**
Surmārā, 302
al-Surmārī, 302, 331
swords, 65–6, 239, 347

*al-Ṭabaqāt al-kubrā* (Ibn Sa'd), 37, 39
*ṭabaqāt* works (biographical dictionaries), 279–84, **281**, **282**, 293, *See also* *manāqib* (biographies)
al-Ṭabarī, 28, 46, 168, 190, 317, 340

al-Ṭaḥāwī
conversion to Ḥanafism, 292, 295, 299
Ibn Abī al-ʿAwwām al-Saʿdī and, 265, 267
*manāqib* of, 285, 291, 292–5, 299–300
on rebellion, 239–40
traditionalisation of Ḥanafī jurisprudence, 338
Ṭāhir b. al-Ḥusayn, 202
Ṭāhirid dynasty, 202–4, 340
al-Ṭāʾiʿ (caliph), 329
Tāj al-Dīn al-Rāwandī, 345
*takbīrāt* (reciting Allahu Akbar), 171
al-Tanūkhī, 112, 302
*Taqdima, Kitāb al-Jarḥ wa al-taʿdīl* (Ibn Abī Ḥātim), 100, 106
*Tārīkh* (Abū Zurʿa al-Dimashqī), 83, 84–5, 88–9, 270
*Tārīkh* (al-Ṭabarī), 190
*al-Tārīkh al-awsaṭ* (al-Bukhārī), 64–7, 195, 245
*Tārīkh Baghdād* (al-Khaṭīb al-Baghdādī), 24–5, 157–8, 165–6, 182, 219, 338
*al-Tārīkh al-kabīr* (al-Bukhārī), 50, 63–4
*tashbīh*, 31, 227. *See also* analogical reasoning (*qiyās*)
*Ta'sīs al-naẓā'ir* (al-Surmārī), 302
*Ta'wīl mukhtalif al-ḥadīth* (Ibn Qutayba), 71, 73
*Ta'wīlāt al-Qur'ān* (al-Māturīdī), 179
textual communities
creation of experiences by, 357
discourses of heresy, 26, 27, 207, 260
exploitation of material, 137
in general, 11, 20, 23–4, 27, 109–12, 350
Ḥanafism as, 300
literacy, 177
*manāqib* works and, 306
*masānīd*, 324
memorising books, 203
orthodoxy/heresy and, 110–12
proto-Sunni traditionalism as, 81, 82, 83, 111–12, 242
al-Thaʿālibī, 238
Thābit (father of Abū Ḥanīfa), 158, 160–2, 272
theology, 235–41, 356
*al-Thiqāt* (Ibn Shāhīn), 229
time, 310
Tirmidh, 161
al-Tirmidhī, 229, 265
topographies, moral, 124, 132, 138, 149
transmitters, 187, 228, 232, 322. *See also* *isnād*s (lists of transmitters)
Transoxiana, 62, 171, 174–5, 179, 339
tribulation, 134–7, 146–7
Troeltsch, Ernst, 114
Tughril (sultan), 345
Ṭūlūnid dynasty, 291
Turner, John P., 256
Turner, Victor, 312
Ṭūs, 289

ʿUbayd Allāh b. al-ʿAbbās al-Muṭṭalib, 271
ʿUbayd Allāh b. al-Ḥurr, 160
ʿUbayd Allāh b. Mūsā al-ʿAbsī, 314
ʿUbayd Allāh b. Yaḥyā b. Khāqān, 69
Ubulla, 143
ʿUmar b. Abī Salama, 269
ʿUmar b. Ḥammād, 161
ʿUmar b. al-Khaṭṭāb (caliph), 137, 147, 148, 185
ʿUmar b. Maymūn, 253
Umayyad caliphate, 149, 185
Umm Salama, 269
*umm walad* (slave-concubines), 213
unbeliever (*kāfir*), 224, 248
unholy regions. *See* regionalism
Upper Mesopotamia, 185
al-ʿUqaylī, 219, 220, 228, 231–2, 337
*Uṣūl* (al-Sarakhsī), 181
usury, 226
ʿUtba b. ʿAbd al-Sulamī, 271
ʿUthmān b. ʿAffān (caliph), 122, 148
ʿUthmān b. ʿAlī b. Muḥammad al-Shīrāzī, 286
ʿUthmān al-Battī, 165–6, 215
ʿUthmān b. Muḥammad b. Abī Shayba, 34
*Uyūn al-akhbār* (Ibn Qutayba), 71

van Ess, Josef, 8, 17, 19, 113, 356, 358
violence, 33–4, 65–6, 239, 347

Wahb b. Munabbih, 349
Wakīʿ b. al-Jarrāh
on Abū Khāzim, 295
on analogical reasoning, 77–8
on attitudes concerning past caliphs, 199
authorship of *Kitāb al-Maʿrifa wa al-tārīkh*, 120
biographical dictionaries, 78
al-Bukhārī and, 62, 173
Isḥāq b. Rāhawayh and, 49
on Medina, 250
on Murji'a, 77
on orthodoxy, 172
proto-Ḥanafism and, 78
on speculative jurisprudence, 77–8
*walā'* (clientship), 159
Walker, Peter, 124

Wansbrough, John, 13–14
Wāṣil al-Shārī, 275
Wāsiṭ, 185
Wāthila b. al-Asqaʿ, 269, 270–1
al-Wāthiq, 95
Webb, Peter, 154
Weber, Max, 117, 243
whipping, 258, 274
Wilken, Robert, 124
Wilson, M. Brett, 19, 356, 358
*witr* prayer, 343
women, 245–6, 355
written communication, 110. *See also* textual communities

Yaḥyā b. ʿAbd al-Ḥamīd al-Ḥimmānī, 314
Yaḥyā b. Abī Ṭālib, 303
Yaḥyā b. Ādam, 221
Yaḥyā b. Aktham, 251
Yaḥyā b. Maʿīn
  ʿAbd Allāh b. Aḥmad b. Ḥanbal and, 90
  on Abū Ḥanīfa's ḥadīth proficiency, 231
  on Abū Mushir, 84
  Aḥmad b. Ḥanbal and, 75
  al-Bukhārī and, 68
  Ibn Ḥibbān on, 337
  Ibn al-Ushnānī and, 319
  Miḥna, 32
  on al-Shāfiʿī, 75
  on Shiʿism, 189
  on speculative jurisprudence, 75–6
  sympathy for Abū Ḥanīfa, 75–6, 234
  on Wāthila b. al-Asqaʿ, 270
  on Yaʿqūb b. Sufyān, 83
Yaḥyā b. Ṣāliḥ al-Wuḥāẓī, 77
Yaḥyā b. ʿUmar, 150
Yamān al-Juʿfī, 169
Yaʿqūb b. Ibrāhīm, 336
Yaʿqūb b. Layth, 122, 150
Yaʿqūb b. Sufyān al-Fasawī, 82
Yāqūt al-Ḥamawī, 330–1
Yazīd b. Abī Ziyād, 186
Yazīd b. Hārūn, 214
Yazīd b. al-Walīd (caliph), 190
Yemen, 284–7
Yūnus b. ʿAbd al-Aʿlā, 299
Yūnus b. Sulaymān al-Saqaṭī, 87
Yūnus b. ʿUbayd, 129
Yūsuf b. Khālid al-Samtī, 230, 232, 321
Yūsuf b. Shāhīn, 268
Yūsuf b. ʿUmar, 177, 185

Zādhān Farrūkh, 177
al-Zajjājī, 182
Zakariyyā' b. Yaḥyā b. al-Ḥārith al-Nīshāpūrī, 288–90
Zakariyyā' b. Yaḥyā al-Sājī, 283
*zakāt* (almsgiving), 59
al-Zamakhsharī, 285
Zaman, Muhammad Qasim, 8, 236
al-Zandawasītī, 179
Zayd b. ʿAlī, 150, 185–90, 297
Zaydism, 318
Ziyārid dynasty, 333
al-Zubayr b. ʿĪsā, 38
al-Zubayr b. ʿUbayd Allāh b. Ḥumayd, 38
Zufar b. Hudhayl, 217, 232, 346
Zūṭā, 158

Printed in the United States
by Baker & Taylor Publisher Services